AMERICAN PROGRESS

"AMERICAN PROGRESS"
designed by George Crofutt
painted by John Gast, 1872

(courtesy Christie's)

AMERICAN PROGRESS

THE GROWTH OF THE TRANSPORT, TOURIST, AND INFORMATION INDUSTRIES IN THE NINETEENTH-CENTURY WEST

seen through

The Life and Times of George A. Crofutt Pioneer and Publicist of the Transcontinental Age

By

J. Valerie Fifer

The Globe Pequot Press

Chester, Connecticut

United Kingdom and European Distributor: Pandemic, Ltd., 71 Great Russell Street, London WC1B 3BN, England.

Library of Congress Cataloging-in-Publication Data

Fifer, J. Valerie.
  American progress.
  The growth of the transport, tourist, and information industries in the nineteenth-century West.

  "Publications of George Andrews Crofutt": p. 403-5
  Bibliography: p. 438-62
  Includes index.
  1. Crofutt, George A. 2. Businessmen—United States—Biography.
3. Transportation—West (U.S.)—History—19th century. 4. Advertising—Transportation—West (U.S.)—History—19th century. 5. Tourist trade—West (U.S.)—History—19th century. 6. Guidebook industry—West (U.S.)—History—19th century. I. Title.
HC102.5.C76F54 1988 338.092'4 [B]   87-32539
ISBN 0-87106-732-3

Printed in the United States by The Nimrod Press, Boston
First Edition/First Printing

CONTENTS

MAPS

ILLUSTRATIONS

CONTENTS

ACKNOWLEDGEMENTS

I wish to thank the staff of the many library and archive collections used in the preparation of this book, and listed in the Sources, for their ready assistance and interest in the project. It has been a great pleasure to work among them at all times.

In addition, I am also most grateful to Ken Longe, Research Specialist, Union Pacific System; to Richard Reed, Niagara County Historian, Lockport, N.Y.; to Lawrence Naukam, Local History Division, Rochester Public Library, N.Y.; to staff of the Chicago Historical Society and the Chicago Public Library (Business/Science/Technology Division), and to many other individuals, for dealing with specific queries so promptly and helpfully. It is a pleasure also to have had the opportunity to talk with Francis Rizzari, of Lakewood, Colo., about his early interest in George Crofutt, and to acknowledge the work of cartographer David Lawes. Further appreciation is expressed for permission to reproduce the following maps: to the Seaver Center for Western History Research, Natural History Museum of Los Angeles County (Map XIII); to Donald Duke in Los Angeles (Map XIV, from his personal collection); and to the Association of American Geographers (Map XV). The book has been published with the aid of a grant from the Simpson Fund. Finally, and especially, I thank my husband for his unfailing encouragement throughout.

J.V.F.

INTRODUCTION

"This is a strange country, this Great American West," observed the French traveller Louis Simonin in 1867, as he crossed the trans-Mississippi region for the first time.[1] Such assessments were not confined to Europeans; the Great West was a strange country for the vast majority of Americans also.

Americans had long been familiar with a succession of 'New Wests' linked to the opening of new routeways, and the expansion of settlement and communication. Tidewater and Western interior had been fundamental geographical and economic realities since colonial times, and federal guarantees for westward expansion were built into the Constitution, and into support for the public domain. Westward territorial expansion had been bold in its demands and continental in scale. The United States secured a boundary on the Mississippi in 1783, along the Rockies in 1803, and on the Pacific Ocean in the mid-1840s; more specifically, in 1846-8 the country had acquired the four key inlets of lower Puget Sound, the Columbia River mouth, and San Francisco and San Diego Bays that together pegged out the Pacific Coast strategy of the Polk administration.

It was no secret that much of the West beyond the 96° W meridian —some five hundred miles or so east of the Rockies — was for many an alien land, dry as well as distant. Yet neither of these obstacles was regarded as insuperable. Although some originally considered that the United States' boundary had gone too far, most Americans were convinced that, if necessary, all environmental problems could be solved, sooner or later. Winning another New West could and would be achieved, provided it was worth the effort. The basic question therefore was not how the West would be won, but what the West was *for*. After the Civil War, Americans began to organize themselves more purposefully towards finding the answer.

This book examines aspects of the development of the American West during the second half of the nineteenth century by means of three related themes: transport, tourism, and the growth of the information and advertising industries. Between 1870 and 1900, the marketing of the West was one of America's greatest national accomplishments. It was based on the construction of the transcontinental railroads and the associated land sales and settlement, but selling the West also depended on the opening of a vigorous new frontier which exploited the region's immense scenic and climatic resources. This involved the promotion of a new type of western exploration, and created the western tourist industry.

The needs of this new tourist industry were often closely linked with those of new settlers in general. The West as a whole faced the tasks of improving transport and accessibility, attracting investment, and satisfying the huge demand for information; the challenge was met in a brief, extraordinarily intense period of western boosting and advertising that was fuelled by the sudden spectacular boom in western data collection and distribution. Together, the transport, tourist, and information industries played a crucial role in Western development, as this analysis of their evolving relationships sets out to show. All brought new settlement and investment into the West, demanded a new awareness of the environment, helped to define the new word 'transcontinental', and stimulated the growth of a new spirit of American nationalism.

"Seeing and Understanding Our Own Land"

Westward expansion had always been both a practical and a symbolic expression of America's Romantic Movement. In physical and intellectual terms, Romanticism was closely associated with personal exploration and discovery, with the inspiration and challenge of the landscape, and with the restless search for change and new experience. In the second half of the nineteenth century, the American West provided a fresh source of ideas and imagery, and new definitions of beauty and form.

Mountains were one of the great universal primary themes of the Romantic Movement. They embodied the force and energy of Nature — grand, powerful and sublime. Lofty peaks, precipitous rock walls, deep gorges, avalanches, cataracts, storms, winds, and wave-battered sea cliffs became important elements in man's emotional and spiritual relationship with the wilderness. For some, Western America was never to be more than a vast, cruel country to search, and to survive. For others, it was Nature in an unfamiliar form but still a Nature to be understood and harmonized. In this case, the quest for fundamental truths about man's relationship with God and the natural world required the same questions to be asked in new surroundings:

> "I come to the West prepared for the distaste I must experience at its mushroom growth," wrote Margaret Fuller, travelling from Boston. Nevertheless, she was determined to reject preconceptions, and to remain open-minded and curious, ... resolved, above all, "by reverent faith" to discover "the mighty meaning of the scene, perhaps to foresee the law by which a new order, a new poetry, is to be evoked from this chaos."

A deep appreciation developed as she came to understand and adjust to the scale of the West ...

2

"I began to love, because I began to know the scene, and shrank no longer from 'the encircling vastness.' It is always thus with the new form of life; we must learn to look at it by its own standard."

The impact of the West was stimulating, disturbing . . .

"*Home!* where is it? It seems as if there was no home, and no need of one, and there is room enough to wander on for ever." [2]

The search for order and the joy of revelation are recurring themes in nineteenth-century America. So too is the theme of continuity with Eastern experience, of adjustment and adaptation rather than fundamental change when transferring to a Western environment, despite the fact that the adaptation often demonstrated that the West had a way, and a mind, of its own. The influence of Romanticism and Transcendentalism was carried far into the West by many travellers, to be carried back again in many cases refreshed and refurbished — or left to grow. After meeting John Muir for the first time in Yosemite, California in 1871, Emerson found him to be "a new kind of Thoreau, a Thoreau browsing upon the cedars and sequoias of the Sierra, instead of upon the scrub-oaks of Concord." [3]

Time and again, a study of the transport, tourist, and information industries reveals the strength and variety of Eastern influence upon the West, not only through federal agencies and economic controls but through a host of cultural and ethnic connections, including schools, colleges, churches, urban institutions, hotels, stores, local and national newspapers, magazines and periodicals, and the spread of mail-order. "The wind blew from the East," as Ferner Nuhn observed; ". . . printing press and letter box were always close on the heels of the hunters." [4]

Record levels of immigration into the United States in the second half of the nineteenth century, coupled with western railroad expansion, brought the West into focus as an Americanizing environment. About half the emigrants settling beyond the 96° W meridian after the Civil War came from the Eastern States, and about half of them directly from Europe. "We may well ask — and with special reference to the West," wrote Josiah Strong somewhat anxiously in 1885, "whether this in-sweeping immigration is to foreignize us, or we are to Americanize it." [5] It was a vital question. The transatlantic passage and the New World had almost always provided in themselves, subtly or strikingly, a powerful Americanizing influence, but for those from the cooler, wetter regions in the East and in Europe, the semi-arid West was to prove one of the most difficult and unpredictable of regions for permanent settlement. In the event, it was also to become one of the most successful Americanizing environments of all.

Technological, commercial, demographic, and intellectual change helped to tie the West into the United States' great Industrial Revolution. And for the majority of nineteenth-century Americans, change was equated with progress. "On the plains and in the mountains the railroad is the one great fact," Nordhoff observed in 1872, en route to California.[6] R.L. Stevenson was to gain the same powerful impression as he headed west a few years later . . . "It seems to me, I own, as if this railway were the one typical achievement of the age in which we live, as if it brought together into one plot all the ends of the world and all the degrees of social rank." [7] "In America . . . ," Maurice Morris asserted, "the railway is the pioneer of all progress. Civilization and settlements follow it . . . Towns and villages grow round it, and to show their gratitude, welcome it daily through their best streets." [8]

Thus a fresh wave of Americans, old and new, rode the rails of the West's latest, remarkable "one great fact" — to see, to know, to chance it. Samuel Bowles from Massachusetts reflected one aspect of the new American mood at the end of the 1860s, as he travelled west on the first transcontinental railroad:

> "The continent is spanned, the national breadth is measured . . . There is no such knowledge of the nation as comes of traveling it, of seeing eye to eye its vast extent . . .
>
> Whatever we go out to see, whatever pleasures we enjoy, whatever disappointments suffer, this, at least, will be our gain, — a new conception of the magnitude, the variety and the wealth, in nature and resource, in realization and in promise, of the American Republic, — a new idea of what it is to be an American citizen." [9]

Another dramatic stage had been reached in the search for "the meaning of America," a new flush of American Romanticism in the West's new technological age . . .

> "My last piece of advice to everybody who is thinking of the California journey is, Go! don't give it up!", wrote Susan Coolidge, back home in New Haven, Conn. after her first transcontinental railroad trip in 1872. "The discomforts . . . the trifling vexations, are soon forgotten; while the novelty and freshness, the beautiful sights, the wider horizon, the increased compass and comprehension, remain fresh to us always." [10]

Seeing and understanding this new land mixed duty with opportunity. The Great West was indeed a strange country. It might be regarded at first glance as uncivilized, unproductive, even ungodly; but it would never now be seen as unAmerican.

Creating Western America's Tourist Industry

The United States was one of the first countries in the world in which tourism played a key role in helping to shape new economic policies designed to combat regional underdevelopment.

The West was brought within the framework of big business in the second half of the nineteenth century. The region's continued reliance on substantial Eastern investment was underlined by the failure of its own Far West; the Pacific Railroad never developed as a major world route for the Oriental trade, despite the fact that the press made much of San Francisco's first east-bound consignment of tea, "despatched as the rails were joined to inaugurate America's new overland trade with China and Japan, 10th May 1869." The opening of the Suez Canal only six months later emphasized the dominance of Old World routeways; the Pacific Railroad was not the important new 'Passage to India', and the 'California Connection' — political, economic, and military — remained the railroad's primary justification.

Given the costs of construction and the thousands of square miles of uninhabited or sparsely populated territory pierced by the Union Pacific-Central Pacific's 1800-mile track, the growth of western passenger and freight revenues depended on a massive injection of Midwestern, Eastern, and European investment — fast inputs of time, money, and human energy. Promotion of Western America's transcontinental tourist industry began in 1869, immediately after the opening of the Pacific Railroad. Tourists were drawn largely from the comfortably-off middle classes at this period, and whether travelling for pleasure, health, education, or part-business purposes, they were often also potential settlers or investors in the West. Tourist promotion by the railroad companies, and by a wide range of other groups and individuals, led to the rapid adoption of Eastern styles and Eastern tastes, along with Eastern investment, as the West moved quickly to satisfy the demands of its new travellers.

"The train . . . ," recalled one tourist in 1871, "was like a slice out of one of the Eastern cities set down bodily in the midst of a perfect wilderness . . . the wild and woolly West." [11] The immediate introduction in 1869 on the Union and Central Pacific Railroads of Pullman and Silver Palace Cars, the heavy investment in first-class hotels, the development of selected tourist resorts, and the growth of the affluent, long-distance excursion trade all help to contradict Edward Ullman's argument that the "frontier of comfort" reached the West for the first time in the 1940s. [12] From the start, Western America's new tourist industry had to fight fierce competition from the Eastern resorts, and was forced to meet the standards and demands of the Eastern market. The varied attractions and accessibility of the Eastern and Great Lakes centres, to say nothing of Europe and the Mediterranean via the new, fast transatlantic passenger steamship services introduced in 1871, all spelled trouble for the virgin tourist territory of the West. Curiosity or patriotism could arouse sufficient enthusiasm for a single transcontinental trip, but the slogan

"See America First", or "Go *West* instead", was virtually worthless if in practice it became "Have Seen Western America Once".

The West had to make a start, however, and in the first place "that seriousness, almost moral earnestness, of the mid-Victorian tourist" drew on deep wells of pride and affection for the American homeland:

> "America ... ," wrote Sarah Hale, "the rudest mountain, and the wildest wood of thy varied landscape is far dearer to my heart, and more inspiring to my imagination than the sublime antiquities and unrivalled natural charms [of Europe]."

...And in 1872, one New Yorker welcomed the creation of the Yellowstone National Park with the comment:

> "Without committing ourselves to the general principle of protection for home manufactures, we may afford to rejoice at any measure tending to encourage the practice of doing our own pleasuring within our own borders." [13]

Tourists to Western America were now encouraged to look for something more than mere imitations of Europe, even though in the early days it was prudent to prime the pump with advertisements for the West's own "American Switzerland", "American Italy", "Egyptian Desert", and "French Riviera". Sustained growth, however, depended on America being true to itself:

> "It goes without saying," wrote Charles Warner, after travelling through the West, "that this is not Europe, either in its human interest or in a certain refinement of landscape that comes only by long cultivation and the occupancy of ages."

But the compensating factor was that the American tourist in the West was abroad in his own country, and often uniquely involved in the possibilities of making money and boosting the Western economy at the same time ... for, Warner continued, since such a tourist travelled "in this new country, which is his own, the development of which is so interesting, and in which the opportunities of fortune seem so inviting, he is constantly tempted 'to take a hand' in it." Indeed, the American citizen touring the West carried with him a responsibility for the progress of the country.[14]

"The West is very wonderful, large and unfinished," concluded R.H. Davis, back home in New York after an extensive trip.[15] For many Americans, and others, the late-nineteenth century West was often a living reminder of the United States' recent pioneering past, a glimpse of strange, raw excitement to world-weary Eastern eyes. "All is bustle, motion, and struggle," wrote Bryce, finding, in 1888, the West to be "the most American part of America." "Confidence goes a long way towards success," and the confidence of Westerners, Bryce discovered, was superb

— a "constant reaching forward to and grasping at the future ... Time seems too short for what they have to do." [16] Many travellers saw the speed of growth in the West as the clearest, least complicated picture they could find of the post-war renaissance of American spirit and purpose, and as a ripe new field of operation for Eastern enterprise, marketing and investment. If this was thinly disguised neo-colonialism, the mandate was the Union's support for the 'westward course of empire'. Whether tourists explored the American West in search of adventure, self-discovery, health, culture, business or pleasure, the general awareness of their coming in addition both as witnesses and contributors to Western development is one of the most persistent and outstanding features of the West's nineteenth-century tourist industry.

Despite periodic financial panics across the United States, tourism remained one of the most successful growth industries in the nineteenth-century West. Three distinct stages of development can be identified, linked closely to transport, and to the expansion of ancillary services. Stage 1, the 1870s, was the decade of primary penetration for the Western tourist industry, with initial site selection, and early market growth. Signs of strong local diversification at key sites appeared quickly, as did the fierce rivalry between California and Colorado, which was to be one of the most important influences on the industry's entire growth pattern across the West.

In Stage 2, the 1880s, the length of Western America's new transcontinental and supporting railroad networks more than doubled, making this a decade of rapid expansion in the tourist industry, both in demand and in range of services. More interconnection, however, led to greater concentration rather than to greater spread of the main tourist traffic flows. This resulted from increased specialization, consolidation, and highly skilful regional promotion. The West sharpened its image and streamlined its services as the numbers of tourists coming from the Eastern and Midwestern States, and from Europe, rose dramatically, and at the same time became more active and demanding. Much of the West's tourist potential in economic terms now had to be gauged in relation to the ease with which any centre could slice off a piece of the passing transcontinental tourist traffic destined for California. For California was the irresistible attraction, and fortunately for Western America's tourist industry it was located on the 'far side' of the United States ..."California," as Henry James discovered, "belonging so completely to the 'handsome' side of the continent," ... "California, ... ever so amiably strong." [17]

In Stage 3, the 1890s, the expansion of Western America's tourist industry reached unprecedented levels, and helped to bolster the economy in certain key areas during financial depression. The 'democratization' of Western tourism accelerated with the growing popularity of

Tourist Pullman Cars, along with other new or improved transport facilities such as electric trolley cars and bicycles. New tourist services and new patterns of recreation were added to, not substituted for, the styles of the Eighties. Increased diversification was thus the theme of the 1890s; with a rapidly expanding market for what the West had to offer and a new boom in the information and advertising industries, tourism soared to new heights in attracting development and business investment. There is a marked correlation, therefore, between the stages of growth in Western America's tourist industry in the second half of the nineteenth century and phases of typical development of transport networks that have been identified elsewhere in underdeveloped countries.[18]

Increased growth of the largest centres, and increased competition between them, characterized the Nineties, particularly now between rival areas within California, and the longer-standing competition between California and Colorado. Indeed, in the thirty years between 1870-1900, the initiatives and influence of these two States continued, directly and indirectly, to shape the patterns of Western America's tourist industry. They gave the lead, as this study shows, in formulating and applying three 'laws' for the successful development of Western tourism that may be defined as: the *Law of Concentrated Effort*; the *Law of the Improved Intervening Attractions-Total Distance Ratio*; and the *Law of the Resort Region* which required the eventual ability of key resort centres to convert themselves into larger, well serviced, and highly distinctive tourist amenity areas.

Although Western America's tourist industry began in the nineteenth century, statistics were not systematically recorded until well into the twentieth century. Even so, much can be gathered from travellers' reports, newspaper files, hotel and boarding-house capacities, building programs, company archives, photographs, scrapbooks, and a wide range of printed trade and business material. What this shows is that Western America's nineteenth-century tourist industry introduced virtually all the basic strategies and options that are often associated only with twentieth-century growth. Many of the introductions in fact came early in the 1870s-1880s period. Twentieth-century developments in the tourist industry were primarily linked to two factors — the new transport modes of automobile and air travel, and the huge increase in volume traffic as shorter working hours, higher factory and farm wages, and paid holidays were gradually introduced. The nineteenth century was extraordinarily inventive, however, and Western initiatives included the rapid introduction of a much wider range of cheaper accommodation and transport facilities near the key coastal and inland attractions than studies focused on tourism's wealthy clientele normally reveal. An 'off-the-peg' tourist trade was quick to copy and adapt the styles of the tourist industry's expensive *haute couture*. The following were all well-established, popular features of Western America's tourist industry by the 1890s:

Package tours
Travel agents; travel couriers and guides
Special excursion and group rates (transport and hotels)
Long-distance rail fare reductions
'Free-to-wander' individual, or family, special Tourist Tickets
Luxury hotels; cheaper boarding-houses; tent cities
'Everything-under-one-roof' resort complexes and country clubs
City tours
Farm and Factory tours
Day Excursions
Special-interest or 'hobby' outings
Sporting parties; beach and picnic parties; riding; pony-trekking
Spas
Health farms
Dude ranches
Desert retreats
Rented cottages, furnished or unfurnished
Climbing
Camping; tents, wagons, back-packing
National Parks and wilderness areas
Pioneer reconstructions; 'What-it-was-like-in-the-Old-Days' trips

          *   *   *

Women of all ages were well represented on Western America's tourist frontier, just as they had been as westering pioneers on the overland trails. "American women are great travellers," agreed two foreign visitors on their first trip to the United States, a fact which never ceased to astonish many male Europeans if the number of times they noted it down is anything to go by. The large proportion of women tourists in the West had been a striking feature since the early 1870s. Their letters, diaries, books, and newspaper and magazine articles make a substantial contribution to the literature, and women continued to play a significant, often a dominant, role in the growth and diversification of the Western tourist industry.

It was an important development. Few women had ever been included in the fashionable European Grand Tours of the seventeenth, eighteenth, and early nineteenth centuries, while for the many American women in the Eastern cities who had never followed the emigrant trails, their first exploration by rail of the trans-Mississippi West must have been like running away to sea. Railroads gave women who could afford to take vacations, however rarely, a new sense of adventure and a new freedom of movement, as well as a new means of security, in travelling through the

9

West — travel not merely to a few especially favoured spots but to many of the more rugged and isolated locations also. Quite apart from their inclusion in large family groups, more and more women travelled on their own — mothers and daughters, sisters, friends, schoolteachers, women joining special parties, women alone.

Analysis of Western America's new tourist industry also reveals a particularly strong New England influence. New Englanders were prominent not only as consumers but as investors, entrepreneurs, tour organizers, promoters, writers, and publicists. Nowhere was their pioneering influence more marked than in the hotel industry. From the start, Western tourism adopted a highly urbanized approach; it was no use turning tourists out of elegant Pullman Cars into ramshackle hotels. New Englanders' business acumen and traditional inn-keeping skills created many of the West's most distinctive first-class hotels — great 'forward capitals' planted at the most active edge of the tourist frontier.

"Le mystérieux *Far West* a disparu devant les *Yankees*," Louis Simonin decided; " . . . le *go ahead* américain a retenti de l'Atlantique au Pacifique." [19]

While New York, Boston, Philadelphia and Chicago all maintained strong controlling interests in much of the West's economic development, Boston's and New England's early involvement in transcontinental tourist promotion is outstanding. The region's maritime trading reach had always been a long one, and its peripheral location in an expanding United States remained a perpetual challenge. As Daniel Boorstin noted in a general context, "The contribution of New England . . . to the new nation was far out of proportion to her numbers or her extent." [20] The tourist industry was no exception.

Judging by the record, few tourists were unduly concerned as to whether they were called 'tourists' or 'travellers'. These often pompous semantics, diverting some to this day, were largely irrelevant both to individuals and to groups who came confidently into the nineteenth-century American West "open-eyed and duster-clad," . . . "with their questions and their notebooks," bent on finding as much truth, inspiration, improved health, or sheer enjoyment as was possible in the allotted time.

Inevitably, those who had cause or disposition to hate tourists dwelt on the insensitive or excruciatingly banal comments made by some of them. Such comments, and the acid criticism they provoked, made good copy, but undue repetition can misrepresent the total picture. Complaints that tourists did only what fashion demanded often means simply that in the early years, the most popular sites were also the only ones readily accessible. The range of activities that soon characterized the nineteenth-century Western tourist industry reveals great diversity of taste; tourists demanded and got what they wanted. Perceptions, attitudes, and purposes varied, but tourists were no different in that respect from others entering the West. As one writer reminded groups of transcontinental tourists, California-bound in the 1880s:

> "The four days' ride from Kansas City, New Orleans, or Omaha, is either dull, monotonous, and desolate, or cheerful, exciting, and instructive, just as each passenger elects." [21]

Facts and Figures: Information-gathering in the West, and the growth of Advertising

The opening of the West in the second half of the nineteenth century coincided with a world-wide period of exploration, scientific enquiry, and classification. The Pacific Railroad Surveys of 1853-54, authorized by Congress, had given an impressive lead. After the Civil War, the United States launched a new series of fact-finding expeditions across the West, and following the Whitney surveys of California in 1860-68, the four great Government-sponsored surveys between 1867 and 1879 represented an outstanding achievement in geological and topographical mapping, resource evaluation, and scientific data-collection. These were the King Surveys along the Fortieth Parallel (1867-72); the Hayden Surveys of Nebraska, the Yellowstone region, and Colorado (1867-78); the Wheeler Surveys West of the One-Hundredth Meridian (1867-79); and the Powell Surveys of the Colorado River and the Colorado Plateau region (1869-79) — all of which paved the way for the creation in 1879 of the United States Geological Survey.

America demanded a constant up-dating of its own geography:

> "No American should be deficient in knowledge of his own country," declared the *New-York Tribune* in 1873, in discussing the West. "As to its geography . . . no excuses are admissible. The country is new, and much of the information about it is recent. . . . The American is expected, and he expects, to supplement the knowledge he obtained at school or college with continual accessions of general information."

The West was being probed and plotted, mapped and measured. So far, so good. But the West was not going to sell itself; that was a different problem altogether. Along with an intensive period of data-collection and distribution, the late 1860s also marked the beginning of one of the most concentrated advertising campaigns and regional promotions the world has ever seen. Much of it was left to private enterprise — to railroad companies, immigration and land agencies, local Chambers of Commerce, roving journalists, and individual businessmen, speculators, and boosters. Local newspapers were vital. "To a stranger who asked in a small Far Western town, how such a city could keep up four newspapers, it was well answered that it took four newspapers to keep up such a city." [22]

Many tourists were themselves born communicators, drawn from a well-educated, articulate middle class. Initially, the literature of the trans-Mississippi West had been compiled not so much by the essayist, novelist, and poet as by explorers' journals, military and trail reports, emigrants' guides, surveyors' notes and scientific records, which together produced much of the early plain prose of the West. In the railroad age, however, a flood of new material poured out of the West as travellers stuffed bulging notebooks into their baggage, and headed back east. Articles commissioned by the major magazines and periodicals, detailed personal diaries, excursionists' 'jottings', messages home, and letters to newspaper editors avid for copy all elaborated the information networks. Notes often formed the basis of popular lecture tours. Many letters and longer articles were collected and reprinted in book form within a few weeks of the traveller's return. Others were reworked into novels, or privately printed and circulated to members of literary societies and discussion groups. Still more were read aloud at socials, sewing circles, church meetings, and in schoolrooms up and down the land. Western America's 'print rush' was one of the most varied and remarkable of all the nineteenth-century bonanzas.

The information explosion was not confined to the written and spoken word; the visual arts made an indispensable contribution. Sketchers, wood-cut artists, lithographers, painters, and photographers were all stimulated by western landscapes, new technologies, and a fast-disappearing 'Old' West. The boom in mass-produced illustration in the second half of the nineteenth century, both in colour and black-and-white, stoked the western information industry, revolutionized its form, and widened its markets on both sides of the Atlantic. Between 1870 and 1900, information-gathering and processing became one of the West's most important extractive industries.

Advertising has always been part of the larger operation of marketing, and marketing Western America involved selling land, climate, goods, services, and ideas. During the second half of the nineteenth century, advertising in general ceased to be largely a reflection of existing needs and habits; it began to *create* demand, encourage new tastes, and accelerate social change. Like those in the Eastern States, Western America's boomers, boosters and drummers knew full well that advertising which promises no benefit to the consumer does not sell.

"In every bar-room lay a copy of the local paper," wrote Rudyard Kipling in Montana, on his first visit to America in 1889, "and every copy impressed it upon the inhabitants of Livingston(e) that they were the best, finest, bravest, richest, and most progressive town of the most progressive nation under Heaven; even as the Tacoma and Portland papers had belauded their readers. And yet, all my purblind eyes could see was a grubby little hamlet full of men without clean collars and perfectly unable to get through one sentence unadorned by three oaths." [23]

Kipling did not yet understand that new settlements could be all these things simultaneously. Western towns were competing fiercely with each other and with everywhere else for just about everything, and "wild advertisement, bunkum and blow" came with the territory. The boomers' overriding purpose was to get people to come at all costs; after that, if newcomers did not find what they were originally looking for, empty pockets and the need to survive by doing something else would keep most of them around long enough to boost business, and so carry on the endless struggle for new growth. As James Bryce noted in the Eighties, in his perceptive commentary on 'The Temper of the West':

> "Prosperity is largely a matter of advertising, for an afflux of settlers makes prosperity, and advertising, which can take many forms, attracts settlers. Many a place has lived upon its 'boom' until it found something more solid to live on." [24]

One of the basic laws of advertising, however, is that it can only persuade people to buy an inferior product once: Profits come from repeat purchases, and increased sales depend on improving the product or expanding the market. Selling Western America depended on both.

Guidebooks in the Railroad Age: New Geographies of the West

Railroads ferried their cargoes of passengers into the West at unprecedented speeds. Handcarts, wagons, and stagecoach had all permitted slower adjustments to be made to new surroundings. Now, railroads accelerated the pace of travel while at the same time insulating passengers for long stretches from genuine contact with the Western environment. On balance, rail travel had enormous advantages, but there was still an important role for a new type of 'trail guide'.

Guidebooks setting out to capture the spirit and purpose of this new age had to bring the West into perspective. As well as being guides for the road, they had also to be travel books in the old and best American tradition — travel books, as Tuckerman described them in the 1860s, striving always "to make one part of our vast country known to the other." [25] The role of the new Western guidebooks was thus to provide light and shade in the great physical and mental transformation scene that marked the opening of the West. They had to match the speed of the transport revolution, and perform swift, clear introductions to the landscape for Americans and Europeans on the run.

Guidebooks introduced order into what was for many an initial chaos of new sights and experiences. Americans in particular, keenly investigating what this latest West was for, needed to feel the pride, and to begin to weigh up the economic advantages, of national home-ownership on such a greatly enlarged scale. Railroad passengers no longer had to worry about physically finding their way across the West, but they still required reliable direction-finders to help them make sense of it all. The new Western guidebooks were catering for a much larger market than the earlier trail and emigrant guides, but they continued to arrange and organize a welter of information about the unknown, the unusual, the untidy. They were simple, dependable interpreters of the scene, sorting confusion without robbing it of the capacity to inspire, invigorate, shock, or delight. As this study shows, the most successful Western guidebooks in this period were, like the old wagon-masters and stage-drivers, trusted fellow-travellers for whom the West was not undis-covered country. Passengers went forward with confidence; Nature and the West were not going to overwhelm them.

The most popular tourists' guidebooks in the 1870s and 1880s thus went far beyond supplying the mere 'nuts and bolts' of travel; they were highly successful geographies of the new American West. They re-sponded to man's basic curiosity about places, and to geography's strength as a field subject, by recording and helping to explain the marvellous complexity of the real world. Above all, these guidebook-geographies had to avoid being admired but unread. With forthright comment, personal observation, anecdote and humour, writers pre-sented concise, vivid descriptions of Western scenery, settlement, land use and resources in language that the man- and woman-in-the-street could enjoy and understand. There was emphasis on the scale and speed of change in the landscape. The 'Work in Progress' notices were being nailed up right across the American West, and within the limits of their size and format, the best guidebooks in this tourists' frontier age used direct observation as the starting point from which to illustrate the dynamic relationships between the physical and human world. As the thousands of new passengers rolled across the plains, the mountains, and the deserts, they were busily learning not merely the answers, but also the questions they could next most sensibly ask about the West.

The West set America buzzing with good geographical writing in newspapers, books and magazines. There was a duty to satisfy the need to know, and for their part, the guidebook-geographies rose to the occasion by marshalling an immense amount of new material, incorpo-rating data from the latest government surveys, monitoring new devel-opment in mining, agriculture, ranching, manufacturing, transport, and settlement, and packaging it cheaply both for the pocket and the reference shelf. With the rapid expansion of railroad networks and settlement in key areas, regional guidebooks soon became a significant additional growth industry, popular not only with tourists but also with the thousands of new settlers speaking to, and learning about each other through these up-to-date regional records. Many of the most energetic and successful of the Western guidebook writers diversified into this field, boosting regional identities and helping railroad passenger departments, local businessmen, land agents, and others to spark a major new boom in the information industry.

On the whole, guidebooks have been a much neglected source for research on Western frontier writing in the second half of the nineteenth century. The fact that they are often ignored both as frontier literature and as travel books conceals their variety as well as their value, in many cases, as a record of Western frontier development from the 1870s to the 1890s. Just as the distinction between 'tourist' and 'traveller' was often artificial, so too was that between 'guidebook' and 'travel book' in some instances, both in Europe and the United States. While few guidebooks possessed great literary merit, the easy idiom, spirited pace, and personal authority of the most popular guides to the West enabled them to make a unique contribution to the region's geographical and travel literature. Writers with the largest sales and the longest runs were not those who, as one nineteenth-century American traveller noted dismissively, "offered information only on the technicalities of journeying." Through keen observation and regular field work, the major writers also offered what were often the only systematic, comprehensive, and repeatedly up-dated summaries of social and economic development in the nineteenth-century West.

In her discussion of frontier influences on American literature, Hazard had discerned by the 1920s a growing tendency to lay more emphasis on the "American" aspect, "and estimate the value of a piece of writing very largely by its fidelity to the American scene, its significance as an interpretation of these States."[26] The new guidebooks to the West in the second half of the nineteenth century were part of America's frontier literature in that sense. They joined the ranks of 'America's Commentators', and in the next few years swiftly carried Tuckerman's judgments of the 1860s right across the United States. . .

"Honest and intelligent books of travel preserve their use and charm because they describe places and people as they were at distinct epochs . . . The point of view adopted, the kind of sympathy awakened, the time and the character of the writer — each or all give individuality to such works, when inspired by genuine observation, which renders them attractive as a reference and a memorial."[27]

The pioneering role of George A. Crofutt in the West's Tourist and Information Industries

The varied and colourful life of George Andrews Crofutt (1827-1907) provides an excellent framework for the analysis of Western America's transport, tourist, and information industries, as well as a fascinating example of individual persistence and achievement in the frontier age. Until now, very little has been known about Crofutt, despite the fact that he was one of the most prolific and widely read writers on the American West in the second half of the nineteenth century. His surviving guidebooks and periodical, *Crofutt's Western World*, are now rare items, scattered across the United States in special collections or on antiquarians' shelves on both sides of the Atlantic. One American on vacation in Europe reported a few years ago finding a century-old copy of *Crofutt's Trans-Continental Tourist* on a bookstall in Rome, Italy. He bought it to add to his collection of rare Americana back in the States but later had to admit, with a colleague, that months of research had yielded no clues about the writer.[28] Others have echoed this problem in brief notes introducing special reprints of the guides. Only recently has the only known picture of Crofutt (born Crofut) been discovered in Colorado, in an old, long-forgotten scrapbook of Western pioneers. His date and place of death have up to now remained unknown, his full name virtually unrecorded.

Crofutt, famous in the field of nineteenth-century Western publications, simply disappeared from the records and the memory. With rare exceptions, and then with only a passing reference, indexes in even the most comprehensive volumes omit 'Crofutt' from the enormous lexicon of the American West. This is partly because guidebooks as a genre, along with their authors, are widely neglected in studies of Western development in the railroad age, and partly because no personal papers or collected documentation exists. There are no short cuts to Crofutt. The details of his long and eventful life must be pieced together from fragments, from hundreds of brief references in newspaper files, in business and street directories, in passenger lists, in pioneers' reminiscences, in old maps and old cemeteries, and in historical society, university, and special library collections right across the United States.

Additional material about his movements and his associates lies buried in company reports, in municipal, County, and State records, and in Federal archives. Given the content, range, and style of the guidebooks themselves, however, they provide, along with Crofutt's other publications, rich primary source material through which to trace his own experiences and wider contemporary developments at the same time. Different editions of his works, even different batches and reprints of the same edition, job-printed insertions, stop-press items, printed correspondence, prefaces, prospectuses, and advertising copy all contain a wealth of detail in abbreviated form. Set into the context of current events, they throw light on Crofutt's activities, as well as on the geography, social history, and economic conditions of his times. Crofutt's life thus becomes a revealing case study in the promotion of the West, both as an individual pioneer, and as one of those closely involved in monitoring and stimulating the growth of Western America's tourist and information industries.

Born in Danbury, Conn. in 1827, Crofutt was to join one of the classic migration flows of nineteenth-century America. As a youth, he left the isolated, small-town environment of the New England interior to seek his fortune first in New York City, and then in Philadelphia, as an editor, publisher, and advertising agent. Bankrupted by the Financial Panic of 1857, he joined the Gold Rush to Pike's Peak and reached Colorado in 1860. Crofutt found no gold; instead, he discovered the West. For the next ten years, suddenly transformed from Eastern businessman to Western pioneer, Crofutt became, among other things, a long-haul freighter over the plains, mountains, and deserts of the West. It was the decade that marked the great post-Civil War boom in freighting before the completion of the Pacific Railroad. Crofutt was actually present at the famous 'Great Event' at Promontory, Utah on 10th May 1869, and towards the end of a life packed with excitement, he recalled that the 'joining of the rails' that day remained the most thrilling scene he had ever witnessed, both in its accomplishment and as a milestone in American development. Crofutt returned immediately to the world of publishing. For the next twenty-five years or so, through his guidebooks, his periodical, his extensive correspondence with prospective settlers, his personal contacts with local editors, railroad agents, publishers, advertisers, artists and illustrators, hoteliers, tour promoters, and not least, through his own energetic travels, Crofutt helped to satisfy the huge demand for reliable information about the West.

It was largely as a result of Crofutt's efforts that the word *transcontinental* was suddenly and widely adopted throughout the United States. Chosen as the title for his first guidebook in 1869, the word *transcontinental* stressed both the physical and the mental connection of the West's new Union Pacific-Central Pacific Railroad with the rest of America. *Transcontinental* immediately became a household word, thrust into everyday language with impeccable timing and unmistakable force. An American invention, the word was born of the railroad and bred in a new phase of travel, economic expansion, and national identity, but within a few months, the bold, unambiguous title of Crofutt's guide for *transcontinental* travellers had sent this new, all-American word spinning round the world.

Crofutt's lifelong conviction that transport was the key to progress was rooted in his boyhood experience in Connecticut. Danbury had struggled in vain to join the canal age, and then laboured hard and long to attract the railroad. Not until 1852 did the railroad push its way up the narrow valley to reach the town, the same year that the first few miles of railroad track were laid west of the Mississippi River. Crofutt travelled on the Erie Canal, and followed the transport revolution into the trans-Mississippi West.

The middle of the nineteenth century had put more and more men who stepped off the railroads, not into the birch canoe, in Turner's phrase, but behind a freight team. Freighting kept one on the move and in contact with the land — trail conditions, gradients, water supply, grazing, crossing points, pioneer communities, small towns, and growing markets. It also gave time for quiet contemplation of the landscape's different scales, shapes, colours, and moods. Crofutt's experience as a freighter and wagon-train escort was to give him that intimate, first-hand knowledge of the West that helped to distinguish his guidebooks from many of more elaborate publications that flooded onto the market in the 1870s and 1880s.

Here was a practical Western pioneer whose theme was always to be, in effect, 'this is my world, and welcome to it'. Crofutt's guides blended authority and realism in a plain, unpretentious style that gave him a special edge over his early competitors, many of whom, Crofutt noted scornfully, "wrote up the West" without ever having crossed the Mississippi, much less the Rockies! The prestigious *Appletons' Illustrated Hand-Book of American Travel* promised to guide its readers "from the cities and palaces of the East to the wildernesses and wigwams of the West," but while it was sound on the cities, it was weak on the wigwams.

Crofutt encouraged his readers to become more involved with the ways of the West, less with each other. His basic message was always "Leave your old self behind, . . . keep your eyes and your minds open . . . Lay aside all prejudices, and for once be *natural* while among nature's loveliest and grandest creations . . . Above all, forget everything but the journey." Guidebooks were travel books, but they were not the "variegated vagabondizing" immortalized by Mark Twain, nor the acutely detailed observations of those who, like R.L. Stevenson, focused on the emigrants, and on the ordeal of the long train journey for much of the way. Yet many of the most popular guidebooks in the West's railroad frontier age were also, like every classic travel book, a story of discovery lived moment-by-moment. They captured the scale of the undertaking, the freshness of personal observation, the sense of a shared experience. Guidebooks looked outwards; the travellers, along with their guide, immersed themselves in the changing landscape and its people, not in the idiosyncracies of their fellow-passengers. "Everything suggests a beyond," wrote one traveller, fascinated by the huge kaleidoscope of the West outside the railroad car.[29]

Scattered reminders of individual journeys can still be found among some of the guidebooks' tattered pages — scraps through which to relive the passing moment, then and now. Dust from the alkali desert still lies trapped between some of the leaves, fine sand or black lava dust between others. Pressed flowers, an old letter, a bookmark, or a list of special items to expand on back at home — all these have kept a place, and a memory, down the years. Marginal notes do the same, a medley of new impressions, reactions and discoveries, scribbled beside the guidebook entries, to store away, discuss, and remember.

*   *   *

Crofutt was an experienced advertiser, and skills learned in the East were applied to the West:

> "Prudent, persistent advertising is sure to produce results," he wrote, "in almost all instances, far beyond expectation . . . Whatever is worth doing at all, is worth doing well. Decide what you wish to do, and then push it intelligently and energetically . . . If you have goods to sell, compel the world to listen to you . . . more fortunes have been lost by modesty than by boldness." [30]

Crofutt's message is as fresh as the day it was written, well over a century ago. In effect, the guidebooks were Crofutt's own counter- and mail-order catalogues of the West. He was in business to sell scenery, climate, farms, mines, appreciation, ideas and opportunity. His guides were "books of positive statements," designed to inform, encourage, but not delude. They extended a personal invitation to the public to go and sample the results of American Progress, to *watch* the Western frontier being transformed — by the railroad, by new perceptions of the environment, and by the changing tastes and demands of the American population.

The first *Trans-Continental Railroad Guide*, and America's first exclusively mail-order catalogue, both appeared in 1869. Three years later, as Crofutt and others continued to advertise the West with such success, Montgomery Ward produced his first mail-order catalogue, with similar reliance on a vigorous, economical writing style. In the mid-1880s, that super-salesman Richard Sears also entered the field, spicing his copy with the same enthusiasm for the product, and again, speaking directly to the individual solely through the pages of the catalogue. As with all successful advertising, the reader had to become quickly involved, be given the vital information, and be encouraged to want the product. Success depended on the skill of the communicator, on human desires for self-improvement, and on the satisfaction of value for money. Effective advertisers knew their product, gave the facts without over-complicating the message, and published testimonials from satisfied customers. Crofutt's Western guidebooks were indeed part of the new American determination to provide 'catalogs for the people'.

"Crofutt has written the field notes of half a continent," wrote one contemporary, marvelling at the range and condensed detail of his work.[31] This remained the product of his own personal travel, collection and compilation. Crofutt, a Connecticut Yankee thrown into the West, became one of the nineteenth-century link men, one of the robust and resourceful army of publicists who extended the country's information networks, and helped to accelerate the West's economic development. If customers did not want what the West was selling, they would not buy; if there, they would not stay. In the railroad age, thousands arrived simultaneously on new frontiers, and as always, there were multiple appraisals of the West. In the event, new technologies, opportunity, immigration, and investment strengthened the United States' east-west connection during a period of unprecedented national change and expansion. Throughout the nineteenth century, Americans came variously to explore, to exploit, to explain, and to enjoy the West. By the end, enough of them had discovered what the West was for, and how it could be won, to bring the great frontier movement in the United States officially to its close.

PART I

PREPARATION IN THE EAST:
THE 1830s-1850s

VIEW ON THE ERIE CANAL
Watercolor by J.W. Hill, c.1830
A small packet-boat and barge, with tow-path team, travelling through upper
New York State.

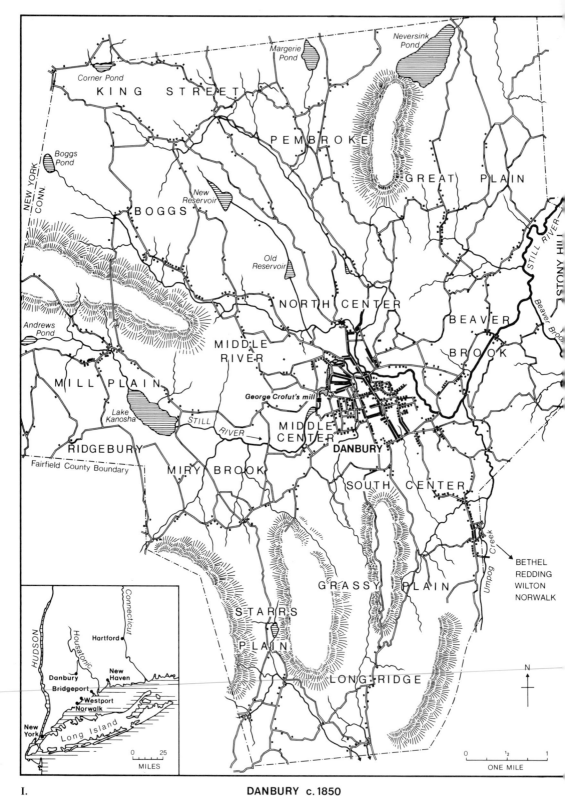

I.

DANBURY c. 1850

The railroad reached Danbury in 1852

Bethel separated from Danbury in 1855

based on maps published in Danbury in 1867, from earlier surveys

The New England Background

Many stories of the American West begin, like this one, in the Northeast. George Andrews Crofutt was born on 13th August 1827 in the small Connecticut town of Danbury, one of the hundreds of early settlements scattered among the mountains and forests of southern New England.[1] Crofutt's home town had been founded in the summer of 1684 when a small group of farmers from Norwalk down on the Tidewater followed an Indian trail inland through the forest and the occasional Indian clearings, looking for a place to plant a "new towne." For several miles the valley remained narrow and almost completely enclosed by steep rocks, sharp buttresses and massive trees, but eventually it widened for a mile or so between the bounding granite ridges and here, in 1684-5, eight families purchased about fifty square miles of land from the local Indians who called the place Pahquioque — their "broad plain." It proved to be a hard land in every sense, however, and Danbury's growth was slow as successive generations struggled to clear the forest, remove stumps, boulders and stones from their fields, and drain the bogs in the valley floor. In the 1820s, George Crofutt's Danbury was still no more than a village, an isolated series of small communities tucked away behind the coast of Connecticut, twenty-four miles from the sea.

The twin ridges of Town Hill to the east and Deer Hill to the west framed the Vale of Danbury. Between them, the Still River wound through the main part of the village, past the scattered farms and the surrounding meadows, before flowing northeastwards out of the Vale to join the Housatonic River twelve miles farther north. Numerous lakes and marshes remained, a reminder that the original settlers had dubbed the area Swampfield. Town Street, the central lane, ran roughly north-south for about a mile-and-a-half, and from it paths led away through garden lots and pastures to the small outlying clusters of population. At the time of Crofutt's birth, Danbury contained about a hundred cottages on Town Street, and another hundred or so dotted among the fields, churches, schools, stores and workshops. The Still River had earned its name because in this section of the valley it was virtually free of the small falls and rapids that whiten the waters of so many New England streams. The

Still's water supply was excellent however, and it was soon dammed to provide water power.

From the end of the seventeenth century, families of Crowfoot, Crofoot, Crowfut, Crofert, Crofut, Crofutt and Croffut were well represented among Danbury's farmers, millers and artisans. While the pronunciation of all these surnames was the same, the spelling varied, not merely with the passage of time or from one branch of a family to another, but often within the lifespan of a particular individual or the text of a single document, as several old Danbury land records show.[2] One of the first steps in trying to trace the details of George Crofutt's background is the discovery not only that he was born Crofut, but that he spelled it thus for more than forty years before he doubled the 't' — the form that will be used consistently throughout this book.

Although one of Danbury's frequent fires destroyed many of the town's early nineteenth-century birth and baptism records in 1850, available evidence indicates that Crofutt was the eldest son of George and Charry (Charity) Hull Crofut who lived on the western edge of the village beside the family's grist mill.[3] Shortly after George was born, the mill burned down and Crofut Snr. went into partnership with another local miller, Charles Starr, to rebuild the mill on the same site beside the Still River. The Starr family, related to the Hulls, already owned a linseed oil mill close by, built in 1812 by Friend Starr, Charles' father, to process locally-grown flax.[4]

Home, Church and School

Daily life was simple for the miller's son. One of George's regular jobs at mid-day would have been to carry his father's dinner across to the mill from the cottage kitchen, and then help out or run messages before returning to his lessons. Youngsters liked to watch the heavy ox-drawn wagons laden with rye, corn, and occasionally with wheat rumble into Crofut's mill yard. Rye flour and corn meal were the local staples; wheat flour was a luxury normally reserved by housewives for making piecrust and finer grades of pastry for special occasions. Most of the flour leaving Crofut's mill was slowly carted to the centre of Danbury by crossing the Still River bridge at White's Pond and then hauling the load over the steep rise in West Lane to reach Town (Main) Street. But George Crofut also did a steady trade in the neighbouring hamlets of Miry Brook and Mill Plain, tucked away 2-3 miles farther up the Still River to the south and west, and relying almost entirely for their supplies on Crofut's grist mill. Several of George and Charry Crofut's relatives lived in Miry Brook and Mill Plain, including members of the Crofut, Hull, Harris and Andrews families.[5]

Away from the noise and dust of the mill, and with household chores and schoolwork completed, George would often spend a summer afternoon, like so many other boys in the village, fishing in the mill-pond or bathing in the river. Occasionally he wandered out on to Deer Hill to look down over the neat pattern of small fenced and stone-walled fields quilting the valley, with the skyline of Town Hill and the ridges beyond. This was the spot to get the best view of Danbury — the lanes, cottages, schoolhouses, and distinctive church spires.

The Danbury of George's boyhood contained six different churches, all Protestant and all playing an important role in the life of the community. The First Congregational Church had been the focus of

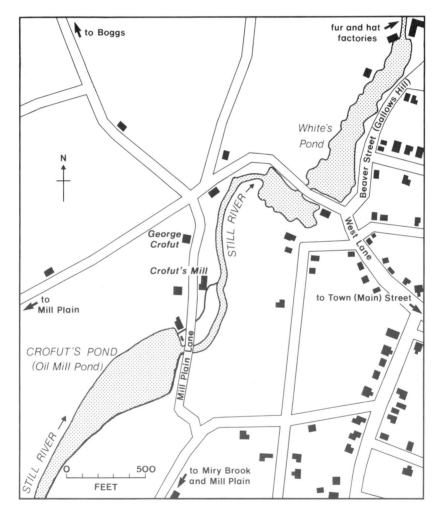

II. **CROFUT'S MILL AND MILL POND ON THE STILL RIVER, DANBURY, c.1850**

based on a mid-nineteenth century plan of Danbury, showing property ownership

2.

DANBURY IN 1835
in J.W. Barber, *Connecticut Historical Collections,* 1836
John Barber sketched this view from Deer Hill, looking east across the village and the
Vale of Danbury.

Annotated sketch of Barber's view

Danbury's religious life, and of its Town Meetings, for more than a century. After assembling in each other's homes for the first ten years, the tiny community had managed to complete its first church Meeting-House on Town Street in 1695.

In the second half of the eighteenth century, Episcopal, Sandemanian, Baptist, Methodist and Universalist churches were all established progressively in Danbury. Indeed, Danbury was one of only eight centres in New England (most of them in Connecticut) of the Sandemanian sect, formed in 1765 as an off-shoot of the old Scottish Presbyterian Church. George would have seen the grave of Robert Sandeman in Danbury's ancient Burial Ground when his father had first taken him to see the

GEORGE CROFUTT'S BOYHOOD HOME, MILL PLAIN LANE
The family cottage, built into the rock wall of the Still River Valley, stands close to the mill in Mill Plain Lane, now known as Oil Mill Road. Already old in Crofutt's day, the cottage is now one of the longest surviving homes in Danbury.

4.   PART OF CROFUT'S POND ON THE STILL RIVER, MILL PLAIN LANE

During the early nineteenth century, several mills and workshops using water power were located at this site with its dam, mill-race and mill-pond — the largest in Danbury. Crofut's Pond was also known as Oil Mill Pond (one mill produced linseed oil), and it became a favourite spot for fishing and swimming in summer and ice-skating in winter. Photographed here in 1909, the pond was drained in the early 1970s.

graves of members of the Crofut family also buried there. Looking down from Deer Hill he could pick out the cemetery set behind the Town Jail and the old Schoolhouse, and dating back to 1684 when some of Danbury's original pioneers had failed to survive their first winter and been laid to rest.

New England society was founded on both preacher and teacher, however. The region's earliest colonial law had its roots in the belief that all children must be able to read and understand the Scriptures and the laws on which their communities were founded, and that they should be brought up to follow some lawful calling or employment. Danburians had always heartily endorsed these principles, and the habits of hard work and perseverance which Crofutt absorbed as a child were to retain a strong influence on him for the rest of his life.

"In Connecticut," wrote Timothy Dwight, a former President of Yale, in 1821, "there is a school-house sufficiently near to every man's door to allow his children to go conveniently to school throughout most of the year . . . There is scarcely a child in this state who is not taught reading, writing, arithmetic and how to keep accounts. Poverty, here, has no efficacy towards excluding any one from this degree of education."[6] Children who lived some distance from the school were not usually sent until they were four; those who were closer often began at two, otherwise at three. Boys of eight, nine or ten would often have to interrupt their lessons to help on the farm or in the family business during the summer, Dwight reported. Girls most commonly left school between the ages of twelve and fourteen.

DANBURY MILL,
THE ORIGINAL SITE OF CROFUT'S GRIST AND SAW MILL BESIDE THE STILL RIVER

In 1882, Peter Robinson's extensive new fur-cutting and hat-felting factory, which still used water power for much of the year, replaced the earlier mills at Crofut's site and operated here until 1917. From 1920 until 1982, the premises were mainly used for storage by the American Hatters & Furriers Co., and finally as a furniture factory.

In 1983, however, the historic industrial use was changed with the conversion of the interior of this fine 101-year-old building into forty-one residential apartments. Seen here on Oil Mill Road, it is now known as Danbury Mill and is included in the National Register of Historic Places. The cast-iron water wheel is housed in a basement.

For older pupils, Danbury Academy had long represented one of the small town's greatest assets. Crofutt would have been among the many youngsters who benefitted from the endowment made by Comfort Starr in 1763 to maintain a school in the centre of town to provide "learned and skilful instruction in the various branches of Good Literature, and in the English, Greek and Latin languages, and in vulgar arithmetic." This was the school originally built on a patch of ground between the town jail and old burial ground — "constantly reminding scholars," in the words of one citizen, "of the uncertainties of life on the one hand and the certainty of death on the other." By Crofutt's time, the school had been enlarged and, as Danbury Academy, moved to a new site nearby on Town Street.

Crofutt's early years appear to have passed uneventfully enough amid the routine of Danbury's workaday existence. Aside from those along Town Street, small clusters of population could be found in various sections of the Still River valley, separated from each other by ponds, marsh or forest, or associated with one of the mills. Crofut's mill site was such a focus — to a small boy, a world-within-a-world. Along Mill Plain Lane were home, a few neighbouring cottages, the river, the dam, mills and mill-pond. Nearby was the Baptist Church and his first school on West Lane, in Danbury's Middle Center School District.[7] Together they provided the fabric of Crofutt's New England childhood.

Earning a Living in Danbury in the Early Nineteenth Century

Plans for the future had soon to be made, however, and no doubt George would have liked to avoid the disappointment he must have caused at home with the news that he did not want to work in the mill and take over the family business. George Crofut & Son, millers, would in due course refer to Crofutt's brother, not himself.

Crofutt had considered the problem of his future scores of times, trying to imagine life in the different occupations that Danbury had to offer. Changes had gradually crept up the valley from the Tidewater during the early 1800s, and those who could were diversifying their businesses; George's own father, for example, now ran a saw mill as well as a grist mill. Diversification in early nineteenth-century New England was often dramatic as merchants and traders from the Tidewater sought out those small waterfalls and dams inland which were capable of providing the power for new factories, and thus the opportunity to introduce new capital and machinery. Danbury was no exception. Crofut Snr.'s own expansion was relatively modest but Crofut's large mill-pond and mill-race attracted a cluster of other industries, since Crofut's great site advantage had always been that he was able to use water power for 8-9 months of the year, needing a steam engine for only 3 months during the worst of the winter.[8] By the 1830s-1840s, along with Crofut's flour, feed and saw mill, and Starr's linseed oil works, one of Danbury's famous fur and hat factories was located at the site, as well as a small furniture factory. The Starr family had other interests too, in tanneries, timber, planing mills, box-making and house-building.

A host of other small industries were to be found in Danbury over this period, taking advantage of the Still River's water power and local supplies of charcoal, and based in many cases on the extraordinarily wide range of skills developed over the years in an isolated, self-contained community. Some crafts failed to survive the competition of increased factory production and larger markets elsewhere. With the exception of hat-making, first formally recorded in 1780, Danbury's local market remained restricted, despite the efforts of local pedlars to sell small items outside the village. At peak, however, Danbury's manufactures had included woollen and linen cloth, shirts, boots and shoes, belts, suspenders, combs, wagons, harness, saddles and other leather goods, paint, paper, furniture, clocks, cutlery, axes and iron nails.

None of these occupations appealed to young George Crofutt apparently; neither did any aspect of the hat-making industry which by then dominated Danbury and offered more openings and apprenticeships than any of the town's other industries. Bonnet-making remained a small cottage industry, but hatting developed rapidly beyond that stage in Danbury after the American War of Independence. By the beginning of the nineteenth century, the village was producing about 20,000 hats a year in small workshops, and had become the single most important hat-manufacturing centre in the United States. Hats had put Danbury on the map, the only one of its many everyday wares for which the village found a substantial market outside the valley. Indeed, Danbury hats were soon being sold from New York City to Charleston, S.C.

In 1835, when Crofutt was eight years old, the art of making silk hats was introduced into Danbury and gave a further boost to an industry already working all hours to meet the demand for wool hats, and fur hats made from beaver, otter, mink, nutria, muskrat, rabbit and hare. After John Barber visited Danbury in 1835, he reported that 289 people were employed in hat-making in 24 workshops, and that between them they were producing 134,000 hats annually, valued at $402,000.[9] Production in the smaller neighbouring community of Bethel, still part of the Danbury township at that time, was almost as great. Many of the workshops at this period were still village kitchens, cellars and farm cottages; as Crofutt grew up he saw several of these scattered small businesses join forces and move to new premises along the banks of the Still River. Before long, large mills and factories rather than tree-fringed banks, marked the winding course of the river through the valley.

New patented inventions characterized this period of growth and experiment. Danbury prided itself on what traditional Yankee ingenuity

31

and know-how could achieve, and looked for ways to expand. Crofutt had always been fascinated to wander along the bank of the Still River and take a roundabout route into town past the mills and factories located on Beaver, River and Elm Streets. Some workshops specialized in sorting skins, furcutting, block-making, trimming, or making wooden cases (hat boxes). Henry Crofut made hats in a large factory in the centre of town; in smaller premises so did a number of other Crofut and Andrews kinsmen living three miles away in Bethel, where the hat trade continued to flourish until the 1850s. Other relatives in the Hull, Starr, Harris and Peck families also worked in the hatting trade, but George probably regarded work in any hat factory as boringly routine and often unhealthy. It was often dangerously so in fact, since many years were to pass before the danger of mercury poisoning from some of the hat-making processes was eliminated. The damage to the nervous system by mercurous nitrate often resulted in severe involuntary twitching movements in the face and body that gave rise to the phrase "mad as a hatter", introduced into the United States through Danbury in 1836.

Agriculture, including horse and cattle raising, was Danbury's oldest industry, but Crofutt lacked both the interest and the experience. Besides, the prospects were extremely poor. Agriculture in the Still River valley, as in many other parts of New England, had remained hard, back-breaking work for little reward. It was true that local outcrops of limestone in the Vale of Danbury produced pockets of more fertile soils among the widespread thin, acid soils derived from the granites, but heavy leaching, poor drainage and the short growing season remained severe limitations. Many nineteenth-century farmers would have found a seventeenth-century report on the Connecticut farming settlements as true as the day was written:

> "The country is mountainous, full of rocks, hills, swamps and vales. What was fit was taken up; what remains must be gained out of fire, by hard blows, and for small recompense." [10]

In the early 1800s, many New Englanders, Danburians among them, had given up the struggle and abandoned their farms. They had taken jobs in the local workshops, or moved down to the coast to find work in the larger mills, yards and factories on the Tidewater. Others for whom life on the land was the only life worth living looked instead for a better return for their labour, and went west to the rich farm lands of Ohio. [11]

Stagecoach to Norwalk:
Danbury's Isolation in the Canal and Railroad Age

For as long as he could remember, Crofutt had listened to his parents and others discussing Danbury's isolation, and the urgent need to improve transport links to the Tidewater. If the town was to grow and hold its own in the face of increasing competition, faster, smoother communication with the coast was vital. If Danbury could lay its hands on nothing better than the stagecoach, and an assortment of slow, heavy wagons lumbering along abominable roads, then the town faced ruin. Danbury provided a good illustration of the isolation that enveloped so many New England communities even a relatively short distance from the sea. Danbury had no navigable water to extend the lifeblood of the coastal economy inland.

Envious glances were cast at the two remarkable river navigation systems flanking the Danbury region — the Hudson River to the west and the Connecticut River to the east. But the Hudson's magnificent waterway was in a class of its own, and the extent of inland navigation on the Connecticut was unique in New England. While Hartford remained the busiest inland port, the construction by 1829 of a series of locks and relatively short canals around the Connecticut's major obstacles had opened the river to small vessels all the way from Long Island Sound to Barnet, Vermont, a distance of some 300 miles. Danbury derived no comfort from the fact that its own landlocked corner of Connecticut lay between the two longest navigable inland waterways in the northeast.

In 1830, as 'canal fever' spread across the States, Danbury mill- and factory-owners, supported by farmers and Westporters, increased their demands for a Westport-Danbury canal. Westport lay on the Tidewater and was already making plans to boost its small population of c. 1800, diversify its existing industries of carriage, cotton, and shoe manufacture, and achieve incorporation from Fairfield County by 1835. As well as being on the Tidewater, Westport was also located at the head of navigation on the Saugatuck River; sloops and schooners could reach Westport bridge, three miles inland from Long Island Sound. If a canal were to extend beyond this point and capture Danbury's trade, Westport would become competitive with Norwalk, a Goliath by comparison.

With enthusiam fired at both ends, the canal survey was urged forward in a mood of great optimism. The route selected began in the centre of Danbury, close to the junction of Elm and White Streets with Town Street. The reliable water supply of Neversink Pond [Map I], four miles north of the town and about twenty feet above canal level at Town Street, was to be the principal feeder for the northern section. From Danbury, the canal was to run south through Bethel and on to Redding. Here it was to swing southeastward, cross the ridge into the Saugatuck valley and continue to Westport.

The surveyors published their report but the project failed to attract enough financial backing. Investors were becoming increasingly wary of the rash of canal schemes that so many towns began putting forward after the spectacular success of the Erie Canal, opened in 1825. The north-flowing Still River was no help in this respect, Danburians reflected gloomily; who wanted to look northward when all the opportunities and the profits lay to the south?

To its dismay, Danbury discovered that the 30-mile canal to Westport was an extremely expensive proposition whichever way you looked at it. The Saugatuck River played a key role in the project since the surveyors had planned to use its small valley for nearly two-thirds of the canal's route. But the difference in levels between Danbury and the Tidewater was still nearly 400 feet and the Redding ridge added another 200 feet which would have to be negotiated by the narrow boats. Costly excavation through the granites and schists, and many locks, would be required. Besides all that, outsiders asked bluntly, where were you when you got there? Danbury's population was still little more than four thousand. By the mid-1830s, support was more readily found for canals which could help to open up the Midwest. Backers were not interested in pouring money up the narrow valleys into the New England interior.

After the failure of the Westport-Danbury canal project, Danburians tried again in 1835 to improve communication with the Tidewater by proposing the construction of a horse-drawn railroad from Danbury down to Norwalk, but nothing came of it. Next they championed the idea of a grand New York-Albany railroad which would pass through Danbury, but once again they were thwarted. The excellent steam navigation service on the Hudson River for 8-10 months of the year helped to postpone the need to complete a rail link between New York City and Albany (the Hudson River Railroad) until as late as October 1851.

As the years went by, Danbury had to make the best of what was available. Bridgeport on the Tidewater scooped the business of the upper Housatonic Valley while Danbury was still struggling to poke a railroad of its own down to the coast. In 1840, the opening of the Housatonic Railroad between Bridgeport and New Milford brought rail transport to Hawleyville, six miles northeast of Danbury. A stage line carried passengers the rest of the way. A year later, Danbury's postmaster decided he could offer a better service by avoiding the break in the journey; he expanded his mail operation and for a while introduced a stage which by-passed the railroad and went all the way to Bridgeport down the Housatonic Valley. Danbury applauded his enterprise and filled his coaches, much to the consternation of the railroad whose dangerous track and rolling stock were already driving enough passengers away. But the postmaster's venture was no more than a temporary challenge to the Housatonic line.

Danbury continued to complain that it was stuck in the stagecoach age. The arrival and departure of the stage might provide a spot of excitement for the youngsters on Town Street, Crofutt among them, but the business community bemoaned their lack of railroad facilities. What they wanted was the sight of a rail depot and freight yards, not a daily reminder of the limitations of horse-power. Transport costs had become a nightmare. Factory owners described themselves as backwoodsmen in every sense, since Danbury's local 'coalpits' were merely charcoal-burning hollows. Indeed, very little coal reached Danbury at all in the first half of the nineteenth century. The steam processes used so extensively in the hatting industry, for example, were forced to rely on charcoal, as the increasingly deforested slopes encircling the town clearly showed.

The town was hemmed in by rugged mountains whose constraints were not so much due to altitude (1000ft-1200ft) as to the obstacles they presented to east-west movement. Danbury was only five miles from the New York State line but its isolation from the lower Hudson Valley was intense. The journey entailed a difficult, cross-country wagon ride of at least ten hours to Sing-Sing in order to reach the nearest point on the Hudson River where vessels bound for New York could be boarded. This route had been opened during the War of 1812, but after that it attracted little traffic from Danbury.

Given the regional north-south grain of the landscape, Danbury's most direct route to the Tidewater remained that of the old Indian and pioneers' trail to Norwalk. New York City was normally reached by taking the stage or sleigh to Norwalk (6-8 hours), and then an overnight sloop along the Sound. The famous showman P. T. Barnum, who was born in Bethel, recalled Danbury's sense of isolation from New York City at this period — "to 'go to York' in those days was thought quite as much of as to go to Europe is now." [12] The Boston-New York stage passed through Norwalk on the busy coast road but it was usually full. Groups from Danbury found that they had to charter a special stagecoach in Norwalk if they wished to avoid the voyage to New York.

No one ever succeeded in making the regular journey by stage down the narrow valley to Norwalk anything more than a test of endurance. Only in summer or early fall was the route through the woods and beside the lakes pleasant enough to take people's minds off the length and discomfort of the journey. At best, the noon stage from Danbury was scheduled to arrive at Norwalk in the early evening, but the rough, twisting road through Bethel, Redding and Wilton was often deep in mud or slush, or flooded, or made treacherous by packed snow and ice. A Snow Warden and teams of oxen were sent out to help cut a way through deep drifts and roll out a smooth surface wide enough for coaches and wagons to get through, but sections of the valley were often completely cut off from the 'outside' during the winter. One of Danbury's flourishing industries was the making of sleigh-bells, at the Miry Brook foundry not far from Crofut's mill.

35

The Printer's Life Begins

The one place in Danbury with its window permanently open to the outside world, Crofutt discovered, was the local newspaper office on Town Street. Most likely he found himself spending more and more of his free time after school hanging round the printing office of the town's newest paper — the *Danbury Times*. Crofutt was fascinated by gadgets and machinery all his life, probably ever since his first glimpse of the great water-wheel at Crofut's mill. The sight now of a room half-filled by the heavy, wooden, Ben Franklin-style press, the neat cases of type, the seeming confusion surrounding the collection and layout of news and advertising copy, and not least the sheer pleasure and satisfaction derived from a well-designed, well-printed page — all this gave him a sense of purpose and excitement.

Danbury's first newspaper, the *Farmers' Journal*, had appeared in 1790, the *Republican Journal* in 1793. Later, the *New England Republican* (1804), the *Danbury Recorder* (1826), the *Connecticut Repository* (1832), the *Danbury Gazette* (1833), and the *Danbury Chronicle* (1836) were among those news-sheets that came and went over the years, merging with or replacing previous publications. Printers in Danbury, as elsewhere, had for generations turned their hands to the production of a small local newspaper in addition to printing the books, pamphlets, sermons, tracts and lectures for which there was such a steady demand.

The first issue of the *Danbury Times* appeared on 5th July 1837, shortly before George's tenth birthday, and it soon became Danbury's most successful newspaper. The four-page weekly was published by Edward Osborne whose skilful blend of local, national and international news, mixed with advertising and editorial comment, and spiced with letters, anecdotes, poetry and humour, proved to be a winner. At first, Crofutt would have helped with the tidying, the errands, the folding and stacking; the paper was printed one side at a time and folded by hand. Crofutt's subsequent apprenticeship to this world of newspaper printing and publishing laid the foundation of his future career. At last he had discovered what he wanted to do.

As an apprentice, George was able to continue to take advantage of Danbury's high regard for books and libraries, founded on the general belief that what little free time was available should be put to good use. Looking back on his boyhood at the start of the nineteenth century in neighbouring Ridgefield, Samuel Goodrich had similarly remembered with pride that while few among the population of 1200 or so subscribed to out-of-town newspapers, "We had a public library of some two hundred volumes." [13]

Danbury's first public library was established in 1770, free to all denominations. This was burned in 1792, a heavy blow to the community, however accustomed people had become over the years to watching workshops, dwellings, churches, inns, barns, stores, jail and schoolhouse go up in flames. Danburians quickly replaced the library as best they could, but by the 1830s they had decided that it needed enlarging, particularly to meet the needs of the town's new factory owners and artisans. In 1833, the local Mechanics' Library Association undertook to overhaul the stock and effectively start afresh:

"A meeting of some of the citizens of Danbury was held at the house of Isaac Ives on the 8th April 1833, to take measures to establish a library in this village . . . the committee resolved to solicit subscriptions for the purpose of purchasing and establishing a library for the use of the inhabitants of the town of Danbury forever."

The normal subscription was to be $2.00 but Article 7 of the Library's Constitution guaranteed that:

"Every apprentice between the ages of fourteen and twenty-one bringing from his employer a certificate of good character and guarantee for safe return of books shall be entitled to the use of books *free of charge*." [14]

Isaac Ives was in the hatting business and a deacon of the Congregational Church, and he moved the work of the committee along at a lively pace. In June 1833, members voted to attach a reading room to the library and, most importantly, to open it in the evenings from 6:30 - 9 o'clock so that people could read there, with warmth and light provided, after the day's work in the field or the factory. Eli Mygatt took charge of the Mechanics' Library and Reading Room in October 1834 and housed all the books and papers in part of his own home on South Town Street. For the rest of his life, nothing gave Mygatt greater satisfaction than his service to the community as Danbury's librarian and mentor.

Crofutt learned to appreciate the educational opportunities Danbury prized so highly, along with the values of self-reliance, hard work, Yankee enterprise, and patriotism. These were the values that shaped many a New England upbringing in many a similar small New England town. As it was, Crofutt came from Danbury and that was where he learned them. By the time he reached his late teens, however, Crofutt was anxious to widen his horizons, and ready to leave.

What settled the matter for an ambitious young man was probably the realization that there was no opening for him on the *Danbury Times*. When the founder, Edward Osborne, moved on to Poughkeepsie in 1845, he passed over the running of the newspaper to his two brothers, Harvey and Levi Osborne. Crofutt would have been left with the routine rather than the responsibility of compiling the paper.[15] It was clear that from now on his opportunities lay beyond the confines of Danbury, and that he must go out and find them. Thousands of others scattered among the small communities of the New England interior, in need of work, better prospects, and more elbow-room, were doing the same.

Danbury in the late 1840s was still without a railroad and many now despaired over the town's continued isolation from the Tidewater and, above all, from easy contact with New York City. Despite the importance of the hat trade, this industry like others was suffering more than ever from poor transport facilities, and thus the high costs of obtaining raw materials and moving finished products. Population growth remained limited, still fewer than 6,000. In 1844, the projected Hartford-New York railroad was routed to pass through Danbury and continue to New York City via White Plains, but once again, the proposal fell through. No railroad reached Danbury until March 1852 when the Danbury and Norwalk Railroad eventually made its way up the valley. By then, however, Crofutt had left his home town for good, to try his luck first of all in New York. The isolation of the New England interior left an indelible impression on him. It was here that Crofutt initially saw the need to improve accessibility, compete for routeways, and attract the railroad. He would find that the problems of the West were often to be the problems of the East writ large.

Crofutt abandoned Danbury, but not the lessons and attitudes he learned there, nor the deep appreciation of a loving, simple and secure home life. Nearly thirty years later, after receiving news of the death of his mother, Crofutt movingly recalled his early days and his old home:

> "Since we bade good-bye to father and mother, since the circle of loved ones has become a thing of the past, since we have said farewell to faces that no more will give back that accustomed look of love, since we have made new homes of our own, or wandered far in search of what we may — or more likely, may not — have found, there is no one spot on all the earth for which the heart finds itself yearning so frequently or so fondly.
>
> That home may have been of the rudest and roughest sort, but if it had a father and a mother, it was home . . . strong hands and warm hearts . . . your room under the roof . . . the uneventful life in the quiet village, with its scores of well-remembered neighbors, whose names are now recalled by headstones in the churchyard.
>
> Today you may have been so long away that it all seems ages ago. No matter, the recollection of father and mother, the soul of the home, fill the picture as your heart has kept it. There is still, and will remain while you live, the love and longing for the dear old spot, where the quiet days of careless joy ran away so soon." [16]

Agent and Publisher: Early Struggles in New York and Philadelphia

As soon as he arrived in New York City, Crofutt made his way into Lower Manhattan to look for work. By the 1840s, Printing House Square, close to City Hall, was already well established as the centre of New York's newspaper publishing and printing trade, and the newcomer from Danbury appears to have learned quickly how to survive there.

Reporters, printers and messengers darted about the Square, hurrying along Spruce, Nassau, Beekman and Ann Streets, or down Park Row and on to Broadway. Crofutt hurried with them, turning his hand from office and errand boy to any small clerking assignment that came his way. A chance remark made many years later suggests that he may have worked briefly at the *New-York Tribune*, which had been founded in April 1841 by the redoubtable Horace Greeley. If so, it was in some minor capacity as Crofutt is not mentioned in the paper's contemporary employment records.

As well as the newspaper offices, most of the major book and magazine publishers were also located close to Printing House Square, mainly on Broadway and Nassau. After innumerable enquiries in one office after another, and much legwork up and down steep flights of stairs, Crofutt at last found a job as a publisher's and bookseller's travelling agent. This involved going from town to town to distribute and promote the sales of the company's list of books, newspapers and magazines. An agent's life was precarious, he soon discovered, never dull, occasionally rewarding. It meant keeping a close eye on the competition, maintaining his existing outlets and ceaselessly searching for new ones in a market fiercely contested by the huge range of weekly and monthly publications.

Ho! For The Erie Canal!
Crofutt's First Western World

Crofutt's sales territory extended deep into the hinterland of New York City. In 1849 he went as far as Buffalo looking for business, travelling north up the Hudson to Albany and then heading west by stage to work his way through the towns strung out along the 230 miles of the Erie Canal between Schenectady and Rochester. He made several side-trips on the turnpikes from Utica and Syracuse, and then took a run through the Finger Lake villages. Beyond Rochester, however, Crofutt decided to continue his journey west on the Erie Canal whose route he had been following, between detours, ever since leaving Albany.

Buffalo was another ninety miles from Rochester — a potentially rich strip of territory for the book and magazine trade since the settlements along the western section of the Erie Canal were now among the fastest growing in the United States. Rochester itself was an eye-opener. Only a village before the Canal pumped life along the routeway, Rochester was a flourishing city of 36,000 when Crofutt arrived there in 1849. With a new annual record in 1847 of 8630 clearances on the Erie Canal, the city had far outstripped Syracuse (whose own population nevertheless was now 22,000, having doubled in a decade). Rochester's advantages stemmed from its combined role as a canal and a road junction, from its proximity to Lake Ontario transport, and from the plentiful water power provided by the Genesee Falls. The town had prospered with the early importance of the Genesee Valley's fertile wheat lands to the south, and from the new western territories and extended eastern markets made accessible by the Erie Canal. As a result, Rochester had become western New York State's major flour- and saw-milling centre.

Crofutt explored 'Flour City', admired the imposing new aqueduct completed in 1842 to carry two-way Erie Canal traffic over the Genesee, and then wandered around the extensive canal basins, quays, ware-houses and boat-yards. Rochester was the most important boat-building centre on the Erie Canal, a supremacy that had only recently begun to be challenged by Buffalo, where some of the Rochester builders were now expanding their operations. Seth C. Jones' yard, one of the largest, had been launching graceful packet-boats on to the Erie Canal ever since the late 1820s, and following the enlargement of the canal, Rochester's boat-yards had climbed out of the recession of 1840-3 and filled their order-books for new packets, freighters and scows.[1]

Crofutt bought a ticket on the Red Bird Line and boarded one of their newest packet-boats, the *Niagara*, for the journey west. It was his first trip on the Canal whose spectacular success he had so often heard being discussed during his boyhood with a mixture of envy and awe by the would-be canal promoters of Danbury. With a real sense of occasion, therefore, Crofutt began an unforgettable journey through the fields, farms and canal towns of western New York State.

The *Niagara* was the latest word in comfort. The packet had been built in Jones' yard in 1846, its sleek cedar hull extended to 100 feet to allow for a redesigned cabin interior. There were separate Ladies' and Gentlemen's Saloons, cushioned seats beside enlarged picture windows, elegant decoration and soft furnishing, dining tables set with fine china and silver plate, a bar and refreshment counter, smoking room, writing desk and library. The sleeping accommodation and washroom facilities, though still cramped, had been greatly improved so that passengers were now invited to travel in leisurely style by stepping aboard "one of the new floating palaces that surpass any thing ever put on the Canal." "Packet-boats are long drawing-rooms," wrote one visitor, "where the traveller dines, sleeps, reads, lolls, or looks out of the window … and all this without perceptible motion, jar, or smell of steam." [2]

There were no locks on the 62 miles between Rochester and Lockport, one of the two remarkably long 'Levels' on the Erie Canal. The packet glided gently along at 4 mph drawn by horses or mules plodding along the tow-path where teams were changed every 10 - 15 miles. The journey was slow but so much more comfortable than the crowded, bone-shaking ride endured on many a stagecoach. It was also an extremely cheap form of travel. Attempts at monopoly and price control among the various packet lines had always met with public protest; even a mid-1840s proposal to set passenger rates as low as 1½ cents per mile with board, and 1 cent without, were howled down and promptly undercut. As Buffalo's canal-boosting *Commercial Advertiser* observed in 1845:

> "The superior cheapness of the packets unquestionably is the principal inducement with some travelers to take that mode of conveyance; but so excellent are the accommodations now offered by the packets, and so infinitely more attractive are they to all who travel merely for pleasure, or who wish to travel in the greatest ease and security, they would do a good business were their prices as high as charged on the railroads. The boats that ply between this city and Rochester and Syracuse and Utica, are comfortable and roomy as the cabin of a steamboat … We can conceive of nothing more agreeable than floating tranquilly through beautiful country, such as the canal route has become, with ability to read, write, or talk as the inclination prompts, and with every thing at command that a good hotel can furnish." [3]

There was no shortage of diversion — conversation, music, or a game of cards could be exchanged for a turn along the upper deck, and a closer view of the canal traffic. Crofutt was seeing the Erie Canal at that significant point in its history when the east-bound cargoes of wheat, flour, cheese, meat, wool and lumber had for the first time surpassed the total volume of west-bound traffic from New York State — mainly emigrants, furniture, tools, and general merchandise. Seth Jones had recently launched a fleet of new giant freighters at Rochester, each with a capacity of 1000 barrels of flour or 4000 bushels of wheat; "the canal is alive … everything that will float is out and doing business."

As the journey proceeded, Crofutt observed repairs being made to bridges, banks and tow-paths, and scribbled away in his notebook on everyone and everything that caught his eye. The *Niagara* slipped through Spencerport, Brockport, Holley, Albion, Medina and Middleport, making its way between low gravel ridges and across the flats bordering Lake Ontario [Map III]. By the 1840s, the main flood of emigrants was sweeping straight through this region to the richer farm lands of the Midwest. Only the more isolated sections of western New York State retained a pioneering atmosphere with new clearances and new farms, although Crofutt sensed a frontier energy all along the waterway, and found that settlements on or close to the Canal were still expanding and diversifying. There was plenty of scope here he noted for an active travelling agent.

Dan Bromley: the "prince of captains" on the Erie Canal

The Red Bird Line on which Crofutt was travelling had continued to fight tooth and nail against its rivals on both the canal and the railroad for the Schenectady-Buffalo traffic; in this fight the popularity of the packet captains often played a decisive role. The most famous of them all was Captain Dan Bromley, and Crofutt soon discovered that as a passenger on the *Niagara*, he had the good fortune to be under the command of "the prince of captains," and King of the Erie Canal. [4]

Most of Daniel H. Bromley's life had been spent moving the world and its goods between Albany and Buffalo. He was born in 1810 at New Haven, Oswego County, N.Y., a tiny, isolated hamlet founded in 1798 on the shore of Lake Ontario during the post-Revolutionary settlement boom in upstate New York. The future 'King of the Erie Canal' was the youngest of four brothers — Hiram, Drayton, Pliny and Daniel, all of whom left New Haven as soon as possible to find work in a less remote corner of the State. Hiram established one of the leading forwarding agencies in Albany, and Daniel began as one of his assistants. Soon after the opening of the Erie Canal, Daniel's skills and boundless self-confidence persuaded a local owner to put him in charge of one of the line packets carrying freight and a few passengers. Still only 16 years of age, his captain's life had begun.

Captain Dan was extraordinarily popular. His whereabouts on the Canal were invariably reported by the local press. He commanded respect, settled disputes, and won people's affection wherever he went. The good captain had the gift of making passengers feel that while each might board his boat as a stranger, they all left him as a friend. "Captain Dan had no faculty for making enemies," recalled one old-timer; "he was forthright but never offensive, a truly noble-hearted character of sterling integrity and generosity who grew in esteem the better he became known. As a go-ahead businessman he had few compeers." [5]

ROCHESTER

AND

ALBANY.

Red Bird Line of Packets,

In connection with Rail Road from Niagara Falls to Lockport.

1843.  1843.

12 hours ahead of the Lake Ontario Route!

The Cars leave the Falls every day at 2 o'clock, P. M. for Lockport, where passengers will take one of the following new

Packet Boats 100 Feet Long.

THE EMPIRE!

Capt. D. H. Bromley,

THE ROCHESTER

Capt. J. H. Warren,

and arrive in Rochester the next morning at 6 o'clock, and can take the 8 o'clock train of Cars or Packet Boats for Syracuse and Albany, and arrive in Albany the same night.

☞ Passengers by this route will pass through a delightful country, and will have an opportunity of viewing Queenston Heights, Brock's Monument, the Tuscarora Indian Village, the combined Locks at Lockport, 3 hours at Rochester, and pass through the delightful country from Rochester to Utica by daylight.

N. B.---These two new Packets are 100 feet long, and are built on an entire new plan, with

Ladies' & Gentlemen's Saloons,

and with Ventilators in the decks, and for room and accommodations for sleeping they surpass any thing ever put on the Canal.

For Passage apply at Railroad and Packet Office, Niagara Falls.

T. CLARK, ⎰ Agents
J. J. STATIA, ⎱

September. 1843.

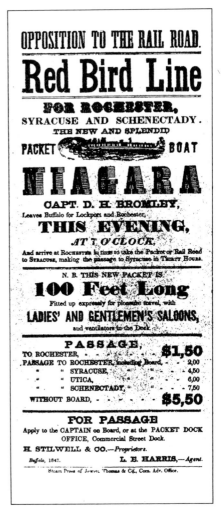

1843

1847

6.

PACKET-BOAT SERVICE ON THE ERIE CANAL

In the fight for business on the canal, broadsides for the Red Bird Line's packets gave prominence to the captain in charge, especially when this was the popular 'King of the Erie Canal', Capt. Dan Bromley.

Dan Bromley's word was law in the Rochester boat-yards. He had run up his personal pennant and taken command of the *Empire* in 1843. In 1846, an even more splendid passenger vessel, the *Niagara*, was built for him in order to boost canal traffic and compete with the railroad:

"A magnificent new packet boat, 100 feet in length, is now on the stocks in Jones' Boat Yard," Rochester's *Daily Democrat* reported. "The boat is being built for Dan Bromley, the Admiral of all Packet Captains, and the Prince of good fellows. The boat will be launched in a few days, and is designed as an Opposition Packet between this city and Buffalo. She will be furnished upon a scale of unequalled magnificence, and cannot fail to become as popular as her commander, for what he doesn't know about accommodating the traveling public isn't worth learning." [6]

The *Niagara* was finished in time to catch the end of the 1846 season before going into winter quarters in Rochester in November and resuming operations the following spring.

In later years, when traffic on the Erie Canal was being lost to the railroads, Captain Dan was not one to wallow in nostalgia. He gave up the packet-boats and worked as a special conductor on the Buffalo & Niagara Falls Rail Road before buying and managing with great success the Clifton House Hotel at Niagara Falls. Eventually, he returned to Rochester and went into partnership with his brother Pliny, running the Osborn House and turning it into one of the most popular and profitable hotels in the region.

Crofutt appears to have met Dan Bromley only once but he never forgot him, nor the immense amount he learned from him about the region during the trip. He kept track of his old acquaintance and years later, shortly before Dan's death in 1876, Crofutt remembered old times as he sped west by rail on the Chicago express in December 1873: "I passed through this country in 1849 with prince of captains, Dan Bromley, ... and should have been glad to grasp him by the hand once more." [7]

"Don't Miss Niagara Falls!"
The Old Strap Railroad From Lockport

Excitement mounted aboard the *Niagara* as it approached Lockport, a town of over 12,000 people that owed its existence to the Erie Canal. At this point, the Erie Canal had been cut through the Niagara Escarpment in a straight, 7-mile trough, 2 miles of it through solid rock. The Lockport 'fives' or 'combines' were five pairs of locks which carried boats up and down the 66-foot rise in the Canal. Completed in 1825, and improved in the 1840s, this double staircase of locks represented the single most spectacular achievement by the Erie Canal's engineers anywhere between Albany and Buffalo. The Lockport 'fives' were also the most frequently pictured feature of the Canal, and everyone was on the look-out for the famous 'water staircase' at the end of the long, level run from Rochester.

Niagara Falls was already the most famous scenic attraction in the New World, the awe-inspiring climax to the travels of many American and European tourists. Business passengers also, travelling on the packet-boats, were encouraged to make a short side-trip by rail between Niagara Falls and Lockport while they had the chance, before proceeding to their destinations. Crofutt and several others on the *Niagara* had decided to do this. Some of the passengers had bought copies of *Johnson's New Map of Niagara Falls and River* published earlier that year in Lower Manhattan's Vesey Street, close to Crofutt's agency offices on Broadway and Printing House Square. The map with surrounding text was a veritable mine of

THE 'FIVES' OR COMBINED LOCKS ON THE ERIE CANAL AT LOCKPORT,
showing the improvements made in the 1840s

condensed information and several on board were able to study the details as the *Niagara* glided towards Lockport. Johnson noted that by 1849 "30,000 from different parts of the globe annually visit the mighty cataract — Nature's masterpiece." With the thrill of anticipation, Crofutt and his fellow excursionists prepared to follow suit.

After disembarking at Lockport, Crofutt spent some time strolling round the town, looking at the shops and businesses, and noting down a few useful names and addresses. He then made his way back to the Canal and climbed the steps between the locks to get a closer look at their construction. The new work on the Lockport 'fives' had cost $600,000. Brightly lit at night, the series of stairways, platforms and iron railings were an impressive sight — "like the ascent to a gigantic temple," an earlier visitor had reported. Finally, Crofutt walked back to the Eagle, which was conveniently located beside the Canal, and linked to it by a covered, illuminated flight of steps between the landing stage and the hotel entrance. After a meal and some conversation with manager Nichols, Crofutt turned in for the night.

Next morning, the group bound for Niagara Falls had an early breakfast before walking over to the Lockport & Niagara Falls Rail Road depot at Chapel and Market Streets, where a small antiquated engine with one car was trying to get up steam. Passengers were informed that there would be a delay, and Crofutt passed the time poking around the depot, the repair sheds and the small hand-operated turntable at the end of the single track. Eventually, the party climbed aboard, already wondering whether they would not have been wiser to take the stage. It was too late now. The tiny train crawled up the steep track in the middle of Market Street, crossed the Erie Canal, and proceeded slowly through the streets of Lockport until it reached open country.

"What a rickety little railroad!" Crofutt recorded. "The road is laid with wooden stringers on which is spiked a flat iron rail about the width of a wagon wheel." The Lockport & Niagara Falls Rail Road was indeed an old strap railroad, one of ten independent railroads that since 1847 had made it possible, if not easy, to do almost the whole journey from Albany to Buffalo by train. The Lockport & Niagara Falls Rail Road had begun as a speculative venture by a few Lockport businessmen in 1833 but it never attracted sufficient funds to put it on a sound footing. After a charter was secured in 1834, there was endless debate over the route and the financing. Appeals to John Jacob Astor (for a loan of $50,000) and to others who had invested in the building of the Erie Canal were unsuccessful; Lockport's dream railroad attracted little interest outside its own remote corner of New York State.

Money was scraped together from local farmers and tradesmen in the villages of Lockport and Niagara Falls, and work began in 1835. "We

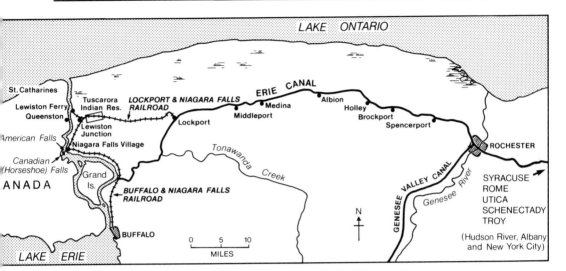

CROFUTT'S ROUTE THROUGH WESTERN NEW YORK STATE IN 1849
ERIE CANAL: WESTERN DIVISION
(based on a map by J.B. Stillson, Divisional Engineer, New York, 1851)
AND
LOCKPORT & NIAGARA FALLS STRAP RAILROAD (1837-51)

laid 24 miles of crooked wooden track," recalled the foreman, Stephen
Sult of Lockport. "There were 300 Canadian, Scotch and Irish workmen
but it took more than two years to finish." This was because there were
scarcely ever more than a handful of men working at any one time.
Horse-drawn service began in 1837 and shortly afterwards, small, wood-
burning, steam locomotives were introduced, but they were inefficient
and a perpetual nuisance to those trying to coax them into life.

The railroad became the butt for much local ridicule. Derailments
were common but rarely dangerous, given the slow speed of the outfit.

"One time," Stephen Sult recalled with a chuckle, "we dumped out the
President of United States. It was sometime along in '37 or '38 that Martin
Van Buren came up on the packet on his way to Niagara Falls, taking the
train at Lockport ... A spread rail ditched the train and the car tumbled
over on its side and the passengers were pitched together in a heap. The
train was going so slow that nobody was hurt. The President crawled out
without a scratch, and didn't look as if he was mad any. He helped tip the
car back, climbed in, and on they went just as if nothing had happened."

"Another time, Mrs. Storrs of Lockport said she'd bet she could walk from
Lockport to Niagara Falls and get there ahead of the train if they'd give her
an hour's start. Mrs. Storrs was pretty spry and a good walker, but the train
folks was kind o' surprised when they got to the end of the 24-mile run and
see her sittin' on the hotel steps waitin' as cool as a cucumber!"

Repairs were rudimentary. "When the track sunk and the strap rails
sagged," Stephen Sult went on, "all you had to do was to pull up the tie and

47

stick under it some clay or mud or anything there was handy . . . Those old rails made us a good deal of trouble. They were forever getting loose at the ends and running up over the car wheels. I remember seeing a passenger considerable surprised once by having the end of a rail come up through the floor of the car and knock off his hat! The engine used to run out of fuel sometimes, but that wasn't anything. All the fireman had to do was to stop and take a few rails from a farm fence." [8]

By the time Crofutt's party ventured on to the line in 1849, Lockport's strap railroad had gone from bad to worse. "The rolling stock was so primitive and delapidated" Crofutt recalled with amusement, "that even on the gentlest rise, all the passengers were told to get out of the car and 'give a hand over the grade.' "

The passengers clung on as the train lurched slowly towards Lewiston Junction, where a horse railroad branched off for Lewiston's steam ferry services to St. Catharines and Hamilton, Ontario. Before reaching the Junction, the Lockport Rail Road ran through the Tuscarora

8.   VIEWING THE AMERICAN FALLS AT NIAGARA IN 1848
(from Table Rock)
'Drawn from nature' by Aug. Köllner; Lith. by Deroy, printed by Cattier

Indian Reservation where, in the early days of the L. & N.F.R.R., groups of Indians amused themselves by riding up alongside the train on their ponies and then overtaking it with derisive whoops. But this bit of excitement had long since palled. The railroad lost money rapidly during the late 1840s and in August 1851, just two years after Crofutt's trip, the L. & N.F.R.R. ceased operation and the track was removed. In 1853, the New York Central Railroad reorganized the small separate rail systems to Buffalo and beyond, but most of Lockport's strap railroad was off the main route and its days were over. Farmers bought some of the small wayside stations for storage or accommodation and ploughed the rest into memory.

Crofutt was not surprised to read later of the closure. Lockport's reaction was more positive — the town was by then heartily sick of the noise, the sparks and the inconvenience of the railroad that wobbled along their main street. Shopkeepers were thankful to be rid of it, complaining that they lost business because horses were frightened by the general commotion and customers avoided the area. The train's final journey down Market Street was celebrated by bonfires and cheering crowds!

The whole journey west of Rochester had been a revelation. It was punctuated by the superb natural wonder of Niagara Falls but for Crofutt the route itself had provided an object lesson in the close relationship of westward expansion, transport development and national growth. It was his first experience of a western world, a series of first-hand impressions that for the time being were stored away. In 1849, the young man from Danbury did not go west; he did not, for example, join the crowds of 'forty-niners' flocking to California. He remained in the eastern States and appears to have continued to work as a local and travelling agent for a number of New York publishing houses.

Off to Philadelphia

Early in 1854, Crofutt arrived in Philadelphia by stage and took a room close to the terminus at the White Bear, a small tavern near the corner of Race and N. Fourth Streets. By that time, Race had become the common name for the old Sassafras Street, and its hectically busy section between Third and Fourth was Philadelphia's main arrival and departure point for stage lines serving all the major centres in Pennsylvania and the East. The White Swan was the most popular hotel on Race as it was next door to the stage-line office, just above Third. But the Swan was often full and Crofutt found the White Bear's cheaper accommodation, just a few doors away, a convenient lodging while he explored the area.

Crofutt's main commission at this time was the sale of a New York publication called *The United States Journal of Mechanics, Agriculture,*

Literature and Amusement, which had been started in July 1849 by the printer and publisher Jesse Milton Emerson. The distribution methods were typical of the period. Emerson's aim was to recruit an expanding network of agents, ideally to have a local agent or correspondent based at every post office. Here, lists of subscribers were kept up to date and the bundles of printed matter received. The agent's job was to serve the existing readership, drum up new business, chivvy the delinquent subscribers, and not least, to send regular reports to the publisher about the locality and its reading tastes. In addition, the agent had to organize display material, distribute circulars advertising the publisher's stocks of new books and special offers, and collect and forward orders. It was also the agent's job to deliver the latest issues of his publications promptly to the local newspapers and to make sure that the delivery was reported, if possible with some favourable comment about the contents.

Book sales were a vital part of the business. Emerson's complete book list, free on request to *Journal* readers, contained over one thousand titles ranging through histories, the classics, European and American novels, wild life studies, adventure stories, and books on favourite pastimes and home improvement. Special offers of a $1.00- or a 50-cent steel-plate engraving, a fountain pen, or small piece of jewellery, often gold- or silver-plated, were available to every *Journal* subscriber or book purchaser. Studs, pins, fob chains, watches, sleeve buttons, rings, bracelets, brooches and ear-drops were all popular items on Emerson's special offer. Gifts, plus commission, were the agent's means of livelihood as he struggled to extend his list of subscribers amid the increasingly cut-throat competition. Like his fellow correspondents across the country, Crofutt was reminded by the publisher that since the goods were provided without any effort on his part, "an enterprising and energetic agent finds a business established for him." Indeed, Emerson advertised for agents under the headline "A Money-Making Business" in which it was claimed an agent could reasonably expect to earn at least $1200 for himself annually. Certainly nothing less than tireless enterprise and energy could achieve success in a market so ceaselessly fought over by the great publishing houses of Boston, Philadelphia and New York. Among the giants, the small firms found a niche or were crushed out of existence.

Individual agents often represented a number of different publishing houses simultaneously, either by arrangement between the publishers themselves or through personal initiative. Large New York publishers and booksellers like Appleton, Wiley, and Putnam, all on Broadway, were continually advertising for local and travelling agents. The rivalry between the Boston, Philadelphia and New York companies grew more intense. Boston and Philadelphia had been early leaders in the printing and publishing field, but since the late 1820s, New York City had challenged both of them ever more successfully for that leadership. This was apparent both in book and magazine publishing in the United States. By 1850, New York's aggregate annual circulation of periodicals was 50 per cent higher than that of either Philadelphia or Boston, and was soon to be nearly three times greater than Philadelphia's alone, its nearest rival.

A few months after Crofutt's arrival in Philadelphia, Jesse Emerson had expanded his activities in Lower Manhattan by forming a new organization with John Emerson and a group of fellow journalists — J.M. Emerson & Co., at 69 Gold Street. In August 1854, the company was responsible for publishing three periodicals: the existing *United States Journal*, the new *United States Magazine* which had been launched three months earlier as a dollar (per annum) monthly on May 15th, and third, for good measure, the *United States Weekly Journal*, which reprinted selections from the other two.

The *United States Magazine* was the fifth publication since 1779 to bear this name. The experienced Seba Smith was made editor of both the *Journal* and the *Magazine*, whose full title, *The United States Magazine of Science, Art, Manufactures, Agriculture, Commerce and Trade* reflected the popular eclectic approach. Seba Smith had begun life as an editor in Portland, Maine back in 1820, and in 1829 had founded Maine's first daily newspaper. [9] His versatility and talent for humour and political satire did much to establish the reputation of the *United States Magazine*. As well as the topics featured in the sub-title, biography, travel, national and international news also received good coverage, while the whole was brightened by large woodcuts printed on coloured stock. Elizabeth Oaks Smith, wife of the editor and well known as a poet, lecturer and critic, became a frequent contributor. Crofutt found the monthly magazine well received; "published in New York" reported Philadelphia's *Sunday Dispatch*, "the *United States Magazine* is handsomely illustrated and contains choice reading matter." For the variety and quality of its content, Emerson's new venture was considered a strong entry into an already crowded field.

Crofutt's arrival in Philadelphia as an Emerson agent had coincided with a crucial period in the city's history, since 1854 was also the year of consolidation. Philadelphia's population was then nearly half-a-million. Consolidation of the old city with its surrounding sprawl of districts, boroughs, and townships was designed to link the mercantile core to the burgeoning suburbs, and thus eliminate restrictive jurisdictional barriers. Above all, in the bitter competition between the eastern seaboard cities, Philadelphia was determined to hold on to its traditional key position in the country's urban, industrial and political hierarchy. Boston continued to fight in its own corner. Competition from Baltimore, particularly for rail routes to Pittsburgh and beyond, was vigorous but manageable. The small, specialized City of Washington, D.C. could be discounted, but New York City could not. It challenged Philadelphia ever more successfully as the financial capital of the United States, as the major port on the Atlantic seaboard, and with its superb routeway through the Appalachian system, New York also challenged Philadelphia for control of the expanding trade with the West.

Philadelphia's population more than doubled between 1840 and 1860, from 258,000 to 566,000, largely as a result of massive Irish immigration following the potato famine of 1845-8, and the flow of central and east European refugees after the political uprisings of 1848-9. The huge, sudden influx of unskilled Irish labour in particular led to sharp cultural conflict, appalling slum conditions, and political and religious clashes,

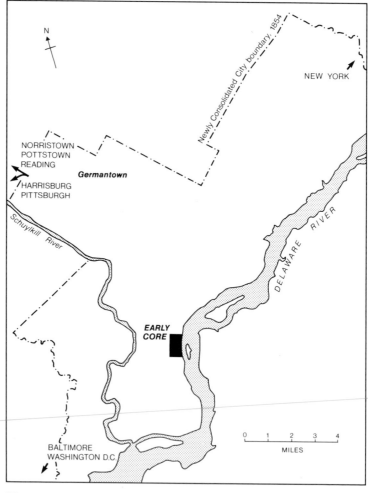

IV.

PHILADELPHIA

The expanded city boundary, 1854

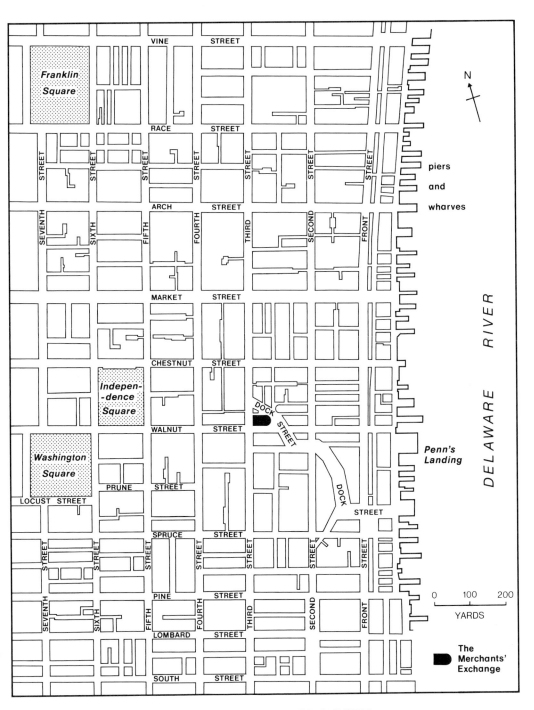

V. **PHILADELPHIA'S EARLY CORE**

The core remained the city's main business and commercial district in the late 1850s.

together with unprecedented waves of rioting and crime whose violence had rocked Philadelphia in the 1840s and early 1850s. Struggling to adjust to these new internal threats to its society, to rapidly changing manufacturing and transport technologies, as well as to external challenges, Philadelphia had to come to regard the consolidation of city and county in 1854 as the basis of recovery, and even as its strongest single weapon in the fight to reassert Philadelphia's authority and influence in the country as a whole.

Up to the Civil War, however, despite suburban expansion, many craftsmen and artisans still lived and worked in the heart of the city — the city of William Penn and Benjamin Franklin. Mechanics and merchants crowded the streets of the old mercantile core, the rectangle little more than half-a-square mile between the Delaware River and 7th Street, Vine and South. Crofutt soon found more permanent lodging at 12 Prune Street, as the extension of Locust was then known. Prune Street was on the "right side" (i.e. the south side) of Market Street, which was an important functional divide in the city's business district. Prune was also much closer than Race to Philadelphia's central publishing quarter with its important concentration of printers, lithographers, artists, engravers, newspaper offices and advertising agencies. Philadelphia was a pioneer in all these fields, not least in advertising. In 1841, Volney Palmer, calling himself an advertising broker, had started on Third Street what is regarded as the first advertising agency in the United States. In 1850 he expanded the business and opened branches of his new American Advertising Agency in Philadelphia, Boston and New York.

By September 1855, however, Crofutt was facing new problems. The Emerson Company's agency was transferred to A. Winch, a bookseller at 116 Chestnut, who was already handling the distribution of several other magazines. Bookstores in established centres like Philadelphia were now increasingly responsible for maintaining subscription lists, and for organizing the circulation and advertising of books, magazines and periodicals. Certain bookshops in Philadelphia had also become popular meeting places for discussion of the contents of the various publications, a club-like atmosphere created by the provision of comfortable seating grouped appropriately in the quiet recesses at the back of the shop.

In 1854, G.G. Evans' magnificent bookstore at Chestnut and Fifth expanded another side of the business, Gift Book sales, which were enormously popular in Philadelphia in the late 1840s and 1850s. Gift Books were richly decorated with ornate bindings, fancy page borders, ribbon pulls, and special plates, and were presented as "personal tokens, souvenirs, mementos, keepsakes, and forget-me-nots." [10]

But G.G. Evans' was a gift bookstore in another sense also; gifts were offered with each book sold at retail price, and more were available to

9. INTERIOR VIEW OF G.G. EVANS' GIFT BOOK STORE, PHILADELPHIA, IN THE 1850s

10.   PART OF G.G. EVANS' PACKING-ROOM

book club organizers. Evans' emporium was thus typical of the new trends in the agency, advertising, and mail-order business. A visitor invited to tour the store marvelled at

> "the piles of letters and dollars received daily with orders from a simple volume to a private library; . . . a single day's business sometimes amounts to over three thousand books, nearly one million volumes per year, besides a large jobbing city trade . . .

> Many orders from ten to one hundred dollars are from clubs in different parts of the country. These clubs are formed by individuals in their own neighborhoods, and it is a certain way of getting a library of books for nothing, besides selling the gifts which accompany the premium books . . . One safe is crammed with jewellery and gold watches ready for despatch!" [11]

Faced with this trend in the larger towns and cities for store-based book and magazine distribution, the free-lance travelling or local agent now found his energies better directed towards servicing the smaller, more scattered communities both in the east and west of the United States.

The Fight for Circulation in the 'Golden Age' of Magazines

Crofutt had to decide whether or not to move on. He liked Philadelphia; despite the fierce competition in the publishing business, indeed largely because of it, he regarded the city as the most favourable environment in which to branch out on his own. The 1830s and 1840s had been decades of massive expansion. Quite apart from newspaper and book publishing, American magazines had increased from ninety or so in 1825 to nearly seven hundred in 1850. Few magazines survived for long, however; the average life was about two years so that probably four or five thousand had been launched during this period:

> "These United States are fertile in most things," wrote the *New-York Mirror* during this 'golden age' of development, "but in periodicals they are extremely luxuriant. They spring up as fast as mushrooms, in every corner, and like all rapid vegetation, bear the seeds of early decay within them . . . They put forth their young green leaves in the shape of promises and prospectuses, blossom through a few numbers and then comes a frost, a killing frost, in the form of bills due and debts unpaid. This is the fate of hundreds — but hundreds more are found to supply their place, to tread in their steps and share their destiny . . . All the failures are no warning. Every spring a new generation arises — with new hopes, new plans, and new titles." [12]

By 1855, Philadelphia alone was publishing ten daily newspapers, thirty weeklies and eighteen periodicals, among them some of the most successful in the country. The *Saturday Evening Post* led Philadelphia's weeklies, but it was Philadelphia's periodicals which had shown the most startling expansion, doubling in number between 1852 and 1853. The most famous monthly magazines were *Graham's, Godey's, Peterson's* and *Arthur's* — household names across the United States. George R. Graham had founded his magazine in 1840 and quickly built an unrivalled pioneering reputation by his brilliant handling of essays, short stories, poetry, biography, reviews, travel and fashion. Excellent original engravings and woodcuts, along with contributors such as Poe, Longfellow, Lowell, Bryant, Cooper, Dana, Holmes and Willis, pushed *Graham's* circulation to more than 60,000 by 1844. Louis Godey and Sarah J. Hale steadily increased the circulation of *Godey's Lady's Book* from 70,000 at the end of 1850 to a high point of 150,000 by 1860. *Peterson's Magazine* gained an even wider circulation, while the accomplished Timothy S. Arthur and Virginia Townsend carved out their own faithful market of up to 30,000 with *Arthur's Home Magazine*.

The competition among these and other Philadelphia 'giants' in the mid-1850s was intensified by the out-of-town publications such as *The Knickerbocker* of New York, the *New York Ledger*, Boston's *North American Review* and *Ballou's Pictorial*, and above all, *Harper's New Monthly Magazine*, which had such an immediate and profound effect on the content of popular American magazines after its first appearance in June 1850 in New York.

Seba Smith had candidly acknowledged the stiff competition faced by the *United States Magazine* at its launching in May 1854:

> "Among more than sixty book and magazine publishers in New York City, *Harper's* is well out in front. They have the advantage of having their own type-setting, stereotyping, presswork and binding, all done on their own premises, which are compact though extensive, and employ 500-600 people." *Harper's* had rebuilt and modernized after a major fire in December 1853; "their great river of operations flows through the channel they have opened for themselves in that spacious building on Beekman Street."
>
> "*Appleton's* is next in volume of business," Smith continued. "Like *Harper's*, the firm (founded by their father Daniel) now consists of four brothers and employs about 500 ... They have a magnificent new bookstore on Broadway, and nearly one million dollars invested in the business, about the same figure as their annual sales ... George Putnam's is not so large *but*," Seba Smith added the compensating factor, "*Putnam* publishes Washington Irving." [13]

As well as these domestic products, all the prominent British periodicals such as *Blackwood's*, the *Edinburgh Review*, and the *Quarterly* were also reprinted in the U.S.A., mainly in New York; some 20,000 copies of *The Illustrated London News*, for example, about 10 per cent of its total circulation, were sold in the States.

Amid this welter of publication, Crofutt, like so many others, worked on the principle that there was always room for one more. As well as transferring his agency for the *United States Journal* and the *United States Magazine*, Crofutt also gave up responsibility for handling the other out-of-town publications on Emerson's exchange list — *Harper's New Monthly*, the '*Knick*', *Littell's Living Age* (a weekly published in Boston), and the reprinted *Blackwood's Magazine*. That done, Crofutt looked for a central location in the heart of Philadelphia's printing and publishing area. He moved from Prune Street to 73 South Fourth Street above Walnut, but soon found that he needed an office even closer to the heart of the business district. Dock Street at Third was to provide the answer.

Life in Dock Street in the Mid-1850s:
Hard Lessons for a New Publisher

Dock Street followed the curving line of the old Dock Creek which had originally flowed into the Delaware River close to Penn's Landing. Penn had regarded Dock Creek as a ready-made canal into the heart of the city, and at first, sloops had regularly unloaded cargo as far upstream as Third. As the creek became more sluggish and polluted, however, plans were authorized in 1765 to cover it and use the extra space for a street market. In the event, the scheme was delayed until after the War of Independence. In 1785, Dock Creek was arched over as a sewer and a new, curving Dock Street introduced into Philadelphia's classic checkerboard pattern, the first of its kind in the United States. The curved street was a striking innovation in the city of straight lines. As one irreverent Bostonian put it: "The streets are so regular that Bostonians long to give Philadelphia a kick which shall disarrange the buildings and make the streets run nowhere, and give the city a home-look."

Land use along Dock Street became highly specialized. The city's fish market and rows of food stalls continued to be found in the lower section, close to the Delaware River and the quays. So too were sail- and rope-makers, tobacco warehouses, flour and saw mills, and other stores. The top end of Dock Street, however, opening on to Third between Walnut and Chestnut became the great merchants' quarter, the hub of Philadelphia's business life. The corner was dominated by the imposing Merchants' Exchange whose marble stairways and Corinthian columns reflected the popular neo-classical designs of William Strickland, the Philadelphia architect who had already achieved a national reputation. Built between 1834 and 1838, the Exchange's ground floor housed the Post Office, two insurance companies, and the Merchants' Coffee House. Commercial Reading Rooms, the offices of the Board of Trade and of the Board of Brokers, and several general meeting rooms were all located in the Rotunda above.

In front of the Exchange, the widened portion of Dock Street became the central terminus for Philadelphia's many omnibus lines; it was also the busiest of the city's three authorized coach and hack stands, serving the business and commercial district. Within a small radius lay the principal banks, wholesale establishments, newspaper offices, printers and publishers, and many hotels, shops and restaurants located along Third and Fourth Streets, Walnut and Chestnut. A distinctive feature of the Dock Street traffic were the railroad wagons rumbling up and down the centre of the street from the local freight yards. Philadelphia's City Railroad had opened between 1833 and 1838, and one of its three lines ran between East Market Street and the Delaware River via Third and Dock. Concern about the dangers of fast trains and fire hazards in the city's congested central area had quickly led to the banning of steam locomotives within the old city limits and to the requirement by city ordinance that animal power be used instead.

Crofutt plunged into the heart of this action, irresistibly drawn to the variety of business around the Exchange and to the opportunities for personal contacts and trade recommendation. Crofutt's lodgings at 73 South Fourth Street had been owned by two brothers, Charles and William Lay, who made printing inks and kept an office on the ground floor. John R. Campbell, who, in the early 1850s, ran his own small printing business at Vaughn and Locust, also lodged there. By 1855, the Lay brothers found that business was booming. They were now one of Philadelphia's five major manufacturers of printing inks and, like Crofutt, were on the look-out for a more central office site.

Towards the end of the year, Charles and William Lay, John Campbell and George Crofutt all left 73 South Fourth and moved to 83 Dock Street, two doors below Third, opposite the Merchants' Exchange. The building was small, wedged in between taller property, with its three floors and an attic running back only a short distance from the street. But it was sufficient for their needs and although the premises were cramped, the location was excellent. No. 83 had been occupied successively by a number of small Philadelphia newspapers including the penny-daily *Native Eagle and Advocate*, and the weekly *Christian Chronicle*. Between 1851 and 1853, the *Sunday Dispatch* had occupied the site until, like the *Christian Chronicle*, it needed to move to roomier accommodation.

Shortly before Crofutt and the others arrived at No. 83, the Post Office had also moved from the Exchange Building; the demand for space had forced it to abandon the ground floor of the Merchants' Exchange in 1854-5, and cross Dock Street to new premises three doors below Third. It was now actually next door to No. 83, and Crofutt considered he had found the ideal location. With the Lay brothers and Campbell working below, Crofutt rented a room at the top of the house, cleared a desk and, at the age of twenty-eight installed himself as proprietor and advertising agent of three new publications.

11.   THE PHILADELPHIA MERCHANTS' EXCHANGE AT DOCK STREET,
WALNUT AND THIRD

'Drawn from nature' by Aug. Köllner, 1848; Lith. by Deroy, printed by Cattier

Coaches, hacks and omnibuses, together with horse- or mule-drawn railroad wagons
carrying coal and other freight through the city centre, made Dock Street Philadelphia's
busiest intersection in the heart of the business district. George Crofutt's workplace at
No. 83 Dock Street, two doors below Third, can be seen on the right, squeezed between
taller buildings, and with its blind out.

The first was called the *Monthly Rainbow*, an enlarged and more
elaborate version of one of John Campbell's publications of the same
name. Crofutt's magazine was a folio journal "elegantly printed on a
double-imperial sheet of fine white paper." It was priced at 6 cents a copy,
50 cents for a year's subscription. Crofutt had purchased the subscription
list of Campbell's old *Monthly Rainbow* (whose circulation was claimed to
be more than 7000 copies), and in addition that of Lay and Brother's
magazine for printers called *Ink Fountain* (circulation c.5500).

The competition among publishers and editors was growing fiercer
by the minute. Many newspapers had recently come and gone, often

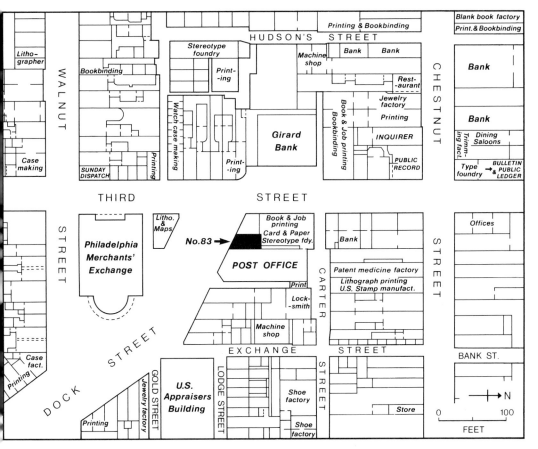

VI.

DOCK STREET AND THIRD

Opposite the Merchants' Exchange and next door to the Post Office, Crofutt's business location at 83 Dock Street was in the heart of the city's newspaper and printing quarter.

based on the Hexamer and Locher survey (late 1850s),
published at 401 Walnut Street, Philadelphia, 1860,
and on other sources

launched in the first place to reflect the enormous variety of political and religious opinion within Philadelphia's social and ethnic groups, and dependent upon these for a regular percentage of their sales. Philadelphia now published 11 dailies, 36 weeklies and 22 periodicals; Crofutt's new *Monthly Rainbow* joined them on Saturday, 15th March 1856. Still printed by John Campbell, the contents covered the traditional ground of current events, general interest pieces, articles on recent inventions and discoveries, fiction, book reviews, and humorous anecdotes. A Manuel M. Cooke was hired as the literary editor, one section continued to be devoted to the printing trade, while Crofutt himself took charge of all the advertising. The front page, however, was under the control of the scientific editor, a Dr. L.L. Chapman, whom Crofutt appears to have met while lodging at 73 South Fourth Street, and who in 1851 had written and published in Philadelphia a small 4-page sheet called *The Rainbow and Monthly Astro-Magnetic Mirror* which he later sold to John Campbell.

Chapman probably provided some of the initial investment for Crofutt's *Monthly Rainbow* but may well have hastened the failure of the enterprise with his pseudo-scientific jargon, and his unconvincing astronomical observations and meteorological forecasts which dominated the front page. Philadelphians were unimpressed. Philadelphia, 'the Athens of America', had long been celebrated for its distinguished achievements in science and medicine. Both the American Medical Association and the American Association for the Advancement of Science had been founded in Philadelphia, and in 1857 the city still published nine-tenths of the medical books issued in the United States. J. B. Lippincott & Co. was Philadelphia's leading publisher of text and reference books, while the famous *Journal of the Franklin Institute*, with its papers on Mechanical and Physical Science, and Civil Engineering, was one of the first and finest publications in its field. In New York, the *Scientific American* had reached a circulation of 30,000 by 1853. The *Monthly Rainbow's* 'scientific editor' had no place here.

Chapman's efforts are worth recording, however, since they represented an interesting attempt to fill a gap between science and theology for the general reader. The first half of the nineteenth century was a spectacular period of scientific and applied scientific discovery. The general public, largely through newspapers and magazines, was aware of the new discoveries and new technologies, and filled with wonder and excitement at the possibilities of scientific advance; but many readers' understanding of the basic scientific principles involved was limited by their lack of experience and scientific education. At the same time, many religious leaders were becoming increasingly perturbed by the growing contradictions between the Bible's and the scientists' explanations of physical phenomena. Vehement opposition often developed between the two.

There was room, therefore, for a third group — those who sought the common ground and an approach which allowed individuals to retain their religious beliefs without rejecting scientific interpretations. Chapman was one of these, although his case was weakened by his own inadequate knowledge of physics and astronomy. He had had some early training in medicine but he could not explain in acceptable scientific terms his main thesis — the linking of "electrical patterns" in the atmosphere with physical and mental health. He set out to forecast on a daily, even an hourly, basis, favourable and unfavourable periods for human activity during the coming month:

"READER! You would not say that your (almost hourly) changes of feeling are without cause! *that would be atheism!* Nor that every change has a supernatural cause — *that would be superstition!* They must then have a *natural* cause.

As electricity is the universal principle of physical vitality, all animated nature will feel in some degree the unfavourable effects of its deficiency . . .

What a world of misery from family discords may be prevented by foreknowing the seasons of greater atmospheric irritation.

Success in life, as far as it depends on the will or agency of others, is dependent mainly upon the states of nature at the *time* in which we choose to transact business with them. For, when persons feel gloomy, or as if something *they know not what* is wrong, they will (of course) feel less disposed to oblige, and more inclined to refuse than when the condition of the atmosphere disposes more to Serenity, and cheerfulness, and to do all in their power to Oblige, and when they will bestow favors, or part with money *at least* with *less* reluctance."

George Crofutt's mistake was to allow Chapman to take over the front page of the *Monthly Rainbow*. Experience shows that kept short and simple, and on an inside page, astrological predictions (the term was abhorrent to Chapman) do help to sell papers.

Crofutt worked hard to push his new *Monthly Rainbow* as a desirable advertising medium with rates as low as eight to ten cents a line. His recent employer, Jesse Emerson in New York, bought space to advertise the *United States Magazine*. Crofutt's younger brother Charles, then aged twenty, also advertised his business in the *Rainbow*. At this time, Charles Crofut had left Danbury to seek his fortune down on the coast in Westport, Conn. There, he opened a small factory making, under patent, portable grist mills, straw cutters and shingle machines. George mean-while struggled on in Dock Street, but despite the publicity he gave his magazine in the Philadelphia press, the *Monthly Rainbow* was a failure. Without single editorial control, it lacked style and cohesion. On a small budget, it became largely an exchange, "scissors-and-paste" job. Even with premium offers, Crofutt's folio and its contents were not thought to be worth 6 cents a copy when 10 cents, for example, could buy the sixteen-page *Frank Leslie's Illustrated Newspaper* which had appeared exactly three months earlier in New York. This was a rainbow indeed, a lively miscellany of news, reviews, fiction, travel and the arts, spiced with large, dramatic pictures. Before long, Frank Leslie was claiming a circu-lation of 100,000 for his dazzlingly successful weekly.

Even the printer's trade section in the *Monthly Rainbow* failed to hang on to its readers. Charles and William Lay had launched their quarterly *Ink Fountain* in Philadelphia in 1852, but by the time they sold it to Crofutt early in 1856, the Lay brothers were already suffering from the competition of the quarterly *Typographic Advertiser*, which began its long-running publication in Philadelphia in 1855, quickly captured the advertising in fact as in name, and went on to become an established leader in its field throughout much of the United States. The Lay brothers decided that they were far better off as manufacturers of printing inks; they enlarged their Eagle works in Philadelphia and opened a branch factory in Cincinnati.

Crofutt's second venture, *The Philadelphia Merchants' Diary and Guide, for 1856*, fared no better. This was a small, paper-backed diary and pocket-book of information for local businessmen, one of a kind printed and distributed by any number of firms in Philadelphia at this time. Indeed, Philadelphia led the way in this type of publication. No other city in the United States produced the hundreds of high quality, illustrated trade cards and booklets for distribution by individual local businesses, shops and factories — a reflection of the city's traditional expertise, and the many skilled engravers, lithographers and printers among its work-force.

A local family of job printers, Henry and Isaac Ashmead, handled Crofutt's guide but there was no profit in it. His modest compilation offered nothing that was not already available in a more detailed and sophisticated form, since in addition to the trade cards, Philadelphia was also notable for its extensive range of Shoppers' Guides, Visitors' Guides, Strangers' Guides, and Merchants' Guides. Businessmen placing an advertisement in Crofutt's publication were given 200 free copies for distribution to their customers on which, as an added inducement, their individual trade cards were printed on the front cover of the guide. Crofutt claimed that he had placed 20,000 copies in the hands of Philadelphia's merchants. Sadly, there was little to show for all this determined legwork. Crofutt's *Diary and Guide* was a useful personal exercise in organization and speed of production, but his 1856 issue was the first and the last.

He tried once more. Early in 1857, still at 83 Dock Street but associated now with a newcomer to Philadelphia, S. M. Bigelow, Crofutt launched a weekly newspaper called *The Nation*. It survived only a few issues before total collapse, its brief appearance unknown or long forgotten by 1865, when the New York weekly of the same name began its long and distinguished career. Charles Lay and John Campbell mean-while stuck doggedly to their trades. Lay & Brother still manufactured inks, while Campbell kept his printing business on the ground floor of No. 83, and thanked his stars he was rid of the burden of trying to make a living in publishing. Let the Crofutts, Chapmans and Bigelows of the world run their own risks. And they did; there was no shortage of hopefuls ready to try their luck. Philadelphia now published no fewer than 12 dailies, 44 weeklies and 40 periodicals, with other United States' and European publications still adding to the competition.

With all the effort that had gone into its production, the ignominious failure of *The Nation* was a hard blow to the publishers' pride and pockets. It was reported that Crofutt and Bigelow had obtained the help of Mrs. E. D. E. N. Southworth as associate editor of *The Nation*. Mrs. Southworth had already achieved remarkable success as a writer for *The National Era* and for Philadelphia's own prestigious *Saturday Evening Post*, whose circulation she had helped to boost to an estimated 80,000 - 90,000 by the end of 1855. "At mid-century," one authority records, "Mrs. Southworth shared with Charles Dickens the palm as the most popular writer for the American middle-class audience." During the 1850s she emerged as the leader in the field of romantic fiction. Her first best-seller was published in Philadelphia in 1852, and in the late 1850s-early 1860s, when three more of her novels each sold more than two million copies, Emma Southworth was set to become the most popular woman writer in the annals of American publishing.[14] The electrifying effect that her serialized stories had upon the sales and subscription lists of those weeklies lucky enough to secure her services gladdened editors' hearts, and Crofutt no doubt hoped that the magic of her name would get *The Nation* off to a good start.

In October 1855, Mrs. Southworth had vacationed in Germantown while recovering from a period of overwork and poor health.[15] Germantown was an old settlement overlooking the Schuylkill river, six miles from the business core of Philadelphia, and a pleasantly cool, wooded retreat away from the downtown area. It had been linked by rail to the city in 1832 when Philadelphia's first line was opened, and by the mid-1850s, hourly rail and stage services made Germantown a readily accessible and convenient centre.

> "I was much impressed in my drive today with the beauty of the country," wrote one local resident at this period. "Germantown, always a respectable, substantial village, (is) now adorned with elegance and supplied with all the conveniences of a city — shops, gas, waterworks, with none of the annoyances of town, but quiet, country scenery, gardens and trees every-where. The railroad and the taste for villa life have done it all, and so manifold are its advantages that the wonder to me is how any can bear to stay in town." [16]

It is possible that Crofutt arranged a meeting with Mrs. Southworth in 1855, talked over his plans and asked for her advice or assistance. There is no evidence, however, that she was ever involved with *The Nation*, or with any of Crofutt's publications. Indeed, in 1857, she agreed under contract to write exclusively for the *New York Ledger* in which several of her best-sellers first appeared in serial form. The *Ledger's* weekly circulation quickly soared to an estimated 400,000, out-distancing all its competitors to become one of the publishing wonders of the age.

More than two thousand American magazines and periodicals are estimated to have died in the 1850s. Crofutt and Bigelow were part of that huge crowd whose "young green leaves" of publication had succumbed to the "killing frost" of debt. They had failed to attract good writers or vital advertising, and were desperately under-capitalized. *The Nation* had avoided party politics but failed to identify and capture a large, faithful, middle- or working-class readership which was the conspicuous feature of the most successful publications. The year 1857 also marked a devastatingly sharp increase in market competition with the introduction of *Harper's Weekly* in New York in January, and *The Atlantic Monthly* in Boston in November. Both were to send shock waves through the world of American periodical publication and quickly achieve national and international fame.

Crofutt's timing for the introduction of a new weekly like *The Nation* was disastrous in other respects, since in August 1857, financial panic swept much of the United States. It was precipitated by the failure of the New York City branch of the Ohio Life Insurance and Trust Co., following over-speculation in railroad securities and real estate. All the Philadelphia banks stopped payment at the end of September 1857. Many banks across the northern States closed altogether and thousands of small businesses were bankrupted. Crofutt's was no exception and he quickly joined the ranks of Philadelphia's unemployed.

Several famous periodicals became casualties of the 1857 Panic; many more were to be shaken to their roots by the combined effects of bank failures, accumulated debts, and the crippling loss of subscribers as unemployment spread. Philadelphia's own *Graham's Magazine*, along with the *New-York Mirror*, the *Democratic Review*, and *Putnam's Monthly Magazine* all failed to survive; *The Knickerbocker* barely did so. *Putnam's Monthly* had gained an excellent reputation since its introduction by George P. Putnam & Co. in January 1853, but it was unable to cope with the double blow in 1857 of competition from *Harper's Weekly*, followed by the financial panic of the summer and fall.

Crofutt's former employer in New York, Jesse Emerson, had been doing well in the mid-1850s and had moved his publishing business from Gold Street, first to larger premises at No. 1 Spruce, and then onto Broadway. In October 1857, J. M. Emerson & Co. took over *Putnam's* and merged it with the *United States Magazine* to produce *Emerson's Magazine and Putnam's Monthly*. It was edited by Seba and Elizabeth Oakes Smith, with a circulation in the region of 40,000. But not for long; the combined magazine ceased publication in November 1858, and

Crofutt read of the loss of the Emerson publications he knew so well, indeed, of the collapse of the entire Emerson organization in New York, as he struggled to salvage a few scraps from his own ruined fortunes in Philadelphia.

Both Crofutt and Bigelow left the city at the end of 1857, owing John Campbell rent for their office accommodation at 83 Dock Street. Charles Lay retired soon afterwards, leaving Campbell to discover that he had not escaped the risks of the publishing gamble after all. Work was increasingly hard to find; quite apart from the newspaper press, in 1857 there were as many as fifty other printing offices in Philadelphia employing anything up to one hundred people each.[17] Campbell hung on as a job printer for nearly three more years but by 1861, he too had left the city.

Farewell to Pennsylvania

Crofutt appears to have gone from Philadelphia to Reading, Pa. Nearly 70 miles from Philadelphia, Reading was a smelting and manufacturing town of some 21,000 people on the edge of northeast Pennsylvania's rich anthracite coalfield, the best source of anthracite in the United States. The Schuylkill Canal had for years provided a slow and increasingly inadequate means of transporting anthracite into Philadelphia, and manufacturers had clamoured for a railroad. The opening of a full passenger service on the Philadelphia & Reading Railroad in 1839, coupled with the long-awaited coal freight service to the Delaware River's Richmond wharves in 1842, had tied the fortunes and the economic development of Philadelphia and Reading more closely together, and boosted trade in the smaller Reading Railroad centres such as Norristown, Pottstown and Pottsville where Crofutt also looked for work.

While in Reading, either in 1858 or 1859, Crofutt was married. His wife was Anna M. Burcker, born in Reading on 7th November 1817.[18] Anna's parents, Henry and Margaret Burcker, had both been born in the United States, although, like nine-tenths of Reading's population, they were of German extraction, descendants of eighteenth-century immigrants from the Rhineland. As a young man, Henry Burcker had served in the United States army during the last part of the 1812-15 war with Britain. Commissioned as 1st Lieutenant, he had marched with a company of Reading men under Captain Jacob Marshall following British attacks on Washington, D.C. and Baltimore, and been stationed at York, Pa. between September 1814 and March 1815.[19] After the war, Henry and Margaret Burcker were married and settled down to raise a family, but after Margaret's death their eldest daughter, Anna, had stepped into her mother's shoes and run the household for several years.

The Burcker family lived on Bingaman Street, below 5th, where Henry Burcker was in business as a coppersmith. His connection with the printing and engraving trade may have been the reason for Crofutt's initial contact with the family. Crofutt may even have lodged with them and had the first real taste of the comforts of home life since he left his parents' cottage in Danbury. Just as Crofutt arrived in Reading, however, major changes were occurring in the Burcker household, changes which left Anna lonely and out of a job. In October 1857, Henry Burcker had remarried and his second wife, Leah Drexel, had come to live at Bingaman Street. A daughter was born to Henry and Leah the following year.[20] However amicable the relationship, Anna must have recognized the fact that Leah was now the mistress of the house and best left alone to develop her role as a new wife and mother. George Crofutt had swept into Anna's life at this critical point. Although he was ten years younger than Anna, and still struggling desperately to make a living, Crofutt's basic cheerfulness, courtesy and engaging personality were a tonic to Henry Burcker's eldest daughter who was now no doubt feeling unneeded, purposeless, and very middle-aged.

Before or soon after their marriage, George and Anna Crofutt appear to have decided to leave Pennsylvania and make a new start in the West. The political situation in the United States was steadily deteriorating; increasingly bitter sectionalism between North and South dominated Congress. To an unsuccessful, virtually penniless agent and publisher like Crofutt, unable to contend with the scale and quality of the East's competition, California had appeared in 1858 to offer the best opportunity for starting afresh. By 1859, however, there was a new source of excitement — the newspapers were full of accounts of gold discoveries near some mountain in the Rockies called Pike's Peak. That settled it. The Crofutts made plans to seek their fortune in the new boom area of Colorado, or failing that, to keep going until they reached California.

PART II

PIONEERING IN THE WEST: THE 1860s

12.   CROSSING THE MISSOURI RIVER AT COUNCIL BLUFFS

Engraved from a sketch by Frederick H. Piercy in James Linforth, *Route from Liverpool to Great Salt Lake Valley, 1855*

Pioneers waiting on the trail under the cottonwood trees for the return of the ferry-boat.

VIEW OF PIKE'S PEAK
Forty miles in the distance.

CAMPING ON THE PLAINS.

13a. TWO ILLUSTRATIONS FROM *THE MINERS' HAND-BOOK AND GUIDE TO PIKE'S PEAK,*
by Parker & Huyett, St. Louis, 1859
The Guide promised "a New and Reliable Map, showing all the Routes, and the Gold
Regions of Western Kansas and Nebraska."

CHAPTER THREE

A New Start in the Trans-Mississippi West

Ho! For the Gold Regions! Ho! For Pike's Peak!

In April 1860, George Crofutt crossed the Mississippi for the first time, looked briefly around the city of St. Louis, checked his money, bought a ticket at the North Missouri Railroad office on N. Fourth Street and without more delay set off again into the West. The plan appears to have been that Anna Crofutt would leave Reading a few weeks later and make the entire journey to the Rockies by railroad and stagecoach. George could afford to go only a short distance further by train. The railroad took him another nineteen miles to the bank of the Missouri River whereupon he and the rest of the passengers got down, surrounded by piles of luggage and freight, and waited for the ferry-boats to take them across the Missouri to the little river port of St. Charles. Thus, Crofutt stepped abruptly out of the world of the rails to begin a walk of nearly a thousand miles to the Rockies of Colorado.[1]

The ferry-boat passengers huddled together against the chill wind blowing off the water. The Missouri River was over half-a-mile wide at this point, with treacherous currents and water levels high with snowmelt and spring flood. Broken drift ice swept past in the rushing waters — was this really the same river they called the Big Muddy? Eventually the passengers, stiff with cold, clambered awkwardly out of the ferry-boat, thankful that the ordeal was over. Crossing the Mississippi on one of the excellent St. Louis steam ferries had been a joy-ride by comparison.

The small settlement of St. Charles straggled along the bluff. It was an old Missouri River trading post founded in 1769, twenty-five miles above the confluence with the Mississippi. Between 1821 and 1826, St. Charles had been the temporary capital of the new State of Missouri, and by 1860 the town's population had reached 3000, but for much of its century-old existence St. Charles had remained little more than the isolated, final departure point for parties setting out to explore the vast wilderness of the upper Missouri basin.

Alongside the ferry-boat landing, some of the freight was being reloaded into North Missouri Railroad cars since the track had been extended to Hudson (now Macon) a few months earlier. Carts and trail wagons were also being loaded for the 230-mile journey west across the State of Missouri to Kansas City, Crofutt's next destination.

Of course there was the possibility of using river transport; more than a hundred Missouri river-boats were now plying between St. Louis, St. Charles and the main outfitting towns strung along the Missouri between Kansas City (Westport Landing) and Omaha [Map VIII]. Side-wheelers could take more than two weeks to cover the 360 miles upstream between St. Charles and Westport Landing — a slow, circuitous journey where delays were common and timing always unpredictable. Walking along the wagon road to Kansas City was usually quicker. Besides, most of the vessels were already crammed with west-bound emigrants — 'Peakers', Mormons and others — who had swarmed aboard some forty miles back in St. Louis. Only gangs of river-boat gamblers from St. Louis made the short trip, disembarking regularly at St. Charles to disappear silently back to base to start work on the next unsuspecting boat-load out of St. Louis.

Crofutt decided to stay on dry land, whatever his mode of travel; the last thing he fancied was to spend any more time on the Missouri River than was absolutely necessary. In any case, the single fare of $25 may have been more than he wanted to part with when he was uncertain of the expenses that lay ahead. Without hesitation, Crofutt joined the first wagon party leaving St. Charles and by the third week in May he reached Kansas City. "I had become a pilgrim on the plains from sunrise to sunset."

Kansas City was now growing fast. A recent visitor had remarked that he found it difficult to tell where the Missouri River ended and the main street began; both consisted of mud and water of similar colour and depth. In 1860, however, Crofutt found a city of c.6000 busily cutting down the river bluffs and grading the streets. The pilgrim on the plains had no time to lose; Crofutt left Kansas City almost immediately, probably on 17th or 18th May,[2] bound due west along the trail to Lawrence, Kansas Territory.

In 1860, the State of Missouri could be crossed by trail, rail or river-boat, but there was little choice when it came to crossing the plains beyond the main Missouri River outfitting towns. The cost of the journey by stagecoach forced the majority into going on foot. The basic stage fare to Denver in 1859-60 varied between $100 and $150, including board. Setting this amount aside to pay for Anna Crofutt's journey had already drained most of the couple's resources. Writing from Leavenworth, another emigrant summarized the position for those who assumed at first that they had neither the patience nor the stamina for the long trudge across the plains:

"We thought at first that we would proceed by stage, but the fare is one hundred and fifty dollars, and we concluded that if we could find a cheaper way without much inconvenience we would go that way.

Tomorrow afternoon a train of seven wagons loaded with provisions, tents, freight, etc, under the charge of the proprietor, Mr. Freeman, of this city leaves for Denver City, the nearest point to the mines. He is to carry our baggage for ten cents per pound, and board us during the journey for twenty-five dollars, and furnish tents for us to sleep under. We are to walk, which we do not think will be over and above pleasant, but still if we can save a hundred dollars by so doing we do not mind it." [3]

After three days' march from Kansas City, Mo., Crofutt reached Lawrence, Kansas Territory, and discovered that the town had rapidly become one of the main departure points for Pike's Peak, and for a dream the Lawrence townsfolk themselves had helped to create. Streets, hotels and saloons were jammed with strangers. On every side, Crofutt heard vivid accounts of the on-off-on-again story of the Pike's Peak gold rush. It was his first close encounter with the speed of change in the West, a phenomenon which was to fascinate Crofutt for the rest of his life.

The newness of the region excited him. Lawrence was the first town to be built in Kansas and had been founded by Bostonians as a 'gateway' settlement on the south side of the Kansas River in 1854 to arrest the westward extension of slavery. The first party arrived in August, "not as adventurers to see how they would like it. They had come to stay and see the thing done ... to make Kansas free." In its brief existence, Lawrence had already suffered blockade, raiding and burning in 1855-6; a new arrival in 1857 found only a small collection of houses which still "seemed to be straggling around on the prairie as if they had lost their way." The population had not lost its way, however, and as a determined, crusading outpost of Massachusetts, Lawrence folk were far from being "the traditional roughs of the frontier." [4]

Gold fever had swept Lawrence in 1858. For decades, mountain men, Indians, and army scouts had occasionally reported signs of gold in creeks near the base of Pike's Peak. In 1850, miners from north Georgia, including a few Cherokee Indians, had joined the gold rush to California and panned any likely-looking stream on the way. Ralston Creek and Cherry Creek had yielded some gold but not enough to deflect the miners from the California trail.

Eight years later, however, some of the Georgians led by Green Russell had returned to the Pike's Peak-Cherry Creek area of western Kansas and been joined in July 1858 by a party from Lawrence — thirty-six members of the newly formed 'Lawrence Gold Hunting Company'! In September 1858 another Kansas group arrived and formed the St. Charles Town Association east of Cherry Creek. Small amounts of gold were again found in some of the South Platte tributaries, and at the end of October, Russell established the settlement of Auraria at the west side of the Cherry Creek-South Platte confluence. A second campsite (soon to be renamed Denver City) was established on the virtually deserted St. Charles claim on the east side of Cherry Creek in November 1858 by a party from Leavenworth led by George William Larimer, who also established a third campsite at Highland, on the north side of the Platte, in December 1858. Scattered between these three sites, a small core of prospectors hung on over winter to explore other streams draining the Pike's Peak area.

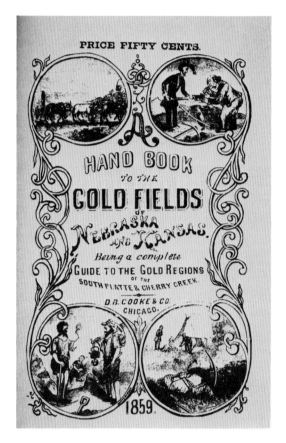

13b.   A HAND BOOK TO THE GOLDFIELDS OF NEBRASKA AND KANSAS,
Published in Chicago and New York, 1859
Written by William N. Byers and J.H. Kellom, this was one of the many 'Goldfields' guidebooks distributed coast to coast in 1859 that boosted the rush to Pike's Peak.

The rest were ill-equipped for winter in the Rockies and returned to Lawrence or to centres in the Missouri-Mississippi region to make plans for renewed exploration in the following spring. Some of them elaborated hastily written field notes and accounts of their "wanderings and adventures" for publication. Despite having virtually nothing to go on, most of them painted a rosy picture of the region's assumed gold deposits. Editors and reporters in the Missouri River towns did the rest. "The latest letter from our Special Gold Correspondent!!" headed a column of one typically resourceful newspaper during the no-news winter of 1858-9, cheerfully ignoring the fact that the luckless Special Correspondent had found no gold at any time throughout the period.

In 1858-9, the fortunes of most of the outfitting towns between Omaha and Kansas City were plummeting with the decline of the 'Mormon War' trade to Utah, a slump made worse by the 1857 financial panic and national economic depression. Far and wide, the boosters spread the glad tidings of a new American bonanza in the Rockies. Guides to the 'Pike's Peak Goldfields' flooded the markets in the East and Midwest before any significant discoveries of gold had been made; the occasional note of caution was lost amid the confident predictions of another great gold rush on the California scale. As many as seventeen books and pamphlets were published in 1859 alone; Lawrence, Kansas even managed to bring one out in December 1858. The eastern States readership was amply supplied — seven 'Goldfields' guidebooks were published or republished in New York City, five in Chicago, two in Cincinnati, and others in St. Louis, Pittsburgh, Washington, D.C., and Boston.[5]

Thousands of hopefuls had beaten the recommended trails to Pike's Peak, clutching at shadows and dreams of another, nearer California — one that avoided the necessity of crossing the Rockies and the deserts beyond.

"Those two little words 'Pike's Peak' are everywhere," marvelled one reporter from St. Louis, after touring the outfitting towns. "There are Pike's Peak hats, and Pike's Peak guns, and Pike's Peak boots, and Pike's Peak shovels, and Pike's Peak goodness-knows-what-all. . . ."[6]

"It is astonishing how rapidly we learn geography," wrote another. "A short time since, we hardly knew, and didn't care, whether the earthly elevation called Pike's Peak was in Kansas or Kamtschatka. Indeed, ninety-nine out of every hundred persons in the country did not know that there *was* such a topographical feature as Pike's Peak. Now they hear of nothing, read of nothing, think of nothing, dream of nothing, *but* Pike's Peak. It is a magnet in the mountains, toward which everybody and everything is tending."[7]

'Peakers' jammed the river-boats, the landings and the stores. Out on the trail, often before winter was over and grass available, 'Peakers' stumbled into the West in 1859, "perfectly ignorant of everything" . . . "fools loose on the plains," as one old hand described a party from the east, "wandering along with their carpet bags, and their ridiculous outfits."

In February 1859, on the first wave of enthusiasm, W.H. Russell and John S. Jones had founded the Leavenworth (City) and Pike's Peak Express Company, and in April begun their ambitious 700-mile stage-coach service across Kansas between Leavenworth (later Atchison) and Denver via the Republican River route.[8] But despite the ballyhoo, no more gold worth speaking of was found in the winter and spring of 1859. The word spread that the "Pike's Peak gold" put on display had really come from California, not from the Rockies. The three small settlements of Auraria, Denver and Highland were almost deserted as hundreds turned for home — "Back to the States" wrote one, "flat busted. We have been to the Pike's Peak diggings and we are disgusted with the God-forsaken country. There ain't any gold to be found." Plenty of other "Go-Backs", destitute and embittered by the guidebooks' rhetoric, howled:

"Hang Byers and D.C. Oakes
For starting this damned Pike's Peak hoax."

The groups straggling homeward passed the crowds still flocking west, many of whom were alarmed by the wretched condition of the returning traffic. As E.L. Gallatin, one of the 'Peakers' who settled in Denver, recalled:

"We met a large number of discouraged stampeders going back who made it a part of their business to discourage all that were coming this way . . . but I argued to go on and see for ourselves and take no man's word."[9]

About half of the estimated 100,000 goldseekers who set out from the Missouri River towns in the spring of 1859 are thought to have turned back before reaching the Rockies, and another 25,000 did so shortly after they arrived. The Pike's Peak boosters had the last word, however. Two men in particular transformed the fortunes of the region — Gregory and Greeley. On 6th May 1859, John H. Gregory, an old Georgia miner returned to a promising site he had found in January 1859 and struck rich gold deposits in Clear Creek Canyon, about 40 miles west of Denver. His was the first discovery of lode gold and this transformed the prospects of the region. Placering soon gave way to hardrock mining.

Exactly one month later, on 6th June 1859, Horace Greeley, editor of the *New-York Daily Tribune*, arrived in Denver; his fellow passenger on the stage was Albert Richardson of the *Boston Journal*. Henry Villard of the *Cincinnati Daily Commercial* had arrived a fortnight earlier. Greeley wasted no time in hiring a mule to take him up to Gregory's Diggings.

"Last Thursday," wrote one astonished miner, "we were honored with a visit from *Horace Greely*. Only think, *Horace Greely*, clambering over these ragged old mountains on a *mule*. He was dressed in black, had an old slouch hat on with the rim drooping down on all sides, and he visited all the sluices. . ."[10]

14. CLIMBING THE TRAIL INTO
THE ROCKY MOUNTAINS IN 1859

*Drawn by George G. White;
Engraved by N. Orr & Co., in A.D.
Richardson,
Beyond the Mississippi, 1867*

"I have come here to lay my hand on the naked, indisputable facts," vowed Greeley, "and I mean to do it." What he saw and heard made newspaper history. His vivid, authoritative dispatches sent back to the *Tribune* dispelled many of the uncertainties surrounding Pike's Peak. By late June and July 1859 there was "an uncontrollable eruption of emigrants — a great river of human life rolling toward the setting sun."

15.   GREGORY'S DIGGINGS, CLEAR CREEK CANYON, COLORADO IN 1859
            Drawn by White; Engraved by Orr, in Richardson, Beyond the Mississippi, 1867

Thousands of emigrants with their handcarts and white canvas-covered wagons formed seemingly endless columns along the trails across Kansas and Nebraska. The special joint statement issued on 9th June by Greeley, Richardson and Villard confirmed the existence of paying quantities of gold. It had been made at the request of B.D. Williams, agent for the Leavenworth and Pike's Peak Express Company, and was published as a hand-bill for distribution along the trails and in the outfitting towns. William Byers, editor of Denver's *Rocky Mountain News*, went one better. On 11th June, with characteristic showmanship, he printed the Greeley-Richardson-Villard report on brown wrapping paper as a *News* 'extra' and gave it wide circulation among the mining camps, along the columns of wagons already crossing the plains, and throughout the Missouri River outfitting towns.

Byers, a farm boy from Iowa, was himself a recent arrival on the scene after a life already crammed with adventure in Oregon, California and Panama. Back in the Missouri River country, Byers had whiled away some of his time by writing *A Hand Book to the Gold Fields of Nebraska and Kansas* without ever having set eyes on them.[11] Still only twenty-eight, he had then set off from Omaha complete with printing press, type, a supply of paper, and some half-completed copy, determined to find success in a new career. His wagons rolled into Denver on 17th April 1859 and only six days later, Byers published the first newspaper in the Rockies, scooping the rival *Cherry Creek Pioneer* by 30 minutes! The latter's forlorn owner, Jack Merrick, sold out to Byers within three weeks. In little more than a month, Denver's ebullient young editor was entertaining Horace Greeley; even Byers could scarcely believe his luck.

The joint report from Gregory's Diggings had cautioned against underestimating the difficulties; success would require capital, experience, and endurance. Greeley, Richardson and Villard begged the press to print their report in full, omitting none of the warnings. Let the foolhardy beware! Greeley's reputation was solid, however, and his reassurance about the existence of gold in paying quantities produced a new spirit of optimism. The news helped to lift the gloom of the 1857-8 financial crisis and made up the minds of many like Crofutt, facing unemployment and depression in the East, that the long journey west was worth the gamble. And the West's own call to them was loud and clear. As one Kansas editor wrote to a correspondent in Pennsylvania:

> "The West is large enough, and its capacities are diversified enough, to absorb all the labor which is turned adrift by the financial embarrassments of the seaboard."

Many of the "Go-Backs" decided to go again; thousands more decided for the first time that the chilling message "Busted at Pike's Peak" was too negative — why, it already had a quaint, historic ring to it! As the trails opened in the spring of 1860, an unprecedented flood of 'Peakers', Crofutt among them, surged across the plains.

Lawrence, Kansas: "Gateway to the West!" "Get Your Outfits Here!"

Lawrence was still jammed with strangers that final week in May 1860 as Crofutt pushed his way through the crowds filling Massachusetts Street. "They're from all parts of United States," observed one of the locals, "and they're all getting ready to leave, going, or gone." Lawrence's main street now ran back from the Kansas River for about half-a-mile before losing itself on the open prairie. Below Henry and Winthrop Streets, it was lined with frame and a few brick buildings — grocery and dry goods stores, drug stores, boarding-houses and saloons.

Lawrence was busy filling its gaps and rising confidently out of the plains. Crofutt passed the fresh stacks of lumber, brick and stone set out ready for building on the town lots, and watched new shade trees being planted. The town had a population of about 2000 and was the last outfitting point on the southern route before the unrelieved isolation of the plains began in earnest.

Crofutt had to check his provisions and find a fresh wagon party to join for the journey. He made enquiries at the different stores. There was Stearns' at No. 27 Massachusetts — Charles Stearns, a cheerful, irrepressible old-timer advertising everything for the miners' and emigrants' outfits "except whisky and tobacco." The earliest land-use sketch of Lawrence (1854-5) shows Stearns' eating house alongside the Emigrant Aid Office. Later, he was well sited next to Babcock & Lykins' bank building, a 3-storey 'brown brick' which was large enough to accommodate Lawrence's smart new City Drug Store, and other offices. As business increased, Stearns expanded by opening an Ice Cream Saloon, and another Diner. Never one to miss an opportunity, Stearns had capitalized on Greeley's visit to the mines by placing a large notice out on the sidewalk to advertise his stock of boots: "just like the boots that Horace wore — stout, heavy and hardwearing!"

Close to Stearns', George Ford had opened his new Empire and Country Store; Bullene & Read, Allen & Gilmore, Raymond & Thompson, H.L. & James Blood, Maltravers Solomon, and half-a-dozen other dry goods suppliers had arrived or expanded since the rumours of gold had swept the country in 1858. Benjamin Franklin Dalton had arrived in Lawrence in March 1858 after ten years in the Boston clothing trade. He brought his stock with him up-river from St. Louis, opened a new store in the Collamore Building on Massachusetts Street and quickly became one of the liveliest businessmen in town. While the Lawrence Party was still making its way uncertainly across the plains towards Pike's Peak in June 1858, B.F. Dalton had been the first boldly to head his advertising copy "Ho! for the Gold Regions! New Store! New Goods!" [12]

Just across the street was the Post Office building and O. Wilmarth's large book and stationery store, its well-stocked counters reflecting the steady, sophisticated local demand. Visiting homes in and around Lawrence, preacher Richard Cordley had discovered that "You would find on the table the best Eastern papers, and the brightest magazines. The table might only be a dry-goods box, but the papers would be there just the same." [13]

OUTFITTING STORES IN MASSACHUSETTS STREET, LAWRENCE, KANSAS, c. 1860

Crofutt found a selection of newspapers at Wilmarth's and flicked through the neat piles of magazines. All the old surviving favourites were there — *Godey's, Peterson's,* and *Arthur's,* along with *Harper's,* the *Atlantic Monthly, Leslie's,* the *Knickerbocker,* the *New York Ledger, Scientific American, Ballou's* and many more. There were several British periodicals. There was even, Crofutt noted wryly, an old advertisement for *Emerson's Magazine and Putnam's Monthly.* But time was short and he still had to make arrangements for the journey.

Meeting Fellow Pioneers

In the spring of 1860, parties of four to six leaving Lawrence reckoned the cost of the trip to the Rockies to be about $75 per man. After several enquiries along Massachusetts Street, Crofutt approached Samuel Tappan's office and warehouse opposite the bank building, and found a wagon being loaded with freight for the Tappan Brothers' new store in Colorado City.

Tappan was a well-known figure. As a youth, Samuel Forster Tappan had worked in Boston but had decided to come out to Kansas with the first party of emigrants which left Boston in July 1854.[14] He helped to found Lawrence and took a prominent part in the Free Kansas movement

17.   WAGONS ASSEMBLING ON THE EDGE OF TOWN IN LAWRENCE, KANSAS, c. 1860,
BEFORE TAKING THE TRAIL WEST

against the 'Border Ruffians'. In 1857, he had been joined by a relative
from Boston, Lewis N. Tappan, who opened a dry goods store on
Massachusetts Street while Samuel concentrated on the insurance business. In 1859, Lewis decided to move on. He contacted his elder brother,
William, who had been prospecting, ranching and trading in California,
Oregon and the Columbia River country for the past ten years, and
together they arranged to head for Pike's Peak and open four new stores
in Denver, Central City, Colorado City and Golden, specializing in dry
goods, hardware and miners' supplies. The younger brother's energy and
determination at such an early stage of Colorado's development marked
Lewis Tappan as the leading pioneer merchant of the region — "He's gone
west again," said one observer in Lawrence, "with his goods, his Puritan
principles, his temperate habits, and his Bible."

Crofutt watched the merchandise being packed and roped, and fell
into conversation with the two young men doing most of the work —
James Tappan, one of the huge clan of "cousins from Boston", and
Benjamin Crowell. Crofutt perhaps had not realized before his arrival the
strength of the town's New England connection: "Lawrence was distinc-
tively a Yankee town", one visitor had discovered in 1857. "The 'melodious
twang' of New England sounded on all the streets." [15]

The New England twang was certainly audible that May morning in

1860 as Benjamin Franklin Crowell struggled with the loading of bales, crates, boxes and barrels, talking animatedly to Crofutt as he did so. Like Lewis and Samuel Tappan, Ben had been born in the small Massachusetts fishing port of Manchester-by-the-Sea, twenty-five miles northeast of Boston. Much to Captain Sam Crowell's disappointment, Ben had decided not to follow in his father's footsteps and go to sea. Crofutt must have recalled the disappointment he had caused his own father on a similar issue. In the late 1840s, Manchester-by-the-Sea had nothing to offer Ben apart from fishing and boat-building; its chair- and cabinet-making industry was dying, businesses were being neglected, and crowds of 'forty-niners' joined the California goldrush. Crowell, aged thirteen and heart-broken by his mother's recent death, went to Boston and found work in a book-bindery until, in 1859, at the age of twenty-four, he caught 'Pike's Peak fever'.

Longing for adventure, Ben wangled the job through the Crowell-Tappan Manchester family connections of helping to freight Lewis Tappan's merchandise across the plains. He travelled directly to Lawrence and met the small team that Samuel Tappan had assembled for the journey west. Two more of the party had just arrived back in Lawrence — Albinus Z. Sheldon and Frederick A. Spencer. Indeed, departure had been postponed until their return from a late commission to survey Indian lands in the Ottawa reservation, about forty miles south of Lawrence. Samuel Tappan had fretted over the delay since he too was planning to leave for Colorado later in the year and was anxious to get the Tappan Brothers' freight safely out of the warehouse and on its way as soon as possible. But Sheldon and Spencer were experienced, and Lewis Tappan had left instructions that their wagons should accompany his own.

Albinus Sheldon, a minister's son from Southampton, Massachusetts, had worked as a surveyor in the Mississippi region since 1855, after completing two years of a civil engineering course at Amherst College. Employed first in Wisconsin and then on the projected Vicksburg-Shreveport Railroad, he had subsequently gone back up-river to Kansas and worked on town surveys along the Leavenworth-Fort Gibson Railroad, including those of Burlington, De Soto and Poland. Sheldon had also platted part of Lawrence and, with his assistant Fred Spencer, been appointed by the Territorial Legislature in 1858-9 to survey the old Santa Fe Trail and recommend how the route could be shortened.

As they worked on this project, Sheldon and Spencer had talked of the new opportunities opening up in the Pike's Peak region; new towns, mining claims, trails and bridges all needed surveyors. The western edge of Kansas Territory was developing a life of its own; before long it seemed, eastern Kansas would acquire statehood, railroads and settlers, support 'Honest Abe' for the Presidency, shake out the footloose, and get back to minding its own business. "Not everyone will make a fortune in the goldfields," a Lawrence editor exhorted his readers, "stick to your farms, look out for that 'one acre more' which Mr. Greeley talked about. Extend the market for our grain and pork, and make even better use of what you cultivate already."

For the moment, however, the footloose still dominated the traffic. "In 1860," Albinus Sheldon recalled years later, "Lawrence was swarming with sterling fellows without occupation, but with stores of energy for any enterprise which proffered either profit or adventure." [16] Lewis Tappan was not the only merchant to follow them to the Rockies; there was simply not enough business to support Lawrence's profusion of dry goods stores. B.F. Dalton, trading close to the steady, prosperous Bullene & Read, longed to see the Pike's Peak region he had advertised so solidly for two years. He had already had a grand sale of surplus stock, packed the rest, and was leaving for Denver at the beginning of June. Next door to Dalton's, Crofutt had found James Dunn, proprietor of the Commercial House. Dunn was similarly impatient to be off and was displaying a large "For Sale" sign, along with a welcome offer to board at reduced prices.

The Tappan party was short-handed; worse than that, it soon became clear even while still stationary in the dust of Massachusetts Street that neither Ben Crowell nor James Tappan had any idea how to handle oxen or wagons, much less how to bring the two together. Sheldon and Spencer were busy elsewhere with their own last-minute preparations.[17] Crofutt had watched Ben's efforts with great amusement and rose to the challenge that perhaps instead of standing there he could do better. Crofutt had already learned the basic skills on the march across Missouri; Crowell's jaw dropped as without fuss George yoked the oxen Tappan had purchased and hitched them to the wagon. Crofutt was one of the party from that moment. Ben Crowell continued to declare that all oxen looked alike to him, so he painted one horn of each of the near oxen bright red in a distinctive pattern, and then announced he was ready to go.[18] Bullwacking would be learned the hard way, on the trail.

Going West on the Arkansas (Santa Fe) Trail

Early next morning, May 26th, the Sheldon-Tappan party walked slowly out of Lawrence and on to the plains. After heading southwest for about twenty miles, they picked up the main trail, crossed the prairies of Kansas and followed the Arkansas River westward towards the Rockies.

The Arkansas Trail was the most southerly and, at about 700 miles, by far the longest of the three main routes to Denver. The Platte route was the most popular and already famous as the principal overland route to

California, Oregon and Utah. The central Smoky Hill Trail was the most direct. It was less than 600 miles, a fact the Leavenworth-Lawrence-Topeka business communities always stressed when attempting to attract emigrants away from their great rivals, the outfitting towns servicing the Platte route farther north. But the Smoky Hill route was short of water and grass over long stretches, and vulnerable to Kiowa Indian attack. It was not recommended for beginners in the freight business, especially as there had been no rain to speak of since September 1859 and the drought persisted through 1860.

The Tappans had chosen the Arkansas Trail on Albinus Sheldon's advice, and because it had become increasingly popular with merchants and forwarding agents supplying Colorado City, Denver, Auraria, and the mining camps behind them. For much of its length, the Arkansas road was part of the old Santa Fe Trail whose eastern terminus became established at Independence, Mo. in the 1820s but which since the 1840s had more often started from Westport Landing, Kansas City, Mo. It attracted early emigrants as the spring grass was available sooner than on the northern route, although the trail's importance was essentially commercial — a freight route, rather than a major path of westward migration. The Arkansas Trail's main advantages were firm level ground, and good supplies of wood, water and grass; when transporting merchandise, these advantages far outweighed the extra distances involved:

> "Let me say one word about Kansas City and the Arkansas road," wrote an experienced freighter. "You have without doubt the best road in the world to the mines... I had positively rather freight for 10 cents over the Arkansas route than get 15 cents on the Platte." [19]
> "The Arkansas is undoubtedly 'the route'," another correspondent emphasized, "the best natural road in the world; grass plenty all seasons of the year ... and not one 'hard pull' on the whole route from Council Grove to Pike's Peak." [20]

The group had been warned of the dangers of Kiowa and Comanche attack, and of North-South border raids, but in the event the Sheldon-Tappan party was unmolested. With no break in the drought, they were thankful to have chosen the Arkansas Trail. The river had dwindled to a narrow silver band in the middle of a great bed of sand but they were never without sufficient water or grass.

The ox-drawn wagons covered an average of 15-20 miles a day, Crofutt recalled: "days of traveling, watching, resting; nights on guard ... as we plodded with the ox-team towards the land of gold." For Crofutt, the immensity of the plains, and the millions of buffalo blackening them at intervals as far as the eye could see, were unforgettable first impressions. Rather than becoming wearied by the monotony, he was captivated by the stillness, the ever-changing patterns of light, and the grandeur and beauty of the prairie. Although another decade was to pass before Crofutt found his particular style, his future as one of the most enthusiastic and prolific writers on the American West dawned on that first journey across the plains. Indeed, Crofutt could echo the sentiments of another pioneer heading into Colorado at this time in an ox-drawn wagon:

> "Days and weeks slipped by as we pursued our tedious journey westward across the plains, but I loved every moment of it, for I was young and it was spring, the prairies were beautiful, and this unknown land gave promise of great adventure." [21]

The Foot of the Rockies:
Colorado City on the Fourth of July, 1860

At Bent's Old Fort (abandoned by William Bent in 1849), Crofutt's party turned off the Santa Fe Trail and continued west beside the Arkansas River to Fountain, near the old Fort Pueblo. This old Mexican frontier fort had been deserted since Christmas 1854 when Ute Indians wiped out the inhabitants. Its large square was enclosed by a low, crumbling adobe wall with a single gateway. In the 1840s and early '50s, however, Fort Pueblo had housed a small, mainly Mexican population raising cattle and corn in the surrounding Arkansas meadows, and it had been a welcome stopping point for traders and others travelling on the Arkansas Trail, or along the mountain front between the North Platte and Mexico.

The Sheldon-Tappan party explored the ruined fort. "There was no Pueblo City in 1860," Crofutt later recalled, "unless *four* Mexican adobe hovels could be called a city." These had been hurriedly built in the winter of 1859-60, using blocks from the old fort, by a small group of settlers from Independence, Missouri, in order to establish a rival to Fountain — a similarly tiny adobe "town" created in 1858 on the opposite side of Fountain Creek. Nearby, the Creek joined the Arkansas River and it was here that Zebulon Pike's party had camped on 23rd November 1806 before heading toward the "Grand Peak", which he sighted but never climbed. By the 1830s, however, military maps had confirmed the name Pike's Peak. A party of 'Peakers' had over-wintered at Fountain in 1858-9 because of the good supplies of grass and cottonwood, but in time Pueblo, on the west side of the Creek, became the principal settlement. Sheldon, Spencer, Crowell, Tappan and Crofutt rested at Fountain for the night before turning north and following the Cherokee Trail along the base of the Rockies towards Pike's Peak. Finally, on June 30th, after five weeks and 700 miles of continuous travel from Lawrence, the wagons rolled into Colorado City.[22]

Colorado City turned out to be a collection of about 300 dwellings and half-a-dozen stores strung out along "Colorado Avenue" which ran parallel with Fountain Creek. "Although a young town, Colorado City is located at the very foot of Pike's Peak, and is growing with wonderful

COLORADO CITY IN THE EARLY 1860s
in Alfred E. Mathews, *Pencil Sketches of Colorado,* 1866
The sketch shows part of Colorado Avenue, the grove of cottonwood trees lining
Fountain Creek, and behind the cleft of Ute Pass, Pike's Peak.

rapidity," the *Lawrence Republican* had reported in March 1860. Of
course, everything was relative. "Out here," sniffed a visitor from the East,
"the word 'city' is attached to every place of more than three houses." But
growth had been rapid since the town was formally established in August
1859; Colorado City had consisted then of a dozen log cabins and a
cluster of tents, and the founding citizens from Lawrence, including
Lewis Tappan and M.S. Beach, were delighted at the progress their town
had made.

Gold prospectors had camped there in 1858 and called the proposed
townsite El Paso since it lay on the high plains at the entrance to the Ute
Pass. This was the well established Indian route to the hunting grounds
in the South Park section of the Rockies, and the geographical importance
of the pass as a gateway into the mountains highlighted the potential of

El Paso (renamed Eldorado and then Colorado City) once gold was discovered at Tarryall, Fairplay, Buckskin, and California Gulch around the edges of South Park [Map VII].

Only a few days before Crofutt and his friends arrived in Colorado City, the wagon road up Ute Pass had been the focus of much local excitement. A company from Eastern Kansas, under a charter from the Territorial Legislature, had attempted to take over responsibility for the road and levy a toll on all traffic between Colorado City and South Park. Since the local inhabitants had already worked hard to repair and improve the road themselves, they insisted it remain free. A group of them tore down the toll gate and burned the cabins of the East Kansas company officials involved. "Last seen they were on their way to Denver," grinned one observer, "proposing to 'sue' in a country where there is no law."

The Sheldon-Tappan party brought their wagons to a halt outside Lewis Tappan's store, the town's first dry goods house. Colorado City was getting ready for its first Fourth of July celebration which was being organized with great enthusiasm by a group of founder members including Melancthon Beach, George Bute, Charles Pearsall, and Anthony Bott:

> "Most were away in the mountains between spring and fall hunting for gold, but there were about fifty people present," Bott recalled.
> "We held a picnic down in the cottonwood grove back of the Stockbridge place. It was a beautiful spread under the trees, and M.S. Beach delivered an eloquent oration on patriotism." [23]

Blacksmith Sheafor attended to the anvil-firing among other diversions, and in the evening a "grand ball" was held in a vacant store, with a fiddler playing long into the night for the dancing despite the fact that Colorado City could muster only six women for the occasion. Crofutt, Crowell, James Tappan, Sheldon and Spencer all had the time of their lives, an exuberant celebration under the stars, beneath the shadowy bulk of Pike's Peak.

"Of course, there were no fireworks," Sheldon added later as he relived the event. "The nearest place from which fireworks could have been obtained then was St. Louis or Kansas City, and people were too industrious and economical to indulge in *luxuries* for a Fourth of July celebration. While we had clothing and provisions, very few had any ready money." Recalling Mel Beach's oration, Sheldon continued:

> "A majority of the people in Colorado City were loyal and ready to celebrate the occasion ... but there had already been mutterings of a secession by the southern states and war was talked of. There were a number of southerners in camp, and while the Union adherents outnumbered them, trouble might have resulted from flag-raisings or other demonstrations." [24]

Looking for Gold

James Tappan, Sheldon and Spencer decided to stay in Colorado City for a while and take stock of the immediate surroundings. Crofutt and Ben Crowell, however, were anxious to push on and explore the latest gold discoveries on the margins of South Park.

They set out on 5th July and followed the valley of Fountain Creek (Fontaine qui Bouille) back into the mountains. To the right, they passed massive, curiously-shaped outcrops of vivid red sandstone; to the left, three bubbling soda springs whose spray had encrusted the surrounding rocks. As the valley steepened, Crofutt and Crowell followed the winding wagon road over Ute Pass (6800 ft), and after several more hours reached the diggings along Tarryall Creek. Crofutt and Crowell found them crammed with prospectors; Hamilton, Fairplay and Tarryall already had a population of about five thousand. Their hearts sank as it quickly became evident that in July 1860, they were late arrivals at the Pike's Peak gold rush.

Hundreds of others were making the same discovery. The Howbert party had also struggled up to the Tarryall Diggings in June 1860. Irving Howbert recorded the scene:

> "Tarryall Gulch was alive with people washing gold from the sands and gravel along the creek . . . Large numbers of gold seekers were arriving every day, and, at the same time, many disappointed ones were leaving for other mining camps."

The Howberts secured a claim at the lower end of the main Tarryall Diggings, but

> "much to our disgust the complete clean-up showed only $6.00-worth of gold for three days' work of three men and a boy." [25]

This was so disappointing that the party immediately abandoned the claim and quit . . . "some owners had drawn the prizes, but apparently we had drawn a blank."

Some sixty miles to the north, Gregory's Diggings had given birth to Mountain City, soon to be overtaken by Black Hawk and Central City, now the focus of hectic regional activity. Many Lawrence citizens were there, including the ebullient B.F. Dalton who with a partner, Edward Ropes, had successfully established a quartz mill at Gregory's Diggings, and also opened a store there, in addition to the extensive new Clothing Emporium he had just opened in Denver. "The number of Lawrence people in the diggings is very large, including many families," a correspondent informed his Lawrence readers in August 1860. "I sometimes feel inclined to wonder while meeting so many of your old familiar faces, whether you have anybody left at home!" [26]

About thirty thousand people were already located at Jackson, Jefferson, Deadwood and Spanish Diggings, and elsewhere within a ten-mile radius of Gregory's original discovery. Even so, less than one-third of the gold seekers were estimated to be making enough to cover their expenses.

> "Work in the diggings is a toilsome and monotonous occupation," wrote C.M. Clarke, prospecting at Clear Creek in July 1860, "and the labor generally poorly recompensed . . . A miner's life is a hard and laborious one, cut off from all the refinements and comforts . . . and surrounded by dirt and filth." At the end of the day, with little or no reward for all their effort, Clarke's party would "return to the tent in no pleasant mood, dissatisfied, disheartened, and the majority about ready to clear out." [27]

The outlook for newcomers needing quick returns was bleak. Thomas Golden, one of the successful prospectors, and principal founder of the town on Clear Creek bearing his name, summarized the position with some crisp advice to the masses: "Stay in the States, and we will bring the gold there."

Crofutt and Crowell had neither the mining experience, nor the funds to engage the services of those who had. They were soon to abandon the idea of gold prospecting and, like many others in a similar fix, turn their thoughts to freighting, the skill they had learned on the trail.

Everything was on the move; mining tools, pipes, machinery, nails, ropes, sacks, blankets and provisions were being hauled into the mountains. Clothing, boots, cooking and heating stoves, tinware, liquor and ledgers all formed part of the cargo bound for the mining camps. The diggings were a confusion of tents, cabins, sluices, carts and wagons, mules, horses and cattle, slaughter houses and saloons, all set against the constant accompaniment of sawing and hammering.

There was an insatiable demand for wood and hay haulage, both at the mines and in Denver. Old Charles Stearns, the Lawrence storekeeper, had been unable to stay away from all the excitement. He toured the gold regions, puffing and blowing up the steep mountain slopes, and missing nothing when it came to pricing goods and gauging profits:

> "Teamsters and day laborers do the best, I think. A man with a good team can get plenty of work hauling quartz and wood over the most horrible roads imaginable. He wants patience and Christian fortitude, together with gentle cattle and stout wagons." [28]

Charles Stearns was right. Crowell and Crofutt decided to cut their losses, return to Colorado City and see what success, if any, Sheldon and Spencer had been having in their absence. Ben hung on a little longer, loathe to give up too quickly and turn his back on all the excitement. He was still up at South Park on 20th July 1860 when the Kansas Territorial Census enumerator, toiling all summer from one mining camp to another, recorded Ben (occupation, Miner!) and four new-found associates from Connecticut, Virginia, Ohio, and Indiana working a section of the Diggings together.[29] Soon afterwards, however, Ben ran out of money and was forced to give up. He made his way down the Ute wagon road back to Colorado City, and to the realities of earning a living.

Crofutt, meanwhile, had pushed on to Denver as he was anxious to be reunited with his wife. A mid-July reunion was much later in the season than the couple had planned, although George felt he had packed at least four years' adventure into the four months since he left Pennsylvania.

First Impressions of Denver

Anna Crofutt had already arrived in Denver, a good six weeks earlier in fact. According to the record, she came in on 1st June 1860, apparently either on the Rice & Parker stagecoach from St. Joseph or by the Central Overland California & Pike's Peak line from Atchison, after making the 650-mile journey across the plains, via the Platte River route, in 6 days 12 hours.[30]

The C.O.C. & P.P. had been reorganized by William Russell during the winter of 1859-60 (this time with the help of Alexander Majors and William Waddell), to replace his bankrupt Leavenworth & Pike's Peak Express Co. Russell had abandoned the Republican River route in late June 1859 and switched to the Platte so that in 1860 he could carry mail and passengers over a greatly extended line from St. Joseph, Mo., Atchison and Leavenworth to Denver and Salt Lake City. The Concord coach rattled into Denver three times a week and unloaded passengers and mail at Bradford's Corner, home of the C.O.C.'s Stage, Express and Post Office at the junction of Blake and G (16th St.).

Anna Crofutt waited in lodgings in Denver for her husband to arrive. In six days, she had been whirled across Kansas and Nebraska from the Missouri River to the base of the Rockies and deposited in a noisy, crowded frontier town of five thousand people, most of them it seemed made up of miners, gamblers, loafers and drunks. In addition, about a thousand Arapahoe Indians were camped in the streets, preparing for a war-party against the Utes which began in mid-June. In the summer of 1860, the first sight of Denver was anything but reassuring.

By this time, several frame and a few brick buildings — banks, stores, the smart new City Druggist, and the Apollo Theater for example, had risen above the sea of cabins, tents and freight wagons. Another traveller offered his own terse description: "Denver's got one large cemetery, two hotels and a hundred liquor stores, with drinking and fighting all the while." Anna Crofutt could discover the rest for herself.

As the capital of the renowned Pike's Peak region, Denver was a shock and a disappointment to many who had crossed the plains — "a most forlorn and desolate-looking metropolis . . . nominally in Kansas but practically as far from government and civilization as central Africa." Vigilante Committees and informal courts had been established by local citizens in most of the towns and mining districts to deal with "the murderers, thieves, rowdies, gamblers and desperadoes bedeviling the Pike's Peak region."

Denver had organized its Vigilantes in September 1859 but the "reign of terror" continued.

> "Our place is infested with hoards of villains," wrote one Denverite to his brother in Wisconsin. "Men are found murdered on the highway, others are robbed, while thefts of stock are of frequent occurrence. . . . A Vigilance Committee in town commenced punishing the rascals in right good earnest; they strung up a few, . . . But what better can we expect in a community without laws? We are neither in the Union or out of it." [31]

Attempts by Auraria-Denver to persuade Congress to go further on the government and law-and-order issue in 1859-60 and establish Jefferson Territory had failed. "Denver remains lively and deadly," another inhabitant wrote in July 1860, "a shooting or stabbing occurs almost daily."

Passengers coming in on the stage had to find room-and-board in town. The Broadwell House (formerly the Pacific House) on Larimer and G did nicely if they could afford it, but most of the wagon parties camped outside on the meadows bordering Cherry Creek, Clear Creek and the South Platte. The river banks and the surrounding pastures were covered with tents, wagons and thousands of grazing animals; "When I first arrived in Denver," Crofutt recalled, "the bottom lands were marked out by the heavy growth of cottonwoods beneath which, where the Union Depot now stands, were camped hundreds of gold seekers."

At first, Auraria on the west side of Cherry Creek was larger than Denver but in April 1860 the rival settlements, together with Highland, consolidated to form Denver City. Denver remained, first and foremost, the port of entry to the mines. As the principal point of interchange between plains and mountain traffic, the town strengthened its position as the main regional service and supply centre for mining communities on both sides of the Continental Divide. In the spring and summer of 1860, while miners thronged the Tarryall, South Park, California Gulch, and Central City-Clear Creek areas, many were probing farther west. Prospectors crossed the Park Range and the main crest of the Rockies to begin working the headwaters of the Colorado system along Blue River; others worked their way along the upper Arkansas and over the Sawatch Range.

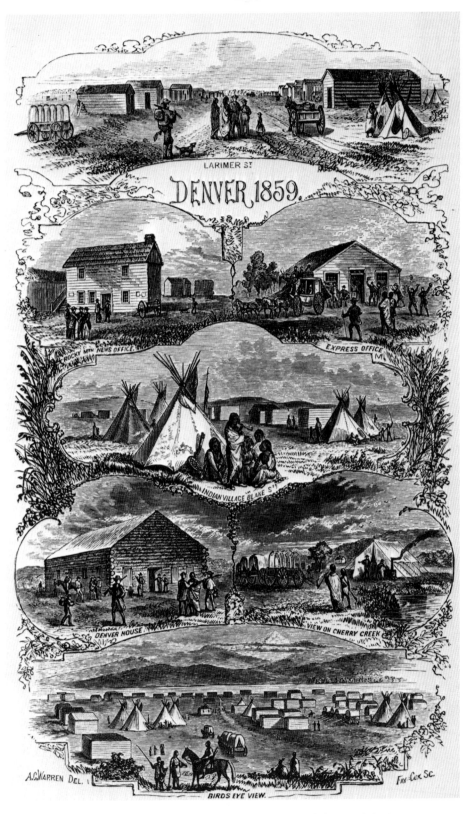

SEVEN VIEWS IN DENVER, 1859 in Richardson, *Beyond the Mississippi*, 1867

We do not know whether Anna Crofutt was able to wait the six or seven weeks in Denver before her husband arrived. By the middle of July, the chances are that she was getting desperately short of money. Already in her forties, Anna may also have found the isolation, discomfort, and lawlessness of Denver a poor substitute for life in Pennsylvania. To make matters worse, the weather seemed as violent and unpredictable as the population. Streets full of choking dust had been transformed at the end of June 1860 by the worst hail and rainstorm many had ever experienced. As lightning struck, water poured through Denver into Cherry Creek and the South Platte, turning the whole of the lower part of the town "into one great reservoir of muddy water." Brick fronts, board walks, and frame supports collapsed into the surging torrents; cellars filled and thousands of dollars-worth of goods were destroyed. The place was a wreck, Anna Crofutt must have decided, gloomily surveying the scene. There is no further reference to her in the early 1860s and the probable explanation is that she returned to the East. Anna is always to remain a shadowy figure in the story.

George Crofutt did not stay long in Denver; he took the wagon road south for some eighty miles along the base of the Rockies, over the Arkansas Divide and back to Colorado City. On the way, Crofutt took stock of his position. He was committed to the West, but why worry over the details of his location in this part of the world? The first question was, should he settle anywhere in the Pike's Peak region? Did not the original idea of going all the way to California still offer him more opportunity? The latest rumour on that count, however, was that passes through the Wasatch Range east of Salt Lake City were already blocked with snow and impassable — a false alarm as Crofutt later discovered. He would think again about going to California in the spring; meanwhile he had to make enough money to see himself through the next few months. He hurried on and was soon back in Colorado City, in the cheerful company of Ben Crowell, Jim Tappan, Al Sheldon and Fred Spencer.

The Development of Colorado Territory in the 1860s: A Freighter's Life in the Pre-Railroad Age

Sheldon and Spencer had found their surveyors' skills much in demand.

> "Laying out and making fine wagon roads up through the passes and sections of the mountains seems to be the order of the day at present," reported one local observer at the start of the 1860s; ... "The prosperity of the valley towns, and of the towns at the immediate *foot* of the mountains, and of those *in* the mountains will be so greatly affected by these roads that parties are willing to sink thousands in making them ... The folks in the States have no idea of the extent and number of towns and cities and settlements scattered ten, twenty, fifty miles apart throughout this country at the present time." [1]

By the time Crofutt returned from Denver, Sheldon and Spencer had already explored the plains and foothill zone around Colorado City. The two surveyors now wanted to investigate the area to the north between Colorado City and Denver, particularly the landscape of the South Platte-Arkansas Divide whose buttes, mesas and plateaux ran out on to the plains from the base of the Rockies for about forty miles. This dark forested belt, rising to more than 7500 feet and known locally as The Pineries, was strikingly distinctive when viewed from a distance. Crofutt was the only one of the party so far to have crossed the Divide, and he relayed his impressions to the others, including that of the obvious lack of good wagon roads each side of the main Denver trail. They decided to get going without further delay. Ben's days as a miner at Pike's Peak fell squarely into the "bust" category, but he was not going to settle for working in the Tappan store; that could be left to Jim Tappan. Like Crofutt, Ben turned to freighting, and the prospects for freighting looked better nearer to Denver.

For the rest of the summer, the group based their activities on the Divide. Near the head of Cherry Creek, deep in the Pineries, they built a rough cabin which was dubbed *Ivan Cracken* — "my first country residence in 1860," Crofutt always described it, half-affectionately, "constructed at the time the rocks were rent." [Map VII] It sufficed as a summer shelter, however, being close to a stream and a strong spring, and surrounded by good hunting within the forest, especially for antelope. Eight miles higher up the creek was George Redman's cabin, the first in this part of the valley. With Jonathan Lincoln and Joseph Gile, Redman had settled beside upper West Cherry Creek (or Redman's Creek as it became known) on 10th July 1860, about three weeks before Crofutt and the others selected their own site. For a while, between them, they had the valley to themselves.

Sheldon and Spencer examined the Divide carefully and made a preliminary survey of routes in the valleys of Running Creek, Cherry Creek and Plum Creek. In the watershed's western section, they rediscovered what was later to be called Summit, Divide, and finally Palmer Lake.[2] This had been spotted in 1820 on Major Stephen Long's expedition,

19. MOUNTAIN AND PLAIN: THE TWO WORLDS OF COLORADO

Looking northeastwards down the lower slopes of the Rocky Mountain Front Range and across the plains to the dark skyline of The Pineries, on the South Platte-Arkansas Divide.

Seen from Mount Manitou; the modern highway approach to Ute Pass appears bottom right.

but Captain John Frémont, who must have passed close to the lake during his expedition to the Rocky Mountains in 1842-3, did not mention it. Neither did Francis Parkman, who crossed the Divide in August 1846 on his way south to Fort Pueblo, nor George Ruxton, who was on the Divide in 1847 during his exploration of the Pike's Peak region in 1846-7. The old trail in front of the Rockies linking Santa Fe, Pueblo, St. Vrain and Fort Laramie crossed the Divide some sixteen miles east of the lake. Various portions and branches of this ancient trackway were known as Trapper's Trail, Jimmy Camp Trail, the Old Divide Trail, the Government or Military Road, and the Cherokee Trail. After the Pike's Peak boom, the section of the trail between Colorado City and Denver was improved to provide a serviceable stage and wagon road, with the twenty-or-so miles over the crest of the Divide graded more gently and brought closer to the mountain front. The road was still about eight miles east of Palmer Lake, however, whose existence remained forgotten to all but the Indians and a few trappers until Sheldon and Spencer found it again in 1860.

Crofutt and Crowell meanwhile cut and baled hay from morning to night. They hired a team and hauled the hay to Denver and into the mountains to Central City where, as winter approached, the selling price climbed rapidly from $50 to $150 a ton.[3] From Central City, Crofutt also took desperately needed supplies of hay and wood out to some of the more isolated mining camps and found that the income from this modest enterprise far exceeded his expectations. It was proving to be an excellent time for small-scale freighters to enter the business.

Both men decided to locate farms with part of their earnings. In these early days, groups of farmers as well as miners protected their interests by forming Claim Clubs and electing their own Recorders to file the details of each member's claim. Farm land, timber lots, town sites and mining property were treated this way. Crofutt chose a quarter-section near the South Platte river just west of Denver.[4] The land was alongside the town's first race course, notorious for its gamblers, shootings and fistfights, but the location looked good for future development. Ben Crowell favoured Colorado City rather than Denver and chose land on the south side of the town, about a mile below the confluence of Cheyenne and Fountain Creeks, on a stretch known as Big Flat. By now, several newcomers were beginning to irrigate sections of bottom land along Fountain Creek. While he continued to haul freight between Colorado City and Denver, Crowell and some of his new neighbours joined forces to dig an irrigation ditch from Cheyenne Creek, and began to raise a variety of crops for sale to the local stores, and to the supply wagons hauling up the Ute trail to the mining camps.

Ben Crowell was also becoming more involved in the civic affairs of Colorado City which in 1860-61 were dominated by New Englanders and

20.   FREIGHT TRAINS CLIMBING UTE PASS
in *Crofutt's Grip-Sack Guide of Colorado,* 1881

by newcomers from New York-New Jersey. One day, shortly after his arrival, Ben found himself elected from among the crowd on main street as one of three judges at a 'People's Court' assembled to try a Mexican charged with horse stealing. The crowd stood and listened to the witnesses, heard the defence, voted the man guilty and within a few minutes watched the hanging. That was that, Ben discovered in amazement, as he watched the crowd quickly melt away and go about its business. In August 1861, Crowell was to become the editor of a new four-page weekly called *The Colorado City Journal.*[5] In less than twelve months, the young man from Boston found he had become a successful freighter, farmer and businessman.

Forests and Farms on the Arkansas Divide: Early Days in the Pineries

At the end of the summer in 1860, Crowell, Sheldon and Spencer returned to Colorado City. Crofutt, however, decided to stay on the Divide and at least for the time being, continue to live in *Ivan Cracken*, the log cabin in West Cherry Creek Canyon, eight miles east of Huntsville and forty-two miles from Denver.

He was now on his own, and during that winter of 1860-61, though not the worst by any means, Crofutt discovered just how harsh the climate of the Pineries could be.

> "The times here are a little the hardest that I ever saw," wrote another pioneer in February 1861. "Everything fairly grinds. The great struggle is to get something to eat, (and) to live through till spring."[6]

That year, 1860, frosts occurred every night from the beginning of September; the temperature, which during the summer had been about ten degrees cooler than in Colorado City, suddenly fell sharply as blizzards and heavy snow swept the Divide. Deep drifts enclosed the cabin and the trails as Crofutt struggled to dig a way through and keep going. Although he ran perilously short of supplies, he survived, and with the coming of spring in 1861 made up his mind to stay put. Albinus Sheldon returned to the Pineries a few weeks later, in charge of one of the Government Survey teams sectioning the new Territory of Colorado, which had been established by Congress on 28th February 1861. While supervising the marking of meridians and township boundaries, Sheldon was able to hear how George had managed to endure the winter, patch up the cabin and keep himself alive.

Crofutt's decision to stay on the Divide was a sensible one as the location provided him with a double source of income. The western section, including the Huntsville area, had begun to attract farmers as early as 1859; the numerous strong springs along the Divide which fed tributaries of the South Platte and the Arkansas made the area popular for stock-rearing in the more rugged stretches, and for dairying, hay and vegetable production elsewhere. New settlers were toiling from dawn to dusk during the short summer seasons to develop the pockets of good soil into fertile meadows for potatoes, root crops, and small grains, as well as for profitable horse and mule breeding. Above *Ivan Cracken*, higher up West Cherry Creek, Joseph Gile was already specializing in turnips, and George Redman in horses, cattle and hay from his extensive fields of sweet timothy and clover.

Freighting for the local farmers in and around the Divide, and putting up hay himself, Crofutt came to know the region well. He carried potatoes, cabbages, turnips, beets, cucumbers, melons, and pumpkins into Denver along with butter, cheese and countless wagon-loads of fodder. Crofutt also did business with "Potato Clark", Rufus H. Clark, a round-the-world sailor from Connecticut who had later decided to cross "the great sea of the great plains" to reach the Rockies. He pioneered potato cultivation four miles south of Denver in the spring of 1859, sold his crop for 20-35 cents a pound that year, and by the early 1860s had 250 acres under potatoes alone.[7]

> "Establishing *ranches* is about the best and most money-making pursuit anybody can engage in out here," wrote one enthusiast about the Huntsville-Cherry Creek-Plum Creek region in 1859. "Farming — raising crops of corn, wheat, oats and potatoes — will pay here next year better than even successful mining. Raising staples and fancy vegetables, such as cabbages, beets, turnips, watermelons, onions, and so forth, would, with certainty, ensure men considerable fortunes by next summer and fall." [8]

There was much truth in this. Denver and the mining communities it served were a rapidly expanding market for local producers, and many were soon anxious to take advantage of it. After eighteen months' prospecting in Colorado, a young easterner assured his brother:

> "No better country . . . can be found for any enterprizing young man, who will come with the expectation of *making this his future home*. He can realize this by any branch of industry he may undertake and *stick* to, but most emphatically by farming." [9]

Travellers noted that the high prices for produce were tempting the disappointed miner to seek in the soil of the valleys what he failed to find in the rocks of the mountains. Local stores longed to reduce their dependence on freighted food supplies from Atchison, Nebraska City and other Missouri River towns, especially flour, corn and wheat. Long hauls and unpredictable trail conditions often resulted in scarcity or glut, and both played havoc with prices.

Crofutt's second reason for settling at the head of Cherry Creek lay in the Pineries themselves, today known as the Black Forest. These extensive stands of Ponderosa pine and scrub oak mantling the Divide's main ridges were one of the best and most accessible sources of timber in the entire Pike's Peak region. The first steam saw mills had arrived in Denver early in 1859. One was installed in the Cherry Creek Pineries by Cooper and Wyatt, two enterprising individuals who were the first to get their lumber and sawn timber to the Denver market. It was stacked ready for sale on 21st April 1859, two days before the first issue of Denver's *Rocky Mountain News*, and in good time for editor William Byers to advertise its arrival! That early Pike's Peak booster, Daniel C. Oakes, built two saw mills in the Pineries, one below Richardson Hill, about 25 miles south of Denver, and another near Huntsville, on East Plum Creek. Others followed and the freighting of timber from the Divide into towns and mining camps became steady, lucrative work.

Many did it as short-term measure. "Looking back," said one, recalling a season's freighting as a youth, "it sharpened my wits and taught me to think for myself in every emergency, and to look ahead and try to avoid possible trouble ... the experience obtained was of the greatest value to me in after years." [10] Two others from Crofutt's home town of Danbury, Conn., Wildman and Andrews, had hauled lumber from a Pineries' saw mill into Denver to make ends meet once their mining claims failed to provide them with more than about $3 apiece per day — "The time for fooling has gone by," Thomas Wildman informed his relieved mother and sister in Connecticut, "I am content to work hard."

Wildman's friend Andrews hated freighting, however, and soon departed to prospect along the Blue River. He was unsuccessful, lost interest in the West, and hotfooted it home to Danbury. Thomas stuck to freighting for nearly three months before getting a job in Denver as a clerk. Within a couple of weeks he had worn out his clothes and written to his mother asking for any of his brother's cast-offs that could be spared. Bullwhacking and freighting admittedly were not the stuff that Western dreams were made on, but men and boys from widely different backgrounds could soon live and look the part if they had the muscle and determination:

> "I stopped at a ranch yesterday to buy some milk to make my dinner off of and the old lady remarked that I did not look much like one who was brought up to drive team. I told her I had not been, but that in this country everybody must work for a living." [11]

Crofutt certainly agreed with that statement but unlike Thomas Wildman, Crofutt soon came to regard freighting as his regular occupation. Between 1861 and 1864, he concentrated on hauling logs, sawn timber and general freight to and from Denver, up to the mining camps in the Rockies or south over the Arkansas Divide to Colorado City and the Cañon City area.

21.   THE OLD PINERIES WAGON ROAD THROUGH WEST CHERRY CREEK CANYON
This was one of Crofutt's regular routes as he freighted over the Divide.

Like Colorado City, Cañon City had been founded in the summer of 1859 as another gateway settlement to the Rocky Mountains, especially to the gold diggings around South Park, California Gulch and the Blue. As he freighted through the town in 1861, Crofutt had watched solid, stone-fronted buildings being erected and the corner lots eagerly taken up. But the nearest placers were soon worked out, and Cañon City lost business to the gateway towns farther north.

Freighting meant long hours and strenuous work in all weathers — yoking and unyoking oxen, maintaining the wagon, heaving, braking, loading and roping timber, seeking business, getting in supplies. One of Crofutt's most difficult hauls was over the steep Mt. Vernon wagon road which ran from Golden to Black Hawk and Central City. Most of the machinery and equipment for the mines, mills and crushers in this busy region was hauled over the Mt. Vernon road which ascended to more than 8000 feet and then had to negotiate very steep gradients down to Black Hawk. "Working in teams," Crofutt recorded,

"we eased the wagons down by ropes secured by a turn or two around huge

102

pine trees beside the road. The peeled bark and the marks of the ropes are still to be seen. It once took ten of us, besides our teams, *nine days* to lower one boiler, the weight of which was a little over seven tons."

Crofutt normally worked alone, however, although he was acquiring plenty of new friends and neighbours among the farmers and stockmen moving into the area. A few stockmen had settled around *Ivan Cracken*, and the small community later became known as Rock Ridge. Horses grazed the lush creek bottom grass but in general, this rugged section of West Cherry Canyon was unsuited to irrigation and had been given over to stock raising. Crofutt continued to cut his hay and ranch his cattle among the surrounding bluffs, stumps and pine forests.[12] In some ways, each small valley seaming the slopes of the Divide was a world apart, a world enclosed between local dividing ridges that separated the different headwaters flowing through the Pineries from the main crest. Crofutt's journeys wove these individual valleys into, for him, a connected and keenly observed landscape, and he came to know the nearly eighty-mile stretch between Denver and Colorado City as his own.

The volume of business with Denver and the mining camps stimulated greater activity on the northern side of the Divide and allowed Crofutt to vary his routes when going in that direction. He became a familiar figure on all of them. The trail down Cherry Creek Canyon took him past Mort Fisher's (Judge Wyatt's) old saw mill, set up in 1859 at Russellville — the site of Green Russell's first discovery of gold (in 1858) in the Pike's Peak region. "Where it all began," Crofutt recalled, before, in the twinkling of an eye, the lodes high in the Rockies pulled their thousands away from the foothills and up into the mines.

A few miles farther on, a small ranching community had developed around the 'Frank's Town' of James Frank Gardner, a live wire who helped to organize the local Claim Club for new settlers along Cherry Creek and who, in 1861, successfully challenged D.C. Oakes by managing to get the first county-seat of Douglas County officially established at 'Frank's Town' instead of at Oakes' Mill. Crofutt would pass Frank Gardner's cabin where all the county business was conducted, make his calls, and go on another ten miles to the ranch at Pine Grove (later Parker). So familiar a figure was Crofutt in these early days that this section of the canyon is still known locally as Crowfoot Valley, the small tributary creek near the forgotten *Ivan Cracken* as Crowfoot Creek, and the steep rise west from Frank(s)town to Castle Rock as Crowfoot Hill.[13]

Nearer to Denver he would pick up that last section of the Smoky Hill Trail used by Russell and Jones in the early days of the Leavenworth & Pike's Peak Express, and follow it over the plain alongside Cherry Creek into town.

Another trail over the Divide, about eight miles to the west, ran

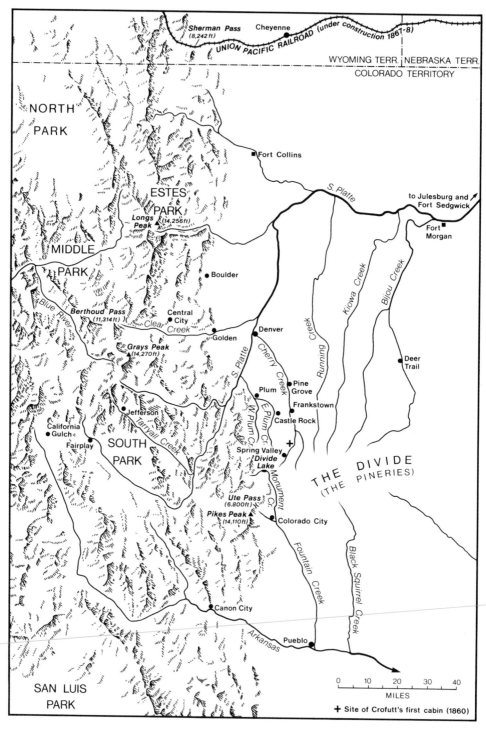

VII. **CENTRAL COLORADO IN THE 1860s**

through the "rough, ragged, bluffy country" of East Plum Creek Canyon. Further improvement of this section of the wagon road which ran along the Rocky Mountain Front, first through West and later East Plum Creek Canyon, had been authorized by the Second Territorial Legislature in 1862, and a few ranches were strung along the nearly eighty-mile stretch between Denver and Colorado City to service the needs of the travellers.

Most freighters called at the Coberly ranch ('Half-Way House') on West Plum Creek for food, rest, and an exchange of news. George Coberly, together with his wife Sarah and four children, had crossed the plains from the East in 1858 after struggling unsuccessfully to survive the effects of the 1857 Panic. They wasted no time looking for gold but turned immediately to farming and ranched on both West and East Plum Creeks — the latter near Huntsville, that prosperous agricultural area where the Coberlys' first neighbour was D.C. Oakes.

In the early 1860s, however, the Coberly place meant Mrs. Coberly's home-sweet-home on West Plum Creek. "Mother" Coberly, as George Crofutt always called her, kept a clean, cheerful, welcoming home. Travellers were warmed and well fed; the air was filled with the smells of fresh baking. Kitchen and stores were stocked with beef and pork cuts, hams and cheeses, and the shelves laden with home-made choke-cherry, plum and gooseberry jams, sauces and preserves. Plain rooms were prettied with needlework, the porch jars filled with wild flowers and berries.[14]

> "Coberly's is the best house perhaps on the whole route [between Denver and Colorado City]," Bishop Talbot recorded in his diary in the early 1860s, as he and his wife journeyed along the trails — "An excellent supper, comfortable sleep, and kind attention quite refreshing." [15]

The Coberly place was known for miles around as one of the few ranches offering overnight accommodation and as such, it became an important source of regional information where talk and entertainment continued long after supper. Mrs. Coberly always greeted Crofutt as an old friend, as indeed he was since they had first met at the Fourth of July celebration in 1860 in Colorado City. She and her elder daughter had helped to prepare the picnic and later danced to the fiddler on that memorable night after Crofutt and his friends had completed the long journey across the plains.

If Crofutt crossed over to East Plum Creek, the wagon road to Denver took him past Old Man Fisher's place where, in complete contrast to the Coberlys' home, the elderly widower and his ranch house survived in an equally dirty, dilapidated condition. Crofutt appears to have carried Fisher's wood from time to time to sell in Denver. Then it was on to Castle Rock, a small community of about fifty settlers, most of them raising beef but with dairy cattle, improved pastures and vegetable gardens marking

22.   ONE OF THE EARLY TRAILS TO DENVER PASSING BENEATH CASTLE ROCK
The prominent landmark of Castle Rock, nearly 6600 feet above sea level, forms the
northern gateway to the Pineries. Tabular sandstones are capped here by the resistant
Castle Rock Conglomerate.

out the rich irrigated bottom lands along Plum Creek. The vivid splashes
of green caught his eye amid the tawny hay fields: "Among the brown
bordering mountains, nestling in the hollows, are miniature prairies —
patches of green on which the rays of the morning sun fall in folds of
yellow light, enveloping them in a flood of golden beauty." How he loved
this land! Crofutt would let his gaze sweep from the Rockies' great Front
Range, across Plum Creek towards the lovely valleys of the Cherry Creek
system unrolling from the Pineries. Above him, the spectacular sandstone
butte of Castle Rock dominated this section of the route, its gaunt,
dun-coloured mass thrust against the skyline. Crofutt never tired of this
strikingly varied landscape between the Pineries, the Rockies, and the
town of Denver.

If he had time, he could call on miner and stockman John Craig who
had pioneered in Happy Canyon in 1859. Craig was the same age as

Crofutt and came from Pennsylvania. Isolation and near-starvation had driven Craig down to work at D.C. Oakes' sawmill in 1860 before he got enough money together to run the ranch in Plum Creek Canyon known as the Round Top Corral, and later to develop the site of Sedalia (Plum).

If time was short, Crofutt headed straight for Denver over Richardson Hill, across the Plum Creek Divide. At the foot of this long steep hill was Oakes' mill, opposite which, beside a spring, was the Richardson ranch. This was known throughout the region as the Pretty Woman's Ranch after Sylvester and Elizabeth Richardson arrived there from Catskill, New York, via Wisconsin and Denver, in June 1861. Mrs. Richardson was described as the most beautiful woman in the Territory, and until the Territorial wagon road was re-routed in 1864 and Richardson Hill by-passed, the grace of the hostess and the excellent food made it a favourite stopping point.[16] Pretty Woman's Ranch was usually Crofutt's last stop going north before the long pull up Richardson Hill, a pause at the top of the Plum Creek Divide to rest his team and enjoy the magnificent view along the Front Range, and then the final twenty miles over the gentler slopes into Denver.

Freighting loads in the opposite direction to Colorado City took Crofutt south through the Pineries, over the crest of the Divide and past Dirty Woman's Ranch (25 miles from Colorado City), near the farming, stock-raising and lumbermen's community of Monument. In 1860-61, the rancher's wife had become a by-word throughout the region for her dirty appearance and slovenly habits; pigs, goats, chickens, dogs and cats wandered freely through the ranch house turning the whole place into a pig-sty.[17] New owners, Henry Walker and his wife, took the place over in 1862 and cleaned it up, although it remained known for miles around as Dirty Woman's Ranch, much to Mrs. Walker's annoyance. After two years, the Walkers moved out and the place was later taken on by a hard-working woman with a young family who ran the ranch and provided simple board and lodging for up to six overnight travellers. Her four small rooms were papered with *Harper's Weekly* and the *Atlantic Monthly*, recorded one visitor in 1867; there was plenty of good food, well cooked and served in plain but clean surroundings.[18] But however unjustly, Dirty Woman's Ranch was never known as anything else. The name Dirty Woman's Creek stuck fast even longer, and survives to this day.

From time to time, George saw Ben Crowell, still raising crops as well as sheep and cattle on his highly profitable irrigated spread at Big Flat. In 1861-2, Ben was also busy editing the weekly *Colorado City Journal* — "A rather spicy affair," said their old trail partner Albinus Sheldon, "as might well be presumed with the name of B.F. Crowell figuring prominently as its editor!" [19] Spurred on by the Tappan brothers, Ben was becoming more deeply involved in Colorado City politics. These were exciting times for the small town. Several months of argument and lobbying had kept the population at fever pitch after Congress had established Colorado Territory on 28th February 1861; in September of that year their efforts were rewarded when Colorado City was made the Territorial capital. In 1862, after the first general election for Territorial and County officers, Ben Crowell became a member of the Board of the El Paso County Commissioners, and was later made Chairman.

Like Ben, Albinus Sheldon had also prospered, and at the same time become increasingly involved in boosting the fortunes of Colorado City. In 1861, as well as leading a survey team on the Arkansas Divide, Sheldon had been in demand up at the mines around Breckenridge, Hamilton and Fairplay. In addition to demarcating claim boundaries and re-routing some of the wagon roads and bridges in the mountains, he had advised miners on drainage problems and also installed hydraulic machinery at Little French Gulch. In 1862, Sheldon became the first County Surveyor of El Paso, a Justice of the Peace, and the president or secretary of numerous committees and organizations in Colorado City.

Political office had no attraction for Crofutt, however. Although struggling to make ends meet, he found life on the trail a never-ending source of fascination. He liked being on the move, visiting mills and ranches, taking the trails to the mining communities, pausing to enjoy the secluded beauty of the Rockies' South Park or to watch the evening sun cast changing patterns of light and shadow along the mountain front and over the plains beyond.

It was curious how little fundamental change Crofutt's new life had introduced. Perhaps that was the secret of his happiness. Of course, he had replaced the selling and distribution of magazines with that of farm produce and cords of timber; he relied now not on the railroad, stage and canal boat but on his own ox-drawn wagon; the style and sophistication of New York and Philadelphia had given way to a raw frontier existence in a new West; the risks of business and bankruptcy in the States had been transferred to the struggle for survival in the Territory of Colorado. But he was still his own boss in a job that kept him in contact with a wide variety of people, places and events.

Crofutt would pass through Golden, Central City or Colorado City, do business, look up friends and acquaintances, note what was new since his last visit, and be ready to move on. In Golden, he always tried to call on George West, a printer from Boston who had arrived in 1859 and towards the end of that year started the *Western Mountaineer*, a splendid little newspaper full of news from the mining camps. Before long, Crofutt found West promoting Golden's interests still more in the spirited new *Colorado Transcript*. Wherever he went, Crofutt's interest and experience kept him in touch with local editors and printers who were starting up all over the place. Every small community intent on boosting its fortunes needed its own little *Chronicle*, *Clarion*, *Register*, *Recorder* or *Gazette*.

The Denver Pioneers, and the Changing Fortunes of the Overland Express

There was more to do in Denver, and Crofutt would occasionally stay in town for a few days, make deliveries, buy in supplies, and when necessary attend to his quarter-section across the South Platte river on the north-west edge of town. Down here on the bottom land, Crofutt's neighbour was Thomas M. Sloan who had arrived in Denver in 1859, claimed, like so many others, a quarter-section in advance of the official filing of owner-ship, and built a successful business raising hay and breeding horses and mules. Sloan had found part of his land to be "as dry as an ash pit" so he dug a well and prepared to irrigate the most parched section. He struck a major aquifer, however; large quantities of water quickly rose to the surface and the "ash pit" was transformed into Sloan's Lake. George Turner, a driver on the Denver, Golden and Central City line of the Overland Stage, recalled crossing the Platte in 1860-1 and "following the road through the wide swale where Sloan's Lake is now. It was a good, dry road then, with no water. When I returned to the route in the early part of 1863, the Lake was there as it is now, covering the right of way." [20]

Having found more water than he had bargained for, Tom Sloan built a large Ice House on the edge of the lake and did a roaring trade freighting ice to local stores and breweries, and to settlements along the mountain front as far north as Fort Laramie. Ice was normally packed in sawdust, and Crofutt freighted this when required from saw mills in the Pineries. Sloan invested much of his profit in town by purchasing Jim Broadwell's first boarding-house and running it as the Sloan House. Broadwell meanwhile had bought and renovated the old Pacific House on the corner of Larimer and G (16th St.), turning it into Denver's smartest hotel — the Broadwell House. For a while, Tom Sloan divided his time between his farm and his boarding-house, but in 1866 he disposed of Sloan House and went back to the land.

Crofutt cut and sold the hay crop from his quarter-section next to Sloan's and occasionally rented out the pasture but did no more than that with his 160 acres. Once business was completed in Denver, Crofutt preferred to stay in town and see what was going on by way of new arrivals and new building. He would buy a selection of newspapers fresh in from the States, stuff them away to enjoy at leisure, and call at the office of the *Rocky Mountain News* for a chat with William Byers. There might be mail to be collected. This meant calling at the Central Overland California & Pike's Peak Express Office at Bradford's Corner — the corner of Blake and G (16th) — and joining one of the lines that tailed back down the street.

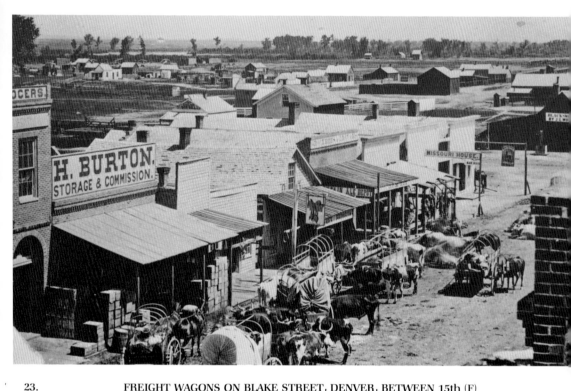

23.   FREIGHT WAGONS ON BLAKE STREET, DENVER, BETWEEN 15th (F)
AND 16th (G) STREETS, IN THE EARLY 1860s

Denver was the major break-of-load point along the Rocky Mountain Front for freight trains arriving from the Missouri River ports. Here, new loads were assembled for the journey to the mining settlements farther west.

At this busy end of Blake Street stand Hiram Burton's storage firm, grocers and provision merchants, liquor stores, a saddlery and harness outfitters, the Missouri Rooming House, and J.L. Woolley's blacksmith works. The view was taken looking north, with the South Platte River in the background.

In 1860, the Overland Express had been bringing in and taking out about five thousand letters a week, and since then, the volume had increased enormously. Collecting mail usually meant hours of patient waiting in line. Some bought a place in the queue and departed on other business. Most whiled away the time talking, gambling or watching the bustle of activity at Denver's busiest intersection. Hinckley's Express Office stood on the opposite corner where, on his first arrival in Denver back in July 1860, Crofutt had watched over $25,000-worth of gold arrive in a single load from the mines, ready for trans-shipment east.

The arrivals and departures of the tri-weekly Concord stage generally attracted crowds of onlookers across the street at Bradford's Corner, which was dominated by the impressive two-story frame building that housed two of William Russell's business interests in Denver — the

24.   WAITING FOR LETTERS AT THE C.O.C. & P.P. EXPRESS OFFICE AT
BRADFORD'S CORNER, DENVER,
AFTER THE ARRIVAL OF THE STAGE (1860)
Drawn by F. Beard; Engraved by J.P. Davis & Speer, in A.D. Richardson, *Beyond the Mississippi,* 1867

general store run by his partner Robert B. Bradford, and the Overland Stage company itself. A reporter watched the excitement:

> "On the corner, a hundred people are gazing at the Concord coach of the Central Overland and Pike's Peak Express Company, about to start for the Missouri river ... The stages have come in from the mountains, crowded with dusty passengers, and bringing the express messengers with their packages of letters and gold dust for the States ... Every seat [on the Concord] is filled, and every passenger known or vouched for, as this is the one day of the week upon which an express messenger is on board with forty or fifty thousand dollars in gold dust. A motley crowd waits to witness the departure ... The passengers receive the ultimate hand-shakings and final valedictions, and the coach rolls away on its long journey." [21]

It was at the C.O.C & P.P. post office window that Crofutt first met Amos Steck, who had been made postmaster by the Leavenworth and Pike's Peak Express Co. shortly after his arrival in Denver in May 1859. Amos had reached Denver after years of travelling back and forth across the States. He was born in Lancaster, Ohio in 1822 of German Lutheran stock but had attended school, and then law school, in Philadelphia. Thrilled by the excitement of gold in California, Amos joined the 'forty-niners' ' overland rush to the goldfields, but he made very little, took to delivering mail to the mines, worked in the post office at Sacramento, and then returned via Panama to Pennsylvania, where he married and moved with his wife Sarah to Wisconsin.

Early in 1859, gold fever struck him again and now as one of the 'fifty-niners', he joined the rush to Pike's Peak. Amos was no more a miner in Colorado than he had been in California but he knew he liked the West and a little over a year later, in August 1860, Mrs. Steck and their five-year-old daughter Isabella arrived in Denver to join him. That month, the Central Overland California & Pike's Peak Express Co. at last acquired the desperately needed Government mail contract, having carried mail as a costly private service for eighteen months since the old Leavenworth company days. Part of the cost had been passed on; the charge was 25 cents for letters and 10 cents for newspapers, in addition to the regular U.S. postage of 3 cents on ½ oz. letters. Complaints about the cost were frequent and bitter. Small wonder that some had to make do with the sight of a letter from home, then turn away from the Express office window without paying to take it and open it. Others would stand, quickly scan their mail and then claim that the letters were not for them in the hope of retrieving their quarters. Pre-payment by the sender was obligatory only on U.S. Mail.

Amos Steck was busier than ever after August 1860 following the award of the Government contract and the increased volume of mail, but he found that the C.O.C. & P.P. was changing its character in other ways. The Pony Express had been started by Russell, Majors and Waddell in April 1860 as a fast mail and messenger service connecting St. Joseph, Mo. and Sacramento, via Salt Lake City, in only ten days. Bold and imaginative as it was, the Pony Express was not awarded a Government subsidy until March 1861, and never became a commercial success. It placed an intolerable financial burden both on the freighting and the stageline operation which, as resources drained away, was forced to become the company's work-horse, cutting first the 'frills', and then the staff and some of the basic services. Russell lost the far western section of the Overland run. He was forced to concentrate on the Missouri River-Denver-Salt Lake City route, and relinquish the Salt Lake City-California business to his rival John Butterfield, whose southern loop to the west coast through Texas and Arizona had been shifted north by Congress at the start of the Civil War.

It was a bitter few months of rapid decline in a time of national political turmoil and changing communications technology. The overland telegraph link coast-to-coast was pushed forward and completed in

PONY EXPRESS AND OVERLAND TELEGRAPH, 1861

in H.T. Williams, *The Pacific Tourist*, 1876

The Pony Express rider hails the competition as construction workers complete the final stages of the Overland Telegraph. After the wires were joined in Salt Lake City in October 1861, the main Pony Express service ended, although short local runs survived for several years.

Williams' engraving was based on a painting by George M. Ottinger, a pioneer artist in Utah, who was also famous as an early photographer of the region. He became a junior partner of photographer Charles R. Savage in Salt Lake City, and later set up his own business.

October 1861, effectively ending the work, if not the image, of the Pony Express. Russell was replaced as President of the company but the financial damage was already done. By the beginning of 1862, the C.O.C. & P.P. was virtually bankrupt — Clean Out of Cash and Poor Pay the employees grumbled — and in March of that year, Ben Holladay took over the company's remaining assets. Depressed by Russell's collapse, Denverites watched the familiar signboards replaced by the Holladay Overland Mail & Express Co. and debated whether this new 'Stagecoach King' would have the same interest in Denver's continuing prosperity that William Russell had always shown.

As the C.O.C. & P.P.'s fortunes went from bad to worse during 1861, Amos Steck gave up his job as postmaster and returned to his law books. The postal service itself was changing. After the creation of Colorado Territory in February 1861, government post offices were gradually

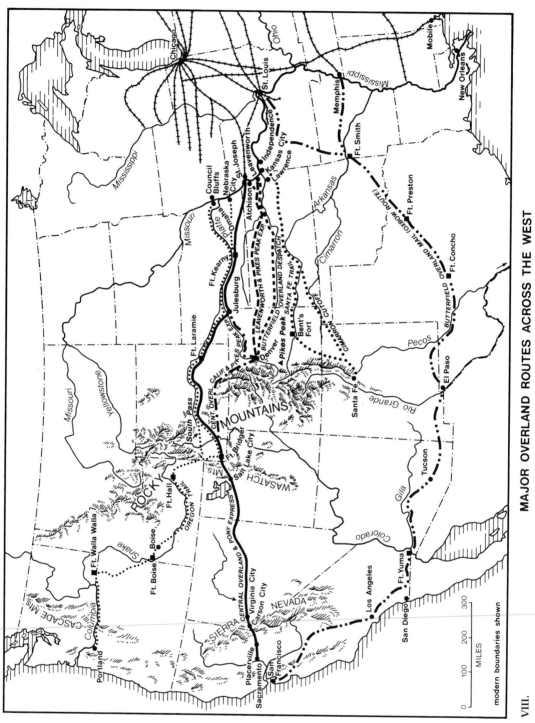

MAJOR OVERLAND ROUTES ACROSS THE WEST DURING ALL, OR PART OF, THE EARLY 1860s

VIII.

introduced. The first to appear on the Cherry Creek Divide, a few miles below Crofutt's place, was opened at Russellville in May 1862 with the dynamic Frank Gardner as postmaster. By September 1862, Gardner had organized the transfer of the post office to his ranch at 'Frank's Town'. On East Plum Creek, in January 1862, Daniel Oakes and his wife were put in charge of the new Territorial post office at Huntsville, where Kansas Territory had earlier been persuaded to locate a post office in May 1860. One way or another, as ranchers took on the job of country postmasters, and the work in town became more routine, Amos Steck decided to stretch his wings. He became a member of Colorado's Territorial Legislature and with the rest of the Denver contingent rode down to Colorado City with his wife for the July 1862 sitting.

Colorado City boosters like Mel Beach, the Tappan brothers, Ben Crowell and Albinus Sheldon had been jubilant over the decision in 1861 to make their town the Territorial capital, but the July 1862 meeting of the Territorial Legislature soon put paid to their plans. Colorado City might have persuaded the voters in September 1861 that its central location in the Territory and proximity to the symbolic Pike's Peak gave it the advantage over Denver, but the Legislature could scarcely find a cabin large enough to meet in, there was no accommodation apart from old Mrs. Maggard's log tavern, there was not enough paper and ink in town to record even one day's business, and there was no printing press nearer than Denver. After three days the members and their visitors could endure it no longer and voted to adjourn to Denver. Mrs. Steck wished she had not bothered to buy a new hat for the occasion.

Amos flourished in Denver and his enthusiasm for the town was infectious. He was elected Mayor in 1863, and subsequently appointed Receiver of Public Monies in the U.S. Land Office, and Judge of Arapahoe County. He was always to value his start as the postmaster, however, saying that it had enabled him to learn the names, faces and business of everyone who had ever filed past his windows collecting mail! Certainly, Steck's local knowledge and prodigious memory for individuals and events were a by-word throughout the region for the rest of his long life. Crofutt spoke with astonishment in later years of Steck's ability to recall minute details about the early days and development of Denver — the man was a jovial, walking encyclopedia.

The security and loyalty of the western States and Territories were both matters of concern in Washington, D.C. at the start of the Civil War. Indeed, it had been the formal organization of the Confederate States under Jefferson Davis on 4th February 1861, and particularly the secession of Texas on 23rd February, that had pushed Congress into the creation of Colorado Territory five days later.

In April and May 1861, two influential newcomers, Henry M. Teller, followed by Bela M. Hughes, arrived in Denver. Each in his own way was determined to help maintain the integrity of Colorado (and its gold) within the Union. Only a few buildings were actually displaying Confederate flags and these were quickly hauled down, but miners from Georgia had been among the earliest prospectors at Pike's Peak, and Southern sympathizers made their presence felt. Bela Hughes was made a member of the Territorial Assembly and began a long association with Colorado. In April 1861, shortly before his arrival in Denver, Hughes had been elected by the stockholders of the C.O.C. & P.P. Express Co. as President in place of Russell. After Ben Holladay's take-over of the company in March 1862, Bela Hughes, who was Holladay's cousin, continued to run the business for another year before becoming Holladay's agent and attorney. Teller, a young lawyer, was also to devote the rest of his life to Colorado, including in due course many years in the U.S. Senate. Soon after his arrival, he began by opening a law office in Central City.

Colorado was made a Military District, and Camp Weld was established in Denver in 1861 as the training base and headquarters of the First Regiment of Colorado Volunteers. Their job was to protect Colorado from Confederate attack, and they helped to repel the Texan invasion of New Mexico in 1862.

Fire, Flood, Famine, and Fighting

Crofutt continued freighting across the Arkansas Divide as well as driving his wagon farther afield to the towns and mining camps sprawling along both sides of the great Continental Divide. He took every opportunity that business offered to stop in Denver, read the latest war dispatches, and look up old friends. Many were feeling isolated, vulnerable and pessimistic about Denver's prospects.

Although far from the heat of battle, Denver had suffered a series of setbacks in the early 1860s. The town's initial failure to become the capital of the new Territory was a blow to its pride and business — a double blow in fact when, after Colorado City's brief glory, Golden secured the prize. In the summer of 1861, a large and totally unexpected volume of freight brought in from Nebraska City had caused a sudden collapse in prices; several of the small-scale merchants, unable to make enough profit, had gone out of business. In and after 1861, Denver's freighting connections were mainly with Nebraska City and Atchison rather than with Leavenworth, and Colorado merchants complained bitterly of being defenceless targets for the speculators, wholesalers and freighters alike, working out of the two rival Missouri River ports.

William Russell was bankrupt and his popular associate, Alexander Majors, just a shadow of his former self. Dogged by creditors, Majors was still freighting out of Nebraska City along the Platte, and Crofutt met him from time to time on the trail and in Denver, where Majors maintained a large warehouse and supply store.

There was increasing alarm over the recall of army units from the Western forts by the end of 1861, once the War between the States took hold. Indian attacks on stage lines, supply posts and ranches raged through the summer of 1862. Crofutt and all his neighbours were constantly on the alert. Congress was forced to reconsider the position and establish its military and political priorities in the West. The result was that vulnerable sections of the Oregon Trail were reinforced by troops in order to encourage Unionist emigrants to continue to move west, and to maintain the loyalty of the Mormons.

In addition, the new telegraph link with Utah and California needed protection, as did Ben Holladay's Overland stage coach and mail service. Denver itself had no telegraph. The town's telegraph link to Julesburg was delayed for two years, until 1st October 1863. Not for the first time, Denver realized that it lay outside the main communication corridor to the Pacific, and well to the south of the Oregon Trail and the thin blue line of army forts. Fort Laramie, the nearest to Camp Weld, was over two hundred miles away. Denver and all who depended on it would have to defend themselves. Some were already pulling up and going farther west; hundreds of miners in 1862-3 went to new gold strikes in Montana and Idaho.

Nothing seemed to be going right. Fire swept through Denver during the particularly dry spring of 1863. The blaze began behind Blake Street in the early hours of Sunday, 19th April. Driven by a strong wind, flames leapt through the Downtown area, jumping streets, devouring blocks (still mostly frame), and wiping out nearly a hundred businesses and ware-houses. Almost half of Denver's stored goods were destroyed, along with every hardware and stove store in town. Huge piles of flour, corn, and bacon continued to burn throughout the following day.[22] Mayor Amos Steck, who had only just taken office on 1st April 1863, was preoccupied for weeks in organizing relief. Whatever the encouraging war news coming from Gettysburg and Vicksburg, Denver struggled with one setback after another. While the Downtown area rose slowly again from the ashes, farmers and stockmen on the plains around Denver were more concerned with the prolonged drought and another plague of grasshop-pers than with anything else.

Freighters and stage drivers arriving in Denver by the main Platte River route via Julesburg were bringing more bad news. The Cheyenne had become more active in the summer of 1863, robbing wagons, stealing horses, and attacking exposed settlements on the plains. So far, these attacks had been concentrated several hundred miles east of the moun-tain front, but 1864 was to change all that. Rumour swept through

Colorado that an alliance of the Cheyenne, Arapahoe, Kiowa and Sioux was planning to wipe out all the settlements and trail posts along the Platte, the Arkansas, and the base of the Rockies in order to put a decisive end to the increasing white penetration and ownership of the plains and the hunting grounds.

To make matters worse after Denver's slow recovery from the fire of 1863, floods devastated an even wider region in May 1864. Cherry Creek was notoriously unpredictable. It was not unusual at this season for stage coaches to rattle the last mile into Denver along the dry bed of Cherry Creek, but on 19th May 1864, the river became a raging torrent. Cherry Creek had an extensive catchment on the Arkansas Divide; snow melt and sudden heavy rains brought floods sweeping down the valley. D.C. Oakes' main saw mill, among others in the Pineries, was carried away; so were many of the ranches — crops, livestock and all. Thousands of sheep and cattle were drowned, four-to-five thousand sheep in the Cherry Creek ranches alone. To the west, bridges and mountain roads were swept away, settlements cut off by landslips and mud.

The floods tore through Denver. Amos Steck described the terror of that night:

> "It was the night of May 19, 1864, and anyone who saw the sight will never forget it. The night was clear as crystal, one of those brisk wintry nights that get mixed up with summer, where the stars are twinkling and the moon is pale, but the air is still balmy.
>
> About ten o'clock that night a faint rumbling was heard. At first we all thought that a thunderstorm had broken loose, but as the sound grew more distinct we knew it could not be that for there was not the least sign of a cloud in the sky. Then one old fellow who lived in the mountains said he reckoned there had been a cloudburst up in one of the canyons and the water was heading this way. The alarm bells in the town were rung and messengers were sent around to warn the people on the bottoms of the coming flood. Many of us flocked to the high ground near Broadway and stood there waiting to see what would happen. The grumbling merged into a rumbling sound and the rumbling swelled into a roar, and then we could see a faint cloud of dust rising in the bed of the creek toward the canyon. As the dust approached the roaring increased until it became deafening.
>
> It was then that we perceived a great crest of water like a seismic wave rushing toward the city. It was fully ten feet high, and I do not know how broad, glistening and sparkling in the moonlight, and in its wake a wide black river. Well, it swept everything before it and flooded the west side so that the cavalry from Camp Weld had to come swimming on horseback to carry the women and children to a place of safety ... That was the worst flood we ever had ... It caused thousands and thousands of dollars-worth of property to be destroyed, besides nearly drowning a multitude of people." [23]

Next day, Denverites surveyed the desolation. Much of the Downtown area had disappeared or been reduced to matchwood. The damage was far more serious than that caused by the June 1860 floods in Denver's earlier days. Since then, buildings had actually been erected in the dry bed of Cherry Creek. The City Hall was swept away, along with the vital records of claims and land titles whose loss would cause so much dispute and litigation in later years. Joe Coberly, who had been lying sick in the house opposite City Hall, was carried out whiter than a sheet from the soup of mud and flood water that had risen to the level of his bed. William Byers' heavy printing press, along with most of the *Rocky Mountain News* equipment, was later found on the sand bars several miles down the South Platte. "Not a *pica* left," said Crofutt.

"There was mud everywhere," recalled Elizabeth Tallman, who arrived two weeks later after crossing the plains in an ox-drawn covered wagon. "We found the citizens of Denver busily digging out. Our house was on Larimer Street between 12th and 13th, and the bridge, if there ever was one over Cherry Creek, had been washed away. So we heaped piles of brush in the creek to serve as a crossing. Several weeks after the mud in the creek had dried, my nephew, while playing in the sand, unearthed a ballot-box which had been lost when the City Hall was swept away in the flood. The box, the first ever used in Denver, was painted green and belonged to B-3d ward. It is still one of my treasured possessions and holds all my souvenirs and mementos of pioneer days." [24]

Crofutt suffered a double blow. As well as the general slump in business, his own hay crop in Cherry Creek Canyon was destroyed in the flood, and more was ruined on his quarter-section down on the bottom land of the South Platte close to Sloan's Lake. Altogether, he estimated that he had lost 100 acres of field crops in excellent condition that season "when the great flood of May took my last few cents to the Missouri River." Crofutt echoed the words of fellow pioneer Amos Steck, that the settlers should have learned from the Indians, "for they would always point high into the trees to the clinging driftwood there and thus show how high the water had been at some time before." [25]

The costs of all supplies in Denver simply rocketed. Flour, for example, was $25 a sack; customers who complained were sharply reminded that Denver's earlier stock of flour, cloth and practically everything else was now six miles down the Platte on the sand bars. Many local farmers, stockmen and mill-owners had been wiped out. There was a devastating plague of grasshoppers. The long hauls across the plains from the Missouri River ports, normally taking about 40 days, were now taking anything up to 3 months and had become much more irregular as Cheyenne and Arapahoe attacked freight wagons and stampeded oxen all along the trail between Fort Kearny and Denver. Alexander Majors and other freighters were forced to take refuge in Fort Kearny. Food was extremely expensive and increasingly scarce right through the summer and fall. In June 1864, fresh Indian attacks along the South Platte threw

Denver into a state of panic, particularly after the Hungate murders, when the scalped and mutilated bodies of the parents and two children were brought into Denver from the Hungate ranch on Running Creek, only thirty miles southeast of the city.

The attacks grew worse until between November 1864 and March 1865, the Overland Stage service was suspended, and Denver, feeling more cut off from civilization than ever before, was forced to send its east-bound mail via San Francisco and Panama. Stockaded forts were hastily constructed in the main towns. Underground tunnels to small hide-outs were run from the most isolated ranches. Caves were explored for use in emergencies. Groups of settlers and small communities built block houses (pierced with loopholes and enclosing a well, spring or stretch of creek) in the surrounding plains and foothill country, into which families could retreat at night, and whenever daylight attacks were anticipated. Following the wagon road along East Plum Creek, Crofutt regularly passed the large fort and block house built in June 1864 near the second Coberly ranch at Huntsville. A fort was built two miles west of Frankstown, while Frank Gardner built another large enough for about eighty people nearer to his main settlement.

But there was not always enough warning for the stockades and block houses to be reached. "Mother" Coberly's husband George was killed later that year in Frankstown during an Indian raid. Bluffs came very close to some of the wagon roads and trails, and Indians swooped suddenly from well concealed gulches and canyons. Crofutt found the Plum Creek Divide particularly dangerous. Indeed, Crofutt and his neighbours knew only too well in the summer of '64 how successfully Indian raiding parties could hide almost anywhere in the Pineries. Several Indians rode over Crofutt's own land but he escaped a major attack. Not so the beautiful, secluded Spring Valley, about eight miles long, half-a-mile wide and part of the West Cherry Creek system. The valley had attracted its first pioneers in July 1860, just before Crofutt and his friends had passed through and built *Ivan Cracken* lower down the canyon. Although the pioneers had built their Spring Valley fort as early as 1860, the entire valley was overrun by Indians in 1864 and several of the settlers were killed. Later, Indians killed both George Redman and Jonathan Lincoln; Joseph Gile survived. All harvesting that summer from Denver to Pueblo was done under close guard and the watchful eye of armed lookouts.

"Despite death and hardship," wrote Mrs. Coberly's grandson when recording the period, "the pioneers couldn't afford to let sentiment loose. They had to go on in the usual manner and put grief behind them. There were memories, of course, but life had to go on, and memories only hindered living."[26]

AN INDIAN ATTACK ON THE OVERLAND STAGE NEAR JULESBURG, 1864
in H.T. Williams, *The Pacific Tourist*, 1876

After John Evans, Governor of Colorado Territory, and General R.B. Mitchell, Commander of the Military District of Nebraska, had failed in their attempt to parley with the Cheyenne, Arapahoe, Kiowa, and Sioux and disband their alliance, matters came to a head in the 'Battle' of Sand Creek, a tributary of the Arkansas. The Third Regiment of the Colorado Volunteer Cavalry was led by Colonel John M. Chivington, whose destruction of the Cheyenne and Arapahoe Indian camp on 29th November 1864 was defended by the overwhelming majority of local settlers but elsewhere earned widespread condemnation as the Chivington Massacre. In January and February 1865, about a thousand Arapahoe, Cheyenne and Sioux sacked Julesburg and cut the overland telegraph yet again, but although freighters and emigrants crossing the plains continued to come under attack, the main large-scale, co-ordinated Indian assaults were over for the time being.

There were more hardships to come, however. To make matters worse, after the floods, famine and Indian fighting, the region was overtaken by one of its worst-ever winters. Small wonder that the Denver area was more preoccupied with its own troubles than with the final stages of the War between the States. The Arkansas Divide was savaged by blizzards and windchill in 1864-65. Deep snow buried the pastures at the end of October, and persistently low temperatures for three months after that kept the grass out of reach of starving animals. Most of the remaining herds were wiped out or severely reduced, and many settlers and cowhands abandoned the area and moved closer to Denver. Crofutt had shifted to the head of Plum Creek, and survived the winter by selling logs in Denver at high prices:

> "The winter of 1864-65 was unusually severe," he recalled years later in conversation, "and it was on that account I was able to sell wood in Denver at $80 a cord. It was probably the highest price ever paid for wood in this city, although I have known of higher prices elsewhere. At that time I was living at the head of Plum Creek and ran out of grub . . . I hitched up eight or ten yoke of oxen to a couple of sleds and started to town with a load of wood. It required four days to travel twenty-five miles. The snow was partly frozen and we were obliged to break a road all the way down the valley.
>
> Arriving on the west side of Cherry Creek I met Alexander Majors. 'We haven't got a stick of wood at our place,' said Majors, referring to his warehouse in Auraria; 'what do you charge for a cord of wood?' 'Well,' I replied, 'I suppose it is worth $50 or $60 a cord.' Majors had to have the wood and he ordered one of the loads to be thrown off at the warehouse. Proceeding further, I met Amos Steck. 'Hello, Crofutt,' shouted Steck, 'what is the price of wood? We haven't a single stick.' I gave $80 a cord as the price. Steck kicked at the price but as his household was out of wood, the remainder of the load went into his backyard and he paid up." [27]

*   *   *

In the spring of 1865, Crofutt decided to move off the Arkansas Divide and concentrate his energies along the trails east and west of Denver. He had never recovered from the 1864 flood, and now no longer wanted to keep a base on Cherry Creek or Plum Creek, or for that matter on his South Platte bottom land. "Everything went down with the waste of waters." He could not afford to hang on and pay the taxes on the quarter-section beside Sloan's Lake, whatever its potential as farm land or real estate. The land's devastated condition, coupled with Crofutt's need for a quick sale meant that, like others in the same predicament, he took what he could get.[28] The deal included three yoke of oxen which not long afterwards were stolen by Indians, who were normally more interested in the theft of horses and mules. Alexander Majors had said that Indians sometimes drove off oxen in order to get a fee for finding and returning them. Not this time. Crofutt knew he could have expected something of the sort since, one way or another, his Sloan's Lake bottom land had been nothing but trouble and disappointment right to the last.

The Civil War ended in April 1865. In shifting the focus of his activities off the Arkansas Divide, and switching the emphasis from north-south journeys along the mountain front to east-west movement across the continent, Crofutt took advantage of the great post-war revival in his western world. The trails across the plains sprang again into life as new waves of emigrants started out for the West. Army forts were expanded and refitted as the Government assigned more troops to protect the wagon trains. The mid-1860s were to become an unprecedented 'golden age' of freighting in that brief post-war, pre-railroad phase.

Pathfinder for David Butterfield

In the summer of 1865, Crofutt widened his horizons dramatically for a few months by becoming a mountain explorer. He was employed to scout possible far western routes for a planned extension to David Butterfield's new stage line.

David Butterfield (no relation to John Butterfield of the old southern Oxbow loop-line to California) was a former Denver merchant who, at the age of thirty in 1864, had become a storage and forwarding agent in Atchison while subcontracting the haulage work. Before long, he became determined to break Holladay's monopoly between the Missouri River and Denver. Butterfield organized the Butterfield Overland Despatch in July 1864 and chose the shorter Smoky Hill River route, despite the problems of its dry sections, and the lack of a government mail subsidy and regular troop escort which helped to protect Holladay's Overland Mail and Express line along the Platte. Butterfield received military protection only during the construction of his line. He established relay stops every 12-25 miles as he was determined to rid the Smoky Hill River route, once and for all, of its deadly tag: "the Unmarked-grave or Starvation Trail". George Crofutt knew the early pioneers on the last twenty miles of Butterfield's route well, since the Twenty-Mile House stage stop was at Pine Grove (later Parker) on his route down Cherry Creek into Denver.[29] The enlarging of the old ranches into a succession of service stations at Seventeen-Mile House, Twelve-Mile House, Nine-Mile House, and Four-Mile House, marked the final countdown of the Smoky Hill Trail's southern loop into town.

David Butterfield's plans included a major expansion beyond Colorado and Utah into Montana, Idaho, New Mexico, Arizona and Nevada, but he began by bidding for the Atchison-Denver traffic. The first stage, with Butterfield on board, arrived in Denver in great style on 23rd September 1865. A welcoming committee travelled out to Four-Mile House to meet him, the band played, and amid cheering crowds, Butterfield was carried off to a splendid civic reception at the Planter's House.[30] Not since William Russell had anyone put Denver's interests so much at the centre of things. Nothing was too good for Dave Butterfield.

> "It was given out amid great rejoicing," Crofutt recalled, "that the line would be immediately extended westward by way of Salt Lake City to Portland, Oregon ... [Earlier], I had been engaged with two other parties to make a personal examination of this line ... it was my first acquaintance with the route directly west from here [Denver] to Salt Lake City ...
>
> I went from Denver by what is now the Argentine Pass, down the Blue River, and through what I suppose now is the vicinity of Steamboat Springs. I followed the Yampa river down to the Green, crossed into Utah into Parley Park, near where Park City is today, and went down Emigrant Canyon, getting my first view of Salt Lake at Camp Douglas. In talking with a number of parties there about the route, it was suggested to me that I return by way of Provo and Provo Canyon, which I did. After a great deal of skirmishing around and prospecting, I reached the Green at the mouth of White River, and followed that river to about where Meeker is today. From there ... past the mouth of the Blue River ... I followed part of the Grand [the Colorado], and came back to Denver over what they now call Berthoud Pass.
>
> The trip took nearly three months. I met a great many Indians, and a few white men who were trapping for beaver. I made my report to the stage company at Denver and learned that General Bela M. Hughes [had organized] a trip [led by Edward L. Berthoud with Jim Bridger] in 1861 or 1862 over, I presume, the same route as mine, for Ben Holladay, with the view of finding a feasible route for the Overland stage. [Hughes organized another expedition in 1865] but none of our explorations resulted in the location of a stage line. Dave Butterfield's company got into financial difficulties and went out of business." [31]

Butterfield was in fact bought out by Ben Holladay in March 1866. Denver gritted its teeth and prudently renamed McGaa Street, between Blake and Larimer, after the triumphant 'Stagecoach King'.

Crofutt's arduous months of exploration, expecially the return journey from Salt Lake City to Denver, had been pushed through some of the steepest, most inaccessible mountain terrain in Colorado. Passes were infrequent and very high (Berthoud Pass, 11,314 ft); the canyons were narrow and winding, with many of the valley heads running blindly into the complex, deeply dissected plateaux west of the Continental Divide. Indeed, the major routes into Utah were never to penetrate northwest Colorado — a scenic paradise as Crofutt always remembered it, but an engineer's hell.

Back in Denver for the winter of 1865-66, Crofutt ran his business from a lumber yard at the corner of Larimer and G (16th St) where he advertised cords of oak wood for as little as $21 a cord. Times were still hard. Denver had so far been unable to shake off the depression of the past three or four years. Worst of all, Denver had actually lost population since the heady days of 1860, and at the end of the Civil War contained only about three thousand.

Nothing had resulted from another of Crofutt's ventures — speculation in toll roads. On 27th April 1865, George Crofutt and two associates, Rufus Clark and Edwin Scudder, had registered a company in Denver to construct and operate a toll road from there to the summit of the Arkansas Divide, to be known as the Denver and Arkansas Air Line Road.[32] Rufus Clark ("Potato Clark"), an old business acquaintance of Crofutt's and the most prosperous of the trio, had already made a fortune in farming and was on his way to making an even bigger one in real estate investments in and around Denver. Clark had been elected to the Colorado Territorial Legislature, and was one of the best known of the early pioneers. Edwin Scudder was a merchant on Cherry Street, between 5th and 6th. In the 1860s, the lack of good roads and shortage of public funds to build them, attracted many to speculate in building toll roads and bridges in Colorado's mining and farming regions. Freighters like Crofutt were frequently involved because of the first-hand knowledge they could offer to city investors.

The Denver and Arkansas Air Line Road required five thousand dollars initial capital. It was to start in West Denver, run south along the west bank of Cherry Creek for about three miles and then make for the Plum Creek Divide close to Richardson Hill. The road was to run on southeastwards to the Lake Gulch road, proceed to Redman's ranch on the Cherry Creek headwaters and end on the Divide, where it would join the existing wagon road to Colorado City and the Arkansas (at Pueblo).

Standard charges on the Colorado toll roads at this period were as follows: [33]

Each vehicle with one span of horses, mules or cattle	$1.00
Each additional pair of draft animals attached	.25
Each horse or mule with rider	.25
Horses, mules, cattle, or asses driven loose ... Per head	.10
Sheep, hogs, or goats ... Per head	.05
Travel for attendance at funerals	Free

Crofutt, Clark and Scudder failed to attract enough capital, but the rule was always: if one venture flopped, try another. Trial, error, disappointment, despair, adjustment, and perhaps next time, success — these were all part of normal, everyday frontier life. Scores of projected toll roads in Colorado were only partly built; many were never started. The Denver and Arkansas Air Line was apparently one of these. Ten months later, however, in February 1866, Frank Gardner, John Jones, Ozro Brackett, George Engl and Joseph Gile, all prosperous ranchers who had pioneered the Divide in 1860, formed a company and successfully built a toll road in the upper Cherry Creek area linking Frankstown, Lake Gulch, and Gile's ranch in Spring Valley.[34] By then, Crofutt was busy elsewhere.

In the spring of 1866, Anna Crofutt visited Denver again. This time she also went up into the mountains, for on 1st March, she travelled to Central City on one of Ben Holladay's Overland stagecoaches which left Denver daily at 7 a.m. for the Central City area.[35] Anna looked out for the places her husband's letters had made so familiar as she crossed the foothill grazing land, stopped briefly in Golden, and then abruptly entered the gorge to be flung around a succession of sharp zig-zag bends, unable to see either the summits or the base of the canyon walls. As another passenger on Anna's route noted shortly afterwards:

> "For hours we climbed up one side of these mountains only to dash down the other . . . [Eventually] we struck the waters of North Clear Creek, some two miles below the city of Black Hawk . . . We were soon in the city itself, amidst structures of every description, a motley string of buildings — stamp-mills, engine-houses, shops, stores, offices, and dwellings — often stuck into the sides of the hills, or located in the valleys, and in some cases even below high-water-mark.

> On through the city we went, drawn by six splendid horses over a road excavated along the abrupt side of a hill . . . Where Black Hawk ended, and Mountain and Central Cities commenced or ended, no one could tell, for they were all alike composed of mills, shops, and dwellings, promiscuously jammed together in every imaginable way. Our stage at last came to a halt in Central City, on Main Street, closely built of log, brick and wood, and we alighted at the Conner House, a wooden structure of no prepossessing appearance, but with comfortable fare." [36]

Central City had only one boarding-house which offered mattresses; the others merely had "hay beds". The Teller House, partly financed by Henry Teller, the successful local lawyer, was not opened until 1872. Mrs. Crofutt stayed in Central City for a little over three weeks, probably while her husband was hauling timber in the region. But on 24th March 1866, she took the stage back to Denver and apparently returned once again to the East.[37]

No doubt they had discussed where Crofutt could best make a living over the next few years, and it would have become clear to both of them that he was now going to have to extend his freighting activities over a very much wider area, picking up business out on the plains, as well as westward into Wyoming and Utah. Journeys ranging across a thousand miles would mean months away from home out on the trail. Denver itself was still a raw frontier town struggling to recover from the disasters and depopulation of the early 1860s. All told, there was nothing to keep Anna Crofutt in Colorado.

The Freighting Boom of the Mid-1860s.

Long Hauls Along the Platte: "Those were the Days and these the Plains that tried Men's Mettle"

The following month, April 1866, Crofutt began to concentrate his efforts down on the plains, freighting over the Platte-North Platte and Platte-South Platte routes from the Missouri River outfitting towns. His final trip that season was out of Nebraska City and past the future site of Lincoln, which became the new state capital in 1867 . . . although in 1866, Crofutt recalled later, "there were no more than three or four buildings in sight in any direction." [38] The Platte valley was to focus the bulk of the business in the second half of the 1860s — supplies for the army forts, the stagecoach stations, the new railroad camps, and the emigrants' service ranches. The term 'ranche' was widely applied throughout the region; arable farms, stock farms, way stations and trading posts along the trail were all included, as well as mail delivery points, regular meal stops, grocery and liquor stores.

Denver was now making more of its relative proximity to the Oregon and California trails. During the Civil War, traffic on the long Santa Fe-Arkansas route had declined, as had the fortunes of Colorado City, although its champions fought hard to keep the town going. One of these, Albinus Sheldon, summarized the problems:

> "In 1860 and 1861, the great thoroughfares of the Arkansas and the South Platte roads afforded about equal currents of travel to Colorado, and Colorado City and Denver were respectively sustained by these currents. But as the War for the Union progressed, the bands of guerrillas, which raided Missouri and Kansas, rendered the Arkansas Valley so unsafe that in 1862 it was virtually abandoned, and the whole line of travel was diverted to the South Platte. Thus the porridge which had been the pabulum of Colorado City was dished up for the fattening of Denver.

> Southern Colorado was thenceforth ignored, and every hotelkeeper and bar-tender (in Denver) became an active partisan for the retention of the advantages thus fortuitously gained. All new arrivals were authoritatively informed that there was nothing south of the 'Divide' worth their seeking, and persuaded to remain in Denver, or to go to the mountains, which were supposed to be limited to the neighborhood of Central City. Thus was the ambitious young town of Colorado City most fatally throttled." [39]

While it was still the centre of a prosperous farming region, Colorado City had to depend in all other respects on its administrative role. The *Colorado City Journal* had long since collapsed, but Ben Crowell continued to take on more responsibilities as an El Paso County Commissioner while still flourishing both as farmer and sheep rancher on Fountain Creek. "Versatility," was Ben's motto: "this today and that tomorrow. The frontier's built by jacks-of-all-trades."

Albinus Sheldon, meanwhile, had been appointed by Territorial Governor Evans during the troubled months of 1864 as one of the first three brigadier generals of Colorado charged with organizing local defence. That same year, Sheldon was elected to the Territorial Legislature. He was still the El Paso County Surveyor and, married to Calanthe Everhart, whose family had arrived in Colorado City from Ohio in 1862, Albinus Sheldon had become a solid, widely respected figure in the town and the Territory.

*   *   *

Freighting along the Platte, Crofutt hauled wood, grain, flour, hay and general provisions to the army forts. Major contractors secured the military's bulk orders and then sub-contracted the work out to a host of small operators like Crofutt.

Profits among some of the middle-men soared. On one occasion, Crofutt sold sixty cords of softwood in Denver to John Hughes for $20 a cord. Hughes' contract price for delivery to the army post at Fort Sedgwick, about 200 miles northeast of Denver, was $105 a cord. The winter of 1865-66 was particularly cold, Crofutt recorded; "Fort Sedgwick's barracks were built of lumber without plaster on the inside — good summer houses, but as cold as a barn in winter." Supplies of timber ran very short. Nearly all the wood used at Fort Sedgwick and Julesburg that winter had to come from the Pineries and the scrub-oak bluffs on the Arkansas Divide, and the Denver contractors were making the most of it. Freight transportation costs from Denver to Fort Sedgwick and Julesburg were anything between $55-$75 a cord that season. Contractors were allowed by the government to put in as much hardwood as they could get, at double the price — $210 a cord. Crofutt's softwood was included in a bulk consignment of hardwood for which Hughes was duly paid $210 a cord when he made delivery at Fort Sedgwick.[40] John Hughes was regarded by some as unscrupulous, by others as "Lucky Jack", and by the majority as Denver's most enterprising and resourceful contractor that year.

Like Alexander Majors who did more than anyone to popularize oxen, Crofutt found them more economical to run than mules when there was no particular urgency on delivery, and a slow steady plod of some two miles an hour would suffice. Heavily laden — with machinery, stoves, presses, and the like — oxen normally covered 12-15 miles a day, and up to 20 miles if the road was good and their feet not sore. Oxen were also tougher for the really long distances, and when properly managed could regularly travel up to 2500 miles in one season. The army preferred to use mules for drayage both on and off the post; as a result, oxen were generally cheaper to buy and more widely available.

Denver had become one of the principal centres in the West for the one- or two-wagon man. The ranks of the old-time freighters were swelled in the post-Civil War period by newly discharged troops and fresh waves of emigrants, all hoping, like others before them, to let a season or two's freighting bank-roll them to better things. In the summer of 1865, it was estimated that 11,220 men and 8960 wagons, drawn by 59,440 oxen and 14,620 mules (involving an investment of $7,289,300 in teams and wagons alone), were transporting 54,000 tons of freight from the Missouri River's forwarding stations into Colorado, Utah and Montana.[41] Freight traffic was even heavier in 1866, a banner year.

> "The business of freighting," wrote another experienced observer, "was performed here on such a scale as to constitute one of the wonders of the West. . . . Thousands of these immense freight wagons, capable of carrying 15,000 to 20,000 pounds of weight each, . . . are scattered from the Missouri River to the Pacific Coast." [42]

Crofutt was an old hand now. It was six years since, still a newcomer to freighting, he had watched Ben Crowell light-heartedly paint the horns of his oxen in the middle of Lawrence, Kansas. By the late 1860s, Crofutt had become one of the best known individual operators in Colorado. He had met most of the region's famous mountain men and plainsmen, including Jim Bridger and Kit Carson.[43] In fact, Carson had been staying in Denver when Crofutt first arrived. A glimpse into the range of Crofutt's knowledge of the main freight routes across the plains and into the mountains in the 1860s is provided by a large, annotated map of the trails which he later compiled, "drawn from personal experience." [44]

At first, he concentrated on the 200 miles of the South Platte trail between Denver and Julesburg, the stage post and telegraph station at the Upper California crossing of the South Platte. Four miles southwest of Julesburg, the army had completed Fort Sedgwick in 1864-5 as part of the new military defences west of Forts Kearny and Cottonwood (McPherson), although Julesburg itself, as noted earlier, had again been heavily attacked by Arapahoe, Cheyenne and Sioux in January and February 1865. Sedgwick was a major fort at a dangerous junction, and a heavy consumer of hay and timber.[45] In 1866, the price for a cord of softwood at Julesburg had increased to $150. Fort Morgan (Wardwell), closer to Denver, was another of Crofutt's regular delivery points since it was located in a poorly grassed, virtually untimbered area. Indeed it was so expensive to maintain that Fort Morgan was abandoned in May 1868, and its garrison transferred. But the freighters made the most of it while it lasted . . . and so did Mark Boughton, Crofutt recalled, with his booming sales of "tangle-foot" whisky at his ranch near the post!

As well as freighting hay, timber and general supplies to the forts, Crofutt also made deliveries to the forward railroad camps. The Union

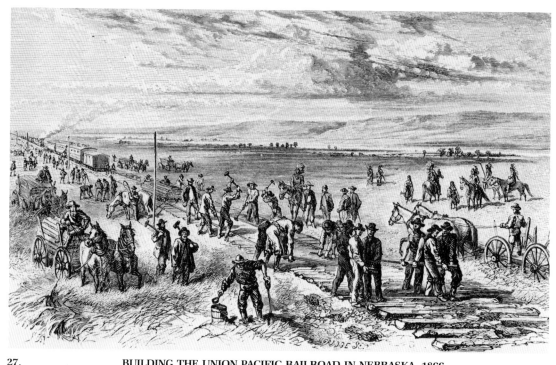

27.

BUILDING THE UNION PACIFIC RAILROAD IN NEBRASKA, 1866

Drawn by Alfred R. Waud; Engraved by James L. Langridge, in A.D. Richardson,
Beyond the Mississippi, 1867

Pacific Railroad reached Kearney, 190 miles west of Omaha in August 1866, and by the end of the year, the tracks were 305 miles beyond the Missouri. The Platte valley was the U.P.'s "great open road" towards Utah. Far ahead were the surveyors, selecting and refining details of the route through the Rockies, the Laramie mountains, the Wyoming basin, the Wasatch Range and so to the Salt Lake Valley. Behind them were the cutters, bridgers, fillers, and graders, and anything up to three hundred miles behind these in some cases, came the track-layers, advancing on average between two and five miles a day in a back-breaking rhythm of 4 rails to the minute, 3 blows to the spike, 30 spikes to the rail, and 400 rails to the mile. Wrote one visitor, recording the U.P. action:

> "We found the workmen, with the regularity of machinery, dropping each rail in its place, spiking it down, and then seizing another. Behind them, the locomotive; before, the tielayers; beyond these the graders; and still further, in mountain recesses, the engineers." [46]

Speed demanded that the Union Pacific often made do in the early stages with ties cut from the soft pulpy cottonwoods along the river banks. Even so, tie-layers aimed to insert a tougher oak, cedar or pitch pine tie with every three specially treated cottonwoods. These had been 'burnettized', i.e. soaked in a preservative solution of zinc chloride. The demand for timber was insatiable as the U.P. track-layers made up for lost time after the terrible winter of 1866-7 and streaked across the plains of Western Nebraska and into Wyoming by the end of that year. Colorado freighters and suppliers like Crofutt, with knowledge and experience of the timber business along the Rocky Mountain Front and its adjacent mining districts, found the U.P.'s passage across the plains in 1866 and 1867 the high point in their trade. Crofutt hauled pine and cedar from Pine Bluffs in Wyoming and, forty miles farther west along the track, watched Cheyenne transformed from the single shack he remembered in June 1867 to a raw railroad frontier town of more than six thousand only a few weeks later.

Crofutt was also frequently engaged to escort emigrant trains from ranch to ranch. He knew well many of the plains station-men, their families and their "square meals" for 50 cents to $1.50. He also knew the hazardous nature of the rivers. The Platte continued to sustain, and to frustrate, newcomers to the plains:

> "At times," Crofutt warned his fellow travellers, "after you pass above Julesburg, there is more fancy than fact in the streams. I remember the drought of 1863 when teamsters were obliged to excavate pits in the sand of the river bed before they could find enough water for their stock. In many places it looks broad and deep; try it, and you will find that your feet touch the treacherous sand ere your instep is under water; another place, the water appears to be rippling along over a smooth bottom, close to the surface; try that, and in you go, over your head in water, thick with yellowish sand.

> The channel is continually shifting . . . Woe to anyone who attempts to cross this stream before he has become acquainted with the fords. In crossing the river before this, if the wagons came to a stop, down they sank in the yielding quicksand until they were so firmly imbedded that it required more than double the original force to pull them out; and often they had to be unloaded, to prevent the united teams from pulling them to pieces while trying to lift the load and wagon from the sandy bed."

Crofutt always distrusted the river while retaining his love of its plains—

> "The first view of the Platte Valley is impressive, and should the traveler chance to see it for the first time in the spring or early summer it is very beautiful. Should he see it for the first time when the summer's heat has parched the plains, it may not seem inviting. Its beauty may be gone, but its majestic grandeur still remains."

Danger from Indian attack remained and troop escorts were increased. The army issued new regulations on the minimum size of wagon trains, but Crofutt recalled some of the practical problems involved. Despite everything, life had to go on:

"In the early spring of 1866, an order had been issued that no less number of persons than 30 should be allowed to pass a government post on the overland road between the Missouri River and Utah, and that they must be well organized and armed to resist any Indian attack . . .

I appeared at the post [Fort Morgan] with a party of 28 men and applied for a pass. Captain 'Mike' Sheridan, brother of 'Little Phil', refused.

Three days passed; no recruits came to our number. Early the following morning . . . [without permission], our 'outfit' rolled down the Platte river 25 miles that day, and I have never seen Captain 'Mike' since." [47]

The fort at Cottonwood Springs had been re-established as Fort McPherson in February 1866. Like other forts at the end of the Civil War where the regular army replaced the volunteers who had been stationed on the frontier during the fighting, it was renamed in honour of one of the war heroes. On another of his journeys, again in 1866, west of Fort McPherson, Crofutt was riding up the Platte Valley ahead of a well escorted wagon train, and moving along the high bluffs on the lookout for signs of Indians. Down in the valley he spotted instead a coach and four horses travelling at high speed in the opposite direction. Back with the wagon train, Crofutt heard one of the drivers swearing that as the coach swept past, he had recognized William T. Sherman as one of the three occupants. And he should know his old commander, the driver assured everyone loudly, as he had marched with him through Georgia to the sea. Having arrived safely with the wagon train at Fort Sedgwick, Crofutt enquired about the solitary coach hurtling across the plains. "Yes," the camp commandant told him, deadpan, "it was General Sherman with one aide and a driver. The general has been claiming there is no danger from the Indians, and that he can ride from the mountains to the Missouri River with nothing but a penknife to defend himself with. He is now testing the truth of his claim!" Sherman got through but earned only brickbats from the locals, and did not repeat the trip without a safe escort. [48]

Sherman's trip was made during a lull in Indian hostilities and this had led him to snub the settlers between Denver and Colorado City who in 1866 had asked him for military protection. [49] In 1867-8, Indian attacks flared again throughout the region—on the stage lines, the railroad camps, the ranches, and the isolated valleys on the Divide. In the summer of 1868, while Sherman remained busy supervising Indian affairs in the region, including the distribution of Congressional funds and the setting up of Reservations, he wrote to Samuel Tappan:

"I have no hope of civilizing the plains Indians. A few may be rescued from destruction, but they will not as a whole work the soil, and must be simple paupers or work. Congress may for a few years support them, but sooner or later will get tired and abandon the effort.

At best we can give them a chance, and so prepare things that our own people may progress in their legitimate routes, and yet not come into violent collision with Indians." [50]

Crofutt was to express a similar view:

"That the Indians have suffered wrongs may not be denied. That they have committed outrages is also true . . . The question is not one of past causes, but of present necessities." [51]

*   *   *

The Union Pacific's track-layers were now racing west across the plains. Freighters flocked to each of the railheads in turn, as one after the other of these makeshift towns exploded into hectic activity as the temporary trans-shipment point between rail and wagon traffic—the Union Pacific's 'hells on wheels'. Crofutt remembered it all vividly:

"The railroad reached North Platte in November 1866 and until the railhead was completed to Julesburg in June 1867, all the freight was shipped from there. In its palmiest days, North Platte boasted a population of over 2000 . . . The gamblers, the roughs and the scallawags lived in clover . . . When the town began to decay, these leeches followed the rails and blighted every camp and community in their path . . . Some enraged individuals took the law into their own hands and hung the villains to the first projection high and strong enough to support their worthless carcasses. But many stayed free and moved on . . .

After June 1867, Julesburg during the 'lively times' had a population of 4000; before it was abandoned as the rail-to-wagon reshipment point, it was the roughest of all rough towns along the Union Pacific line . . . it is said that morality and honesty clasped hands and departed from the place. We have not learned whether they ever returned, and really we have our doubts whether they were ever there."

Passing through in 1869, an English traveller recorded the desolation:

"Julesburg seemed to consist of about three and a half dilapidated board shanties stuck down in a treeless waste of yellowish-brown buffalo grass . . . the prairie was littered for miles with old tin cans and empty bottles. On the outskirts of what had once been the town, there stood almost a forest of little wooden crosses sticking up at all sorts of angles, survivors of more that had fallen down." [52]

As the Union Pacific pushed on beyond Cheyenne, and the track-laying race with the Central Pacific grew more desperate, thousands more freighters were employed by the U.P. to carry supplies along the graded road bed. In 1868, the Union Pacific laid 425 miles of track, and freighters based in Denver who stayed the course found their journeys first becoming shorter and then lengthening again as their destinations, controlled by the needs of the U.P. construction gangs, chased the sun into the west.

Denver's Railroad Fever

Denverites had never quite recovered from the shock of discovering that the Union Pacific Railroad's chief engineer and surveyor, Grenville M. Dodge, had selected the gentler slopes of Sherman Pass (8242 ft) in Wyoming in 1866 for the first part of the route through the Rockies, rather than the difficult Berthoud Pass (11,314 ft) behind Denver, and that as a result, the "nothing place" of Cheyenne would reap the main-line benefits that Denver regarded as rightfully its own.

Back in September 1865, at one of his special receptions in Denver, David Butterfield had drawn rousing cheers from the audience of more than a hundred when he forecast that

> "as sure as anything in the future could be, the Smoky Hill route would be the route for the great Pacific Railroad . . . The Union Pacific would soon be leaping over the prairies along the Smoky Hill!" [53]

General Grenville Dodge was also in the audience on 26th September. He listened as the Denver boosters, toasting Butterfield, confidently celebrated the city's location on both the new stage line *and* the coming Pacific Railroad with all the certainty of knowing that night follows day. Dodge wisely kept his own counsel. Only a few days before, he had been with an army patrol in the Black Hills of Wyoming and discovered the gentle gradient down to the plains of what later became known as Sherman Pass, west of Cheyenne.[54] He and his engineers never found anything better.

The fact was that apart from curving briefly into the extreme northeast corner of the Territory at Julesburg, the Union Pacific avoided Colorado altogether. After his formal appointment to the company in May 1866, Dodge had personally examined the main passes behind Denver, and talked with those who knew them well, Crofutt included. One by one, however, the proposals had to be rejected as being too high, too steep or too readily blocked by snow. Denver's lofty Rocky Mountain Front Range, soaring to more than 14,000 feet, was a magnificent scenic backdrop, but the Union Pacific needed its mountains in smaller doses, and demanded a less dramatic passage to the west. Wyoming obliged.

In the fall of 1867, as the U.P. reached Cheyenne, Denver organized its first Board of Trade. John Evans, editor Byers, and a host of local businessmen and traders, including Crofutt, had been pressing hard for such an association for months. Some Denverites had already dismantled their stores and shifted them to Cheyenne. As the city grew increasingly anxious about the disastrous consequences of being by-passed by the Pacific Railroad, there was overwhelming pressure to get something done.

Golden had earlier led the way by organizing Colorado's first railroad, the Colorado Central, in 1865. William Loveland and Henry Teller had masterminded that scoop and employed Capt. E.L. Berthoud as their surveyor. Crofutt remembered the first ground being broken at Golden in May 1867, but it was not until September 1870 that the mere 15 miles between Golden and Denver were completed. Denver would defeat Golden in the railroad war just as it had eventually done, in 1867, in the fight to become the Territorial capital. But first, Denver had to build its own railroad to the main line at Cheyenne, 106 miles to the north, and the Board of Trade made the 'Denver Pacific' its top priority.

At the same time, however, Denver grew excited about the possibility of building a series of narrow-gauge railroads into the Rockies in order to replace the wagon roads, reach the mining centres, and introduce a new age in Denver's industrial and commercial development. Many local speculators switched their interests from toll roads to mountain railroads. Now, no one was more enthusiastic than Crofutt over the possibilities of a 3-ft narrow-gauge network, and in 1868 he was involved in launching three new railroad companies based in Denver.

The first, the Arapahoe, Jefferson and South Park Rail Road Co. was organized on 30th January 1868 by eight Denverites, including some of the town's earliest pioneers: Amos Steck; George Crofutt; Richard Whitsitt, who had been one of the original Leavenworth party led by General William Larimer, and who was now a successful realtor; Jacob Bright Smith, a prominent lawyer, who had been Chief Justice of the proposed Jefferson Territory in 1859; Francis Gallup, joint owner of a saddle and harness store; Loyal Nye, a mining agent; John Nye, a miners' outfitter turned saloon keeper; and George Boutelle, a surveyor.[55] The projected railroad from Denver into the timber belt had been suggested originally by Crofutt in order to supply the Denver Pacific line to Cheyenne with ties; an estimated 200,000 ties were needed. A preliminary survey of the route was made, but shortly afterwards the contract for the ties was placed in Omaha so at this stage, much to Crofutt's and his associates' disappointment, plans for the South Park Rail Road were dropped. In fact, Omaha had just been linked to the eastern rail system through the extension of the Chicago & Northwestern to Council Bluffs in 1867, and oak ties for both the Union Pacific and Denver Pacific could now come from Wisconsin and Michigan.

On 1st April 1868, Crofutt, Francis Gallup and John Nye launched the Miners' Rail Road Co. which was to run from Golden to Black Hawk and Central City, the route planned originally by Loveland and Teller as the narrow-gauge mountain section of the Colorado Central.[56] The following day, Crofutt, Francis Gallup and Aaron Shallcross, a local druggist, registered the Denver and Turkey Creek Rail Road Co. but none of these

28.   GEORGE A. CROFUTT
This is the only known photograph of Crofutt, and was probably taken in Denver c.1867,
when he was forty.
The picture was discovered in an old scrapbook dating from the 1870s kept by Caroline
Frazer, one of the children of William Frazer who died in a blizzard in the Pineries (Black
Forest) in 1862. Frazer probably met Crofutt in the early 1860s up on the Divide, and
although Mrs. Frazer remarried in 1864, Crofutt may well have kept in touch with the
family when in town. Caroline labelled her picture 'Geo Crowfut'.

speculative ventures attracted the necessary capital.[57] At the time, all were simply three more casualties of the 'narrow-gauge fever' which swept through the Denver region in the late 1860s. The first priority was the Denver Pacific, the city's standard-gauge lifeline to Cheyenne. Costly, tortuous, narrow-gauge railroads into the Rockies would have to wait.

An End to Freighting in Salt Lake City, and a New Start

With the failure of his Denver-based railroad ventures, Crofutt left town and returned to long-distance freighting in the summer of 1868. He followed the line of the Union Pacific and hauled timber and general supplies through Wyoming into Utah, where Salt Lake City became his base.

Crofutt's absence from Denver in the second half of 1868 confirmed the cancellation of his appointment as an official Road Overseer, in this case for District No. 2, Arapahoe County. On 2nd February 1869, the County Board of Commissioners declared the office vacant and appointed George W. Snell in his place.[58] The system had been established by the Colorado Territorial Assembly on 11th March 1864, when an Act was passed requiring county commissioners to divide their counties into Road Districts.[59] A Road Overseer was to be elected annually by each District, and in the late 1860s, counties slowly got around to doing something about it.

The duties of these part-time Road Overseers were to keep open the roads and bridges in their Districts, and to supervise the removal of obstructions, the cutting of drains and ditches, and the purchase of timber, gravel and stone for all necessary repairs and maintenance. The Overseer also supervised the erection of signposts at all forks in the road, and checked that they gave clear directions and distances to towns and public places. The general rule was that all able-bodied men between the ages of 18 and 50 who fulfilled prescribed county residence qualifications had to give, or send a substitute to provide, two days' work annually on the public highways under the direction of an Overseer. Failure to do this resulted in the demand for a $5 road tax. Overseers were also authorized to require an individual to lend his team of horses, mules or oxen, and a wagon, cart, scraper or plough, with reasonable compensation, in order to get the work done.

Overseers had to put up a bond ($500 appears to have been standard at this period in Arapahoe County), and were paid for their services — the same amount per day as was allowed to their county commissioners. Overseers were also required to submit an annual report of road poll taxes collected, worked out, or delinquent, along with a record of all road district receipts and expenditures. Crofutt's familiarity with the roads and the local inhabitants in many of the Districts had made him an obvious choice for election, but he may have become bored with the job, or had difficulty in raising the bond. In any event, in the summer of 1868, Crofutt decided that business looked livelier in Utah.

Even before the approach of the railroad, Salt Lake City was an important freighting and agricultural supply centre for much of the intermontane West. Now, freighting reached a frenzy of activity.

The Wasatch Range, towering above the great Salt Lake Valley on the northeastern threshold of Utah, provided the most serious barrier to the final stages of the Union Pacific's construction. Echo Canyon and Weber Canyon tested every skill of the surveyors, engineers, tunnellers and trestle-bridge builders. Mormon President Brigham Young signed a

29. FREIGHTING SUPPLIES TO THE UNION PACIFIC RAILROAD CONSTRUCTION CREWS
IN ECHO CANYON, UTAH, 1868
The newly graded track is seen on the right.

contract with the U.P. to do the grading through Echo and Weber Canyons, and huge convoys of teams and wagons laden with workmen, tools and supplies headed east from the Great Valley. Ground was first broken in Utah at Weber Canyon in June 1868, and Crofutt appears to have seen this work in progress and to have supplied some of the advance parties of cutters and graders. By the end of 1868, the Union Pacific had finished grading to the mouth of Weber Canyon and was ready to lay the rails down Echo Canyon. In April 1869, Congress and the railroad companies finally put an end to the race between the Central Pacific and the Union Pacific (whose graders now overlapped for 200 miles in Nevada-Utah) by establishing Promontory Point, Utah, fifty-six miles west of Ogden, as the meeting place of the Central Pacific and Union Pacific Railroads. The Union Pacific completed its track to Ogden on 8th March 1869.

Salt Lake City, like Denver, was by-passed by the main line. Investigation by U.P. surveyors, and by Grenville Dodge himself, had confirmed the superiority of the route north of the Lake despite the pressure brought to bear on the Union Pacific for the Salt Lake City and south-shore alternative, both by the majority of Mormons in Salt Lake City and by Gentiles anxious for other reasons to destroy the Mormon's isolation. For his part, Brigham Young had done everything he could to persuade the U.P. and, failing that, the C.P., to route through Salt Lake City. He frequently observed that he "did not care anything for a religion which could not stand a railroad." [60]

> "If I could direct the route [of the railroad]," Brigham Young said in June 1868, "I should have it down through Echo and Weber Canyons, and from there through the lower part of Salt Lake City, and then pass the south side of the lake to the Humboldt ... We are willing to do our share of the work provided we get well paid for it ... I would like to hear the whistle and the puffing of the iron horse every evening and through the night, in the morning and through the day." [61]

Salt Lake City by now had a population of about 13,000, a bustling regional metropolis and by far the largest city Crofutt had been in since he had passed through the great Mississippi river-port of St. Louis (pop. 160,000) in 1860. The Tabernacle, still unfinished, had been opened for public worship in October 1867, and its huge single oval-span roof dominated the tree-lined avenues. Although the railroad was being run forty miles north of Salt Lake City, Crofutt found the city full of optimism about the boost the Pacific Railroad would give to the Valley, and the prospect of the branch line to the city from Ogden. The line from Ogden, to be known as the Utah Central Railroad, was already planned. Indeed, work on it started exactly one week after the Pacific Railroad's rails were joined.

Crofutt had always made a point of getting to know the local editors and newspaper offices wherever he went. In Salt Lake City, in the fall of 1868, he found Edward L. Sloan hard at work on the production of a new city business directory, the first of its kind in Salt Lake. The *Deseret Almanac* had been published in Salt Lake City between 1851 and 1865; it was a miscellaneous collection with only a few business entries. In 1867, George Owens had compiled and published a 135-page Salt Lake City Directory, with business entries also for Provo, Springville and Ogden. But Owens had left to live in New York, the Mormons disliked him and his directory, and sales were negligible. The way was open for a larger volume with wider appeal.

Sloan was a local journalist and the city's official phonographer (shorthand-writer). During 1868, he had been struggling single-handed to publish his new directory at the beginning of 1869, before the completion of the Pacific Railroad and the branch line to Salt Lake City, but the amount of work involved was proving too much. At the *Deseret News* office on the corner of Main and South Temple, where Sloan was assistant editor, Crofutt would find him buried in half-completed returns, ready to admit defeat.

Listening to Sloan's problems, and thumbing through the familiar lists and files cluttering every corner of the office, Crofutt was suddenly back in his mind's eye in Philadelphia where, twelve years earlier, he had produced *The Philadelphia Merchants' Diary and Guide, for 1856.* The heyday of freighting was over so far as Crofutt was concerned. He did not see his future as a small-time freighter operating in the more remote areas beyond the railroad tracks, be they standard or narrow gauge. Without more ado, he offered to help Sloan to collect and sort the information still needed, and to assist in the production.[62] Sloan was greatly taken with Crofutt's enthusiasm for the idea and the speed with which he pinpointed what still had to be done. Crofutt was a tireless worker and surprisingly knowledgeable, Sloan discovered, about layout and general presentation.

Together, they decided to have the Salt Lake City directory printed in Chicago, and to increase income and sales in both cities by incorporating a 22-page business house and advertising supplement entitled "Chicago: its growth and trade." Crofutt worked quickly, first in Salt Lake City and then in Chicago. Utah's Territorial historian, the surveyor general, Salt Lake's city recorder, the postmaster, and the Weber County Clerk all helped.

Sloan and Crofutt had their copy ready by the beginning of 1869, but plans were frustrated when Crofutt found his journey to Chicago delayed by heavy snowstorms in the mountains in February and March. Unlike the Central Pacific Railroad in the Sierra Nevada, the Union Pacific had not originally thought it would be necessary to build long snowsheds on any section of the route through the Rockies and west into Utah. Snow fences, for the most part, were meant to suffice. Extra protection had to be added in 1869, but after even heavier snowfalls and longer delays in 1871-2, the U.P. was forced to construct snowsheds at all the most vulnerable points. Eventually on his way in the spring of 1869, Crofutt travelled by the Union Pacific to Omaha, a fascinating run over the rails for a thousand miles, often within sight of his old haunts and familiar wagon roads. Although he had been part of the changing scene for nearly a decade, the speed of that change never ceased to astonish him.

Once he had completed the journey to Chicago, Crofutt took a room at the Briggs House, a popular first-class hotel at the corner of Randolph and Wells that could accommodate 450 guests. This was the first time Crofutt had been east of the Missouri River, and back to the turmoil and tempo of big-city life, since he left Pennsylvania in 1860. Now, the volume of traffic swirling through the Briggs House in downtown Chicago was a powerful reminder of a large hotel's particular contribution and value to the local business community. Crofutt, like thousands of others, was to make good use of that fact for the rest of his life, and it is worth noting why the Briggs, and hotels like it, played such an important role in American society.

Large, first-class American hotels had been dubbed "the palaces of the public" in the *National Intelligencer* as early as 1827. Their huge lobbies were impressive, and frequently out of all proportion to the resident guest capacity. Hotel lobbies, restaurants and bar-rooms were open to non-residents, and became indispensable centres of business and social activity. Introductions, discussions, negotiations, deals — all were part of the hotel's communication network, and the hotel lobby's invisible earnings. Established figures met there, surrounded by reporters and, in a special sense, by 'lobbyists'. Newcomers mingled with the crowds, asking questions and planning their next moves. Many hotels lost money on their guest-rooms, except at peak periods, but made up the loss in their bar-rooms, dining-rooms, and adjacent meeting areas. There were cardrooms and billiard rooms. In large hotels, shops, banks, ticket agencies and information booths were located around the lobby. Hotel reading-rooms were free to guests, with a small fee charged to outsiders; here, a variety of local and out-of-town newspapers, magazines, and business reports were available, providing another reason why so many called in regularly to their favourite hotels for an up-date on news, gossip, local politics, market trends, and a spot of personal business advertising.

Europeans were often astonished by the size of many American hotels, by the number of outsiders swinging through the doors "as if they owned the place," and by the "vastness" and elegance of the lobbies and public rooms. As Doris King observed, the American hotel very soon in its history became a peculiarly American institution, "for the story of the development of the first-class hotel is part of the story of the Rise of the Common Man." [63] Certainly, business that in England, for example, would have been discussed outside the office in private homes, private clubs, or at house parties would in America just as readily have been sealed in a hotel. Many in fact booked into a hotel and established home and office there. Permanent boarders — judges, lawyers, storekeepers, salesmen, and others, often brought their families to live there. Vividness, sociability, and the housing shortage all contributed to the popularity of hotel life, noted Jefferson Williamson in a pioneering study on the American hotel; "the hotel habit" was easy and ideally suited to a restless, opportunity-seeking society continually on the move. No other nation in the world consistently made such general use of its hotels as did America.[64]

Crofutt's choice in Chicago, the Briggs House, had been built by William Briggs in 1851 and during the 1850s became Abraham Lincoln's favourite hotel. Now run by Benjamin H. Skinner, the Briggs House maintained its high reputation for smoothly professional hotel-keeping and personal service, along with the added advantage of proximity to Chicago's Chamber of Commerce and central business district. Here, Crofutt rapidly concentrated his efforts on thirty-three firms which were already trading into Utah or anxious to expand their business there in the coming months. While Crofutt put the Chicago supplement together, the printers got on with the Salt Lake material. Rounds & James, a large printers and binders at 46 State Street, handled the work quickly and efficiently, and before long, copies of the *Salt Lake City Directory and Business Guide for 1869* were neatly stacked and ready for distribution.

The pace and pressure of life in Chicago had been a shot in the arm. Crofutt was tingling with new energy and excitement as he headed back into the West over the rails. He returned to Salt Lake City early in May to find preparations almost complete for celebrating the joining of the Union Pacific and Central Pacific Railroads. Excursion parties were fully booked. Edward Sloan was going up to Promontory Point to report the event for the *Deseret News*. No sooner had Crofutt unpacked his bag, and brought Sloan up to date on the successful completion of the work in Chicago, than they were off to join the other press representatives for the Great Event.

PART III

PATTERNS OF WESTERN EXPANSION AND EAST-WEST CONNECTION: THE 1870s-1900s

30.   GATEWAY TO THE WEST IN THE NEW TRANSCONTINENTAL AGE
The Union Pacific Railroad's depot at Omaha, Nebraska in W.H. Rideing, *Scenery of the Pacific Railways*, 1878

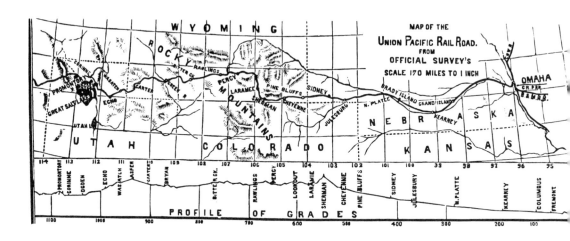

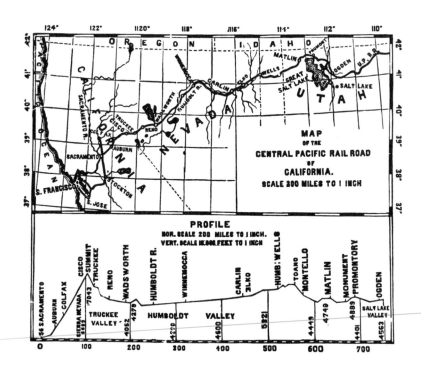

Maps, with Profile Grades, of the Union and Central Pacific Railroads
in the first edition of the *Great Trans-Continental Railroad Guide,* 1869

CHAPTER FIVE

Transcontinental:
Crofutt Spreads The Word
Across America

The Golden Spike ceremony to mark the joining of the rails had originally been scheduled for Saturday, 8th May 1869, but torrential rain, washouts, and a last-minute wage dispute delayed the arrival of the official Union Pacific representatives by two days. As a result, 10th May passed into American history as the day of the Great Event.

California's special contingent, unaware of the delay, had arrived on the Friday afternoon in a downpour, to find virtually no signs of activity on Promontory's bleak plateau. The Central Pacific Railroad party, led by President Stanford, eventually spent the weekend sightseeing, with one night at Ogden as guests of the Union Pacific. The press reporters followed them round, making the most of the splendid luncheon at Taylor's Mills on the Saturday — "a bountiful collation and oceans of champagne,"[1] and then a short excursion into Weber Canyon.

So great was the national significance of the Pacific Railroad, the major newspapers from coast to coast had already had their Special Correspondents "at the front" for some time, falling over themselves to find human interest stories to include in their regular on-the-spot dispatches about the final stages of the work. Press representatives from New York, Boston, Springfield, Mass., Chicago, Omaha, Sacramento and San Francisco were on hand, as well as those for the Associated Press, an alliance originally formed in 1848 by six New York newspapers which had subsequently developed into a nation-wide agency news service.

There were about a dozen official representatives from Salt Lake City, including journalists Edward Sloan, J. McKnight, T.B.H. Stenhouse (of the *Telegraph*, recently transferred to Ogden), and photographer C.R. Savage. Mingling with the crowds, Crofutt saw no familiar faces from Denver, which did not surprise him. Although a few were in fact present, most Denverites were more intent on getting their own track completed to Cheyenne than willing to stand on some desolate, unlovely spot called Promontory in the wilds of Utah, and be reminded yet again that the U.P.'s main line had passed them by.

Crofutt had one strong reminder of his freighting years, however, in the shape of Alexander Majors, who was employed as a railroad grading contractor in 1868-69. His son Benjamin had worked with him, and both attended the celebration.[2] Like so many others in the late 1860s, Alexander Majors had passed swiftly from the freighting into the railroad age. In 1867, he had sold his freighting business in Nebraska City and moved with his family to Salt Lake City, later to begin work for the Union Pacific. Majors' reputation as a freighter, and his old association with the famous Pony Express, made many in the crowd want to meet him and shake him by the hand.

Crofutt found the press corps a cheerful, no-nonsense bunch. He slid easily into the general conversation with tales of newspapers in Colorado, and of their editors' early struggles among the mining camps. The enforced delay in the Golden Spike celebrations had the newspapermen swopping stories long into the night, and Crofutt found himself chatting with H. Wallace Atwell, who was reporting for San Francisco's *Daily Morning Chronicle*. "He's better known as 'Bill Dadd, the Scribe'," Sloan told Crofutt as he introduced them.[3]

The San Francisco *Chronicle* had a reputation for crisp, incisive editorials and talented writers. It began in 1865 as the *Dramatic Chronicle* under Charles de Young, and quickly became noted for its investigative journalism, and as the fearless champion of the people. Its squibs attracted the attention of Mark Twain who made the *Chronicle* one of his haunts in San Francisco, and paid for his desk by writing occasional pieces. Twain attracted others like Bret Harte. In September 1868, just eight months before the completion of the Pacific Railroad, the paper had become the *Daily Morning Chronicle*, and achieved such immediate success that the proprietors wagered and won their challenge a few weeks later that they had swept the board and grabbed the largest circulation in the city.[4] Atwell, the *Chronicle's* man, could hold his own among the Promontory pressmen.

After Edward Sloan's introduction, Crofutt began discussing an idea with Atwell that had grown stronger in his mind in recent months. It had taken shape when, as Sloan's assistant in Salt Lake City, he had made a modest return to the world of printing and publishing, and had dominated his thoughts ever since the trip to Chicago with the new, exhilarating, 1000-mile journey to and from Omaha.

The idea was simple enough — a complete guidebook to the new Pacific Railroad from Omaha to Sacramento, with added information about the San Francisco region. The book must be inexpensive, handy for the pocket, concise in its detail and yet have something to say about every station and point of interest along the entire 1800-mile route. Atwell was enthusiastic. Given the importance of being the first on the market, the two men appear to have decided then and there to divide the route between them, each drafting the section he knew best. Atwell, long resident in California, initially took on all or part of the Central Pacific line; there is no evidence that he knew or had ever travelled the U.P.'s rails east of Utah. Crofutt had already "been over every foot of both roads . . . on all kinds of conveyances — engine, hand-cars, construction train, in the saddle, and sometimes on foot." For the moment, however, he was to be responsible for the Union Pacific route, much of which he knew intimately from his freighting days.

Guidebooks had already played their part in opening the New World. They had assisted emigrants across the Atlantic and into the United

UNION PACIFIC RAILROAD PHOTOGRAPH CAR,
near Point of Rocks, Wyoming, 1868
As construction work proceeded, both the Union Pacific and the Central Pacific Railroads employed photographers to publicize the scenery along their routes. Point of Rocks was 805 miles west of Omaha. Good coal supplies had been discovered nearby and were already being worked by the Wyoming Coal Co.

States; they had led others across the plains and through the mountains to Oregon, California, Utah, or Pike's Peak. The eastern States were well served with railroad guides and travel handbooks. *Harper's New York and Erie Rail-Road Guide Book*, for example, published in 1851 with 136 small, original engravings, had set a high standard, while notable earlier guides and handbooks had been written by G.M. Davison, R. J. Vandewater, N.P. Willis, W. Williams, and T. A. Richards.

The Central Pacific and Union Pacific Railroads had begun to organize their own elaborate publicity campaigns through special 'end-of-track' excursions, often with descriptive guides to match. The C.P. started with a Fourth of July run from Dutch Flat to Sacramento in 1865, while the U.P. hit the headlines with its celebrated excursion in October 1866 to mark the railroad's arrival at the 100th meridian, 247 miles west of Omaha.[5]

A number of small publications already provided information at local or regional level. In California, for example, Bancroft's monthly guides for travellers printed basic timetable and mileage details. But Crofutt and Atwell wanted to capture the reality and continental significance of the new railroad's "one unbroken line."

"The Pacific Railroad — Done! Done!"

The rain stopped during the night and Monday, 10th May dawned cold and cloudless. Before long, the sun was up — "A clear and beautiful day, the grassy plain, the green-clad hills, and the snow-clad summits of the Wahsatch Mountains forming an unforgettable scene."

The two engines, the U.P.'s 'Rogers 119' and the C.P.'s 'Jupiter' No. 60, steamed forward to face each other across the short gap in the rails. Officials and their guests assembled. Sketchers moved from group to group, while the photographers selected their vantage points and worried about how best to arrange all the dignitaries. The telegraphers checked the special apparatus they had prepared for transmitting the hammer blows on the last spike by telegraph to a waiting nation. Soldiers from Fort Douglas, and others from the 21st U.S. infantry battalion on their way to the Presidio at San Francisco, marched into place.

> "All was excitement and bustle that morning," Crofutt recalled, "men hurrying to and fro, grasping their neighbors' hands in hearty greeting, as they paused to ask or answer hurried questions . . . There were the lines of blue-clad boys, with their burnished muskets and glistening bayonets, and over all, in the bright May sun, floated the glorious old Stars and Stripes, an emblem of unity, power and prosperity.[6]

Promontory's isolation reduced the thousands of spectators that had been predicted, although millions across the United States were present in spirit. The most accurate estimate of the crowd was probably 600-700, entertained by stirring selections from the military band, and the Tenth Ward Band from Salt Lake City. The crowd grew noisier and more impatient as noon approached, the hour when the rails were to be joined. Spectators swarmed over both engines and jostled the workmen putting the finishing touches to the track. Reporters strained to catch the speeches, thankful to be able to fill in the gaps from the official texts that had been distributed in advance.

The encircling crowd prayed, "got done praying," and then watched with glee or embarrassment as the C.P.'s President Stanford and U.P.'s Vice-President Durant both swung, and missed, the final spike. No matter; the telegrapher clicked three dots over the wires at 12: 47 p.m. to signal that the spike was driven home and the country's celebrations could begin. San Francisco had already been celebrating for three days, having received the news of the 8th May postponement too late to change its plans! The telegrapher completed his work: "The last rail is laid, the last spike driven. The Pacific Railroad is finished."

"Twenty or thirty prominent newspapers have reporters here," wrote one of the army officers present. "Everybody who is sober enough is scribbling; some are cheering, some laughing and throwing up their hats — it is a festive scene. The speeches are good and our band played pretty well until they had taken too much ardent spirit." [7]

Crofutt's interest in the Pacific Railroad was probably first sparked in Philadelphia in the 1850s. Just opposite No. 83 Dock Street, the Philadelphia Board of Trade's meeting-room in the great Merchants' Exchange had contained a valuable map collection, including a large chart showing five possible routes for a railroad to the Pacific Ocean. The surveys for a Pacific Railroad had been commissioned by Congress in March 1853 and completed in 1853-54. Crofutt often met his business contacts in the Board of Trade's offices, where there had been much debate about the different lines to the Pacific, boldly marked across the map through the huge, empty spaces of the West. Now he was at Promontory, the dream was reality, and Crofutt was to remember the Great Event as the most thrilling day of his life.

Crofutt had worked his way through the crowd and, being tall, managed to get a good view. He could still recall it vividly more than thirty years later:

"The most exciting scene I ever witnessed was the completion of the Pacific Railroad. I have seen many stirring events, have been present at floods and fighting and executions where men's blood was up and every nerve strained to its utmost, but the driving of the last spike in the railway spanning the continent was the grandest and most exciting event my eyes ever beheld. Perhaps we were over-strained in our estimates at the time, but we felt that the work there being concluded meant more to this nation and to the advancement of civilization than anything else that could be imagined . . . Great mass meetings were held in the principal cities, but at Promontory Point, when the men standing on the cow-catchers of the two engines reached forward and shook hands, the crowd sang and danced and shouted with a delirium of joy never to be known but once in a lifetime." [8]

There was a strong sense of theatre about the scene, both in the physical setting and in the dramatic impact of events. The crowd, the two locomotives and the rails formed the centrepiece, set upon a huge otherwise empty stage. The stark desert arena, framed by mountains, dwarfed yet drew attention to the momentous action taking place below.

Edward Sloan was also busy capturing local colour for his *Deseret News* readers:

32.   JOINING THE RAILS AT PROMONTORY, UTAH, 10th MAY 1869

One of the famous photographs of the Great Event taken by the U.P.'s chief photographer, Andrew J. Russell. The Central Pacific engine is on the left, the Union Pacific on the right. The telegrapher's small table can be seen centre-right.

"The thermometer stood at 69° in the shade of the Central Pacific telegraph car...Half an hour sufficed for the photographers to take views of the scenes from every available standpoint — they will be much sought after.

The succeeding moments, prior to 6 p.m., were vigorously applied to refreshment and hilarity — mirth, good humor, and more champagne... Hail to the day thus commemorated and immortalized by the completion of the Pacific Railroad." [9]

President Stanford and the C.P. party left at 5 p.m. to begin the journey west; the Union Pacific contingent were homeward-bound an hour later. Within forty-eight hours, the first train from the east had passed over the link and was on its way to California.

"How to Go! What to See!" The New Book Leads the Way

Crofutt lost no time in starting work on the guide. Drawing on his recent experience with Sloan's Salt Lake City Guide, he headed straight for Chicago, put up once again at the Briggs House, and rented an office close by in the Larmon block, at the corner of Clark and Washington. He formed a new publishing company, Geo. A. Crofutt & Co., adopting the new spelling of his name for the first time. Atwell was the sole partner. Next he hurried over to Rounds & James, the printers and binders at 46 State Street and discussed production costs. Sterling P. Rounds was particularly taken with the idea. He was a live wire in Chicago's printing trade, always on the look-out for new business and advertising outlets; his highly successful *Rounds' Printer's Cabinet* had been going since 1856. Rounds had been especially excited by the West since 1861, when he had printed the notes made by Charles Clarke on his adventure-filled trip to Pike's Peak during the gold rush. Together with his brother, H. E. Rounds, Sterling had also strengthened the Chicago connection by investing money and materials in a number of newspapers starting up in the West in the 1860s, including funds to expand Denver's *Rocky Mountain News*.

Crofutt began assembling the statistics, timetables, details of land for sale to settlers by the railroad companies, and other data needed for a guide which was to be "correct, concise, comprehensive and thoroughly reliable." At the same time, it had to convey to the traveller the sense of new opportunity, and the magnitude of the railroad's achievement as one of the greatest national enterprises of the century.

Before long he was travelling west again from Omaha, working closely with the railroad personnel (including the Union Pacific's President Ames, General Superintendent Hammond, and Ticket Agent Budd), and in their mutual interest, constantly seeking support for as many different outlets for the Guide as time would permit. He made notes en route, weaving in his own experiences of freighting days. He jotted down points where the "old emigrant road" ("old" so soon!) could be spotted, as

151

well as a whole geography of bridges, ferries, fords, army forts and service ranches, several of which were already deserted with the passing of the stagecoach era. The immediacy of the plains section distinguished the Guide from the outset, and the ability to convey this sense of *knowing* rather than merely *seeing* the landscape was carried right through to the end. As Crofutt and Atwell were to emphasize:

> "The book is the result of our personal experience . . . one of ten, the other of twenty years west of the Missouri river. . . . The Guide is prepared from *actual observation* over the whole line, and *not* a rehash of old, unreliable newspapers and hearsay accounts."

Travelling west to California, Crofutt passed Promontory once more and watched while yet another souvenir-hunter cut a piece from the "last tie." Crofutt did not have the heart to tell him that the last tie had already been replaced several times as enthusiasts continued to carry fragments away in triumph.

Atwell and Crofutt quickly made their final arrangements. The authorship, however shared, would be credited entirely to the well-established and more experienced Atwell, using his regular pseudonym "Bill Dadd, the Scribe". H. Wallace Atwell had already written a number of newspaper and magazine articles under this byline, and achieved considerable success. He was born in Woodstock, Vermont and as a youth of seventeen had joined the California gold rush in 1849. After several months without reward he abandoned prospecting, took odd jobs and then, from 1854-64, worked in a lumber mill in Mariposa County. Ready for a change, Atwell next worked for a printer in Mariposa County, and then for a succession of small newspapers, before being employed by the *Daily Morning Chronicle* in San Francisco. By the time he met Crofutt, Atwell was thirty-seven and had been in California for twenty years.

Crofutt was content at this stage to identify himself solely in the role of publisher. Even so, he personally checked and amplified the far western section of the route, and wrote the whole of the central and eastern sections, letting the realities of his life as a freighter on the plains, the perils of Indian attack, and the courage of the emigrants flow on to the pages. Here was no "maudlin sentimentalist or sober-faced broad-brim," no deskbound city publisher, but one of the pioneers talking to the new railroaders.

Travellers were quickly enveloped in the plains of Nebraska and urged to appreciate the finer details as well as the broad brush strokes of this huge, seemingly uniform landscape. Dramatic tales of the hardships and isolation endured by many of the emigrants were not allowed to obscure that special quality about the plains which Crofutt loved. Far from being a drab, depressing vista, the plains could lift the spirit with their stillness and inspiring sweep of land and sky. "There is beauty on every hand . . . for the traveler who admires nature in all her phases," not least "among the wild prairie flowers when their thousand different hues and varieties are spangled with showers or morning dew." Despite the grandeur of the mountains still to come, Crofutt told his readers, you will find that the quiet, graceful beauty of the prairies goes on lingering in the mind with an effect all its own.

Following the guidebook, otherwise unseeing eyes were helped to spot the features that had mattered so much to the early pioneers and the wagon trains. Apart from the basic supplies of water, wood and grass, railroad passengers began to pick out the details of gradient, the critical width of streams and firmness of river banks, and the dangerous location of bluffs or sloughs which at certain points had forced the emigrants away from the river, sometimes into miles of loose, barren sand. Already, the journey was a revelation.

Linking plains and mountains, Crofutt expanded the section on Colorado to remind travellers of the delights that lay to the south, pointing out to them the graded road bed just short of Cheyenne that would in time carry the tracks of the Denver Pacific Railroad. "Volumes would not suffice to do justice to Colorado Territory," but Crofutt made sure that his readers had their appetites whetted for the delights awaiting the tourist, and the opportunities for the settler:

> Imagine yourselves on a mountain viewpoint in the great Front Range . . . "the vast scene is before you — wild, rugged, and grand. Away to the east, like some great ocean, lies the vast, grayish expanse of the plains. . . . Look south towards majestic Long's Peak, Gray's Peak and Pike's Peak, all over 14,000 ft . . . inhale long draughts of pure mountain air . . . find streams stealing away through beds of tiny, delicately tinted mountain flowers . . . gaze at the high, bold masses of granite piled one on the other in wild confusion."

Farther on, the bleakness and awful grandeur of the Sherman Pass (8242 ft) had earlier made an unforgettable impression on Crofutt; now he told his readers:

> "At Sherman Pass, the tourist, if his 'wind is good,' can spend a long time pleasantly in wandering amid some of the wildest, grandest scenes to be found on the continent. There are places where the rocks rise higher, where the chasms are far deeper, where the surrounding peaks may be loftier, and the torrents mightier in their power — and still they do not possess such power over the mind of man as does the wild, desolate-looking landscape around Sherman . . . in no place I have ever visited have I felt so utterly alone, so completely isolated from mankind, and left entirely with nature, as at Sherman, in the Black Hills of Wyoming."

Then would come a change of mood — a touch of melodrama straight out of the pages of the dime novel. Readers could shudder over the story of Joseph (Jack) Slade, a hired tough who had begun as a freighter and trail boss for Russell, Majors and Waddell in 1859, and later been employed by 'Stagecoach King' Ben Holladay in the early 1860s as a division superintendent based at Julesburg. Here he was given a free hand to protect and maintain the service along some 200 miles of Holladay's Overland Stage line. Slade's increasingly ruthless exploits and wild drunken outbursts made him notorious throughout Colorado, Wyoming, and finally Montana where in March 1864 he was hanged by vigilantes in Virginia City —"a short shrift and a stout rope" ended Jack Slade's grisly career.

In eastern Wyoming, passengers could either admire or be scared out of their wits by the great Dale Creek bridge, a huge trestle 650 feet long and 128 feet high spanning the creek from bluff to bluff:

33.   THE DALE CREEK TRESTLE BRIDGE, WYOMING

photograph by A. J. Russell

Built in 1868, the great wooden trestle was not replaced by an iron structure until 1877. After further work in 1885, the track was eventually relocated and a new crossing of Dale Creek made in 1900-01, using fill instead of bridgework.

"The bridge is the grandest feature of the road," Crofutt assured them, ". . . securely corded together, it presents a light, airy and graceful appearance when viewed from the creek." But now, look down! "The beautiful little stream looks like a silver thread below us, the sun glinting its surface with a thousand flashes of silvery light."

What an enthusiastic writer! thought one traveller in 1869, clutching his guidebook, and confessing that several passengers dared not look down from this all too airy-looking trestle bridge. Expressions of admiration were saved until all the cars were safely over.[10]

A few miles beyond the brash new railroad town of Laramie, travellers were on the look-out for the isolated block of Sheep Mountain, over 9000 feet in the Medicine Bow ranges of the Rockies; the adventurous tourist would find that "the road is rough and the ascent toilsome but the view when once on the summit will well repay the trouble." Crofutt described the climb, and the magnificent final panorama:

Near the peak, "in the center of a green grassy lawn, lies Crystal Lake, a circular lake nearly a mile wide, its clear cold water glistening in the rays of the sun and reflecting, as in a mirror, every object on its banks. . . . The scene is one of unsurpassing loveliness around you, while the view in the distance is grand, aye, sublime — beyond the power of words to depict."

Crofutt outlined the main features, and then added, "stepping from the sublime to the useful . . . That immense pile of railroad ties we saw in Laramie came from these pine forests — floated down the river when the spring freshets filled the low banks with the melted snow. During the building of the railroad, thousands were floated down to Laramie, and thence hauled along the line."

Travellers eventually left Wyoming loaded with information about the grazing, lumbering and mining potential of the region they had crossed, as well as its landforms, soils, vegetation, and wild life. Along the way, Crofutt had continued to tie the package with memories of his own freighting days, the old stage stations, and finally the sudden burst of activity at the Union Pacific's temporary trans-shipment points between rail and wagon traffic, the notorious 'hells on wheels'. Beyond North Platte, Julesburg and Cheyenne, the U.P. had reached Benton, Wy. at the end of July 1868, and that summer large quantities of freight were transferred to wagons heading into Montana, Idaho and Utah:

"There were high old times in Benton then . . . a town of canvas tents and 3000 people — roughs, thieves, petty gamblers (the same thing), fast women, and the usual accompaniments of the railroad towns . . . All the water used was hauled two miles from the Platte River — one dollar per barrel or ten cents per bucketfull. . . ." But as the rails pushed on to Bryan, the entire population of Benton packed its tents and disappeared, "leaving only a few old chimneys and post holes to mark the spot of the once flourishing town."

155

On went the travellers, following Crofutt through increasingly rough and broken country, covered with sage-brush and flecked with alkali, to discover the surprisingly easy Rocky Mountain pass at Creston — just 7100 feet and part of the main Continental Divide, although more than 1000 feet lower than Sherman Pass. Soon they began to descend the long narrow valley of Bitter Creek, once again reminded, as the train eased them round the tortuous bluffs for 60 miles, of those who had so recently struggled on foot or by wagon:

> "The stream is small, and so strongly impregnated with alkali as to be almost useless for man or beast. The banks and bottoms are very treacherous in places, miring any cattle which attempt to reach its fetid waters. This section was always a terror to travelers, emigrants and freighters, for nothing in the line of vegetation grows thereon excepting greasewood and sage-brush. The freighter who had safely navigated this section . . . would swear that he was a 'tough cuss on wheels from Bitter Creek.'"

New sights and impressions came tumbling in as the passengers penetrated ever more deeply into the Western Cordillera and became aware for the first time of the colourful complexity of the ridges, spurs, ranges and plateaux lying beyond the Rockies. Cliffs and cuttings gave Crofutt the opportunity to include a brief description of the geology along the route. Then there was information about the gold and silver mines being developed in the Sweetwater district, some 80 miles away from the railroad, as well as the discovery of oil-bearing shales, and the exploitation of the coal measures that the U.P. had been fortunate enough to find at half-a-dozen points along its route. At the same time, Crofutt always added a personal touch; he would name a settler in an isolated ranch visible from the train, draw attention to sections of the old overland road, tell his readers about the famous mountain man and guide Jim Bridger (and the army fort named after him), recount the violent end of the Bear River desperadoes, and then tune to a different western note and recommend the best places he had found to fish for trout, to hunt deer, bear or buffalo, and to collect moss agates.

The entry into Utah was dramatic. Past the massive red sandstones of Castle Rocks, and the walls of conglomerate and granite, the train rattled into Echo Canyon,

> "amid some of the grandest and wildest scenery imaginable. We do not creep on it as though we mistrusted our powers, but with a snort and roar we plunge down the defile, which momentarily increases to a gorge, only to become, in a short distance, a grand and awful chasm."

Domes, precipices, buttresses, and the famous Hanging Rock above the old overland stage station, towered in places up to 2000 feet above the train.

"On goes the engine, whirling us past ravines which cut the rocks from crest to base, shooting over bridges, and flying past and under the overhanging walls. When, after crossing Echo Creek thirty-one times in twenty-six miles, we rush past the Witches' Cave and Chimney Rock, our engine gives a loud scream of warning to the brakeman, who throws on the brakes and brings the train to a stop."

As the journey continued beside the Weber River, Crofutt pointed out where the old stage road to Salt Lake City turned off for Parley Park. He had first seen this beautiful valley in 1865 when exploring routes for David Butterfield, and by now it contained several hundred Mormon farms. The old stage station had been turned into a fine hotel by William Kimball, Crofutt told his readers, and tourists were advised to make a point of sampling Parley Park's delightful scenery, and rich stocks of fish and game. "It is one of those pleasant places where one loves to linger, regrets to leave, and longs to visit again."

Soon the passengers were on the look-out for the One Thousand Mile Tree (1000 miles from Omaha), before plunging deeper into Weber Canyon, past Devil's Slide and Devil's Gate, and through a breathtaking sequence of tunnels and torrents, bridges and rock buttresses, perilous ledges, and endless cutting and filling. Here and there they caught sight of a sliver of cultivation before "the massive walls close in again and crush out the green meadows." Then with a final shriek of the whistle, the train escaped from the dark Wasatch Mountains on to the sunlit plains of the Great Valley of Salt Lake.

Curiosity about the Mormons and the popularity of side-trips to Salt Lake City required an expanded section on Utah Territory. There were descriptions of Brigham Young, Salt Lake City, the nearly-completed 37-mile spur of the Utah Central Railroad which linked the Mormon capital to the transcontinental line at Ogden, and details of the highly productive irrigated agriculture in the Great Valley. Crofutt had all this and more at his finger-tips, having assisted Edward Sloan on the compilation of the Salt Lake City Directory a few months earlier.

Beyond Corinne, passengers watched farmland gradually give away to alkali beds, "white, barren, and glittering in the sun with a hard gray light, very disagreeable and wearying to weak eyes." But the arrival at Promontory (4532 ft) was the next major event, and as they prepared to change from the Union Pacific to the Central Pacific Railroad, passengers could spend a little time reading Crofutt's description of the 'joining of the rails', and try to imagine those few hours of excited celebration on 10th May 1869. Standing now amid the sage-brush, travellers looked forlornly along Promontory's main street — a bleak collection of about thirty board and canvas shacks, mainly saloons and small dining-rooms whose nearest water supply was a spring four miles south of the railroad.

The enormous size of the Great Salt Lake (max. length c.84 miles, width c.45 miles) was not readily grasped from the railroad, so Crofutt set the scene by describing a climb he had taken one spring morning to the top of one of the prominent peaks close by:

> "After an hour's toilsome walking through sage-brush and bunch-grass, then among sage-brush and rocks . . . then among more rocks, stunted cedars, tiny, delicate flowers and blooming mosses, we stood on the summit of the peak, on a narrow ridge of granite not over four feet wide, and there, almost at our feet — so steep was the mountain — lay the Great Salt Lake . . . glittering in the morning sun like a field of burnished silver. Mile after mile it stretched away, placid and motionless.

> By the aid of the glass, the islands could be distinctly seen . . . lone sentinels in the midst of this waste of waters . . . The principal islands are Antelope (15 miles long), Sheep's [Fremont], Hat, Stansbury, Carrington and Egg. They possess many charming summer retreats, many natural bathing places, where the gravelly bays intrude among the grass-covered points and hillocks. The water is so buoyant, that it is difficult for the bather to sink therein, and so strongly impregnated with salt, that if allowed to dry on the body it falls off like scales . . .

> Away beyond these islands rise the white-crested Wahsatch Mountains . . . and we think we can pick out the curve in their brown sides where nestles Salt Lake City. Far away to the southward the range blends with the sky and water; dim, indistinct lines of green, brown, blue and silver blend into one . . . sweeping down in one waving mass of vanishing color which slowly recedes in the dim distance until the eye can follow its course no farther . . .

> Away to the west, Pilot Knob rears its crest of rocks from out the center of the great American Desert. Do not look longer in that direction — all is desolation; only a barren plain, hard gray rocks, and glinting beds of alkali meet the vision.

> One more view to the north, one look at the lines of green hills and greener slopes which sweep down toward the sandy, sage-clad plateau on which stands the station; another and last look at the placid lake, and now, cooled and refreshed by the mountain breeze, we pluck a tiny moss bell from the cleft in the highest rock and then descend the rugged mountain."

The Central Pacific Railroad took the passengers from Promontory across the western deserts of Utah and Nevada, and past Humboldt Wells around which the weary emigrants and their teams rested after their journey across a particularly harsh sand and alkali section. Then the blessed relief of the Humboldt Valley system — "the transition from the parched desert and barren upland, to these green and well-watered valleys is so sudden, that it seems like the work of magic." At Elko, Nev., some 5000 feet above sea level and 470 miles from Sacramento, the train made another of its regular 30-minute "eating stops". Elko is still built of wood and canvas, Atwell told his readers, and reminds me of the early days of Sacramento, with the long trains of pack mules moving along main street to those mining camps still inaccessible to the freight wagons.

When they stopped at Argenta in central Nevada, passengers got

34.   HUMBOLDT HOUSE, NEVADA

in *Crofutt's New Overland Tourist, and Pacific Coast Guide,* 1884

One of the original 30-minute "eating stops" on the Central Pacific Railroad. "The
meals are the *best* on the road," Crofutt reported. West-bound passengers took
supper, East-bound passengers breakfast.

Early in 1871, Samuel Smiles Jr. travelled east from San Francisco, and arrived at
the Humboldt House at 7 a.m. for breakfast. He notes in his journal:
"On descending, I find a large, well-appointed refreshment room, with the tables
ready laid; and a tempting array of hot tea and coffee, bacon, steaks, eggs, and
other eatables . . . a 'regular square meal'."

down to eat at the Railroad House, beside the freight yards and the
stage-line office. Wells, Fargo and Hill Beachy both ran daily coaches to
Austin and the rich Reese River-White Pine silver mining region lying one
hundred or so miles to the south. Most of the passengers had heard of
Wells, Fargo, but they were now told about one of the West's most famous
stage-line owners, Hill Beachy —

> "a household name from Sacramento to Oregon, from the Rocky Mountains
> to the Pacific. Thousands of poor devils who rush off after wild excitements
> and 'get broke' have reason to bless Hill Beachy and his stages, for want of
> funds never kept a man in a strange land; if he could reach Beachy, he was
> sure of being passed home again . . .

> Hill Beachy looks every inch the pioneer and rambling, restless Western
> stage man. The Indians, among whom he has been running his stages for

years, call him 'bad medicine', and keep out of his way most of the time. Asked which State he claimed as home, Beachy replied, 'Well, I don't know. You see I was born in Pennsylvania, and when I was ten years old I ran away and went to Ohio, and since then I have not lived anywhere. I have been on this coast as long as any of them, so I suppose I belong here.'"

As the train rolled through western Utah and Nevada, travellers who had kept their eyes peeled were now beginning, with the help of the Guide, to see the significant variations in the desert landscape. There was no uniformity here either; instead, an astonishingly complex geography in form and colour — gravel spreads, sand hills, alkali beds, lava flows, gaunt ranges, sculptured bluffs, dry creeks, flash flood rubble, old lake shorelines, mineral workings, springs and sinks, and the vital signs of the presence of salt or sweet water. And all this was yet another part of America, to be seen and comprehended:

> "To the careless passer-by, the country appears devoid of interest. But the seeker after knowledge, who wishes to delve into nature's mysteries, can here find pleasant and profitable employment. The whole sum of man's existence does not consist in mines, mills, merchandise and money. There are other ways of employing the mind beside bending its energies to the accumulation of wealth; there is still another God, mightier than mammon ... and among the works of His hands — these barren plains and brown hills."

Beyond the Truckee meadows, where emigrants and their teams had rested after crossing the desert, the train ran on to Reno, a motley collection of cabins housing a population of some six hundred. Reno was important as the nearest point on the railroad to Nevada's fabulous Comstock Lode, and the rich silver-, gold-, and copper-mining centres around Virginia City, Gold Hill, and the Pea Vine district. Reno's connecting stage lines and freight wagons did a roaring trade. Dyer's stage ran to Washoe and Carson Cities, while the Sage-Brush Stage Line and Wells, Fargo both ran daily services to Virginia City and Gold Hill, whose combined population was about twenty thousand.

In addition to its railroad and stage-line interests, Reno was also the terminal for a surviving spur section of the legendary Pony Express, which ran south to Virginia City with the express material Wells, Fargo sent ahead of the mail. Alerted by the Guide, passengers watched in fascination as the special mail bags were thrown from the cars before the train had stopped, and then transferred swiftly to the waiting horses, their "light, wiry riders" already in the saddle. In less time than it took to tell, the Pony Expressmen had disappeared in the dust of Reno's main street towards the first of the three relay points. It was yet another vanishing page of Western history, another fleeting reminder of the speed of change in the extraordinary decade of the 1860s.

Beyond Reno, the air became cooler, more invigorating, and filled with the aroma of spruce and pine in the Sierra Nevada. Travellers could appreciate the story of a lumberman from "away down in Maine,"

> "who had been very sour and taciturn during the trip across the plains, refusing to be sociable with any of his fellow travelers. But when he entered within the shades of the forest, he straightened himself up for a moment, looked around, and exclaiming, 'Thank God, I smell pitch once more,' sank back in his seat and wept for joy."

Truckee City, California must certainly have delighted him. It was a major depot for the Central Pacific Railroad, and the most important lumbering centre in the region — "One can hardly get around the town for the piles of lumber, ties and wood which cover the ground in every direction." A few miles away, there were the tourist attractions of Tahoe and Donner Lakes. Amid all the beauty, passengers read the harrowing tale of the Donner Lake tragedy (1846), but before long they were on the look-out for reminders of the goldrush pioneers — the signs of their diggings, their patched-up cabins, and the old emigrant road. Part of the charm of these older mining towns, wrote Atwell, as he described the gold placers and hydraulic methods used around Dutch Flat, Little York, You Bet, Red Dog and Gold Run, is the way every miner's cabin if at all possible has its small irrigated garden decked with flowers and fruit trees.

The magnificent view at Cape Horn provided the single most spectacular scene of all, the narrow track climbing high above the chasm of the American River:

> "When the road was in course of construction, the groups of Chinese laborers on the bluffs looked almost like swarms of ants, when viewed from the river . . . When the road-bed was constructed around this point, the men who broke the first standing ground were held by ropes until firm foot-holds could be excavated in the rocky sides of the precipitous bluffs."

There was more to say about the gold-bearing quartz belt and prosperous lode-mining in the Grass Valley-Nevada City region, but beyond Newcastle, Atwell was again urging passengers to catch a glimpse of 'the past' among the old placers and old-timers he knew so well:

> "Look off to the right . . . there is a miner's cabin under yonder tree, with the little patch of garden and, yes, a rose bush in front. The old '49-er comes to the door, pipe in mouth, twenty years' beard, and gazes on the passing train . . . He admits the fact that the railroad has got ahead of *his* time, and is sending its loads of rosy-cheeked women into the country to disturb *his* peace and quietness."

After Rocklin and Junction, the foothills were left behind and the railroad began to cross the rich farm and stock lands of the Central Valley, en route for Sacramento. Atwell delighted to contrast the wealth of Californian agriculture with the laborious life of many of the New England

35a.

SUMMIT TUNNEL, CALIFORNIA

At 7017 feet above sea level and c.1700 feet in length, Summit was the highest point on
the Central Pacific Railroad, and the longest in a series of tunnels built by the C.P.
through the Sierra Nevada.

farmers he had known in his youth. He quoted an old friend, on a visit
from Maine, gazing across the Central Valley:

> "So this is California! What on earth can you find to do? No brush to grub
> up, no timber to clear off, no stone to pick up and put into walls." With such
> an easy life, his friend wondered. "How do you pass your time?"

Atwell enlarged upon California but could give no more than a taste of it:

> "To speak of all her towns, rivers, cities, mountains, vineyards, etc., would
> fill a far larger volume than this, and then the half would not be told ... But
> jump into Doc Tucker's stage and see a portion of the fairest of all fair
> lands."

Atwell lived in Woodland, a thriving farming town of some 1200 inhabitants, and the county seat of Yolo County. In summer, Yolo was "one vast
wheat field stretching almost as far as the eye can reach." California's
importance as a major wheat producer had begun after the devastating

35b.   BUILDING SNOWSHEDS ON THE CENTRAL PACIFIC RAILROAD

in *Great Trans-Continental Tourist's Guide,* 1870

The C.P. built nearly fifty miles of snowshed in the Sierra Nevada. Following demands from passengers, 'windows' were cut at intervals to provide look-outs and relieve the monotony.

163

36. ROUNDING CAPE HORN ABOVE THE NORTH FORK OF THE AMERICAN RIVER

in *Great Trans-Continental Tourist's Guide,* 1870

The California gold rush had been sparked a few miles south of this point at Sutter's saw mill, on the South Fork of the American River. There, in January 1848, James Marshall discovered flakes of gold in the mill-race and by May 1848, the rush was on to pan for gold in the wilderness of canyons and gullies draining the Sierra.

droughts of 1862-5 which had wiped out many of the State's three million cattle and ended for ever the dominance of cattle ranching in the Californian farm economy. At first, large-scale wheat production was concentrated in the Sacramento Valley where, among a dozen or so major growers, the giant was Dr. Hugh Glenn whose huge wheat ranch of 55,000 acres stretched for nearly twenty miles along the west bank of the Sacramento in Colusa County, adjacent to Yolo. "The wheat lands and the harvesting process are a sight to behold," observed Atwell. On the Glenn ranch, ploughing often involved using a hundred Stockton Gang Plows at once, each drawn by an eight-mule team; fleets of harvesters moving through the sea of grain were no less impressive.

Wheat was sent down-river to the flour mills at Sacramento which, before the construction of the transcontinental line, was already a local railroad centre as well as a river port. Wheat also moved by rail and river to the grain elevator at Vallejo, on San Pablo Bay — "the only one on the coast and the chief pride of the city." Bulk handling was soon to be introduced. With its excellent sheltered deep-water anchorage and local railroad services, Vallejo was competing strongly with San Francisco at this time for shipping business. "Many claim that Vallejo is the natural point for a commercial metropolis," Atwell commented, since the city focused railroads and deep port facilities. "The present enormous rates of wharfage in San Francisco, and the high price of real estate for depots, etc. have forced companies to look elsewhere for a point where the largest ships can come alongside their wharves and discharge their cargoes into the railcars, and vice versa, without rehandling or reshipment."

California was now on the threshold of what became known as its Bonanza Wheat Period, 1870-90. During the decade 1860-70, the population of the mining Counties had fallen by 25 per cent, while that of the agricultural Counties had doubled; indeed, in the 1870s, the value of the wheat crop was to overtake that of gold. The completion of the transcontinental railroad suddenly extended California's domestic grain market far beyond the local urban, mining and ranching communities, and in addition to its overseas exports, the State also became a national wheat centre. Towards the end of the nineteenth century, however, Californian wheat growers faced crippling competition from the prairies and the Great Plains, as well as from cheaper foreign imports, and so turned increasingly in the 1890s to the spectacular development of irrigated fruit and vegetable production for the eastern markets. Improvements in long-distance, refrigerated freightcars, in general handling and selection, in new crop varieties, and not least in high-pressure advertising all assisted California to market its glorious climate in a sensational new economic bonanza.

In his concise descriptions of the landscape, Atwell provided a summary of the varied soils, drainage, agriculture, vegetation, and land use in the Sacramento region, both along the valley floor (including the tules [bulrush marshes] and the delta), and in the foothill zone. He spoke to tourist and emigrant: "Go among the homes and the harvest fields—eat of the fruits and drink of the wines of this sunny land." There was no mistaking his own enthusiasm for "the wealth, the beauty, the richness of the soil and the salubrity of the climate in California."

Swing on down to San Francisco! The authors neatly packed the information on hotels and places of interest in the city whose population had almost *trebled* to 150,000 during the 1860s. There was a tempting range of side-trips by ferry, river steamer, and stagecoach for farmer, tourist and emigrant.

37.   SETTLERS!   TOURISTS!
The Union Pacific and Central Pacific placed these advertisements in the first edition of the *Great Trans-Continental Railroad Guide,* 1869. Other advertisers included manufacturers, banks, stores, and hotels in New York, Chicago, Omaha, and San Francisco.

"But first, after choosing your hotel, look over the newspapers, for everyone reads them who wishes to become acquainted with life in California." Both Crofutt and Atwell had provided their readers with information on every local paper worth reading at the main stops all the way from Omaha. "Gobble up the local news ... newspapers are the histories of the present."

Not surprisingly, "Bill Dadd, the Scribe" had more to say about the San Francisco press. There was the independent, long established *Bulletin*, which specialized in marine and business news, and the *Alta California*, the largest, as well as one of the oldest (it began in January 1849), with more foreign correspondence than any other paper published in the city. Then came a puff for the *Alta*'s main rival: "Do you want a lively, piquant, local newspaper ... all life, vim and earnestness? Then read the *Morning Chronicle*," he advised loyally, before adding a few words about the *Morning Call*, and *Examiner*, the *Times* and the *Herald*. After listing various literary journals, and the *California Farmer*, Atwell called it a day. "If among these papers you can find nothing to suit you, nothing new — why then, we advise you to read the Bible, and profit by its teachings."

After whirling around San Francisco and the Bay area, tourists and potential settlers were taken through the fertile wheat fields, orchards and vineyards of the Santa Clara, Napa, Sonoma, and lower San Joaquin Valleys, and encouraged, if they had time, to visit the summer resorts — Yosemite, the Mariposa Grove of Big Trees, the Big Trees of Calaveras, Mount Diablo, Calistoga and the geysers, and Mount Tamalpais, for example — not forgetting the twelve-mile ferry ride to San Quentin, that "well known place of summer and winter resort for the noted characters of the State."

Now, America's first trans-continental railroad journey was done. As part of its introduction to the West, the Guide had promised "to tell you what is worth seeing — where to see it — where to go — how to go — and whom to stop with while passing over the Union Pacific Railroad, the Central Pacific Railroad, their branches and connections by stage and water." Crofutt and Atwell signed off ...

"We have come with the traveler from the East to the West, and here, on the sunny shores of California, we take leave of our fellow travelers — our readers, and the public generally, with a cheery Goodbye, until we meet again."

Trans-Continental: "Inspired!"
"The Right Title At The Right Time"

The word 'overland' had been the universal term for describing the old trails to Mexico, Utah, Oregon and California. In the 1850s and 1860s, beyond the navigable waterways and railroad networks in the East, a massive increase in the cross-traffic to California, and then to Colorado, gave the word 'overland' new currency, strongly boosted by the stage lines and by Government action. In 1858, John Butterfield's Overland Mail began the first mail stage service authorized by Congress between the Mississippi (St. Louis and Memphis) and California (Los Angeles and San Francisco). At best, the journey took three weeks and, until it was re-routed at the start of the Civil War, made a great southern loop through Texas, New Mexico and Arizona [Map VIII].

Soon, the Central Overland California & Pike's Peak Express (1859), Holladay's Overland Mail & Express (1862), and David Butterfield's Overland Despatch (1864) had all written the word 'overland' into the language of the pre-railroad, trans-Mississippi West. The Pony Express and the Overland Telegraph underlined it. Plans for the railroad, first mooted in the 1830s, struck a different note — the *Pacific* Railroad rang out clear and true.

The word 'transcontinental' appears in none of the early railroad reports, none of the advance publicity, and none of the Golden Spike ceremonial. It seems to have been invented in New York City in 1853; the March issue of *Harper's New Monthly Magazine* noted in its Current Events column "the proposal of a company, embracing the wealthiest of New York capitalists, to construct a trans-continental railroad from New York to San Francisco," provided the Government would grant right of way. But Congress had just authorized the official Pacific Railroad Surveys and this private, speculative type of project now attracted little support.

The word 'transcontinental' (first with, later without the hyphen) was scarcely used again in the 1850s. A long Memorial to Congress from the Pacific Railroad Convention held in San Francisco in Sept.-Oct. 1859 used it once, but the term attracted no attention. Occasional references can be found in the late 1860s among writers seeking to vary their prose after over-indulgence in the adjective 'Pacific'. Albert Richardson, for example, spoke only twice of the "trans-continental" journey throughout his voluminous account of travels *Beyond the Mississippi*, published in 1867. Edward Bliss did so briefly early in 1869 in F.B. Goddard's *Where to Emigrate and Why*.

Nowhere is the omission of the word 'transcontinental' more marked than in Congress, where decades of speeches and discussion in both

38. COVER ENGRAVING OF CROFUTT'S ORIGINAL *GREAT TRANS-CONTINENTAL RAILROAD GUIDE*, 1869

The design reflects the importance still given at this stage to the railroad's role in the future development of Oriental trade with Europe and the United States.
But while this idea soon faded, the word *trans-continental* was an immediate success.

169

chambers had produced a vast body of literature on the subject of the Pacific Railroad. Yet, a detailed examination of the official record reveals that the word was apparently used for the first time in Congress as late as February 1868, when Senator John Conness of California spoke of the importance of the "great Pacific railroad, the great trans-continental railroad" to the development of east-west commerce across the American continent.

In the final days before the Great Event, the editor of San Francisco's *Daily Morning Chronicle* began to show interest in the word. On 8th May and 9th May 1869, whatever the delays at Promontory, San Francisco had begun its celebrations on schedule, and matching this, the *Chronicle* on both the 8th and 9th headlined the completion of the Trans-Continental Railroad! The term was not included in Atwell's own dispatches. Adjacent columns in the *Chronicle* continued to run the more familiar Pacific Railroad banner but within a couple of days, the rival *Daily Alta California* and the *Chicago Tribune* had also used the word 'trans-continental', although in both cases it was tucked away in columns flagged by the familiar term, Pacific Railroad.

A celebratory issue in June 1869 of San Francisco's popular new magazine *The Overland Monthly* contained a reference to trans-continental travel, although it was Bret Harte's poem "What the Engines Said", which appeared in the same issue, that immediately caught the public's attention. The poem was reprinted from coast to coast and like so many other pieces in similar vein, captured the spirit but not the word 'transcontinental.'

Atwell's editor on San Francisco's *Daily Morning Chronicle* had given the word a Californian airing. Back in Chicago, Crofutt may have discovered that the Chicago Board of Trade had passed a series of resolutions on 'the trans-continental railway' on 20th May 1869. On 24th June, engineer John A. Poor used the term to introduce a lecture given at Rutland, Vermont.

During the whole of the summer of 1869, nothing more than isolated and widely scattered references such as these are to be found, virtually four months after the completion of the Pacific Railroad. This makes Crofutt's and Atwell's role in bringing the word 'transcontinental' into *everyday* American usage at a stroke all the more remarkable. Crofutt in particular appears to have appreciated the freshness and potential of the word. After conferring with Atwell and collecting his share of the copy, Crofutt registered the title of the new publication in Chicago on 22nd July 1869; it was to be America's, and the world's first *Great Trans-Continental Railroad Guide.*[11]

Throughout August, Crofutt worked day and night assembling the contents, adding footnotes, timetables, maps and advertisements, and discussing the final layout with the ever-encouraging Sterling Rounds. Crofutt spent his life dashing between his office in the Larmon block at the corner of Clark and Washington, the printers on State Street, and his room at the Briggs House where one day he managed to chat briefly about old times with David Butterfield, who was passing through Chicago on a new business venture. "Not dead yet!" Butterfield told Crofutt cheerfully, having put the collapse of his Overland Despatch well and truly behind him.[12]

The *Great Trans-Continental Railroad Guide* was published on 1st September 1869.[13] With its bold title, and distinctive cover drawn for Crofutt by artists George and Angelo Fasel, and engraved by William Baker, the Guide quickly became a familiar sight along the entire route.

There was advice to travellers about lunch counters, baggage checks, and transfers. The more you travel, the less you carry. Suitable clothing was important; some hints were direct and down-to-earth:

When the car is crowded . . .

> "It is not customary, it is not polite, it is not right or just for a *lady* to occupy one whole seat with her flounces and herself, and another with her satchel, parasol, big box, little box, bandbox and bundle . . . The woman who indulges in such flights of fancy as to suppose that one fare entitles her to monopolize three seats should not travel until bloomers come in fashion." [14]

The Guide offered nearly 250 pages for 50 cents and was sold on all the railroad cars, as well as at the news-stands, bookstores and railroad stations. It managed to communicate a passionate enthusiasm for the West, and an explicitly transcontinental concept of American progress by combining the spirit of 'Manifest Destiny' with a practical 'do it yourself'. The pages fairly crackled with exhortations to *go*, to experience the sense of space, the vistas, the wonders but also the realities of the West at first hand.

The Guide, like the railroad, had cut a huge slice out of the centre of Western America for all to see. For most, it was their first sight of the country's arid and semi-arid environments, and while passengers would discover that the western half of the United States sprawling between the Missouri River and the Pacific Ocean was not a totally empty, howling wilderness, the Guide made no attempt to gloss over the worst stretches. Nor did it mislead the unwary into thinking that farms without irrigation could succeed on land suited only to grazing. And grazing land itself should not be oversold. Near Wahsatch, in the Wyoming-Utah border country, Crofutt gently put down some of the local boosters . . .

> "Grass in abundance covers the hills, and it is claimed by those who reside there, that the small grains can be grown successfully. We agree with them

on this point, merely remarking that the smaller the grain is that they attempt to raise, the more it will resemble the crop produced."

During daylight hours, the harshest sections of the landscape would intrigue and fascinate some — repel, weary, or disillusion others. But the Guide would help to sort the multitude of new impressions, as well as meet the demand for basic facts and figures, as it spun its continuous thread of western geography, geology, statistics, recent history, anecdote, sentiment without nostaglia, inspiration, and practicality. After that, the new pioneers could strike out on their own.

*　　　　　*　　　　　*

The *Great Trans-Continental Railroad Guide* was an immediate success. Within a few days, the first batch of reviews appeared in the leading Chicago papers, to be followed by more from across the West. Chicago's *Tribune*, *Times*, and *Republican* set the ball rolling:

> "The new trans-continental guide is the most complete railroad reference we have ever seen . . . and apart from its value as a guide-book, the style makes it a very entertaining work. It is indispensable to the traveler who desires to go to the Pacific."

> "The title and the book come at the right time — a vast amount of information prepared by gentlemen of long experience in traversing the States and Territories through which this great national thoroughfare passes ... One very useful feature is the complete and comprehensive time-table, inserted in such a manner that it can be withdrawn and a new one substituted whenever there are any changes. By this plan, the guide-book will always be new and fresh."

> "It is more than a guide ... every point of interest in the vicinity of the railroad is described in a racy way, which makes the book readable and deserving of credit for a peculiar humor, which reminds us of California and the plains in almost every sentence."

> "As a work of interest and benefit to the general Western traveling public, the 'Guide' is far in advance of any other work ever published. It is also well filled with valuable statistics relating to the trade and commerce of the West. If you have a fifty-cent stamp the book is dedicated to you."

> "The character of the book is in its title."

> "Neither too little or too much, but precisely what the traveler, whether tourist or stay-at-home, wishes to know."

> ". . . aiming rather at a clear, truthful statement than an overdrawn picture."

"The Great Trans-Continental Railroad Guide is a worthy herald of such an achievement as the Pacific Railroad," reported San Francisco's *Golden Era*, which had been founded in 1852 and become the most successful, influential, and widely circulated of all California's literary weeklies. "Beside being a complete and authentic Guide in the strict sense of the term, it possesses the charm of a book of travels."

"The Guide is a credit to the publishers and the continent across which the line passes ... It tells you how to enjoy yourself, in fact everything of importance on the road or get-at-able from the line. It is capitally written and should be in the hands of everybody who travels — in an age when all travel. Buy it, and read it for yourself."

Crofutt was overjoyed and overwhelmed by the success of the Guide. He toiled away in the cramped room in the Larmon block, dispatching the mail-orders coming in directly to his office. The Guide had been stereo-typed "and succeeding editions will be published as the demand requires," but Crofutt was quite unprepared for the rush that occurred in the fall. Printers Sterling Rounds and Edward James were all smiles, reprinting rush orders for the Chicago outlets as well as for the railroad companies and other distributors all along the route.

The word 'trans-continental' now fitted like a glove; it was *the* word for describing the railroad, the journey, and the achievement. Following the Guide's huge success, the Union Pacific Railroad formally adopted the word for the first time in their December 1869 timetables and it was soon in regular use, both on the Central and Union Pacific, the Kansas Pacific (1870), and on the eastern railroad networks which advertised connections to 'the trans-continental'.

The Boosters From Boston

The Guide and the word 'trans-continental' received another boost when the Boston Board of Trade announced its intention to make a Trans-Continental Excursion from Boston to San Francisco and back between 23rd May and 1st July 1870. The party numbered about 130 — Board of Trade members and their families together with George M. Pullman whose Pullman Pacific Car Co. was based in Chicago, and whose new Pullman Palace Day and Sleeping Cars had been developed in 1864-67. Five thousand Bostonians came to cheer them off. A bottle of sea water filled in Massachusetts Bay was ceremoniously put on board Boston's first through train to the Pacific. There was to be a reenactment, this time on the continental scale, of the historic Great Lakes-New York Harbor water-pouring celebration in 1825 at the opening of the Erie Canal.

The train consisted of eight elegant Pullman Palace Cars, a specially promoted 'Pullman Hotel Express' comprising the most elegant drawing- and dining-rooms, stylish furnishings, carpets, silver and cut glass, ornate gas lamps, carved and inlaid panels ... "the list is endless" passengers reported, much impressed, "a first-class hotel flying through the country at 40 mph."

39.

SUNDAY ON THE UNION PACIFIC RAILWAY
The Illustrated London News, March 20, 1875

Sunday church services were an early feature of the transcontinental railroad, just as they had been on transatlantic passenger ships and Mississippi river-boats.

There were two well-stocked libraries and two Burdett organs; concerts, sing-songs, readings and church services were regular features. One of the saloon cars was set aside at certain hours for children's leapfrog and other games — "We are like one great family, full of fun and frolic, and having a good time."

A unique feature of this combined business and pleasure trip was the decision to print and publish a daily newspaper on the train during the journey, a 4-page sheet called *The Trans-Continental*. It was the first time any American newspaper had been produced this way, and the issues quickly became collectors' items. A Gordon printing-press was placed in the baggage car and the editor's desk squeezed into the Smoking Car, which also had to find room for the bar, wine room, and the hairdressing and shaving saloons. W. R. Steele of Chicago was the editor, his usual office located at 46 State Street, in the same building as the Trans-Continental Guide's printers and binders. Sterling Rounds was delighted with the idea; he had by now expanded his business into the next-door premises and, also in 1870, become President of Chicago's Taylor Printing Press Co.

The Trans-Continental's editor lost no time in bringing out his paper as the train began to move. "Incidents of this trip gladly welcomed," Steele encouraged the passengers in Boston, "remember brevity, please, and pass forward the items."

Crowds turned out at every station to catch sight of the splendid Trans-Continental Excursion train and wave it through. There was an especially elaborate reception by the Chicago Board of Trade. George Pullman returned to his office at this point, leaving his brother Albert to accompany the party for the whole journey. The train sped on and crossed the Mississippi on the new iron bridge, although work was still to start on a permanent bridge over the Missouri between Council Bluffs, Iowa and Omaha, Nebraska. Excitement mounted as the journey west of Omaha began. Crowds were still gathering at every major station to wave the train through. The Boston party now made full use of the *Great Trans-Continental Railroad Guide*; many had brought their own, and additional copies were available on the train. Crofutt could not have hoped for a better blaze of publicity.

Editor Steele was publishing *The Trans-Continental* on the train every day, or every other day. He included items of foreign news and advertisements but the journey across the plains and the "real West" now rivetted everyone's attention. Most of the passengers were contemplating their new surroundings with a mixture of awe and inspiration, and several were busily writing poems, articles or short stories as they rolled along. "But remember," begged the editor, "the articles should not be, like our bottle of Atlantic water, far-fetched."

LET EVERY STEP BE AN ADVANCE.

Vol. 1. Grand Island, Nebraska, Wednesday, June 29, 1870. **No. 10.**

The Trans-Continental.

Published Daily on the Pullman Hotel Express,
Between
Boston and San Francisco.

W. R. STEELE, *Editor.*

☞ *Communications and Exchanges for this paper should be addressed,* TRANS-CONTINENTAL, *46 State Street, Chicago.*

Notes from our Log Book.

Sunday, June 19.—All the members of the second division of the Yo-Semite party reached Knight's Ferry this evening, after riding fifty-two miles from Bower Cave, and there lodged. Before reaching the hotel, we crossed the Stanislaus river on the new covered bridge recently built, in place of the ferry formerly run by DENT & GRANT—the latter now President of the United States. The toll-keeper generously supplied the party with a basket of ripe pears from his orchard on the side of the river, as a free treat.

Monday, June 20.—The second division rode by four-horse wagons, a distance of thirty-eight miles from Knight's Ferry, to the city of Stockton, which they reached before 11 o'clock, after a cool and pleasant morning ride. There they took rooms at the Yo-Semite House, and others visited the century plant, in blossom in the Court House yard, while all roamed around the city on tours of observation. Lunch, amounting to a dinner, was served at noon, and at 1:40 P. M., all embarked on a special car kindly provided for our party through the thoughtful kindness of John Corning, the Assistant General Superintendent of the Central Pacific Railroad, and reached San Francisco before 6 P. M., after a glorious trip. About twenty of the first party to the Yo-Semite, who reached San Francisco on Friday last, started at

4 P. M., by steamer, and over the Napa Valley branch of the California Pacific Railroad for the Geysers, and lodged this night at Calistoga Springs.

Tuesday, June 21.—The last party to the Geysers made a pleasant visit to those natural wonders. Other excursionists were in San Francisco or its vicinity, variously engaged. Many visited Woodward's Gardens, to see the flowers and wild animals.

Wednesday, June 22.—The last party to the Geysers returned to San Francisco, where nearly all the excursionists had collected, and were preparing for the start homeward Friday night. A few of the excursionists had already left for the East; a few left on Thursday, and a few will remain in California for several months. Small parties, this week, visited San Jose, the Almaden mines, Oakland, and other places, not far from San Francisco. Others visited mutual friends at their country seats in the immediate vicinity of the city.

Thursday, June 23—Was chiefly occupied in private visits, shopping, and sight-seeing at the city. During the evening, a farewell dinner, already mentioned in this paper, was given by several of the members of the excursion to gentlemen of San Francisco, who had been prominent in showing signal attentions to our party.

Friday, June 24.—This, our last day in San Francisco, was a busy one with nearly every one of the party. Many were the last things to be done; collections of photograph views, to be selected or made complete; friends to be called on, and little remembrances packed away for loved ones at home. A magnificent sunset lighted the waters and hills of the great bay of San Francisco, and lingered as a beautiful and effective final picture of the "Sunset Land" upon the memories of our excur-

sionists, and when the morning sun arose on the 25th, we were swiftly pressing eastward and homeward surrounded by all the comforts of our favorite Pullman train.

OUR TRAIN.

At Cheyenne, those of our party who had preceded us again joined our train, and the Pullman drawing-room and sleeping car "Northwest" was coupled on, making one more house in our rolling village. Commencing at the engine, we have now—

1. Baggage car.
2. Provision car, including printing press.
3. Smoking car, including printing office, wine room, and barber's shop.
4. Commissary and dining car, "Saint Cloud."
5. Palace sleeping and drawing-room car "Marquette."
6. Palace sleeping and drawing-room car "Palmyra."
7. Commissary and dining car "Saint Charles."
8. Hotel car "Arlington."
9. Hotel car "Revere."
10. Drawing-room and sleeping car "Northwest," and we do not believe that a train equal to it in size, beauty and convenience ever existed before, up to this present point, in the history of the world. As improvement is, however, the order of the day, what may we not expect from Mr. Pullman in the future.

—Yesterday as we journeyed across the apparently boundless Laramie Plains, herds of swift antelope were seen coursing with nimble feet, sometimes keeping up with, and at others running from our train. Grouse were also seen in comparatively plentiful numbers.

40.

THE FRONT PAGE OF *THE TRANS-CONTINENTAL,*

29th June 1870, printed aboard the train. It records the busy program of visits and excursions in California undertaken by the party from the Boston Board of Trade.

176

As the train crossed the plains and made its way through the mountains, the travellers lifted their eyes to the hills. Images and emotions produced a new, deep pride in America, and captured that Yankee perception of a sublime presence in the magnificence of Nature. One of *The Trans-Continental's* contributors caught the prevailing mood:

> "If there be anywhere an American heart that is sluggish in its patriotism, or anywhere a soul that is dull in its sensibility to the beneficence of our country's God, let him come out upon a journey like this, where he shall see his flag as the emblem of progress and of peace, and in the boundless acres the matchless heritage of ourselves and our posterity."

The Boston party spent nearly a week in San Francisco, where they were treated to an exuberant reception; they poured the Atlantic water into the Pacific amid loud cheers, undertook a hectic round of meetings, sightseeing and shopping, and listened to themselves and their excursion repeatedly described as "trans-continental". After a last lingering look at the magnificent sunset in this 'Sunset Land', the main party was homeward bound, and ready to fill the final issues of *The Trans-Continental* with their impressions and delight:

> "From the open page of nature, lessons of pleasure and improvement are before us! ... The trans-continental railroad has literally blended all the States into *one nation*."

Crofutt Fights the Competition: "Secure the Best Seat You Can and Prepare to Be As Happy As You Know How!"

"Within ten years," Horace Greeley had said in 1859 after toiling up a wagon road in the Rockies, "the tourist of the Continent will be whirled over a far easier road . . . and will sip his chocolate and read his New York paper — not yet five days old — . . . in utter unconsciousness that this region was wrested from the elk and the mountain sheep so recently as 1859." [15]

Ten years later, in August 1869, an English traveller on the new Union Pacific railroad made the journey from Omaha to Cheyenne with nothing but memories of his school atlas for reference, on which the plains he was crossing were still marked as the Great American Desert. The following month, the *Great Trans-Continental Railroad Guide* could have been in his hand, that "complete and indispensable *vade mecum* over an enormous line."

In the summer of 1869, before the Guide's publication, several reporters and magazine writers also made the journey west on the U.P. and C.P. Railroads, since editors all over the country were demanding follow-up pieces to the Great Event. Horace Greeley dispatched A.D. Richardson, now working for the *New-York Tribune*, on a trip to San Francisco, and Richardson's characteristically vivid copy provided a series of nine articles under the heading 'Through to the Pacific.' [16] It is significant that none contained the word 'trans-continental'.

Unlike most, if not all, of the other reporters on the same assignment, Richardson had already made seven trips into the West during the pre-railroad decade. Now, as he sprawled at ease in the Pullman Car, he reflected that "the gain is wonderful in time and comfort; the loss irreparable in romance and picturesqueness." Most of Richardson's earlier trips West had been relatively short, weeks fizzing with adventure and excitement. A sense of lost romance, of nostalgia, accompanied Richardson's appraisal of the West at the dawn of the railroad age. For Crofutt, on the other hand, ten years of freighting, and the experience of the heavy, day-to-day work load that he had shared with so many of his fellow western pioneers evoked neither a romantic nor a nostalgic view of the past — a past to be known, explained, respected, and then simply recognized for what it was — one of the many stages in America's continuous program of change: in transport, in opportunity, in new economic growth, and in new national awareness and integration.

Before long, the entire transcontinental journey could be done, if necessary, in about six days. The first through-car from California arrived in New York City on 24th July 1869; so many had wanted to travel that the whole train had been sold out for the complete 3,167-mile trip to New York shortly after the ticket office opened.

As traffic from the eastern States expanded, two trains a day each way were soon needed to cope with the excursion parties, family groups, and individuals all impatient to ride the world's newest, longest, and highest railroad. Times and technology had changed, but the new iron trail across the West was still made up, like the old routes, "of hope, anticipation and desires."

William Humason was typical of this new breed of pioneers. Eager to get going, he had started his journey from New England to the Pacific on 6th May 1869, four days before the rails were joined at Promontory. Now as he crossed the plains, looking ahead, Humason could scarcely contain his excitement:

> "This was my first sight of the famous Rocky Mountains. My boyish dreams were realized. For hours, at the school desk, have I pondered over the map, and wandered, in imagination, with Lewis and Clark, the hunters and trappers and early emigrants, away off to these Rocky Mountains, about which such a mystery seemed to hang, — dreaming, wishing, and hoping against hope, that my eyes might, some day, behold their snow-crowned heights. And here lay the first great range . . . distant, to be sure, but there it lay, enshrined in beauty." [17]

The Rockies, soaring out of the plains, were the magnificent gateway to America's Mountain West, a dramatic encounter in which emotion and intellect could both be stirred by an overwhelming sense of awe and power, present but unseen. Relatively few had visited alpine Europe, Mexico, or South America — or, for that matter, the Blue Ridge in southern Appalachia, the highest mountains in the East, yet below 7000 feet. The Appalachians, Catskills, Adirondacks, and White Mountains all left travellers unprepared for what lay beyond that strange and magnificent scale-adjustment provided by the Great Plains.

For the vast majority, the Rockies were a totally new experience. For many New Englanders in particular, that same sense of harmony between nature, God, and the individual was now inspired by the mountains — just as earlier, the woods around Concord had inspired the young Emerson:

> "In the woods, we return to reason and faith. There I feel that nothing can befall me in life . . . which nature cannot repair . . . My head bathed by the blithe air, and uplifted into infinite space — all mean egotism vanishes . . . I am nothing; I see all; the currents of the Universal Being circulate through me; I am part or particle of God." [18]

Thirty years later, Fitz Hugh Ludlow saw the Rockies for the first time:

> "I confess," he wrote, "that my first view of the Rocky Mountains had no way of expressing itself save in tears . . . a sudden revelation of the truth, that the spiritual is the only real and substantial; that the eternal things of the universe are they which afar off seem dim and faint.
>
> In the East there is nothing to illustrate the Rocky Mountains by . . . they are full of infinite suggestion. Their presence makes a thoughtful man wish to sit down and learn from them . . . such genius, . . . colossal, sublime . . . man a wanderer, a guest, not a master. . . .
>
> To see the Rocky Mountains in bright sunlight, to drink from the vast, voiceless happiness which they seem set there to embody, is one of the strangest mixtures of pleasure and pain in all scenery." [19]

For some, as Crofutt had envisaged, the plains remained a uniquely haunting prologue to the mountains, a vast national transition-zone linking the humid East and the arid West:

> "To my eyes, to all my senses . . . they silently and broadly unfolded, " wrote Walt Whitman in 1879. "While I know the standard claim is that Yosemite, Niagara Falls, the upper Yellowstone and the like, afford the greatest natural shows, I am not so sure but the Prairies and the Plains, while less stunning at first sight, last longer, fill the esthetic sense fuller, precede all the rest, and make North America's characteristic landscape." [20]

*   *   *

41.   THE NEW YORK POST OFFICE UNDER CONSTRUCTION IN LOWER MANHATTAN
Harper's Weekly, October 23, 1869, *from a photograph by Rockwood*
Broadway is on the left, Park Row on the right, City Hall and Park just to the north of the
construction site. The massive Post Office building was completed in 1875.

The demand for the Trans-Continental Guide was so great, and the
potential market in the eastern cities so enormous, that in 1870 Crofutt
decided to move from Chicago to New York City and make the country's
biggest publishing centre his own. Before leaving, however, he brought
out a temporary revised edition of the Guide in January 1870 with the
assistance of B.D.M. Eaton, a journalist newly arrived in Chicago. Eaton's
help had apparently been enlisted once Crofutt became swamped with
orders. They worked in the same small office in the Larmon block, at the
corner of Clark and Washington, and published this edition of the *Great
Trans-Continental Railroad Guide* under the imprint of Crofutt & Eaton.

Then it was on to New York. Crofutt went straight to Lower
Manhattan's Printing House Square where, over twenty years earlier, he
had looked for work as a young hopeful from Danbury, Conn. Now,
Crofutt had a success on his hands. He rented an office at 21 Park Row,

the imposing terrace in the heart of the newspaper and magazine district. Within a stone's throw were the New York *Post, World, Herald, Times, Tribune,* and *Sun* buildings, as well as the Chamber of Commerce, the main railroad and shipping offices, and the Post Office in the Middle Dutch Church building on Nassau Street.

Directly opposite, the huge new Post Office was under construction, on the island-site between Broadway, City Hall Park, and Park Row. All in all, it was an ideal location, Crofutt decided, not unlike his old one at the top end of Dock Street, Philadelphia in many ways. But one thing was different. He had now found a national market and the means to supply it. Failures in Philadelphia, indeed all his varied experiences to date in both the East and the West seemed to have been preparation for his new work.

Crofutt brought out the 1870 New York edition with one change in the title; instead of *Railroad,* it was now the *Great Trans-Continental Tourist's Guide,* containing thirty-six illustrations, up-dated information, and a new map of the route. Paper-bound copies were still 50 cents, but a cloth-bound edition was available at $1.00. For the first time, the Guide was handled by the American News Co., "czar of the news-stands and the distribution business." Distribution networks had always been crucial. In the late 1830s, middlemen had started to collect papers at central distributing points and to supply them to carriers and other retailers at a slightly higher price (instead of carriers and dealers having to run from office to office themselves). These middlemen in turn formed wholesalers' combines and monopolies with city-wide, and later nation-wide, connections. In New York City, A.S. Tuttle's firm began its agency operation in 1854 and became the American News Co. ten years later.

Crofutt and "Bill Dadd, the Scribe" now went their separate ways. Atwell appears to have had no desire to get more deeply involved in the regular revision and production side of the business. He loved California, particularly the more leisured, small-town life of the Central Valley. Atwell was more than content to let Crofutt supervise even the San Francisco end of the Guide's distribution; indeed, there is no record of Atwell undertaking further work for the *Chronicle* or for any other newspaper in San Francisco. Nor in the future does he appear ever to have claimed either sole or joint authorship of the *Great Trans-Continental Railroad Guide,* a fact which tends to confirm that Crofutt had written most of it.

After the flurry of activity in 1869, Atwell returned to Woodland, Yolo County, where he started work for C.P. Sprague, a prosperous attorney and landowner whose law practice and real estate interests, as well as his vineyards, orchards and wheat acreage, had made him one of the richest men in Yolo County. Sprague was planning to produce a *Commercial Directory for the State of California* on a county basis, including details of property ownership and investment interests among the business communities. Atwell was engaged to collect and sort the necessary information. He took a room at the Capital Hotel and became increasingly depressed by the size of the task and the lack of cooperation; "great expense and no small amount of annoyance" faced the compiler of such a tome. With growing weariness and frustration, Atwell struggled to bring out a 602-page volume for Yolo County by November 1870, but it was the first and the last in this over-ambitious project.

Atwell moved to Sacramento, and in February 1873 found a job that sent him north to the California-Oregon border country to report the Modoc War (1872-3), a struggle for land rights involving settlers, the Modoc Indians, and government troops. As special war correspondent for the *Sacramento Daily Record*, Atwell provided a series of detailed dispatches between February and June 1873 under his usual pseudonym, "Bill Dadd". After that, Atwell came south once more, moved briefly to Stockton, and then for the next fifteen years made a modest living writing poetry and short stories, compiling two immigrants' land directories for part of southern California, and editing a variety of local newspapers in the San Joaquin Valley, especially in Tulare County.

Three thousand miles away in New York City, Crofutt's life was filled with orders, promotion, travelling, checking, proof-reading, and in maintaining contacts with the railroad companies and with the whole network of nation-wide wholesale outlets. Eli S. Denison was his general agent on the Central Pacific and on all the California railroads; Crofutt had first seen Denison at Promontory at the Great Event celebration when Eli had been in charge of the Central Pacific's special excursion train.

With the enormous success of the Guide and its title in 1869, Crofutt suddenly found himself faced with fierce competition on all sides. The city of St. Louis, Mo. was quick off the mark, thanks to double-dealing by B.D.M. Eaton, Crofutt's former temporary associate in Chicago. J.L. Tracy's *Guide to the Great West* was published by Tracy and Eaton in St. Louis in 1870. Apart from the emphasis it gave to the St. Louis and Missouri railroad connections with the U.P.-C.P. line, the text relied heavily on Crofutt's and Atwell's original. After bringing out the Crofutt & Eaton edition of the *Great Trans-Continental Railroad Guide* in Chicago in January 1870, Eaton had gone straight off to St. Louis and repeated the performance a few weeks later with a new-found associate, Joshua L. Tracy. Tracy and Eaton set up as publishers at 510 Pine, but the 1870 edition was their only venture and they quickly went out of business. Tracy drifted about, dabbled in writing, and for a while found a job first as manager of the St. Louis Fair Museum, and then as one of the city's promoters of the Texas & Pacific Railway. Eaton went back to reporting, and specialized in river and commercial news for various St. Louis papers. Crofutt was outraged by Eaton's action over the Guide: "Our imitator from St. Louis — a petty, swindling, advertising dodge — is beneath notice."

The California press was particularly anxious not to let the guide-book market become dominated by the East, and even more impatient to capitalize on the popularity of the word *Trans-Continental*. It was a winner; the Boston Trans-Continental Excursionists had removed any doubts on that score. Much to Crofutt's anger and despair, both the style and key title word of the *Great Trans-Continental Railroad Guide* were-closely copied in 1871 in San Francisco by the MacCrellish Company's *Alta California Pacific Coast and Trans-Continental Rail-Road Guide*. Even Eaton had not stooped so low, Crofutt fumed. "It's double robbery . . . we *paid* the *Alta* in 1869 to advertise *our* guide!"

Fred MacCrellish had led the California press party at Promontory's Great Event celebration. He was a Philadelphian who had gone out to California in 1852, joined the *Alta* two years later, and before long assumed control of the paper as editor and proprietor. The *Alta* complained that Californians were forced to read the existing guide-books *backwards*! when making *their* trans-continental journey!! So the *Alta* discovered that its duty lay in rectifying this injustice by putting first things first!!! More than half of the 300 pages were devoted to California — its agriculture, mining, commerce, cities, railroads, hotels, tours and travel. Why wait until the end of a trans-continental guide to acquire "the much-needed information about California, the place of greatest interest on the whole journey?"

Crofutt fought back with characteristic energy and determination. Major publishers were now entering the fray — *Appletons' Hand-Book of American Travel: Western Tour*, and Rand, McNally's *Western Railway Guide: the Travelers' Hand Book to all Western Railway and Steamboat Lines*, both revised and expanded, appeared in 1871. Crofutt met the competition head on by revising his text twice a year, by clear layout and indexing, by skilful advertising and promotion, and by keeping a close personal eye on every stage of the production and distribution process. The Guide was now printed in the Herald Building at the corner of Broadway and Ann (just a few doors away from Crofutt's Park Row office) by the Metropolitan Book and Job Printing and Engraving Establishment. This firm was able to handle the full range of material — text, new illustrations, new maps (including a coloured map of the world), and a series of large fold-ins that greatly increased the advertising space. Crofutt was attracting advertisers so successfully that he employed William McLaughlin, close by at 83 Nassau, to take charge of that section of the business.

By September 1870, Crofutt had already travelled over the entire transcontinental route four times.

> "The public does not want a *big book*," wrote Crofutt, assessing the market, "guide-books that make a little go a great way, use *large type*, *thick paper*, *glittering generalities but no reliable facts*." Quite the reverse, and with the railroads' blessing, Crofutt served up "a book of positive statements," complete, straightforward, and as accurate as possible. "If I hear of rumored changes, I immediately investigate before publishing so that the guide, at the time it is published, is correct. As proof of this, refer to the Railroad Companies' endorsements, and the recommendation of the guide to the public, which is printed on all their time cards."

In 1869, the authors of the *Great Trans-Continental Railroad Guide* succeeded where a fellow New Englander had, on this occasion, been overwhelmed. Samuel Bowles, the distinguished editor from Springfield, Mass. was one of the half-dozen or so Easterners whose accounts of earlier personal trips to the West by stage, or rail-and-stage, before the joining of the rails had become classics of the 1860s. In 1869, however, Bowles also produced "a Guide for travel to and through Western America" entitled *The Pacific Railroad — Open*. But this time, Bowles' small volume about his journey was in fact no more than an introductory essay on the route across the West which, he argued, was far too wide and too wonderful to be captured by a guide-book:

> "The field is too broad, also the variety of experiences to be had too great, the forms and freaks of nature too strange and too numerous, — the whole revelation too unique and too astonishing, — to be readily catalogued and put into flexible covers for one's overcoat pocket." [21]

Nonsense! cried Crofutt, as the railroad companies and the travelling public demanded and got what they wanted.

The text of the *Great Trans-Continental Tourist's Guide* had a deceptively simple economy of style that was easy to achieve, others thought, until they tried to copy it. Some of the way-side stops had little intrinsic interest and Crofutt did not hesitate to say so. Anticipation for what "really was worth looking at" merely increased. Travellers relished Crofutt's ability to involve them in the scene and to communicate vividly from personal experience the speed of change in the West ... "Two years ago, ... one year ago, even less, he would tell his readers, it was thus and thus — Now what do we find? ..." Nor were readers left in any doubt about Crofutt's continuing personal commitment to keeping up to date — no armchair traveller he, despite his New York office. A conversational Note in his Guide would tell them "Shall be off in a few weeks to the Pacific Coast ... to breathe the pure air of the Rocky and Sierra Nevada mountains, broil an antelope 'jerk', fly a trout, taste the sparkling vintage

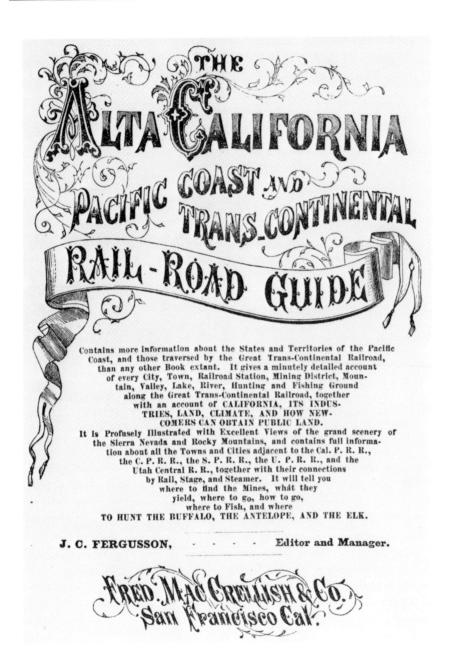

THE ALTA CALIFORNIA
Pacific Coast AND Trans-Continental
RAIL-ROAD GUIDE

Contains more information about the States and Territories of the Pacific
Coast, and those traversed by the Great Trans-Continental Railroad,
than any other Book extant. It gives a minutely detailed account
of every City, Town, Railroad Station, Mining District, Mountain, Valley, Lake, River, Hunting and Fishing Ground
along the Great Trans-Continental Railroad, together
with an account of CALIFORNIA, ITS INDUS-
TRIES, LAND, CLIMATE, AND HOW NEW-
COMERS CAN OBTAIN PUBLIC LAND.
It is Profusely Illustrated with Excellent Views of the grand scenery of
the Sierra Nevada and Rocky Mountains, and contains full information about all the Towns and Cities adjacent to the Cal. P. R. R.,
the C. P. R. R., the S. P. R. R., the U. P. R. R., and the
Utah Central R. R., together with their connections
by Rail, Stage, and Steamer. It will tell you
where to find the Mines, what they
yield, where to go, how to go,
where to Fish, and where
TO HUNT THE BUFFALO, THE ANTELOPE, AND THE ELK.

J. C. FERGUSSON,   · · · · ·   Editor and Manager.

FRED. MAC CRELLISH & CO.
San Francisco Cal.

42.   TRANS-CONTINENTAL GUIDEBOOK COMPETITION, 1871

This was one of many guidebooks published in the early 1870s that copied Crofutt's
general style, and his use of the word *trans-continental*.

of the 'Sunset Land', and view the wonder of wonders in the West. Reader, will you go along?"

The reviews continued to enthusiastic. *The Times*, London, noted that "the condensed form and fund of valuable information contained in this little volume is really wonderful." Samuel Morse recommended it. Others found it "spirited, fresh, and real" and unmatched for reliability, completeness and delight. *The New York Times* admired the typography and presentation, adding that as well as everything else, "the Guide has a decided and unique value as a reference book." It had indeed earned a place on America's reference shelves, and was more widely read than even the soaring sales could indicate. Because of this, by 1871, Crofutt claimed an annual readership of over two millions, one-quarter of them Europeans. The Guide was enjoyed by many who never made the journey except through its pages: "Everybody cannot make this delightful tour *by rail*," Crofutt read in a letter from Illinois, "but everybody can make the journey, at home, by reading your excellent Guide."

The world-wide publicity was reflected in correspondence to Crofutt in 1872, published in the Guide:

> "When in Bombay last year, I presented my copy of *Crofutt's Trans-Continental Tourist's Guide* to the Manager of the Oriental Bank. The gentleman writes that his business friends have begged the privilege of reading it, until it is now nearly worn out, and that the little book has excited such a lively interest in this trans-continental route, that the English residents there are planning their future trips to England via the Pacific Railway."

In 1871, the Union Pacific and Central Pacific Railroads ordered several thousand copies of the Guide for circulation in Europe as an advertisement for their "trans-continental" line. Some editions were translated for sale abroad, but the title word *Trans-Continental* had already become universal. The word, along with the guidebook, had been sold to America and to the rest of the world.

The trains hauled their cargoes of passengers in starkly contrasted styles — we were all variously "sorted and boxed for the journey," as one of them put it. Most American and foreign emigrants travelled west in appalling discomfort — dirty, weary and overcrowded in plain, wooden-benched box cars. The railroad offered quick, cheap transport to a new life in the West, the journey itself mostly misery and endurance. But although emigrant wagon trains survived locally until well into the 1880s, the cheapest rail-fare in the early years from Omaha to Sacramento (nearly 1800 miles) was as low as $40, and many travelled shorter distances. The first-class through-fare was $100 (Pullman Palace service about $4 a day extra), and the second-class, $75.

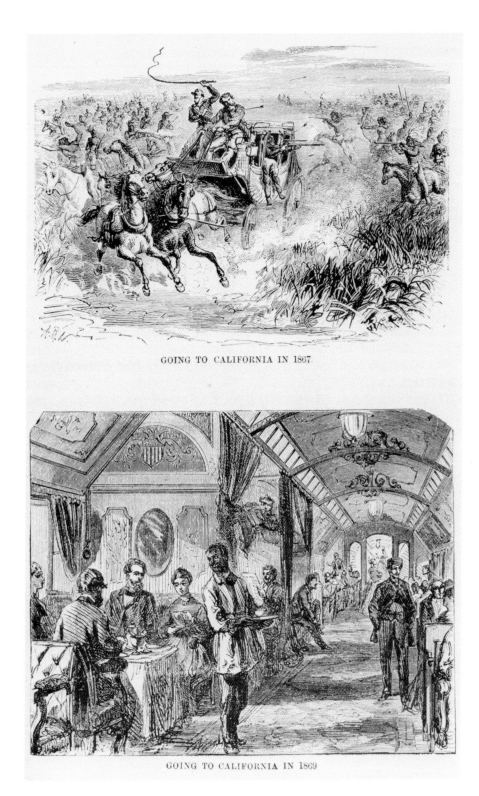

GOING TO CALIFORNIA IN 1867.

GOING TO CALIFORNIA IN 1869

43. THE SPEED OF CHANGE IN TRANSPORT ACROSS THE WEST — 1867 AND 1869
Drawn by Alfred R. Waud in A.D. Richardson, *Garnered Sheaves*, 1871

187

Tourists from home and abroad, relaxing in the Pullman Cars, were to provide the railroads with an increasingly important source of revenue. George Pullman had been quoted as saying "Americans who travel don't care what they are charged for comforts, if they can only get their money's worth." Certainly, the enormous success of his Sleeping, Parlor, and Dining Cars played an indispensable role in developing long-distance routes. No time had been lost; Pullman Sleeping and Parlor Cars had been attached to the Union Pacific train which left Omaha on 13th June 1869, only five weeks after the completion of the Pacific Railroad. Before long, George Pullman added extra facilities. He negotiated a weekly through service with the Union Pacific and Central Pacific that avoided the necessity of changing trains at Promontory, Utah and also added a Dining Car to his special 'Pullman Hotel Express', with full breakfast, lunch and dinner service. The Central Pacific had now completed their track from Sacramento to Oakland-San Francisco so the journey was non-stop, save for fuel and water, between Omaha and the West Coast. The fare was $168 for Drawing Room and Sleeping Car, with meals an additional $1.00-$1.50 each.

The first of these special weekly Pullman Hotel Express trains left Omaha on Tuesday, 19th October 1869, and began the fast return trip from San Francisco on the following Monday, 25th October. Most Pullman services of course continued to use the regular "eating stops". All told, the response was staggering. Company reports show that by 1870, the Union Pacific was running a fleet of thirty-one Pullmans, in addition to its nineteen First Class passenger cars. The Central Pacific Railroad also quickly discovered that it had overestimated freight and underestimated passenger traffic, and immediately rushed through more orders for its own Silver Palace Cars.

Americans from the Eastern States who might otherwise visit Europe became the target for vigorous "Go *West* instead" promotion. Europeans with money and opportunity came to regard travel on "America's trans-continental railroad" as a new dimension to the fashionable Grand Tour. Jules Verne neatly adapted the idea in *Around the World in Eighty Days*, published in 1873, when Phileas Fogg saved precious time by taking the trans-continental train from San Francisco to Kearney, Nebraska, short of Omaha. The possibility of such a trip had been advertised much earlier in California; on 20th September 1869, H.S. Crocker, a publisher in Sacramento, had announced: "Now that the Pacific Railroad is complete, few of our readers are aware that *a journey around the world can be made in eighty days*." Crocker proceeded to tell them how to do it.

As the market and the competition increased, Crofutt issued an expanded edition of the Guide in 1871, and for the first time called it

Crofutt's Trans-Continental Tourist's Guide. With his own name in the title, Crofutt now swiped at his competitors for all he was worth:

> "We were the *first* to stake our *dollars* and *time* on the venture, since when our imitators have been numerous. To 'Our Own Correspondents' across the continent the Guide has proved a perfect 'God-send.' It enabled them to describe minutely the wonders of the trip equally as well in the *night* as in the day-time, while sleeping soundly in a palace car.
>
> All these we could tolerate, but when *great big* DEAD BEATS, like Appleton's of this city, employ penny-a-liners to sit in their office — *never go out of New York City* — and compile "Guides" and "Books of Travels" by robbing us, and all the others who travel and spend their money collecting reliable information, — and when the *Alta* man of San Francisco steals even the "good name" of our book — to say nothing of such as Rand & McNally, Gilbert, Eaton, Tracy, and a score of other *catch-penny swindles* — we begin to think that the race of honorable writers and publishers is nearly *run out.*
>
> We now issue the Guide as *Crofutt's Trans-Continental Tourist's Guide.* Let us see if they won't go for *Crofutt* next!" [22]

The public lapped it up. Through a mixture of directness, enthusiasm, persuasion, and an appeal for fair play, Crofutt developed a rapport with his readers both through his style and his content. Atwell had been a more established figure, but

> "I realized that I was unknown to the 'newspaper world' — having spent *ten* of the best years of my life on the plains and in the mountains — that mine was a 'backwoods' style, and that I had nothing to expect but severe criticism. Judge my surprise upon receiving the complimentary notices of the Guide, recommending it to the public, from over 200 of the best journals in the country." [23]

By 1872, *Crofutt's Trans-Continental Tourist's Guide* comprised 224 pages, fifty illustrations and eleven maps, including the large, steel-plate, coloured map of the world which linked America's transcontinental railroad into round-the-world travel. The price was now increased to $1.00 paper covers, $1.25 cloth (flexi- or hard-bound). But this is real value for money, Crofutt assured the public — "facts, names, dates, distances, illustrations, and condensed telegrams, in *the smallest possible space* and for the *least possible money.*"

He would supply all the necessary details for obtaining a ticket on a Palace Sleeper and then add "But as we cannot all afford to ride in Palace Cars, do the next best thing — secure the best seat you can, and prepare to be as happy as you know how!"

Crofutt had found his public; they journeyed together, always fellow-travellers, observing, sharing experiences, constantly aware of the speed of change in their new West. Some were depressed by the wilderness;

more often they were exhilarated and humbled by the scale and variety of the American landscape.

"One word more before we go —
As you leave the busy hum and ceaseless bustle of the city for the broad-sweeping plains, the barren patches of desert, and the grand old mountains — for all these varied features of the earth's surface will be encountered before we reach the Pacific coast — lay aside *all* city prejudices and ways for the time; leave them in Omaha, and for once be *natural* while among nature's loveliest and grandest creations. Having done this, you will be prepared to enjoy the trip — to appreciate the scenes which will rise before you.

Above all, forget everything but the journey, for in this consists the secret of having a good time.

The bell rings — the whistle shrieks — 'All aboard,' and we are off!"

CHAPTER SIX

The New Age of Western Promotion: Life in New York in the 1870s

"Another book on the West! Yes, and why not?" wrote J.H. Beadle in his preface to *The Undeveloped West* in 1873. "There ought to be a new book on the West, by some careful observer and thorough explorer, at least once a year; for so many and so various are the changes, so important the new discoveries, that a volume is but thoroughly read before the facts it narrates are old."

The early 1870s set a cracking pace in the race to win the West in print. There was an enormous increase in demand for information; farmers, miners, tourists, artisans, traders, speculators and investors — hopefuls of all kinds and from all quarters — clamoured for facts and figures, and devoured what was offered. The West, in its turn, needed selling, quickly and efficiently, once the transcontinental line was completed. The railroad companies, alarmed at the thought of tiny revenues from a western wilderness, were powerful promoters of the information industry. The efforts paid off as a huge new travelling population of men and women, rich and poor, came to look at or live in the West. In 1870, the first full year of operation, nearly 150,000 travelled on the U.P.-C.P. line between Omaha and Sacramento as through- or way-passengers; by the end of the decade on that route alone, the figure approached one million. This vital source of revenue had quickly been established. On the Union Pacific, for example, gross passenger earnings outstripped gross freight earnings for the first time in March 1870, and continued to do so for the remainder of the financial year. Even in the mid-1880s, gross passenger earnings on the U.P. system were still as much as one-third of those from freight traffic, and on the Central Pacific nearly one-half. On the Southern Pacific Railroad of California (Northern and Southern Divisions), gross passenger earnings were as high as 70 per cent of gross freight earnings at that time.

Crofutt soon found that even the twice-yearly revision of *Crofutt's Trans-Continental Tourist's Guide* was inadequate to record the speed of change in the West, much less to handle the sheer volume of new information becoming available. "The *Guide* is too slow for George now!" wrote one of his friends, as Crofutt announced his intention to expand his business at the end of 1871 and launch a new, 8-page, dollar (per annum) monthly newspaper called *Crofutt's Western World.*

Double Success: Crofutt Goes "Booming Along"

Crofutt gave up his office at 21 Park Row and instead rented an extra room at the Park Hotel nearby to serve as his registered office accommodation. He had been staying at the Park since his arrival in New York from Chicago in 1870; the hotel's convenient location at 138 Nassau, on the corner of Nassau and Beekman Streets, together with its bar and restaurant, made the Park a regular haunt of printers, editors and reporters in the heart of New York's newspaper and magazine publishing district around Park Row and Printing House Square [Map IX].

Crofutt's Western World began in November 1871, and both the November and December issues remained 8-page. To Crofutt's delight, however, demand was so good that he doubled the number of pages in January 1872 and advertised widely that here was now a paper as big as *Harper's Weekly,* devoted entirely to the trans-Mississippi West—its railroads, settlers, miners, tourists, local industries and kindred interests ... "Concise ... plainly written ... try it!"

This was still the age of 'personalized' newspaper production, an era of individuality which towards the end of the nineteenth century made way for greater use of the syndicated column, new technologies, and increased standardization. Given his experience with the *Trans-Continental* guidebooks, it had not taken Crofutt long to discover that neither the titles of publications nor particular words, however catchy, were subject to copyright protection. Even so, the inclusion of the proprietor's or the editor's name in the title of a newspaper or magazine could get round the problem to some extent, and at the same time help to sharpen the image of the periodical in the public's mind. Graham, Godey, Peterson, Arthur, Harper, and Frank Leslie were among those who had exploited the "name-in-the-title" in their sales promotion with outstanding success. By the end of 1871, Crofutt had followed suit in the titles of both his publications, and the timely addition of his name to the *Trans-Continental Tourist's Guide* allowed his success in that field to spill over, by association, onto his newspaper. "Crofutt" was now a by-word for an ability to grasp what people wanted to know, and to present the basic essentials in simple, clear and dependable terms. Wrote one Westerner in 1872:

"George A. Crofutt, the Bismarck of railroad literature ... has launched a newspaper of his own on the deep sea of public favor.

The new journal is called *Crofutt's Western World,* which is enough, for here there *is* something in a name that not only commands popularity but will fill George's coffers with very hard cash." [1]

The virtually single-handed production of this new monthly chronicle of western development was an ambitious undertaking and, together with the *Guide*, demanded every ounce of Crofutt's energy, speed, and organizational ability. Apart from the basic literature supplied by the railroad and other agents, Crofutt used five methods to gather information and keep his copy lively and up to date:

(i) As part of his regular revision of *Crofutt's Trans-Continental Tourist's Guide*, he continued to make his own trips from New York City to the Pacific coast, in order to renew his contacts, record changes, and add new itineraries and side-tours.

(ii) He worked an extensive exchange list with many of the small newspapers scattered throughout the West.

(iii) He made direct requests through the columns of *Crofutt's Western World* and the exchange papers, for regular, reliable reports from correspondents.

(iv) He dispatched reporters and others from New York on special fact-finding expeditions.

(v) He invited his western readers, when visiting New York, to make a point of calling at his office in the Park Hotel to talk about old times, and new times, in their own particular corners of the West.

The wealth of information contained in the exchange lists provided the bread-and-butter business. Western newspapers began to flood into the Park Hotel where, surrounded by stacks of loose sheets, pamphlets, and mountains of correspondence, Crofutt read and clipped his way through the "histories of the present," sorting the cuttings, condensing and re-writing the material where necessary for crisper copy. "I gather the items," said Crofutt, "and play havoc with pencil and shears in rehashing them for the *Western World* readers to devour."

In June 1872, the Rev. Sheldon Jackson summed up the double success:

> "Three years' almost constant travel on the Union Pacific Railway has more and more impressed me with the reliability of Crofutt's Trans-Continental Tourist's Guide ... Now, Mr. Crofutt appears with a monthly paper, remarkably full of condensed news about the far west, apparently the cream of the local column of hundreds of western papers." [2]

Western news was sucked into Crofutt's office to be filtered and poured forth. West spoke to East, but West also spoke to West through his pages, for many of the small western papers starting up in the early 1870s used Crofutt's network both to listen and to be heard. All were part of the phenomenal increase in the number of newspapers in the United States at this period, a breathtaking response to the soaring circulations triggered by the Civil War, and sustained after that by rising immigration and westward expansion. By 1870, America had more than one-third of the world's newspapers. The boom continued during the 1870s when, despite a financial depression, the number of newspapers in the United States almost doubled.

"America is the classic soil of newspapers," observed one English writer in 1871, "everybody is reading." Parties, sects, societies, associations, new settlements — special interest groups of all kinds — were catered for and publicized in the country's astonishing "universality of print."[3] The West was fertile ground both for its own and the East's publications:

> "I have read in books," wrote one Kansas homesteader, "that the people of the frontier kept moving ever westward to escape civilization. But if my experience counts for anything, such people were the exceptions. So eager were we to keep in touch with civilization that even when we could not afford a shotgun and ammunition to kill rabbits, we subscribed to newspapers and periodicals, and bought books."[4]

> Back numbers were saved and circulated. "How eagerly we all read the stale news," recalled one army wife stationed on the western frontier of Kansas, Colorado and New Mexico between 1867 and 1877; "With what anticipation every item was scanned. Newspapers were begged and borrowed and read and passed down the line."[5]

Crofutt cast his net right across the trans-Mississippi West, ranging from the recently purchased Alaska to Texas, from California to Dakota. As a result, many readers found that the *Western World's* combination of digestible detail and geographical spread made it the most convenient monthly synopsis of western development available. Crofutt reported major events such as the opening of the Union Pacific's long-awaited Omaha bridge over the Missouri River in March 1872, and the disastrous fire in downtown Portland, Oregon in August 1873. He monitored progress on the new railroads clawing their way west (the Texas & Pacific Railway, for example, where Grenville Dodge was in charge of operations), and, in his Condensed Items, made handy packages of news from a host of western towns. Crofutt highlighted the rapid growth of San Diego (c.3000 in 1873 and growing fast), and steady progress in the new village of Phoenix, Arizona. Few details escaped his eye wherever local opportunity for development was concerned; so, for example, he reported plans for a new apple and apricot cannery at St. George, Utah, as well as the temporary closure of schools around Vermillion, Dakota, in order that teachers and children could help to harvest the bumper wheat crop. Here was a pointillist at work on the huge canvas of the West.

There were notes of everything from the price of hay in Reno, Nevada to the spring drought in Kansas, from the new narrow-gauge railroads in Colorado and Utah, to the proposed improvements to navigation on the Upper Missouri and Red Rivers. Crofutt broadcast the cry from Oregon's

Willamette Valley for more emigrants, and the latest mineral strikes everywhere from Alaska to Arizona. Short items were mixed with longer pieces and trade statistics for prospective settlers and investors to study at leisure—an analysis, for example, of California's grape, hops and dried fruit harvest, its wine industry, and the expanding acreage for longstapled cotton in Kern, Fresno and Merced Counties. There was news of trees breaking under the weight of the orange crop in Old San Bernardino, along with notes on Los Angeles' first Board of Trade and the highly favourable outlook (May 1874) for crude petroleum production in Ventura County. This was a significant forecast; both the San Fernando and Ventura districts expanded production in the late 1870s. Drilling had begun in a small way in the 1860s, but it was not until the late 1890s that California began to develop as a major oil producer.

Crofutt's Western World, directed more towards settlers than tourists, quickly established itself as an impressive contribution to the western information industry. Whichever western region he was describing, Crofutt always gave meticulous attention to developments in mining, manufacturing, irrigated agriculture and transport — the last not only over the railroads and their new branch lines but also on improved wagon roads and cattle trails.

*　　　　　　*　　　　　　*

"Reams of paper and gallons of ink . . . and still the reading public asks for more. And there is always more to be said," wrote one Cincinnati reporter, "[about] the ever-varying circumstances of Western life . . . beyond the Mississippi."[6]

Sales were booming. In April 1872, Crofutt set off on his own trip west, and appointed William Crane Jr. as editor of *Crofutt's Western World* while he was away. The work load in producing the monthly publication was so heavy that Crofutt had promised to go for just a "short run west." But he found so much new development that he extended his travels. Crane buckled under the weight of work, unable to match Crofutt's speed and capacity for organization; by August he was forced to give up, ill with worry and exhaustion. Crofutt rushed back to New York and immediately "pitched in" — his own laconic phrase for toiling day and night to clear the backlog of work, restore order, answer letters, pay bills, meet deadlines, and avoid any break in publication. The trip west had been a tonic, however; Crofutt had brought back so much material that he added a special supplement to his 16-page *Western World!*

Meanwhile, Crofutt had also sent others off on fact-finding expeditions. As soon as he doubled the size of *Crofutt's Western World* in January 1872, Crofutt had begun by dispatching Edwin Q. Bell on an extensive trip through the West as his roving reporter. Bell was well known in the newspaper world. He had been on the staff of *De Bow's*

Review for many years and in 1867-8 become co-editor of this famous old magazine, founded in New Orleans in 1846 as the *Commercial Review of the South and West.* Bell was De Bow's brother-in-law, and with him had struggled for years to steer the magazine through its many financial and political storms. *De Bow's* revival after the Civil War was short-lived, and Bell, facing hard times in the early 1870s, seized the chance to go out west on Crofutt's behalf.

Another of Crofutt's roving reporters was to be the self-styled 'Professor' Stephen James Sedgwick, a New York schoolteacher who in the 1860s had developed his skills as a 'magic lantern' lecturer on a wide range of scientific, cultural, and foreign travel topics. In 1869 and 1870, however, looking for adventure he had gone west and worked as one of A.J. Russell's photographic assistants during the making of the official record of the building of the Union Pacific Railroad. Sedgwick, son of a glass-maker, made a set of more than a hundred glass slides from the U.P. and C.P. photographic collections and by 1873, the 'Professor' was giving a series of immensely popular lantern lectures in and around New York City. He provided his own commentary as, scene by scene, he took his audience on an imaginary journey all the way from Omaha to Sacramento.

It was a dazzling performance. In what became a set of four 1½ -hour lectures, Sedgwick skilfully mixed long-shots and close-ups, quoting vividly throughout from his own experiences, as well as from *Crofutt's Trans-Continental Tourist's Guide.* Indeed, his emphasis was very much on tourism, on the wonders of visiting and viewing, rather than on settlement and migration to the West. Sedgwick's gifts as a speaker and the breathtaking realism of the projected photographic slides enthralled his audiences, and brought a unique experience of western travel into countless public halls and lecture rooms in the East. At least 20,000 people are estimated to have attended Sedgwick's meetings. Crofutt heard him and was greatly impressed. In June 1873, he commissioned Sedgwick as a travelling correspondent for *Crofutt's Western World,* and throughout the summer and fall of that year, Sedgwick toured the Far West and produced long and detailed reports for the *World* readers.[7]

Reports of another kind were also being solicited with great success. Crofutt offered one column each month free of charge for one year to all the Governors of the western States and Territories, or to authorized Immigrant Commissioners, so that they could publicize the resources and opportunities of their respective regions. Those few who were tardy in responding found themselves hauled over the coals in the columns of the *World* by a remorseless editor!

In addition to these reports, in July 1873 Crofutt also began publishing extracts from the Hayden geological and topographic reports on the American West. Professor F.V. Hayden had led the first successful scientific expedition into the Yellowstone country in 1871 and been a major influence in the Congressional decision to create the Yellowstone National Park, the first in the United States. Crofutt's support for Hayden's efforts is recorded in letters he wrote to Hayden in February 1872 which are now held in the National Archives.[8] In 1873-6, Hayden turned his attention to Colorado, and one of the details in an early report especially caught Crofutt's eye: with his own memories of the Territory in the 1860s, Crofutt told his readers that Hayden had sent as many as 227 different kinds of grasshopper found in Colorado to Washington, D.C.'s Natural History collection!

Crofutt kept up a lively exchange through his columns, fielding brickbats as well as bouquets, and chatting to old friends. It made excellent copy, emphasized the personal approach, and balanced the longer reports and surveys. "How are you, old man? and how is the *World* thriving?" asked Edward L. Sloan in 1873 from Salt Lake City, where he was now editor of the *Herald*. And Crofutt replied "We've just swallowed *The West* ... not bad eh?" Crofutt was indeed "booming along." In June 1873, *Crofutt's Western World* took over *The West*, an 8-page monthly which was published in San Francisco by John H. Carmany & Co. *The West's* editor had been Dana C. Pearson, and Crofutt decided to devote a special section of the *World* to Pacific Coast affairs under Pearson's editorship while he continued to handle the rest from New York. From now on, *Crofutt's Western World* was published both in San Francisco and New York. At first, Carmany's own press printed the western editions, while in New York, printer George Yates had the ideal location for Crofutt—right next door to the Park Hotel at 16 Beekman Street.

Crofutt now claimed a circulation of 17,500, almost certainly an exaggeration which was partly the fault of the chaotic state of *The West's* subscription lists. An earlier estimate of 9000-10,000 was probably nearer the mark. There was to be a big increase in sales throughout the spring and summer of 1873, however, by which time, according to the record, *Crofutt's Western World* was being sent to subscribers in every State and Territory in the Union, as well as to sixteen foreign countries on all five continents.

Crofutt announced that so much "valuable, varied and spicy material" was flowing in each month that he was considering making the *World* a weekly, or at least a semi-monthly. Mail was now being delivered *five times a day* from the Post Office to Crofutt's room in the Park Hotel. The introduction of free delivery service within the major cities of the United States had been part of important new legislation on postal charges authorized by Congress in the Act of 3rd March 1863. This Act had established a uniform letter rate of 3 cents per ½-ounce regardless of distance, and also introduced 'classes' of mail which allowed cheaper postal rates for newspapers and other printed material. One way or another, all three introductions had boosted western and transcontinental mail in general, and businesses like Crofutt's in particular. Other ancillary services sprang up to speed the dispatch of bulk orders; in December 1873, Crofutt reported that James Brady's New York Mailing Agency was a marvel of efficiency in folding, addressing and posting many of the city's weekly and monthly publications.

Meanwhile, Crofutt was constantly encouraging his readers to put pen to paper, assuring them that he would publish letters

> "from a prospector, miner, ranchman, stockherder, muleskinner or bull-whacker who *knows* whereof he writes ... but they must contain *facts*, plain common-sense facts concerning the country ... those written by sentimental and emotional tourists, who go thundering across the continent in six days, three-fourths of the time sleeping in a Palace Car, would be rejected at first glance."

Despite this comment, Crofutt appears elsewhere to have maintained a stimulating correspondence with many of the tourists he met on his travels and through his guidebooks, but he had little sympathy with those who wasted the opportunity to learn about the West, and who made little serious effort to understand as well as to enjoy their new surroundings.

*   *   *

Crofutt extended a standing invitation to his readers to call and see him at the Park Hotel. As a result, a stream of old friends and new faces appeared at the door of his office.

> "We hope that none of our many friends from the Great West will ever visit Gotham without making himself known at our sanctum; the latch-key is always on the outside!"

Not surprisingly, several of his visitors stayed at the Park Hotel, probably at special rates. It was western hospitality in the heart of Lower Manhattan.

A welcome visitor was James M. Hutchings who always found time to call when in New York on one of his popular lecture tours. Crofutt did the same whenever he was in California. Hutchings was famous as the first successful magazine publisher in the Far West. *The Pioneer; or, California Monthly Magazine*, launched in 1854, claimed to be the first literary periodical in the region but it could not survive Hutchings' arrival on the scene. Between 1856 and 1861, *Hutchings' California Magazine* had provided a vivid picture of the Golden State. Hutchings, a 'forty-niner', was a lively writer and a tireless promoter of California; he also knew the advantage of having his own name in the title of the publication. As owner and editor, Hutchings filled the well-illustrated, monthly magazine with his personal experiences as a miner, traveller and guide. In 1855, he had led the first party of tourists into Yosemite, the valley he loved and with which he was to be associated as a writer, naturalist, hotel-keeper and publicist for the rest of his life. Hutchings had written to praise *Crofutt's Trans-Continental Tourist's Guide* when it first appeared, and the two became firm friends.

Bret Harte may also have called on Crofutt from time to time, since they had mutual acquaintances in San Francisco and some of Harte's pieces, together with reports of his movements, appeared in the *Western World.* Harte had been editor of California's *Overland Monthly* for its first two years (1868-70), and with his own highly popular short stories and poems, he had boosted circulation to 10,000 and helped to establish the *Overland's* reputation as one of the country's finest literary magazines — a western *Atlantic Monthly.*

> *"The Overland Monthly,"* observed a British writer in 1870, "is already one of the best periodicals which America produces ... It is entitled to the rare distinction of being readable from cover to cover and yet to be able to maintain its place without being propped up by an instalment from a novel." [9]

Bret Harte had assumed that his talent would find wider recognition in the East so, aged thirty-five, he left California in 1871 and spent the next seven years based in or near New York City. The spark was gone, however, and Harte's popularity rapidly declined. Riddled with debt, he lived a hand-to-mouth existence, hating the grind of the lecture tours on which he depended.

Harte's resignation from *The Overland Monthly* had had an equally disastrous effect on its publisher in San Francisco, John Carmany, from whom Crofutt bought *The West* in 1873. Carmany struggled to keep the *Overland* going, lost about $30,000 in the process and suspended publication in 1876. It was a terrible tale of dazzling success turned sour, both for Harte and the publishers. Competition on the west coast had always been fierce; J.M. Hutchings had noted back in 1859 that nearly ninety newspapers and periodicals were published in California. Expansion had continued unabated in the 1860s. Crofutt emphasized the point with the dry observation that in some parts of the United States "a criminal condemned to death may choose whether he would be shot or hanged. In California he has no choice — he is simply buzzed to death by reporters."

"Enterprise, Energy, and Advertising, Advertising, Advertising — Persistent and Long-Indulged!"

Advertising agencies, born in Philadelphia in the 1840s, grew rapidly in the major northeastern cities after 1865; New York soon led the field. Crofutt kept a close eye on advertising, both his own and that of others buying space in *Crofutt's Western World*. Experience in Philadelphia had taught him that newspapers, like most businesses, depended on advertising to survive the everlasting battle for circulation. Newspapers had three main sources of revenue. The first, sales and subscriptions, was the least profitable. The second, job printing, provided regular income for many newspaper establishments, especially as at this period most of the journalists and the smaller weeklies still had their background in the printing trade. Above all, however, advertising provided the principal source of revenue; this was the lifeline and at best, the real money-spinner. Crofutt's message was simple:

> *"All good fellows advertise.* The business man that don't advertise *today* will, twenty years hence, be the old man on the corner selling peanuts to the children of those who *do* advertise." [10]

> "Although an advertisement is of necessity transitory in its nature, ... advertising has proved the most efficacious, the most speedy, and the least expensive means of making known the wants of mankind to each other.

> ... Who would succeed must apply the rules of common-sense and exercise judgment ... But of one thing there can no longer remain a doubt: that prudent, persistent advertising is sure to produce results, in almost all instances, far beyond expectation ...

> Whatever is worth doing at all, is worth doing well. Decide what you wish to do, and then push it intelligently and energetically ... If you have goods to sell, compel the world to listen to you ... more fortunes have been lost by modesty than by boldness." [11]

The basic theory of advertising has never been summarized more clearly. Despite the huge growth in the American advertising industry in subsequent years — in markets, media, research, and investment — the simple fundamentals remained unchanged. Crofutt's piece could have been written yesterday.

"Picture It !" The Boom in Mass-Produced Illustration

"A picture's worth a thousand words" and Crofutt was now caught up in the mid-nineteenth century boom in mass-produced illustration. During the 1840s and '50s, steel and copper engravings had been a striking feature of magazines like *Graham's* and *Godey's;* despite the costs involved, plates had become an indispensable weapon in the never-ending struggle for sales. Production costs were certainly high, anything from $300-$1000 apiece, so that publishers often found original engraved plates to be more expensive than the magazine's entire literary content. Not surprisingly, plates were regularly exchanged, or bought second-hand by the smaller periodicals.

The high quality and immense popularity of woodcuts began in the 1850s with the pioneering work of *Harper's New Monthly Magazine,*

Harper's Weekly, and *Frank Leslie's Illustrated Newspaper*. Out on the west coast, artist George H. Baker captured a large slice of the California woodcut trade. He was a 'forty-niner' from Boston, but he soon abandoned the search for gold and worked in Sacramento art jobbing and mapping mining claims, before moving in 1862 to San Francisco. There, with his bold style, speed and versatility, Baker became one of the most prolific producers of maps and illustrations for guidebooks and other publications, for the rest of the nineteenth century.

Lithographs had also steadily increased in popularity during this period, following the introduction of the process from Germany by the early 1820s. Lithography involved printing onto paper, ready for hand-tinting if desired, drawings done on special flat, highly polished stone, using special water-repellent crayons. Production costs easily undercut those for copper and steel engraving. Nathaniel Currier learned the technique in Boston, and then moved to Philadelphia and on to New York, where in 1835 he started a business on Wall Street. A year later he shifted to Nassau Street, added a factory on Spruce, and in 1852 was joined by James Merritt Ives.

In 1857, Currier & Ives became partners. With premises in the heart of the printing and publishing district, the two men and their team of artists went on to acquire a national reputation for inexpensive, hand-coloured lithographs depicting many aspects of American life.[12] Some 7000 different prints were produced: landscapes and seascapes, homesteads and mansions, historical and sporting scenes, portraits and political cartoons, steamboats and wagon trains, railroads and vistas of westward expansion. Currier & Ives lithographs captured American hearts and American dreams, and adorned American homes from coast to coast for more than fifty years. In their Nassau and Spruce Street works, Currier & Ives were surrounded by their New York competitors, to say nothing of rivals located in Philadelphia and Boston, but they held their lead and outlasted them all.

During the 1860s, hand-tinted lithographs were increasingly replaced by chromolithographs, an important development introduced in 1864 which used a separate stone for each colour, and thus provided a new and relatively fast method of colour reproduction. Favourite oil or watercolour paintings were copied, but in many cases paintings were specially commissioned for the purpose. The quality of these 'chromos', as they were known, varied with the time and the skills applied to them, but the advent of cheap chromos, usually between 50 cents and $3, gave a huge boost to the popularity of lithographs for home decoration and for advertising in the second half of the nineteenth century.

Crofutt already offered special clubbing terms and ran a premium book list for subscribers to *Crofutt's Western World*, but in 1872 he decided to add a chromo to his gift offers. Working in the Park Hotel on the corner of Nassau and Beekman Streets, and with Currier & Ives only a few doors away at 125 Nassau, Crofutt was surrounded by artists and illustrators coming and going through the printing and publishing quarter of Lower Manhattan. Among them, Crofutt had met John Gast, an artist and lithographer who rented a small studio at 116 Fulton Street, and lived in Brooklyn. Fulton Street led down to one of the busiest ferries in the United States, and Gast was one of the thousands who regularly crammed the Fulton Ferry linking Brooklyn to Manhattan. There was plenty to look at on the way over. Construction work on the Brooklyn Bridge had begun in 1870 and three years later, Roebling's two granite gothic towers, wonders of the age, began rising above East River.

Crofutt discussed his ideas for the chromo with Gast. Sketches, photographs, paintings, and allegorical pictures of the opening of the West by wagon, Pony Express, telegraph and railroad had become

44.   BROOKLYN BRIDGE UNDER CONSTRUCTION IN 1873
Harper's Weekly, November 1, 1873, from a sketch by C.E.H. Bonwill

The view from the Brooklyn tower across East River, Lower Manhattan and Governor's Island, to the Hudson River and New Jersey shore. The bridge's new Manhattan tower rises on the other side of East River, which is crowded with sailing ships, sidewheel steamers, barges and ferries. Brooklyn Bridge was completed in 1883.

increasingly popular during the 1860s. Emanuel Leutze's *Westward the Course of Empire takes its Way,* painted in 1861 as the study for the giant mural in the nation's Capitol building, typified the spirit of Union expansion and consolidation. In 1869, the cover of Crofutt and "Bill Dadd's" *Great Trans-Continental Railroad Guide* had projected the same theme. Now Crofutt wanted a new visual expression of the multiple development of the western frontier in space and time, clear in its message and attractively colourful to the eye.

Crofutt had decided to call the chromo *American Progress.* It was to be unmistakably patriotic, a vision of the future based on what the United States had already achieved. The panoramic view swept centrally from coast to coast, and Crofutt listed the items he wanted Gast to include. Significantly, everything in the picture was drawn from Crofutt's personal experience. Every element in the composition he knew first-hand, or by close association, from his pioneering years in the 1860s. Although the iconography of westward expansion had been selectively featured in several paintings, and in popular prints by Currier & Ives (e.g. 'Across the Continent', 1868), and also *Harper's* (e.g. 'The Course of Empire', *Harper's New Monthly Magazine,* June 1867), none of them included quite as many different aspects of the westward movement in one picture as did Crofutt's design for *American Progress.* This was meant to instruct as well as to decorate, to form a comprehensive record as well as a work of art.

On the right of the picture, the Atlantic seaboard contains a simple composite representation of the major ports, cities and manufacturing industries of the Eastern States from which, advancing westward, move the agents of progress — some pushing forward in isolation, others overtaking earlier stages of westward pioneer penetration. As Crofutt well knew, there was no strict sequence of pioneering activities at any one place, no uniform progression of economic development and transport technology common to all the highly contrasted landscapes and resource frontiers of the West. The picture of *American Progress* provides a broad pattern incorporating hunters, prospectors and farmers, an early cabin, the covered wagon, stagecoach and Pony Express, and, by 1872, three transcontinental railroads completed or under construction. The American Indians, along with their buffalo, are in retreat as the frontier of settlement presses rapidly westward. Overhead, wearing the "Star of Empire", floats the symbolic figure of national enlightenment, carrying two of the most important tools of progress, Crofutt stressed — education and rapid communication. In one hand, the central figure grasps the common school book; in the other, the wire of the expanding telegraph system.[13]

Thus, in 1872, twenty-one years before Frederick Jackson Turner delivered his influential essay on "The Significance of the Frontier in

American History," Crofutt's design for *American Progress* was helping to illustrate and to project the popular theme of continental infilling and the procession of civilization. Here were some of the individuals and groups of actors in the great American drama who had thrown themselves into the wilderness and, with changing methods of transport and communication, moved westward across the stage.

John Gast painted a small picture in oils, 12¾ " × 16¾", from which chromolithographs in nineteen colours were produced. The annual subscription to *Crofutt's Western World*, with the chromo included, was raised by 50 cents to $1.50 in 1873: "A give-away price — the picture alone is worth $10!" announced Crofutt blithely, greatly taken with the total effect. While Crofutt acknowledged that "the country is flooded with chromos," *American Progress* proved extremely popular and undoubtedly contributed to increased sales in 1873. Some readers backed the chromo with canvas and varnished it before hanging. Crofutt decided to commission R.S. Bross to make a steel engraving based on Gast's original, so that as well as distributing the chromo, Crofutt also used the black-and-white reproduction of *American Progress* as the regular frontispiece in his other publication, *Crofutt's Trans-Continental Tourist's Guide,* and in most of his later guidebooks.

John Gast did not name the painting that Crofutt had commissioned, and a century later it was still listed in the Smithsonian Institution's *Inventory of American Paintings executed before 1914* under three different titles: *Westward Ho!* or *Manifest Destiny* or *Spirit of the Frontier.* The painting itself first attracted widespread attention in 1976 when, on loan from a private collection, it was included in the major exhibition 'America as Art', mounted at the National Museum of American Art (National Collection of Fine Arts) in Washington, D.C. as part of the Bicentennial celebration. Although some time later it was noted that Gast's painting of 1872 had been used for Crofutt's lithograph of 1873, Crofutt's link with Gast, and his initiating role in the design of Gast's picture, have hitherto remained unknown.

John Gast meantime was doing splendidly out of the boom in chromos; while keeping his home in Brooklyn, he worked virtually full time as an artist for the next five years, and moved from Fulton Street to roomier premises in Park Place, just off Broadway. Chromos, together with engravings, and packets of photographs and stereoscopic views, now figured prominently alongside book lists in publishers' advertisements.

This was an extraordinarily exuberant age for mass-produced illustration. The introduction of photo-engraving stimulated wood-engravers in their search for greater subtlety of tone. Stereo photography was enjoying an enormous boom of its own. By 1875, there were more than a hundred American photographers each maintaining, in addition to their other work, trade lists of more than 1000 different stereo views.[14] Hundreds of different models of hand and table stereoscopes, together with trays and cabinets to store the views, appeared in homes across the country during the next few years. As the business of illustration increased, Crofutt bought an interest in the International Publishing Co., a little farther south off Broadway at 93-95 Liberty Street, and opened an extra office there. The firm specialized in advertising and distributing American and imported books and pictures.

Crofutt copyrighted *American Progress*,[15] taking advantage of the copyright protection made available for the first time under the Act of 8th July 1870 to paintings, drawings, sculpture, and designs for works of fine art. Copyright had already been extended to photographs and their negatives by the Act of 3rd March 1865; as part of the 1870 legislation, many copyright procedures were improved and the business was centralized in the Library of Congress.

Cook's Tours in America: The Start of a New Westward Movement

Crofutt met Thomas Cook for the first time in October 1872.[16] Ever since Cook had organized his first excursion train over the twelve miles from Leicester to Loughborough, England in 1841, he had been outstandingly successful as the pioneer of cheaper travel by means of specially chartered trains, hotel coupons, and 'through' tickets. Thomas Cook had started a new business — the travel industry. He expanded his activities in Britain, the Low Countries and the Rhineland in the 1850s, and more widely in Europe, particularly in Switzerland, France and Italy, during the early 1860s.

In April 1865, Thomas Cook opened his first London office and turned it into a tourists' supermarket. In addition to tickets and passport services, Cook sold a wide variety of travellers' accessories, including guidebooks, baggage, footwear, umbrellas, walking sticks, telescopes and water purifiers. Leaving his son in charge of the business, Thomas Cook was soon off on a new venture, reviving his earlier idea of developing operations in America. He embarked on his first visit to Canada and the United States in November 1865, seven months after the end of the Civil War, and covered thousands of miles in preparing excursions. These began the following year, and included one of the Civil War battlefields.

By now, Cook's personally conducted Tour System was world famous and when he met Crofutt, "the trans-continental man", in New York early in October 1872, Thomas Cook, aged 63, was getting ready to depart on the second leg of what he regarded as the climax of his career — the first Around-the-World Cook's Tour. Cook's party had just crossed the Atlantic, and the excited passengers, basking in the attention they were attracting in the press, were now bound from New York, via Niagara Falls, Chicago and Salt Lake City, to San Francisco. Cook had not been present at the "joining of the rails" at Promontory, Utah in May 1869, but six months later he had been a guest at the elaborate ceremony in Egypt to mark the opening of the Suez Canal. There and then he had begun to plan his Around-the-World Tour.

Cook discussed with Crofutt details of the western Union Pacific-Central Pacific railroad journey, including the availability of side-trips. Cook's Around-the-World Tour was not a race against the clock, and lasted not 80, but 222 days. Crofutt was impressed by Cook's latest idea, the Circular Note or Traveller's Check, introduced in New York in 1872. As a means of carrying money, Cook's Traveller's Check was an instant success. It could be exchanged for cash at the current rate of exchange at any of the ticket agents, banks, and hotels participating in Cook's Tour System, and was thus an extremely convenient addition to his existing services of 'through' or circular tickets, and hotel coupons.[17]

Crofutt had received a letter from one traveller in Europe extolling the advantages of Cook's Tour System:

"Mr. Cook delivers coupons for travelling by railways, steamers, and diligences (stagecoaches) in all the countries of the world. Besides that, he issues hotel coupons, representing the price of lodging, breakfast, dinner and service in first-class hotels in all countries. On the cover of the ticket-case are printed the names of the hotels where Cook's coupons are accepted, all first-class hotels, from which you can take your choice.

If you arrive in an hotel and it is full, you have simply to show Cook's Tourist Ticket-case, and you are certain to be lodged in a neighboring hotel, or in a private lodging if there is no room at the hotel. One need not trouble himself about any details, as one knows beforehand what he is to spend exclusive of extras, such as wine and various other drinks. The coupons are available everywhere, and the instant you have one for each day you intend staying *en route*, you are certain never to find yourself in a difficulty. If these are not sufficient they will renew your supply at the hotels, and if you have too many, they will take them back and return the value, less a slight percentage."

Cook had thus invented the package tour. The idea was to catch on with American operators, although no serious competitor to Cook emerged until the beginning of the Eighties. The major stage-line and express companies in the United States had of course extended their own travel networks in the 1850s and 1860s, but it was Thomas Cook who found a gap, filled a need, and first captured the tourist market with his range of special services and conducted excursions.

"America *will* travel, any how or any way!" Crofutt was reminded by one of his western correspondents who had just endured an exhausting journey by stage across the deserts of southern California and Arizona. But the West also bred its winners; the Pullman revolution prompted one well-seasoned traveller to observe that "the Western States are gradually teaching those of the East to carry passengers from place to place in perfect comfort."

Thomas Cook had been forced to work extremely hard, however, to sell his ideas in America in the early years, and to challenge the view that he would be better employed confining his efforts to escorting Americans around Europe, rather than around the United States. As one commentator observed:

> "Arrived in America, the nation did not lay itself down at the feet of Mr. Cook; on the contrary, the press, and the railway folks, and the ticket agents, said, with characteristic frankness, "Who are you?" Some good folks did not scruple to say they did not see the scheme in the same light as the originator, and would be glad to know why he couldn't leave them alone to do their own touring." [18]

Cook became more determined than ever in the face of opposition, and by the early 1870s, increasing numbers of Americans and others enjoyed being "Cooked" about the United States and Canada. By 1872, American business prospects both to and from Europe were so good that Thomas Cook opened a New York office (Cook, Son & Jenkins) at 261-2 Broadway [Map IX], followed by branches in Boston, Philadelphia and Washington, D.C. In March 1873, he published the first American edition of his monthly *Cook's Excursionist*, "devoted to the interests of tourists and travelers." Cook was planning a major expansion of his tour system right across the United States. Four million people had already travelled with Cook's in the Old World; now Cook announced, "We want to do the same thing in America, for pleasure seekers, that we do in Europe. We want to open up new routes."

The company advertised frequently in *Crofutt's Western World* in the early Seventies, as well as in the *Trans-Continental Tourist's Guide*.

> "Cook's has grown to be one of the indispensable institutions of the present day," observed Crofutt, adding the clincher ... "Thomas Cook is an enterprising Englishman with Yankee ingenuity!"

The Financial Panic of 1873

On 18th September 1873, the collapse of one of the country's leading securities firms, Jay Cooke & Co. precipitated a crash on the New York stock market and, along with other failures, sparked off one of the worst financial panics the United States had ever experienced. Although certain underlying factors could be traced world-wide, the major causes of the collapse in the U.S.A. were over-investment in railroads, severe currency and credit inflation, government waste, and an adverse trade balance.

High protection had been a feature of the Civil War and it continued until 1872; overproduction, shortage of markets and falling prices combined with disastrous effect in 1873.

The Jay Cooke company itself had become heavily overcommitted to the building of yet another transcontinental railroad, the Northern Pacific to Tacoma on Puget Sound. After the heady years of the early 1870s, the crash checked, and in some cases put a stop to the West's ambitious railroad construction program for the rest of the decade. It was a shattering experience for the likes of Grenville Dodge, chief engineer on the Texas & Pacific Railway which had been organized in 1871 to link New Orleans and Southern California. About 500 miles were built through Louisiana and Texas, Dodge recalled, but work stopped and the line was never completed as planned. To us, the Jay Cooke failure came "like a clap of thunder out of a clear sky." [19]

Another early casualty of the 1873 panic was the former 'Stagecoach King', Ben Holladay, who in the mid-Sixties had sold out at a handsome profit to Wells, Fargo and switched his interests to developing railroads and steamboats in the Northwest. In a series of increasingly risky and often shady deals, Holladay had speculated and borrowed heavily on Wall Street, and in Europe, before the bubble burst. Not that warnings about the mania for investment in railroad stocks had been lacking. *The Atlantic Monthly* and *The Nation*, for example, had drawn attention to the increasing power and self-interest of the railroad companies, and to the dangers of blind faith in railroad investment, especially given its huge popularity in the early 1870s in the United States.

Jay Cooke & Co. had advertised regularly in *Crofutt's Western World*, including the September 1873 issue which had been parcelled and dispatched three weeks before the firm collapsed. Crofutt described "the appalling crisis" that had hit Lower Manhattan as he went on working to bring out his October number as usual:

> "Banking houses, enjoying a world-wide reputation, whose credit seemed so firmly established as to be able to withstand the worst financial shock, came toppling down on the heads of their founders like pasteboard edifices; corporations, established on an apparently sound basis, and which controlled millions of capital, became suddenly bankrupt; stocks and stock-brokers were involved in unutterable ruin, and it seemed as if the 'bottom' had fallen out of everything." [20]

By the end of the year, Crofutt reported that although several New York publications had put up the shutters or were struggling along more dead than alive, *Crofutt's Western World* had so far weathered the storm. The fact that the paper was also published in San Francisco (still at J.H. Carmany's premises at 409 Washington Street), undoubtedly helped to cushion the blow and maintain circulation. Until the mid-Seventies, businesses on the west coast often claimed to be little affected by the eastern panic, but competiton for Pacific Coast readership became stronger than ever. As J.H. Carmany was forced to cut back, struggling with the mounting losses on *The Overland Monthly*, Crofutt took the opportunity while on his annual trip to California at the end of 1873 to transfer the *Western World's* publication to Riley and Edwards at 113 Leidesdorff Street, San Francisco. This house was already publishing the *Coast Review*, among other periodicals, and in February 1874, John G. Edwards severed the final link with Carmany's company by replacing Dana Pearson as the western editor of *Crofutt's Western World*.

No effort was now spared to win new readers and even more importantly, to persuade existing ones to renew their subscriptions for 1874.

> "If on account of hard times, you had thought to let it go," Crofutt addressed his readers, "before deciding to do so, answer honestly and fairly, can you *afford* to do without it?"

Many subscribers found that they had no choice. The mid-1870s was a period of dull trade and low prices. The crisis of 1873 and the depression that followed it led to wage reductions and unemployment; by 1875, half-a-million men were out of work in the United States.

Nevertheless, *Crofutt's Western World* continued publication both in New York and San Francisco, and the 1874 issues went out undiminished in size, price, advertising, variety of content, and geographical coverage. The paper was still a mine of information in the opinion of one faithful reader from Montana, with Crofutt himself, as always, "brim-full of life and enterprise."

What was news? Granger movements were reported to be sweeping across the plains, and Crofutt noted the conditions which had encouraged the new vitality and effectiveness of 'Granger votes'. During the depression which followed the Panic of 1873, western farmers suffered badly from low prices for grain while their costs remained uniformly high, particularly the monopoly freight and storage rates charged by the railroads for moving grain and supplies. John Beadle, travelling through southern Kansas in 1873, found that grain worth sixty cents in New York was selling for only fifteen cents in Kansas. Kansas had been

> "railroaded to death," he reported, with more lines constructed than business would demand for another ten or twenty years. "Except perhaps the one through line, none of the roads were paying more than running expenses. . . . The capital invested in the railroads was a dead loss, as far as present dividends were concerned. But stockholders insisted on some returns, and the managers attempted to squeeze out a few dollars by cutting down their employees on one side and raising freights on the other. It took three bushels of corn to send one to the sea-board." [21]

The National Grange of the Patrons of Husbandry (better known as the Grangers) had been founded in 1867 as a farmers' social and educational movement, but local Granger meetings soon became the natural focus of grievance, and then of organized political pressure on the railroads. Active during the depression years, the Grangers provided the first significant challenge to the railroads' price-fixing practices and to their inter-State control.

Increasing Competition and Investment in the Western Guidebook Industry: Crofutt Changes Course and Meets with Disaster

For the most part, *Crofutt's Western World* found its readership in the early 1870s among the thousands of new settlers to the West — small-scale farmers, miners, store-keepers and mechanics from the Eastern States or Europe who were on their way, thinking of going, or already there. So far as tourists were concerned, Crofutt remained better known nationally and internationally for his *Trans-Continental Tourist's Guide* which was revised annually and, in addition to direct mail-order, was sold on the railroad cars, in the ticket halls, and at news-stands, agencies, and major bookstores.

Crofutt held his own in the early years. The most blatant imitators had acknowledged defeat and retired from the fray. On the other hand, competitors who credited quotations taken from Crofutt or who recommended his Guide in their own publications could be good for business. *Nelson's Pictorial Guide-Books* were a case in point. So too was Charles Nordhoff, sailor, journalist and travel writer, whose popular *California: for Health, Pleasure, and Residence. A book for travellers and settlers* was first published by Harper in New York in 1872. Nordhoff's illustrations included a "Bird's-eye view of the Trans-Continental Route," and he advised tourists to take with them to the west coast "Crofutt's excellent Trans-Continental Guide."

Descriptions of individual trips to the west coast continued to flow onto the market as travellers returned home bursting to see their diaries, letters and notebooks in print. Some of these accounts were described as guidebooks, e.g. John Lester's *The Atlantic to the Pacific. What to see and how to see it*, which was published in 1873. While competently written, the book (based on letters to Rhode Island's *Providence Evening Press*) was in fact a once-only, descriptive personal itinerary of the 'What I did, and what I did next' variety although, like others of this genre, it encouraged more people to make the trip, and thus helped to boost rather than reduce the regular guidebook sales.

The real competition was regrouping, however, and much of it was adopting a more specialized and more lavish style of production. Not only were teams of writers being employed under the guidance of a general editor to produce the text, but publishers fought to outdo each other over the amount and quality of their illustration. In 1873, for example, *Harper's Weekly* sent two artists off to the West for a whole year on a sketching expedition, with instructions not to rely exclusively on the more familiar scenes but to ride into the more remote areas in their search for a new, true and vivid record of the West.

One monumental undertaking of the period set a new standard, both in its extensive coverage of American scenery and its superior workmanship . This was Appletons' great project, *Picturesque America*, published in New York in two volumes between 1872 and 1874. With hundreds of steel engravings and woodcuts made from original drawings specially commissioned from major artists of the time, nothing had so far equalled the style and quality of *Picturesque America* in presenting American landscape as popular art. The illustrations alone cost $100,000, the total outlay, $250,000. William Cullen Bryant edited the accompanying text to this pictorial encyclopedia of America. Published in parts, and totalling well over a thousand pages, it became a national record to be bought, bound and treasured for the years to come, both at home and abroad. Nearly one million copies of *Picturesque America* were sold, and it was widely regarded as one of the great publishing successes of the decade.[22]

One of the best examples of a guidebook modelled on this new, more elaborate scale was *The Pacific Tourist. Williams' Illustrated Trans-Continental Guide of Travel, from the Atlantic to the Pacific Ocean.* The word 'trans-continental' was public property now, but oh, how it boosted sales! The guide was edited and published in New York in 1876 by Henry T. Williams and was the product of a team of writers (only a few of whom rated special mention on the title page), as well as eight principal artists and engravers. In fact, over forty people were to be involved in compiling Williams' *Pacific Tourist* — "the most elaborate, the costliest and the handsomest Guide-Book in the world!"

Williams' formidable competition was still to come, but Appletons' company was already hard at work preparing a new series of guidebooks. In any case, Crofutt knew it was time to elaborate his own *Trans-Continental Tourist's Guide*. In 1873, the 5th edition (4th annual revision), published both in New York and Chicago, still contained 224 pages, 50 illustrations, and eleven maps, including the large coloured map of the world; 50,000 copies were reported sold that year alone, priced at $1.25, cloth-bound. Crofutt decided, however, that the hard times and consequent sales resistance of 1874 were best met with a new enlarged format. He reduced the number of pages but increased the page size of his 6th edition to 7¼ "× 10¼", and doubled the number of illustrations to one hundred, several of them full-page. . . . "Neither pains nor money spared

Yes, You Do!

STAY AT HOME, OR TRAVEL,
YOU MUST HAVE IT!
CROFUTT'S

Trans-Continental Tourist!

For 1874. Sixth Annual Volume,

Containing a full and authentic description of over Five Hundred Cities, Towns, Villages, Stations, Government Forts and Camps, Mountains, Lakes, Rivers, Sulphur, Soda and Hot Springs, Scenery, Watering-Places, and Summer Resorts; where to look for and hunt the Buffalo, Antelope, Deer, and other Game; Trout Fishing, etc., etc.; in fact, to tell you what is worth seeing, where to see it, where to go, how to go, and whom to stop with while passing over the

Union Pacific R. R., Central Pacific R. R. of Cal.,

Their branches and connections by stage and water, from the Atlantic to the Pacific Ocean

Enlarged,

Revised,

Re-written.

Engravings and Maps cost $10,000!
One large colored Map of the World!
Tinted Paper, 160 Pages, Flexible Cloth Covers.

Magnificent Views of Scenery in
Colorado, Wyoming, Utah,

Montana, Nevada, California,

Oregon, Etc., Etc.

BEAUTIFUL ILLUSTRATIONS,
Size, 6½ by 9 inches,

Wonderful Yellowstone Country,

Yo-Semite Valley and Big Trees,

The Geysers, Cape Horn, Etc.

ALSO,

ECHO AND WEBER CAÑONS,
GARDEN OF THE GODS,

Donnar Lake, the Columbia River Country,

SUMMIT SIERRA NEVADA MOUNTAINS, ETC.

It is the most Complete, Elaborate, and Comprehensive TOURIST-BOOK published in this or any other country.

Sent, **POST-PAID,** to any address in the United States on receipt of the price, $1.50; and to any part of the World for $1.75.

Address,

GEO. A. CROFUTT, Publisher,

No. 93 LIBERTY STREET, NEW-YORK CITY.

No. 113 LEIDESDORFF ST., SAN FRANCISCO, CAL.

45.   ADVERTISEMENT FOR *CROFUTT'S TRANS-CONTINENTAL TOURIST,* 1874
in *Crofutt's Western World,* May 1874

to thoroughly revise, enlarge and embellish *Crofutt's Trans-Continental Tourist* for 1874!" It was published in New York and San Francisco, the price was raised to $1.50 post-paid ($1.75 abroad), and distribution reports indicate that it sold well, both in Europe and the United States.

Once the guide for 1874 was published, however, as usual on 1st May, Crofutt felt desperate for a change. The effects of the Panic of 1873 — recession, growing unemployment and reduced immigration, had hit the sales of *Crofutt's Western World*. 'Subscription Expired' had been stamped on more and more copies sent out in the spring of 1874; chasing delinquent subscribers was a thankless task, the familiar story of publishers needing to cut their losses yet loathe to strike out names from the list. Keeping up the vital exchanges with other newspapers was another burden in hard times. To cap it all, the steady grind of editing a monthly publication had become a terrible chore. The volume of work had already forced Crofutt to employ more sub-editors in the spring and summer of 1873, a mixed blessing so far as he was concerned. He knew he needed to stay close to the editing and production side of the business, yet in August 1873, with booming sales and so far, not the slightest hint of financial panic from Wall Street, Crofutt yearned to get out of New York and go west:

> "Would to God I could get out of this dull, dusty, hot city and its india-rubber, pestilential atmosphere, and once more breathe the cool, pure air of the Rockies. But O! I'm here, and I fear *forever*."

*   *   *

Crofutt found time during those long, hot summer days in 1873 to try his hand at something new; he developed and patented what he called 'Crofutt's Life Protector', a simple breathing mask designed for use by firemen and miners. 'Crofutt the writer and publisher' was also 'Crofutt the inventor' at heart. His long-standing interest in mechanics and gadgetry was nourished at this time apparently by the proximity of the *Scientific American* offices at 37 Park Row. This influential, well-established weekly was 'the inventors' paper' since it published the official list of patents received regularly from the U.S. Patent Office. As a result, through their advice columns, a huge correspondence, and a steady stream of visitors, the *Scientific American's* staff maintained contact with inventors of all sorts — from the successful and famous to the disappointed thousands who remained in obscurity.

'Crofutt's Life Protector' consisted of a hard rubber mask with flexible, close-fitting edges, a glass visor or double eye-piece, and a 'curtain' of softer material to be drawn in below the chin and around the neck. The fabric was to be kept wet so that while the wearer could breathe through it, smoke particles would be trapped. A wet sponge placed inside, over the nose and mouth, gave added protection. Crofutt patented the first design (registered as Improvement in Eye and Lung Protectors) on 9th December 1873, and a second, modified version on 23rd June 1874.[23] He advertised his Life Protector for sale at $5, emphasized its wider uses, for example, in foundries, mills, lead works, dry quartz crushers, and guano ships, advised travellers and hotel guests to carry one in their baggage, and published an endorsement from the Montreal Fire Department.

Major fires occurred with alarming frequency; lives and property were lost as cities, towns, shipping, forests and farms blazed away. Large sections of Chicago, Portland, Oregon, and Boston had recently been gutted while in New York, City Hall's district warning fire-bell rang with monotonous frequency. More efficient fire-fighting and fire-escape procedures had become matters of national concern. Improved pieces of equipment — fire extinguishers, high self-supporting ladders, fire-proof materials, and the like — were widely reported in the press, as well as in the specialized insurers' and investors' journals. In Lower Manhattan, new designs of fire-engine and other equipment were often displayed and tested in front of City Hall, just a few steps away from the Park Hotel.

It was against this background, therefore, that Crofutt concentrated on patenting an improved protector "against smoke, steam and noxious gases." One of the greatest hazards in fire-fighting was the danger of suffocation by smoke, and smoke-masks of one sort or another had been in use in Europe since the eighteenth century. But none of these smoke-masks, including Crofutt's, removed the danger from the odourless, highly toxic and non-filterable carbon monoxide gas, which is present in varying amounts at every fire. In fact, reduction of the smoke hazard alone could actually increase the danger because it allowed the period of exposure to the gas to be prolonged. 'Crofutt's Life Protector' was no more successful than earlier smoke and dust masks; samples were widely distributed but it never appears to have gone into production. Not until the invention in Germany (1901-04) of a marketable self-contained breathing apparatus using an oxygen cylinder, were firemen and others able to move at will through smoke, gases, and oxygen-deficient atmospheres.

Crofutt the inventor gave up for the time being. What about Crofutt the writer, editor and publisher? Here too, the decision was the same. By the end of 1874, Crofutt had resolved to make a clean break from publishing. So far as his newspaper was concerned, after the boom years, *Crofutt's Western World* had never recovered the ground lost in the aftermath of the Panic of 1873, and Crofutt had no desire to try to spend his way out of trouble by revamping the paper and aiming hefty but expensive blows at his competitors. Despite the depression, the competition was intensifying. For every door that closed, more were opening to mop up the business and create new markets. Not only were the 1870s boom years for American newspapers; the number of magazines and periodicals in the United States, having nearly doubled between 1865 and 1870, doubled again during the next decade.[24]

Crofutt ceased publication of his ailing *Western World*, but the annual *Crofutt's Trans-Continental Tourist* was a different matter. This could be subcontracted as a going concern and Crofutt did so, transferring the publishing rights to George W. Carleton & Co. of Madison Square, New York, and to Sampson Low & Co. in London, who specialized in the distribution of American publications.

Carleton's was a major publishing house which already handled a number of guides and travel books among its extensive interests. The company announced the forthcoming 7th edition (6th annual revision) of "Crofutt's celebrated Guide Book" for 1875 with the confident prediction that the circulation would exceed even that of previous years. . . .

"owing to the extraordinary demand, the value and interest of its contents, and its low retail price of $1.50."

Carleton then addressed potential advertisers:

"It is usual for guide-books to contain a large number of advertisements interspersed throughout the works; in fact it would be impossible for such a book as the present one will be, to be sold without a revenue from this source.

We do not advise parties who only solicit retail trade to use this book as an advertising medium, but confidently commend it to connecting Railroad, Steamboat and Stage Lines, or Manufacturers, Jobbers, and others, who are able and desirous to do business with people from all parts of the world.

Advertisers shoud bear in mind that CROFUTT'S TRANS-CONTINENTAL TOURIST goes into the hands of the wealthy people of the world — those who can afford to travel — those who have the means to purchase what they want. Many of these books will be bought by people who reside west of the Missouri, but far the greater number by capitalists, manufacturers, merchants, jobbers and others from the Eastern portion of the United States, and from the Old World. . . .

PRICES FOR ADVERTISING SPACE are invariably as follows:

One-fourth of a page, one year	$100
One-half of a page, one year	$150
One page, one year	$275

Small *prominent* spaces on maps, from $50 to $75 each.
Cards in BUSINESS DIRECTORY, under appropriate headings, one year $10; or $5 a line (more or less twelve words to a line)."

*   *   *

Thus with heavy promotion and expensive advertising rates, Carleton & Co. took over the publication of *Crofutt's Trans-Continental Tourist* in 1875 with a strong bid for a share of the affluent and expanding European market, as well as a new sales drive in the eastern United States. This was to include wider distribution of the guide on the railroad routes out of New York. Crofutt meanwhile came to terms with the fact that once before, nearly twenty years earlier in Pennsylvania, he had been forced to change job and direction after the Panic of 1857; he must do so again now to escape the doldrums of the mid-Seventies. This time, however, he would not go West but stay put in New York City, capitalize on his immediate surroundings, and start a new career. He chose the hotel business.

Running a first-class hotel was the ambition of many successful American businessmen in the nineteenth century. For Crofutt, who had spent so much of his time continually on the move, running a hotel of his own held many attractions. From coast to coast, friends and acquaintances were already doing the same. In March 1874, for example, railroad ticket agent William Knowland had, with a partner from Delmonico's restaurant, opened the new, elegant St. Omer hotel at Manhattan's fashionable 23rd Street and Sixth Avenue. In recent years, there was nothing Crofutt had liked more than the bustle and variety of life at the Park Hotel — the comings and goings of old friends and correspondents from the West, along with the buzz of news and gossip from the editors, reporters, artists, printers, agents, and city businessmen milling around the lobby, dining-room and bar.

Crofutt was a lively talker and good listener; his drive and enthusiasm were the characteristics that most people remembered — "Chock-full of ideas and energy" recalled one, while another recorded Crofutt typically welcoming or looking up old friends, moving round a room, or along the street, shaking hands and exchanging news. In any event, Crofutt reasoned that once he was free of the demands of editing and publishing, he could derive both pleasure and profit from devoting all his time to the Park Hotel. In December 1874, the lease was transferred from Albert A. Durand, who had been the Park's proprietor and manager for some years, and Crofutt, full of new plans, celebrated the New Year with boundless optimism.

The Park had been built in the late 1840s and contained 140 rooms in its six-story block on the corner of Nassau and Beekman Streets, always a popular location just behind New York's 'Newspaper Row'. One of Crofutt's first decisions was to employ B.H. Skinner as his hotel manager. Benjamin Skinner was the old friend from Chicago whom Crofutt had first met in 1869 when he was there putting the finishing touches to Sloan's *Salt Lake City Directory*, and staying at the Briggs House while he did so.

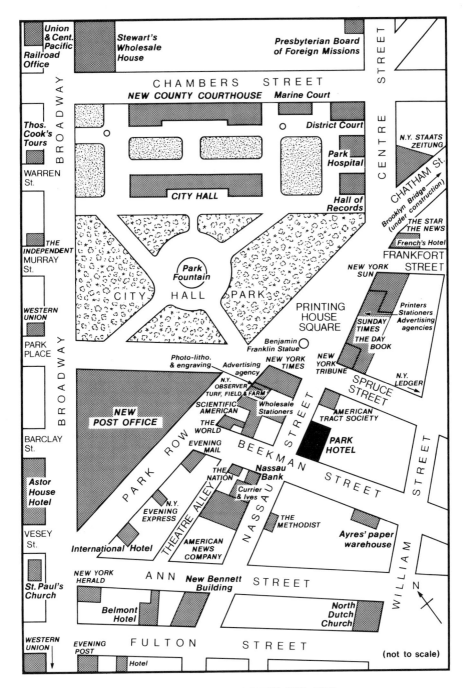

Union & Cent. Pacific Railroad Office

Stewart's Wholesale House

Presbyterian Board of Foreign Missions

STREET

CHAMBERS STREET

NEW COUNTY COURTHOUSE Marine Court

District Court

BROADWAY

Thos. Cook's Tours

Park Hospital

N.Y. STAATS ZEITUNG

CENTRE STREET

WARREN St.

CITY HALL

Hall of Records

CHATHAM St.

Brooklyn Bridge (under construction)

THE STAR THE NEWS

THE INDEPENDENT
MURRAY St.

French's Hotel

FRANKFORT STREET

NEW YORK SUN

WESTERN UNION

Park Fountain

CITY   HALL   PARK

PRINTING HOUSE SQUARE

Printers Stationers Advertising agencies

SUNDAY TIMES

THE DAY BOOK

PARK PLACE

BROADWAY

Benjamin Franklin Statue

SPRUCE STREET

N.Y. LEDGER

Photo-litho. & engraving

NEW YORK TIMES

NEW YORK TRIBUNE

Advertising agency

N.Y. OBSERVER
TURF, FIELD & FARM

NEW POST OFFICE

SCIENTIFIC AMERICAN

Wholesale Stationers

AMERICAN TRACT SOCIETY

STREET

BARCLAY St.

THE WORLD

EVENING MAIL

BEEKMAN   STREET

PARK HOTEL

STREET

Astor House Hotel

THE NATION

Nassau Bank

Currier & Ives

NASSAU

PARK ROW

N.Y. EVENING EXPRESS

THE METHODIST

VESEY St.

THEATRE ALLEY

AMERICAN NEWS COMPANY

Ayres' paper warehouse

WILLIAM

International Hotel

St. Paul's Church

NEW YORK HERALD

ANN   New Bennett Building   STREET

N

WESTERN UNION

Belmont Hotel

North Dutch Church

EVENING POST

FULTON   STREET

(not to scale)

Hotel

IX.   LOWER MANHATTAN IN THE MID-1870s:
BROADWAY, CITY HALL, AND THE PRINTING DISTRICT

based on the Insurance Maps of the City of New York, surveyed and published
by Perris and Browne, 164 Fulton Street (survey dated June 23, 1875);

on Crofutt's map of the Park Hotel and its surroundings (1876);

and on other sources

Skinner had been in the hotel business in Chicago for more than twenty years, first as manager of the Metropolitan, and then as proprietor and manager of the Briggs. After the great Chicago fire of October 1871, which destroyed nearly all of the city's finest hotels, the Briggs House, like the Grand Pacific, the Palmer House, the Tremont, the Sherman and others had been speedily rebuilt. Some of Chicago's biggest hotels had only just been completed before the fire wiped them out, but the Briggs was twenty years old and the opportunity was taken to modernize it completely during reconstruction. In May 1873, Skinner had returned as hotel manager, before being attracted by Crofutt's offer to come to New York in 1875 and manage the Park.

After more than twenty-five years, however, the Park Hotel was itself badly in need of renovation. It had no elevator, and the furniture, fittings

46.   PRINTING HOUSE SQUARE, LOWER MANHATTAN, LOOKING SOUTHWEST
Lith. by Endicott & Co., c.1865

Crowds have gathered in the heart of New York's printing and business district to watch a parade of Union troops through Lower Manhattan. Park Row and St. Paul's Church can be seen on the right, the end of Nassau Street to the left of the *New York Times* building. The Park Hotel lies farther down Nassau, adjoining the block visible but one story higher. Currier & Ives' workshop is shown at the junction of Nassau and Spruce Streets.

and decorations were faded and old-fashioned. Albert Durand had been content with the comfortable, "lived-in" look of the place but Crofutt now decided that in New York in the mid-1870s, something a lot smarter was required. Even the legendary Astor House on Broadway was currently closed for extensive modernization.

In the early months of 1875, Crofutt invested heavily in making internal structural alterations to the Park Hotel. He had an elevator installed and with the help of a small army of builders and decorators quickly refurbished throughout with new furniture, carpets, bedding, curtains, paint and wallpapers. By the summer of 1875, the proud new proprietor of the Park advertised that he was now ready

> "to meet all his old friends from the Trans-Mississippi country, from the South and from other parts of the world, and would do all in his power to make their stay in New York City pleasant, and if possible, profitable.
>
> The Park Hotel is located in the very heart of downtown business, within one block of City Hall, the new Post Office, close to Printing House Square, and the great publication offices of the city ... near the *Herald, Times, Tribune, World, Sun,* and other leading journals, with *Horse-Cars* from the door to all parts of the city — places of amusement, all depots, all steamboat landings, all ferries. It is just the place for merchants and businessmen to stop.
>
> The prices are also an inducement as good rooms range from $4.00 to $14.00 per week. Transient guests from 75 cents to $2.00 per day. European Plan affording superior comfort at reasonable terms."

A rare, probably unique photograph illustrating the excellent central location of the Park Hotel appears in the great Panorama taken in 1874 by William W. Silver from the top of the new Post Office building, which was then still under construction. Other major new building and development projects in Lower Manhattan were also going ahead all around — from the Brooklyn Bridge, to the new Western Union offices, and the flamboyant bulk of the *New York Tribune* whose tall new tower block on Printing House Square was, in every sense, one in the eye for the *Trib's* competitors.

Despite all Crofutt's efforts, however, indeed partly because of them, business prospects by the end of 1875 were going from bad to worse. In less than two years, Crofutt's hotel venture would become a total disaster. The prevailing economic conditions blighted general confidence and growth; recession, unemployment and wage cuts in the wake of the 1873 Panic became worse in the mid-Seventies, coast to coast. By 1875, half-a-million were out of work, while in 1876-7, more than 18,000 companies failed in the United States. Not until 1878-9 did the depression begin to lift for many industries and small businesses.

Only a trickle of visitors and old friends now arrived from the West to see Crofutt, and to stay at the Park Hotel. Indeed, across the country, few people were travelling at all unless they had to, and even the local non-resident trade declined miserably. Crofutt was to discover the hard way that hotels are always among the first casualties in any financial depression. Added to the loss of trade was the fact that Crofutt's ambitious renovation of the hotel during the slump had placed an intolerable financial mill-stone around his neck. Ironically, Benjamin Skinner may have made matters worse in this respect with talk of the latest post-fire improvements to the Briggs House in Chicago, a 'new look' hotel he had managed but not had to pay for.

Crofutt's own savings, along with the large sums he had borrowed for the renovation, were swallowed by the Park Hotel. With increased running costs, and so much capital invested in the new elevator and in up-graded bedroom accommodation, Crofutt may only then have begun to appreciate how much the old Park, located in the centre of Lower Manhattan's crowded business district, had depended on its bar and restaurant receipts. The Park was not small, there was steady competiton from other hotels and boarding-houses close by, and its room occupancy was never sufficient to allow Crofutt to break even, much less show a profit. The bar and restaurant trade could not save the day.

Few local merchants, banks, or businessmen were in a position to extend long-term, low-interest credit during the depression of the mid-1870s, and Crofutt soon owed money to grocers, butchers, wine and spirit merchants, and a host of others. The Centennial year of 1876 was, for Crofutt, one long dismal catalogue of promissory notes, chattel mortgages, rent demands, and unpaid bills. The manager and officials at Crofutt's bank, the Nassau, had literally watched over the renovations to the Park in 1875 and the mounting debt that followed, for the bank was directly opposite the hotel, on another corner of Nassau and Beekman Streets. By a curious coincidence, the Nassau Bank occupied the same site on which showman P.T. Barnum had once opened an office as a publisher's agent and advertising copy-writer, soon after his arrival in New York from Danbury, more than thirty years before.

By January 1877, Crofutt lacked the cash even to pay the wages of the hotel's live-in staff; cooks, clerks, elevator-boy, bell-boy, chambermaids and maintenance men were all hammering on his door. Overwhelmed by debt, Crofutt was declared bankrupt the following month on his own petition.[25] "Hotel-keeping," his old boss, publisher J.M. Emerson had once reported, noting the competition, "Hotel-keeping in New York has become a great business, requiring a large capital, a knowledge of the world, intelligence, liberality, and an enterprising spirit." Emerson was right; capital first, Crofutt had discovered, invested in better times and with better judgment.

Following Crofutt's petition for bankruptcy in February 1877, and the subsequent official announcements, thirty-eight creditors duly presented their claims to New York's Southern District Court on Fulton Street during the succeeding months. At a meeting of the Court in June 1877, Crofutt was found to owe a total of $32,685 to creditors who had proved their debts, $12,850 of which was owed in rent arrears to Sidney E. Morse, who had taken over the lease of the Park Hotel in May 1876.

In July 1877, the creditors appointed John H. Platt, a Wall Street lawyer, as Assignee of the bankrupt's estate and effects, but three months later Platt had to report to the Court that the case was one of 'No Assets', there being no money to hand, and no property of the bankrupt from which any money could be immediately realized. Small sums had been available to pay the hotel staff under Section 27 of the Bankruptcy Act (March 2, 1867), which in establishing a much-needed uniform procedural system for bankruptcy throughout the United States, authorized priority payment of wages due from a bankrupt "to any operative, clerk, or house servant to an amount not exceeding fifty dollars."

Crofutt's personal possessions were few — only clothing valued at seventy-five dollars. Although we cannot be certain, his wife, Anna Crofutt, does not appear to have been present, nor involved in any way in the hotel venture. Some of the creditors, impressed by Crofutt's established reputation as a writer and publisher, and by his air of optimism at all times, alleged that Crofutt must have illegally transferred his assets in advance. Examination of the available records, however, suggests that the creditors were misled by Crofutt's earlier exaggerated claims about the value of his 'Life Protector' patents, which were in fact worthless, as well as by his earlier speculative ventures in twelve, mostly mining, joint stock companies whose shares, likewise, had little or no value in the mid-1870s.

Crofutt meanwhile did not stay in New York while his affairs and his reputation were worked over in the Bankruptcy Court. He was one of many; bankrupts and creditors, tied together by failure, were streaming through the courts as thousands went out of business. The law permitted a bankrupt to apply for a discharge from his debts within one year of the adjudication of bankruptcy, and if no assets had come into the hands of the Assignee, the onus was then on the creditors to appear and to show cause why a discharge should not be granted. This was the best that Crofutt could hope for. Several friends had rallied round with hospitality and small loans to keep him going while he got back on his feet. Taking risks and going broke were typical of the times, and Crofutt appears to have suffered no lasting damage or personal defamation after the crash. Having completed all the Court statements, Crofutt placed his affairs in the hands of a solicitor and left New York at the beginning of June 1877. Where was he going? Back to the West, of course!

WHEN IN CHICAGO,

DO NOT FAIL TO STOP AT THE OLD-TIME

BRIGGS HOUSE.

LOCATED ON THE ORIGINAL SITE,

RANDOLPH STREET, CORNER FIFTH AVENUE,
CHICAGO, ILL.

This is one of the largest Hotels in the City or the West—having hot and cold water in every room, and all the modern improvements, passenger elevator, suites of rooms, and rooms with baths, etc., while the charges have been reduced to the nominal price of only $2.00 to $2.50 per day.

J. E. CUMMINGS,   J. H. CUMMINGS,
    Chief Clerk.   Proprietor.

ADVERTISEMENT FOR THE BRIGGS HOUSE, CHICAGO
in *Crofutt's New Overland Tourist, and Pacific Coast Guide,* 1878-9

CHAPTER SEVEN

Western Expansion in the 1870s and 1880s

New Demands For Information, Advertising, and Investment

Transport ▪ Tourists ▪ Health Seekers ▪ Settlers

"Never say you *can't* do a thing — and never cry 'broke' till you are dead." [1]

The robust philosophy of Phineas T. Barnum, that Universal Yankee, was helping him to forge his own way through the disasters and triumphs of the nineteenth century. George Crofutt, another Danbury man, was equally determined never to admit defeat.

"Flat-busted" in the east, and now aged fifty, Crofutt set out to follow the advice he had given so often during the 1870s to the many correspondents and visitors in New York who asked him:

"Where can I go in the West to make money?"

Crofutt's answer had always been the same:

"You can make money ANYWHERE in the great West, if you will peel off your coat and go to work . . . If you have any ambition and self-reliance, and will work at the first opportunity — and will hunt around for the opportunity —will let gambling, whiskey and kindred vices alone, you can make 'a bushel of money' in a few years, anywhere.

Make a good reputation — that is the main qualification . . .

Begin at the bottom of the ladder and climb up, learn gradually the ways of the country, to be able to take a step ahead *understandingly*. Don't wait for someone to proffer you nuggets of gold; remember, it must be your own industry, your own energy, and your own good manner that will bring success." [2]

It was a classic restatement of what many regarded as fundamental American values — a sober work ethic that would be applied by increasing numbers of immigrants to the New West. For some, it produced instant success, for others, modest but steady reward; for others again, especially small farmers from the humid East struggling to come to terms with the dry plains environment, hard work was not always enough. New legislation, new technology, and a new "understanding" would indeed be necessary to step ahead successfully into the late-nineteenth century West.

Leaving New York, Crofutt travelled first to Chicago, probably in the company of Benjamin Skinner, his former hotel manager who, after the New York débâcle was also now homeless and unemployed. In Chicago, Skinner quickly found work as a steward at the Palmer House, Potter Palmer's huge hotel on State Street; routine as it was, the job would keep him going until, with any luck, he could re-establish himself as a hotel manager.

Crofutt, for his part, was determined to return to writing and publishing as quickly as possible. He was not about to dispute the wisdom of Longfellow's conclusion that the "talent of success is nothing more than doing what you can do well." After spending the summer visiting some of his old haunts in the Rocky Mountain region and the Southwest, Crofutt returned briefly to Chicago and made plans to launch a new publishing company. He headed straight for his old stamping ground downtown, the northeast corner of Clark and Washington where, eight years earlier in a small room in the Larmon block, he had produced his first resounding success — the *Great Trans-Continental Railroad Guide*.

The Larmon block had been gutted in the Chicago fire of 1871, but a new office block, the Ashland, had been built on the same site. For convenience, and probably also for luck, Crofutt reserved an office in the Ashland block and then went off to stay at another familiar address, the Briggs House, on the corner of Randolph and Wells (Fifth Avenue).

He was not, however, going to let the disastrous year of 1877 end without seeing his name restored to the publishers' lists. Early in November 1877, Crofutt copyrighted a new periodical, *The American Patent Exchange, devoted to the interests of inventors and owners of patent property*, to be published by George A. Crofutt in New York, Chicago and San Francisco.[3] Nothing more was to come of this journal. It could scarcely have been thought of as a money-spinner, given the competition from the *Scientific American*, and it is unlikely that Crofutt himself at this stage regarded the copyright application, accompanied by the title-page, as anything more than a symbolic gesture to lift his spirits, and somehow maintain the continuity of his name in the publishing field during the dark days. He had other plans for the longer term.

Crofutt left Chicago again in mid-November 1877, and spent the next few months on an exhaustive fact-finding tour through the West to the Pacific. From dawn to dusk he filled one notebook after another with details of new settlements, new hotels, times, routes, distances, side-trips and a flood of new impressions. Once again, he found the West was acting as a tonic, new every morning. Portions of the West were on the threshold of great change, including a major tourist and rail transport revolution. If he could not bury his ruined fortunes from back East, once and for all under the open skies of opportunity in the West, it would not be for want of trying.

Crofutt returned to Chicago in the early part of 1878, opened his office in the Ashland block, announced the formation of a new company, the Overland Publishing Co., and immediately set about producing his trans-continental guidebook under his own imprint once again. But there was one significant change; Crofutt dropped the word 'trans-continental' from the title and replaced it with 'overland'. As a result of the enormous popularity of 'trans-continental' in the new western railroad age, 'overland' was acquiring a rarity value!

More specifically, Crofutt was forced to acknowledge that since the appearance of Henry T. Williams' elaborate and highly publicized trans-continental guide of 1876, Williams' book had grabbed the headlines, and the word-association — to say nothing of the lion's share of the sales also. What could you do when Williams assured readers that *his* Trans-Continental Guide contained more material than Crofutt, Nordhoff, and *Picturesque America* combined! Williams had also taken the unusual step, prior to publication, of circulating the proofs of his new guidebook in February 1876 so that he could print the favourable notices received inside the guide, as part of the first issue. Carleton and Low had both published *Crofutt's Trans-Continental Tourist* in 1875 and 1876, but Williams' success in '76 was decisive; Crofutt's publication was immediately dropped and the contract between him and the publishers severed. It was just one more nail in the coffin of 1877.

The Western guidebook market remained dominated in 1876 and 1877 by *The Pacific Tourist*. Williams' *Illustrated Trans-Continental Guide of Travel, from the Atlantic to the Pacific Ocean*. Ironically, Henry Williams was on Beekman Street in Lower Manhattan, only a few doors away from Crofutt's failed Park Hotel, now empty and boarded up as the crowds hurried past.

Eight hundred miles farther west in Chicago, Crofutt worked feverishly on his new guidebook, involving himself in every aspect of production in order to keep up the pace and make sure he did not miss the vital summer sales season. He made certain, as always, that his Index was comprehensive and well organized, and again kept the main text clear and uncluttered by placing additional background information in a separate Annex, also indexed and cross-referenced. By the end of April 1878 everything was ready and the new book was published as *Crofutt's New Overland Tourist, and Pacific Coast Guide . . . over the Union, Central and Southern Pacific Railroads, their branches and connections, by rail, water and stage . . ., 1878-79*. Nearly one hundred illustrations were included, with several of the engravings based on photographs from the well-known western specialists Charles R. Savage of Salt Lake City, and Carleton E. Watkins and Thomas Houseworth of San Francisco.

The *New Overland* was meant to be regarded as a continuation of Crofutt's earlier *Trans-Continental* series (of which, Crofutt reminded his readers, some 344,000 copies had been sold). He had taken time and trouble during his travels in 1877-8 to renew his network of contacts in the trans-Mississippi West, among them the railroad agents, wholesale distributors, hoteliers, stage-line operators, printers and local newspaper editors. He was still well known. Few knew or cared about his bankruptcy; anyone would tell you that most folks making a fresh start in the West were escaping from trouble of one sort or another.

Crofutt's New Overland Tourist, and Pacific Coast Guide. The Expansion of California's Regional Rail Network in the 1870s

Crofutt cut the price of his new guide to 75 cents for flexible cloth covers ($1.00, hard back), and then, once again, welcomed his fellow-travellers to the ever-changing West. Off they went together through the pages of the *New Overland Tourist*. The paying public would have to decide whether or not Henry T. Williams remained the unchallenged 'King of the Guidebook trade'.

As usual, passengers were involved from the word go in the multitude of changes, large and small, that lay behind the scenes. Regular improvements on the main Union and Central Pacific Railroads had already produced a new batch of western railroad 'antiquities' for travellers to identify; traces of the very recent past could be spotted where sections of track had been realigned, earlier temporary structures rebuilt, and some of the service centres and "eating stops" relocated. It is easy to forget how busy these places were just a short time ago, Crofutt told his readers, when all that is left for you to see now is a water-tank and a bit of side-track.

In western Nebraska, Crofutt recalled the early days of the Pony Express with the story of his old pioneering friend, James A. Moore, who had recently died. Before settling down as a trader at the military post near Sidney, Jim Moore had made one of the famous record-breaking rides by the Pony Express. On 8th June 1860, he had ridden from the Midway relay station on the south side of the Platte, 140 miles west to Julesburg. On arrival, he found an urgent dispatch just in from the Pacific. After resting *only seven minutes*, wrote Crofutt, and *without eating*, Jim returned to Midway, "making the 'round trip' — 280 miles — in fourteen hours and forty-six minutes." It was among the great classics of the Pony Express, an outstanding feat of speed and endurance.

Old stage stations, ranches, and the emigrants' and freighters' roads still formed an essential part of the total picture, but at Big Springs, near Julesburg, an area already notorious for danger and violence from the 'old days', Crofutt could now add news of a daring train robbery. Crime had also moved with the times:

> "On Sept. 18th 1877, a party of twelve masked men, armed with guns and revolvers, took possession of Big Springs station, bound and gagged the men, cut the telegraph wires, and when the western train arrived ... secured $65,000 from the express car, and $1300 and four gold watches from the passengers. Then the robbers mounted their horses, that had been hitched near by, and allowed the train to proceed. No person was killed or injured, but *all* experienced much difficulty for days in getting their hair to *lay down*; and, it is said among the railroad men, that even *now* a sudden shout of 'hands up' in the hearing of that express messenger will send his hat up three feet from his head ...

> Immediately after the robbery, a reward of $10,000 was offered for the arrest of the perpetrators; three have been caught and have paid the penalty of the crime with their lives. About one-half of the money has been recovered."

Despite the size of the reward offered by Wells, Fargo, little more of the money (mostly freshly minted gold coins) was ever recovered. The hold-up was the work of the Sam Bass gang, and other reports list six rather than twelve robbers. The three dead recorded by Crofutt were Bass's partner, Joel Collins, Bill Heffridge and Jim Berry. Later in 1878, Sam Bass died in Texas of gunshot wounds, on his twenty-seventh birthday. As the train rolled on from Big Springs' small, otherwise nondescript station, built opposite a line of bluffs and row of water-tanks, passengers could look about them and relive what was to remain one of the richest single train robberies in Western history.

There was a 30-minute "eating stop" at Cheyenne (population c.3500), the mid-point on the Union Pacific Railroad, and the largest town between Omaha and Ogden. Crofutt included a review of recent events in the relatively little-known Territories stretching away to the north of Cheyenne — from Crow Creek to the North Platte and the Powder River, in Wyoming, Montana and Dakota.

After the end of the Civil War, the 1860s had been a period of increasing confrontation between the Government and the Indians. Renewed hostility was triggered by the arrival of the Union Pacific Railroad and the creation of the town of Cheyenne in 1867; the late Sixties had seen the establishment of new army forts, the abandonment of others (Crofutt supplied the details), and the setting up of Indian reservations.

Pressures became worse in the 1870s. There had been rumours of gold deposits in the Black Hills region of Dakota Territory for many years, but nothing definite was known until Colonel George Custer's expedition to the Black Hills in 1874 reported abundant gold, as well as good soils, timber, and water supply. The whole area had been guaranteed by treaty to the Sioux but Custer's statement sparked a gold rush which began in 1875 and which was at its height in 1876-78. Crofutt again supplied the details. Passengers stretching their legs at Cheyenne could see part of the huge quantities of freight which were now being shipped northward from Cheyenne, the nearest point on the railroad, over the 260-mile wagon road to the mines and farms in the Black Hills. A daily stage also ran from Cheyenne to Deadwood.

But to those whose total knowledge of the region, and the issues, began and ended with outrage at the death of Custer and over 250 men under his command in the battle with the Sioux and Northern Cheyenne at the Little Big Horn in Montana, in June 1876 — Crofutt had this to say:

> "When gold was discovered in the Black Hills — *acknowledged* Indian country — and the white man commenced to invade it, the Government attempted to prevent their trespassing, and to keep faith with the Indians ... Finally, the Government 'winked' at emigration which it could not, or would not prevent.

47.   A PARTY OF GOLD MINERS SETTING OUT FROM CHEYENNE FOR THE
BLACK HILLS, DAKOTA TERRITORY, 1877

Frank Leslie's Illustrated Newspaper, October 6, 1877

This striking double-spread was one of the series of nearly two hundred illustrations made on 'The Frank Leslie Transcontinental Excursion to the Pacific Coast', April-June 1877. The pictures were published regularly in Leslie's weekly from July 1877 to July 1878. His staff artists on the trip were Harry Ogden and Walter R. Yeager, his staff photographer W.B. Austin. Frank Leslie and his wife led the party.

What see we now? The white man has *taken* the Indian's country, . . . and *driven* the Indians out, beggars as they are, with only the bread that the Government chooses to toss to them.

We are no 'Indian Lover', but if the Government . . . treated with the Indian, as an equal, where is our boasted 'civilization', when, though the lands do contain gold, we *take* them without a 'thank you', as the elephant would crush a toad. Does *might* make *right*?"

*   *   *

Crofutt's up-dating of the text on new settlement and new mineral strikes included the latest information on the narrow-gauge railroads that had sprouted from the main lines during the 1870s in Colorado, Utah and Nevada. Crofutt had checked the routes of the narrow-gauge, and added his own observations and background knowledge to the bare bones of distances and grades supplied by the railroads themselves.

Close to the border of Colorado and New Mexico, for example, on a new stretch of the Denver & Rio Grande railroad, Crofutt chatted his passengers through the magnificent mountain scenery around Spanish Peaks in typical style. At La Veta, on the south branch of Cuchara Creek and nearly 7000 feet above sea level, passengers watched an extra locomotive being added to the train and all spare cars left behind at the station.

For a while, the old Sangre de Cristo wagon road could be seen near the track, winding its way around the mountain. Before long, however, at Ojo, eyes were glued to the window to catch sight of an isolated tree on the skyline, directly ahead of the train, at the top of Dump Mountain:

"Now, notice the long reddish line encircling that mountain near its top. Do you see it? That is our road, and there, in front of that tree, we will be in half-an-hour, looking down at this station . . .

Up! up we go! On your right, that peak is Veta Mountain, 11,512 feet . . . Now keep your eye to the left — there is the road — can we ever get up there? The gorge narrows and darkens for nearly 3 miles before we reach the great Mule Shoe Curve . . ." Heads were swivelling in all directions. "The higher we go, the grander the view. Onward-upward. Ah, we have it! Look away down that little, narrow valley, and see *little Ojo* station, where we stood only a few minutes ago, and looked *up* — looked at the tree first — then located our present position."

Crofutt and his fellow-passengers drank in the beauty of the Spanish Peaks and the Sangre de Cristo mountain panorama before the train puffed its way up to the bleak summit of Veta Pass (9382 ft), where the only building was a small, stone-built station sheltered by a grove of trees. At this time, Veta summit was the highest railroad pass in the world. Then came the equally steep journey down through the pine and spruce

48. CROSSING THE SANGRE DE CRISTO MOUNTAINS ON THE DENVER &
RIO GRANDE RAILROAD
in *Crofutt's New Overland Tourist, and Pacific Coast Guide, 1878-9*

forests, via Garland, to San Luis Park, and to the rich farmland and stock-raising country around Alamosa on the Rio Grande, at the end of the line.

This spectacular narrow-gauge route had been pushed through the Sangre de Cristo Mountains with much of the road-bed nothing more than a ledge blasted from the walls of the ravines; the steep track was closely tied and double spiked. It had been built in less than two years. Work only started at Cucharas in May 1876, Crofutt reminded his readers, yet the railroad reached Garland in August 1877 and Alamosa in June 1878. But the cost had been crippling. Short of funds in the wake of the Panic of 1873, the Denver & Rio Grande could for the moment no longer pay its bills, and later in 1878 was leased to its new and powerful rival in south Colorado, the Atchison, Topeka & Santa Fe, until that particular railroad war was settled in 1880.

After exploring the scenery and excitements of this, and other narrow-gauge railroads, passengers were returned to the main line to discover what changes had occurred along the Union and Central Pacific routeway. The settlements of Wells and Elko in Nevada, for example, were expanding dramatically, thanks to discoveries of silver, copper, lead and iron ore about 35-40 miles southeast of Wells, and to the new silver bonanza in the Cope and Tuscarora districts, 50-80 miles north of Elko. In addition, there had been significant development in cattle ranching along this upper section of the Humboldt Valley.

Argenta, on the other hand, was now just a ghost station. Hill Beachy, the popular stage-line proprietor, had died in San Francisco in 1875 and Argenta no longer focused the region's stage and freighting business. The Central Pacific's former "eating stop" had been relocated, and the cluster of buildings, once so full of activity, now stood empty and echoing around an unimportant side-track.

Passengers instead took their meals at Battle Mountain Station twelve miles farther west, and the main stage and freighting centre between the railroad and the mining districts scattered to the south for the best part of seventy miles. There were several new stores, hotels, restaurants, saloons, and warehouses in Battle Mountain. Ranches had spread north of the town — "the country is alive with herds of cattle," Crofutt noted, adding that cattle buyers from California were now appearing regularly in town. Indeed, ranching and hay production was a major growth industry in this precious well-watered strip running across the Nevada desert. Crofutt reported that in 1878, the numbers of livestock along the Humboldt River and the adjacent valleys were estimated at 353,000 cattle and 30,000 sheep, and that in one year, 486 car-loads of cattle had been shipped to San Francisco, and 20 car-loads to Chicago.

49.   WOOD-HAULING IN NEVADA, BETWEEN GOLD HILL AND VIRGINIA CITY

in *Crofutt's Trans-Continental Tourist,* 1874

"The ten-mule team," Crofutt explained in a footnote, "is hauling three wagons coupled together like a train of cars — 'trail wagons' — on which are loaded twenty-four cords of wood."

Rich new silver strikes were made in the early Seventies in the Comstock region, where freighting had been boosted rather than reduced by completion of the Virginia & Truckee Railroad from Virginia and Carson Cities to Reno in 1871.

Crofutt packed his pages with facts and figures, impressions and tidbits all the way to California — and then proceeded to tackle California with gusto. There had been a whirlwind of change spinning through California along the tracks of the Central Pacific Railroad. By 1872, the all-powerful Central Pacific had gained control, one way or another, of California's several small independent railroad companies, including the California Pacific, the Western Pacific, the California & Oregon, and the Southern Pacific — the name later applied to the whole system. The 'Railroad Kings'' monopoly was not confined to railroads, wharves, and real estate, however; through their purchase of the California Steam Navigation Company, the 'Big Four' (Huntington, Stanford, Crocker and Hopkins) controlled the bulk of the State's river traffic, while their ocean steamship line, the Occidental and Oriental, organized in 1874, was to dominate the Pacific coastal trade within six years.

Competition was obliterated on all sides of the Bay Region — north, south, east and west — and single management extended along the routes of operation. Crofutt's guide neither concealed nor laboured the fact of the railroad's monopoly. In any case, few were fooled by the fiction of separate management and control among the variously named transport companies. As Grace Greenwood reported to the *New York Times* in 1872, putting the development dilemma in a nutshell:

> the town of Merced's business had been greatly increased thanks to "the elegant new hotel El Capitan, built by the Central Pacific Railroad Company, — that dreadful monopoly that brings about so many beneficent improvements." [4]

Yet the scale of the economic and political power exerted by the Central Pacific-Southern Pacific organization was greater than many visitors and new arrivals realized, since the freedom from competition it enjoyed had few parallels elsewhere in the United States at this period. Amid the general wave of prosperity brought by the railroad — new towns, new farms, new businesses, new markets — individuals and small communities could be crushed in the grip of the giant railroad and landowning bosses.

Earlier material from *Crofutt's Trans-Continental Tourist* on the towns and cities, local excursions, soils, agriculture, industry, etc. was reworked and updated. Despite the huge increase in information that California's growth had generated, Crofutt's clear organization provided a succinct yet comprehensive survey; judged in terms of what it set out to do, the guide is as instructive and fascinating to read today, when following the same routes to record a century of change, as it was at the beginning of the railroad era. *Crofutt's New Overland Tourist* handled a wide-ranging western agenda, and was not intended to compete with books, periodicals, and other literature devoted exclusively to the Golden State. Even so, concise description and interpretation of the patterns of settlement, agriculture and industry around San Francisco and San Pablo Bays, together with the Contra Costa, Sacramento, Central Valley, and Coast Range regions, and beyond, were all skilfully woven, using a multitude of short threads, to reveal to Crofutt's fellow-travellers the varied and colourful fabric of Californian life.

San Francisco was uniquely cosmopolitan; visitors said so, and San Franciscans boasted of it. The city region was a world of its own. Many San Franciscans, if they thought about it at all, regarded the greater part of California's Central Valley as remote backland — landlocked and unfamiliar, both in climate and economy. The southern end especially

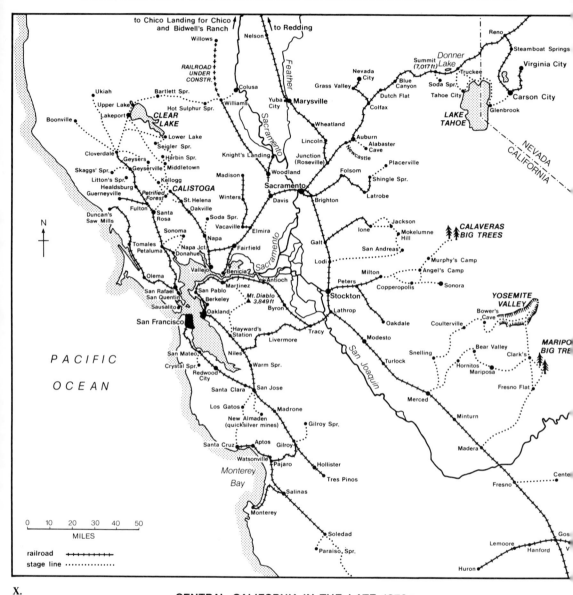

CENTRAL CALIFORNIA IN THE LATE 1870s
RAILROADS, STAGE LINES, AND MAJOR TOURIST ATTRACTIONS

based on *Crofutt's New Overland Tourist and Pacific Coast Guide* (1878-9)

was their own frontier, California's own 'Wild West'. If Crofutt's readers wanted to glimpse how California had changed in the 1870s, then among everything else on offer they would have to follow the railroad south from Sacramento, into the valley of the San Joaquin.

Stockton (pop. c.13,000) was the gateway to the southern section of the Central Valley, a huge lowland which, in all, stretched nearly 500

234

miles north-south and 50 miles east-west. The city was both a railroad junction and the head of river navigation on the San Joaquin for vessels of up to 200 tons; shallow-draught steamboats could normally go a further 150 miles upstream to Firebaugh. Stockton's early focus had been eastward, since its original interests were linked to the placer mining communities on the slopes of the Sierra Nevada. Now, Stockton more often looked south, for California's 'Windmill City', as Crofutt and others described it, had become the regional service centre for the San Joaquin Valley's expanding wheat trade, which had spread south from the Sacramento Valley and consolidated California's great wheat belt. "For a country so recently settled," Crofutt commented, "the amount of grain and stock raised in the San Joaquin Valley, and the hundreds of smaller ones tributary to it, is almost incredible."

The Central Pacific Railroad had pushed south through the San Joaquin Valley at top speed in the early 1870s. Plans to build along the coast had soon been dropped once the 'Big Four' had discovered that much of the land they required was already in private ownership under old Mexican land grants, whereas the San Joaquin Valley was still largely publicly owned. This gave the Central Pacific a virtually free hand in selecting its right of way and locating its land grants and services — a magic wand in the shape of a railroad track, which could create new towns, revitalize old ones, or isolate the few that could not, or would not, meet the railroad's demands.

The Central Pacific followed the eastern side of the valley, which was well watered by rivers from the High Sierra. The Coast Range to the west sheds only two small permanent streams into the southern section of the great Central Valley, and the almost complete lack of urban settlement on the western side of the plain was in sharp contrast to the eastern fringe. But this had had its advantages for another giant operator, since it was over the western and central floor of the valley that a second huge property-owning enterprise had been located — the ranch lands of Henry Miller and Charles Lux.

In a different section of the guide, Crofutt had drawn his readers' attention to Miller's home at Bloomfield, near Hollister, and to Lux's spread at Baden, twelve miles from San Francisco. Lux managed most of the firm's interests in the city, while Miller, the major force, organized company growth, and supervised much of the field and ranch work. Between them, these two 'cattle barons' would acquire grazing and water rights stretching for more than one hundred miles along both banks of the San Joaquin River, a fifty-mile stretch along the Kern River, and much else besides in California, Oregon and Nevada. By the end of the 1870s, Miller & Lux ranch hands were driving 1800 cattle into San Francisco every month, and in time were able to graze their stock each night on

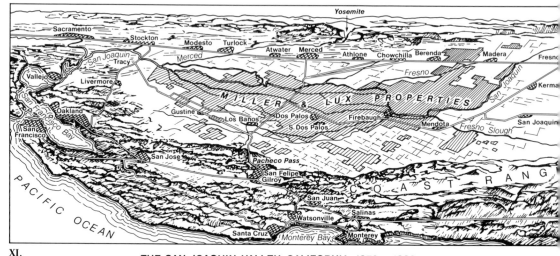

XI.

THE SAN JOAQUIN VALLEY, CALIFORNIA, 1870s–1880s
RAILWAYS, ROADS, AND THE MILLER & LUX PROPERTIES
Source: Wallace Smith, *Garden of the Sun* (1939), with minor amendment

company land along the full length of the trail from Los Angeles to San Francisco. At its height, as Miller continued to expand after Lux's death in 1887, this cattle-and-wheat empire owned more than a million head of livestock and well over a million acres of land in the Far West.

Passengers were now beginning to get the hang of the San Joaquin Valley. Wheat lands and storage elevators stretched away into the far distance as trains rumbled through Morano, Modesto and Atwater, and on to Merced, where town lots had been laid out and quickly sold by the Central Pacific on 8th February 1872. The railroad's hotel was named El Capitan as a reminder that Merced was one the main starting points for excursions to the Yosemite Valley [Map X].

James Hutchings' pioneering work in publicizing Yosemite had begun in 1855, and during the 1860s, painters, sketchers, photographers, surveyors and geologists had all helped to boost Yosemite's reputation as one of the most breathtaking sights in the United States. Its towering granite walls and plunging waterfalls perched high above a mosaic of forest, lake and meadow covering the valley floor, were sheer poetry to the eye, and an inspiration to the soul. Yet in the nine years between 1856 and 1864, Yosemite had a total of only 653 registered visitors, and even after the Civil War, there was no dramatic increase. Many Easterners and Europeans who were keen to explore this Californian wonderland were not prepared to cross the West by stagecoach in order to do so.

"I have just finished six days and nights of this thing [stagecoach travel]," wrote Demas Barnes in 1865, tired and irritable after completing only the first week of his overland journey through the West. "Until I forget a great many things, ... I shall not undertake it again."

He pressed on "over the most wretched of roads," a lively and observant traveller who nevertheless saw no particular virtue in 'roughing it'. "Dust, deep and thick, is the staple production of this country."

In California, the dust merely changed colour. "I endeavoured to be romantic, but I could not."

Barnes returned to New York via Panama, glad to be home after "an interesting, but not a pleasant trip" across the West.[5]

The completion of the transcontinental railroad changed all that. Central California's major scenic attractions located on, or within a day or so's journey from the main line, soon felt the effect.

THE FIRST KNOWN PICTURE OF THE YOSEMITE VALLEY, CALIFORNIA

in C.P. Russell, *One Hundred Years in Yosemite*, 1931, from the Yosemite Museum

One of the original pencil sketches made by Thomas A. Ayres, an artist who accompanied James Hutchings on the first tourist excursion into the Valley in June 1855 and helped to publicize the outstanding beauty of the region.

El Capitan is on the left, Bridalveil Fall and Cathedral Rocks on the right.

51.   STAGECOACH AND FREIGHT WAGONS TRAVELLING THROUGH THE
SIERRA NEVADA IN 1865

Drawn by A.C. Warren; Engraved by James L. Langridge, in A.D. Richardson,
Beyond the Mississippi, 1867

The artist omits the choking clouds of dust, but includes a water-cart attempting to lay
some of it, bottom left!

"When our pleasure-seekers on the Eastern coast," prophesied another New York in 1867-8, "can reach in a week such objects of wonderful grandeur and beauty as the Yosemite, Lake Tahoe, and the High Sierras, there will be crowds taking the summer trip."[6]

In 1869 alone, Yosemite recorded a total of 1122 visitors, and the extension of the Central Pacific Railroad along the San Joaquin Valley in the early Seventies sent fresh waves of tourists from Europe and the Eastern States surging into Yosemite and the Mariposa Grove of Big Trees. In 1875, 2423 visitors were recorded. By the end of the 1870s, there were as many as seven competing routes into the Valley starting from various points on the railroad. In Merced, the El Capitan hotel accommodation was soon inadequate, and the proprietors used Silver Palace Sleeping Cars to handle the overflow while new building went ahead.

By 1878, Crofutt found Merced to be in the centre of one of the richest and most varied agricultural regions in the San Joaquin Valley. Not only was its wealth based on wheat, barley, corn and rye; increasing vegetable, tobacco and cotton production reflected the extension in the mid-1870s of a network of irrigation canals branching from the new, 100-mile-long San Joaquin Valley & King's River Canal.[7] Rivers brimmed with snow-melt from the Sierra Nevada. More canals were planned. Techniques of diverting water long distances by flumes and sluices had been learned by the gold miners; before long, similar techniques were being applied to agriculture, where they revolutionized land use in the south Central Valley. Large-scale canal work had started here in 1871-72. It was the beginning of what became an increasingly ambitious system of water transfers from water-surplus to water-deficient areas within and outside the Valley; in time, it developed into one of the most remarkable irrigation projects in the world.

As the train rolled on, travellers noted some of the other sources of water supply for this thirsty land. At Stockton and elsewhere, Crofutt had drawn attention to the windmills and the cupola-covered water tanks on the tops of the houses, from which pipes supplied domestic needs, irrigated the gardens, and then ran any surplus into adjacent fields. Beyond Fresno, windmills were raising good water from wells at depths of 15 to 40 feet, and new irrigated lots were being laid out as farming colonists arrived. It was not only the physical size and weight of California's crops that astounded everyone; the sheer *variety* of produce was breathtaking, a veritable dictionary of fruit, dried fruit, vegetables, nuts, vines, cereals and fibres needing only a guaranteed market to explode into increased production.

Recent railroad settlements were just out of the stagecoach age, and many now had a dual role as railroad town and trans-shipment point for the surrounding stage and freight lines. Visalia, the Tulare County seat, had about 1500 people; Tulare itself, still a wool clip and sheep ranching centre, only about 500, although its new function as a railroad division link had brought fresh employment, a round house, and extensive workships screened by rows of eucalyptus trees.

Beyond Lerdo (where, readers learned, some 40 miles away to the southwest oil could be found seeping into ditches and holes in the ground in the Buena Vista district), the train ran close to Bakersfield. This was the Kern County seat, still with a small population of c.800 but busily expanding its livestock production and irrigated cropland with a network of canals from Kern River, and from wells and windmills.

Soil fertility was exceptionally high; matching the excellent climate to a good water supply, one rancher (H.P. Livermore), whom Crofutt had met nine miles from Bakersfield, was getting four to six crops of alfalfa annually from his land. The ranch covered 7000 acres and contained two strongly-flowing artesian wells (260 ft and 300 ft deep) which were discharging over 80,000 gallons of water a day into 150 miles of canals and irrigation ditches. On this ranch, along with the rancher's second spread nearer to Bakersfield, 3500 acres were under alfalfa, and 3000 acres under wheat and barley. The livestock totalled 8000 sheep, 4300 cattle, 1500 hogs, 350 horses, 100 oxen and 70 mules. Then there were the prodigious irrigated crops of pumpkins, sweet potatoes and other vegetables close by!

Right, left and centre, readers were staggered by the uniqueness, wealth and future potential of Californian agriculture. California is like that, Crofutt observed cheerfully — we could fill the guidebook with astonishing figures. "But, for the moment, enough of this," as he hurried everyone on towards Los Angeles.

The last spike on the railroad linking San Francisco and Los Angeles had been driven as recently as 5th September 1876 — near Lang, in the wild, bear-hunting country between the Tehachapi Mountains and the Mojave Desert. Crofutt had met John Lang, after whom the small, last-spike station was named, in January 1878. Lang was a rancher in the rugged, 25-mile Soledad Canyon which was otherwise populated mostly by Mexicans. Before the Southern Pacific railroad pushed through to end its isolation, Soledad Canyon was better known as the "Robbers' Roost", hideout of the notorious Vásquez gang. But several of these bandits are now dead, Crofutt added reassuringly, including their leader, Tiburcio Vásquez, who was captured near Los Angeles in May 1874, and hanged at San Jose on 19th March 1875. "Later, a band of a dozen or more raided Caliente . . . and with all they could carry returned to *this*, their rendez-vous. By a shrewd plan, five were captured, and lodged in jail at Bakersfield, from which they were taken by the citizens and hung without much expense to the county." Passengers gazed nervously at the steep, gloomy walls of the canyon, slashed by narrow crevices, half-expecting to see signs of the villains still lurking behind the rocks. John Lang, however, had been left alone by the gang, given his reputation as a well-armed hunter of the region's giant grizzlies. Lang and his wife in fact stayed put for the rest of their days, and with the coming of the railroad, turned 'Lang's Springs' nearby into a noted health resort.

Beyond the canyon, the journey continued through cattle and sheep ranches, and a small but potentially rich oil-producing region. Dry, dun-coloured landscapes were again bridging the way to the rich greens of irrigated agriculture. Once past the two oil refineries at Andrews, and the long San Fernando tunnel, passengers prepared themselves for the delights of Los Angeles (pop. c.11,000). Essentially, for the time being, it was a railroad company town, but "completely embowered in foliage . . . irrigated by the Los Angeles River, and by windmills. Vineyards in and around Los Angeles are equaled only by the number of orange, lemon, and fruit orchards . . . It is a city of gardens and groves."

THE SOUTHERN PACIFIC RAILROAD PASSING THROUGH CITRUS GROVES AND CATTLE RANCHES NEAR LOS ANGELES, LATE 1870s

Readers were guided through the miles of tropical and semi-tropical fruit lands stretching south and east of the city, and through the small surrounding settlements — some newly served by the railroad, others still by stagecoach. Beautiful, sheltered Santa Monica had been laid out as a town as recently as 1875, and with its formerly independent 18-mile railroad to Los Angeles now controlled by the Central Pacific, its fine firm sandy beach, safe swimming and balmy air, Santa Monica was fast establishing itself as a spa and tourist resort. Santa Monica had another asset, Crofutt added, a highly enterprising booster called L.T. Fisher who edited Santa Monica's weekly newspaper — the *Outlook*.

Tourists were spoilt for choice between the delights of the Pacific coast, scenic drives through the mountains, excursions to old mission sites, or the chance of taking a closer look at the farm lands or the desert country. Prospective settlers found water supply and transport the controlling factors on farm prices. Given the high productivity and multiple harvests on irrigated land, sub-divisions of 7½, 15 or 30 acres were selling well at the Indiana Colony of Pasadena, some ten miles northeast of Los Angeles — "it was just an adobe ranch house five years ago," Crofutt recalled. Land without water could be picked up for a song, but at the Riverside Colony, for example, near San Bernardino, highly productive irrigated land was now worth $100 - $150 per acre, and prices were rising.[8]

Santa Ana, 33 miles southeast of Los Angeles, was at the end of the track. San Diego was marooned another 100 miles farther south, and had to make do with a daily stagecoach service to and from the railhead. Work on the Texas & Pacific Railway had still not been resumed in the aftermath of the 1873 Panic. The track was stuck at Fort Worth, Texas, and San Diego's population (a mere 2500 or so) had watched the plans, and all the optimism of the early 1870s, fizzle out. "The citizens are exceedingly anxious," wrote Crofutt. "By act of Congress, San Diego is the western terminus of the Texas & Pacific railroad, but *when* the road will be built, if ever, is the problem."

In fact, the Texas & Pacific Railroad was never to be built as planned. The 'Stay in Texas Railroad' would have been a better name, for that was to be the result of the financial Panic of 1873, coupled with the Southern Pacific's determination not to allow any competing railroad into California. The Texas & Pacific had clearly meant business in the early 1870s, and presented a real threat to the 'Big Four's' expanding monopoly. The Texas & Pacific quickly made their presence known, striding about their western routeway, shipping supplies into a jubilant San Diego, and starting work outside the town. At Yuma, a bridging point for the railroad over the Colorado River was also surveyed. For California's 'Railroad Kings', none of this would do at all.

As the financial depression deepened in the wake of the Panic, the 'Big Four' seized their opportunity. Huntington's skilful lobbying in Washington, D.C. successfully defeated the attempts by Thomas A. Scott, of the Pennsylvania Railroad, to get a subsidy bill for the Texas & Pacific through Congress.[9] In the late 1870s, therefore, it was the Southern Pacific that raced to the California-Arizona boundary at Yuma, bridged the Colorado River, and established a regular freight and passenger steamer service along 365 miles of the Colorado, water levels permitting.

The Southern Pacific Railroad went on to reach Tucson in 1880, and El Paso, Texas in 1881, where it connected with the stump of the Texas & Pacific. In 1881, the Southern Pacific also made a connection with the Atchison, Topeka & Santa Fe at Deming, New Mexico. The Southern Pacific thus dominated the first southern transcontinental line in the United States, and by January 1883, its own 'Sunset Route' extended all the way from San Francisco and Los Angeles to New Orleans.

It was not until the Atchison, Topeka & Santa Fe Railroad, in cooperation with the Atlantic & Pacific, managed to break into Southern California at The Needles in 1883-4 that San Diego was rescued from oblivion, and not until November 1885 that the town was able to celebrate its through connection to the eastern rail networks. All this was years ahead; in the late 1870s, San Diegans gazed out across their magnificent bay in despair, feeling that on the landward side the railroad appeared to have abandoned them for ever.

After seeing for themselves the effects of railroad politics in San Diego's isolated 'stagecoach corner' of the State, Crofutt and his fellow-passengers returned to Los Angeles and then travelled southeastwards to Yuma, beyond which the Southern Pacific Railroad in 1878-9 could take them nearly 200 miles further into Arizona, towards Tucson. The trip through southeastern California to the Colorado River was captivating to the end, with spectacular contrasts in landform, vegetation, and land use. The eye could sweep from high mountains down into depressions below sea level. Colours were splashed about in dazzling variety — the vivid greens of irrigated acreage; the amber tints of dry ranching; the varied shades of palms and cactus, mesquite and sage; the dappled-greys of old mission buildings; and the red tiles and white dust of small adobe villages drowsing in the American-Mexican borderland.

The speed of change in California had been a dominant theme, astonishing the passengers ever since they had crossed the State line and rolled through the lumbering town of Truckee, in the High Sierra. Indeed, the passengers on the railroad — tourists, merchants, settlers, drifters — were all ingredients of that change. It was hard to keep pace. Real old-timers on the Pacific coast, those who had pioneered in the 1830s and early 1840s, vowed that California had been going to the dogs ever since

1849. In turn, 'forty-niners' and the like, if too old or too unwilling to change with the times, complained that the real rot had set in in 1869!

Inevitably, the lessening of California's isolation by the completion of the transcontinental railroad had required rapid adjustments to be made; it was not roses all the way. Local merchants and manufacturers, for example, were exposed to intense competition from the major companies in Chicago and the Northeast, and San Francisco's hopes of becoming an important new gateway for world trade from the Orient had been killed by the opening of the Suez Canal. Nevertheless, despite panics, the 1870s were a decade of phenomenal growth in California; by 1880, the State's population had soared to nearly 865,000 (over one-quarter of them in San Francisco), an increase of more than 54 per cent since 1870. Though future growth rates varied in northern and southern California, the Sunset Land was to remain a unique economic and demographic miracle, in both the perceptions and the realities of American life.

*   *   *

Crofutt had advertised his *New Overland* guidebook as "the cheapest and the best." At 75 cents (or $1.00 hard-bound), sales were soon climbing, carefully nourished by widespread promotion. Crofutt had attracted two new local investors in Chicago, H. Montgomery White and Charles Tuerk, and had set enough money aside to advertise the *New Overland Tourist* in selected major towns and cities right across the United States. Advertisements were fundamentals, not frills; new products had to be launched with a bang, not with a whimper.

To supplement the main distribution from Chicago, Crofutt had arranged for extra copies of the guide to be printed in Omaha and Denver. Crofutt still had several contacts in Denver, but in Omaha he was delighted to find Henry Gibson, a Colorado pioneer he had first met in the early 1860s. Gibson now ran the largest printing works in Omaha, and with seventy workers supplied customers as far west as Utah and Montana from his Herald Book and Job Printing House and Book Bindery on Farnam Street.

All the effort proved worthwhile. The reviews of the *New Overland Tourist, and Pacific Coast Guide* were like rays of sunshine, lifting the spirits and highlighting the qualities that made Crofutt's guides so popular. Once again, the press praised the authenticity, the coverage, and the wealth of detail provided. Here was a guidebook that was comprehensive and factual, yet readable; its material was manageable, not overwhelming. New York, San Francisco and Chicago set the ball rolling once again:

> *"What Crofutt has left untold in his New Overland Tourist seems unnecessary for the traveler to know,"* wrote The American Bookseller in New York; *"it's*

up to date and describes with telegraphic conciseness. Its convenience and value have been tested for a decade, and have brought it a reputation it needs no words of ours to confirm."

"Mr. Crofutt is abundantly able to furnish us with information regarding the country along the routes described, having traveled over it ere a railroad was thought of, and afterwards going carefully along the lines getting facts and data, and refreshing his memory with associations among once-familiar scenes and faces." (*Pacific Coast Review*) Added San Francisco's *Daily Post:* "It is indispensable to the railroad traveler . . . while to those who have been unable to make the overland journey, it comes nearer giving a vivid idea of what there is to be seen than any other work."

"The information in the New Overland Tourist is the result of actual observations and acquaintance on the part of the author. Mr. Crofutt has made the compilation of this and similar books his business for many years, and he speaks of that whereof he knows, and describes that which he himself has seen . . . From our own observation of fellow-travelers following the facts of Crofutt's Guide, station by station, we know such a book to be not only a luxury but almost a necessity for the unacquainted tourist or emigrant." (The Advance, Chicago)

Westerners welcomed his return, happy to see their own resources boosted through the efforts of "Crofutt, the popular pioneer Coloradoan . . . No tourist, east or west, aye, no western or eastern center-table, should be without the *New Overland Tourist . . .*" advised Denver's *Rocky Mountain Herald,* while James Hutchings wrote again to Crofutt from Yosemite: "What puzzles me is this . . . How you could gather so many interesting facts, and put them invitingly into so small a space."

"Crofutt's New Overland Tourist and Pacific Coast Guide should be in every family and school library, every business office and every reading room in the Union."

"It simply gives the answers to all the questions the traveler will naturally ask . . . taking the reader along and showing him not only everything of interest along the route of the Pacific railroads, but a thousand things which no traveler who clings to one route alone would ever see."

The *Kansas City Times* concluded that "Mr. Crofutt has now a most enviable reputation for his guide, which is the most concise and valuable publication of the kind ever produced in this country."

"It is one of the most sensible, practical guidebooks we ever found," reported the *St. Louis Evening Tribune. "It tells the traveler just what he ought to know, and leaves out useless matter."*

Thus, in 1878, the guide was back on the railroads, the news-stands, and at several of the major bookstores from coast to coast; in 1879, Crofutt moved from the Ashland block to more spacious accommodation at Chicago's first-class Grand Pacific Hotel on La Salle, Jackson and Clark, so as to handle the orders and distribution of the second edition (vol. 2), for 1879-80. Sales demand had outstripped even the most optimistic forecasts, and successive reprints that year reveal not only the growth of the market but also the care with which each reprint was updated, where appropriate, with the latest developments.

Once again, Crofutt spent the winter and early spring ('78-'79) travelling extensively in the West, checking and expanding the text, riding the rails and the stage lines, walking and climbing the trails, finding viewpoints, asking questions. A study of the clips of widely scattered local news reporters, assigned to the regular chore of waiting in railroad stations, stage-line offices, or hotel lobbies to record the new arrivals in town, helps to reveal the speed and range of Crofutt's travels, as well as his enormous physical energy. Fresh in from one journey, the writer of the *New Overland Tourist* guide would be reported as off in the next day or two on another lengthy trip, collecting material and, as usual, "combining business with pleasure." Crofutt's ceaseless round of arrivals and departures always appears to have left the clear impression that besides having to make a living, he roamed the West as a labour of love.

There was good news at last from New York. Undercut by Crofutt, *Williams' Illustrated Trans-Continental Guide* ceased to be a major competitor after 1878. Williams' guide, which sold at $2, or $1.50 for the flexibly-covered Railroad Edition, was twice the price of *Crofutt's New Overland Tourist*, and the price war was undoubtedly one factor in Williams' decision to withdraw. Williams had, after all, stressed the expense involved at the start of his Preface, which had deftly knocked any individual author as being unequal to the task, while boosting the advantages of team effort:

> "Few can form an adequate idea of the immense field required to be covered by a Trans-Continental Guide. The amount of labor, personal travel, and research, all of the utmost faithfulness and accuracy, is beyond expression or terms of comparison."

Crofutt must have spluttered over every line! But it was soon clear that the production costs of Williams' elaborate publication were too high to allow for regular annual revision, a fatal weakness in an era of such rapid change.

Not that Williams' guidebook disappeared immediately from the stands. It was reprinted in New York for the next few years, first by Adams & Bishop, then in 1882-83 by J.R. Bowman, and for the last time in 1884, again by Adams & Bishop. One of the original sub-editors, Frederick E. Shearer, inserted additional material on California in 1879, probably in response to Crofutt's extended coverage in 1878 in the *New Overland Tourist*. But for the most part, Williams' first edition went out unchanged. Readers must have found it disconcerting, to say the least, still to be reading in the 1881 reprint of developments that had "just" taken place "last year (1875)", or of new rail extensions to be laid "during the present year (1876)"! Shearer did not in fact delete these, and other, giveaways until 1882, and the updating, apart from the California supplement, remained minimal.

Henry Williams himself had been working on other projects for some time, in particular a variety of publications to meet the growing demand in the second half of the nineteenth century for ideas and information on home improvement, interior decoration, and house and garden design. Indeed, Williams' books now revived a range of interests he had shelved in part for more than ten years, after publishing his more characteristic *Suburban Homes for City Business Men* in 1867 in New York.

In 1878, the *Denver Tribune* had observed that *Crofutt's New Overland Tourist, and Pacific Coast Guide* was likely to continue for years to be the standard work of its kind in the country. This was to be the case, despite strong competition from major publishing houses such as Appletons' and Rand, McNally. As the national economy began to revive at the end of the 1870s, and western passenger travel increased, Crofutt's persistence paid off, and his *New Overland Tourist, and Pacific Coast Guide* settled into regular publication in this format for the next six years.

A study of contemporary books and articles shows that many travellers used *Crofutt's New Overland Tourist, and Pacific Coast Guide* to plan their routes and to provide general background for their own personal reminiscences about the West. T.S. Hudson, for example, went so far as to acknowledge the assistance of two guides. He made a rapid tour across the United States and part of Canada in 1882, using Appletons' guidebook for the eastern section and Crofutt's for the west. Hudson incorporates a number of Crofutt's informal comments and impressions, and responds to them in making his own observations along the way. Once he reaches Los Angeles, however, Hudson also adds that

> "This is an appropriate point for me to make my bow to Mr. Crofutt and to thank him for the assistance of his useful book, without which, and Messrs Appletons' invaluable *General Guide*, I could not have directed my route so as to have seen so much without a much greater expenditure of time and money." [10]

*   *   *

An important new trend in guidebooks to the West was now emerging, closely linked to the growth of regional rail networks, the development of regional tourism, and the endless competition for new business and more settlers. Specialized regional guides were growing in popularity, and in 1878, as soon as the first issue of *Crofutt's New Overland Tourist* went on sale, Crofutt announced the new delights he had in store. He and his readers would again be travelling companions, this time on a more leisurely exploration of the wonderful West. Four new illustrated regional handbooks were planned, each to be priced at 50 cents:

CROFUTT'S UTAH AND THE GREAT BASIN
CROFUTT'S COLORADO AND NEW MEXICO
CROFUTT IN THE BLACK HILLS
CROFUTT BEYOND THE SIERRAS, including Southern California and Arizona.

With his publishing base re-established, Crofutt left Chicago in the summer of 1879. On his way through Omaha, he checked that the *New Overland's* production was still going smoothly in Henry Gibson's capable hands; that done, he headed west again to Denver.

Growth Along the Rocky Mountain Front:
Pioneering A New Frontier of 'Instant Civilization' in the 1870s

Only those who had known Denver in its early years could fully appreciate how the place had been transformed during the Seventies. The dire conditions of the Sixties had, by 1870, left Denver a virtual ghost town of only 4759 people, just ten more than the recorded population for 1860. "All the old excitement has ceased," wrote a visitor in the summer of 1869; the "quiet little village" was almost at a standstill, riddled with places to let, "while business rushes past on a railroad a hundred miles north." [11] Recovery from the trough of the mid-1860s was indeed very slow, but the arrival of the railroad had a sensational effect.

The completion of the 106-mile Denver Pacific Railroad on 22nd June 1870 linked Denver at last to the main Union Pacific line at Cheyenne. General William Jackson Palmer had watched the boisterous celebration, and then said it all in a few words:

> "Denver was much excited today ... the whole town was out. Poor creatures, it was an event, indeed, for them. They have been so long out of communication with the rest of the world, — I suppose most of the children had really never seen a locomotive." [12]

Palmer had been in town supervising the final stages of construction of another railroad, the Kansas Pacific, which crossed the plains and reached Denver just two months later. This was an important addition to the Union Pacific-Denver Pacific line since the K.P.'s direct link to Kansas City and St. Louis now gave Denver a double connection with the Eastern rail network. In September 1870, Denverites still had a few cheers left for a third arrival, the standard-gauge section of the Colorado Central Railroad which had finally managed to complete its 15-mile run from Golden.

Denver had joined the transcontinental railroad age in the nick of time, before the Panic of 1873 stopped so much western railroad construction dead in its tracks. The Denver region thus scraped home to share in the national boom of the early Seventies, and reached a new high

DENVER, 'GATEWAY TO THE ROCKIES', ENTERS THE RAILROAD AGE, 1870
Denver Station, with the Kansas Pacific, Denver Pacific, and Colorado Central Railroads.
The Kansas Pacific Depot (left) served all three railroads until the new Union Station
opened in 1881.

spot when Colorado acquired statehood in 1876, Centennial year. By 1880,
Denver's population had soared to well over 35,000, with new banks,
business blocks, stores, hotels, restaurants, theatres, and suburban resi-
dences marking the new age of prosperity. Here, Denver claimed, frontier
energy was combined with eastern style:

> "There is a dash and animation to the place," wrote Frank Fossett in 1879,
> "along with a finish and elegance . . . that give the Queen City of the plains
> and mountains this doubly attractive appearance." [13]

A streetcar system, new gas lighting and improved water supply had all
been part of Denver's first wave of modernization between 1871 and 1873.
Several of Crofutt's old friends and associates, including Amos Steck,
Richard Whitsitt, Bela Hughes, William Byers, Francis Gallup, and Rufus
"Potato" Clark, had been actively involved in boosting Denver's urban
development schemes, and when Crofutt arrived towards the end of 1879,
a second building boom was in full swing.

Mining had made a spectacular recovery, and on the northern edge of the city sprawled the new Argo Smelter, which had been enlarged and shifted from Black Hawk in 1878. In the Downtown area, the massive Tabor business block had just opened on 16th and Larimer, the tallest on the city skyline and complete with Denver's first elevator. Horace Tabor, wealthiest of all the new Leadville 'Silver Kings', had struck it rich in May 1878 and was now pouring money into Denver's development. In 1879, he bought a spacious town house and began his political career with a 4-year term as Colorado's Lieutenant-Governor. Two more major projects downtown were nearing completion as Crofutt arrived: the Windsor Hotel on 18th and Larimer, which at its opening in January 1880 was hailed as the finest hotel in the Mountain West, and Tabor's magnificent Grand Opera House on 16th and Curtis. The new University of Denver and the new Court House were planned and in their early stages, while the impressive new Union Station was well advanced, an elaborate gothic pile set in twelve acres on the right bank of the South Platte. This was to be the grand terminus tying the Rockies to the plains, one of the new cathedrals of the railway age. All Colorado's railroads would run to, but not through, Denver. It seemed only yesterday that an Arapahoe Indian camp and thousands of Pike's Peakers' wagons had covered the same site.

The Union Depot was thus designed to coordinate all Denver's railroad services, including the three-foot narrow-gauge mountain railroads which were now enjoying a boom of their own as fresh mineral strikes deep in the Rockies helped to fuel Colorado's economy. The Colorado Central Railroad had by 1877 completed its narrow-gauge tracks west from Golden to Black Hawk, Central City and Georgetown, and with its various branches to the Union Pacific and the Kansas Pacific, the Colorado Central (soon to be controlled by the U.P.) provided valuable additional cross linkage in the northern part of the State [Map XII].

A second narrow-gauge, the Denver, South Park & Pacific Railroad, had by 1878 wriggled its way up Platte Canyon towards the timber reserves and mining centres around South Park, the area that Crofutt and seven associates had hoped to reach back in January 1868 with their short-lived Arapahoe, Jefferson and South Park Rail Road Co. The silver bonanza farther west at Leadville in 1878-9, on the site of the earlier gold strikes at California Gulch, threw the Denver & South Park Railroad into a frenzy of construction as it raced to tap new payloads. Until the Leadville silver carbonate strike, Gilpin and Clear Creek Counties to the north had been supplying two-thirds of Colorado's gold and silver production; before long, spurred by the urban building boom, the Denver & South Park's freight revenues from precious metals were boosted by car-loads of lime and sandstone from Morrison, and eventually by the marble and granites from Gunnison County.

SOUTH PARK IN THE ROCKY MOUNTAINS, SEEN FROM KENOSHA HILL
in *Crofutt's Grip-Sack Guide of Colorado,* **1881**
Scene of frenzied activity in 1859-60 during the Pike's Peak gold rush, the placers around
the edge of South Park were soon worked out or abandoned as prospectors moved on,
or turned to ranching.
In the late 1870s, mining revived and with the coming of the railroad, interest in tourism,
hunting and camping brought new life to South Park. The narrow-gauge Denver, South
Park & Pacific Railroad is seen here on its way to Leadville.

Meanwhile, a third major narrow-gauge, the Denver & Rio Grande,
had been injecting new life along the Rocky Mountain Front. The old
familiar eighty-mile stretch between Denver and Colorado City that
Crofutt and others had known so well in the 1860s was now centre-stage
in Colorado's new age of development, thanks to a determined new
regional builder and booster, William Jackson Palmer.

Back in the 1850s, while Crofutt was a struggling publisher in
Philadelphia, Palmer was also working in Pennsylvania, as a young
railroad surveyor and engineer. Later, he spent a few months studying
railways in England and France. After Civil War service as a brigadier-
general in the Union cavalry, he was appointed in 1867 to take charge of

the surveys for the Kansas Pacific Railroad, a project which like many others carrying the 'Pacific' banner more in hope than expectation, never became an independent transcontinental line. The Kansas Pacific followed the Kansas and Smoky Hill river routes to end in Denver, and during the summer of 1869, Palmer took a break from work out on the plains to explore the Rocky Mountain Front in more detail. The scenery south of Denver, he decided, was even finer than that to the north; for Palmer, it was to be the climax of a voyage of discovery:

> "After crossing the plains westward, and reaching in Colorado and New Mexico the foothills of the great range known as the Rocky Mountains, . . . it is as though one had crossed the sea, and reached the shores of a new country, full of novel attractions and advantages unknown in the land from which we had set sail." [14]

For this new country and its novel attractions, Palmer began planning an ambitious scheme of regional development which was to absorb him for the rest of his life. The project was based on the construction of a north-south, narrow-gauge, axial railroad running south from Denver along the Rocky Mountain Front and through New Mexico to El Paso on the Rio Grande, with a possible extension into Mexico itself. Palmer's north-south railroad was to be a lifeline linking the great east-west transcontinental routes, a line studded with new towns, mines, manufacturing centres, ranching and agricultural colonies. Westward, long fingers of narrow-gauge would poke up into the mountains to promote new mines, new farms, new tourist resorts, new freight traffic and new markets. "Narrow-gauge is the only one fitted to the peculiar conditions of the Rocky Mountains," Palmer stressed, "and permits a 33 per cent economy in the cost of construction." [15] Economy was a vital consideration whatever might be the other advantages of 3-foot narrow-gauge, since Palmer's railroad was not subsidized by Government grants and bonds, and had been refused any more public domain land than a strip 200 feet wide along its right-of-way, with 20-acre tracts for depots at 10-mile intervals.

As soon as the Kansas Pacific Railroad reached Denver in August 1870, Palmer was free to push ahead with his own schemes. He founded the Denver & Rio Grande Railway Company in October 1870, attracted investors, bought land, and within twelve months had laid 76 miles of track running south from Denver, over the Divide, to the new site of Colorado Springs. Pike's Peak itself was to be the focus of a new resort complex developed around its base whose amenities would include an important health spa, new villas and hotels, scenic excursions through the Rockies by railway, improved wagon roads and pony trails, a choice of steep climbs or leisurely rambles — and everywhere, glorious lungfuls of Colorado's clear, sparkling air.

Palmer, the young entrepreneur, was determined, energetic and impatient. Everything had to be done at once — expansion and consolidation. As railroad construction continued south towards Pueblo, Palmer authorized the purchase of land around the mineral springs of Manitou, beside the old Ute trail; there, late in 1871, a spa for tourists and health-seekers began to take shape five miles from his new town of Colorado Springs. The 'Springs' referred to Manitou, but Colorado Springs was to be the major settlement, located on the plains at the foot of Pike's Peak. 'Pike's Peakers' in 1858-60 had been chasing gold; now a new wave of 'Peakers' would come in search of health and recreation.

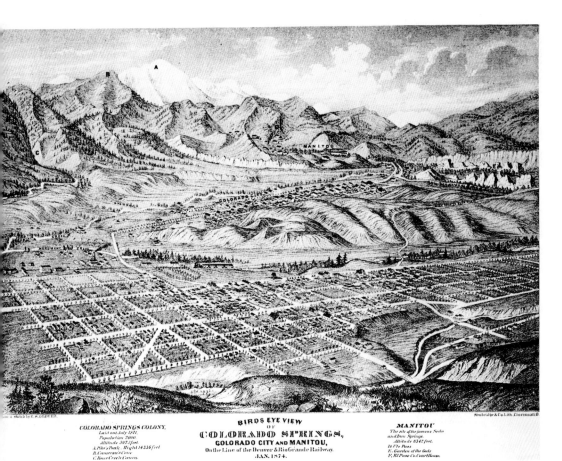

55.

BIRD'S-EYE VIEW OF COLORADO SPRINGS, JANUARY 1874
including the pioneer line of the Denver & Rio Grande Railway, Colorado City ('Old Town'), Manitou Spa, the Garden of the Gods, Ute Pass and Pike's Peak.

With the help of two enthusiastic local supporters, Alexander Hunt and Irving Howbert, General Palmer had by 1871 pieced together and bought up more than 9300 acres in the mountains, canyons and plains around Pike's Peak.[16] On the new, 2000-acre town site beside Fountain and Monument Creeks, two miles east of old Colorado City, Palmer established the Colorado Springs Co. (organized in Denver in May 1871 as one of the several 'specific projects' subsidiaries), and began selling lots for his Fountain Colony on 1st August. Palmer, brought up as a Quaker, wanted to create an enterprising, teetotal community developed by colonists with some capital behind them; residential lots selling at $50 and business lots at $100 were available to "any person . . . possessed of a good moral character and of strict temperance habits" who paid the initial $100 fee to become a member of Fountain Colony. Mountain vistas, wide, tree-lined avenues, comfortable homes, ample water supply for irrigated gardens and parks, new colleges, libraries and a range of major urban amenities were to set the style. Palmer's Colorado Springs Hotel opened on New Year's Day, 1872, coinciding with the start of regular railroad passenger service from Denver on the D.&R.G., and ready to cope with the first wave of tourists and prospective settlers.

Old Colorado City was now little more than a village, ignored by the new Denver & Rio Grande railroad, and with nothing to do but hang on forlornly to the scraps of business derived from its role as the El Paso County seat. General Palmer could not build Colorado Springs fast enough for the most go-ahead of the old Colorado City pioneers who were still around, including Crofutt's former trail partners Ben Crowell and Albinus Sheldon. Both held official county posts but spent most of their time away from a squalid, saloon-ridden 'City' which had no part to play in Palmer's Mountain Base Improvement scheme. In 1873, the El Paso County seat was officially transferred to Colorado Springs, by then a resort and residential town of some two thousand inhabitants.

Palmer favoured concentrated effort at selected sites along the railroad, beads of "capital, influence and organization" large enough to ensure that settlement was rapid, systematic, and permanent. Colorado's mineral wealth was the foundation of the State's economy but most mining boom towns came and went if no other reason for existence could be found. Elsewhere, slow, piecemeal development often resulted in imbalance, duplicated effort and wasted resources, Palmer argued, mindful of his own need to generate passenger and freight traffic. But the issue was wider than stockholders' interests and company profits. Transcontinental railroads were lining up to cross the United States; uniqueness, style, specialization, and skilful advertising of its resources were what Colorado would need to prosper in a West increasingly in competition with itself for settlers and investment from Europe and the eastern United

States. A Pennsylvanian editor had made the point while visiting the 'new frontier' at Pike's Peak in 1874:

> "In the old times, a settler would have had to wait many years, perhaps a lifetime, to have gathered around him for himself and his children the comforts and conveniences which are here at Colorado Springs. Now we go West, and find civilization ready-made to order, waiting to receive us." [7]

The 'Health Rush' begins:
Colorado versus California in the 1870s

Colorado boosters knew that California was the one they had to beat. California could boast a head start, extraordinarily attractive climatic and regional variety, a rich resource base, dynamic promotion, and a population explosion unique west of the Mississippi. Colorado had to sharpen its image and challenge California for a share in the new wave of tourists, health-seekers and settlers travelling west in the early 1870s.

The celebrated journalist Bayard Taylor, long impressed by the beautiful landscapes of central and southern California, whose air he described as "a fluid balm," had later also sung the praises of the Rockies' magnificent scenery and exhilarating atmosphere in his popular book *Colorado: a summer trip*, published in 1867 from earlier correspondence to the *New-York Tribune*. In 1869, New England editor Samuel Bowles had called Colorado *The Switzerland of America*, a European sobriquet that was suddenly in vogue.

On the west coast, no one had done more to promote California at the start of the 1870s than Charles Nordhoff, 'king of the boosters', with his *California: for Health, Pleasure, and Residence* (New York, 1872). Who could ignore his skilful and engaging introduction, with its continental framework and strong national appeal?

> "There have been Americans who saw Rome before they saw Niagara; and for one who has visited the Yosemite, a hundred will tell you about the Alps, and a thousand about Paris. Now, I have no objection to Europe; but I would like to induce Americans, when they contemplate a journey for health, pleasure, or instruction, or all three, to think also of their own country, and particularly of California, which has so many delights in store for the tourist, and so many attractions for the farmer or settler looking for a mild and healthful climate and a productive country.
>
> When a northern American visits a tropical country, be it Cuba, Mexico, Brazil, or Central America, he is delighted with the bright skies, the mild climate, the wonderful productiveness of the soil, and the novel customs of the inhabitants; but he is repelled by an enervating atmosphere, by the dread of malarious diseases, by the semi-barbarous habits of the people, and often by a lawless state of society. Moreover, he must leave his own country, and is without the comfort and security he enjoys at home. California is our own; and it is the first tropical land which our race has thoroughly mastered and made itself at home in . . . the delights of the

tropics, without their penalties; a mild climate, not enervating, but healthful and health-restoring; a wonderfully and variously productive soil, without tropical malaria; the grandest scenery. . . ." [18]

With Nordhoff's sales soaring, there was no time to lose. Colorado's boosters surveyed their assets, marshalled their forces and went into action. Appropriately, General Palmer led the assault.

Together with the construction of the Denver & Rio Grande railroad, Palmer made the creation of Manitou spa his first priority for rapid development along the Rocky Mountain Front. While Palmer pressed ahead with his regional strategy, however, Dr. William Bell, a young London physician who had worked with Palmer on the Kansas Pacific railroad surveys in the late 1860s, was left to get on with the details of organizing the town of Manitou Springs. Bell was enchanted with Colorado. Both as Palmer's financial associate and life-long friend, he became a key figure during the '70s and '80s in attracting English investment, supplementing the work of Colorado's Board of Immigration during its Territorial period, and promoting colonization and tourism along Colorado's Rocky Mountain Front.[19] The Colorado Springs area was dubbed 'Little London'; Colorado itself, 'England beyond the Missouri'. *Out West*, published in Colorado Springs, was launched as a weekly newspaper in 1872, and as a 24-page monthly magazine in 1873 when it began to concentrate exclusively on boosting the farming, mining, tourist, and health potential of the region. *Out West* was widely distributed, and several early copies can still be found in London, as well as in the United States.

Many visitors to Denver in the early 1870s took a special excursion south on the narrow-gauge to see how Colorado Springs and Manitou were progressing. It all helped to boost the 'health belt's' reputation, especially when visitors included the inimitable P.T. Barnum, who bounced into Denver on the Kansas Pacific Railroad in 1872, inspected the first stage of development along the Rocky Mountain Front, visited his cattle ranch forty miles from Pueblo, and announced:

"I never saw so many disappointed people as at Denver ... Half the inhabitants came invalids from the East, expecting to die, and they find they cannot do it. Your charming climate will not permit it! And it is a fact. I am charmed with Colorado, the scenery and delightful air." [20]

Famous names helped to promote business. Rose Kingsley and her brother Maurice, who was Secretary of the Colorado Springs Co., were both active in the area in 1871-2; their distinguished father, Charles Kingsley, visited the spa in 1874.[21] Mrs. Helen Hunt (Jackson), the celebrated and widely travelled writer from Newport, R.I., arrived at Manitou in 1873; her health improved, she remarried and remained in Colorado Springs for the rest of the decade, becoming a powerful publicist for the region. President Ulysses Grant, Jefferson Davis and John D. Rockefeller all visited the resort in 1875, although the Grant family was to be more closely associated with California, notably San Diego.

In the early days, there were six major mineral springs at Manitou (nearer fifty after later drilling and development), most of them containing carbonates of soda and iron. Crofutt could remember the times while freighting in the early 1860s when he had mixed the bubbling water of the soda springs with a little cream of tartar to leaven his bread and flapjacks as he camped along the trail.[22]

By 1872, more than 400 villa sites had been laid out at approximately 6300 feet above sea level around the confluence of Fountain and Ruxton Creeks, in the sunny, sheltered basin at the foot of Ute Pass. The settlement was laced with winding paths, rustic seats and bridges, and picturesque summer houses. Strolling from one spring to another was to become a fashionable and recommended activity for both tourists and invalids:

> "A walk of five or ten minutes before breakfast, in the sunshine, or a jaunt to the Iron Springs, and a refreshing draught of its sparkling waters, will serve as a sharp and effective tonic." [23]

Ornamental pavilions at the principal springs quickly became centres of social life at Manitou. Other major facilities introduced in 1872 as part of the initial planning included a heated bath-house, and a bottling plant for Manitou's sparkling table waters, which were now widely advertised by a handsome new arrival, Dr. Boswell Anderson from Virginia.

The founders were convinced, however, that the success of the entire venture would depend on the provision of ample, first-class accommodation. No tentative half-measures would do. Palmer and Bell favoured the rapid construction of large, elegant hotels as the foundation of their frontier of 'instant civilization' at Manitou Springs. The first major hotel, their own stylish Manitou House, was completed in August 1872, with forty-eight of its fifty-eight rooms filled on the opening day. Eastern fashion had been planted confidently into the American West. As one of the first visitors discovered in 1873, the hotel was full of "Saratoga trunks, pianos and fiddles . . . the war-dance and scalp-dance are seen no more, but the 'Boston Dip', and the 'New York Glide' can be beheld almost any night in the halls of the *Manitou*." [24]

The Cliff House, enlarged in 1873, grew into one of the biggest and most popular hotels in Colorado. The same year, Dr. Bell opened his Manitou Park Hotel, and in 1875, his even more elaborate hotel, The Mansions, landscaped in its own 10-acre park. One traveller, astonished by the crowds visiting the Pike's Peak region in the early 1870s, conveyed the spirit of the new age:

"The world is storming the Rocky Mountains. Like the great sea ... civilization is surging around them — rushing through their wild passes, and now and then throwing a wave over their loftiest summits." [25]

As visitors settled comfortably into the large hotels and villas, or into the many boarding-houses, apartments and cottages that soon clustered around the slopes of Manitou, both the energetic and the invalid could explore happily at their own pace ...

"[Off] in an open buggy through blinding sunshine, to the Garden of the Gods. Cold vanished, the glories of mountain mesa and distant plain caught me by the throat ... I laid my heart that day at the feet of the Sun God of Colorado." [26]

For many, gentle exercise on the croquet lawns, a game of cards, bowls, tennis or billiards, dancing, listening to band concerts, visiting a peacock farm, watching ostrich racing, or simply cultivating new business and social contacts were all pleasant diversions. Some retired or invalid businessmen from the East boosted growth by bringing important investment capital and entrepreneurial skills to Manitou and Colorado Springs, whose American links remained firmly "with Boston, Philadelphia and New York," recalled one resident; "the Middle West said little to us." [27]

There was plenty to see in the immediate vicinity, thanks to the area's geological complexity and colourful, weirdly-shaped rocks; the Garden of the Gods, the Cave of the Winds, canyons and crests, look-outs and lakes — all were the rich raw material of the tourist industry. Excursions into the Rocky Mountain parks and to the jewel in the crown, Pike's Peak, were immensely popular. By 1874, as many as fifty a day in summer were hiking at least half-way along the seventeen-mile Bear Creek Trail to the summit of Pike's Peak. Pony-trekking to the top was a 'must' for many tourists.

"There they go," said one, watching a group move off from Manitou in fine style, "a gallant mounted party — not soldiers or mountaineers — but brave tourists, for the larger part ladies, galloping off over the foothills, to take the new trail to Pike's Peak." [28]

Another day, another group, this time from Colorado Springs. Early one morning in the summer of 1873, Eliza Greatorex spotted a cheerful party gathering in front of the hotel to go up Pike's Peak, to see the sunrise ... "five gentlemen, and at least ten ladies. Among them I notice one old lady quite as gay as the young ones, and who threatens to outdo them all. She must be sixty-five, and I am astonished at her courage." [29]

Less dramatic, but often equally memorable, was the chance to ride through the mountains and plains, call at ranches, meet local working Coloradans, and sample a not-too-wild West. Though not on the scale of Isabella Bird's remarkable journey through the Rockies in 1873, such trips, made easier by reliable transport from a comfortable resort centre, were

56.   THE GARDEN OF THE GODS AND PIKE'S PEAK

in *Crofutt's Trans-Continental Tourist,* 1874

The brilliant red, vertically-tilted sandstones of Gateway Rocks
frame the pink granites of Pike's Peak.

a bonus not found at other major spas. As one traveller based at Manitou and Colorado Springs recalled with pleasure:

> "The very world seemed young in Colorado . . . Smart people of leisure and fashion touched shoulders with builders of the nation, miners and cowboys, where simplicity prevailed." [30]

For the seriously ill, however, sunshine, rest, and tranquil surroundings were themselves powerful physical and psychological restoratives. A Californian doctor, whom Dr. Bell had met in the late 1860s, wisely advised his patients not to "wear themselves out sight-seeing":

> "*If you are after lost health, attend to that, and don't convert yourself into a tourist or a picnicker* . . . Make it your sole business to attend to what you left your home and friends for — the regaining of your health. Keep out of crowded halls, churches, and parties; eat regularly, go to bed regularly, dress conveniently, live generously, be patient; do not expect to be transformed into a Samson or a Goliath in three weeks; expect ups and downs; stay in the open air as much as possible; be rational." [31]

As the main promoter of Manitou Springs, Dr. William Bell was well aware of the rival attractions of Southern California's 'Sanitarium Belt', especially its many hot springs, and varied coastal, valley or mountain facilities around the four major centres — Santa Barbara, Los Angeles, San Bernardino, and San Diego. Indeed, Bell's preliminary Kansas Pacific Railroad surveys with General Palmer along the 35th and 32nd parallels had revealed other potential spa sites for treating tubercular, bronchial and rheumatic conditions in both New Mexico and Arizona. Centres in Texas, Arkansas, South Carolina, Florida, New York, as well as the European spas, all had their attractions.

In 1874, Bell invited another London physician, Dr. Samuel Solly, a specialist in pulmonary diseases, to visit Manitou, and help to boost the spa and his own failing health at the same time. Solly quickly turned his attention to a detailed analysis of the principal mineral springs, and went on to make strong claims for the benefits to be derived from drinking and bathing at the different springs in the treatment of a whole variety of blood, kidney, bronchial, rheumatic, digestive and bowel disorders. Solly also stressed the advantages of mountain as opposed to coastal environments for tubercular sufferers. He published *Manitou, Colorado, U.S.A.; Its Mineral Waters and Climate* in 1875, a timely and highly effective contribution to the massive publicity campaign now being launched for Manitou Springs — the Saratoga of the West.

Though immersed in other projects, General Palmer still found time to publish pamphlets and articles in the eastern States and in London, boosting the attractions of Manitou and Colorado Springs. Persistent advertising was essential to combat the charms of California, now seductively labelled as 'the Italy of America'. In 1874, a make-or-break year, the major resorts in Southern California, already competing fiercely among themselves as well as with others, each launched a vigorous promotional campaign. They emphasized climate, scenery, improved hotel and boarding-house accommodation, and in some areas, agriculture, the ideal side-line for semi-invalids working their way back to good health. Local enthusiasts already called the San Gabriel Valley and its eastern extension the 'Great Orange Belt and Sanitarium'.

Nearby was one of California's most famous and beautiful health retreats, Sierra Madre, founded in 1872 by Nathaniel C. Carter of Lowell, Massachusetts. That year, with a small party from Boston, Carter had promoted the first of his regular winter excursions from New England to Southern California. Always one jump ahead, Carter, a health-seeker as well as a booster and entrepreneur, had a picture made showing himself before and after he was cured of tuberculosis in Southern California. Entitled "Before and After Taking", the picture was displayed by Carter wherever he went, and when asked what the remedy was, he replied, "California climate!" [32]

Santa Barbara also developed a strong New England connection. Its popularity was sparked by Charles Nordhoff's glowing account in 1872 of Santa Barbara's sheltered location and picturesque surroundings. The smaller resort of Nordhoff, named in his honour, was laid out in 1874 in the nearby Ojai Valley. Santa Barbara was a dream, where bitter north-eastern winters were replaced by the sheer pleasure of being able to stay out-of-doors in warmth and sunshine . . . "In Santa Barbara there were not a dozen days during the whole winter in which a baby I know of did not play on the sea-beach." Already, Nordhoff noted, its "pleasant society . . . is, in fact, a cozy nest of New England and Western New York people, many of whom originally came here for their health, and remain because they are charmed with the climate." [33]

What Santa Barbara lacked was first-class accommodation for well-to-do Yankees now showing a sudden surge of interest in the region. The town took the initiative by building the Arlington, Southern California's first luxury resort hotel, which opened in 1875. Financed mainly by a wealthy local rancher, Col. William W. Hollister, the Arlington was managed by the ebullient Dixie W. Thompson, a former sea captain, gold miner and cattle rancher whose colourful personality was as much a part of the Arlington's atmosphere as that of the captains on the old canal packets and the Mississippi river-boats.

Most visitors to Santa Barbara arrived by steamer; special carriages or streetcars took them from Stearns Wharf for a mile or so along State Street to the grandeur of the Arlington, which rose incongruously out of the small, dusty town. A California newspaper editor, born in Santa Barbara in 1876, later recalled that when he was a boy, the Arlington Hotel and the old Spanish mission (1786) were the two most prominent landmarks in town.[34] In many ways, Arlington society was a world of its own, but tourists and health-seekers also wanted to explore their surroundings, and in addition to indoor diversions, 'Captain Dixie' organized bathing parties, picnics, hunting trips, tally-ho excursions, flora-and-fauna expeditions, ranch visits, and a great variety of rambles, wagon rides and other amusements for those who felt up to it.

Hollister and Thompson were both keen to extend 'the season' beyond the popular winter months into the summer, when those who had not returned to the East tended to migrate to San Francisco. There, the vast new Palace Hotel had also opened in 1875; exceeded in size in America only by the United States Hotel at Saratoga Springs, San Francisco's Palace was at once one of the largest and most elegant hotels

57.

THE PALACE HOTEL, SAN FRANCISCO

in Crofutt's New Overland Tourist, and Pacific Coast Guide, 1878-9

Opened on 2nd October 1875, the Palace Hotel covered an entire city block between Market, New Montgomery, Annie and Jessie Streets, and was designed to accommodate twelve hundred guests. The hotel had its own supplementary water supply from four artesian wells, and was built around three interior courtyards.

58.   **THE GRAND COURT OF THE PALACE HOTEL**

Frank Leslie's Illustrated Newspaper, June 29, 1878, from a photograph by Leslie's staff photographer, W.B. Austin

"No picture can quite give an idea of the sunshiny lightness and brightness of effect which is one of the strongest attractions of the Grand Court," wrote Leslie's reporter. This central court was enclosed by glass and widely regarded as the Palace Hotel's most spectacular feature. The six tiers of balconies became fashionable promenades from which to watch the constant comings and goings below. They were decorated with banks of tropical plants and lit by gas, later electric candelabra — a scene that offered a pleasing contrast to the magnificent panoramic views from the hotel's roof and external windows over the city, bay and mountains.

As Emily Faithfull noted: "When all the six galleries are lighted up at night, and the band is discoursing sweet music in the courtyard below, while the gaily-dressed ladies walk about the twelve-feet-wide corridors belonging to each story, the effect is very striking."

in the world. Two years later, E.J. Baldwin, better known as "Lucky" Baldwin, grabbed a share of this lucrative trade by opening his sumptuous Baldwin's Hotel, also in San Francisco.[35] Baldwin owned the famous Santa Anita ranch near Pasadena, as well as six others in the vicinity, business property in and around Los Angeles, and one of the finest racing stables in the United States. Now with his own hotel, Baldwin had expanded his investments in both northern and southern California, and followed the fashion of becoming one of America's wealthy businessmen-hoteliers at the same time.

In the face of competition from any quarter, Southern California's centres merely redoubled their efforts to attract all those "in pursuit of climate." Santa Barbara, for example, opened three new medium-range hotels in the late 1870s, several popular boarding-houses at $6-$10 per week, and unfurnished or part-furnished houses for rent (usual rates: 4-6 rooms for $5-$10 per month). Many visitors pitched tents in summer beside the beach, a practice even more widespread at Santa Monica and farther south. The quieter summer season and dull trade remained a problem, however, until Santa Barbara established itself firmly as a favourite permanent residential spot for rich and retired professional families from New England and New York.

Hard on Charles Nordhoff's heels came another outstanding California booster, the Yankee Major Benjamin C. Truman, with the first of his many publications advertising the Golden State. *Semi-Tropical California: Its Climate, Healthfulness, Productiveness, and Scenery*, a 'say-it-all-in-the-title' winner, was published in 1874.

While the Golden State glowed invitingly on the far western horizon, the Welcome Mat had also been fluffed up on the doorstep of the Rocky Mountains. Boosters there worked hard to emphasize California's 'disadvantages' when compared to Colorado. General Palmer focused on California's distance and isolation from the major centres of population, the relative ease of reaching and exploring the Rockies in the 1870s by standard and narrow-gauge railroads, and the exhilaration of Colorado's bracing air and sparkling snows. California, alas, wrote Palmer, warming to his theme, experienced none of the pleasures of changing seasons; worse still, it had to endure the miseries of winter rain.[36] California was unperturbed by the recital. San Diego, for example, rejoiced in the fact that its average annual rainfall total is only 10 inches (254 mms), with a December-February maximum, and gloried in its mild winters and high year-round sunshine records without excessive heat. Indeed, San Diego has a remarkable mean annual temperature range of only 15°F (8.3°C), one of the smallest in the United States. Denver's mean annual temperature range is as high as 41.8°F (23.2°C), although the annual precipitation is only 14.3 inches (363 mms), with an early summer maximum. Palmer did his best, claiming that Colorado Springs had a reliable 320 fine, clear days a year. But Southern California could field Palmer's "No seasons" gibe and toss back a different interpretation: "Winter and summer are terms that in Southern California lose their ordinary significance," wrote one delighted visitor, "their place being taken by what may almost be called a perpetual spring."

A more practical approach perhaps in the California v. Colorado rivalry was that of guidebook writer Henry Williams, who acknowledged the greater scenic variety of California, including the magnificence of Yosemite and the High Sierras, but who worked on the principle 'if you can't beat them, join them':

> "Those who wish to include both Colorado and California in a pleasure trip will do well to visit California first, during April, May and June, and then on return spend July and August leisurely in the cozy little home resorts of Colorado ... Living in Colorado is more nearly like New England customs than in California, and to those who seek Western travel for health, the climate of Colorado is much more favorable than that of California." [37]

Despite the widespread praise for Colorado's 'elastic air' and stimulating climate, Williams' assurance of its therapeutic superiority when compared to California had no basis in fact. Competing claims directed specifically at health-seekers rather than tourists came thick and fast, but in a decade when, for example, the cause of tuberculosis (the major killer) was still unknown, it was impossible to make accurate definitive statements about the exclusive medico-climatological advantages of any particular State. Recommendations about the 'climate cure' often depended on Eastern physicians' preferences, on personal experiences, advertising, transport, and the availability of reasonably-priced accommodation if a long stay was contemplated. Individual sufferers tried out different locations to suit themselves — coastal or inland, breezy or sheltered, moist or dry, hilly or flat, high or low altitude. If they had not left it too late, tubercular and other invalids usually worked out their own salvation. Many then decided to stay on; Captain John Codman, touring Southern California in 1878, reported that he could find no invalids planning to go home again after they were cured, except "for a visit." [38]

Although it cannot be verified, the most common (and reasonable) estimate is that as many as one-quarter of Southern California's and one-third of Colorado's total population originated as health-seekers in the later nineteenth century. The line between health-seeker and tourist was often a fine one. In the early 1870s, General Palmer estimated that 6000 tourists were visiting Colorado annually. In 1876, however, the new Centennial State received a unique boost at the United States' Centennial Exhibition in Philadelphia, which included reports of F.V. Hayden's western surveys from 1871-6, and a striking display of photographs of the Rockies in Colorado by Hayden's official photographer, William H. Jackson.

Ironically, 1876 was a disastrous year for western railroad travel. In addition to the national economic depression, the Centennial Exhibition in Philadelphia had been such a star attraction that west-bound tourist and business travel on the transcontinental routes, and on the Denver & Rio Grande Railway, was cut by two-thirds.[39] But the publicity of '76 boosted traffic in 1877, and by 1878, the Pike's Peak resort area was breaking all records; nearly 20,000 visitors were registered in the hotels of Colorado Springs and Manitou, with an additional 13,000 or so in the towns' many villas and boarding-houses. That year, Denver registered over 100,000 visitors, and more than double that number in 1879-80.[40]

59.

CAMPING OUT IN COLORADO

The Graphic, September 27, 1879

"In Colorado, camping-out among the mountains is extremely popular during the summer months," the reporter discovered. "There are two kinds of camps, one, the rough and ready . . . the other a much more elaborate affair . . . a home in the wilderness, combining simplicity with comfort."

TOSSING THE FLAPJACK.

ADJUSTING THE PACK.

60.

CAMPING IN COLORADO IN 1874

in E. Ingersoll, *Knocking Round the Rockies*, 1883

Tourists and health-seekers were well represented, and many visited both Denver and Colorado Springs.

These two centres also serviced increasing numbers of campers, for in central Colorado, as in Southern California, camping became extremely popular during the 1870s ... Campers were "strewing the whole country with the great North American *tin can*," thundered one outraged visitor. Denver, born to outfit the early mining camps, soon learned that it could do the same for tourists. Men, women, and children were moving from one place of interest to another, recorded one visitor, travelling in canvas-covered wagons or pitching tents while they explored the mountains, and the peaceful joys of sketching, fishing, "geologizing", and "botanizing". Some families went "cottaging" for $4 to $8 a month, depending on the size and standard of the accommodation, and the length of their stay. Others relied on the ranches, generally only for short stops by individuals or small groups wanting to keep on the move, although some ranchers built extra cabins for summer boarders at cheap rates, which attracted both tourists and health-seekers to what they were content to regard as the 'true' West ...

"Here [in Bergen Park, 1873], we are enjoying the most 'realizing sense' of true ranche life. Sitting at breakfast, near, but not *in* the log house, the table

267

of rough pine boards adorned with red cloth and a fresh bouquet of exquisite prairie flowers, mutton-chops, potatoes mashed and browned to perfection, coffee and milk and cream; near us are cows and horses, and the beautiful, graceful antelopes; broad slopes of green pasture, . . . skies of purest blue, and mountains — mountains all around . . . Our 'apartments', a supplementary log house, the second story reached by a ladder from the outside. . . . But it is in the evenings . . . before turning in, round our blazing camp fires, that we feel the full magical delight and romance of our life.

Families who would see Colorado more freely, naturally and inexpensively than they can in the hotels, can here settle for the whole season in an enchanting home, supplied with pure and wholesome food, with fishing, hunting, and endless attractions of scenery." [41]

The beautiful mountain valley of Estes Park (6800 ft), ten miles north of Long's Peak, was also famous for its hunting, trout fishing, "transparent air", and scintillating atmosphere. In addition to its popularity with

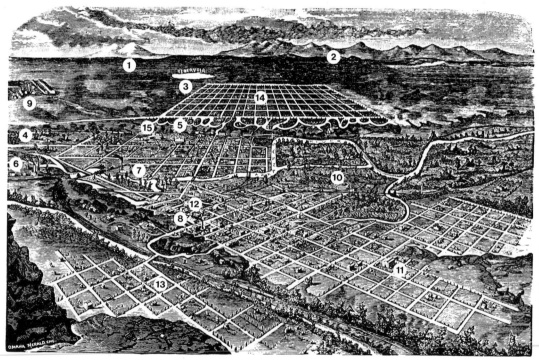

BIRD'S EYE VIEW OF PUEBLO, AND SOUTH AND EAST PUEBLO.

No. 1, the Spanish Peaks; 2, Greenhorn Mountains; 3, Reservoir; 4, Artesian Well of Mineral Waters; 5, Union Depot; 6, Smelting Works; 7, City Flouring Mills; 8, *Chieftain* office; 9, Steel Works; 10, Atchison, Topeka & Santa Fe Round House; 11, County Buildings; 12, Atchison, Topeka & Santa Fe Offices and Depot; 13, East Pueblo; 14, South Pueblo; 15, Denver & Rio Grande Round House.

61.   BIRD'S-EYE VIEW OF PUEBLO

in *Crofutt's Grip-Sack Guide of Colorado*, 1881

campers, Estes Park boasted a fine hotel owned by Lord Dunraven; with its tourists, invalids and resident physician, a visiting Englishman reported in 1880, the place "is what the Americans call a 'health resort' . . . For the first time since leaving New York, we wondered whether we ought to dress for dinner — and this in the Rocky Mountains!" [42]

The development around Pike's Peak and Colorado Springs, however, boosted southern Colorado, and went some way to challenging the dominance of the Denver region. Three of Manitou's principal hotels could, by the late 1870s, between them easily accommodate over one thousand guests, and expansion was already under way.

> "Of course we went to Manitou," wrote one visitor in 1880, "for everyone goes thither . . . One may see men and women walking about, and enjoying life, who long ago, if they had stayed in the East, would have, in Western parlance, 'gone over the range' . . . 'Why, they keep me here for an example of the effects of the climate,' said a worthy and busy man at Colorado Springs; 'I came here from Chicago on a mattress!' " [43]

*   *   *

While one of Palmer's major centres of "capital, influence and organization" along the Rocky Mountain Front was thus being securely pegged to the base of Pike's Peak, the Denver & Rio Grande railroad had reached Pueblo in June 1872, and within the next four months completed a branch west to the Labran-Florence coalfields near Cañon City. South Pueblo was one of the D. & R.G.'s most important new towns, the site of Palmer's subsidiary Colorado Coal & Iron Company. In 1880-81, Bessemer steel mills were introduced to supply an annual 30,000 tons of steel rail for the D. & R.G.'s new building program; as a result, using local raw materials assembled by rail, South Pueblo developed into a major integrated iron and steel manufacturing centre, the only one in Colorado, and one of the first in the West. In 1878, *Crofutt's New Overland Tourist* drew attention to the growth of smelting works, rolling mills, foundry and machine shops at South Pueblo, along with the town's banking and mining interests in the South Park, San Juan, and Trinidad regions. But Palmer's dream that his independent, narrow-gauge 'North and South' railroad would complement not conflict with the great east-west transcontinentals for routes and payloads, was ended by the Atchison, Topeka & Santa Fe while Palmer was still reeling from the effects of the financial Panic in 1873.

Although the Denver & Rio Grande had netted over $100,000 in passenger and freight traffic in 1872, construction costs had been enormous.[44] There were already local complaints that fare and freight rates were too high. In terms of regional development, Palmer was torn between pushing south as fast as possible via Santa Fe to the Mexican border, and interrupting the completion of his main north-south axis in

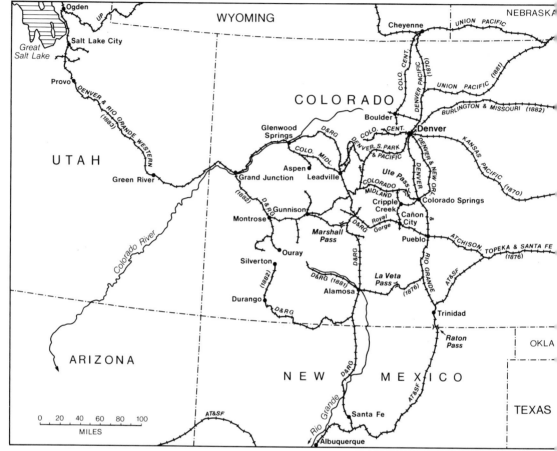

XII.

COLORADO'S REGIONAL RAIL NETWORK, 1870–1901

In 1887-8, the Atchison, Topeka & Santa Fe, and the Missouri Pacific Railroad, began their own services along the Rocky Mountain Front to compete with the Denver & Rio Grande, particularly between Denver and Pueblo.

By 1890, the Chicago, Rock Island & Pacific Railroad had reached Denver and Colorado Springs.

order to build branch lines west into the Rockies. Either way, extension required a steady flow of investment and after the Panic, funds dried up. Except for a 9-mile track completion to Cañon City in July 1874 (partly paid for by the town), Palmer was forced to stop all railroad construction for four years between 1872 and 1876, and this delay lost the D. & R.G. its monopoly and its initiative in southern Colorado and New Mexico. Not only did the Atchison, Topeka & Santa Fe recover more quickly from the Panic and win the race to Trinidad, Raton Pass and New Mexico; the A.T. & S.F. also pursued Palmer into the Rockies.

The Santa Fe Railroad had reached a jubilant Pueblo in February 1876, and following the Leadville silver bonanza in 1878 had quickly challenged Palmer for right-of-way along the narrow Royal Gorge route west of Cañon City, the best southern approach to Leadville's booming new region. Still desperately short of funds, Palmer was forced to lease the Denver & Rio Grande railroad in October 1878 to the Atchison, Topeka & Santa Fe. Legal battles raged while rival company crews grabbed pistols and shotguns. When the war between the two railroads was eventually settled in 1880, they divided their spheres of operation, and Palmer was left for the next three years to look west instead of south, and concentrate on providing Colorado and Utah with nearly 1600 miles of the most spectacular narrow-gauge network in the world.

"Vim, Vigor, and Push": Boosting and Building in the 1880s.

The Expansion of Colorado's Regional Rail Network, and the Growing Demand for Regional Guidebooks

Immediately after his arrival in Denver late in 1879, Crofutt began to plan the first of his projected regional handbooks — a comprehensive guide to Colorado. The new State's impressive growth during the 1870s, coupled with his own knowledge of the region since pioneer days, made Colorado the obvious choice. Frank Fossett's long and detailed study of Colorado, published in 1879, had concentrated primarily on the mines, with shorter sections on farming, history and tourism. Indeed, Fossett's valuable work was essentially a reference book for home, office or library.

So far as guidebooks were concerned, the field was wide open. California had continued to dominate the output of specialized western regional handbooks during the Seventies. There were several short surveys of Colorado, such as Rand, McNally's *Illustrated Guide to Colorado, New Mexico and Arizona* (1879), and collections of articles in book form, such as *Hayes's New Colorado* (1880), reprinted from *Harper's New Monthly Magazine*. Henry T. Williams had announced in 1876 that he was about to follow his grand *Trans-Continental Guide* with a new publication, *The Colorado Tourist*, but Williams dropped his western projects in the late 1870s, and the book never materialized.[45] Crofutt was determined to fill the gap left in particular by Fossett's volume with a wide-ranging, up-to-date, well-illustrated survey of his own that would appeal both to visitors and residents; first published in 1881, it became *Crofutt's Grip-Sack Guide of Colorado. A Complete Encyclopedia of the State*. As the title indicated, the guide was 'packed to go', but at the same time detailed enough to form a major work of reference.

Crofutt spent much of 1880 travelling the length and breadth of Colorado, including a three-month trip of nearly 3500 miles through the new mining and farming settlements in the south and southwest. He went on foot, on horseback, by stage, by wagon, and by railroad, riding on top of the boxcars where lines were still under construction. Much of what he saw reminded him of the Territory's early boom period twenty years before:

"People are scattered all over the country, prospecting, mining, stock raising, cutting grass, building bridges and wagon roads, publishing newspapers, building smelting works and mills, erecting large business blocks." Spearheading the development were the remarkable achievements of the narrow-gauge railways, "spanning gorges, climbing mountains, running to mines, laying out cities." Everywhere he went, Crofutt discovered Coloradoans "prosecuting all kinds of business enterprises with a *vim, vigor* and *push* that says: 'This country is good enough for us. We have come to stay.'" [46]

After a general introduction to Colorado and to Denver, the *Grip-Sack Guide* presented a series of eight railroad tours which between them revealed the growth taking place along the foot of the Front Range, and the enormous variety and wealth of resources lying behind it. Make sure, Crofutt had always advised visitors to Colorado, make sure that you "do more than 'doing' Denver." "Get out and about . . . Views of great scenic beauty are within reach of all, yet many of our people never visit them, but sigh for a tour to foreign lands."

As usual, Crofutt's blend of facts and figures, comprehensive coverage, personal reminiscence, short anecdote, and clear, economical style helped passengers to interpret what they saw, and to remain alert to the speed of the changes going on all around them. Change on the railroads too; Crofutt briefly summarized the histories of Colorado's principal railroads. Several of the standard- and narrow-gauge pioneer lines of the late 1860s and 1870s in northern and central Colorado had, by the end of 1880, passed into the divisional control of the Union Pacific and the powerful Jay Gould, including the Denver Pacific, the Kansas Pacific, the Colorado Central, and the Denver, South Park & Pacific. Farther south, General Palmer's Denver & Rio Grande had survived the 'railroad war', however, and was poised for major expansion into Colorado; just how far south and west the giant strides of the rival Atchison, Topeka & Santa Fe would march was still guesswork.

Crofutt had no patience with local critics of the D. & R.G.; "the company has brought more money into Colorado and done more to promote the general prosperity of the state than all other railroad companies and individual promoters combined." Although he never gave blanket endorsement to all the actions and operations of the western railroad companies, Crofutt's usual response to complaints about charges and profits was to talk also of risks and rewards — sometimes adding the terse reminder that from the train one could often still see the old, time-consuming wagon roads; the dissatisfied were welcome to try using them again, behind a team or on foot.

After describing the highlights of the eight selected railroad tours, the *Grip-Sack Guide* moved on to its main section — information on "every city, town, village, station, post office, post road, medicinal spring, resort,

62. ROLLING DOWN CLEAR CREEK CANYON ON THE COLORADO CENTRAL RAILROAD
(U.P.) NARROW GAUGE

in *Crofutt's Grip-Sack Guide of Colorado,* 1881

and important mining camp in the state of Colorado." This formidable
undertaking contained nearly one thousand entries and remains a
unique and indispensable record of Colorado's settlement and transport
patterns, wage rates and employment opportunities. Here was a picture
of the State's economic development in the 1880-81 period. As well as
nearly eighty illustrations, a coloured fold-in map, scaled at 16 miles to 1

inch, was also included: *Nell's new Topographical and Township Map prepared expressly for Crofutt's Grip-Sack Guide of Colorado*. This in itself has proved to be a valuable contemporary record of many small settlements and roads, some of them later abandoned. The cartographer's sources included F.V. Hayden's excellent *Atlas of Colorado* published in 1877.

Items were listed alphabetically, with extensive cross-referencing, so that readers could quickly find additional information on places, fares, distances and choice of conveyance when travelling on any of the recommended tours, or planning one of their own. A glossary of mining terms and, where appropriate, a note on the poor condition of the trails, were also included. Throughout, readers' awareness of Crofutt's personal knowledge and first-hand experience helped to make the speed of Colorado's development come alive. At the now-deserted settlement of Hancock, for example, perched at c.11,000 feet in the Sawatch Range on the Continental Divide, Crofutt told his readers that while preparing the *Grip-Sack Guide* . . .

> "on the 3rd August 1880, I rested over night with two prospectors, in a lone log cabin. The prospectors claimed to have 'just struck it rich', and would visit Gunnison City next day to buy 'grub'. Time passed, and on Oct. 20th, chancing again over the same route, what did I behold? The lone log cabin was the 'recorder's' office of a new mining district, where 732 claims had been recorded. There were eighty-four new buildings, including hotels, stores, and private residences, and over 500 inhabitants; a town had been laid out, smelting works in progress of construction, and a daily newspaper contemplated. *All* within less than three months." [47]

By 1880, however, isolated log cabins often served tourists as well as miners. Beyond the thriving silver-mining centre of Georgetown, for example, c.8500 feet and reached by the Colorado Central's narrow-gauge, travellers were encouraged to take a carriage on to Silver Plume and Brownsville, and then for the last six miles follow Grizzly Gulch up to Kelso Cabin (c.11,000 ft), whence the energetic could "take saddle or 'foot it'" to the summits of Gray's Peak (14,270 ft) and Torrey's Peak (14,267 ft).

This was all part of the lofty Berthoud and Argentine Pass region which Crofutt had explored briefly in the mid-Sixties. In 1865, three prospectors, Fletcher Kelso, Richard Irwin and John Baker had discovered silver at this point, and the site had been developed by the Sonora Mining Co. In the mid-1870s, however, the company's cluster of log and frame cabins had been bought by a Mrs. Z.M. Lane who, with her son, converted them into tourist accommodation for about fifteen travellers. Captain Lane guided tourists to the peaks while Mrs. Lane's excellent cooking and warm, comfortable mountain lodge attracted many to one of the remotest tourist spots in Colorado. John Beadle found Kelso's "a gem in the mountains." [48] Crofutt told his readers that the "cabin" was the best

63.

KELSO CABIN AND GRAY'S PEAK

in *Crofutt's Grip-Sack Guide of Colorado,* 1881

of its kind in the entire region, with Mrs. Lane keeping everything "as neat and nice as wax." Here was the place, if time allowed, to spend a few weeks climbing, gazing, and enjoying the incomparable scenery along the central spine of the Rockies.

Leadville was on nearly everyone's list. Crowds drawn by curiosity, adventure or business flocked to see Colorado's most recent rags-to-riches spectacular. By 1880, its population was over 15,000, second only to Denver in the Centennial State. Rival railroad companies had clawed their way towards Leadville's glittering prizes once the silver bonanza of 1878 had topped off earlier lead discoveries made in the mid-Seventies. In 1880, both the Denver & Rio Grande and the Denver, South Park & Pacific narrow-gauge railroads were operating into "what is now, at the close of 1880," Crofutt informed his readers, "one of the most cosmopolitan cities. Here meet and jostle the people of nearly every land and clime, the rich and the poor, the miser and the spendthrift, the scholar and the fool, the preacher and the bawd, the morose and the jolly . . .

Leadville is one of those extraordinary productions peculiar to a mining country; one of those places that from a lone cabin, becomes a village in a night, a town in a week, a city in a month, and a 'booming' metropolis the first year." [49]

Indeed, in the early 1880s Leadville was fast losing the 'wicked wild west' image that tourists expected to find there:

"I do not think my anticipations have ever been so completely upset as in Leadville," complained Phil Robinson. "All the way from New York I have been told to wait 'till I got to Colorado' before I ventured to speak of the rough life . . . but not only is Leadville not 'rough'; it is even flirting with the refinements of life." [50]

Crofutt's Grip-Sack Guide helped travellers to savour the enormous contrasts in Colorado, from a lonely camp tucked away in Gunnison County, near Maroon Mountain, and still nothing more than "two cabins and great expectations," to the flourishing mining-cum-spa centre of Idaho Springs, just a short spin from Denver on the Colorado Central (U.P.) railroad, whose observation cars could now carry tourists through the majestic Clear Creek Canyon to see a living history of the early gold rush days.

The plains country was not forgotten. Out in eastern Colorado, for example, lay the tiny post-road station of O.Z., a reminder, Crofutt explained, of the early pioneer rancher Old Zounds, who had signed his original application to the post-office department with just two initials, since when no one had bothered to do any more about changing the name. Out west on the mining frontier came an up-date on the new towns. Among them was Durango, created by the Denver & Rio Grande Co. in 1880, its population already c.2000, and planned by General Palmer and Dr. Bell as the future rail and regional centre of southwest Colorado. It promised a richly diversified economy based on metals, coal mining, manufacturing, timber, irrigated agriculture and livestock production. Track-laying north to Silverton was about to begin [Map XII].

Ouray, however, was still waiting for the 'civilizing rails'. "If the miners at Ouray *pray* at all," Crofutt commented, "it is for the coming of the 'Iron Horse' . . . A wagon road south to Red Mountain and Silverton has been completed at a cost of $100,000; now they are after a railroad." [51] Ouray's thousand-or-so miners were located in a deep isolated mountain amphitheatre above Uncompahgre Canyon. It was a wild and awesome setting:

"a wreck of matter, an exploded world piled up, dug out, and scattered about in strange and reckless confusion; the fiercely seamed red peaks above lending a brilliant contrast to the long stretches of timber, and the golden shade of the valley of the Uncompahgre, lying far below."

The high quality of Ouray's silver ores had encouraged miners to send them south by *burro* and mule train to Silverton, at a cost of $25 a ton, before the wagon road was constructed. Crofutt found plenty going on in and around the town which was vigorously boosted by its two weekly newspapers, the *Ouray Times* and the rip-roaring *Solid Muldoon*. Ouray, like Silverton, was located in the rich silver, lead, copper and gold-mining region of southwest Colorado known broadly as San Juan, which sprawled over more than 15,000 square miles of the tangled, deeply dissected mountain terrain west of San Luis Park. Beneath the surface, networks of shafts, tunnels, adits, and cross-cuts followed the major lodes, while above ground, mills, crushers, sampling works and straggling camp sites marked out the mining landscape.

The economic potential of the San Juan region was both a magnet and a huge engineering challenge to the Denver & Rio Grande railroad, which was about to begin a dramatic new phase of westward expansion. By 1880, the southwest, together with the Leadville and other strikes, had pushed the value of Colorado's annual mineral production to over $22 million; it was the start of two decades of increasing output which climbed to $50 million by the end of the century.[52] "Coloradoans have got so accustomed to hearing of and seeing 'big strikes'," noted Crofutt, reflecting the mood of the early 1880s, "that it would almost take a mountain of solid gold to excite their surprise."

As well as informing visitors, tourists and potential settlers from out-of-State, the *Grip-Sack Guide* was of course also introducing resident Coloradoans to each other. The general tone was enthusiastic, but Crofutt hit out at anything he felt revealed missed opportunity or a lack of enterprise. Overall, a clear impression could be gained from the sweeping list of entries as to how and where the State was expanding, along with its progress, prospects and ambitions.

"Our aim in writing the Guide," wrote Crofutt, "has been to decide in our own mind the wants of the public — of all classes —, anticipate their questions, and then to answer them, in as concise and comprehensive a manner as possible." Certainly, the Guide's handy format and wealth of condensed information on Colorado as a whole provided a broadly balanced framework for the huge increase in the number of travel books on the region that flooded onto the market in the 1880s, as individuals "roamed", "rambled", "wandered", "rode", "climbed", "camped", or "round-tripped" their way through the American West. Much of this travel literature highlighted particular cities, routes, adventures, and individual encounters. Some of it is superficial and uneven but, as with earlier accounts, the records are often perceptive, articulate, amusing, shrewdly observed, and vivid in their revelations of place, achievements and attitudes.

*　　　　　*　　　　　*

Crofutt published his *Grip-Sack Guide of Colorado* (1881), priced at $2.50, in Omaha and Denver, and distributed it for sale at the major bookstores, railroad agencies, and news-stands throughout the United States. From Chicago and St. Louis west to the Pacific, the Guide was also available on all the main-line passenger trains, where it was sold by train-boys or 'peanuts' — live wires who went up and down the cars selling newspapers, books, view-cards, fruit, nuts, cough-sweets, lollipops, and cigars, as well as running errands, taking messages and generally making themselves useful. They worked hard to win over those passengers who, initially or invariably, found train-boys tiresome and obtrusive. A distinctive feature on American railroads, train-boys were employed by general news agents who in turn had leased their rights to sell a variety of goods from the individual railroad companies. Crofutt gave a boost to his 'peanuts' in 1881, adding that in the twelve years they had been handling his publications, the 'peanuts' had sold more than 450,000 copies, and that he was yet to lose the first dollar by their dishonesty or failure to pay.[53]

Crofutt's Grip-Sack Guide was warmly welcomed in the press as the most accurate, complete and convenient source of information available anywhere on the Centennial State. The Denver Board of Trade also passed a special resolution to this effect, and the publicity afforded both to Crofutt and the Guide drew attention to his role as one of Colorado's earliest pioneers, now happily back again as a respected and sought-after member of Denver's business community.

One immediate result of Crofutt's success was an invitation to assist in the organization of the forthcoming National Mining and Industrial Exposition, which was to be opened in Denver in August 1882. A huge new Exposition Hall was under construction on South Broadway, and galleries, models, and displays illustrating western resources and development were being prepared on a lavish scale in order to attract visitors from all over the United States. Silver millionaire Horace Tabor was president of the Exposition's Board of Directors and Planning Committee, and with Crofutt back in their midst, members decided to create a special Bureau of Tourist and Excursion Affairs as part of the Exposition's attractions. Crofutt was appointed to organize excursions and special trains, and to advertise and handle all the arrangements.[54] From March 1882 onwards, he worked on the preparations from a special office in the Denver *Times* building, and in April travelled East to discuss details of

278

new special excursion rates to Denver with the superintendents of all the major railroad companies. That summer, so many crowds flocked to the Exposition, and to the side-trips in Colorado, the show was repeated in 1883 and 1884.

Meanwhile, Crofutt found time to pursue a wide range of other interests. He was an active member of the Denver Board of Trade (replaced by the Denver Chamber of Commerce in 1884), and in May 1882, for example, was invited to speak to his fellow businessmen on the economic advantages of establishing a paper factory in Denver. There was an insatiable demand for news, wrapping, tarred and building papers in the region, and urgent need to reduce the heavy burden of freight charges, which were found to be about one-quarter of the total cost of supplies coming from the Eastern States.[55]

Crofutt was also busy reviving an earlier dream to build, with a small group of associates, his own narrow-gauge railroad into the mountains west of Denver. His extensive reconnaissance through Colorado in 1880-81 while preparing the *Grip-Sack Guide* had been an object lesson in what narrow-gauge systems could achieve by their penetration of rough, steep, virtually inaccessible country; Crofutt's message was always "Colorado only needs to be known to be appreciated."

On 14th August 1882, with four business colleagues, Crofutt incorporated the Denver & California Short Line Railway Co. which proposed crossing the Continental Divide near Argentine Pass (13,100 ft), via the base of Green Mountain, Mt. Vernon Canyon, Bergen Township, Vance Creek and a point near Mt. Evans (14,264 ft).[56] A branch line to Georgetown was proposed, and later another to Leadville. Beyond Decatur, Summit County, little detail was supplied, although Crofutt apparently planned (Article VI) to run the Denver & California a little to the south of that section of northwest Colorado he had explored in 1865 while scouting David Butterfield's proposed stage line to Salt Lake City. A site for the railroad's depot in Denver had been secured between 15th Street and Zang's old brewery, close to Union Station.[57]

The company's proposals also included a telegraph, and a water transport system of pipes and irrigation ditches to supply mines, mills, farms, towns, and industries. As one historian wrote more than forty years later: "The plan to bring water thru the Moffat Tunnel [opened in 1928] from the Western Slope in order to supply domestic users in Denver was anticipated by Crofutt as long ago as 1882."[58]

Crofutt was kept busy for the next few months of 1882-3 arranging tourist excursions for visitors to the National Mining and Industrial Exposition, followed by his regular trip through the West to the Pacific to prepare the annual revision of his *New Overland Tourist*. After that, Crofutt was free to resume work on the railroad project. He checked the route from Denver to the Argentine Pass in more detail, and in 1883-4 completed a preliminary survey for the first division of 71 miles. Beyond southern Utah and Nevada, nothing if not hopeful, Crofutt examined Walker Pass (5248 ft), south of the High Sierra, as a feasible approach to Bakersfield, his projected railroad terminus in California. Crofutt worked hard to secure finance in Philadelphia and New York but for several reasons, the scheme was a total failure.

In the first place, during the early 1880s railroad competition in Colorado had ended the initial free-for-all; it had sorted out the survivors, and eliminated most of the small independent operators. Building new railroads without federal subsidy was a rich man's game, played for the most part by those with personal fortunes or by companies expanding an established regional network. Even then it was a risky business. David Moffat, one of the early pioneers who became a wealthy local banker was, like William Byers, Bela Hughes and John Evans, also one of Denver's earliest railroad enthusiasts, having helped to promote construction of the Denver Pacific north to Cheyenne, and the narrow-gauge Denver, South Park & Pacific. In 1881, Moffat backed a proposal for a new narrow-gauge — the Denver, Utah & Pacific — which was to run up South Boulder Canyon and tunnel under Rollins Pass (11,680 ft). Before long, however, the Burlington & Missouri Railroad, which completed its line across the plains of Nebraska and Colorado to reach Denver in May 1882, bought up the Denver, Utah & Pacific Co., found its proposed route through the Divide impracticable, and abandoned the project.

Twenty years later, Moffat was to sink his entire fortune into yet another attempt to build a direct east-west rail link from Denver to Salt Lake City — the standard-gauge Denver, Northwestern & Pacific Railway. It crossed Rollins Pass (which became the highest railroad pass in North America), and pushed on through Middle Park to reach Steamboat Springs in 1908. Moffat died three years later, financially and physically exhausted. The line eventually crawled along the Yampa Valley in 1913 to end at Craig, where the railroad was finally buried in a northwest Colorado landscape still as beautiful, and as gruelling, as Crofutt had found it fifty years before.

While David Moffat wore himself out in the vain attempt to build a direct rail link between Denver and Salt Lake City, the Denver & Rio Grande, and the associated D. & R.G. Western Railroad, had already linked the two cities in 1881-3 by a long, more roundabout route via Marshall Pass (10,856 ft), Gunnison, Grand Junction, Green River and Provo [Map XII]. In May 1883, General Palmer and Dr. Bell celebrated the completion of their new 'transcontinental' link to California (via the Central Pacific Railroad connection at Ogden), predicting that it would snatch at least one-half of the passenger and tourist traffic away from the

Union Pacific, and, despite the narrow-gauge, syphon off an appreciable amount of the U.P.'s freight traffic into the bargain.

Fierce rivalry between the Denver & Rio Grande, the Union Pacific, and the Atchison, Topeka & Santa Fe Railroads, as well as others waiting in the wings, dominated the action. But this was not all. While Crofutt carried on regardless, extending his own railroad survey in 1883-84 between Denver and the Argentine Pass, a new character had appeared on the stage. This was James J. Hagerman, a wealthy mine-owner and banker from Michigan who had arrived in Colorado Springs in 1884 suffering from the advanced stages of tuberculosis. His health improved. Instead of dying, Hagerman took on a new lease of life. He became engrossed in the development of Colorado, investing in silver mines at Aspen, coal near Glenwood Springs, and above all in a plan to build a railroad from Colorado Springs up the Ute Pass, and across South Park to Leadville. Not only would it follow a more direct route than either the Denver & South Park (U.P.) or the Denver & Rio Grande, this new Colorado Midland Railroad was to be standard-gauge. If it could be built at all through mountainous terrain hitherto regarded as negotiable only by narrow-gauge, the Colorado Midland would handle heavier pay-loads, and save time on transfers to the main standard-gauge tracks. A new line west into the Rockies, added to the existing D. & R.G. north-south railway would also boost Colorado Springs and Manitou, and carry tourists quickly and easily up to the meadows, wild flowers, lakes and picnic spots in South Park.

Comfortably installed in his rival's resort at Colorado Springs, Hagerman directed his explosive energies into wheeling and dealing his railroad over the Rockies into western Colorado, where he was determined to break the monopoly of the D. & R.G. In 1886, the Colorado Midland's standard-gauge swept triumphantly into Leadville, while in 1887-8, the D. & R.G. and the Colorado Midland both raced into Aspen, the centre of Pitkin County's rich silver mines, smelters and stone quarries. The Denver & Rio Grande, with a narrow-gauge system, was forced into a track-widening program on its main lines. In 1890, Hagerman would again thwart the opposition by selling his Colorado Midland Railroad to the Atchison, Topeka & Santa Fe, under the noses of the D. & R.G.:

> "This sale . . . will forever prevent the D. & R.G. from controlling the railroad system of Colorado," wrote Hagerman. "The Denver & Rio Grande were cock-sure of gobbling up the Midland, and gave it out publicly that the trade was about to be closed . . . To say that the D. & R.G. crowd in Denver are crazy with rage, chagrin (and) disappointment is putting it mildly." [59]

In such circumstances, there was little prospect for new railroad promoters with bold ideas but slender means. Crofutt and his associates on the

Denver & California Short Line were not in Hagerman's league, nor even that of Otto Mears, the celebrated wagon toll-road builder who switched his interests to narrow-gauge railroad construction in the Silverton area in the late 1880s. Crofutt made some progress with promises of funding from the American Loan and Trust Company in New York, but the bonds were not taken up; opposing interests, it was said, got wind of the scheme and deterred potential investors, while the short but sharp financial Panic of 1884 helped to put an end to the entire project. No track had been laid. A few years later, adding a curious twist to the story, Crofutt sold his 71-mile survey between Denver and the Argentine Pass to an old acquaintance from New York, "Brick" Pomeroy, whom he had first met as a fellow-editor in the early 1870s in Lower Manhattan.

At that time, while Crofutt had been busy publishing his *Trans-Continental Tourist's Guide* and *Crofutt's Western World*, Mark M. ("Brick") Pomeroy was working a few doors further along Nassau Street as owner-editor of the *New York Daily Democrat* and *Pomeroy's Democrat*, a pungent weekly founded in 1869 that had quickly reached a circulation of over 100,000 — one of the highest in the United States at that time.[60] In the mid-1870s, however, Pomeroy lost money; like Crofutt, he worked his way west to Denver in 1879, and immediately flung himself with boundless enthusiasm into a host of new projects.

One of these was for a proposed Atlantic and Pacific Mining and Railway Tunnel, some 5 miles in length, to be built through the Continental Divide near Georgetown, under Gray's Peak, Kelso Mountain and Loveland Pass (11,992 ft). David Moffat's proposal to tunnel under the Divide at Rollins Pass, a few miles to the north, had been shelved, but Pomeroy began work on his Atlantic and Pacific Tunnel in 1880-81, stressing the wealth from the silver, gold and lead ores that a tunnel at this location would expose. Through widespread promotion in Europe and the United States during the 1880s, Pomeroy gradually raised enough money to complete about one mile of tunnel under the Divide, but the project collapsed completely around the turn of the century, hit by the financial Panic of 1893, Pomeroy's death in 1896, mounting costs and severe technical problems.[61]

After his own abortive efforts in 1884, Crofutt wasted no more time in railroad speculation. Instead, he spent the latter part of the year preparing a second edition of his *Grip-Sack Guide of Colorado*, travelling extensively through the State and then returning to his new office in the Windsor block in downtown Denver to up-date the text. First-edition sales had been excellent; tourists and other out-of-State visitors had snapped it up, while Colorado's own small farming and mining communities were delighted that someone had taken the time and trouble to come and see what they were doing, advertise their efforts and put them

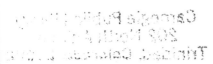

on the map. Favourable comments had continued to flow in from local Coloradoans ... the Guide was "chuck full of information"; "free from gloss or 'taffy' so often found in works of this kind"; "in condensed form, all the traveler or tenderfoot needs to know about the wonderful land that surrounds us"; "a model of its kind ... by an author who knows and is capable of seeing and describing." Crofutt and Colorado were working together, appreciating and boosting each other to their mutual advantage.

> "Colorado is no place for drones," Crofutt had said with breezy matter-of-factness at the start. "If you are ... such a person, *stay away* from Colorado, and let your friends, if you have any, support you in idleness."

The *Grip-Sack Guide*, again priced at $2.50, was available as a hard-bound 'library' edition or with tough flexible-cloth covers for those on the move. Crofutt kept pace with the latest railroad extensions and other developments in the second edition, expanding the Tours section and adding more than two hundred new settlements, mines, and farming and ranching areas. It was published in Omaha in April 1885 by Crofutt's Overland Publishing Co. and, together with an up-dated folded map, was ready once again for the spring and summer tourist invasion that year to the Centennial State.

Crofutt never wrote the set of four regional handbooks he had announced in 1878; production of the encyclopedic guide to Colorado had presumably taken too much time and energy, given the amount of

SALT LAKE CITY, FROM THE WAHSATCH RANGE
in W.H. Rideing, *Scenery of the Pacific Railways*, 1878

detail and personal investigation Crofutt liked to include. He did, however, visit Montana in the fall of 1885, where he compiled the detailed *Crofutt's Butte City Directory, including Walkerville, Meaderville, Centreville and Burlington. Also, Anaconda, Deer Lodge and Dillon . . . for 1885-6*, which was published in Butte City in November 1885.

A few months earlier, as he began his travels through Utah and Montana to record development along the latest extensions to the Union Pacific rail system, Crofutt had spent June and July 1885 in Salt Lake City, looking up old friends and producing a new City Directory while he did so — *Crofutt's Salt Lake City Directory for 1885-6*, priced at $2.50. Sixteen eventful years had passed since he and Edward Sloan had toiled together over Salt Lake's first successful city directory, published in those wild, heady days at the dawn of the transcontinental age. Crofutt was struck now by how little Utah was doing to attract tourists and health-seekers:

"Few, if any, ever think of Utah and its attractions. Why? True, the overland traveler 'takes in' Salt Lake City while en route across the continent,

65. LAKE PARK HOTEL AND BATHING PAVILION, GREAT SALT LAKE, UTAH
in *Crofutt's Overland Tours,* 1890
The Denver & Rio Grande Western Railroad's new bathing resort was opened in Utah in the mid-1880s.

spending a day or two, seldom more. One never sees or hears of any of these thousands with their 'summer houses', 'family cottages', and tented camps in Utah. Why is it? Is it for the want of natural attractions? or the climate? or the difficult access? or the markets? or the cost of living? We answer No! to all these questions . . .

Within a radius of fifty miles from Salt Lake City there are a greater variety of natural attractions, including hot, sulphur, soda, and medicinal springs, grand mountain scenery, . . . the great Salt Lake, . . . than can be found at (many of) the now famous and well patronized summer resorts . . .
But who knows of these things outside of Utah? Every resort in the world advertises its attractions but Utah." [62]

Salt Lake City remained impervious to the appeal to try harder. Other visitors, including government geologist F.V. Hayden, had already noted the attractions of Utah's climate for tubercular and bronchial sufferers, but the number of health-seekers drawn to Utah was never large compared with other centres in the West and Southwest. Salt Lake City had welcomed the new D. & R.G. rail link to Colorado in 1881-3, above all, as a new trade route for marketing Utah's coal, iron, and other minerals, and its agricultural products, as well as for the boost it gave to new Mormon settlement, business and industry. Tourism was merely a by-product. Short-stay visitors ebbed and flowed through Salt Lake City, intrigued to see Mormon life at close quarters. Indeed, the prompt completion of the 37-mile Utah Central Railroad in January 1870 had made Salt Lake City the first, and forever the most popular of all the side-trips on the original Union Pacific-Central Pacific transcontinental journey.

The city's Continental, Walker, White, Cliff, and other smaller hotels, coped with this traffic. In addition, the Walker House, under the same ownership as the huge Zion's Cooperative Mercantile Institution (Z.C.M.I.), ran a free guided tour service around town, and arranged business introductions and excursions for any visitors seeking more information.

But the concept of the specialized tourist resort, which figured so prominently in the growth strategies of California and Colorado, was not encouraged in Utah. Significantly, the one notable exception, Lake Park, 22 miles north of Salt Lake City, had been created by the Denver & Rio Grande Western railroad after Palmer and Bell's basic policy of planting new towns along their tracks was punched into Utah.

Lake Park had been developed in the mid-1880s as a large, elegant bathing resort on the Great Salt Lake, complete with first-class hotel, dressing-rooms, bathing attendants, and shower cabins for rinsing off the brine from the lake. There were restful lounges, libraries, boating facilities, and band concerts. At night, electric lights transformed the buildings and grounds into a delicate fairyland sparkling beside the shore. During the height of the season, 'bathing trains' ran almost hourly from Salt Lake City and Ogden to Lake Park. The success of this resort prompted the Union Pacific Railroad to take a leaf out of the D. & R.G.'s book in 1887 and develop the old bathing station of Garfield, 18 miles west of Salt Lake City. Lake Park and Garfield Beach, however, were to remain the only models of their kind in Utah during the Eighties.

Recording New Growth in the Far West in the Late 1880s:

"Crofutt Has Written the Field Notes of Half a Continent"

The population of the United States west of 95° W had more than doubled in the 1870s. In the 1880s, it nearly doubled *again*, as did Western railroad construction, in a decade of phenomenal expansion.

As the Eighties progressed, Crofutt decided to give up the publishing side of his business, and concentrate exclusively on travelling and writing the guides. *Crofutt's New Overland Tourist, and Pacific Coast Guide* had continued to sell well. Already, total sales of Crofutt's *Trans-Continental* and *New Overland* guides were reported to have topped 800,000, and in the late 1880s there was an enormous new wave of western development demanding attention. Crofutt was now sixty years old but he tackled the job, and the joy, of recording the ever-changing scene of American Progress in the West with characteristic energy and enthusiasm. In 1887, Crofutt closed his Overland Publishing Co. in Omaha, went to Chicago and put his forthcoming publication in the hands of the Arthur H. Day Co. at 126 Washington Street.

New transcontinental railroads and expanding regional networks were pouring farmers, ranchers, miners, merchants, clerks, mechanics, bankers, bricklayers, storekeepers, teachers, tourists, sales promoters, and the like into yet another 'New West' — into new settlements scattered along the corridors of railroad land, or into the thickening clusters of the few key centres. Colorado and the Pacific States cradled the sparsely settled landscapes of the Mountain West. In the late Eighties, Crofutt could record in addition to the newest sites, the spectacular recent growth of Kansas City, Omaha, Denver, and San Francisco — 'gateway' cities to the Great Plains, the Rockies, and the Pacific, and the four largest centres of population west of the Missouri River.

Crofutt spent much of 1887 and the first few months of 1888 on extensive travel through the West, filling notebooks with evidence of the latest phase of growth and consolidation.[63] Back in Denver in the spring of '88, he sorted through the mass of material collected, organizing, discarding, amending, up-dating, re-writing, expanding earlier records where appropriate, and working non-stop to deliver his copy to the publisher in Chicago, ready for the summer season. It was to be a comprehensive and reliable guide for tourists and emigrants along 10,000 miles of the American West.

The book was now called *Crofutt's Overland Tours. Consisting of nearly Five Thousand Miles of Main Tours, and Three Thousand Miles of Side Tours. Also Two Thousand Miles by Stage and Water;* there were just over 250 pages in a completely new layout, with illustrations, and a folded map showing all the tour routes in colour. Priced at $1.00, the guide was bound in flexible cloth, and fitted inside a stiff Manilla case. "Special effort has been made to avoid generalizing," Crofutt stressed . . . "and to express all the information in as plain and concise a manner as possible, using only such language as all can readily understand — booming no personal scheme, railroad, corporation or individual."

Once again, among the many practical hints for travellers in the opening pages, Crofutt reminded everyone to bring an open mind into the West, leaving prejudices and preconceptions behind, including any formed from the "Wild Bill" Hickok imagery of the dime novels or the new travelling Wild West shows (introduced in 1883 by "Buffalo Bill" Cody). "*Come along with us!* but first lay aside the dress-coat of style and don the wrapper of simplicity and ease . . . be natural, be on the alert with eyes and ears . . . enjoy the trip."

Crofutt retained his knack of enlivening the present with touches of the past. Readers were reminded as they read his introductory summary on the development and mobility of the American frontier that they were travelling through the West with a pioneer who had trudged across the plains for the first time nearly thirty years ago. A few lines were enough in places to recall the hazards of life there in the mid-1860s. On Pole Creek, Nebraska, near the site of Sidney, Crofutt told his fellow-passengers:

> "The mouldering headboard still stands — I see it many times each year, and we are again going that way, through the midst the 'buffalo range' of 25 years ago . . . There lie two of the 'noble redman's' numerous victims . . . I buried them both in one grave, rolled up in their blankets. A wagon seat served as a tombstone to mark the place, upon which a jack-knife carved their names. 'Farewell' was the last word — it was a low whisper.

> Two arrows and a rifle bullet . . . The Indian that did the deed . . . is now on a reservation, taking his rations regularly . . . and those trying times have passed, never to return."

Across the plains, through Colorado, Wyoming and Montana to the Pacific Northwest; through Utah and Nevada, or New Mexico and Arizona, into California; through Northern California and Oregon . . . By a combination of main line, side-trips and detours, *Crofutt's Overland Tours* explored the new ways through the West — through the contrasted landscapes, economies, and population patterns of a huge region now coming to the end of its primary frontier stage.

Nowhere was the evidence of recent growth more stunning than in Southern California. The Southern Pacific Railroad alone had brought c.50,000 settlers and tourists in 1885; the rate war that then developed with the Atchison, Topeka & Santa Fe, which by 1885 had built or leased its way into San Bernardino, San Diego, Los Angeles and San Francisco, resulted in over 250,000 immigrants and visitors coming to California in 1886-7. At the height of the rate war on 6th March 1886, the Southern Pacific offered a *$1-ticket* between Los Angeles and the Missouri! The Santa Fe held at $8! These rock-bottom prices were short-lived, but very low fares persisted on the rival carriers until well into 1887. Railroads reported that in 1887-8, 95 per cent of their passengers to Southern California were on one-way tickets (15% first-class; 80% second-class).[64] The President of one local Chamber of Commerce rejoiced at the news:

"Second-class are the bone and sinew of the country."

There was an unprecedented land boom in Southern California; sixty new towns were created between 1887 and 1889, thirty-six of them in 1887 in the San Gabriel Valley.[65] [Map XIII] As one of many examples, Crofutt noted the boisterous beginning of Azusa on the Santa Fe Railroad's route from San Bernardino to Los Angeles:

"It is near the head of San Gabriel valley, in the center of the Azusa ranch, one of the most famous of the old-time Spanish-Mexican estates. The town was opened to settlement early in 1887, and it is said, the rush made to buy lots exceeded anything before experienced in the development of California.

The people actually waited in line *all night* in the street and in the hallways in front of the company's office in Los Angeles in order that they might be able to make an early selection in the morning. Over $200,000-worth of lots were sold the first day, and improvements went ahead with a rush in the new town . . . and so it goes in this country."

There were brief but vivid references to other links in the chain of new or expanded settlements lining the route, including North Ontario, Claremont, North Pomona, Monrovia, Arcadia and Pasadena. Along the foothills of the Sierra Madre (San Gabriel Mountains), Crofutt again drew attention to the sharp contrasts in colour and land use. On the one hand, the irrigated tracts with their towns, shade trees, vineyards, orange groves, and orchards producing an abundant variety of fruits, berries and nuts; on the other, the unirrigated scrubland, and the long, dry gravel fans strewn with the boulders and rubble washed down from the mountains in times past. But the whole area was alive with new development, the 60-mile route from San Bernardino to Los Angeles closely staked and vibrant with growth:

"Many times, it is difficult to tell when you leave the borders of one town and enter the other. Should the ratio of settlement for the last year — 1887

— continue for the next ten, the valleys between San Bernardino and the Pacific Ocean will be *one continuous city.*"

The forecast would prove before long to be remarkably accurate although, in the next decade, the dizziest days of the late-Eighties land boom in Southern California were over.

Throughout, personal observations were stitched into the whole cloth of this enormous western reconnaissance. New armies were on the move. The guidebook's readers were not only carrying their basic equipment for the foray into the West — details about the scenic attractions, the wild life, the city centres, and all the how-to-get-there-where-to-stop-and-what-it-costs material that forms the 'nuts and bolts' of the tourist information industry. Crofutt's forces also clutched his "essential extras" for their Western expeditions — on-the-spot briefings about crop yields, grazing capacity, irrigated agriculture, lumber yards, grain elevators, mills, canneries, new mines, new smelters, new Chambers of Commerce, new schools, new churches, new theatres, new street lighting, new cement sidewalks, and the countless other growth points jabbed into the American West. These were the workaday emblems of progress, not to be missed or taken for granted.

> Civilization has literally rolled across the continent, Crofutt reminded his readers . . . "At the present time (1888-89), there are over nine hundred cities and towns — west of the old Missouri frontier — each with populations from 300 to 25,000, that have sprung into existence within the last twenty-five years."

*   *   *

The enthusiastic press notices and public support for *Crofutt's Overland Tours* showed that there was still a substantial market for a good comprehensive guidebook to Western America, especially for one that, while condensed, contained ample basic regional coverage for tourists and prospective settlers at the same time.

> "*Crofutt has gone across, up and down, and all over the Far West,*" wrote one Chicago journalist in 1888. "No-one can have *Crofutt's Overland Tours* in hand and not feel a strong impulse of desire to visit regions which are here so minutely, so accurately depicted."

> "'Crofutt' is now, as always, an indispensable part of the outfit of a trans-continental traveler. . . . It has been the favorite companion of tourists for many years, . . . but carry it for business or pleasure," advised the *Santa Barbara Independent.*

> "*Crofutt's Overland Tours* . . . a combine of history, biography, topography, geography . . . and statistics of the western half of the continent. . . . The book is of great value to all classes of people, whether they travel or not." (*Field and Farm,* Denver)

"All the necessary information for intelligent sight-seeing in California," was the verdict of the *Los Angeles Tribune,* particularly pleased that the guide was up to date with details on Southern California's new railroads and new towns. "George A. Crofutt is the Baedeker of California."

Judge Goodwin, of Salt Lake City, had no doubts about what he considered the strengths of the guide:

"*Crofutt's Overland Tours* covers the country traversed by the Union Pacific, D. & R.G., Atchison, Topeka & Santa Fe, and Central and Southern Pacific, and their kindred roads . . . every point on 8000 miles . . . making a traveler's encyclopedia of nearly the whole West. It merges in one volume a perfect guide-book and a book of travels. If one picks it up for information he will find himself forgetting what he was seeking for in following through an enchanting story; if he searches for something to interest himself with, he will be sure to stumble upon half-a-dozen important facts of which he was before ignorant. The wonder grows all the time how so much could be condensed in a form so compact and pleasing.

It contains the field notes of a mathematical eye taking a bird's-eye-view of half a continent. It is a mental topographical map . . ." [66]

Revised and enlarged editions of *Crofutt's Overland Tours* were published regularly until 1892, and continued to be sold by all the major railroad and navigation companies working the West. In 1889, the guide was published in both Chicago and Philadelphia by H. J. Smith & Co., while in 1890, Rand, McNally & Co. (Chicago and New York) published the work in two companion volumes, *Crofutt's Overland Guide* and *Crofutt's Overland Tours,* complete with illustrations and fold-in maps, and priced at $1.00 each. Crofutt supervised the Rand, McNally production himself, staying in Chicago in 1890-91, as usual at his favourite hotel, the Briggs House.

In the 1888 edition of the guide, Crofutt had invited anyone who needed more information or advice about the West to write to him in Denver, or via the publishing house in Chicago. In 1890, however, he finally announced that he could no longer manage to keep up his correspondence service; having personally answered up to twenty letters a week for the last twenty years, he told his readers, along with all his other activities, he now had to retire from this demanding sideline. It was a sideline which, nevertheless, had been one of Crofutt's most valued contributions to the West's information industry.

The Indispensable Attraction: California Shapes the Patterns of Western America's Tourist Industry in the 1880s

Central and Southern California's tourist centres and health spas responded dramatically to the railroad boom of the Eighties as the State surged into the lead in the race to expand the Western tourist industry. With new hotels, expanding rail networks, new tour operators, and competitive excursion rates, the resort concept became increasingly attractive to visitors, residents and investors.

Like the boosters along Colorado's Rocky Mountain Front, California's entrepreneurs adopted the strategy of pouring investment into a small number of key attractions. It was the 'Law of Concentrated Effort'. Other business would follow, ripples would spread — but first, the big splash. The 'Two E's', Europe and the Eastern United States, still dominated volume traffic of the kind the West had to win. Given its isolation in time and distance, California went all out to stimulate a strong, steady flow of tourists and long-term visitors, anchored by a well-to-do middle class demanding, as always, value for money. In the 1880s, the Far Western destination had to be a more reliable crowd-puller than the journey itself, however comfortable and diverting this could still be made after the initial excitement of making the journey for the first time had worn off. To travel hopefully was fine, but it was never to be better than to arrive, if the California resort developers had their way.

The Great Hotels

More than ever, first-class hotels pegged the resorts into place. The State's original 'railroad resort' was the elegant Hotel Del Monte on Monterey Bay, "the largest and most complete all-the-year-round Sea-Side Resort on the Pacific Coast," as Crofutt had described it. This delightful "world-

THE HOTEL DEL MONTE, MONTEREY, CALIFORNIA
in *Crofutt's Overland Tours*, 1890

of-its-own," covering in time some 7000 acres, had been built at the southern end of the bay, one mile from the old town of Monterey, by the Southern Pacific Railroad — specifically through its construction subsidiary, the Pacific Improvement Company. Opened in June 1880, the Hotel Del Monte not only attracted San Francisco society but immediately became a popular focus for winter and summer rail tours, with special extended-stay rates, for visitors from the Midwest, the Eastern States, and from Europe.

The hotel, accommodating about 750 guests, was set in the heart of 200 landscaped acres, an important feature of the resort as Crofutt explained to his readers in the *Overland Tours:*

> "In the grounds are immense live-oaks, stately pines, spruce, cypress, fan-palms, banana, cactus, pampas ... with lakes, drives, walks, ten-pin alley, swings, tennis and croquet grounds, slides, etc., together with conservatories, plants and vines, flower mounds and beds in great variety, from temperate, semi-tropical and tropical regions.

> Here can be visited a Labyrinth Hedge or Puzzle - the only one in this country. The hedge is of cypress, about seven feet high and four feet wide, with gravel walks of about the same width. The walks are half-mile to the center if followed directly, but we walked over an hour and never *did* reach the center, and then near another hour before we could get out. We are told that a number of instances have occurred where parties have wandered into this puzzle in the evening, could not find their way out, and not wishing to make an outcry, remained in over night — others cut the hedge and crawled out. This puzzle affords much amusement at times to the old *habitués*.

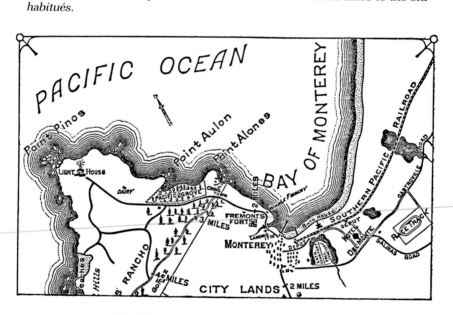

OLD MONTEREY AND THE HOTEL DEL MONTE
Part of a map published in 1883

THE RAYMOND HOTEL, PASADENA, CALIFORNIA
in P.C. Remondino, *The Mediterranean Shores of America.*
Southern California, 1892
This illustration had been regularly featured in Raymond & Whitcomb's prospectus, *A
Winter in California,* since 1886-7.

Farther south, the magnificent Hotel Raymond opened in 1886 in Pasadena. The Boston-based travel agency of Raymond & Whitcomb had been
founded in 1879 as a domestic competitor to Thomas Cook, whose Boston
branch office had already been doing a roaring trade since 1873 only a few
doors away on Washington Street. Boston was always a key city in the
development of transcontinental travel. Walter Raymond, a young Harvard graduate, was anxious to expand the California side of his father's
business through resort development, and came west in 1883 to find a
suitable location for a new hotel.

Offered his pick of the sites along the projected Los Angeles & San
Gabriel Valley Railroad, Walter chose a low hill rising above the floor of
the valley at Pasadena. It lay in the heart of the old Marengo Ranch, five
miles from the foot of the Sierra Madre, and surrounded by farmland and
orange groves. There, complete with its own railroad station, Raymond
planted one of the great new palaces on Southern California's tourist

frontier. "The transcontinental traveler stops at the very door." The head gardener at the Hotel Del Monte had been hired to landscape the grounds, while the manager and staff of the Crawford House, Raymond's hotel in the White Mountains of New Hampshire, were brought out to Pasadena for the winter months, returning regularly to New England for the summer season.[67] The Raymond placed an unmistakably Boston-styled punctuation mark in the San Gabriel Valley, and the response was staggering. In its first season, the hotel entertained thirty-five thousand guests in the fall, winter and spring of 1886-7.[68] Bostonians who sought changes geographical, not social, could now shuttle happily across the continent from one Hub to another. As one of them observed with great satisfaction:

> "You are taken from a snow storm in Boston and a few days later find yourself in a Boston hotel . . . amid the orange groves of the Pacific summer land." [69]

68.   VIEW OF THE SIERRA MADRE MOUNTAINS AND PASADENA, FROM THE
VERANDA OF THE RAYMOND HOTEL
in W. Lindley and J.P. Widney, *California of the South*, 1888

The huge Hotel del Coronado opened in February 1888 near San Diego, and effectively marked that city's long-awaited entry into the transcontinental tourist age. In a great burst of energy, the Coronado had been built in less than a year, a vast "fairy-tale palace" rising from the ocean. Despite its size, the hotel quickly achieved the enviable reputation of high style in a relaxed, even intimate atmosphere. The general verdict was that, astonishingly, the Hotel del Coronado was "mammoth yet homelike," wherever you wandered:

> "The dining-room may safely be called roomy," said one visitor, "as it seats a thousand guests, and your dearest friends could not be recognized at the extreme end. Yet there is no dreary stretch or caravansary effect, and today every seat is filled, and a dozen tourists waiting at the door." [70]

In addition to every conceivable indoor amusement — games, lectures, lantern-slides and talks on California's tourist, business and investment opportunities, plays, dancing, minstrel shows, sketching, singing and instrumental classes, and more — the sunshine and balmy air beckoned the guests outside for hours on end. Facilities for sea-bathing, fishing, yachting, rowing, archery, tennis, hunting rabbits, shooting game birds, playing polo, riding to hounds, or quietly dozing, left many visitors booking their next trip before they left, the perfect arrangement for establishing a loyal, long-distance clientele ready to 'cut and come again' to their favourite resort. The Coronado entertained more than 350,000 guests in its first seven years. [71]

Given its isolated location, the hotel's instant success was a triumph. Vigorous, nation-wide promotion of the deserted peninsula had begun in 1886, when a well-directed advertising campaign encouraged thousands of potential investors to take the free ferry-rides provided across San Diego Bay to view the site of the planned new town of Coronado and the projected great resort hotel alongside. The promoters reached out to the Great Lakes and the Atlantic seaboard. Daily temperature statistics for the San Diego region began to be listed in the Eastern newspapers, and progress reports on the hotel's amazingly swift construction appeared regularly in the Midwestern and Northeastern press. Indeed, guests made the first room reservations at the Coronado from the architects' drawings, five months before the hotel was completed.

After the opening, the Hotel del Coronado gave a powerful boost to local residential development. As one observer noted in 1888:

> "One year ago, the Coronado Beach peninsula was a barren waste; today, a prosperous town with hundreds of pretty cottages, with beautiful shrubbery and flower-gardens, attractive parks, and delightful drives. There are now several stores, several fine churches, and a good school-house. Arrangements have been made for the most complete historical and scientific museum on the Pacific coast, and added to these is the Coronado, ... the largest hotel in Southern California." [72]

69.   THE HOTEL DEL CORONADO, NEAR SAN DIEGO, CALIFORNIA

This photograph was taken soon after the opening of the Coronado in February 1888. Elisha S. Babcock (in foreground, with dogs) was a health-seeker from Evansville, Indiana who, as co-founder of the Coronado Beach Co., bought and began to develop the peninsula in 1885 as the railroad neared San Diego, and quickly built the largest beach resort hotel in Western America.

Red-roofed turrets, white woodwork, spectacular architectural design, and electric lighting installed under Thomas Edison's personal supervision, all helped to create the legend. Climate, facilities, and masterly promotion did the rest.

Essentially unchanged today in function and appearance, the magnificent century-old Coronado is thus the longest surviving grand Victorian resort hotel in the West. It is a National Historic Landmark, and the largest all-wooden building in the United States.

70. ENJOYING THE SUNSHINE AND SEA AIR AT THE CORONADO

in Charles D. Warner, *Our Italy,* 1891

Back in New York, Warner wrote: "The stranger, when he first comes upon this novel hotel and this marvellous scene of natural and created beauty, is apt to exhaust his superlatives. I hesitate to attempt to describe this hotel — this airy and picturesque and half-bizarre wooden creation of the architect. Taking it and its situation together, I know nothing else in the world with which to compare it, and I have never seen any other which so surprised at first, that so improved on a two weeks' acquaintance, and that has left in the mind an impression so entirely agreeable."

Other first-class hotels were opening in this extraordinarily active period for new, or re-styled, tourist resorts in Southern California. The Arcadia opened at Santa Monica in 1887, and work started on the great Redondo Hotel, part of the Redondo Beach resort development financed largely by two San Francisco businessmen, J.C. Ainsworth and R.R. Thompson, on the old Sausal Redondo ranch, sixteen miles south of Los Angeles. Long Beach, twenty-three miles from Los Angeles on the Wilmington branch of the Southern Pacific railroad, catered for "people of refined tastes," . . . "no saloons . . . nothing loud . . . much that is aesthetic." Also in 1887, the Southern Pacific extended its track from Los Angeles to Santa Barbara, bringing a surge of new tourists, health-seekers and residents to a resort which, until then, had made do with steamship and stagecoach. By 1888, there were seventy-nine major hotels in Southern California, open or nearing completion, along with a substantial increase in the number of boarding-houses that had opened in the previous two years.

71.

REDONDO BEACH, NEAR LOS ANGELES

The scene shows three classic components of Southern California's new seaside resorts in the late 1880s and 1890s: the railroad, an extensive beach, and a first-class hotel. The Santa Fe brought its car-loads of passengers right to the shore to enjoy the beach, the promenade, the Redondo Beach Hotel (opened in 1890), and the steamer and fishing pier, just off the left of the picture.

THE ST. ANGELO HOTEL, LOS ANGELES

Built in 1887 at Grand Avenue and Temple Street, the St. Angelo helped to meet the sudden demand in the late Eighties for more medium-size hotels and boarding-houses in the city of Los Angeles.

Boosters continued to act as California's independent or semi-official Land and Immigration Agents. Some were invited west, and then sponsored and financed by the railroads, the large hotels, or by local newspapers and Chambers of Commerce. Others were individual entrepreneurs, restored invalids or city merchants bent on regional growth and market expansion, and gifted with a flair for publicity. Handbooks, magazines, novels, short stories, and ingenious advertising copy flowed from the presses into the libraries, newspapers and homes of the Midwest, the Eastern States, and Europe. Major Ben Truman, masterminding much of the promotional literature of the Southern Pacific Railroad, published numerous books and pamphlets in the Eighties, building on the reputation he had gained as a lively and versatile writer ever since the Civil War. *Occidental Sketches* appeared in 1881, and in

73.   A SCENE IN THE MARIPOSA GROVE
THE SEQUOIA GIGANTEA — OR BIG TREES
in B.C. Truman, *Tourists' Illustrated Guide to the Celebrated Summer and Winter Resorts of California,* 1883

1883, his influential *Tourists' Illustrated Guide to the Celebrated Summer and Winter Resorts of California,* along with *Homes and Happiness in the Golden State of California.* Ben's ebullient personality is stamped all over them. Referring to Truman, and to Colonel Tom Fitch, a New Yorker who made a name for himself in California as an editor, booster, and land auctioneer, Walker wrote in his *Literary History of Southern California,* that both "performed with a frontier flourish and boisterous humor quite absent in the men who succeeded them." [73]

The expansion of Cook's Tours and Raymond & Whitcomb Excursions

Thomas Cook had pioneered the package tour in the United States in the 1860s, and laid his groundwork in Western America during the 1870s. After the departure of his first Around-the-World Tour in 1872, followed by the introduction of the American edition of *Cook's Excursionist* in March 1873, Cook began a period of hard bargaining with American railroad companies coast to coast for reduced rates and 'through' tickets. [74] In 1876, Cook's elaborate display pavilion at the Centennial Exhibition in Philadelphia had attracted huge crowds. As business between Europe and the Eastern States was expanding, the company chose 1876 to launch *Cook's Special Personally-Conducted Tour to California* (July-August), departing from New York and Philadelphia. It included San Francisco, Merced, Yosemite, the Mariposa goldfields and Big Trees, Clark's Ranch (Wawona), parts of the Central Valley and Napa Valley, as well as the petrified forest, geysers and springs region between Calistoga and Cloverdale [Map X]. Cook's Western American tours never looked back.

During the 1880s, while Niagara Falls, Hudson River and the Catskills, Saratoga, the Adirondacks, and the White Mountains remained the rich top dressing on Cook's feast of eastern attractions, the key western centres railroaded their way into the catalogues. Tickets on Cook's pioneering *Grand Annual Excursion to California* were soon validated for up to six months so that tourists could extend their stay in California, and return home independently. Cook's Tourists, with their guide, always travelled together once the party had collected all its members from the various assembly points on the eastern seaboard. But many wanted to linger in California, to return to favourite locations, do some business in San Francisco, or, by the early Eighties, savour the delights of an autumn at the Hotel Del Monte on Monterey Bay, before finally heading back home.

California remained the focus of Cook's Western American, Canadian and Mexican tour system — the indispensable attraction. Of the thirty branch offices Cook maintained in North America during the 1880s, in

HARPER'S WEEKLY.

JOURNAL OF CIVILIZATION.

Vol. XXX.—No. 1561.
Copyright, 1886, by Harper & Brothers.
NEW YORK, SATURDAY, NOVEMBER 20, 1886.
TEN CENTS A COPY.
$4.00 PER YEAR, IN ADVANCE.

74.   THE ANTLERS HOTEL, COLORADO SPRINGS, WITH PIKE'S PEAK

Drawn by Charles Graham, Harper's Weekly, November 20, 1886

General Palmer opened The Antlers in Colorado Springs in 1883. Nation-wide advertisement like this on the front cover of *Harper's* was invaluable. Charles Graham, a regular contributor to *Harper's Weekly* throughout the Eighties and early Nineties, was one of the most versatile and popular artists of the American West. Inside, readers learned more about the appeal of Colorado Springs:

". . . clear skies, bright sunshine, . . . attractive homes, an excellent hotel, no saloons, broad tree-lined and irrigation-ditched avenues, delightful society, and magnificent scenery are the distinctive features of this Western resort."

addition to his New York headquarters on Broadway, only two were located in the West — the first in San Francisco at the Palace Hotel, and later, another in Denver. Most of the increasing but still relatively small amount of tourist traffic to Oregon and Alaska, by rail and steamer, was organized from San Francisco, even after the northern transcontinental railroads reached Puget Sound.

The pulling power of the Golden State never slackened. Throughout the Eighties, the highly popular *Cook's Grand Annual Excursions to California* (May-July, from New York, Boston, Philadelphia, Baltimore, or Washington, D.C., via Niagara Falls), continually added new approach routes across the continent, and extra side-trips. In 1887, for example, the inclusive cost for Pullman travel, first-class hotels, carriage-drives, all incidentals, and side-trips which included Puget Sound and British Columbia, was just under $9 a day. On the southern flank, *Cook's Pleasure Tours to California and Mexico* by the late 1880s were offering six departure dates annually between December and March. Most of the time was spent in California, with full advantage taken of the new southern resort hotels. In Mexico, the Pullman Palace Cars substituted for hotel accommodation, except in Mexico City.

With California so firmly established by public demand as the one essential western destination, Cook proceeded to follow another of his own basic rules for successful long-distance tour operation, what may be termed the 'Law of the Improved Intervening Attractions-Total Distance Ratio'. "Next to California," Cook wrote, "Colorado contains grander natural scenery and more varied attractions than any other part of the Union," and he kept a close eye on General Palmer's railroad and resort developments. For tourists and tour operators, the choice of transcontinental routes to California was to depend heavily on the relative merits and variety of *passing* and *short-stay* attractions strung along the track. Indeed, the ratio of these intervening attractions to the total length of the journey had continually to be increased if the tourist industry was to go on bringing dollars into the West.

Although Colorado's success in attracting tourists and health-seekers remained second to that of California, the Centennial State boosted business dramatically in and after 1883 through the popularity of the D. & R.G. Western Railroad, and the spectacular alternative route it offered to those heading west to California via Salt Lake City. Colorado had finally taken sweet revenge. In the mid-1860s, Grenville Dodge and the westward-bound Union Pacific engineers had shunned the great wall of the Front Range in Colorado. Now the tourists made different assessments. They favoured towering peaks, steep passes, and narrow gorges; they wanted their Rocky Mountains high, all around them, and seemingly impenetrable — provided that in fact they were nothing of the sort, and

75.

MANITOU AND PIKE'S PEAK

in *Crofutt's Grip-Sack Guide of Colorado,* 1885

Manitou House, seen on the right, had opened in 1872 and set the style demanded by
General Palmer and Dr. Bell for first-class hotel accommodation at their new spa. Other
large hotels, as well as boarding-houses and cottages, were soon added.

that the way ahead had already been opened safely, comfortably, and
with the minimum of delay.

Cook quickly boosted the packaging of Colorado and California. As
the Eighties progressed, virtually every Cook's Tour to California went via
Colorado, either on the outward or return journey. Thomas Cook's son,
John Mason Cook, was equally keen to expand and consolidate their
American business. The company highlighted the route through Colorado for west-bound tourists who had arrived in Denver from St. Louis
and Kansas City, or from Omaha, and stressed how much more could
now be enjoyed by the D. & R.G.'s through-line to Utah. There were not
only the splendours around Colorado Springs, Manitou, Pike's Peak and
the Garden of the Gods, but also Pueblo, Cañon City, the Royal Gorge of
the Arkansas River, Marshall Pass, the Black Cañon of the Gunnison,
Montrose and Grand Junction. After this magnificent 'detour', passengers
were whisked on to Salt Lake City, Ogden and Sacramento. Although the
Union Pacific's shorter route from Cheyenne to Ogden could still be

Raymond & Whitcomb Prospectus for the Annual Spring Trip to California, 1888. By this time, the company was running tours to California continuously throughout the year.

76. CALIFORNIA AND COLORADO DOMINATE THE TOURIST INDUSTRY OF WESTERN AMERICA IN THE 1880s

requested, the only standard recommended Cook's Tour to California that omitted Colorado was the great Western Perimeter Route — through El Paso, Texas on the Southern Pacific Railroad to Los Angeles, with the return via the Yellowstone National Park, Wyoming, and the Northern Pacific Railroad. In 1883, Thomas Cook's grandson, Frank H. Cook, had spent several weeks exploring Yellowstone on horseback and planning excursions in advance of the Northern Pacific's grand opening ceremony to which this third generation of the company had been officially invited. The first Cook's Tour to Yellowstone was offered in 1884.

Yellowstone was the pride of the Northern Pacific. Indeed, the creation of the United States' first National Park in 1872 had been powerfully lobbied by railroad financier Jay Cooke who wanted a share of the West's new tourist traffic, and saw Yellowstone as his answer to California's Yosemite. Yellowstone's gorgeous colours, and its astounding landscape of geysers, hot springs, caves, canyons and terraces, had been widely publicized in the 1870s through the fine watercolours and oil paintings by Thomas Moran, and the popular sets of chromolithographs based on them. Both Thomas Moran and photographer William H. Jackson had accompanied F. V. Hayden on the official survey of Yellowstone in 1871, and their work had strongly influenced Congress in its decision to create "a public park or pleasuring-ground for the benefit and enjoyment of the people" which was to be preserved in its "natural condition."[75]

With the eventual completion of the Northern Pacific Railroad in 1883, tourists could reach Cinnabar, Montana, about six miles from the northern boundary of the Park. The whole line was advertised as the "Wonderland Route to the Pacific," but in fact, overall, the Northern Pacific's 'Intervening Attractions-Total Distance' ratio was comparatively low, and even in Yellowstone, the major wonders were widely scattered within the Park. Given the federal government's determination to preserve the wilderness, which, by statute, had been "reserved and withdrawn from settlement, occupancy, or sale," the concept of large-scale resort development conflicted with official policy, and private corporations like the speculative Yellowstone Park Improvement Company were actively discouraged. The Park had been placed under the exclusive control of the Secretary of the Interior, who was authorized to grant only short-term leases (not exceeding ten years) "of small parcels of ground at such places in said park as shall require the erection of buildings for the accommodation of visitors." On his first visit to the United States in 1889, Rudyard Kipling found Yellowstone Park's Mammoth Hot Springs Hotel to be just "a huge yellow barn," and the other hotels mostly "wooden shanties."[76] Kipling had arrived at Yellowstone on the Fourth of July, and found himself overwhelmed, much to his disgust, by a large, exuberant

Raymond Excursion party. "Aren't you one of 'em?", asked the stage driver. "No," said Kipling, . . . "I do not know Mister Rayment [*sic*]. I belong to T. Cook and Son." [77]

Transport within the Park remained a problem. Back in 1872, soon after the creation of Yellowstone Park, a contributor to *Scribner's Monthly* in New York had confidently forecast that "Yankee enterprise will dot the new Park with hostelries and furrow it with lines of travel." [78] But federal decisions had quickly squashed the idea, and internal improvements to the Park's hotels and highways were only slowly introduced. It was not until the Army Corps of Engineers completed a 145-mile road circuit through the Park in 1891 that Yellowstone's popularity grew significantly. Even then, travelling by buggy, surrey or stagecoach, some visitors still thought the long drives between the major attractions "tedious," and

7.   ON THE ROAD THROUGH YELLOWSTONE NATIONAL PARK IN THE 1890s
"A tight squeeze," noted one of the party, "between our stage and a hauling team on the narrow road."

much of the scenery separating the marvels "disappointingly dull." John Aubertin, visiting Yellowstone in 1886, saw a young man who had just been round the Park standing at the station, ready to leave. Aubertin, preparing to go in, asked what it was like. "It is very fatiguing," came the reply; "you have a long way to go for everything you have to see." Aubertin tried again — was it worth all the bother? The young man was politely lukewarm: "Um-m-m-m — yes; oh, yes, it's certainly worth going to see, and particularly as you have come so far." [79]

Except for those tourists with the time and money to make a grand regional reconnaissance through the West, including both the perimeter and the central routes, the Northern Pacific Railroad could do little to capitalize on the soaring popularity of California when advertising its own tourist attractions. By contrast, Colorado was able to do so primarily through the extra business California-bound passengers brought to the Denver & Rio Grande Western's highly scenic route to Ogden, Utah. After 1883, the D. & R.G. was widely advertised as "the most beautiful way to reach California," and "the *only* trans-continental line passing directly through Salt Lake City." And nothing pleased the company more than to hear California-bound Easterners and Europeans booked through on the D. & R.G. system tell their friends that they were going to travel from Omaha to Utah "via the Rockies," as though the Union Pacific had somehow now found other mountains to cross.

The D. & R.G.'s highly publicized "Colorado Loop" to Ogden, via Denver, Grand Junction and the valley of the Great Salt Lake, was nearly 900 miles long, almost twice the length of the Union Pacific's route from Cheyenne to Ogden. But the 'Intervening Attractions-Total Distance' ratio was increased at least ten-fold, not only by the cities and resorts studding the Rocky Mountain Front, and the dramatic route through the gorges behind it, but also by the opportunity for a closer look, from the train, at the Mormon settlements and irrigated farms in the Great Valley, as passengers rolled on towards Salt Lake City, and a special city tour.

The D. & R.G. had invested heavily in Pullman Palace Cars, Horton Reclining-Chair Cars, and special Observation Cars for their "scenic route across the continent." *Cook's American Tours* increased their offers of specially-reduced tickets to Colorado between 1st May and 31st October, in association with the D. & R.G., and built the reductions into their California program at the same time. This was an important development since fares and side-trips on the Denver & Rio Grande had, up till then, been relatively expensive. While the introduction of new Intervening Attractions was vital to the buoyancy of the tourist industry, economic considerations involving travel time and ticket costs could never be ignored in this highly competitive market.

*   *   *

78a.   UNION PACIFIC ADVERTISEMENT IN *COOK'S EXCURSIONIST,* MARCH 1885

This advertisement appeared in every issue of *Cook's Excursionist* from March 1885 to March 1886 as part of the Union Pacific's fight against increasing competition for the Western tourist traffic. The U.P.'s business was severely affected by the Denver & Rio Grande Western's 'Colorado Loop', and by the completion of the Southern Pacific's and Santa Fe's transcontinental routes into Southern California.

The fact that the Union Pacific now had to advertise itself as the 'Pioneer Transcontinental Line' reflects the widespread adoption of the word *transcontinental* by the West's expanding rail system.

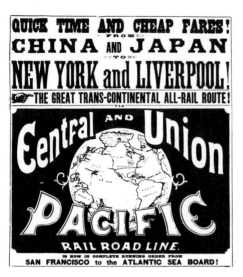

(i) Central and Union Pacific poster, 1870

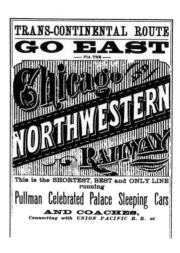

(ii) Chicago and Northwestern Railway folder, 1875

(iii) Rock Island Railroad— Rand McNally folder, 1875

(iv) Northern Pacific Railroad panel, 1883

78b.   TRANSCONTINENTAL: THE 'ALL-AMERICAN WORD'

Following the success of the *Great Trans-Continental Railroad Guide,* the Union Pacific adopted the word officially in December 1869. Others soon followed.

Cook's major American competitor, the Raymond & Whitcomb Co., organized their first transcontinental excursion to California in 1881. Founded in Boston in 1879 by Emmons Raymond and Irvine A. Whitcomb, the firm had its roots in New England's railroad and hotel trade. Emmons Raymond was President of the Passumpsic River Railroad, with interests also in the Boston & Montreal, Boston & Maine, and Vermont Railroads. Whitcomb, born in Swanzey, N.H. had started work in a stationery store in Lawrence, Massachusetts, and later become a conductor on the Boston, Concord & Montreal Railroad.[80] Emmons' son, Walter Raymond, was eager to diversify the firm's interests beyond its original concentration on the White Mountains excursion and hotel business. He saw the West as an essential element in the company's growth, a potentially rich slice of the market that could not be left wide open to English competition in the shape of Thomas Cook.

Boston was already fertile ground for transcontinental tourists and health-seekers. Nathaniel Carter had been promoting trips to Southern California since 1872, and had worked in association with Whitcomb in the mid-1870s. Carter's beautiful health retreat at Sierra Madre, however, fourteen miles from Los Angeles and "in the midst of an orange grove," was to remain isolated from the railroad. Unlike Thomas Cook & Son, Raymond and Whitcomb invested increasingly heavily in the hotel business, and they continued to link their American tour operation, wherever possible, to their own company hotels. When Walter Raymond led his first excursion to California in 1881 and saw the Hotel Del Monte, he knew that the excursion business would take off like a rocket if ample first-class hotel accommodation could be paired with Southern California's matchless climate. During the late 1880s, the Raymond & Whitcomb excursions expanded from eight, to ten, and finally to twelve different winter tours annually to California. The magnificent Raymond Hotel in Pasadena had sealed their success, although the other resort hotels were all incorporated into the year-round excursion program.[81]

Prices, packaging, choice of routes, and flexible return-ticket arrangements were similar to those of Thomas Cook, as both companies kept a close eye on any new features or popular 'extras' introduced by the competition. One European visitor to the American West in the mid-Eighties, watching the tour operators and ancillary services at work, was continually impressed by "the concentration of attention given in the States to keep everybody moving about, with all sorts of information at hand besides."[82] At the end of the decade, Raymond & Whitcomb, much like Cook, were offering a week in Yellowstone Park as part of a transcontinental, 36-day excursion that went west on the Northern Pacific Railroad, and returned east on the latest attraction, the Canadian Pacific Railway. The cost, however, worked out at nearly $10.50 a day, considerably more than Raymond & Whitcomb's blockbusting *Grand Western Tour*, which combined a week in Yellowstone with the Pacific Northwest, an extended stay in the indispensable California (with many side-trips between San Francisco, Yosemite, and Southern California as far south as San Diego and the Coronado Hotel), and a return journey through Arizona, New Mexico and Colorado. Then it was back to Boston, via Chicago and Niagara Falls, after a memorable two months priced, all-in, at $8.60 a day. The annual *Colorado and California Spring Tour* from Boston cost about $7 a day.

On top of all this, Raymond & Whitcomb still found it necessary to run annual *Grand Trips to Southern California by a Direct and Expeditious Route* (the Atchison, Topeka & Santa Fe). California's great resort hotels, established during the 1880s, remained responsive to demand. Indeed, California now contained some of the best and cheapest hotels in the United States. The Hotel Del Monte at Monterey, opened in 1880, was enlarged after a fire in 1887 in order to accommodate the huge increase in business, especially long-term visitors, organized by Cook's, Raymond & Whitcomb, and smaller, regional tour companies. While seeking to attract the comfortably-off, with the time and money to spare, the Del Monte was nevertheless careful not to price itself out of the market. By 1889, for example, Raymond & Whitcomb, still clearing their own profit, were offering their well-established 6-month winter trips to California, including 5 months' stay at the Hotel Del Monte and first-class Pullman Palace Car rail travel, for what amounted to only $3.50-$4 a day. The daily (24-hour) cost of travel on the Pullman Palace Cars alone at this period, with Parlor and Sleeping Car accommodation, and meals, was about $20.

Raymond & Whitcomb excursionists were "entirely relieved from the ordinary cares, responsibilities, and petty annoyances of traveling." The company treated every group as special guests, well-cushioned from the rough elements of society, and from all avoidable delays and interruptions to the advertised schedule. It also avoided "any ostentatious display, which would naturally be obnoxious to persons of quiet tastes. Members of our parties move from place to place as private travelers, and are received at hotels as private guests. ... In the cars they form a select company, and are relieved of the annoyance of being placed in proximity to strangers, and, as it often happens in the common way of traveling, undesirable people." Women travelling alone were advised that they could do so in secure and congenial surroundings, and many took advantage of making at least their first trip west with Raymond & Whitcomb. Souvenir lists of the members of each party were printed, along with other mementoes.

The general verdict was that the firm gave value for money. Mary Wills, travelling independently, "not a member of a Raymond excursion, nor under any obligations to praise it," concluded after regular observation that here were "shrewd, sharp Yankee conductors ... neither philanthropists nor conducting business for love. They make money ... They make bargains, and can by their fiat make or unmake a resort." But Mrs. Wills approved the system; "You will go in first-class style, and a little cheaper than you can travel alone" (i.e. at the same standard). Between the resorts, Raymond & Whitcomb's vestibuled trains had their own dining-car, so whatever the delays, she commented, "and whether in a mountain or a morass, the meal is always forthcoming at the proper time." [83]

Susie Clark had had a marvellous time on her first transcontinental excursion from Boston to California with Raymond & Whitcomb, at the end of the Eighties. Here was the authentic New England note, as fresh and clear as it had been at the dawn of the transcontinental railroad age twenty years before:

> "What a glorious journey it is to sweep across our American continent from the Pacific coast to Atlantic shores ... what a rich experience! Can one ever realize the tremendous extent of this country, or its wonderful resources, its mineral and agricultural wealth until he views it thus from shore to shore?

Susie briskly dismissed the gibe that all organized tourists were helpless fools.

> "No one who has any brains ever travels with the Raymonds," she was told. "Blessed then are the brainless ones," she retorted, "or those who having used their brains to good purpose, have earned now the right to such reposeful recreation."

In any case, the critics had missed the point:

> "Brains do not lie fallow while travelling. Plentiful opportunities occur for storing the mind with valuable information, every hour suggesting new thought, broadening the range of mental vision, which is all the clearer because not absorbed in petty cares concerning that which is least." [84]

Like Thomas Cook's special excursion trains, Raymond & Whitcomb's "hotels on wheels" included well-stocked libraries of transcontinental and regional travel books, as well as magazines and fiction. The company's prospectuses and tour programs listed a selected few, noting by the end of the Eighties that regional guidebooks and "books of travel and adventure relating to the Pacific coast ... are legion. Of the comprehensive books covering the long transcontinental lines, Crofutt's is unquestionably the most complete and comprehensive."

*   *   *

The Eighties consolidated the groundwork on which the expansion and diversification of Western America's tourist industry during the Nineties would depend. The two largest and most successful tour operators, Thomas Cook and Raymond & Whitcomb, followed the railroads across Western America and, with hammer blows, helped to demarcate its new frontiers of 'instant civilization'.

The tour operators' insatiable demands for special services, special rates, and high standards of hotel accommodation enabled the West's far-flung attractions, given overall market expansion, to compete effectively with the great Eastern States' and European resorts. The major hotels, particularly in California, became tourist attractions in themselves as concentrated effort boosted the appeal of favourite destinations, and intervening attractions en route were exploited, wherever possible, to tap the business flowing past them to the Golden State.

Group travel by hand-cart and wagon trains had been an early feature of the West. In the Eighties, the first decade of major expansion by the tour operators, the affluent transcontinental Pullman excursionists were to form their own distinctive element in western group travel whose influence far outstripped their actual numbers. Most of them were urbanized, fastidious, well-educated and well-heeled. Even so, while these organized, escorted groups of tourists were self-contained, they were not cocooned. Local suppliers of transport, livery, information and other services flourished at points along the routes, and around the resorts. Thousands of other tourists and health-seekers travelled quite independently of the tour operators, but along the same tracks. They boosted trade at the great palace hotels and also sustained the growth of many smaller establishments, boarding-houses, and local businesses, strengthening the networks and speeding development on the tourist frontier.

Thomas Cook and Raymond & Whitcomb, however, were important stabilizers of the Western tourist industry through their contacts, initiatives, organization, and bargaining power. They operated on the continental scale, from strong core areas in Europe and the Eastern States, at a time when the American West was a remote, thinly populated periphery with rough edges and tiny local markets. The great tour operators, with the railroads, created a special type of demand in the Eighties, and then satisfied it. They encouraged forward planning in the tourist industry. They supplied regular trade, powerful incentives, standardized procedures, and widespread advertisement. They pumped nourishment around the system, and sent a significant flow of prosperous new tourist-explorers into the West, as temporary or permanent investors in its future.

The 1890s: Competition Intensifies in the Transport, Tourist, and Information Industries

The New Age of Diversification
California and Colorado Increase Their Rivalry and Expand Their Markets

George Crofutt was still in Denver in 1893, the year when Colorado, along with the rest of the country, was rudely reminded that financial panics and disasters were by no means a thing of the past. Colorado had been predominantly a 'Silver State' for more than twenty years, the average value of silver produced having risen to about three times that of gold. Indeed, in 1890, Colorado's silver was nearly five times the value of its gold.[1] Even so, while silver output had soared, silver prices had been falling slowly since demonetization under the U.S.A.'s Coinage Act in 1873. In 1872, silver was $1.32 an ounce; in 1889, 84 cents. Greater efficiency of production had become essential; the emphasis was now on large-scale mining and smelting operations, extended railroad linkage, cheaper transport of raw materials and finished products, and a steady supply of skilled miners. Anxious to keep the issue of silver coinage alive, Denver hosted the first National Silver Convention in 1885, and by 1893, some 220 Silver Clubs had been organized throughout the State.

The Financial Panic of 1893, however, with its national economic depression, political upheavals, and the virtual world-wide adoption of the Gold Standard, sent silver prices tumbling. Major export markets like India were lost. In less than a week in the spring of 1893, silver slumped from 87 cents to 62 cents an ounce. Western hopes were finally dashed when Congress repealed the Sherman Silver Purchase Act in November 1893. Many mines closed; shops and small businesses were bankrupted, and half the banks in Denver ceased trading. The city's streets were jammed with unemployed workers from all over the State.

Foreclosures and tax arrears haunted many families who had invested a lifetime's effort in the region. Like so many others, Amos Steck, one of Denver's earliest pioneers, had been forced to rebuild his savings after the Panic of 1873; now, in the aftermath of the Panic of 1893, he wrote to a friend:

315

"My family are all well. I — 75 years and 7 months old; my good wife 73. The hard times [of 1893] struck us badly but we have health and bear up with courage and hope. All our holdings have shrunk 50-75 per cent, and no sale for any property . . . We are poorer than we have been for 30 years." [2]

Yet experience had always taught Steck to be tough and philosophical: "I've seen Denver rise and fall, go down and get up again, but every time it rose, it went on a notch higher, and even now it's only learning to climb." [3]

New Growth at the Rocky Mountain Front

There was one significant exception to Colorado's widespread economic recession — a gold mining bonanza which had started in 1891 at Cripple Creek up in the Rockies, less than twenty miles southwest of Colorado Springs. Pike's Peak was having the final word in this last of the region's great gold rushes, since Cripple Creek, long disregarded, was only 9 miles from the summit of the mountain! In the Panic year of 1893, when more than 10,000 people swarmed into the district, Cripple Creek produced $2 million-worth of gold. By the end of the century, annual output was over $18 million, with nearly 500 mines in operation in a district containing twelve towns and a population of more than 60,000 — 2nd largest in the State.

Colorado Springs was swept along in this sudden turbulent period of growth, its traditional calm ruffled by the early shock waves from Cripple Creek — struggles between mineowners and miners' union, and the hordes of strangers from many walks of life who surged through the town in transit for the mines. But Colorado Springs' middle-class majority benefitted enormously from their proximity to Cripple Creek whose gold was reputed to have made over thirty millionaires. Business boomed, both in the Springs and in Colorado City (Old Town) where reduction works were built for Cripple Creek ores. Many of the mines, mills, real estate, and transport services in the Cripple Creek area were owned, or part-owned, by residents of Colorado Springs, including Winfield Scott Stratton, James J. Hagerman, Spencer Penrose, Charles L. Tutt and Irving Howbert.

In 1894, 77 mining companies and brokers opened offices along Tejon Street. By 1896, there were as many as 245 brokers crammed into Tejon and the adjoining streets, and the Colorado Springs Mining Exchange, plus two other stock exchanges in the downtown area, could barely cope with the rush.[4] In contrast to the financially Panic-stricken world around them, no banks were closing in Colorado Springs.

The gold bonanza also triggered a late boom in Colorado's mountain-railroad construction. By 1894, the narrow-gauge Florence and Cripple Creek reached the mines, hotly pursued by the standard-gauge

79.   **THE PIKE'S PEAK COG RAILWAY, OPENED 1891**

Onward and Upward! Following the new track on foot for all or part of the way to the summit became a popular activity in the 1890s. Many tourists like these were still determined to be able to say that they had climbed to the top of Pike's Peak.

Midland Terminal in 1895. By 1901, a third railroad, the standard-gauge, 46-mile Colorado Springs & Cripple Creek District Railway (the Short Line) had been completed. Two electric inter-urban lines also served the mining communities during this extraordinary final outbreak of railroad mania [Map XII].

Tourists and health-seekers were also booming and blooming in Colorado Springs and Manitou spa in the 1890s and early 1900s. General Palmer, still a local resident, watched his pioneering resort complex move with the times. He remained a force to be reckoned with, since he controlled the Colorado Springs Co. which still owned half the land in and around the city. Palmer and others embarked on a new program of urban improvement, including additional gardens and parks, library and college extensions, and new tourist attractions. In 1893, Colorado Springs introduced its popular annual Flower Parade. The first carriage-way to the summit of Pike's Peak was completed in 1889-90, just as another remarkable new feature was being curled around the mountain. The spectacular Pike's Peak Cog Railway (starting at Manitou) opened in 1891 with outstanding success, while in 1908, cable-cars on the Manitou Incline Railway took crowds of visitors for the first time close to the summit of Mt. Manitou (9440 ft), an excellent local viewpoint overlooking Manitou spa and the dramatic junction of the Rockies and the plains.

One of the golden rules for successful resort development at this period was to make the going easier for the thousands who did not want to climb, or to start learning to ride a horse. Queues jammed the entrances to the Cog Railway and the Manitou Incline. "A New Adventure! Stand on the Peaks!! All the Fun with None of the Toil!!!" Excited crowds disturbed the stillness for a few, but the day was made for many who could not otherwise have enjoyed scaling the heights.

An enterprising journalist installed himself part-way up the Pike's Peak Cog Railway and published *The Daily Pike's Peak News*. As one tourist reported:

> "Before the train leaves Manitou, the names of the visitors are 'phoned up to the editor, and by the time your car reaches the half-way house the sheet is published, and in it appears your name as one of those who had that day ascended Pike's Peak. You willingly part with ten cents for a copy of the paper. The Daily Pike's Peak News has proven a veritable gold mine to its publisher." [5]

To handle the huge growth in demand for accommodation in the Pike's Peak region, and at the same time compete with the latest luxury hotels that had appeared in Denver before the crash, General Palmer completely remodelled his most famous hotel, The Antlers, in 1898-1901, after fire destroyed much of it. The original had been opened in Colorado Springs in 1883, attracted 11,000 guests in the first season, and immediately established itself as a front-runner in the perennial race with California. As business expanded, the all-important D.&R.G. railroad station behind the hotel was enlarged in 1887, and in 1890, The Antlers itself was almost doubled in size to handle the enormously increased demand of the Eighties.[6] Rebuilding at the end of the Nineties nearly doubled the size of The Antlers yet again, a palatial symbol of the continuing success of one of the first regional tourist resort developments in Western America.

The gold rush settlements at Cripple Creek were themselves a major attraction, another 'must' for the sightseer. In 1901, tourists were flocking to ride the Short Line from Colorado Springs to Cripple Creek through some of the most beautiful scenery in Colorado. The Short Line became one of the State's major tourist attractions, carrying well over 50,000 tourists in the summer of 1902.[7] Special picnic outings and Wildflower Excursion trains became a widely-publicized feature of both the Short Line and the Midland railroads, as trains stopped from time to time in the

0. A WILDFLOWER EXCURSION ON THE COLORADO MIDLAND RAILROAD IN THE 1890s
The photograph was taken near Green Mountain Falls, c.15 miles northwest of Colorado Springs.

mountain meadows so that passengers could pick armfuls of flowers. And not only flowers; trains stopped obligingly at well-known spots for fossil collection, or to enable passengers to inspect special feats of railroad engineering, to enjoy famous viewpoints, or to have everyone out for a group photograph, one of the most popular souvenirs among railroad excursionists at this period. The Colorado Midland ran a 115-mile 'Daily Wildflower Excursion and Scenic Trip' for $1.00 from Colorado Springs and Manitou during the season, and fought a vigorous rate war with the Short Line, which at one stage dropped its fare for a similar excursion to 25 cents for the round trip!

As a result of this highly concentrated booming economy around Pike's Peak in the 1890s and early 1900s, the population of Colorado Springs almost trebled from 11,000 to over 30,000, its prosperity soaring on the twin thrust of the mining and tourist industries.

But the Colorado Springs-Cripple Creek bonanza shone like a good deed in a naughty world. For the majority, the Panic of 1893 triggered deep depression across the United States. By the end of that year alone, nearly 500 banks and over 15,000 businesses were reported to have failed. An early casualty, the Philadelphia & Reading Railroad, collapsed in February 1893 and by the end of the year, sixty-five railroads had gone into liquidation, in all, nearly 20 per cent of the country's railroad network. Before the turning-point was reached in 1897, almost one-third of the total railroad mileage in the United States was in the hands of the receivers.

In retrospect, the years between 1873 and 1897 were to be identified by economists as a 'long-wave' depression, a period of steadily falling prices linked to rapid technological advances in agriculture, manufacturing, transport and communication. Increased mechanization and productivity on a world scale brought a sharp rise in both foreign and domestic competition, and this was matched in the United States by a huge concentration and consolidation of big business — the growth of monopolies, trusts, cartels, and tariff protection, and, at this period, by only limited effective labour union organization.

The 'long-wave' depression, however, had been pricked by vigorous up-swings in the economy, notably in 1878-82 and 1885-90. There was widespread conviction that even when the depressions were deep they were not lasting, and that the growing strength of the United States as a world industrial power would provide resilience and long-term buoyancy to the national economy. The Denver region was no exception. In the wake of the catastrophic slump in silver mining, in railroad freight revenues, and in banking, commerce, savings, and property development, Denverites began sorting through their economic baggage to find which pieces had survived the battering. One vitally important enterprise to do so was the Denver & Rio Grande railroad network which, to the envy of its rivals, came through virtually intact. During the Panic, the D. & R.G. had expanded its freight traffic in coal, coke and agricultural produce, and thus cushioned the blow of lost revenue from the silver trade. Though its income declined, the company rode out the storm.

"This Way to the Scenery!" The Boom in Free Railroad Literature

The survival of the Denver & Rio Grande rail network carried a magnificent bonus. It saved Colorado's tourist industry, and signalled the start of a massive publicity campaign in the 1890s to advertise the mountain resorts, together with a range of special railroad excursions through the scenic wonderland of the Rockies.

During the Eighties, competition for passenger and freight traffic had become more intense than ever — from California, from new transcontinental railroads, and from rival lines in Colorado itself. So far as passenger traffic was concerned, regional guidebooks on sale to the public (such as *Crofutt's Grip-Sack Guide of Colorado*) were now increasingly supplemented by 'give-aways'. The D. & R.G.'s own promotional literature, like that of its major competitors, began to be widely distributed free of charge in the late Eighties, and increasingly in the Nineties, throughout many parts of Europe and the United States. Responsibility for this advertising lay with the D. & R.G.'s general passenger and ticket agent, a key post which from 1880-84 was held by F.C. Nims. In 1881, his well-illustrated publication *Health, Wealth and Pleasure in Colorado and New Mexico* provided a detailed guide to the D. & R.G.'s 'Scenic Line of America', and, with other work, set a high standard for Nims' successor to maintain. Since this turned out to be the enterprising 'Major' Shadrach K. Hooper, there was no need to worry.

Hooper was Colorado's answer to California's Major Ben Truman. For the next two decades, the sheer quantity and variety of his publications on the attractions of Colorado in general, and the D. & R.G. in particular, rivalled the output even of giants like the Southern Pacific, the Union Pacific, the Northern Pacific, and the Atchison, Topeka & Santa Fe. Passenger traffic gave lifeblood support to the western railroads. Tourists were vital; so too were settlers, who not only increased way-traffic but also generated freight. The combined flood of railroad posters, pamphlets, books and brochures designed to sell land, and lead (or sometimes mislead) new settlers into the West, remains one of the most colourful, imaginative, and staggeringly successful contributions to the information and advertising industries that the United States has ever known.

Like that of his rivals, Hooper's law was 'never let up'. Hundreds of thousands of free booklets, pamphlets and souvenir albums in prose, verse and picture were circulated, many running into several editions, as a growing library of 'little gems' flowed from Hooper's pen into homes, hotels, clubs, schools and offices around the world. Among the most popular were:

The Story of Manitou (with W.A. Bell and S. Wood, 1885);
Tourists' Handbook of Colorado, New Mexico and Utah (1885);
The beautiful Denver and Rio Grande: Scenic Line of the World (1886);
Rhymes of the Rockies; or, What the Poets have found to say of the beautiful scenery on the Denver & Rio Grande Railroad (1887);
Souvenir of the Denver and Rio Grande (1887);
Official Guide to Cities, Villages and Resorts on the line of the Denver & Rio Grande Railroad (1888);
Gems of the Rockies (1889);
Around the Circle (1889);
Valleys of the Great Salt Lake (1890);
Among the Rockies (1890);
The Natural Resources of Colorado (1893);
The Opinions of the Judge and the Colonel as to the Vast Resources of Colorado (1894);
The Geography of Colorado (1895);
Slopes of the Sangre de Cristo (1896);
The Gold Fields of Colorado (1896);
Sight Places and Resorts in the Rockies (1899);
A Honeymoon Letter from a Bride to her Chum describing the Beauties of Colorado (1899);
The Fertile Lands of Colorado and northern New Mexico (1899);
What may be seen Crossing the Rockies en route between Ogden, Salt Lake City and Denver (1903);
Camping in the Rocky Mountains (1903);
With Nature in Colorado (1904)
Salt Lake City: the 'Zion' of the New World (1904);
Ancient Ruins of the Southwest (1909).

Such a list, by no means complete, helps to reveal the impressive contribution to the West's information industry made by individual railroad companies. Collectors anywhere in the United States or Europe could obtain any, or all, of the D. & R.G.'s publications free of charge simply by writing to the nearest local agent. Many of the titles recorded print runs of between 250,000 and 500,000 copies, and occasionally more, through the successive editions. They averaged sixty-or-so pages, but a few were much longer, and with maps and statistics supporting the detailed text and copious illustration, they formed major books of reference on the geography and economy of Colorado, and adjacent regions. The *Official Guide to Cities, Villages and Resorts on the line of the Denver & Rio Grande Railroad*, for example, ran to 286 pages, and, like all the other publications, was distributed free of charge.

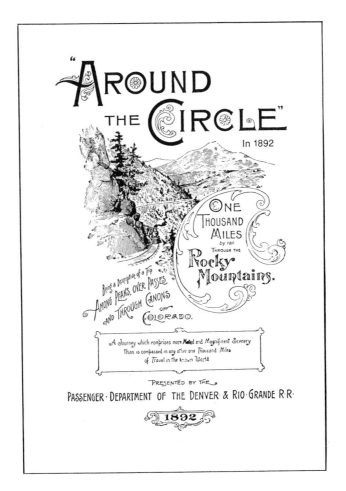

81. ONE OF THE EARLY "AROUND THE CIRCLE" RAILROAD
GUIDEBOOKS, DISTRIBUTED FREE BY THE DENVER & RIO GRANDE

First published in 1889, *Around the Circle* was one of the most popular booklets ever produced by the Denver & Rio Grande Railroad, and new editions were regularly issued for more than twenty years.

> "My aim," Hooper told his readers, "is to show the life, the hopes, the things done, the things now doing, and the things next to be done . . . in the hope that this may attract you, hold your interest for a space, delight you, and in the end instruct you."

Tourists were often also potential settlers or investors, and Western America was hunting all three. As part of the drive to boost trade in the Nineties, the D. & R.G.'s Passenger Department was given an annual advertising budget of $60,000, out of which it commissioned a series of illustrated lecture tours, and expanded its newspaper promotion in the Eastern States. The company even provided the celebrated photographer William Henry Jackson with a private train from which to take dramatic new views of Colorado.[8] In the wake of the Panic, western railroads needed every scrap of business they could find. While Hooper increased his department's output of publications, he also looked for new ways of enticing tourists, traders and settlers into the region.

82.

OVER THE ROCKIES IN AN OBSERVATION CAR

Drawn by Charles Graham; Harper's Weekly, July 18, 1891

One of the most effective of Graham's Western illustrations, it emphasized the latest improvements made by the railroads to their Observation Cars . . .

"Once we looked through a plate-glass window two feet square, and enjoyed the prospect; then the window grew gradually larger, until now the Observation Car has come, consisting of nothing but windows on either side, and reaching to the top. . . . You may ride over the Rockies and take in their grandeur, see the everlasting snow that crowns the summits, and be as comfortable as you desire."

Another important new development was the 'Kodak' camera, introduced by George Eastman in 1888, and widely advertised as the 'Tourist's Camera'. This highly successful invention of a simple, hand-held box camera, loaded with roll-film for 100 exposures, priced at $25.00, and supported by a developing and printing service, triggered the new age of amateur photography. Adjustable focusing was unnecessary, with everything from about three-and-a-half feet to the far distance adequately sharp. Larger hand-held models were produced in 1889 and 1890 (seen at left of picture). In 1891, daylight-loading Kodak cameras were introduced, to be followed by a series of even smaller and cheaper models during the next decade, including the $5.00 Pocket Kodak (1895), and the popular $1.00 Brownie (1900).

First he coaxed them to Denver. Convinced that there was no business like showbusiness, Hooper proposed the introduction of some spectacular annual event in the State capital to publicize Colorado's resources and pull in the crowds. California had been quicker off the mark. Santa Barbara organized its first Floral Pageant in 1886, and began the annual Floral Festival in 1891. Pasadena elaborated the idea and introduced its New Year's Day Tournament of the Roses in 1890, a title which said it all to the blizzard-swept multitudes farther east. San Francisco had mounted the California Midwinter International Exposition in Golden Gate Park in 1893, and Los Angeles, La Fiesta de Los Angeles in 1894, both as part of a concerted effort to drag business away from the traditional 'World's Fair and Convention country' of the Eastern and Midwestern States.

California kept chipping away at the barriers of time and distance. In November 1894, the Southern Pacific Railroad introduced a new 'Four Days to California!' — a weekly service from New York to Los Angeles on the Sunset Limited. The dynamic Los Angeles Chamber of Commerce, re-established in 1888, organized the famous 'California on Wheels' travelling railroad exhibit, which toured the United States displaying the range of resources, including the superb climate, of the Golden State. An estimated one million people visited the imaginative layouts advertising life and opportunities in California during the special train's two-year tour. Elaborate exhibits were also organized for the World-style Fairs in Chicago, Atlanta, Omaha, and St. Louis, and for every State Fair in the Midwest. The Los Angeles Chamber of Commerce itself housed a well-publicized permanent free exhibition of Southern Californian products, including samples of fruit and other agricultural produce, wine-tasting, maps, models, pictures, information, and tours. By the early 1890s, the exhibition was attracting more than 100,000 visitors annually.[9] Dozens of associations were invited to Los Angeles and lavishly entertained. By 1900, Los Angeles was known as the best advertised city in America.

Colorado could not afford to relax. The Colorado Springs-Cripple Creek region was doing very nicely of course, raking in the profits from the mines and the tourist attractions around Pike's Peak. Not surprisingly, Hooper's proposal to blow Denver's trumpet more loudly gained strong local support and resulted, in October 1895, in the city's first 3-day Festival of Mountain and Plain. It was a resounding success and with its parades, fun and razzle-dazzle, became a regular annual attraction for thousands of visitors until the turn of the century.[10] Reduced rail fares were offered, just as in 1882, Crofutt had negotiated special excursion rates on all the major railroad routes into Denver for the National Mining and Industrial Exposition. "Colorado is and long has been the best advertised of the Rocky Mountain states," reported Denver's *Rocky*

Mountain News, with immense satisfaction.[11]

Elaboration of the D.&R.G.'s popular 'Around the Circle Tour' in 1896 kept up the momentum. Passengers were offered an All-Rail (or a more adventurous Rail-and-Stage) Tour of a Thousand Miles through the Rockies for $28, and found that they could take anything from four days to sixty days over it. The breathtaking scenery, opportunity for stopovers, and numerous side-trips at specially reduced rates helped to make the 'Around the Circle Tour' one of the great classics of Western America. It offered maximum flexibility to an increasingly demanding market. It was short enough in duration for those who wanted nothing more than a 'Highlights of the Rockies' detour on the way to or from California; it was long enough for others to linger, for example, at Denver, Colorado Springs or Manitou, to visit fashionable new tourist attractions like mining camps and Indian pueblos, or to hunt, fish, ramble and sketch at leisure among the mountains.

In 1893, Walter Raymond, busily supervising hotels from Boston to Pasadena, had strengthened the New England-Colorado-California connection still further by creating the first major resort centre on Colorado's Western Slope. That summer he opened his large, elegant Hotel Colorado at Glenwood Springs, which was served both by the D.&R.G. and the Colorado Midland railroads [Map XII]. Given this double advantage, Walter Raymond had built in his characteristically grand manner, with accommodation for 600 guests.

The Rocky Mountain State of Colorado would never acquire one of California's greatest assets, firm sandy beaches and sea bathing, but Glenwood Springs got next best, the world's largest outdoor Hot Springs Pool, where year-round swimming became a unique and famous addition to the spa's other scenic and sports amenities. The Raymond & Whitcomb excursions, complete, like Cook's Tours, with their own travelling representatives, added Glenwood Springs to their choice of itineraries to and from California; although most of the visitors moved on after a few days, the spa also attracted a loyal band of longer-term vacationists and health-seekers. Glenwood Springs lay well to the north of Colorado's popular central route to Salt Lake City, and away from the 1000-mile 'Around the Circle Tour' through the Rockies. Thus it formed an important new outlier of Colorado's tourist industry, ready for immediate action in the years of cut-throat competition that followed the Panic of 1893.

So far as the California trade was concerned, *brief* stop-overs in Colorado, Utah or New Mexico were actively encouraged by the popular transcontinental 'limited' tickets offered on all the major railroad routes serving the west coast. 'Limited' tickets permitted no stop-overs before crossing the Missouri River, after which an extra week was allowed for touring the Rockies, or elsewhere, before continuing the journey to

California. As one Southern California promoter advised airily, determined not to let his readers get side-tracked in any sense:

> "One week gives ample opportunity to visit Denver, Salt Lake City, Santa Fe,
> and other points of interest . . . all the time usually desired."

It was a ding-dong battle. Southern California's climate was a priceless
asset, its warmth and light like softly spun gold. Reviewing all the major
'climatic resorts' in the United States in the early 1890s, the prominent
New York physician, Dr. Edmund C. Wendt observed:

> "Southern California has, perhaps, the most delightful climate in the world.
> The air is genially warm and dry, yet not enervating as in more tropical
> climates, and more salubrious general conditions can nowhere be found."

Many in Europe and the Eastern States, hankering for the West, demol-
ished distance in their mind's eye and thought first of California —
thoughts, as Frémont recalled, that "were flooded with its sunshine." One
Southern Californian summed up the economic importance of tourism:

> "Last year [1893] tourists brought more money to California than the entire
> fruit crop amounted to, and this portion of the State got the most of it." [12]

California's location and powerful appeal continued to determine the
basic structure of the entire Western tourist industry. Without the
long-distance tourist traffic from the Eastern and Midwestern States, and
Europe, generated by California's reputation, magnificent climates,
regional variety, and ceaseless promotion, the volume of traffic to all the
other tourist attractions scattered across Western America between the
plains and the Pacific would have been greatly reduced. Some intervening
points could not have been developed at all at this period without the
California connection.

The New Tourist Pullman Cars

Western railroad companies were the cutting edge of the tourist trade, as
they were of land sales and settlement expansion. The widespread
introduction of Tourist Pullman Cars at the end of the 1880s enabled
thousands of new travellers, family groups and excursion parties to visit
the West for the first time in the Nineties. These new Day and Sleeping
Cars were more functional, but the price cut was dramatic — they were
less than half the cost of the Pullman Palace Cars. Simple furnishings
replaced the elaborate decoration and lavish services still obtainable in
first-class, but Tourist Pullmans were comfortable, not spartan, and they
bridged the gap between the best and the worst in long-distance rail
travel.

A comparison of charges for Palace and Tourist Pullman Cars
explains the latter's enormous impact on increasing the volume of trans-
continental passenger traffic in and after the late Eighties. In 1889, the

Union Pacific and its connecting lines, for example, offered double berths in their Pullman Palace Cars for $13 on the stretch between Omaha or Kansas City and San Francisco or Los Angeles. (Drawing-room/Parlor Car accommodation and meals were extra). Crofutt provided the latest on the new Tourist Pullman 'Family Sleepers' in his *Overland Tours* for that year:

> "This company runs family sleeping cars on the Pacific Express daily for second-class passengers. These cars are fitted up complete with mattresses, curtains, blankets, pillows, etc. . . . and are provided with uniformed porters who keep them in good order and look after the wants of the passengers. No smoking is allowed in these cars, and none but second-class passengers are permitted to occupy them. The charges are $5 for a section between Council Bluffs/Omaha and Los Angeles (double berth), or $2.50 for lower or upper double berth. Intermediates are charged 50 cents a night."

83.   THE DISCOMFORTS OF TRAVEL — WEARY PASSENGERS SETTLING IN FOR THE NIGHT
Frank Leslie's Illustrated Newspaper, February 9, 1878
The misery of the long rail journey across the West for those without Sleeping Car accommodation was captured by one of Leslie's artists on the transcontinental excursion of 1877.

Free Emigrant Sleeping Cars had been available for several years, 'free' in the sense that no extra charge was made for the sleeping-car service. The

THE MODERN SHIP OF THE PLAINS

Drawn by Rufus F. Zogbaum, 1885; Harper's Weekly, November 13, 1886

Following the Central Pacific Railroad's initiative in 1879, Emigrant Sleeping Cars were introduced on all the major Western railroads in the 1880s. Zogbaum's sketch shows emigrants travelling west on the Northern Pacific Railroad. Most of the upper berths in the Emigrant Sleeper have been folded back into place, but two of them remain down and occupied.

Crofutt had visited the Central Pacific Railroad's works at Sacramento in 1879 to see the first twenty-five Emigrant Sleeping Cars under construction, and he included a detailed description of them in *Crofutt's New Overland Tourist, and Pacific Coast Guide,* 1879-80.

"To cherish, aid, and ameliorate the condition of the emigrant," Crofutt stressed, "is to hasten the settlement of the vast amount of unoccupied land, and the development of the enormous mineral and other resources of the great West . . . The honest, industrious and enterprising emigrant is the *germ of life* in our trans-Missouri country . . . Families emigrating should have the *special* care, attention, and *protection* of the railroad companies . . . together with all the comforts and conveniences possible, and at the *lowest* rates of fare."

wood-slatted seats let down and the upper berths folded up in the standard manner, but no upholstery or bedding was provided. The forty-eight passengers per car made do with the cooking stove, water, and toilet facilities supplied, and then with whatever comfort could be squeezed from their own bundles and baggage. But the 'Free Emigrant Sleepers' were a big improvement on earlier conditions, and after their introduction on the Central Pacific in 1879, they soon became a feature on all the major Western railroads.

Before long, Tourist Pullman Cars had also become an effective weapon in the fight for western passenger traffic. Colorado was keenly aware of the temptation offered by the cut-price comfort on the Tourist Pullmans to travel further, make it a transcontinental journey, and go all

85.   A TOURIST PULLMAN SLEEPING CAR, c.1897

Tourist Pullmans and Tourist Pullman Sleepers provided upholstered leather or rattan-covered seats and plainer decoration than the Palace Pullmans. But bedding and porter services were included at less than half the price of first-class, and Tourist Pullmans brought thousands of new travellers into the West in the late 1880s and 1890s.

the way to California. To counteract this, after a successful experiment in 1883, the Denver & Rio Grande Railroad ran free Tourist Pullmans in the late Eighties and early Nineties as part of their effort to boost business . . .

> "Whole families bound for Rocky Mountain resorts loll about on the wicker or leather seats," reported a writer in *World's Work*; "one or two people are heating coffee on the range at the end of car; . . . heads project from the open windows: everybody is happy. In porter service and plush these people are not so well provided as the parlor-car passengers, but to discomfort they will not own. They contend that their berths are as snug as those in the first-class car behind." [13]

Tourist Pullmans had their own cooking facilities and ice chests, although the Northern Pacific Railroad still prided itself on the company's special Pullman Dining Cars which served excellent meals at a flat rate of 75 cents. Light snacks were also brought along the train. In the case of the Atchison, Topeka & Santa Fe, in addition to its well-appointed Tourist Pullmans, the company's high reputation for catering rested on the famous Fred Harvey railroad depot restaurants and hotels, as well as on the Harvey Dining Cars.[14]

The new Tourist Pullman age triggered the growth of new tour operators, busily seeking untapped markets and offering cheaper rates than Thomas Cook and Raymond & Whitcomb. In one form or another, these newcomers opened in most of the major cities of the Northeast and Midwest, where a longing for California's warmth and sunshine had been reinforced by a particularly bitter winter in 1887-8. In 1888, the new firm of A. Phillips & Co. opened on Boston's Washington Street, in a blaze of publicity, as specialists in 'Boston and California Excursions.' By 1892, one of Phillips' partners, John C. Judson, had expanded into a new business a few doors away, again specializing in transcontinental excursions, and cheaper bulk tourist traffic to California.

Southern California welcomed any move to keep it competitive with Florida, and any enterprise which helped to make it almost as easy in time and money to reach the Golden State as to roll down to the Sunshine State, a name for Florida banished from the lips of all self-respecting Californians.

> "As to the various ways of coming [to Southern California]," wrote Kate Sanborn in 1893, "I greatly prefer the Southern Pacific in winter and the Atchison, Topeka & Santa Fe in spring or summer. Either will take you from New York to San Diego and return for $137, allowing six months' stay. The 'Phillips' Excursion' will take you from Boston to San Francisco for fifty-five dollars. But in this case the beds are hard, and you provide your own meals." [15]

There was now no shortage of advice on cheaper ways to reach Southern California, or "The Land of the Afternoon," as Ratcliffe Hicks called it, back home in 1898 in Springfield, Massachusetts. Wondering "why any intelligent farmer in New England stays there," Hicks recommended that the best way for those with moderate means to reach Southern California ("where they sell the climate and throw the land in"), was "to go by the Tourist Cars which leave Boston every Saturday and go through to Los Angeles without change in about six days, via Kansas City . . . Fare $67." [16]

Newcomers swelled the ranks of the great boosters of the Seventies and Eighties. John Hanson admitted in 1896 that, irritated by all the ballyhoo, he left Chicago to visit Southern California for a few weeks "in a skeptical mood." Before long, he announced himself to be yet another case of "he came, he saw, he was conquered." "It is the only land I have ever seen where it seems enough just to live and breathe." [17] Like many converts, Hanson rushed into print, eager to share the good news, and convinced that book titles should have a plot of their own, with a clear beginning, middle, and end. He chose *The American Italy: the scenic wonderland of perfect climate, golden sunshine, ever-blooming flowers and always-ripening fruits. Southern California.* Hanson was a writer after Ben Truman's heart!

Although Southern California's late-Eighties land boom had peaked before the end of that decade, and then been followed by the economic recession of the early Nineties, the region showed great resilience. Tourists, retired farmers and businessmen from the Northeast (and increasingly from the Midwest), and young families, were all part of a ceaseless migration. Accountants and agents, hoteliers and storekeepers, prosperous merchants building west-coast outlets, aspiring lawyers and doctors, and crowds of health-seekers continued to favour the area — even though, in the last instance, the 'sanitarium' image was given less publicity. The 'Tourist Pullman Revolution' had its most significant effects in California, where the increases in passenger traffic during the Nineties were maintained by constant advertising, and by close cooperation between the railroad companies, the well-established and the new package tour operators, and by price-cuts at the major resorts. In 1895, the leading California hotels were offering an extra 50 cents-a-day reduction on their regular rates to long-distance excursionists. Several hotels in Colorado followed suit.

In the 1890s, the western railroad companies increased their special offers both on cheaper 'limited' tickets, with the emphasis on 'fast-to-destination' service, and on an even greater variety of 'tourist' tickets. These had the twin advantages still of enabling travellers to visit favourite spots at greatly reduced rates, and allowing them to break their journeys as often as they liked over a period normally of up to six months. "You are not bound to swallow the whole dish at a sitting," wrote one appreciative holder of a 'tourist' ticket. "You have licence to stop here and there to take breath."

The freedom offered by 'tourist' tickets and their immense popularity were often ignored by critics who chose instead to mock or pity the hurrying, 'so-many-miles-a-day' sightseer gathering a "multitude of mixed, novel impressions rapidly piled on one another [to] make only a dreamy, bewildering, swirling blur, most of which is unrememberable." [18] In fact, what tourists demanded was the freedom to choose, and railroads, along with others, learned to please a variety of tastes.

> "We want you all!", the Southern Pacific Railroad reminded the public yet again in 1892, crowning Western America's attractions with the glint and sparkle of California . . . "Tourists, Invalids, Capitalists and Homeseekers — WELCOME!!"

The Regional Concept in Resort Development: Diversification of Transport and Services, and the Rise of the Day Excursion

While the turbulent 1890s confirmed the dominance of California and Colorado in Western America's tourist industry, the decade also marked a period of transition in that industry, as in so many other aspects of American life. This was not yet the age of mass tourism, which began to develop in the 1920s and 1930s through wider automobile ownership, a range of lower-cost services, and eventually, paid holidays and shorter working hours. Even with price reductions and increased traffic, most tourists at the turn of the century were still drawn from the more prosperous middle class. But middle-class tastes were changing, at least in part. In addition to the great resort hotels and the special excursion parties, the increasing popularity of smaller resorts, boarding-houses, cottages, ranches, campsites, tent cities, picnic parks, climbing clubs, and wilderness trails was diversifying the pattern. New branch railroads, cogs and cables, electric rail and trolley lines, and the bicycle craze all helped to open up the way.

Transport provision remained a matter of life or death to the tourist industry, but after getting their carloads to the end of the tracks, the railroads began to help their passengers down from the train and into the great outdoors. In the 1890s, the Southern Pacific was advertising special campers' fares and free checking of tents, stoves, and other camping equipment.[19] The Denver & Rio Grande soon followed. Indeed, the Union Pacific (Colorado Central division) had already given a lead in the mid-1880s by selling round-trip tickets for $9 "from Denver to the top of Gray's Peak." The cost included the spectacular narrow-gauge railroad trip to Graymont, and horse and guide from Graymont to the summit (14,270 ft, 3-4 hours). "The horses are safe and the guides experienced," Crofutt had reported in 1885; "Ladies may make the trip assured of care and attention." [20]

Railroad agents in Colorado in the late Eighties and Nineties even helped to recruit individuals for camping parties in the Rocky Mountains, and offered the inexperienced a few guidelines once they had left the train for "the freedom and leisure of a camping tour." Together with a strong, light covered-wagon, advised one agent, "You want a good-natured driver who can cook and be a man-of-all-chores at camp." . . . "Do not rush nor feel in a hurry; if you do, better take the first train . . . Take it easy, . . . be prepared that when you want to rest, the others will all want to go. When you want to climb, they will want to fish. There will be times when everybody seems to be a rusty file." Four to six campers were considered to be the ideal number, especially if they were all strangers to each other. This was a more common occurrence than might be expected, and a most welcome opportunity for some tourists travelling alone to try something they had never dreamed of tackling before. One woman, determined to take nearly everything in her stride, set off from Boulder to camp "with eleven others, all strangers, saying that she had made up her mind 'to complain of nothing if they would only keep the brush out of the butter.' "[21]

Western railroads also catered for the growing popularity of outdoor life and cheaper accommodation in the Nineties by freely distributing lists of small hotels, boarding-houses, ranches and farms willing to take visitors and accessible from the railroad stations. The Denver & Rio Grande, for example, listed seventy-eight such places accommodating anything between five and fifty guests (ten to twenty was most usual), in hotels, cottages, cabins or tents, and included details of the daily, weekly, and monthly rates. Mrs. Henry B. Walker, that unwilling occupant of the Dirty Woman's Ranch in the early 1860s, turns up again thirty years later at Husted, some ten miles north of Colorado Springs and one mile from the D. & R.G. railroad station. Happily settled at the Walker Ranch for many years, Mrs. Walker was now offering accommodation for six guests, with full board, for $6 a week.

In California, in the early Nineties, the Southern Pacific railroad went a stage further by building a number of three-room cottages for consumptives at Indio, thus providing both transport and accommodation well away from the major tourist resorts.[22] Elsewhere, railway picnic parties and wildflower excursions were as popular in California as they were in Colorado, and railroads carried picnickers into the redwood forests or into fields ablaze with California poppies with equal ease.

Above all, once the transcontinental railroads had deposited their passengers among the mountains or along the Pacific shore, the challenge was to keep them there as long as possible. The continued expansion of Western America's tourist industry depended on the rapid growth of distinctive resort regions, full of internal variety in scenery, amusement, local transport, and styles of accommodation. The great hotels like the Del Monte, Raymond, or Coronado, for example, with their own landscaped gardens, walks, picnic spots, bathing beaches, and a huge range of indoor and outdoor activities, were resort worlds of their own — the heart of their appeal. Thousands flocked to these indispensable king-pins of the industry. More were opened in the early Nineties, among them the palatial Hotel Green in Pasadena, staffed by the Raymond & Whitcomb company. And to confirm the trend, after Pasadena's famous pioneering Raymond Hotel burned to the ground on Easter Sunday 1895, Walter Raymond immediately planned and built an even larger, more elaborate 'Raymond' on the same site, which opened in December 1901. Far from declining in popularity as the tourist market diversified, the palace hotels, and the Cook's and Raymond & Whitcomb excursions, were coping with a huge increase in demand for their particular style of service. Both companies opened new branch offices in Los Angeles in the early Nineties.

Others were hard on their heels. One of Thomas Cook's early competitors, the London-based company of Henry Gaze & Son, which hitherto had concentrated its business in Europe and the Old World, decided that it could no longer afford to ignore the lucrative tourist trade within the United States. In 1891, Gaze opened his first American Tours office at 113 Broadway, New York City. Meanwhile, the major Eastern railroad companies, such as the Pennsylvania Railroad, were busily expanding their own programs of escorted and unescorted tours to California in the early Nineties.

Creating the Los Angeles Resort Region

Resort regions worked on the same basic principles as the resort hotels, enlarging the scale of their operation but never losing sight of the need to tempt visitors to extend the length of their stay. In the mid-Eighties, for example, a group of New Yorkers who were making their own western tour were advised that there was enough to interest them in and around Los Angeles for at least a week, but that the city's own hotel accommodation left much to be desired.

Los Angeles soon put that right as part of Southern California's great hotel-building and improvement program in the late 1880s, which included L.A.'s first-class Nadeau, St. Elmo, Westminster, and Hollenbeck Hotels. Then the city set about applying the 'Law of Concentrated Effort' in the context of the Nineties.

One week would never again be long enough to begin to do justice to the Los Angeles resort region, which alone was half the size of Connecticut, and sprawled from the Pacific Ocean's beach playgrounds to the San Gabriel Mountains and adjacent valleys. Some of these already contained flourishing tourist attractions of their own. The aim now was to produce a well-defined, well-integrated economic region, geared to tourism (along with other resource development), and tied by a network of flexible internal connections. Crucial to these were the regional amenities, their distribution pattern, and the efficiency of their transport services. The Los Angeles resort region concentrated on providing, as part of its total package, a wide variety of day-trips by road and rail, made up of 'Rounds and Radials'. 'Rounds', as round-trips were known, stressed the appeal of "Always Something New!" . . . "No Repetition!!" 'Radials' promoted fast, direct service to major local attractions like city parks, zoos, boating lakes, well-publicized spas and resort hotels dotted about the region, and especially, to the Ocean's sand and surf. At some points, 'Round' and 'Radial' were combined in a day-trip, like a brightly coloured flower on the end of a stalk.

In the Nineties, Outings and Day Excursions blossomed as never before. Los Angeles pioneered its regional pattern with the 'Grand Round', which was a day's drive from the city that began with a trip through orchards and orange groves on the way to Pasadena, and a visit to the Raymond Hotel. After the hotel burned down, carriages continued to drive up to the site to enable tourists to see the famous view extending from the Ocean to the San Gabriel Valley and the Sierra Madre, as well as to allow them to watch Raymond's rebuilding operations. Then it was on to the Sierra Madre Villa for lunch, before going on to tour "Lucky" Baldwin's Santa Anita Ranch, the Sunny-Slope Vineyards, Winery and Distillery, and finally the San Gabriel Mission (1771). The 'Grand Round' was a 'must' for tourists, and a development model for the entire region.

'Rounds' came in all shapes and sizes. Day-trips on Los Angeles' street-railways took visitors sightseeing around town for 5 cents on the special "Seeing Los Angeles" observation cars, complete with guide, which ran almost continuously to cope with the demand. Further afield, day-trips were also a feature of several towns strung along the new railroad tracks in the San Gabriel-San Bernardino Valley, where the parallel routes of the Southern Pacific and the Santa Fe, and their subsidiaries, were only 2-5 miles apart.

San Bernardino, sixty miles from Los Angeles, nevertheless formed part of the Los Angeles resort region, with an hourly train service to the city. A popular day's carriage drive from San Bernardino began with a tour of Frank Hinckley's gardens and citrus groves in Old San Bernardino. Tourists were given a sense of the past with reminders of the early Spanish ranch site and the pioneering Mormon settlement of 1851-57, followed by a glimpse of the future with a trip through the new towns of Redlands, Lugonia and Highland. Then they were ready to bowl up to the new Arrowhead Springs Hotel for lunch. The 'Round' continued with an optional tour of the Harrison Ranch close by, before returning to San Bernardino via the celebrated Rabel and Harlem Hot Springs. For many tourists, this was an unexpectedly varied day, full of colour, progress, and achievement. Dramatic contrasts in vegetation, land use, and irrigated agriculture patterned the valley and surrounding slopes. The region still attracted sufferers from tuberculosis, asthma, bronchitis, and rheumatism, and many health-seekers had taken up citrus growing, horticulture or viticulture, full- or part-time. The whole 'Round', indeed, was an object lesson in frontier expansion, and in the successive stages of cultural and economic development in this part of Southern California.

6.

LOOKING TOWARD REDLANDS AND THE SAN BERNARDINO MOUNTAINS
ACROSS THE IRRIGATED CITRUS GROVES AND FARMS IN THE
SAN BERNARDINO VALLEY IN THE 1890s

Located at the eastern edge of the Los Angeles resort region, the 'Round' from San Bernardino was one of the most popular day-trips in the 1890s. Amid superb scenery, it gave impressive evidence of the new growth and opportunities in Southern California.

XIII.   PROMOTING SETTLEMENT AND TOURISM IN THE LOS ANGELES REGION
Part of a colourful information folder on Corona, Riverside County, prepared by the
Colonization Department of the Santa Fe Railway System at the turn of the century in
co-operation with the Corona Chamber of Commerce. Pamphlets and other material
were produced by the railroads for virtually every town along their routes. Maps, pictures,
facts and figures were skilfully arranged to help newcomers familiarize themselves
quickly with the region.

Another very popular day's outing from San Bernardino was to
Riverside, ten miles south, where pioneering work in the cultivation of
seedless navel oranges in the 1870s had revolutionized production and
laid the foundation for Southern California's national and world reputation in the industry in later years. Five trains a day linked Riverside to San
Bernardino and Colton on the Santa Fe and Southern Pacific Railroads,
while yet another rail link to Los Angeles was available via Anaheim.
Tours could be taken through Riverside's orange groves and packing
sheds, where, by the late Nineties, fifty million oranges were boxed
annually. A quiet stroll through local gardens and orchards, a drive along
the twelve-mile Magnolia Avenue, and a visit to Riverside's elegant Rowell

Hotel or Glenwood Tavern, were all additional tourist attractions which helped to highlight this northeastern corner of the Los Angeles resort region.

Competition for the tourist trade was fierce, and 'Rounds' were a regular feature of virtually every settlement in the Los Angeles basin and connecting valleys that had geographical and cultural variety to offer, and go-ahead local residents ready to organize trips from the railroad stations. Pasadena and San Fernando were two such examples, only 30-40 minutes by rail from Los Angeles, and with frequent service throughout the day. The proximity of the Santa Fe route (the former California Central Railroad, reorganized in 1889 into the company's Southern California Railway System), to the base of the Sierra Madre also made the new, valley-edge rail towns between Duarte and Claremont the recommended departure points for camping trips up into the canyons behind. The picturesque, well-shaded San Antonio Canyon was especially popular with ramblers, botanists, and health-seekers; with climbers also, since this was the route to Mt. San Antonio ("Old Baldy"), over 10,000 feet and the highest peak in the Sierra Madre.

"The tendency nowadays to wander in wildernesses is delightful to see," wrote John Muir in 1898. "Thousands ... are beginning to find out that going to the mountains is going home; that wildness is a necessity; and that mountain parks and reservations are useful not only as fountains of timber and irrigating rivers but as fountains of life." [23] The Nineties had seen the creation of four forest reserves in Southern California — San Gabriel, San Bernardino, San Jacinto, and Trabuco Canyon. Muir regarded them as major assets, not in this case for their timber, but for their wild life, and their protection of vital headwater systems. In addition, Muir continued,

> "As quickly available retreats from dust and heat and care, their value is incalculable. Good roads have been graded into them, by which in a few hours lowlanders can get well up into the sky and find refuge in hospitable camps and club-houses, where, while breathing reviving ozone, they may absorb the beauty about them, and look comfortably down on the busy towns and the most beautiful orange groves ever planted since gardening began." [24]

New transport networks stoked the tourist industry. The dramatic expansion of electric railways and trolley lines in the mid-Nineties around Los Angeles reinforced many of the popular 'Rounds' pioneered by the carriage trade. The Pacific Electric's famous 'Kite-route' through the vivid colours and contrasts of the Los Angeles resort region helped to delineate as well as promote this outstanding tourist attraction. The panorama of orange groves, vineyards, orchards, wells and windmills, new settlements, flower-decked stations, and stylish hotels, all bathed in

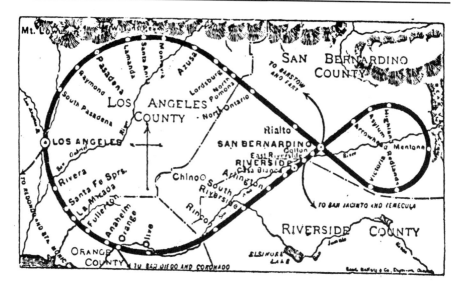

87.   THE FAMOUS STYLIZED MAP OF THE FIRST 'KITE-SHAPED ROUTE'
       (SANTA FE RAILROAD) AROUND THE LOS ANGELES REGION
       in J.W. Hanson, *The American Italy . . . Southern California*, 1896

sunshine and backed by the steep wall of the Sierra Madre, proved a
winner; thousands gazed in effortless delight from the cars at the
geographical variety of 'instant' Southern California passing by. The
'Kite-route' carried some of the highest-density round-trip excursion
traffic in Western America.

Since rival railroad tracks parallelled each other so closely, the giant
companies were already advertising 'Kite-routes' of their own. The A.T. &
S.F. had pioneered the idea. The Day Excursion dominated the market,
and the Santa Fe Railroad offered a 166-mile 'Kite' trip for $2.75 that left
Los Angeles at 8:30 a.m., and included a lunch-stop at Redlands and two
hours at Riverside. Special Sunday Excursions were packed with local
family parties. The Santa Fe also offered an extended 'tourist' ticket on its
'Kite' route for $3–$4. Not to be outdone, the Southern Pacific promoted a
similar 150-mile excursion over its own lines, 8:55 a.m.–6:30 p.m. out of Los
Angeles, which it dubbed the 'Inside Track Flyer'.

Electric rail service opened to Pasadena in 1895 and to Santa Monica
in 1896. Trolleys ran almost continuously between Los Angeles and Santa
Monica during the summer, sweeping both tourists and local residents
down to the ocean on the fast inter-urban shuttle. Santa Monica was soon
linked to Los Angeles by as many as five steam or electric railways;
passengers often went out on one route and returned on another, for a
round-trip fare of 50 cents. In fact, the Pacific Electric system sent 50-cent
round-trips spinning all round Los Angeles, wheels-within-wheels speeding business and pleasure, and rolling around the perimeter of the resort

OPENING DAY ON THE FIRST ELECTRIC TROLLEY SERVICE FROM LOS ANGELES TO SANTA MONICA, 1st APRIL 1896

region from Santa Monica, Redondo Beach, San Pedro, and Long Beach on the one hand, to the San Fernando, San Gabriel, and San Bernardino Valleys on the other. Many centres could reap the benefits of cut-throat competition. Pasadena's half-hourly service into Los Angeles, for example, operated from early morning until nearly midnight, using three steam railroads plus the Pacific Electric. The single fare dropped to 25 cents; 35 cents return.

Before long, expansion of the Pacific Electric's train and trolley system had produced one of the most complete and comprehensive networks of inter-urban and suburban electric transport in the United States. With this system, the Los Angeles Chamber of Commerce reported in 1895, "farmers residing in almost any portion of the County will soon be as favorably situated as suburban residents, being able to run up to town at any time of the day, and have their mail delivered to their door."

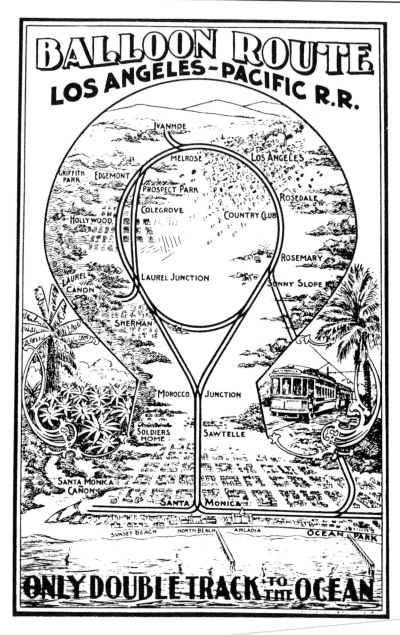

89.   "ALL DAY FOR $1.00!"
AN ADVERTISEMENT FOR THE 'BALLOON ROUTE' TROLLEY TRIP,
ONE OF THE PACIFIC ELECTRIC'S MOST POPULAR 'ONE-DOLLAR SPECIALS'.

Morocco Junction was renamed Beverly Hills. The Arcadia Hotel, opened in 1887, is shown facing the Ocean. Ocean Park was a new town and bathing resort laid out on land purchased by Abbot Kinney and Francis G. Ryan in 1892. In 1900, Kinney went on to develop Venice, adjoining Ocean Park to the south. The Lagoon Line trolley service was extended from Santa Monica in 1901, and a new direct route from downtown Los Angeles opened in 1902. Major construction work at Venice began in 1904.

Farmers were indeed running up to town, along with their produce. Freight, mail, commuters and tourists were all whisked about the Los Angeles region by the Big Red Cars of the Pacific Electric, whose services were consolidated and expanded by Henry E. Huntington (nephew of railroad magnate Collis P. Huntington) between 1901 and 1910, into a fast, comfortable and inexpensive regional transport system.

Fares went as low as one-half to three-quarters of a cent per mile, and trolley cars were often chartered for special tourist excursions, school parties, Sunday-school picnics, and moonlight outings. Never was a transport system more effective in promoting that great pleasure of the Nineties, the Day Out. In addition to the many standard 50-cent round-trips, the Pacific Electric 'One-dollar Specials' also attracted huge crowds, particularly the daily 'Balloon Route' which included Santa Monica, Ocean Park and Redondo Beach; the 'Triangle Trip' between Los Angeles, Long Beach and Santa Ana; and the 'Old Mission and Orange Grove Trip' along the San Gabriel Valley. What with these, the comprehensive 'Kite-route', and the twice-weekly 'Orange Empire Excursion' to San Bernardino, Redlands and Riverside, Los Angeles showed how old favourites, enticingly labelled, never lost their appeal.

OCEAN VIEW HOUSE, SANTA MONICA

Ocean View House was opened in the 1890s at the north end of Ocean Avenue. It was an attractive example of the many medium-size hotels and boarding-houses that spread so rapidly in Southern California during the Nineties.

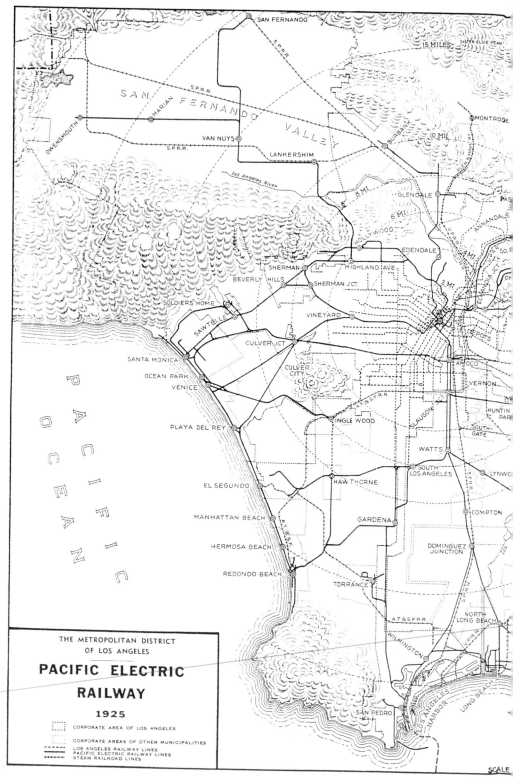

XIV.

THE LOS ANGELES RAIL NETWORK

The size and density of this rail network, one of the finest regional systems in the United States, resulted from the boom in both steam railroad and electric trolley construction in the Los Angeles basin during the late-nineteenth and early-twentieth centuries.

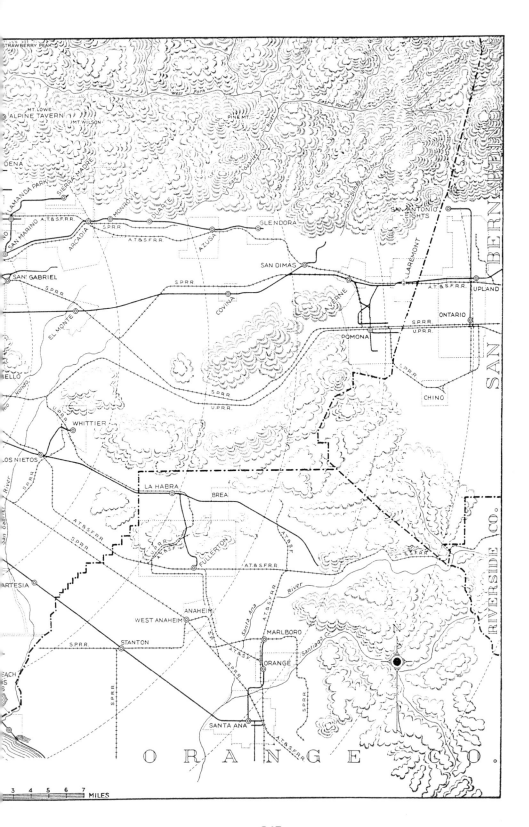

Los Angeles, mid-way between the beach at Santa Monica and the Pasadena-Sierra Madre country (both were about fifteen miles from the L.A. city centre), became increasingly important as the regional pivot — for transport, trade, tourism, administration, and a much sought-after manufacturing base. About half the Los Angeles County population lived in the city, which by 1890 had boomed to more than 50,000 and to more than double that figure during the next decade. The Los Angeles resort region, pegged and strung across the southern part of Los Angeles County, and neighbouring sections of Orange, Riverside, and San Bernardino Counties, attracted an estimated annual influx of tourists that in peak years was at least twice the size of the resident population. Tourists were both spectators and participants in the region's economic development, and when, by 1895, some three hundred oil wells and a forest of derricks had sprouted within the Los Angeles city limits, short trips to view them were organized with the same speed and enthusiasm that carried tourists off to admire the orange groves.

Santa Monica, Redondo Beach and Long Beach all boosted their investment in tourism once the Los Angeles 'harbor war' had been finally lost to San Pedro in 1898. The Pacific Electric did its bit by adding yet another round-trip 'Special' from Los Angeles known as the 'Great Surf Route': '100 miles for $1!' This concentrated on the coastal features, ranch lands and orchards between Santa Monica and Long Beach, included a steamer trip from Long Beach to San Pedro, and, characteristically, provided information on port development and changing land use all along the way. That Congress had been persuaded to construct an artificial port for Los Angeles anywhere at all was a triumph. As the Committee Senator from Maine had observed dismissively at the outset, when inspecting the open shore:

> "The Lord has not given you much to start with, that is for certain . . . If you Los Angeles people want a harbor, why not move the city down to San Diego? There is a good harbor there." [25]

Angelenos did not need to be reminded.

Los Angeles pushed the margin of its resort region even farther out into the ocean during the Nineties with the development of Santa Catalina Island. Angeleno George R. Shatto bought the island in 1887, opened its first hotel the following year, and added another round-trip to the collection. Daily steamer trips ran from San Pedro and Redondo, with frequent rail connections to Los Angeles. After the Banning brothers of Wilmington and L.A. bought Santa Catalina in 1892, business boomed as never before. Between 1893-5, the hotel was enlarged, others were built, cottage and tent accommodation was extended, and Avalon became one of the most popular resorts in Southern California. Penetration roads were pushed into the mountainous interior, where hunting wild goat offered an unusual alternative to fishing, swimming, shell-collecting, wildflower excursions, and trips along the coast in glass-bottomed boats. Many Angelenos liked the free-and-easy atmosphere of Santa Catalina for cheap, longer holidays of one or two weeks; about five thousand were reported to be camping on the island in the summer of 1895. Many local residents, however, as well as most out-of-State tourists favoured the indispensable round-trip, especially the one from Los Angeles to Santa Catalina Island, including 24 hours at the hotel, for the all-in price of $5. Tourists usually left with a souvenir copy of the island's newspaper, since Avalon was credited with having started the first and only newspaper, *The Wireless*, entirely dependent on wireless dispatches sent daily by its correspondent in Los Angeles.

While Santa Catalina made its mark on the southern margin of the Los Angeles resort region, the opening of the Mount Lowe Cable Railway in 1893 notched up another success sixty miles away in the Sierra Madre, on the region's northern perimeter. Born in New Hampshire, Thaddeus Sobreski Coulincourt Lowe had arrived in Southern California in 1888 after an adventurous career as a Civil War balloonist, scientist and inventor. Lowe quickly decided to bring a few thrills into Los Angeles' horizontal life-style. From Altadena, north of Pasadena, the Mount Lowe Electric Railway ran to Rubio Falls, whence the Great Cable Incline lifted visitors to the summit of Echo Mountain (3500 ft).

There, Lowe built a stylish hotel, Echo Mountain House, an Observatory, and a small zoo. Nearby, he added the powerful searchlight brought west from the 1893 Chicago World Fair. At night, the light could be seen from many parts of the Los Angeles basin, and for several miles out into the Pacific, becoming a famous regional landmark. Beyond Echo Mountain, with breathtaking curves and magnificent views, Lowe's Mountain Railway trolley cars swept on for another five miles to Mount Lowe, where, by 1895, Thaddeus had built his second hotel, Ye Alpine Tavern (5000 ft), just below the summit at the end of the line. Although not on the scale of Colorado's Pike's Peak Cog Railway opened in 1891, Lowe's varied and exciting 'Trip of a Lifetime' was for many years one of California's major tourist attractions. Return trips from Altadena (home of health-seeker Andrew McNally, of Rand, McNally & Co. in Chicago), as far as the popular viewpoint of Echo Mountain, cost $3; to the Mount Lowe summit, $5. Before long, daily round-trips from Los Angeles, 9 a.m. - 6 p.m., were pulling the crowds with special all-in excursion fares of $2.50.

"Los Angeles, that good old tourist town;
From the ocean to Mount Lowe
Sight seein' we did go —
Rode them trolley cars for miles and miles around." [26]

91. THE 'TRIP OF A LIFETIME' TO MOUNT LOWE, NEAR PASADENA
THE GREAT CABLE INCLINE, MOUNT LOWE RAILWAY

Trolley cars ran to Altadena, whence the first stage of Thaddeus Lowe's Mountain Railway took tourists to Rubio Canyon. Here, passengers have left the trolleys at Rubio Pavilion (left) and are ready to ascend 3000 feet on the Great Incline, opened on the Fourth of July, 1893.

92.   ECHO MOUNTAIN HOUSE AT THE TOP OF THE GREAT CABLE INCLINE

The spectacular views from the Incline and the summit of Echo Mountain, together with the variety of attractions Lowe provided there, encouraged many visitors to spend the whole day at this site. The well-appointed Echo Mountain House even published its own newspaper, the Mount Lowe *Echo*. At night, the panorama across the Los Angeles basin became a carpet of light.

93.   THE 'ALPINE DIVISION' OF THE MOUNT LOWE RAILWAY

The final stage provided a thrilling ride in open, narrow-gauge trolley cars to Ye Alpine Tavern, near the summit of Mount Lowe (6100 ft). Echo Mountain House and part of the 'Alpine' track can be seen below on left. This section of the famous 'Trolley Trip to Cloudland' swept over 18 trestles and around 127 curves.

The cost of daily excursions, the life-blood of the industry, was closely watched. The network woven by Los Angeles' interlocking system of 'Rounds' and 'Radials' remained taut yet flexible, and the city wooed year-round tourists to what was confidently claimed as "one of America's busiest centers for short trips." Certainly, internal competition between rival doorstep attractions made the Los Angeles resort region one of the most practical, price-conscious and go-getting promoters of the tourist industry in the whole of the United States.

Los Angeles was always ready to push its luck. The superb climate and variety of attractions in the Los Angeles resort region, the popularity of daily jaunts, and the relatively easy gradients and good suburban roads

94.

THE MONDONVILLE HOTEL, LOS ANGELES, c. 1896

Located in the midst of irrigated orchards and groves at Washington Street and Arlington, Los Angeles, the hotel also served as the Mondonville Club House. It offered rest and refreshment at all hours to cyclists enjoying the 'bicycle craze' in the ideal surroundings of the Los Angeles basin during the Nineties.

all combined to make this area a perfect setting for the bicycle craze, which, in the Nineties, created an astounding burst of new business among tourists and local residents alike. Between 1885-89, rapid improvements in bicycle design, notably in wheel size, safety frames and pneumatic tyres (patented in 1888), opened up a mass market in the following decade. In 1896, there were an estimated 2,500,000 bicycle-riders in the United States, with a combined investment of some $75,000,000 in manufacturing, and still more in the spin-off economy of repair shops, tourism, guidebooks, clubhouses, special clothing, and a wide range of sundries.[27]

Bicycle-parties and bicycle-tours were all the rage. Although the urbanized northeastern United States dominated the movement, the bicycle's popularity in California was unique in scale west of the Mississippi. Cycling was strongly recommended to invalids during the 1890s as good exercise and pleasant therapy. It appealed to health-seekers who, alone or in groups, could go for a spin at their own pace and rest whenever they wanted in that significant transitional period of personal transport between the age of the horse and the automobile. Health-seekers, however, simply swelled the volume of men and women, young and old, who pedalled California into the record books in the 1890s. The Census Reports for the Year 1900 list as many as 234 bicycle repair shops in California, a figure not equalled elsewhere in the United States outside the densely populated manufacturing regions of the Northeast and Midwest. More bicycles were sold in proportion to the population in Los Angeles than in any other city in the world.[28]

As well as being mid-way between the ocean and the Sierra Madre, Los Angeles was also roughly equidistant from Santa Barbara and San Diego, each about one hundred miles from the city. Although neither formed part of the Los Angeles resort region, both were securely linked to it by the late Eighties, and a significant proportion of their business expansion in the Nineties came via Los Angeles. This was particularly true of Santa Barbara, whose link to Los Angeles by the Southern Pacific railroad, completed in August 1887, brought a new age of prosperity to this 'old' pioneer resort of the Seventies. Indeed, the railroad journey was a twice-daily attraction in itself, with special 'tourist' tickets sold in Los Angeles for about $3 to allow for stop-overs on the way to Santa Barbara at such celebrated spots as the San Buenaventura Mission (1782), and the beautiful health resorts of Nordhoff and the Ojai Valley. The final thirty miles of the journey were equally memorable, a "sea-voyage on rails." The track hugged the cliffs for much of the way . . . "At times, on looking from one side of the car, nothing can be seen but the deep-blue sea, and . . . the ocean-surf can be heard beating under the train as though it were against the sides of a ship."

95.

PART OF TENT CITY ON CORONADO BEACH, NEAR SAN DIEGO,
WITH THE HOTEL DEL CORONADO IN THE BACKGROUND

The World's Work, August 1902

"People rent furnished tents here for from $3 to $5 a week, or they may bring their own tents and camp free."

Tent Cities were a popular feature of Southern California's tourist industry in the 1890s and early 1900s. Catalina Island, Redondo Beach, and Coronado Beach were three of the best known.

At Coronado Beach, tents had originally housed construction workers for the Hotel del Coronado in 1887-8. Ten years later, the idea was revived and advice sought from the tent-city developers on Catalina Island. In Nov. 1899, *The San Diego Union* reported that work had begun on "a miniature town — a tent town — with electric lights, a modern water and sewer system, walkways, roadways and electric trolley cars."

Enquiries poured in. The original plan for 500 tents was quickly expanded so that by Opening Day, 10th June 1900, Coronado Tent City had been born. By 1901, the Santa Fe and Southern Pacific Railroads both offered special excursions and reduced fares to Tent City from all points on their routes. The Santa Fe ran the 'Tent City Flyer' from Los Angeles to San Diego, and advertised the new beach resort as part of a major promotion tour about California across the West and Midwest. Tent City agencies were opened from New York to San Francisco, and brochures widely distributed in the industrial Northeast.

Coronado Tent City spread along the Silver Strand and doubled its tourist population in less than a year. By 1902, more than 1400 canvas tents and palm cottages were in place. Band concerts, dancing, vaudeville shows, children's sports and a circus were featured throughout the summer, and over 4000 tourists arrived for the opening of the 1903 season. But there was also space to get away from the crowds, move well down the beach, and enjoy nothing but the sand, the sun, and the ocean.

Accommodation, trolley-car services, and general maintenance were all handled by the Hotel del Coronado, some of whose guests sampled camp life for a week or two. Other tourists based themselves in Tent City but joined in many of the activities of the hotel. All tents were provided with beds, rocking and camp chairs, kitchen utensils, linen and laundry services, and electric light. Ice boxes were extra. A restaurant was added, although the grocery store and kitchen tents remained popular with those who wanted to do their own housekeeping. One contented visitor summed it up: "Life in Tent City is a perfect mixture of metropolitan and backwoods existence."

Thousands of new visitors arrived on America's 'Riviera' coast during the Nineties, and a new phase of hotel construction began in Santa Barbara, 'America's Mentone'. Biggest of all, at the end of the decade, came the magnificent Potter Hotel, which was built near the water's edge and could accommodate 1000 guests in palatial style. Its appearance coincided with the completion in March 1901 of the Southern Pacific's popular direct coast route between San Francisco, Santa Barbara and Los Angeles, which stimulated a major new surge of tourists into Southern California from the Golden Gate. Milo M. Potter already owned Los Angeles' Westminster Hotel as well as the Van Nuys, by then the largest hotel in the city. Guests began filling his new Potter Hotel in Santa Barbara in December 1902, although the official opening was in January 1903. Bookings came thick and fast. Accommodation at the Potter Hotel and Country Club, "set in a Floral Park 1000 feet from the Sea," was soon increased to cater for 1600 guests. The resort hotel was only five minutes' walk from a new railroad station, and the Southern Pacific offered free 'break-of-journey' tickets to allow stop-overs at the Potter Hotel. With the help of the railroad, linked advertising, and complementary attractions, Milo Potter was outstandingly successful in expanding both his city and his seaside hotel business in Los Angeles and Santa Barbara.

Elaborating the San Francisco Resort Region

The growing rivalry between Los Angeles and San Francisco was reflected in the tourist industry, as in almost everything else. Both were united in the 'Come to California' movement, but after that it was a free-for-all in which Los Angeles, the late-comer, quickly learned the basic moves and then fought for a slice of the Bay Area's tourist trade.

Even after the completion of Southern California's first rail link to San Francisco by the Southern Pacific in 1876, and the staggering growth triggered by the arrival of the Atchison, Topeka & Santa Fe in 1885, Los Angeles found that in the Nineties and the early years of the twentieth century, despite setbacks, San Francisco had no difficulty in keeping ahead. Indeed, the advantages of San Francisco's key position as the terminus of America's central transcontinental route had been reinforced in the 1880s by the construction of the Denver & Rio Grande Western Railroad, whose scenic alternative through Colorado to Salt Lake City and Ogden merely pumped tourists back into the central corridor, and carried them on to the Golden Gate. Los Angeles fought hard and successfully for its own direct rail link to Utah. Completed in 1905, and under Union Pacific control, the new San Pedro, Los Angeles & Salt Lake Railroad shortened L.A.'s link to Chicago by about three hundred miles, encouraged Southern Californian investment in new mining areas, and boosted freight and passenger revenues to the new port-city of Los

Angeles. But compared to San Francisco, Los Angeles still retained a 'small-town', unsophisticated air.

San Francisco was hard to beat, especially as the Bay Area had pioneered Western America's tourist industry. The gold rush had stimulated the development of a regional transport network during the Fifties, Sixties, and early Seventies, and the web of rail, stage, and ferry systems, along with sea and river navigation — all connecting the Bay Area to its hinterland — had been greatly strengthened by the 'Big Four's' powerful monopoly. This integrated transport system, together with the magnificent setting, stimulating climate, commercial growth, and available investment capital, had produced a vigorous and highly distinctive San Francisco resort region with a radius of ninety-to-a-hundred miles from the city centre.

The region extended as far as the Calistoga-Cloverdale-Clear Lake country in the north, curved through the State capital of Sacramento and the Central Valley, and then swung south to include the stylish Hotel Del Monte, the Seventeen-mile Drive, and the beautiful surroundings of Monterey and Carmelo Bays. The hotel was only three hours from San Francisco on the Del Monte Limited, advertised as "The Fastest Passenger Flyer West of the Missouri River." As before, the Del Monte maintained strong ties with San Francisco society, and many of the city's newspapers kept reporters there to detail the comings and goings, and the fashion news. But the Del Monte's appeal had always been much wider than as a unique type of wealthy Bay City 'suburb'. By the end of the Nineties, the Del Monte could accommodate as many as two thousand guests, and had earned the reputation among many American and European tourists and tour operators of being both one of the finest, as well as one of the most reasonably priced, resort hotels in the world.

Although Lake Tahoe had continued to improve its facilities since the 1860s, and become a fashionable outpost of the San Francisco resort region by the 1890s, the region's most important outlier remained Yosemite, portions of which in 1890 became a National Park. Tickets for the round-trip were sold in San Francisco at the Yosemite Stage and Turnpike Co. office on Market Street, and cost $60; this included railroad and stagecoach transport both ways, together with hotel accommodation and tours by carriage or saddle-horse during the three days spent in the Yosemite Valley. This route followed the Southern Pacific's main line to Berenda, and then the 22-mile rail spur to Raymond. The Santa Fe Railroad sponsored a rival stage line, the Yosemite Transportation Co. based in Merced, with its own combined rail-stage tour office on San Francisco's Market Street.

In the Nineties, however, tourists were becoming increasingly accustomed to being able to 'ride the rails' all the way to their favourite attractions. For some, the long journeys by stagecoach from any of the half-dozen railroad departure points strung along the San Joaquin Valley were sheer misery — journeys of 60 to 90 miles on poor roads just to reach Yosemite, let alone explore it.

In 1891, Charles Dudley Warner championed their cause, rejecting the fad that crowds inevitably lowered the tone and debased the natural environment:

> "I believe that the pilgrims who used to go to the Yosemite on foot or on horseback regret the building of the stage road, the enjoyment of the wonderful valley being somehow cheapened by the comparative ease of reaching it. It is feared that a railway would still further cheapen, if it did not vulgarize it . . . But the romance for the few there is in staging will have to give way to the greater comfort of the many by rail . . . Yosemite will remain."

By 1890, between 4000 and 5000 visitors were making their way to Yosemite each year, but thousands more were awaiting the railroad. "Help people to reach the great wonders of the West," Warner urged . . .

96.

THE STONEMAN HOUSE (1886-96) IN THE YOSEMITE VALLEY
The Stoneman House was built by the State of California to meet the growing demand in the Eighties for better hotel accommodation at Yosemite, a State Park since 1864. In 1885, the State Legislature appropriated $40,000 for construction; another $5000 was secured for water supply and furniture. The hotel could take about 150 guests. It was destroyed by fire in August 1896.

"scenery must be made accessible." [29] In 1907, the railroad was extended to El Portal, the main entrance to the Yosemite Valley.

Meanwhile, camping and the pleasures of outdoor life were gaining popularity among men and women of all ages. In August 1895, in Yosemite, John Muir's party passed a group of girls who radiated "health and enjoyment, every step telling the exhilaration of the spicy mountain air. They were followed by a large spring wagon laden with camp equipments, drawn by a pair of horses driven by a woman ... Never before have the mountains seen so many young people camping in the hospitable, life-giving gardens and glens. It is a hopeful beginning. May their tribe increase." [30] In 1892, Muir and a group of supporters in San Francisco had founded the Sierra Club, a society as much concerned with

97.   THE CLIFF HOUSE AT POINT LOBOS, SAN FRANCISCO, WITH SEAL ROCKS, 1870
Frank Leslie's Illustrated Newspaper, June 18, 1870, *from a photograph by Thomas Houseworth & Co.*

Although a succession of Cliff Houses had stood here since 1850, the first famous one (above) was built in 1863. Damaged in 1887, it was later completely destroyed by fire on Christmas Day 1894. Work on a replacement began immediately, for Cliff House was part of a San Francisco tradition. Taking breakfast, and viewing the seals, sea-lions and coastal sights before fog began to roll in through the Golden Gate, was the first stage on one of San Francisco's earliest and most popular day-trips.

the protection and appreciation of wilderness areas as it was with mountaineering.

At the heart of the resort region, however, San Francisco developed its own tourist industry from a strong city base and a magnificent range of Day Excursions. Round-trips exploited the striking regional variety of bays and ocean, springs and spas, forested sierras and rich agricultural valleys, goldfields and vineyards, urban excitements and peaceful backwaters. Several of the city's round-trips had been going strong since the 1860s. Cabs and hacks swarmed all over San Francisco, and information for tourists about fares and the coupon-ticket system had been included in Crofutt and Atwell's original *Great Trans-Continental Railroad Guide* in 1869. After 1873, when San Francisco's cable-cars were introduced,

98.

THE CLIFF HOUSE, c.1898, WITH OCEAN BEACH

The Sutro Castle Cliff House was built in less than two years, and opened in 1896. This huge, highly fashionable chateau-like structure housed a hotel, restaurant and shops. It was owned by Adolph Sutro, who developed the site still further in 1896 by opening the celebrated, glass-covered Sutro Public Baths. These were hot and cold sea-water baths, tubs and plunges that could accommodate two thousand swimmers. A theatre, restaurant, aquarium, and landscaped gardens were added attractions.

Many tourists and local residents now chose to spend the whole day sampling the varied pleasures of Sutro Heights. Cliff House survived the 1906 earthquake virtually unscathed, but was destroyed by fire in 1907. The tradition continued, however, and building work on a new Cliff House started immediately.

tourists found that they could go almost anywhere along the routes for the single fare of 5 cents, thanks to the elaborate system of transfers.

The earliest round-trip remained one of the most popular. It included the view of Seal Rocks from Cliff House at Point Lobos, a visit to San Francisco's old Mission Dolores (1776), panoramic views over the city and the Golden Gate from Telegraph, Russian, or Clay Street Hills, or from Twin Peaks, and visits to San Francisco's famous fruit and vegetable market, as well as to Chinatown.

Local railroads carried thousands on special outings to beauty spots and picnic grounds. Crofutt recommended tourists to allow time for a run on the North Pacific Coast Railroad, a narrow-gauge which could be boarded at Sausalito after an impressive ferry-ride across the bay. Beyond the prosperous little town of San Rafael, the track wound through pine, spruce, and redwood forests, picnic glades, dairy farms, and lumber camps, with dazzling glimpses of bay and ocean on the way to Cazadero and Duncan's Saw Mills. Loggers in the region were making huge inroads into the redwood forests for the San Francisco market. Saddle-horses and later, a 12-mile wagon road from San Rafael, had long enabled tourists to reach the summit of Mount Tamalpais (2606 ft), one of the finest viewpoints on the Pacific Coast. In 1896, however, a winding mountain railway was opened from Mill Valley, on the North Pacific Coast Railroad, to within a few feet of the summit, and the Tavern of Tamalpais became an added tourist attraction. The mountain top could now be reached in two hours from San Francisco, and all-in trips combining ferry, narrow-gauge, and mountain railway were offered for as little as $1 single, $1.40 return. Carriages and saddle-horses could still be hired, and proved to be a popular 'extra' to the Day Out, which delighted tourists and others with the many different modes of conveyance that stitched the excursion together.

While the San Francisco resort region elaborated old attractions, and continually added new ones, the city itself remained the great focal point. It was unique in this respect; no other city west of the Mississippi could hold a candle to the Golden Gate metropolis as a national and international tourist attraction in its own right. No trip to Western America was complete without a visit to San Francisco. By 1900, its population was approaching 350,000 — the ninth-largest city in the United States — and still well over three times the size of Los Angeles, despite the latter's rapid transformation from remote adobe cow-town to the new regional head-quarters of Southern California. With the shoreline cities, the Bay Area now contained a population of more than half-a-million, its core city wealthy, confident, full of contrasts, and highly ambitious. San Francisco offered visitors a range of facilities unmatched elsewhere in the West, not only in hotels, restaurants, shops, theatres and opera houses but also in libraries, galleries, and cultural societies: literary, scientific, historical and geographical. Thus, between them, the San Francisco and Los Angeles resort regions provided a new scale and diversity to California's tourist industry, and a powerful stimulus to the United States' west coast economy.

Consolidating the Rocky Mountain Resort Region in Colorado

More than four hundred miles separated San Francisco and Los Angeles. Contrasts in their size, location, and economic opportunities encouraged competitive styles and separate identities. Only seventy-five miles separated Denver from Colorado Springs — a mere two hours by rail. Despite different backgrounds and undoubted rivalry, as a response to the unstoppable growth of California's tourist industry, the two largest tourist centres in Colorado quietly sank their differences, pooled their resources, and forged a unified Colorado Rocky Mountain resort region, with a single clear cutting edge.

The north-south boundary of the region along the Rocky Mountain Front remained firmly pegged to Denver at one end and to the Colorado Springs-Manitou-Pike's Peak cluster at the other, despite strenuous efforts by the Pueblo Chamber of Commerce in the Nineties to advertise the town as a winter tourist resort, at the junction of routes to Salt Lake City and New Mexico. By the end of the decade, however, Pueblo had faced reality and sharpened its own unique image. The city was now advertised enthusiastically as 'The Pittsburgh of the West', and, defiantly distancing itself from the tourist trade, Pueblo adopted the slogan 'Watch Our Smoke!'

Development of the Colorado Rocky Mountain resort region was to concentrate on the Denver, not the Pueblo, side of Colorado Springs, even though most of the intervening seventy-five miles was still dead ground in tourist terms. This was to change; new life was injected into the Pineries, the watershed area between the South Platte and Arkansas drainage systems, as well as the traditional divide between the social and economic interests of Denver and Colorado Springs. Symbolically, Denver, Colorado Springs, and the D. & R.G. Railroad gave their blessing to the creation of a new, watershed resort centre at Palmer Lake, and nourished it with the body-building diet of the late Eighties and Nineties — the Day Excursion.

Palmer Lake (7238 ft) was perched on the western crest of the South Platte-Arkansas drainage divide, fifty-two miles from Denver and twenty-three from Colorado Springs. It was the old 'Divide Lake' that George Crofutt remembered so well from his first summer in Colorado back in 1860, when two of his trail partners, Albinus Sheldon and Fred Spencer, had rediscovered the lake while surveying the Divide. In 1869, pioneers

D.C. Oakes and the Bennet family had built a ranch at the lake, near the stage road. After General Palmer ran his first Denver & Rio Grande railroad track south to Colorado Springs in 1871, the area began to attract more attention, but it was not until the mid-Eighties that it was decided to develop the site into a major playground resort.

The D.&R.G. began with the railroad station itself, dismantling the showpiece they had specially built to display in the grounds of the National Mining and Industrial Exposition, held in Denver in 1882-4, and reassembling it at the new 'Palmer Lake'. The station was one of the prettiest in Colorado. Charmed with the effect, the D. & R.G. pushed ahead rapidly with the business of transforming what until then had been a workaday timber-loading depot at the crest of the Pineries. The company built a stone embankment and promenade along the edge of the lake, a well-equipped boat-house, a dance pavilion, and a large refreshment hall where lunch-baskets could be purchased and picnics spread if the weather outside turned cold or wet. Surrounding the lake were grassy meadows and pine glades beneath the towering Rocky Mountain Front Range, where the crowds could disperse to ramble, picnic and play. Many visitors, however, never moved far from the water's edge. The lake itself was the recreational focus, a priceless natural asset in this dry plains/mountain front geographical junction zone . . . "Sparkling like a diamond in her emerald setting," wrote an early booster, "Palmer Lake is a delightful surprise to the tourist; a rare and unlooked for feature in the landscape." [31]

The Denver & Rio Grande railroad placed the emphasis on Day Excursions, and the company did not build a hotel. More to the point, rail fares were cut and shuttle services increased to boost day-trips from Denver and Colorado Springs. In 1881, *Crofutt's Grip-Sack Guide of Colorado* noted that the single fare from Denver to 'Divide' was $3.40 (i.e. more than 6½ cents a mile); by 1885, the fare had dropped to 5 cents a mile. But this was still absurdly expensive compared to the cheap runabout fares in California. Once the D. & R.G. had come to grips with the Day Excursion strategy at the end of the Eighties, and even more firmly in the Nineties, special return-trip fares were offered to Palmer Lake at less than 1½ cents a mile. "Palmer Lake is an ideal spot for Sunday School Outings," advised 'Major' Hooper, happy to advertise an easily accessible beauty spot with ample facilities, where the young could let off steam and tire themselves out. "Sandwiches provided!"

Palmer Lake was also popular for Church and Club Outings, and with civic and military organizations arranging outdoor Socials, band performances, and suchlike. Special 'family' tickets were made available, good for ten round-trips, and their stimulus to the daily traffic to and from Denver (where the offer was originally promoted), led the D.&R.G. to encourage the growth of daily or week-end commuting by Denver and Pueblo businessmen, who could now send their families off to spend the summer in villas or cottages at Palmer Lake. Denver was only a little over an hour's rail journey from Palmer Lake; Colorado Springs was less than an hour away, Pueblo normally two hours. Before long, competing railroads were all offering cheap, 3-month summer-commuter tickets to Palmer Lake from these centres, the three largest cities in the State.

The demand for Commutation and other special Day Excursion tickets grew rapidly during the Nineties. Business boomed as never before in this once-isolated regional frontier between the worlds of Denver and Colorado Springs, drawing both of them into a sparsely populated region that even many local residents had never explored. Neither Denver's nor Colorado Springs' streetcar system ran out this far, but as a subsidiary resort and recreational area, Palmer Lake's main-line service by steam railroads was unrivalled in Colorado, and was now one of the best in the whole of Western America.

Competition between rival railroad companies had resulted in new construction or shared track agreements that by the early Nineties had made the Denver-Colorado Springs-Pueblo section, a total distance of some 120 miles, the most famous 'railroad corridor' in the Mountain West. By the late Eighties, Crofutt reminded readers in his *Overland Tours* that at least twelve passenger trains a day stopped at Palmer Lake, and by the early Nineties, the number had soared to between twenty and thirty every 24 hours. The Atchison, Topeka & Santa Fe had built its own track parallel to that of the Denver & Rio Grande, and added its own picturesquely turretted station to the railroad architecture of Palmer Lake. The trains of the Colorado Midland used the A.T. & S.F. track between Denver and Colorado Springs, while the Denver & Rio Grande made the best deal it could in the face of crippling competition, and offered joint trackage agreements with the Missouri Pacific, and the Chicago, Rock Island & Pacific, between Denver and Pueblo. "So superior is Palmer Lake's rail service and system of connections," rejoiced E.C. Gard in 1894, that from this resort, "a train can be taken at almost any hour of the day or night for any point on any road in the country." [32] Meanwhile, the fare structure remained crucial, and the Denver & Rio Grande learned to cut its prices, not merely through doorstep competition but through constant lessons from the West Coast. 'Major' Hooper was, after all, one of California's most shrewdly observant visitors during the Nineties.

Away from the main crowds near the promenade, boat-house, pavilion, and refreshment rooms, a cluster of new villas, cottages, boarding-houses, and a few hotels began to appear at the far side of Palmer Lake. The Glen House in neighbouring Glenwood Park was opened at a weekly rate of $12 for room and board, and a meals-only service was available for health-seekers and others living in cottages or tents close by. By the 1890s, a wider choice of cheaper accommodation was available in two hotels and some half-dozen small boarding-houses, where rates were normally $1 a day. Buggy rides to visit local cattle and horse-breeding ranches, and the celebrated local potato farms, were a popular activity, along with back-packing, camping, pony-trekking, and the hiring of saddle-horses to explore the canyons and striking rock formations south of Palmer Lake as far as Monument and the Garden of the Gods near Colorado Springs. The Divide offered splendidly varied riding country, and this soon became one of its major attractions, both for day and week-end outings.

Although Palmer Lake was promoted by its earliest residents as a year-round summer and winter resort — "The lake is for boating and bathing in summer, for skating in winter," announced one of them, determined to make the most of this tourist oasis—the area in fact remained a summer playground, a pleasant and easily accessible retreat from the heat of the plains. More money was made in winter by exporting the ice from Palmer Lake than from skating over it. The D.&R.G. built large ice houses by the lake, and hundreds of car loads of ice were widely distributed annually by the railroad. Indeed, when Leadville was constructing its huge Ice Palace in November-December 1895, ready for the opening of the city's spectacular Ice Carnival on 1st January 1896, extra supplies of ice were cut from Palmer Lake and sent up to Leadville on the Denver & Rio Grande railroad.

The fact that Palmer Lake made such a significant contribution to the consolidation of Colorado's Rocky Mountain resort region in the 1890s was based on its ability to complement rather than compete with the tourist attractions in and around Denver, Colorado Springs, and the centres on the Western Slope of the Rockies. Denver and Colorado Springs gave little support, for example, to Finley Thompson's earlier efforts to acquire English investment to build a large, elaborate sanatorium complex at Palmer Lake that would rival the facilities available at Manitou and elsewhere. The end-product of Thompson's unsuccessful venture was a relatively small, more modest construction that became the Rocklands Hotel. Even so, with accommodation for eighty guests, it was eventually to be the largest hotel in Palmer Lake.

Denver and Colorado Springs were encouraging a different type of growth on the Divide. The older Glen House and Glenwood Park development gave way at the end of the Eighties to the new Glen Park Residential and Recreation Area. The Park was landscaped informally with trails, rides, look-out points, shady seats, and scattered building lots for cottages and villas. Central to the enterprise, the town's promotion company had built a concert and conference auditorium capable of seating a thousand, together with a dining hall, and simple hostel and tent accommodation in a secluded area of the park. Given Palmer Lake's excellent railroad services and spacious setting, Glen Park had also been designed as the Chautauqua Assembly Ground for the States of Colorado and Wyoming. Annual summer camps had become a feature of this religious and intellectual movement which took its name from the original Assembly at Lake Chautauqua, New York, in 1874. Known as the 'College of the People', the Assemblies quickly spread across the United States, establishing regular summer-resort centres of adult education that were often located close to, but separate from, the fashionable tourist resorts.[33] Palmer Lake regarded its selection to host the Rocky Mountain Chautauqua Assembly as "a valuable adjunct" to its resort facilities, and advised other long-term summer visitors, if they got tired of "swinging in hammocks doing nothing," to take advantage of some of the lectures,

9.

SLOAN'S LAKE, DENVER, IN THE 1890s

Tom Sloan and George Crofutt located neighbouring quarter-sections here in the early 1860s. The lake formed naturally in 1862 after Sloan struck an aquifer while digging a well. In the 1890s, Sloan's Lake and the Manhattan Beach Amusement Park, seen here along the shore, became one of Denver's most popular local playgrounds. The skyline of the Rocky Mountain Front is in the far distance.

readings, discussion groups, and concerts available just a short walk away in Glen Park.

While Palmer Lake made the most of its distinctive 'back-up' position within the Rocky Mountain resort region, Denver and Colorado Springs were busy strengthening the region's northern and southern bastions with increased vigour and determination. Denver, with a population of over 106,000 by 1890, had greatly expanded its tourist attractions and first-class hotel accommodation in the boom years of 1890-92 — a major investment which helped to sustain this sector of the economy after the Panic of 1893. The Metropole (1890), the Oxford (1891), and the Brown Palace (1892) took their places, with superb timing, in the list of Western America's most stylish hotels.

As the fourth (soon to be third) largest city west of the Missouri River, Denver's desire to diversify and offer more 'fun-of-the-fair' attractions in the Nineties resulted in the opening of Elitch's Zoological and Pleasure Gardens in 1890, and the Manhattan Beach Amusement Park in 1891.

100.   GOING UP BOULDER CANYON BY WAGON ROAD AND NARROW-GAUGE
                                RAILWAY (U.P.)

                          in *Crofutt's Overland Tours*, 1890

The railroad's Sunset branch followed the Boulder River for 13 miles into the mountains. "This section is devoted exclusively to mining and lumbering," Crofutt noted, "but the scenery is noticeably wild and romantic . . . and affords some magnificent views well worth a visit by the tourist."

101. THE PICNIC PAVILION AT BEAVER BROOK STATION, CLEAR CREEK CANYON

in *Crofutt's Grip-Sack Guide of Colorado,* 1881

Beaver Brook was the first stop out of Denver (22 miles) on the Colorado Central Railroad (U.P.). The company built a picnic pavilion above the station, and ran extra trains at reduced rates for school parties and group excursions in the Eighties and Nineties.

from a photograph by William H. Jackson

The Georgetown Loop was built to freight minerals in the 1880s but made more money
carrying tourists in the 1890s.

The Colorado Central (U.P.) narrow-gauge railroad pushed westward over the Loop to
Silver Plume and Graymont in 1884 in an effort to reach the silver boom town of
Leadville. The Panic of 1893 put an end to that dream, and attention switched to
developing the Georgetown Loop into Denver's most popular day-trip. The railroad built
a lunch pavilion at Silver Plume, and also allowed tourists to break their journey on the
Loop to visit the main tunnels of the Mendota Mine nearby, with guides provided.

Manhattan Beach Park lined the northwest shore of Sloan's Lake, next to
Crofutt's old quarter-section located in the early 1860s across the South
Platte. On the south side of Denver, Rufus "Potato" Clark's first quarter-
section, which Crofutt also knew so well, had now become part of
Overland Park, and was already popular for horse-racing, camping, and
golf. Trolley cars carried Denverites and tourists to Elitch's Gardens and
Sloan's Lake; the narrow-gauge Denver Circle Railroad swept them down
to Overland Park. Crofutt had watched this railway being built in 1881 and
then extended in 1883 to connect the site of the National Mining and
Industrial Exposition with the proposed pleasure-ground development
on land bought from Rufus Clark. "The Denver Circle railway," wrote
Crofutt, "... running south from the city for several miles ... is a kind of
a *string* to a real estate kite." [34] The fare was cheap, just five cents.

Denver's first 3-day Festival of Mountain and Plain in 1895 kept up
the momentum. But while many of the Rocky Mountain regional attractions serviced from Denver required more time to be reached and
savoured (Estes Park was only one example), the city went all out to
extend its Day Excursion program. Bicycle clubs played their part, and
Denver "wheelmen" pushed Colorado into a leading position during the
bicycle craze in the 1890s, second only to California west of the Missouri-
Mississippi River line.[35] Short railroad trips into the mountains were the
greatest single tourist attraction, however, and here by far the most
popular excursion from Denver was pointedly advertised as "A Day in the
Rockies." This was the Colorado Central (U.P.) railroad's magnificent
120-mile round-trip through Clear Creek Canyon and Idaho Springs to
the Georgetown Loop. Not only was the journey an impressive field study
of Colorado's changing mining landscapes; the completion in 1884 of the
spectacular Georgetown Loop between Georgetown and Silver Plume,
above South Clear Creek, had passengers crowding the observation cars
for a breathtaking climax. "This tour", wrote Crofutt, "is one of the most
attractive and cheapest that can be made from Denver." "Silver Plume, *two*
miles by wagon road from Georgetown, requires *four-and-a-half* miles by
rail," he reported in a vivid description of the entire route. "The whole
scene changes with every revolution of the wheels, and to be sure not to
miss any grand views, one must keep alert and watchful all the time." [36]

Once the Colorado Midland Railroad had extended its service to Denver via the A.T. & S.F. route, the company's delightful Wildflower Excursions, pioneered from Colorado Springs, became enormously popular. The excellent passenger train service in the Nineties between Denver and Colorado Springs added not only Palmer Lake but many of the tourist attractions around booming Colorado Springs and Cripple Creek to Denver's choice of Outings. In practice, it was a two-way exchange along seventy-five miles of the Rocky Mountain Front that produced a genuinely functional resort region.

The Colorado Springs-Manitou-Pike's Peak area invested so heavily in elaborating and advertising its tourist industry in the 1890s (see pages 316-20), that one Easterner voiced a widely-held opinion when he noted that "Colorado Springs is becoming so well known and famous that no trip to the West or the Pacific Coast is considered complete without a visit to the Springs." [37] The Antlers remained the flagship of an expanding fleet of hotels, boarding-houses and villas, but once again, the variety and cost of the Day Excursion miscellany provided the real battleground among the Western regions for new growth in the Nineties' tourist trade.

Simple, traditional pleasures were not neglected. A detailed list of Daily Walks was available, always a distinguishing feature of the Colorado Springs-Manitou region since the creation of the spa in 1871-72. On the latest major attraction, the return fare to the summit of Pike's Peak, whether by the Pike's Peak Cog Railway or the new carriage-road, was $5. This was the same as the original fare charged on Los Angeles' Mount Lowe excursion, although special rates soon halved the cost of that memorable Southern Californian day-trip. Fares to many of the local tourist attractions around Colorado Springs were often two or three times as much as those in California. Striking exceptions to this resulted from the rate war between the Colorado Midland and the Colorado Springs & Cripple Creek District Railway (the Short Line) on their competing daily Wildflower and Scenic Excursions. The Short Line also made a special effort to attract long-distance tourists; the company offered its normal $5 10-day return tickets up to the mountain meadows and Cripple Creek country for only $2.75 to those passengers who were also holding a current transcontinental train ticket.

One of the cheapest and most popular day-trips around Cripple Creek was the 25-cent Circle Tour by the High Line and Low Line electric tramways. This inter-urban system had been built to link the scattered mining camps and communities, and now boosted its business by providing tourists and others with a unique survey of the whole area.

103. ADVERTISEMENT FOR ONE-DAY MOUNTAIN EXCURSIONS IN COLORADO

Following a series of mergers in the 1890s, the Colorado & Southern Railway Co. began operation in January 1899. An enticing range of Day Excursions had become an essential weapon in the fight for business between rival Western tourist centres by the 1890s-1900s.

In Denver, electric trolley services were consolidated in 1899 into the Denver City Tramway Co., and this gave a boost to the 'Seeing Denver' trolley excursion. Another popular half-day trip from Denver was the 'Wishbone' Tour of the Rocky Mountain Foothills (i.e. along the Clear Creek and Ralston Creek Valleys to Golden, Arvada and Leyden). But both of these trips worked out at more than twice the price of the rail and trolley-car 'Specials' in California.

104.
                        THE GROWING POPULARITY OF OUTDOOR LIFE
FAMILIES CAMPING OUT IN COLORADO IN THE 1880s AND 1890s:
In Bear Creek Canyon, 1884

"One can *radiate* so well from Denver and Colorado Springs,"
enthused a Coloradan tourist promoter in the 1890s. But geography
clearly shaped that radiation field. Unlike California's opportunity to
exploit both mountain and ocean, Colorado's mountains-and-plains
country produced a strikingly unsymmetrical resource base. The concept of being "at sea on the plains" was lyrical but valueless; the plains
were barren ground to the tourist industry, and no golden beaches
marked their junction with the great Front Range. The Denver-Colorado
Springs axis lay on the eastern edge, not at the centre of the Rocky
Mountain resort region. Yet from this strong, consolidated base-line,
development continued at selected sites as far west as Glenwood Springs
(1893). Within the confines of the Rockies, the railroads had been forced
to weave a resort region of remarkably open texture, but the fabric was
well knotted, and proved to be one of the toughest and most durable in
the American West.

At Fall Creek, 1888

105.

106.

In Estes Park, 1890

Other Centres

The 1890s saw some reduction in the old-style 'Health Rush' to the West. The discovery that tuberculosis was a communicable disease with a highly infectious stage gradually put an end to sufferers being advised to travel and to mingle freely with the West's resident and tourist population. Consumptives were to become unwelcome almost everywhere except at isolated camps or purpose-built cottages and sanatoria.

None of this, however, lessened the appeal or the promotion of the climates of Southern California and Colorado for settlers, tourists, and general health-seekers. Colorado was particularly active in this respect, partly because it lacked the range of alternatives which braced the Californian economy. Essays and articles praising high-altitude health resorts were regularly commissioned by the Chambers of Commerce in Denver and Colorado Springs.

Denver physician Dr. Charles Denison, who had been one of the founder members of the American Climatological Association in Washington, D.C. in 1884, lectured and published widely on the medical advantages of Colorado, and became the Association's president in 1890. Dr. Samuel Fisk, like Denison, an early tubercular sufferer from New England, worked in Denver between 1883 and 1898, and was one of the region's most powerful promoters. Dr. Samuel Solly, still based at the booming Manitou and Colorado Springs, was renowned on both sides of the Atlantic for his medical practice and his research; he became president of the American Climatological Association in 1895. No one would be left in any doubt as to the characteristics and benefits of Colorado's climate while these three were around, and no counter-claim from California was ever allowed to go unchallenged.

Physicians from Arizona, Texas and New Mexico also continued to publicize the climatic advantages claimed for the southwest, although none damaged the lead of California and Colorado for first and second place among the West's great spa and tourist resorts. The magnificent Montezuma Hotel, opened at Las Vegas Hot Springs, New Mexico in 1882 by the Atchison, Topeka & Santa Fe Railroad, had flourished during the Eighties, despite a temporary setback caused by fire. But it could not survive the depression of the Nineties, nor the crippling competition from the California-Colorado tourists' box of delights, neatly packaged by the railroads, and by the Eastern and European tour operators.

The lavish Montezuma resort hotel had obeyed the first 'Law of Concentrated Effort', but not the rules requiring improved 'Intervening Attractions-Total Distance' ratios, and *regional* resort development. The Atchison, Topeka & Santa Fe route across New Mexico and Arizona had a low 'Attractions-Distance' ratio; there were too many miles of unrelieved desert. Interest in the old Spanish-Mexican frontier towns of Santa Fe and Albuquerque, in Indian pueblos, and in the art, crafts, and beauty of desert landscapes characterized the twentieth, rather than the nineteenth century. But what the A.T. & S.F. Railroad lost on the swings of the Montezuma Hotel in New Mexico in the 1890s it gained on the round-abouts of the Grand Canyon in Arizona a few years later. In 1901, a branch line was extended from Williams to the south rim of the Canyon, replacing the exhausting two-day, 76-mile stage journey from Flagstaff. Few tourists had endured it. "No work has been done on the road," one of them reported in the early Nineties: "it is made simply by driving over it. There are a few miles here and there of fair wheeling, but a good deal of it is intolerably dusty or exceedingly stony, and progress is slow." [38] Most of the route across the desert was uninhabited, and water scarce. The railroad cut the journey to three hours, with a daily train each way; the return fare was reduced to $6.50, less than half the cost by stagecoach.

With the coming of the railroad, and the opening of the new luxury resort hotel, El Tovar, in January 1905 in the classic Santa Fe Railroad-Fred Harvey House tradition, the Grand Canyon entered the tourist age. Indeed, the strategy and style of its entry belonged more to the nineteenth than to the twentieth century, even though the Santa Fe acknowledged the new interest in Indian culture and crafts by building the Hopi

House and a Curio Shop opposite the entrance to El Tovar, ready for the hotel's first visitors on opening day. Such was the scale and magnificence of the Grand Canyon, it quickly became a resort region of its own, with a variety of round-trips to look-outs along the rim, saddle-horse tours to the floor of the canyon, and additional Fred Harvey Lodges. Some tourists still preferred to 'do' the Grand Canyon from the balconies and picture-windows of the El Tovar, but growing numbers spent one or two weeks

107.   HOTEL EL TOVAR ON THE SOUTH RIM OF THE GRAND CANYON, ARIZONA, 1905

photograph by L.C. McClure

In 1901, the Santa Fe built a branch railroad to the rim of the Grand Canyon, and Fred Harvey's organization soon followed with the first-class, regionally-styled Hotel El Tovar. "All the way on the Atchison, Topeka & Santa Fe," wrote one visitor appreciatively as he settled in to the El Tovar, "with the great Fred Harvey catering from end to end."

The sight of the Grand Canyon was overwhelming . . . "a system, not a mere object of scenery . . . The sheer vastness of the chasm into which one gazes . . . different in this regard from anything ever seen, and being on so stupendous a scale it overpowers, impresses, dominates to the full capacity of the human mind . . . Here lies a miracle of sublimity and majesty, architecture and color."

exploring the area. Many came to regard it as an outlier of Southern California's tourist complex.

Utah had kept its own eye on the progress of Western America's tourist industry. Salt Lake City greeted the increased tourist traffic in the Nineties by opening three new hotels in 1891, notably the Knutsford, which immediately became the most popular first-class hotel for through-passengers spending a few days 'side-tripping' in the city. Improved hotel accommodation was only part of the new development program, however. The success of the Denver & Rio Grande Western's Lake Park resort and the Union Pacific's Garfield Beach had by now encouraged local Mormon leaders to enter the lakeside tourist industry themselves. In June 1891, they formed the Saltair Beach Company to build a new bathing resort on the Great Salt Lake, just twelve miles west of the city and linked to it by the new Saltair Railway, whose name was soon changed optimistically to the Salt Lake & Los Angeles Railway.

The huge, Moorish-styled Saltair Beach Pavilion opened in 1893, its spectacular central complex housing a large dance-hall and a restaurant capable of seating one thousand visitors with ease. Two piers curved out over the lake, complete with a thousand bathing cabins, and bath and shower facilities. Bathing costumes and shade hats could be hired. Saltair Beach was the nearest beach resort to Salt Lake City, and trains rattled to and fro on the 30-minute shuttle crowded with local residents and tourists. Extensive hotel accommodation was not provided at Saltair since the city was now vigorously exploiting the tourist potential of shoreline development by means of the Day Excursion. "For the season of 1893," announced the Salt Lake Chamber of Commerce, "Salt Lake City will have, within twelve to twenty-two miles of the city, three of the most elegantly appointed bathing resorts in the world, all reached by quick and frequent railway service." [39]

Utah's tourist attractions in the late nineteenth century did indeed remain closely associated with Salt Lake City and its immediate surroundings. Essentially, development represented an elaboration of the time-honoured city side-trip for transcontinental tourists, and most of the new amenities introduced in the Nineties catered as much for the business interests and recreation of the local population as for the through-passenger traffic. Although a popular spa was developed at the nearby hot sulphur springs (to which Crofutt had drawn attention in 1885), the Mormons made no attempt to create a diversified resort region in this desert environment. Both by choice and force of circumstance, Utah's 'Law of Concentrated Effort' was applied instead to maintaining its religious values, and to the steady promotion of regional economic development based on irrigated agriculture, livestock, commerce, mining, and related processing and manufacturing.

The Pacific Northwest was a relatively late entrant to Western America's tourist industry, overshadowed by California's wider appeal, more varied climates, early transcontinental railroad link and resort hotel development, and by the Golden State's larger population, more broadly based investment, and peerless promotion. Although Portland, Tacoma and Seattle were all graced by first-class city hotels in the 1890s, the Pacific Northwest failed to develop a clearly identifiable, well-integrated resort region in the nineteenth century. The major urban clusters were set well back from a thinly populated coastline. The relative isolation of the lower Columbia-Willamette Valley area, the intricacies of Puget Sound, and the distance of the steamer route to Alaska all tended to disperse rather than to focus land and sea transport networks. The season was short. Given the local popularity of summer cottages and boarding-houses, summer camps, fishing, hunting, hiking and mountaineering, tourist resorts as such remained small and widely scattered.

In 1894, Frances Victor reported the region's limited coastal resort development after returning from an extensive tour:

> "Owing to the rough and broken character of the mountains, communication between the coast and the interior is difficult. Good harbors affording sea approaches are rare, and owing to these joint obstacles to settlement, an otherwise delightful portion of the Northwest is but slowly coming into favor."

Several of the most beautiful beaches were very exposed, she discovered, and littered with driftwood. "Astoria has no beach . . . no means, in fact, of touring for pleasure except such as depend upon boating of some sort." "Seaside, on Clatsop Beach, is the oldest fashionable summer resort on the Oregon coast," but it was still, like the newer Gearhart Park, Nestucca, Yaquina and Newport, small and quietly informal. There was no shortage of place-names, just a shortage of people:

> ". . . Salmon River, Alseya Bay, Siuslaw River, Umpqua River, Coos Bay, Coquille River, Port Orford, and several smaller inlets, have attractive features, which in time will make them better known to tourists and pleasure-seekers. Meanwhile there is room for all who come." [40]

*   *   *

Two popular fictional characters, Aunt Pheba and Uncle Hiram Harrison, took a trip to the west coast from their farm in Nebraska at the turn of the century. Back home, Aunt Pheba announced firmly: "I don't think much of the country between here an' California, except little spots around Denver an' Salt Lake City." [41] Californians reading Sara White Isaman's humorous *Tourist Tales* noted approvingly that many a true word is spoken in jest.

Although new wonders were discovered and developed in the intervening regions, California and Colorado remained the two end-pegs which fixed and stabilized the tourist industry of Western America. Together, these two States represented for many the quintessential West — the wide threshold of the plains, the picturesque magnificence of the Rockies in classic form, mountain meadows, high sierras, giant *sequoias*, irrigated orchards, sun-drenched beaches and the dramatic finale of the Pacific coast.

California and Colorado had no complaints if their twin attractions wooed fresh crowds of tourists, determined to fill every minute and to see as much as possible in a limited time. But these two western States were not going to carry complementarity too far. "Visit California in winter and Colorado in summer" was never their slogan; each went all out for permanent settlers, steady growth, and a year-round tourist trade. The basic rivalry between them persisted, providing a constant stimulus to greater efficiency, and to the rapid adoption of new styles and services in the American tourist industry. Competition for the expanding Western tourist market was not confined to California *v.* Colorado but this remained the pace-setter — fast and furious in a sparsely populated West fighting distance and isolation by every means at its disposal.

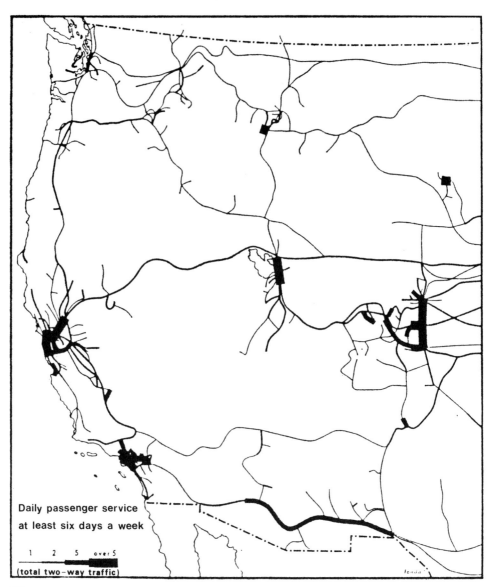

Daily passenger service
at least six days a week

1   2   5   over 5

(total two-way traffic)

XV.

PASSENGER SERVICES AND REGIONAL RAILROAD SYSTEMS IN WESTERN AMERICA AT THE END OF THE NINETEENTH CENTURY

Sources: *Official Guide of the Railway and Steam Navigation Lines in the United States, Canada, and Mexico* (September 1897); and D.W. Meinig, *Annals of the Association of American Geographers* (June 1972)

During the 1880s–1890s, the pattern of Western passenger services
became increasingly dominated by four regional rail networks focused on
San Francisco, Los Angeles, Salt Lake City, and the Rocky Mountain Front
in Colorado between Denver, Colorado Springs and Pueblo.

THE GROWTH OF TRANSPORT AND TOURIST FACILITIES
IN YELLOWSTONE NATIONAL PARK, 1883-1905

08.

GARDINER STATION, 1904

The Northern Pacific Railroad reached Cinnabar, six miles from the Park, in 1883. In 1903, the line was extended to Gardiner at the Park's main entrance and this, along with heavy promotion, brought a surge of new visitors to Yellowstone. Relatively few used the alternative Oregon Short Line Railroad approach of the Union Pacific. In 1903, over 13,000 tourists entered the Park via Gardiner, nearly twice the number recorded at the Yosemite Valley, California that year. Of course, thousands of tourists had already visited Yosemite over the years, so that Yellowstone was for many a newer attraction. But the fact remained that in 1903, the entrance to the Yosemite Valley was still a full day-and-a-half by stagecoach from the nearest railhead.

109.   THE YELLOWSTONE NATIONAL PARK TRANSPORTATION CO.

The company was formed in 1891 to coincide with the completion of the 145-mile road
through the Park by the Army Corps of Engineers. Here, tourists prepare to leave from
the Mammoth Springs Hotel, originally called the National and opened in 1883.

10.

THE YELLOWSTONE LAKE HOTEL
The demand for more and better hotel accommodation in the Nineties resulted in the opening of the Yellowstone Lake Hotel in 1891. Columns, gables and mouldings were added in the colonial-style remodelling of 1903 after the railroad reached Gardiner, and tourists showed new interest in visiting the wonders of the Park.

111.
LAKE TOURS
Passengers disembarking at the West Thumb boat-landing on Yellowstone Lake from
the wood-burning steamer *Zillah,* c.1898.
The 20-mile steamer trip between the Thumb and Yellowstone Lake Hotel was highly
recommended, particularly for the panoramic views near the centre of the lake over
forested slopes and distant ranges, including the Tetons. The trip cost $3. Fishing boats
and fishing tackle could also be hired, by the hour or the day.

12.

TOURISTS AT THE NORRIS GEYSER BASIN IN 1903

The number and variety of the geysers, and the dazzling colours in the Norris Basin
(which was crossed by the stage road), made it one of the main attractions in the Park.
By now, many more tourists were becoming aware of the rarity value of Yellowstone —
the world's largest concentration of geysers and hot springs.

113.   CASTLE GEYSER AND OLD FAITHFUL INN, 1905

This cone-type geyser erupted every 4-10 hours with average bursts of up to 80 feet for 15-60 minutes, although at the turn of the century Castle Geyser also played occasionally at heights of 150-200 feet.

In the background stands Old Faithful Inn, opened in 1904 as part of the major hotel-building program designed to attract more tourists to the Park. By this time, it was widely acknowledged that Yellowstone had lagged too far behind California and Colorado in developing its potential in the West's expanding tourist industry. Besides these two front-runners, the Grand Canyon of Arizona was also becoming a major competitor, thanks to the new facilities and vigorous promotion provided by the Santa Fe Railroad. As a result, Yellowstone improved its services and advertised as never before.

The uniform hotel charge at Yellowstone at this period was $4 a day for the first week, and $3 a day thereafter. The Northern Pacific Railroad now offered a Circular Excursion Ticket to Yellowstone National Park from Seattle/Tacoma/Portland or Minneapolis/St. Paul/Duluth to Livingston and Gardiner for $81.00. This included 6 days' board and lodging at the Park Hotels, and the stagecoach tour. The same Northern Pacific excursion in 1893 had cost $120.00 per person.

Cheaper accommodation in tents owned by the Wylie Permanent Camp Co. based at Gardiner, with food provided, was also available at different sections of the Park.

114.

BEDROOMS AT THE OLD FAITHFUL INN

To vary their appeal, the Yellowstone Park hotels each adopted a different style and identity in the search for new business. Old Faithful Inn, the largest log hostelry in the United States, was an immediate success with its regional image of the Old West backed by twentieth-century comfort.

The Inn's great hall and small 'log cabin' bedrooms recaptured the spirit of the pioneer and the American frontier for thousands of city-dwellers who were strangers to both.

115.   **INTERIOR OF H.E. KLAMER'S CURIO STORE**

Piles of bear skins, geological specimens, pictures, rugs and carvings crowd the store. A wide variety of Indian craftwork is displayed, revealing both the growing interest in Indian culture at the turn of the century and, in some cases, the romanticized image it had already acquired.

The Baedeker Age

Crofutt's Overland Guide and *Crofutt's Overland Tours* were published for the last time in 1892. His retirement from regular writing and revision, together with the Financial Panic of 1893, finally ended a publication run of nearly 25 years following the first appearance of the *Great Trans-Continental Railroad Guide* in 1869. At least one million copies are estimated to have been sold; the readership was many times that figure.

Apart from the post-1892 economic depression, two other developments undermined the sales of many established guidebooks in the Nineties. One was the ever-increasing amount of free literature distributed by the railroad companies. All the major lines were by now giving away stacks of detailed, well-illustrated guides and pamphlets produced by their Passenger Departments . . .

> "marvels of paper and typography," wrote one expert, after examining the output of the large railroad companies right across the United States, "with really charming illustrations and a text that is often clever and witty enough to suggest that authors of repute are sometimes tempted to lend their anonymous pens for this kind of work. But even the tiniest little 'one-horse' railway distributes neat little 'folders' showing conclusively that its tracks lead through the Elysian fields and end at the Garden of Eden. A conspicuous feature in all hotel offices is a large rack containing packages of these gaily coloured folders, contributed by perhaps fifty different railways for the use of the hotel guests." [42]

Coupled with the descriptive material distributed by the large tour operators like Cook's and Raymond & Whitcomb, and by many Chambers of Commerce, the market was saturated with free, eye-catching copy publicizing hundreds of different scenic attractions. A sales gap was left only for the most complete and comprehensive type of guidebook, and here the most influential development in the Nineties was the appearance, in 1893, of the first *Baedeker Guide to the United States*.

Baedeker's encyclopedic Handbook for Travellers contained over 500 pages, all of them clearly organized, packed with detail, and illustrated with 39 coloured, fold-in maps and city plans. Background information about the United States, including travel hints but excluding advertisement, was amplified by a series of introductory essays by experts in their fields. These included a short history, a survey of the Constitution and United States' politics (by James Bryce), and accounts of the country's geography, Indian cultures, fine arts, sports, education, and major manufacturing industries.

The guide was edited by James Fullarton Muirhead, an old hand on Baedeker's production team. Muirhead had made a brief initial visit to the United States in 1888, and then spent nearly three years there in 1890-93, travelling extensively, commissioning and collecting material, and writing up the guide in the standardized Baedeker style. Our original idea, Muirhead later explained, had been to ask an American to write the book for us, but in the end it was thought preferable to rely on the experience of the Baedeker staff, and "the stranger's point of view." Besides, Muirhead admitted, "so far as my own voice had aught to do with this decision, I have to confess that I severely grudged the interesting task to an outsider." [43] In the event, *Baedeker's United States* was generally well received, Muirhead recalled; "Whatever other defects were found in it, reviewers were almost unanimous in pronouncing it fair and free from prejudice. Indeed, the reception of the Handbook by the American press was so much more friendly than I had any right to expect." [44]

Priced at 12 marks (approx. $3.00), and published in time to catch visitors to the World's Fair in Chicago in 1893, *Baedeker* presented a powerful, direct challenge to guidebook publishers throughout the United States, including giants like Appleton, and Rand, McNally. Though guidebook specialists since the 1850s, Appletons' had begun in 1879 to model their *General Guide to the United States and Canada* ($2.50) on Karl Baedeker's famous European guidebooks, closely copying his style and layout, and even including Baedeker's own distinctive practice, first introduced in 1844, of marking places of special beauty or interest, both natural and man-made, with one or two asterisks. While Appletons' openly acknowledged the imitation, this may well have been another reason why the Baedeker company took complete charge of their new work. As one of the most important additions to a distinguished series, *Baedeker's United States* was an outstanding production, more detailed than anything else available and, together with *Baedeker's Canada* (introduced in 1894), it soon captured the lion's share of this specialized market, both in Europe and the United States.

In its way, Baedeker's guide was another reminder that the American frontier had officially closed. Henry Gannett, the Geographer in charge of mapping the results of the United States' Eleventh Census (1890), had assisted Muirhead in the production of the Baedeker maps and was already well aware, in his own words, that "In 1890, . . . the settled area has become the rule and the unsettled area the exception. There is no longer any frontier line." [45]

Baedeker, among others, reflected this new age. With all its detail, Baedeker's guide is not the place to look for the dynamics of Western frontier development. By contrast, emphasis on the almost unbelievable speed of change since the 1860s had been a vital characteristic of Crofutt's guides — changes in transport, settlement, Indian lands, farming, mining, journalism and tourism, for example. Crofutt's publications monitored the progress achieved through the countless adjustments to a new environment made by individuals and communities scattered across the West. Now, though much remained to be done, the age of transition had effectively ended; the surviving pioneer landscapes were off the beaten track. In the 1890s, guidebooks no longer urged their readers to keep a look-out for the old emigrant trails, the early camp sites, the pioneer settlements, and the innumerable other traces of a national heritage and a recent past. Such traces emphasized the swift development of the American West, but they were yesterday's markers, crowded out by those of today. In any case, by this time, the compilers of the Baedeker, Appleton, and Rand-McNally guides no longer knew themselves where the old markers lay.

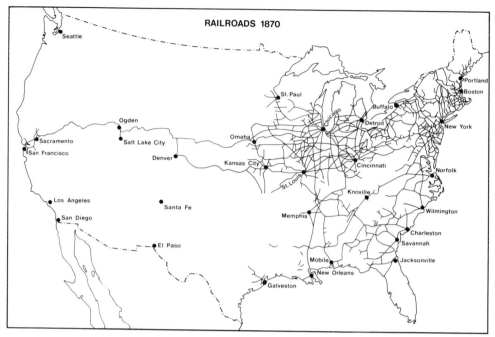

XVI. RAILROAD EXPANSION AND POPULATION DENSITIES
IN THE UNITED STATES, 1870-1890

(outlying territories not shown)

based on the U.S. Dept. of the Interior, Census Office Reports,
and the *Statistical Atlas of the United States* (1898)

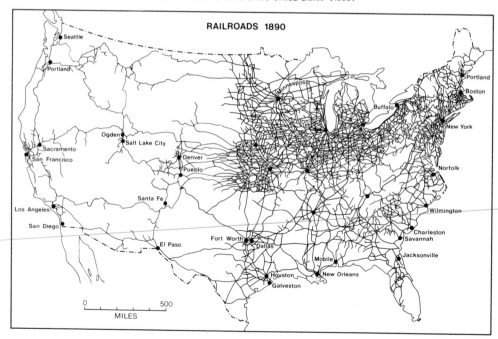

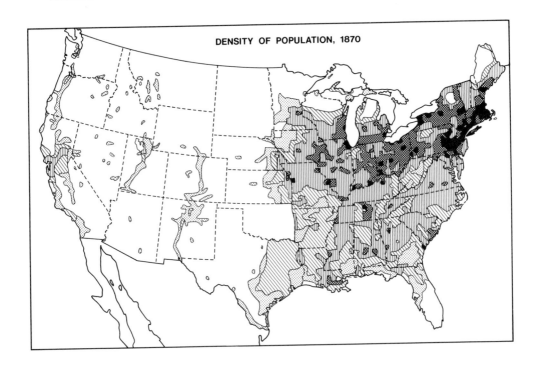

DENSITY OF POPULATION, 1870

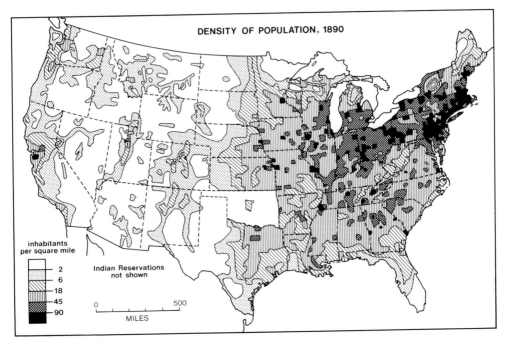

DENSITY OF POPULATION, 1890

inhabitants
per square mile

2
6
18
45
90

Indian Reservations
not shown

0   500

MILES

116.   BIRD'S-EYE VIEW OF THE TRANS-CONTINENTAL ROUTE

This popular illustration, based on *Crofutt's Trans-Continental Tourist's Guide* (1871 edition), was first published in Nordhoff's *California: for Health, Pleasure, and Residence* (1872).

Closing The Frontier

Old Pioneers 'Grow Up With The Country':
Work, Dreams, and Destinations

"The men I met were men of business," reported one astonished New York in 1892, after his first visit to the West . . . men who would rather talk of the new court-house than the first log cabin.

"Neither did I find the West teeming with 'characters'," he added sadly, upset to find the Wild West party over before he arrived. The 'characters', he discovered, "have been crowded out, or have become rich and respectably commonplace, or have been shot, as the case may be." [1]

In many ways, Crofutt and his fellow pioneers had formed a cross-section of western mining frontier development. The Pike's Peak bonanza had pitched them together in one swift, chaotic action. As order emerged from confusion, they had gone their separate ways, and helped to build a West that was now, despite its still wide open spaces, filling in and filling out. The spectacular growth of Western America's transport, tourist, information and advertising industries in the late-nineteenth century had kept Crofutt working non-stop on the production of his guidebooks, but during his extensive travels in the Eighties and Nineties, he had continued to follow the progress of his old trail partners and early associates in Colorado with particular interest. They were now part of a distinctive group of veteran Colorado pioneers, sharing a unique set of memories and anchoring the modern development into a vanishing frontier past.

Crofutt found that Amos Steck was still a major force in Denver, despite the severe financial blows he had suffered, like so many others, in the Panics of 1873 and 1893. Steck, the prodigious "Memory-man", had resumed his law practice after serving as the Probate and County Court Judge of Arapahoe County from 1875 to 1880, the year when, as Colorado's delegate, he also attended the National Republican Convention in Chicago. There was scarcely an urban improvement scheme in Denver with which Steck was not involved over the years — railroads, streetcars, water supply, fire insurance, schools, Sunday schools and hospitals. From 1891 to 1894, Judge Steck, as everyone still called him, was a State Senator. In contrast to his extensive early travels, Steck after 1859 lived the remaining fifty years of his life in Denver; "Steck stuck," as Crofutt put it. Their mutual friend, the pioneering editor and booster William N. Byers, underlined Steck's extraordinary qualities, as impressive as ever in the 1890s, despite the setbacks:

> "Judge Steck is a most remarkable man. His memory of books and men and events is marvelous. Whatever he reads he absorbs . . . He owns one of the best private libraries in the State and has read the books. He never forgets, and for that reason is one of the most thoroughly and widely informed men that ever lived in the State . . . He is a living, moving encyclopedia." [2]

Early pioneers like Amos Steck, William Byers, and Rufus "Potato" Clark were among the many Denverites with whom Crofutt could still talk over old times; all of them had seen Denver grow from a confusion of tents, cabins and wagons in 1859-60, into a city of almost 135,000 people by the turn of the century, the third largest west of the Missouri River.

A few old-timers from Crofutt's early years remained scattered in the small settlements up on the Divide, ranching, dairying, and raising hay, potatoes and small grains in the more sheltered valleys. There were still about 100-150 settlers in and around Rock Ridge, the village that had grown around Crofutt's cabin, *Ivan Cracken*, built in 1860 at the head of West Cherry Creek Canyon. The valley was losing population, however, in the 1890s. The post office at Rock Ridge was closed on 22nd March 1892, and handling of the mail transferred to Castle Rock. By the turn of the century, the village had become abandoned, and Rock Ridge was not listed in the *Colorado Gazetteer* published by Henry Gannett in 1906. This stock-raising region in the heart of the Pineries was still wagon country, a land of saddle-horse, buggy, and cart. Although the railroad was less than ten miles away, the world of fast trains, and easy contact with excursion centres like Palmer Lake, or with Denver and Colorado Springs, was not part of everyday existence up on the Divide. Not for the first time, Crofutt found the Pineries a tightly-knit world of its own.

Two of Crofutt's trail partners on the long trudge across the plains from Lawrence, Kansas in 1860, A.Z. Sheldon and B.F. Crowell, were to be found prospering in Colorado Springs. The other two had gone. Jim Tappan had soon moved on from the family store in Colorado City, but what happened to Fred Spencer, Sheldon's old survey assistant, remains a mystery. Crofutt reported briefly in 1881 that Fred had "skipped the country," but who (if anyone) was on his heels is not revealed. Sheldon and Crowell, however, had stayed put, given the rest of their lives and their energies to the Pike's Peak region, and helped to build the flourishing city of Colorado Springs.

As El Paso County Surveyor, Albinus Sheldon had continued to take a prominent role in local affairs, while his extensive knowledge of the region and sound reputation had resulted in an invitation to write the geography and history of the County in the authoritative *History of the Arkansas Valley, Colorado*, published in 1881 in Chicago. In 1887-88 he built an elegant stone mansion in a 10-acre plot on Colorado Avenue, at the boundary of Colorado City (Old Town) and Colorado Springs, and there he remained, strong and active until 1913 when, after an illness, he moved to San Diego. He died there two years later, aged 82, but was buried in Colorado Springs.

Benjamin Crowell, on the other hand, was not merely comfortably off; he was rich! Ben, who never did things by halves, had made a fortune in middle-age in the Leadville silver bonanza of 1879, the high spot in what had been an increasingly exciting decade.

After the rapid decline of Colorado City during the 1860s, General Palmer's concept of a new growth zone along the Rocky Mountain Front had been a godsend, and Ben Crowell had been one of the keenest supporters of the Fountain Colony development in 1871. Indeed, as one of the three El Paso County Commissioners, Crowell signed the formal order on 2nd September 1872 incorporating the new town of Colorado Springs. Ben was still a lively jack-of-all-trades. Service in the Territorial Legislature and as County Treasurer during the 1870s was fitted in with his farming and sheep ranching enterprises. Added to this were his increasing responsibilities in the El Paso Masonic Lodge, first as Senior Warden and then, in 1875-6, as Master.[3] "Crowell keeps his Yankee wits about him," said an admiring colleague; "he is extraordinarily level-headed, keen-sighted, and shrewd . . . of quick perceptions and sound judgment. . . an influence for good throughout the community."

Early in 1879, Ben hit real paydirt. Through his friend and business associate, Irving Howbert, a young pioneer at the Tarryall Diggings in 1860 who was by now cashier, and soon to be president, of the First National Bank of Colorado Springs, Crowell acquired a share in the Robert E. Lee silver mine at Leadville. Almost immediately, startling new strikes were made, prompting Frank Fossett to report:

> "The Robert E. Lee is the latest wonder of this wonderful district. A bonanza of surpassing richness has been discovered there this summer [1879]. The ore is from ten to twelve feet thick, and said to yield $200 to $400 a ton, being the highest average grade of any in the district." [4]

Fossett was so impressed that he returned to the Robert E. Lee mine a few months later:

> "The Lee has given the largest yield for a single month and a single day of any mine in the country outside of Nevada. The mine had yielded a round million up to February 1880, a period of only six months after active work fairly began. Probably nine-tenths of that sum was clear profit." [5]

Ben Crowell was one of seven owners of the mine, four of them in Colorado Springs, three in Leadville. Crowell and Howbert both sold their interests in the Robert E. Lee later in 1880, and then, jointly or independently, plunged into a wide variety of new business and political activities.

With a third associate in the Leadville venture, J.F. Humphrey, they began by using part of their windfall silver profits to build "a gem of an Opera House", as Crofutt described it, which opened in April 1881 on Tejon Street in Colorado Springs. Ben became a city alderman and ever more deeply involved in urban improvement schemes (including public utilities, fire brigade and streetcars), in banking (as a director and vice-president of the First National Bank), and, in 1886, in James J. Hagerman's Colorado Midland Railroad.

Ben Crowell represented Colorado at the Republican National Convention in 1884, and is said to have repeatedly refused nomination for State Governor. He did, however, in 1883, accept appointment to the seven-member Board of Directors created to supervise the planning and construction of the State Capitol building in Denver, which, after interminable delays, had in 1881 finally won the State-wide election for Colorado's capital city. Ben took this new assignment very seriously; with some of his fellow Directors, he toured Capitols in the Midwest before extending his own travels around the United States to compare styles and layouts of the different Capitol buildings. Eventually, from the range of designs submitted, the Board of Directors chose that of Elijah E. Myers, an experienced Detroit architect, and the initial building phase was completed between 1886 and 1895, after weathering the depression of the early Nineties and a series of financial storms.

Ben remained a bachelor. He and his two surviving sisters, Emily and Susan, formed a closely-knit family unit after their father died in 1867, by which time it was clear that Ben was more determined than ever to stay out west in Colorado. The fine old Massachusetts sea captain's house in Manchester-by-the-Sea was turned into a boarding-house for summer visitors as the two women struggled to keep the place going. They loved this small New England port, and the view across the bay — and so did Ben, who, homesick for the sea, regularly came to stay for a few weeks in the summer. In 1872, however, Emily and Susan sold up and joined Ben in the new town of Colorado Springs, although later, the three of them usually spent their summers in their old home town, renting a house and living in quiet contentment. In 1885 they broke this tradition; deciding they needed a change, Ben, Emily and Susan spent a year abroad on a grand European tour, which included visits to Russia and Turkey.

From his earliest days as a penniless pioneer, Ben's ability, boundless self-confidence and sense of humour had made him one of the region's most popular boosters and builders. His untimely death in 1897 at the age of sixty-two shocked the local community and desolated his two sisters. Ben was 'taken home' for burial in the family grave in

Manchester-by-the-Sea, where, using part of Ben's fortune, a large memorial chapel was later erected and given to the town by Susan Crowell. It stands there today in this quiet corner of New England — Colorado silver in a Massachusetts field — and a reminder of just one of the many nineteenth-century American pioneers whose restless energy helped to build the West.

*　　　　*　　　　*

George Crofutt remained a travelling man. At heart, he was as eager to explore the West at the turn of the century in search of new opportunities as he had been to discover an earlier West on an Erie Canal packet-boat, or to drive a freight wagon over the plains and the Rocky Mountains. With the end of his publishing career, Crofutt, like most Denverites in the wake of the Financial Panic of 1893, was looking for new ways to make money. Settling down in order to do so, however, was not part of his plan. What could the West now offer him? What could he offer the West?

As silver mining slumped, Colorado made strenuous efforts in the Nineties to boost agriculture as part of a general diversification program, particularly the expansion of cattle and sheep ranching, irrigation, and the cultivation of new crops, notably sugar beet. After the wetter years of the early Eighties, a severe dry cycle began in 1887, with a devastating drought in 1892-94. Drought stimulated interest in dry farming techniques, but official determination to extend the State's irrigated acreage prompted a burst of experiment and speculation in new projects, and probably sparked Crofutt's own renewed interest in the subject in the 1890s. He had been impressed with the potential of irrigated agriculture ever since his freighting days; now was as good a time as any to give the matter more thought. Crofutt left Denver in 1893, and appears to have spent several months travelling through the West, and developing his ideas on irrigation techniques, water pumps, and power supplies.

Part of the time he may have been in Oregon since at the turn of the century Crofutt lists himself as author of *A Round-up of the Chinook Jargon*. Chinook Jargon was a lingua franca of some five hundred words developed among Indians living along the Columbia River and for almost a thousand miles along the Pacific coast into southern Alaska. Knowledge of the Jargon declined rapidly in the 1890s through compulsory schooling and the greater use of English in Indian households, one reason perhaps why Crofutt, and others, attempted to record it. No copy of this "Round-up" has been found, nor any further information about its compilation discovered. It may have remained in manuscript form. There is no evidence that Crofutt was involved in the Alaska gold rush of 1897-1902.

In December 1900, Crofutt was back in Denver and staying at the Markham, a popular hotel on the corner of Lawrence and 17th Streets in the heart of the business and commercial district. The Markham had been especially busy ever since Denver's oldest newspaper, the *Rocky Mountain News*, had taken over part of the ground floor in 1897 while new offices were being built on Welton Street. Crofutt took the opportunity to look up old friends and attend the annual meeting of the Colorado Pioneer Association. He was one of five hundred Colorado pioneers (of 1858-60) who at the end of the century were officially listed as still living in the State. Indeed, Crofutt was also on another list compiled by the Secretary of the Colorado Pioneer Association — that of "the 161 prominent pioneers still following business pursuits in 1901, despite having spent much of life before enduring the hardships and privations of the frontier 42 years ago." [6]

A reporter from the *Rocky Mountain News*, chatting with Crofutt at the Markham Hotel, decided that here was

"A historic character of the West . . . tall, dignified, educated, with the grace of the polished gentleman and a fund of information on any subject that can be presented . . . Few men living have been more active in advancing the true interests of the West." [7]

Between trips, Crofutt's main base in the late 1890s was back east in Hoboken, N.J., where he and his wife rented a small apartment on Washington Street. Over the years, available evidence suggests that Anna Crofutt made only occasional visits to the West, the last one perhaps in July-August 1888, when she was 70. On that occasion, George Crofutt's arrival in Denver from Chicago was reported in the press, along with the fact that "Mrs. Crofutt accompanied him." [8] Such reports about Anna Crofutt were extremely rare. Her name does not appear again in any records of arrivals and departures — in this case, the only reliable clues to her movements in the West. If the relevant hotel registers had survived, more frequent visits might have been revealed, but it is unlikely that Anna Crofutt ever stayed very long in the West.

As Anna's health began to deteriorate, Crofutt spent more time in Hoboken. At 1204 Washington Street, the Crofutts would have been next door on the block to one of the city's most famous residents, the eccentric Hetty Green, otherwise known as 'the Witch of Wall Street'. This brilliant financial broker travelled daily by ferry and trolley car to her desk at New York's Chemical Bank, and in 1900-10 was estimated to have an annual income of between five and ten million dollars. Despite her wealth, Hetty lived frugally, penny-pinching all the way; what the Crofutts made of her, we shall never know.

George Crofutt was working busily on his new irrigation project, listing himself in the New Jersey and Hoboken Directories at this period as an inventor. He filed his first patent application for a 'Continuous Power-Chain of Water-Lifts' on 29th January 1901, a scheme based on lines or grids of small wells and electric pumps. During the spring and early summer of 1902 Crofutt was back again in Denver, staying at what was now called the New Markham Hotel. As soon as the *Rocky Mountain News* had shifted to its new premises in 1901, the hotel had been reorganized and smartened up with a row of hotel shops fronting part of the sidewalk. Crofutt was now nearly 75, but he remained a ball of energy, bounding about, and as eager to talk about plans for the future as he was to chat about the past. Said one reporter, after meeting him in March 1902:

> "Mr. Crofutt today possesses more vigor than many men twenty-five years less his age. He is bright and alert, always full of business." [9]

While in Denver in 1902, Crofutt published a new *Glossary of Terms and Phrases connected with the Mining Industry*. He had expanded one of the sections in his *Grip-Sack Guide of Colorado* into a small book priced at $1.00, and made special arrangements for its advertisement and distribution through a local mining journal, *Ores and Metals*, published at 17th and Stout Streets. Mining might be down, but it was not out. Cripple Creek was still booming, one reason perhaps why Crofutt, in and out of Colorado Springs, gave a personally inscribed copy of the book "to my much esteemed friend, General W.J. Palmer." [10]

Crofutt's main purpose during his stay in Denver, however, was to form a new company to promote his latest invention for water-lifts. On 24th June 1902, he incorporated the Colorado Electric Irrigation Co., in association with Pelimon A. Balcom and Albert S. Whitaker.[11] Balcom, born in Halifax, Nova Scotia, and a company promoter in Denver for nearly fifteen years, had made money in both the Leadville and Cripple Creek mining booms, and was currently involved in helping to finance David Moffat's Denver-Salt Lake City railroad project. Whitaker, who was Mark "Brick" Pomeroy's son-in-law, had been Secretary and Treasurer of Pomeroy's unsuccessful Atlantic and Pacific Tunnel Co. which had finally collapsed after Pomeroy's death in 1896. The Colorado Electric Irrigation Co. set out an ambitious development program in addition to the promotion of Crofutt's own water-lifts, including proposals for the purchase of other patents and real estate on which to expand irrigated agriculture and encourage new colonization.

As soon as the company was formed, Crofutt left Denver again and returned to Hoboken where, two months later on 6th September 1902, his wife died at home at the age of 84. Once the funeral was over and arrangements completed, Crofutt gave up the apartment on Washington Street and returned to Denver, where, instead of hotel accommodation, he now took rooms on a more permanent basis at 1755 Lawrence Street.

He was back in the heart of the business district and not far from Denver's Chamber of Commerce.

As President of the Colorado Electric Irrigation Co., Crofutt devoted all his energies to promoting land and investment deals, and to improving his water-lift invention, for which he was awarded patents in October 1903.[12] But three factors worked against the project. Basically, Crofutt's design for the 'Continuous Power-Chain of Water-Lifts' was unsatisfactory. The series of small individual electric pumps that he envisaged, each lifting water to the surface independently, would have been costly and inefficient compared with water distribution over the same acreage from a smaller number of larger wells and pumps. It is significant that Crofutt did not follow the common practice of including a model of his invention along with the specification and drawings he submitted to the U.S. Patent Office.

A second problem was the proliferation of new irrigation development companies at this period, each of them anxious to purchase patents, acquire land and extend irrigation. The Colorado State records of company registrations in the late-nineteenth and early-twentieth centuries include several small speculative ventures like Crofutt's in the Denver, Greeley and Fort Collins area. All are virtually identical in their aims, their shortage of capital, and their failure to survive. The successful expansion of irrigation in Colorado now lay in large-scale, federally-assisted projects. A third, painfully familiar problem also haunted the enterprise — the short but sharp financial crisis in 1903 which tightened cash and discouraged speculators.

Crofutt remained in Denver until the summer of 1905 when at the age of 78, and with no prospect of financing the Colorado Electric Irrigation Co., he made his farewells and returned east for the last time. Back in New York City, he headed for Lower Manhattan and rented a room at 199 Washington Street, opposite Washington Market and less than half-a-mile west of his old stamping ground around Park Row, Nassau and Beekman Streets. Crofutt was still active, and no doubt frequently walked through the area he had known for more than fifty years. The famous printing and publishing district was changing fast. The *New York Herald* had been the first of the giants to move farther north (to Herald Square) in 1894; now, in 1905, the *New York Times* had also gone, having left its historic site on Printing House Square the year before to move into midtown, and the new Times Square.

Crofutt was here for a little over twelve months. At the end of December 1906, he was admitted to New York Hospital where, after a short illness, he died in his eightieth year on 27th January 1907.[13] Apparently, he had already made arrangements to be buried with his wife. This writer's long search ended with the discovery that George and

Anna Crofutt lie in an unmarked grave in the Greenwood Cemetery in Brooklyn.

*   *   *

Crofutt had been part of a dramatic continental mass movement, and a huge Americanizing process. His own life had continually bounced back and forth between the Eastern and Western States and Territories during the sweeping social and economic changes of nineteenth-century America, and he became as much at home with the Western pioneers as with the Eastern business community. After early struggles, he made money, lost it, and made more. Financial Panics across the United States rocked every decade of his working life. He was, in his own words, "a football of fortune, kicked unceremoniously about." Survival required persistence, courage, and stamina to cope with hard times and repeated failure. 'Making it in America' demanded perseverance in the McGuffey mould— solid work, long hours, self-reliance, and the determination to 'Try, Try Again.' Poverty was a disgrace only if you accepted it without a struggle, being knocked flat only disastrous if you stayed down. Like thousands of others, Crofutt took chances, seized opportunities and remained versatile — he had been printer, agent, publisher, pioneer, prospector, freighter, explorer, guide, escort, farmer, writer, hotelier, and inventor at various times during his long life.

From New England to California, Crofutt saw the United States transformed by the rapid changes in transport and communications — wagon, canal, stagecoach, railroad, telegraph, and telephone. He was born only two years after the opening of the Erie Canal, the dawn of the canal age, when the United States' population was fewer than 12 millions, its society overwhelmingly rural, and its farthest boundary still located in the Rocky Mountains. When Crofutt died, the population was over 90 millions, the frontier phase had officially ended, America's Manufacturing Belt was one of the world's major industrial regions, and the country was at the dawn of both the automobile and the air age. As the individual responsible for first publicizing the word *transcontinental* at the start of the Western railroad era, Crofutt lived long enough to see two other far-reaching developments take place, both of them in 1903 — the first transcontinental automobile trip from San Francisco to New York City, and the pioneering flight by the Wright brothers at Kitty Hawk, N.C.[14]

In the original 'transcontinental age', invented by the railroad, Crofutt set out to convey and share something of his own wonder and enthusiasm for "the beauty and variety of the United States from the Atlantic to the Pacific Ocean, the drama of its progress and the achievement of its people." To this end, he travelled thousands of miles, advanced Western interests for more than thirty years, and was read by millions. Crofutt never lost the personal touch, the direct style, or the voice of experience that together helped a generation to understand and appreciate the American West. He made an important individual contribution to the wider task—one of the greatest national challenges facing the United States in the second half of the nineteenth century—that of promoting railroads and attracting settlers to the West, boosting new business, including the new tourist industry, collecting and packaging information about Western America, and consolidating new political and economic relationships from coast to coast. This had been Crofutt's vision of American Progress. It represented a huge, concentrated outburst of energy, collective effort, and technological development, and has remained one of the most rapid and spectacular regional transformations the world has ever seen.

PUBLICATIONS BY GEORGE ANDREWS CROFUTT

Monthly Rainbow, Philadelphia, 1856.

The Philadelphia Merchants' Diary and Guide, for 1856. Prepared and Published by George A. Crofut [*sic*]; printed by Henry B. Ashmead, Philadelphia, 1856.

The Nation (weekly), with S.M. Bigelow, Philadelphia, 1857.

Great Trans-Continental Railroad Guide, containing a full and authentic description of over five hundred cities, towns, villages, stations, government forts and camps, mountains, lakes, rivers, sulphur, soda and hot springs, scenery, watering places, summer resorts; where to look for and hunt the buffalo, antelope, deer, and other game; trout fishing, etc., etc. In fact, to tell you what is worth seeing—where to see it—where to go—how to go—and whom to stop with while passing over the Union Pacific Railroad, Central Pacific Railroad of Cal.; their branches and connections by Stage and Water, from the Atlantic to the Pacific Ocean. Illus., Maps. [Author listed as "Bill Dadd, the Scribe", (H. Wallace Atwell), but in fact much of the Guide was written by Crofutt], 1869. (Chicago: Geo. A. Crofutt & Co.).

Great Trans-Continental Railroad Guide containing . . . Pacific Ocean. Illus., Maps. Temp. rev. edit., January 1870. (Chicago: Crofutt & Eaton).

Great Trans-Continental Tourist's Guide, containing . . . Pacific Ocean. Enlarged; Illus., Maps, etc. 1st fully rev. edit., 1870. (New York: Geo. A. Crofutt).

Crofutt's Trans-Continental Tourist's Guide, containing . . . Pacific Ocean. Illus., Maps, etc. 3rd vol., 2nd annual rev., 1871. (New York: Geo. A. Crofutt).

Crofutt's Western World (monthly), 1871-74. (New York: Geo. A. Crofutt; April and May 1873 issues also published in Chicago by Geo. A. Crofutt. Starting in July 1873, published in New York: Geo. A. Crofutt, and San Francisco: J.H. Carmany, later Riley and Edwards).

Crofutt's Trans-Continental Tourist's Guide, containing . . . Pacific Ocean.Illus., Maps, etc. 4th vol., 3rd annual rev., 1872. (New York: Geo. A. Crofutt).

Crofutt's Trans-Continental Tourist's Guide, containing . . . Pacific Ocean. Illus., Maps, etc. 5th vol., 4th annual rev., 1873. (New York and Chicago: Geo. A. Crofutt).

Crofutt's Trans-Continental Tourist, . . . over the Union Pacific Railroad, Central Pacific Railroad of California. Their branches and connections by Stage and Water, from the Atlantic to the Pacific Ocean. Illus., Maps, etc. 6th vol., 5th annual rev.; new enlarged format, 1874. (New York and San Francisco: Geo. A. Crofutt).

Crofutt's Trans-Continental Tourist, . . . from the Atlantic to the Pacific Ocean. Illus., Maps, etc. 7th vol., 6th annual rev., 1875. (New York: G.W. Carleton & Co.; London: Sampson Low & Co.).

Crofutt's Trans-Continental Tourist, . . . from the Atlantic to the Pacific Ocean. Illus., Maps, etc. 8th vol., 7th annual rev., 1876. (New York: G. W. Carleton & Co.; London: Sampson Low & Co.).

Crofutt's New Overland Tourist, and Pacific Coast Guide, containing a condensed and authentic description of over one thousand two hundred cities, towns, villages, stations, government fort and camps, mountains, lakes, rivers, sulphur, soda and hot springs, scenery, watering places, and summer resorts; where to look for and hunt the buffalo, antelope, deer and other game; trout fishing, etc., etc. In fact, to tell you what is worth seeing — where to see it — where to go — how to go — and whom to stop with while passing over the Union, Central and Southern Pacific Railroads, their branches and connections, by rail, water and stage, from sunrise to sunset, and part the way back; through Nebraska, Wyoming, Colorado, Utah, Montana, Idaho, Nevada, California and Arizona. Illus., Maps. Vol. 1, 1878-9. (Chicago: The Overland Publishing Co.).

Crofutt's New Overland Tourist, and Pacific Coast Guide, containing ... over the Union, Central, and Southern Pacific Railroads, their branches and connections, by rail, water and stage ... Illus., Maps. Vol. 2 (rev. edit.), 1879-80. (Chicago: The Overland Publishing Co.).

Crofutt's New Overland Tourist, and Pacific Coast Guide, containing a condensed and authentic description of over one thousand three hundred cities, towns, ... over the Union, Kansas, Central and Southern Pacific Railroads, their branches and connections, by rail, water and stage ... Illus., Maps, etc., 1880. (Omaha, Nebr.: The Overland Publishing Co.).

Crofutt's Grip-Sack Guide of Colorado. A Complete Encyclopedia of the State. Resources and condensed authentic descriptions of every city, town, village, station, post office, and important mining camp in the State; soda, sulphur, hot and medicinal springs; summer, health and pleasure resorts; the mining, stock raising and farming interests; where to hunt, fish, and view the most magnificent scenery in the world. Altitudes, distances, routes, and fares. Illus., Map. Vol. I, 1881. (Omaha, Nebr.: The Overland Publishing Co.; Denver, Colo.: Alvord & Co.).

Crofutt's New Overland Tourist, and Pacific Coast Guide, ... over the Union, Kansas, Central and Southern Pacific Railroads, their branches and connections, by rail, water and stage ... Illus., Maps, etc., 1882. (Omaha, Nebr. and Denver, Colo.: The Overland Publishing Co.).

Crofutt's New Overland Tourist, and Pacific Coast Guide, ... by rail, water and stage ... Illus., Maps, etc., 1883. (Omaha, Nebr. and Denver, Colo.: The Overland Publishing Co.).

Crofutt's New Overland Tourist, and Pacific Coast Guide, ... by rail, water and stage ... Illus., Maps, etc., 1884. (Omaha, Nebr. and Denver Colo.: The Overland Publishing Co.).

Crofutt's Grip-Sack Guide of Colorado. A Complete Encyclopedia of the State, Illus., Map. Vol. II (rev. edit.), 1885. (Omaha, Nebr.: The Overland Publishing Co.).

Crofutt's Salt Lake City Directory for 1885-6, including Prefatory, Street and Business Directory, Names, Advertising Index, and a new map of Salt Lake City, 1885. (Salt Lake City: Herald Job Department).

Crofutt's Butte City Directory, including Walkerville, Meaderville, Centreville and Burlington. Also, Anaconda, Deer Lodge and Dillon. With a Classified Business Directory. For 1885-6. Montana Territory. (Butte City, Montana: Office of the Daily Inter-Mountain, November 10, 1885).

Crofutt's Overland Tours. Consisting of nearly Five Thousand Miles of Main Tours, and Three Thousand Miles of Side Tours. Also Two Thousand Miles by Stage and Water. Illus., Maps, etc., 1888. (Chicago: Arthur H. Day & Co.).

Crofutt's Overland Tours. Consisting of over Six Thousand Miles of Main Tours, and Three Thousand Miles of Side Tours. Also Six Thousand Miles by Stage and Water. Illus., Maps, etc., 1889. (Chicago and Philadelphia: H.J. Smith & Co.).

Crofutt's Overland Tours and *Crofutt's Overland Guide. Consisting of over Six Thousand Miles of Main Tours, and Three Thousand Miles of Side Tours. Also Six Thousand Miles by Stage and Water.* Illus., Maps, etc. Published in two companion vols, 1890. Sub-titles vary slightly. (Chicago and New York: Rand, McNally & Co.).

Crofutt's Overland Tours and *Crofutt's Overland Guide* ... Published in two companion vols, 1892. (St. Louis, Mo.: Charles E. Ware & Co.).

Glossary of Terms and Phrases connected with the Mining Industry, in common use in the mining regions of America, compiled and arranged by George A. Crofutt, 1902. (Denver, Colo.: The Smith-Brooks Printing Co.).

NOTES

Introduction

1. Louis L. Simonin, *Le Grand-Ouest des Etats-Unis*, Paris, 1869, p. 20. (Trans. by W.O. Clough as *The Rocky Mountain West in 1867*, Univ. of Nebraska Press, Lincoln, 1966, p.14).

2. Margaret Fuller (Ossoli), *At Home and Abroad; or, Things and Thoughts in America and Europe*, edit. by Arthur B. Fuller, Boston, 1874, pp. 21, 26; manuscript note, p. 27. (First published Boston, 1856).

3. John Burroughs, "The Spell of the Yosemite", *The Century Illustrated Monthly Magazine*, New York, vol. 81, 1910, pp. 47-53. Reported on p. 48.

4. Ferner R. Nuhn, *The Wind Blew from the East: a study in the orientation of American culture*, New York, 1940 (reissued 1967), p. 2.

5. Josiah Strong, *Our Country: its possible future and its present crisis*, New York, 1885, p. 45.

6. Charles Nordhoff, *California: for Health, Pleasure, and Residence*, New York, 1872, p. 32.

7. Robert Louis Stevenson, *Across the Plains: leaves from the notebook of an emigrant between New York and San Francisco*, London, 1892, p. 49. Published as part of *The Amateur Emigrant*, London, 1895. Stevenson made the journey in 1879.

8. Maurice O'Connor Morris, *Rambles in the Rocky Mountains: with a visit to the goldfields of Colorado*, London, 1864, p. 4.

9. Samuel Bowles, *Across the Continent*, Springfield, Mass. and New York, 1865, pp. 1-2; and *The Pacific Railroad — Open*, Boston, 1869, p. 116.

10. Susan Coolidge, *pseud.* (Sarah Chauncy Woolsey). "A Few Hints on the California Journey", *Scribner's Monthly*, New York, vol. 6, 1873, pp. 25-31. This reference p. 31.

11. Lord Dunraven, *Past Times and Pastimes*, London, 1922, vol. 1, p. 73.

12. Edward L. Ullman, "Amenities as a factor in regional growth", *The Geographical Review*, New York, vol. 44, 1954, pp. 119-32. This reference p.119.

13. Esther Moir, *The Discovery of Britain: the English Tourists, 1540-1840*, London, 1964, p. 156; Sarah J. Hale, *Sketches of American Character*, Boston, 1829, p. 8; "The Yellowstone National Park", *Scribner's Monthly*, New York, vol. 4, 1872, pp. 120-1. This reference p. 120.

14. Charles Dudley Warner, *Our Italy*, New York, 1891, pp. 69-70.

15. Richard Harding Davis, *The West from a Car-Window*, New York, 1892, p. 242.

16. James Bryce, *The American Commonwealth*, London and New York, 1888, pp. 830, 837.

17. Henry James, *The American Scene*, London and New York, 1907, p. 412.

18. E.J. Taaffe, R.L. Morrill, and P.R. Gould, "Transport Expansion in Underdeveloped Countries: A Comparative Analysis", *The Geographical Review*, New York, vol. 53, 1963, pp. 503-29.

19. Louis L. Simonin, *Les Pays Lointains. Notes de Voyage*, Paris, 1867, p. 100.

20. Daniel Boorstin, *The Americans*. Vol. 2, *The National Experience*, New York, 1965, p. 4.

21. Walter Lindley, in W. Lindley and J.P. Widney, *California of the South*, New York, 1888, p. 76.

22. James Bryce, *op. cit.*, p. 836.

23. J. Rudyard Kipling, *From Sea to Sea: Letters of Travel*, New York, 1899, London, 1900, vol. 2, p. 68.

24. James Bryce, *op. cit.*, p. 836.

25. Henry T. Tuckerman, *America and her Commentators*, New York, 1864. p. 371.

26. Lucy L. Hazard, *The Frontier in American Literature*, New York, 1927, p. xvii.

27. H.T. Tuckerman, *op. cit.*, p.1.

28. Preface to reprint of *Crofutt's Trans-Continental Tourist* (1874) by Pottsdam Associates, Boston, 1975. Two other guides have also been reprinted: *Great Trans-Continental Railroad Guide* (1869) by Black Letter Press, Grand Rapids, Mich., 1971; and *Crofutt's Grip-Sack Guide of Colorado* (1885) by Cubar Associates, Golden, Colo., 1966, 1981.

29. Isabella L. Bird, *A Lady's Life in the Rocky Mountains*, London, 1879, p. 31. (In Letter III, 8 September 1873).

30. *Crofutt's Western World*, May 1874; extracts from his editorial on the "Value of Advertising".

31. Judge Goodwin, *The Salt Lake Daily Tribune*, 20 May 1888.

Chapter One. The New England Background

1. Crofutt never records his middle name beyond the initial 'A'. It is not included in Library of Congress and most other library catalogues.

Three copies of his guidebooks held at Harvard University, however, contain apparently contemporaneous pencilled additions of the name 'Andrews' on their title pages. As a result, Harvard College Libraries catalogue the full name. Crofutt's full name is also recorded in *A Mormon Bibliography, 1830-1930*, edit. by Chad J. Flake, Salt Lake City, 1978, p. 186. Crofutt was not a Mormon, but Flake's Bibliography, using a variety of local and other sources, also includes selected authors whose work provides valuable detail on Mormon life. (Flake, p. xi).

The date and place of his birth were recorded by Crofutt on arrival in Denver, 1860; in *Register of Men who arrived in what is now Colorado prior to February 26, 1861*, held in the Genealogical Department, Denver Public Library.

Some of Crofutt's later comments and asides scattered among his publications have assisted this outline reconstruction of his early years.

2. *Land Records*, Town Clerk's Office, City Hall, Danbury.

3. Author's field investigation of headstone inscriptions in Danbury's first Burial Ground and in Wooster Cemetery. Also Burial Records, Danbury Scott-Fanton Museum and Historical Society, Danbury. Some additional cross-referencing has been possible using the 1830 and 1840 Census Schedules for the Danbury area, National Archives, Washington, D.C.

4. *History of Danbury, Conn. 1684-1896*, from notes and manuscript left by James Montgomery Bailey, compiled with additions by Susan Benedict Hill, New York, 1896, p. 133 and *passim*.

5. Headstone inscriptions; also documentary and cartographic records of property ownership, City Hall archives, Danbury.

6. Timothy Dwight, *Travels; in New-England and New-York*, New Haven, Conn., 1821-2, vol.1, pp. 178-9.

7. By 1791, Danbury and its surrounding hamlets were divided into twelve School Districts. Maps show that the Crofuts' end of Mill Plain Lane lay in Middle Center District.

8. Recorded in a mid-nineteenth century advertisement for Crofut's grist and saw mill.

9. John Warner Barber, *Connecticut Historical Collections*, New Haven, 1836, p. 364.

10. Report made to British Commission by the General Court of Connecticut, 1680. Included in J.M. Bailey's notes and manuscript, *op. cit.*, p. 2.

11. In 1786, Connecticut had joined other eastern States in ceding its claims to the western territories to the proposed new Federal govern-

ment, but unlike its neighbours, Connecticut had been allowed to retain some 5000 square miles in the northeastern corner of the present State of Ohio. This area became known as the *Connecticut Western Reserve*. In 1791, the Connecticut legislature designated part of the Reserve as Fire Sufferers' Lands, and later sold them off to help meet the demands for compensation from several towns, including Danbury and Norwalk, whose property had been burned by British troops during the Revolution. The sale of the remainder of the Western Reserve helped to support Connecticut's schools.

Many of those who left the Danbury area for Ohio in the late-eighteenth and early-nineteenth centuries settled in the old *Connecticut Western Reserve*, as well as in the Dayton region.

12. Phineas Taylor Barnum, *The Life of P.T. Barnum, Written by Himself*, New York and London, 1855, p. 22.

13. Samuel Griswold Goodrich, *Peter Parley's Own Story*, New York, 1864, pp. 31-2.

14. Danbury Public Library archive collection.

15. Certain events can be inferred, although some gaps in Crofutt's record remain through lack of reliable evidence. The *Danbury Times* is a valuable source of contemporary local events; Crofutt kept in touch with it since snippets from the paper (which merged with *The Jeffersonian* in 1870 to become the *Danbury News*) are included from time to time in *Crofutt's Western World*.

16. *Crofutt's Western World*, January 1874.

Chapter Two. Agent And Publisher: Early Struggles in New York and Philadelphia

1. *Rochester Daily Advertiser*, 19 April 1830; *Rochester Daily Democrat*, 24 April 1843.

2. Nathaniel Parker Willis, *American Scenery*, London, 1840, vol.1, p. 119.

3. *Buffalo Commercial Advertiser*, 25 June 1845.

4. Recalled in *Crofutt's Western World*, January 1874.

5. *Rochester Union and Advertiser*, 2 October 1876.

6. *Rochester Daily Democrat*, 5 September 1846.

7. *Crofutt's Western World*, January 1874.

8. Stephen Sult's recollections are taken from Raymond F. Yates' paper, "The Old Lockport and Niagara Falls Strap Railroad", *Occasional*

Contributions of the Niagara County Historical Society, Lockport, N.Y., no. 4, June 1950, 45 pp. These references pp. 29-33, *passim*.

9. Mary A. Wyman, *Two American Pioneers*, Columbia Univ. Press, New York, 1927, pp. 141-2; see also, for general background, the comprehensive standard work by Frank Luther Mott, *A History of American Magazines*, Harvard Univ. Press, Cambridge, Mass., 5 vols, 1930-68. Vol. 1, 1741-1850; vol. 2, 1850-65.

10. Special Collection, The Library Company of Philadelphia.

11. *Ibid.*

12. *New-York Mirror*, 15 November 1828.

13. *United States Magazine*, New York, 15 May 1854.

14. Frank L. Mott, *Golden Multitudes: the Story of Best Sellers in the United States*, New York, 1947, p. 136.

15. Regis L. Boyle, *Mrs. E.D.E.N. Southworth, Novelist*, Catholic Univ. of America Press, Washington, D.C., 1939, p. 11. This study provides the most detailed record of Mrs. Southworth's life and work.

16. Sidney George Fisher, 7 August 1857. *A Philadelphia Perspective. The Diary of Sidney George Fisher, 1834-71*, edit. by N.B. Wainwright, The Historical Society of Pennsylvania, Philadelphia, 1967, p. 277.

17. Edwin T. Freedley, *Philadelphia and its Manufactures: ... in 1857*, Philadelphia, 1858, p. 173.

18. The date and place of Anna's birth, also her parentage, have been compiled from two sources: her death certificate (State of New Jersey); also, with adjustment for known errors, the *Register of Women who arrived in what is now Colorado prior to January 1, 1861*, held in the Genealogical Department, Denver Public Library. (The State of Pennsylvania did not require records of Births, Marriages, and Deaths to be kept before July 1860).

19. Historical notes on Berks County, Pa., in Regional Reference Dept., Public Library, Reading, Pennsylvania.

20. *Christ Episcopal Church Records* (Marriages and Baptisms), Reading, Pa., The Historical Society of Berks County, Reading, Pennsylvania.

Chapter Three. A New Start in The Trans-Mississippi West.

Ho! For The Gold Regions! Ho! For Pike's Peak!

1. Recalled in *Rocky Mountain News*, Denver, 26 December 1900.

2. Calculated from Crofutt's report in his *Grip-Sack Guide of Colorado,*
   1881, p. 68, that he reached Pueblo (some two days short of Colorado
   City) after forty-one days on the trail from Kansas City. Crofutt gives
   the date of his arrival at Pueblo as 2nd July 1860, although other
   evidence from fellow travellers supports arrival there a few days
   earlier, probably 28th June.

3. Thomas G. Wildman to his sister Lucy Starr Haskins, Leavenworth City,
   Kansas, 25 April 1859. (See *Reports from Colorado, The Wildman
   Letters, 1859-1865,* edit. by L.R. Hafen and A.W. Hafen, Glendale, Cal.,
   1961, p. 25).

4. Richard Cordley, *Pioneer Days in Kansas,* Boston, 1903, pp. 58-61.

5. In addition to surviving original copies, the Pike's Peak guidebooks
   have been reprinted as a facsimile series by Nolie Mumey, Denver,
   Colo., with notes by LeRoy Hafen. See also, *The Pike's Peak Goldrush
   Guidebooks of 1859,* edit. by L.R. Hafen, Glendale, Cal., 1941.

6. *Daily Missouri Republican,* St. Louis, Mo., 10 March 1859.

7. *St. Louis Evening News,* 17 March 1859. (One copy survives in the St.
   Louis Mercantile Library Association's collection.)

8. The first stage arrived in Denver on 7 May 1859; see account in the
   Rocky Mountain News, 14 May 1859. It began as a daily service (except
   Sunday), and broadly followed the middle branch of the Smoky Hill
   Trail. West of the Republican River, the route crossed Beaver, Bijou and
   Kiowa Creeks before striking Cherry Creek twenty miles above its
   confluence with the South Platte at Denver.

9. E.L. Gallatin, *Reminiscences* (36 pp.), Denver, *Special Research Collections,* Colorado Historical Society, pp. 8-9. Gallatin owned a harness
   shop from 1860-75, and was one of Crofutt's early acquaintances.

10. David F. Spain to his wife Ella in South Bend, Indiana, Gregory's
    Diggings, 12 June 1859. (See *The Colorado Magazine,* vol. 35, 1958, p.
    108).

11. W.N. Byers, and J.H. Kellom, *A Hand Book to the Gold Fields of
    Nebraska and Kansas,* Chicago and New York, 1859. Both men, respec-
    tively from Ohio and New York, had lived for some years in Omaha,
    Neb., which is presumably why Nebraska was listed first in the title
    despite the fact that most of the reported gold discoveries were in
    Kansas. The guide was biased in favour of the Nebraska outfitting
    points and the Platte River route (which Byers had followed earlier in
    the 1850s on the trail to Oregon). Neither Byers nor Kellom had visited
    the newly reported gold fields.

12. For this, and other advertisements, current events, and voting registers,
    see successive issues of the *Lawrence Republican* and *The Kansas
    Herald of Freedom,* Lawrence, both weekly newspapers.

13. Richard Cordley, *Pioneer Days in Kansas*, Boston, 1903, p. 61.

14. See original pioneer lists and memorials displayed in Lawrence; also Cordley's *A History of Lawrence, Kansas, from the first settlement to the close of the rebellion*, Lawrence, 1895, *passim*; and letters by S.F. Tappan (New York, February 1901), in the Kansas Collection, Kenneth Spencer Research Library, Univ. of Kansas, Lawrence.

15. Albert D. Richardson, *Beyond the Mississippi: from the Great River to the Great Ocean . . . 1857-1867*, Hartford, Conn., 1867, p. 50.

16. Albinus Z. Sheldon, "El Paso County", in *History of the Arkansas Valley, Colorado*, Chicago, 1881, p. 418; and *The Colorado City Iris*, 1 January 1898.

17. Sheldon and Spencer were boarding at the Whitney House, on New Hampshire Street, close to the Kansas River ferry . . . See *Sutherland's Lawrence City Directory, 1860-61*, Elizabeth M. Watkins Community Museum and Archive Collection, Lawrence, Kansas.

18. Ben Crowell's memory of the horn-painting incident is one of those recounted later to his friend Irving Howbert, and included in Howbert's *Memories of a Lifetime in the Pike's Peak Region*, New York and London, 1925, pp. 239-40.

19. John W. Lee to McCarty & Barkley, forwarding and commission merchants in Kansas City, Mo., Auraria City, 24 August 1859. (See *Reports from Colorado*, edit. by L.R. Hafen and A.W. Hafen, *op. cit.*, p. 131).

20. Rufus E. Cable to I.N. White of Wyandotte, Kansas, Denver City, 30 July 1859. (*Ibid.*, p. 134).

21. Elizabeth J. Tallman. "Early Days in Colorado", *The Fowler Tribune*, Fowler, Colo., 24 July 1936. (See also *The Colorado Magazine*, vol. 13, 1936, pp. 141-9.) Mrs. Tallman, born in New York, was 95 at the time of this interview — alert, active, and Colorado's oldest living pioneer. (Castle Rock, Colo. Library archive).

22. Crofutt recalls arrival at Colorado City, 1860 (with B.F. Crowell and A.Z. Sheldon) in *The Colorado Springs Gazette*, 7 August 1880; Sheldon recalls crossing the plains and arriving in Colorado City on the last day of June 1860 (in the company of Ben Crowell, George A. Crofut [*sic*], Fred Spencer and Jim Tappan) in *History of the Arkansas Valley, op. cit.*, p. 468; and in *The Colorado City Iris*, 8 January 1898.

23. Anthony Bott, *The Colorado City Iris*, 8 July 1904.

24. Albinus Z. Sheldon, *ibid.*

25. Irving Howbert, *op. cit.*, pp. 24, 26.

26. A.D. Richardson, dispatch to the *Lawrence Republican*, 23 August 1860.

27. Charles M. Clarke, *A Trip to Pike's Peak, and Notes by the way*, Chicago, 1861, pp. 93-4.

28. Charles Stearns to editor of *Lawrence Republican*, "from the Gold Regions", 11 April 1861.

29. Population Schedules of the Eighth Census of the United States, 1860. Kansas Territorial Census: Arapahoe County.

30. *Register of Women who arrived in what is now Colorado prior to January 1, 1861*, held in the Genealogical Department, Denver Public Library. The *Rocky Mountain News*, unlike the Register, does not list Anna M. Crofutt among the Emigrant Arrivals; however, it states in June 1860 that lack of space "compels us to omit the greater portion of the names registered."

31. Sidney B. Morrison to A.M. Morrison of Ft. Atkinson, Wisc., Denver, 16 September 1860. (See *The Colorado Magazine*, vol.16, 1939, p. 92).

Chapter Four.   The Development of Colorado Territory in The 1860s: A Freighter's Life in The Pre-Railroad Age

1. Extracts from an "Observer's" report, dated 1 December 1859, sent to the *Missouri Democrat* from Auraria-Denver, published 12 December 1859. (See *Reports from Colorado, op. cit.* pp. 215-24; this reference pp. 219-20).

2. Document Division of the Denver Museum, *The Real Pioneers of Colorado*, biographical work by Maria Davies McGrath, 1934, vol. 3, A.Z. Sheldon entry, pp. 238-9. This collection is one of the primary sources of information on some 1400 early Colorado pioneers. Biographies of thousands more have not been available, Mrs. McGrath reported in her Foreword. There is no entry for Crofut(t).

3. G.A. Crofutt in *Rocky Mountain News*, 26 December 1900.

4. SW quarter of Section 32. See Sectional Map of Township 3, South of Range 68, West of 6th Principal Meridian, Surveyor General's Office, Denver, Colorado Territory, October 15, 1861. Crofutt (George A. Crofut) purchased this quarter-section of 160 acres from Daniel Candy (Warrant No. 102343); see U.S. Dept. of the Interior, *Records*, Bureau of Land Management, Colorado State Office.

5. Only one copy is known to have survived (November 28, 1861). It was part of pioneer Irving Howbert's personal collection (see his *Memories of a Lifetime, op. cit.,* p. 61), and is now on loan to the Old Colorado City Public Library, Colorado Springs.

6. Sidney B. Morrison to cousin J.F. Morrison, Leavenworth Gulch, 17 February 1861, *op. cit.,* p. 93.

7. Crofutt includes many brief references to his pioneering days in the 1860s at the appropriate place-entries in his guidebooks, *passim.* These have been used for the basic initial reconstruction of his movements in this period. Throughout, where direct quotations from Crofutt are used, minor variations in wording between different guidebook editions are ignored unless significant.

8. Report, Auraria-Denver, 24 November 1859, *Missouri Democrat*, St. Louis, Mo., 10 December 1859. (See *Reports From Colorado, op. cit.*, p. 209).

9. Matthew H. Dale to David W. Dale in Daleville, Pennsylvania, Nevada City, Colorado Territory, 12 March 1861. See "Life in the Pike's Peak Region: the letters of Matthew H. Dale", edit. by R.G. Athearn, *The Colorado Magazine*, vol. 32, 1955, pp. 1-24. This reference p. 20.

10. I. Howbert, *op. cit.*, p. 58.

11. The Wildman Letters, *op. cit.*, p. 71.

12. The northern boundary of Crofutt's ranch became part of the line dividing two of Douglas County's original seven School Districts; it was the only individual property boundary used for this purpose. Records begin 1 September 1865: "School District No. 2, including all of Frank(s)town Township north of the north line of Crofut's Ranch. School District No.3, including all of Frank(s)town Township south of the north line of Crofut's Ranch". See Grace I. Lamb, County School Superintendent, "History of Douglas County Schools from Early Records", *Record-Journal*, Douglas County, March 1949.

13. See modern street maps of the Castle Rock-Parker area, Douglas County; also Margaret Long, *The Smoky Hill Trail*, Denver, 1943 (3rd edit. 1953), p. 152; Josephine L. Marr and Joan M. Kaiser, *Douglas County, A Historical Journey*, Castle Rock, 1983, pp. 35, 36, 50, 52. The name of Frankstown was changed to Franktown in the 1870s.

14. Letter from Carroll H. Coberly, son of Joseph G. Coberly, grandson of George and Sarah Coberly (who had two sons and two daughters), 10 October 1961, Colorado Historical Society Collection. Also, the Carroll H. Coberly manuscript, *Early Colorado*, 112 pp., Denver Public Library, Western History Department. There are many references to the Coberlys' Half-Way House scattered among travel accounts in the 1860s.

15. Bishop Joseph C. Talbot, extracts from his diary quoted in *The Colorado Episcopalian*, Denver, June 1959. Talbot's extensive travels to the numerous small towns and mining communities earned him the title "Bishop of the Out-of-Doors".

16. The Richardsons and Pretty Woman's Ranch are described by Fitz Hugh Ludlow in *The Heart of the Continent*, New York, 1870, pp.

148-51. See also the James Grafton Rogers Collection, Colorado Historical Society.

17. Mrs. Byron N. Sanford, diary entry for 28 December 1861, in "Life at Camp Weld and Fort Lyon in 1861-62: an extract from the Diary of Mrs. Byron N. Sanford", *The Colorado Magazine*, vol. 7, 1930, pp. 132-9. This reference p. 134.

18. Alexander Kelly McClure, *Three Thousand Miles through the Rocky Mountains*, Philadelphia, 1869, pp. 116-118. Mrs. McClure visited Dirty Woman's Ranch in May 1867. Before this, the ranch had been occupied by the Garlick family, who took over from the Walkers c.1865. Fitz Hugh Ludlow called briefly on Mr. P. Garlick at Dirty Woman's Ranch, once again in poor condition, while travelling south over the Divide to Colorado City in the mid-1860s; Ludlow, *op. cit.*, pp. 160-2.

19. *History of the Arkansas Valley, Colorado, op. cit.*, p. 440.

20. A longer account by George F. Turner appears in *The Denver Post*, 20 October 1908.

21. A.D. Richardson, *Beyond the Mississippi, op. cit.*, pp. 298-302, *passim*.

22. *Rocky Mountain News*, 20 April 1863; also report in Denver City Directory, 1866.

23. Amos Steck, *The Denver Field and Farm*, 20 May 1905.

24. Elizabeth J. Tallman, "Early Days in Colorado", *op. cit.*

25. Amos Steck, *op. cit.*

26. Carroll H. Coberly, *Early Colorado, op. cit.*, pp. 111-2.

27. G.A. Crofutt, *Rocky Mountain News*, 30 December 1900.

28. A record of the sale (to C.L. Williams) is found in the U.S. Dept. of the Interior, *Records*, Bureau of Land Management, *op. cit.* The General Land Office entry, Washington, D.C. is dated 20 March 1867. That Crofutt was still thought to be the owner is revealed by an announcement, made in his absence, of a proposed Sheriff's Sale of this quarter-section, *Rocky Mountain News*, 12 March 1871.

29. See Edith Parker Low, "History of the Twenty-Mile House on Cherry Creek", *The Colorado Magazine*, vol. 12, 1935, pp. 142-4; Elizabeth J. Tallman, "Early History of Parker and Vicinity", *ibid.*, vol. 23, 1946, pp. 184-6; Jane Melvin, "The Twelve Mile House", *ibid.*, vol. 12, 1935, pp. 173-8. Also Marr and Kaiser, *op. cit.*, chapter 9.

30. *Rocky Mountain News*, 25 September 1865.

31. Edited extracts from interview given by G.A. Crofutt, *The Denver Times*, 25 March 1902. (An account of the Berthoud-Bridger expedition of 1861, and some others, appears in L.R. Hafen, "Pioneer Struggles for a

Colorado Road across the Rockies", *The Colorado Magazine*, vol. 3, 1926, pp. 1-10).

32. This company registration was discovered not in Denver, however, but at Castle Rock, in the earliest Land Records ledger in the County Clerk & Records Division, Douglas County. The incorporators were Rufus Clark, George A. Crofut [*sic*], and Edwin Scudder, and registration was officially entered on 19 May 1865.

This ledger also records, *inter alia*, some of the land holdings of Mrs. Sarah E. Coberly (1866); this is the only source known to the author that gives Mrs. Coberly's own name. Other Colorado records refer to her as Mrs. George Coberly, and later as Mrs. William Krull.

33. Arthur Ridgway, "The Mission of Colorado Toll Roads", *The Colorado Magazine*, vol. 9, 1932, pp. 161-9. This reference p. 168.

34. Marr and Kaiser, *op. cit.*, p. 48.

35. Passenger list, Holladay's Overland Stage Line, *Rocky Mountain News*, 1 March 1866.

36. A.W. Hoyt, "Over the Plains to Colorado", *Harper's New Monthly Magazine*, New York, vol. 35, 1867, pp. 1-21. This reference p. 8.

37. Passenger list for Sat. 24 March, 1866, published in *Rocky Mountain News*, 26 March 1866.

38. *Crofutt's Western World*, June 1873.

39. A.Z. Sheldon, *History of the Arkansas Valley, Colorado, op. cit.*, p. 424.

40. Throughout, unless otherwise noted, all extracts from Crofutt's *Trans-Continental* and *Overland* guidebook series are taken in context from their appropriate place-entries. This account, therefore, is located in the Julesburg-Fort Sedgwick section; pagination varies. Minor variations in wording in revised editions are ignored unless significant; 1st person singular has occasionally been substituted for Crofutt's more customary use of 1st person plural, where this clarifies the point being made.

41. Crofutt, *Great Trans-Continental Railroad Guide*, 1869, p. 35.

42. Ferdinand V. Hayden, *Sun Pictures of Rocky Mountain Scenery*, New York, 1870, p. 33.

43. G.A. Crofutt, *Rocky Mountain News*, 26 December 1900.

44. *The Rocky Mountain Trails, of ye long ago! drawn from personal experience by Geo. A. Crofutt*. Undated, but probably made in Denver in the early 1880s; size 60cms × 51cms. Annotation to 1867. Crofutt, using a later base map, indicated all those "Forts, Cities, Towns, Ranches, etc. which were not in existence when these trails were located, when '*Wood, Water*, and *Grass*' were prime factors." Colorado Historical Society, Denver.

45. The importance of Fort Sedgwick, and the volume of freight passing through it in the mid-1860s, is shown, for example, in the "Consolidated Report of Trains passing Fort Sedgwick, Colorado Territory, from February 1, 1867 to September 28, 1867", Report of Secretary of War, *House Executive Documents*, No. 1, 40th Congress, 1st Session (1867), Serial No. 1324, Washington, D.C., pp. 62-4. See also pp. 57-61 for general conditions in the region at this time.

46. A.D. Richardson, *op. cit.*, p. 567.

47. *Crofutt's Overland Tours*, 1890, p. 35.

48. G.A. Crofutt, *Rocky Mountain News*, 26 December 1900.

49. I. Howbert, *op. cit.*, pp. 211-2.

50. William Tecumseh Sherman to Samuel F. Tappan in Manchester-by-the-Sea, Mass., St. Louis, Mo., 6 September 1868; and Fort Leavenworth, Kansas, 13 August 1868. *Special Research Collections*, Colorado Historical Society.

51. G.A. Crofutt in *Crofutt's Western World*, March 1874.

52. Richard B. Townshend, *A Tenderfoot in Colorado*, London, 1923, pp. 2-3.

53. *Rocky Mountain News*, 25 and 27 September 1865.

54. Grenville M. Dodge, "How We Built the Union Pacific Railway", *Senate Documents*, 61st Congress, 2nd Session, vol. 59, Serial No. 5658, Washington, D.C., 1910; also J.R. Perkins, *Trails, Rails and War: the Life of General G.M. Dodge*, Indianapolis, 1929 (journal entries for period 18-22 September 1865), pp. 187-90.

55. Articles of Incorporation, *Company Registrations*, Arapahoe County Records, Colorado State Archives and Public Records, Denver.

56. *Ibid.*

57. *Ibid.* Crofutt is registered, and signs, as Geo. A. Crofut [sic] in each case.

58. Session Laws of the Colorado Assembly, Board of County Commissioners for Arapahoe County, *Minutes Book*, meeting of February 2nd, 1869, Colorado State Archives and Public Records, Denver.

59. Session Laws of the Colorado Assembly, pp. 127-9, *An Act Concerning Roads and Highways*, March 11th, 1864, Colorado State Archives and Public Records, Denver.

60. William Fraser Rae, *Westward by Rail: the New Route to the East*, London, 1870; the 2nd edition (1871) dropped the second part of the title and substituted: *A Journey to San Francisco and Back, and a visit to the Mormons;* p. iv.

61. Brigham Young, at mass meeting held in the Tabernacle, Salt Lake City, 10 June 1868, "that expression might be given to the popular feeling relative to the railroad coming past this city." See O.F. Whitney, *History of Utah*, Salt Lake City, 1893, vol. 2, pp. 231-2.

62. Crofutt's assistance on the production of E.L. Sloan's 1869 Directory is recorded in *The Salt Lake Herald*, 2 August 1885.

63. Doris Elizabeth King, "The First-Class Hotel and the Age of the Common Man", *The Journal of Southern History*, Southern Historical Assoc., vol. 23, 1957, pp. 173-88. This reference p. 173.

64. Jefferson Williamson, *The American Hotel*, New York, 1930, pp. 116, 130. See also Russell Lynes, *The Taste-makers*, New York, 1954, chapter 6, "Palaces for the People"; and D.J. Boorstin, *The Americans*, vol. 2, *The National Experience*, New York, 1965, chapter 18, "Palaces of the Public".

Chapter Five. *Transcontinental:* Crofutt Spreads The Word Across America

1. *The Daily Morning Chronicle*, San Francisco, 11 May 1869; "From Our Special Reporter, Promontory Point, 8 May, 10 p.m.".

2. Alexander Majors, *Seventy Years on the Frontier*, Chicago and New York, 1893, p. 267.

3. Lists of those present at Promontory for the Great Event are all incomplete, and sometimes also inaccurate. The most useful single source, compiled from several contemporary reports, is Hugh F. O'Neil, "List of Persons Present, Promontory, Utah, May 10, 1869", *Utah Historical Quarterly*, Utah State Historical Society, vol. 24, 1956, pp. 157-64.

   Edward Sloan, however, is the only reporter to identify H. Wallace Atwell as "Bill Dadd, the Scribe". The origin of the pseudonym appears to be Bildad, in The Book of Job; Edwin L. Sabin refers to "Atwell, who was better known as 'Bildad the Scribe'," in *Building the Pacific Railway*, Philadelphia and London, 1919, p. 217.

4. *The San Francisco Chronicle and its History, 1865-1879*, San Francisco, 1879, in San Francisco City Archives, Main Library, Civic Center.

5. Silas Seymour, *Incidents of a Trip through the Great Platte Valley . . . and an account of the Great Union Pacific Railroad Excursion to the One Hundredth Meridian of Longitude*, New York, 1867; and E.L. Sabin, *op. cit.*, pp. 275-85.

6. *Great Trans-Continental Railroad Guide*, 1869, p. 133.

7. Lieut. John Charles Currier, 21st U.S. Infantry, diary entry, quoted by L.R. Mayer and K.E. Vose, *Makin' Tracks*, New York, 1975, p. 205.

8. G.A. Crofutt, *Rocky Mountain News*, 26 December 1900.

9. Edward L. Sloan, *The Deseret News*, Salt Lake City, 19 May 1869.

10. W.F. Rae, *op. cit.*, p. 90.

11. *Copyright Record Books, District Courts, 1790-1870*; vol. 24, Records of Illinois — Northern District, Clerk's Office, Dec. 1868 – April 1870, Entry No. 3963, Copyright Office, Library of Congress. The original ledger is held in the Library's Rare Book Room.

12. Crofutt often added short footnotes to the Guides, changing them frequently in reprints and new editions to record meetings, brief exchanges, quips, and supplementary information. His meeting with Butterfield is noted on p. 225 of the *Great Trans-Continental Railroad Guide*, 1869. David Butterfield was murdered five-and-a-half years later in Arkansas, 28 March 1875, aged 41.

13. The erroneous catalogue entry in the Huntington Library Rare Book Collection giving *1st August* as the Guide's publication date appears to have been based on the dating of the railroad timetable that Crofutt inserted with the Guide. All first editions were published at the beginning of September 1869, and coast-to-coast distribution of the guidebook achieved during the next two weeks.

14. *Great Trans-Continental Railroad Guide*, 1869, p. 32.

15. Part of a Greeley dispatch to the *New-York Tribune*, quoted in Henry Villard's *The Past and Present of the Pike's Peak Gold Regions*, St. Louis, Mo., 1860, p. 50.

16. *New-York Tribune*, 29 May: 5, 22, 25, 26 June; 12, 19, 28 July; 2 August 1869.

17. William Lawrence Humason, *From the Atlantic Surf to the Golden Gate*, Hartford, Conn., 1869, p. 12.

18. Essay on *Nature*, 1836.

19. F.H. Ludlow, *The Heart of the Continent, op. cit.*, pp. 131, 142-3, 158.

20. Walt Whitman, *America's Characteristic Landscape*, see *Walt Whitman: complete poetry and selected prose and letters*, edit. by E. Holloway, London, 1938, 8th impression 1971, p. 764.

21. Samuel Bowles, *The Pacific Railroad — Open*, Boston, 1869, p. 6.

22. Extracts from Preface, 1871. Gilbert is unaccounted for, but may be Curtis F. Gilbert, a reporter living close by at 154 Nassau Street in 1870-1 who moved away in 1872.

23. End-paper panel, 1871.

Chapter Six. The New Age of Western Promotion:
Life In New York In The 1870s

1. *Crofutt's Western World*, January 1872.

2. *Rocky Mountain Presbyterian*, Denver, June 1872. The Rev. Sheldon Jackson, born in New York, travelled widely in the West in the 1860s – 1880s, establishing Presbyterian churches and schools.

3. *The British Quarterly Review*, London, vol. 53, January 1871, p. 3.

4. Elise Dubach Isely, *Sunbonnet Days*, as told to her son Bliss Isely, Caldwell, Idaho, 1935, p. 180.

5. Alice Blackwood Baldwin, *An Army Wife on the Frontier: the Memoirs of Alice Blackwood Baldwin, 1867 – 1877*, edited by R.C. and E.R. Carriker, Univ. of Utah, Salt Lake City, 1975, p. 74.

6. J.H. Beadle, reporting for the *Cincinnati Commercial*. See *The Undeveloped West*, Philadelphia, Chicago, etc., 1873, p. 126.

7. *Crofutt's Western World, passim*; see also William D. Pattison, "Westward by Rail with Professor Sedgwick: a Lantern Journey of 1873", *Quarterly*, Historical Society of Southern California, Los Angeles, vol. 42, 1960, pp. 335-49.

8. G.A. Crofutt to F.V. Hayden, New York, 16 and 19 Feb. 1872, *Records of the Geological and Geographical Survey of the Territories ("Hayden Survey"), Letters Received 1867-79*, RG 57, M623, National Archives, Washington, D.C.

9. W.F. Rae, *Westward by Rail, op. cit.*, p. 320.

10. *Crofutt's Western World*, May 1872.

11. *Ibid.*, May 1874.

12. Currier & Ives were variously located at 2 and 33 Spruce Street; 152 Nassau (until 1872); 125, 123, 115 Nassau; 108 Fulton.

13. Crofutt provides details of the design for *American Progress*, and states that it is his own, in the Annexes to subsequent editions of his guidebooks. See also *Crofutt's Western World, passim*.

14. William Culp Darrah, *Stereo Views: A History of Stereographs in America and their collection*, Gettysburg, Pennsylvania, 1964, p. 8.

15. *Copyright Records*, Copyright Office, Library of Congress.

16. Reported in *Crofutt's Western World*, November 1872.

17. Circular Notes or Letters of Credit for the use of travellers abroad were of course well established but, unlike Cook's Traveller's Checks, they

could normally be exchanged for cash only at one of the bank's foreign agents.

18. *Our American Relations*, reprinted by T. Cook & Son, London, New York and Boston, 1874, p. 21.

19. G.M. Dodge, *op. cit.*, p. 102.

20. *Crofutt's Western World*, November 1873.

21. John H. Beadle, *Western Wilds, and the men who redeem them*, Cincinnati, Chicago, etc., 1878, p. 132. Report of tour made in August 1873.

22. Grant M. Overton, *Portrait of a Publisher, and The First Hundred Years of the House of Appleton, 1825-1925*, New York, 1925, pp. 58-60. So successful was *Picturesque America* that Appletons' followed it with *Picturesque Europe*, edit. by Bayard Taylor, and *Picturesque Palestine*, edit. by Henry Codman Potter.

23. *United States Patent Office Records*, Patent Nos. 145,337 and 152,215.

24. Frank L. Mott, *American Journalism. A History: 1690-1960*, New York, 3rd edit. 1962, pp. 395, 411. Also *A History of American Magazines, op. cit.*, vol. 3, 1865-85, p. 5.

25. *Bankruptcy No. 5773*, District Court of the U.S., for the Southern District of New York. Documents, claims and correspondence relating to the bankruptcy are filed at the Federal Archives and Records Center, General Services Administration, Bayonne, N.J.

Chapter Seven. Western Expansion In The 1870s and 1880s:

New Demands For Information, Advertising, and Investment.

Transport · Tourists · Health Seekers · Settlers

1. Phineas T. Barnum, *op. cit.*, p. 180. *Struggles and Triumphs: or, the Life of P.T. Barnum, Written by Himself* was later edited by George S. Bryan, New York and London, 2 vols, 1927. Barnum regularly updated his own life story, publishing expanded editions of his first autobiography (1855) until two years before his death in 1891. The work was usually sub-titled *A Map of Busy Life, its Fluctuations and its Vast Concerns.*

2. *Crofutt's Western World, passim.*

3. *Copyright Records*, Copyright Office, Library of Congress.

4. Grace Greenwood, *pseud.* (Mrs. Sara Jane Clarke Lippincott). *New Life in New Lands: Notes of Travel* (Letters to the *New York Times*, 1871-72), New York, 1873, p. 303.

5. Demas Barnes, *From the Atlantic to the Pacific, Overland*, New York, 1866, pp. 8, 47, 71, 89.

6. Charles Loring Brace, *The New West: or, California in 1867-1868*, New York, 1869, p. 185.

7. The first 40 miles of the canal had been completed in 1872 as part of a new large-scale irrigation and reclamation project financed in San Francisco. This followed a reconnaissance of the San Joaquin Valley made in 1871 on behalf of the company concerned by R.M. Brereton, an English engineer who had worked on irrigation projects in India. See Charles Nordhoff, *op. cit.*, pp. 128-9, 226-7; also Robert G. Cleland, *From Wilderness to Empire: A History of California, 1542-1900*, New York, 1944, p. 327.

8. Pasadena ('Crown of the Valley' or 'Key of the Valley') was founded in 1874 by a small group of pioneers from Indiana, led by Thomas B. Elliott, an army surgeon from Indianapolis.

   Riverside was established in 1870-72 by the Southern California Colonization Society, organized by John W. North as an agricultural community and settled mainly by health-seekers. It became famous for the introduction into Southern California in 1873 (by one of the colonists, Mrs. L.C. Tibbetts) of the seedless Washington navel orange, imported originally from Bahia, Brazil.

   In 1870, dry grazing land at the future site of Riverside was selling for about 75 cents an acre. North offered small irrigated farms for $2.50 - $20 an acre. Crofutt's figure shows more than a seven-fold increase in best land values by 1878, and this had risen to at least a ten-fold increase by the end of the 1870s.

9. The conflict between the two companies is examined, *inter alia*, by Julius Grodinsky, *Transcontinental Railroad Strategy, 1869-1893*, Univ. of Pennsylvania Press, Philadelphia, 1962; Stuart Daggett, *Chapters on the History of the Southern Pacific*, New York, 1922; Cerinda W. Evans, *Collis Potter Huntington*, Newport News, Va. 2 vols, 1954; David S. Lavender, *The Great Persuader*, Garden City, N.Y., 1970.

10. T.S. Hudson, *A Scamper Through America or, Fifteen Thousand Miles of Ocean and Continent in Sixty Days*, London and New York, 1882, pp. 183-4.

11. William H. Brewer, *Rocky Mountain Letters, 1869; "Letters written to my wife during a trip to the Rocky Mountains, July to September, 1869"*, Denver, 1930, p. 14. Brewer accompanied Prof. J.D. Whitney, head of the Hooper School of Mining and Practical Geology at Harvard, who was leading a field class in the Rockies. Two of the four students in the party, preparing to graduate in 1870, were Henry Gannett, who became the official Geographer to the United States (see Note 45, Chap.

423

VIII), and William Morris Davis, later Professor of Geology at Harvard University and founder of the influential Davisian School of Geomorphology.

12. William Jackson Palmer to his fiancée Mary ('Queen') Lincoln Mellen, in John S. Fisher, *A Builder of the West: the Life of General William Jackson Palmer*, Caldwell, Idaho, 1939, p. 187.

13. Frank Fossett, *Colorado*, New York, 1879, p. 33.

14. William Jackson Palmer, *The Westward Current of Population in the United States*, London, 1874, p. 11.

Details on Palmer's Kansas Pacific Railroad survey work are found in *Report of Surveys across the continent in 1867-68, on the thirty-fifth and thirty-second parallels, for a route extending the Kansas Pacific Railway to the Pacific Ocean at San Francisco and San Diego*, by Gen. William J. Palmer, December 1, 1868, Philadelphia, 1869; also in William Abraham Bell, *New Tracks in North America*, 2 vols, London, 1869.

15. W.J. Palmer, *The Westward Current of Population in the United States*, *op. cit.*, p. 48.

16. I. Howbert, *op. cit.*, pp. 220-2. Howbert had been elected County Clerk of El Paso County in 1869. Alexander C. Hunt was a former Governor of Colorado Territory (1867-9).

17. Letter to W.J. Palmer, and quoted by him in Colorado Springs, March 1874. See *The Westward Current of Population in the United States*, *op. cit.*, p. 27.

18. C. Nordhoff, *op. cit.*, Preface. In fact, malaria *was* found in California at this time, particularly in parts of the Central Valley. See *Reports*, State Board of Health of California, Sacramento, *passim*; also Kenneth Thompson, "Irrigation as a menace to health in California: a nineteenth century view", *The Geographical Review*, vol. 59, 1969, pp. 195-214.

19. William Abraham Bell, *The Colonies of Colorado in their relations to English Enterprise and Settlement*, London, 1874. See also Colorado Historical Society's *Special Research Collections*, W.A. Bell. The Colorado Territorial Board of Immigration was established in 1871; William N. Byers took charge of its operation in 1872. Thousands of booklets and pamphlets were produced, immigration agents appointed in England, Germany, and throughout the United States, and reduced passage and rail fares arranged.

20. Phineas T. Barnum. See edit. George S. Bryan. *op. cit.*, vol. 2, p. 685.

21. Rose Georgina Kingsley, *South by West; or, Winter in the Rocky Mountains and Spring in Mexico*, London, 1874. Preface by the Rev.

Charles Kingsley. Also *Letters from Charles Kingsley*, Colorado, 1874, 1st publ. London, 1876.

22. *Crofutt's Overland Tours*, 1890, p. 95.

23. Shadrach K. Hooper, *The Story of Manitou*, Chicago and Cincinnati, 1885, p. 55.

24. Grace Greenwood, in Introduction to E. Greatorex, *vide infra*, p. 10.

25. *Ibid.* p. 11. Regular reports of growth in, and visitors to, the Manitou and Colorado Springs area appear in *Out West*, later the *Colorado Springs Gazette*, the weekly newspaper which began 23 March 1872.

26. Frances Metcalf Wolcott, *Heritage of Years . . . 1851-89*, New York, 1932, pp. 69-70.

27. *Ibid.* p. 132.

28. Grace Greenwood, in Greatorex, *vide infra*, p. 8.

29. Eliza Greatorex, *Summer Etchings in Colorado*, New York, 1873, p. 41.

30. F.M. Wolcott, *op. cit.*, pp. 113, 85.

31. Peter Charles Remondino, *The Mediterranean Shores of America. Southern California: its climatic, physical, and meteorological conditions*, Philadelphia and London, 1892, p. 127.

32. Carey McWilliams, *Southern California Country: An Island on the Land*, New York, 1946, pp. 123-4.

33. C. Nordhoff, *op. cit.*, pp. 113, 114.

34. Thomas M. Storke, *California Editor*, Los Angeles, 1958, p. 49.

35. The Palace Hotel was built at a cost of nearly $5 million by William C. Ralston, founder of the Bank of California which had made a fortune from the Comstock silver mining bonanza in Nevada. Ralston and the Bank crashed in August 1875, sparking a severe financial panic. Shortly before, E.J. Baldwin had sold his shares in what was soon to become the nearly worthless Ophir Mine in Nevada to Ralston, thus avoiding Ralston's fate — hence "Lucky" Baldwin. Ralston was drowned at the height of the Panic in 1875, (whether by accident or suicide is unknown) after being forced to resign from the Bank. The Palace Hotel was completed, however, and opened just five weeks after Ralston's death. It remained famous and enormously successful until it was destroyed in the great San Francisco fire of 1906. The huge hotel was quickly rebuilt and back in business after a grand reopening on 15th December 1909.

36. W.J. Palmer, *The Westward Current of Population in the United States*, *op. cit.*, pp. 34-6.

37. Henry T. Williams, *The Pacific Tourist*, 1876, *op. cit.*, p. 75.

38. John Codman, *The Round Trip*, New York, 1879, p. 64.

39. James William Barclay, *The Denver and Rio Grande Railway of Colorado*, London, 1877, pp. 11, 19.

40. F. Fossett, *op. cit.*, p. 35; Crofutt, in his *Grip-Sack Guide of Colorado* (1881) reported that the arrivals at the hotels in Denver were averaging over 600 a day (p. 31).

41. E. Greatorex, *op. cit.*, pp. 77-8, 82, 95. See also S. Anna Gordon, *Camping in Colorado*, New York, 1879, pp. 141-2, 155-6; and Isabella L. Bird, *op. cit.*, *passim*.

The 1870s marked the effective beginning of 'dude ranching', as individual ranchers in favoured localities began to supplement their incomes on a regular basis by accommodating tourists and health-seekers. The term 'dude' was not introduced in the United States until 1883; after that, 'dude ranchers' and 'dude wranglers' were those who gave increasing attention to operating a ranch as a tourist attraction, mostly for city-dwellers vacationing in the West.

42. Daniel Pidgeon, *An Engineer's Holiday, or notes of a round trip from Long. 0° to 0°*, London, 1882, vol. 1, pp. 172-3. Estes Park was discovered by Joel Estes, a pioneer from Missouri, during a hunting trip in October 1859. The Estes family lived in the Park from 1861 to 1866. See *Special Research Collections*, Colorado Historical Society.

43. Augustus Allen Hayes, Jr., *New Colorado and the Santa Fe Trail*, New York, 1880, pp. 111-2.

44. Robert G. Athearn, "The Denver and Rio Grande and the Panic of 1873", *The Colorado Magazine*, vol. 35, 1958, pp. 121-38; p. 121. For a comprehensive history of the railroad, see Athearn's *Rebel of the Rockies: A History of the Denver and Rio Grande Western Railroad*, Yale Univ. Press, New Haven, Conn., 1962; repr. Univ. of Nebraska Press, Lincoln, 1977.

45. All that appeared was a small, localized *Williams' Tourists' Guide and Map of the San Juan Mines of Colorado*, New York, 1877; 47 pp., paper covers, price 50 cents.

46. *Crofutt's Grip-Sack Guide of Colorado* (1881), pp. 24, 25.

47. *Ibid.*, p. 52.

48. John H. Beadle, *Western Wilds, op. cit.*, p. 457; *Crofutt's Grip-Sack Guide of Colorado* (1881), pp. 102-3.

49. *Crofutt's Grip-Sack Guide of Colorado* (1881), p. 60.

50. Philip (Phil) Stewart Robinson, *Sinners and Saints. A Tour Across the States, and Round Them; With Three Months Among the Mormons*, London, 1883, p. 45.

51. *Crofutt's Grip-Sack Guide of Colorado* (1885), pp. 126-7. The wagon road from Ouray to Red Mountain was completed in 1882, and extended to Silverton in 1883. It later became known as the Million Dollar Highway. Built by Otto Mears, "the Pathfinder of the San Juan", it was part of the 'Mears System of Toll Roads' for miners, freighters and stage lines in southwest Colorado. The first road opened in 1867 over Poncha Pass, and the system in time covered nearly 400 miles. Arthur Ridgway, *op. cit.*, p. 169, reported that Otto Mears had personally told him "that with possibly one exception, the Ouray-Silverton road, the tolls were not even moderately remunerative."

52. Production Statistics by value, *Bulletin No. 3*, Bureau of Mines, State of Colorado, Denver, 1899.

53. *Crofutt's Grip-Sack Guide of Colorado* (1881), p. 182.

54. General statement on proposed Exposition made by H.A.W. Tabor *et al*, *Denver Tribune*, 9 January 1881.

    Announcement of Crofutt's appointment made by H.A.W. Tabor, The National Mining & Industrial Exposition Association, President's Office, Denver, 7 March 1882.

55. *Rocky Mountain News*, 13 May 1882.

56. Articles of Incorporation (with Amendments, 10 April 1883), *Company Registrations*, Colorado State Archives and Public Records, Denver. Crofutt's original four fellow directors were H. Montgomery White of New York City; H.J. Sisty of Clear Creek County, Colo.; James A. Fleming and Hamilton S. Wicks of Denver. Wicks had originally been Frank Leslie's business manager on Leslie's famous promotional transcontinental trip from New York to San Francisco in 1877; in 1881, Wicks became one of the Directors of Denver's proposed National Mining and Industrial Exposition which opened in 1882.

57. G.A. Crofutt, *The Denver Times*, 25 March 1902.

58. Edgar Carlisle McMechen, *The Moffat Tunnel of Colorado*, Denver, 1927, vol. 1, p. 69.

59. James J. Hagerman, letter dated 21 September 1890; quoted by J.J. Lipsey in "How Hagerman sold the Colorado Midland in 1890", *The Brand Book of the Denver Westerners*, Denver, 1956, pp. 267-86. This reference p. 283.

60. F.L. Mott, *A History of American Magazines*, *op. cit.*, vol. 3, pp. 7, 11, 269.

61. "Fortunes in Colorado — the Atlantic-Pacific Tunnel", *St. Louis Illustrated Magazine*, October 1881, pp.375-82; *Denver Republican*, 14 September 1883; *Denver Times*, 1 June 1896.

62. *Crofutt's Salt Lake City Directory for 1885-6*, Prefatory, pp. 11-12. At this time, the Copyright Office did not provide official application forms and letters served as applications. Crofutt wrote to the Library of Congress, placing the copyright of the Salt Lake City Directory in his wife's name: A.M. Crofutt. *Copyright Records*, Copyright Office, Library of Congress.

63. Although their paths probably never crossed, Crofutt's former associate H. Wallace Atwell ("Bill Dadd, the Scribe") was also busy at the beginning of 1888 promoting his newly published guide and directory for the Southern Pacific Railroad, *The Sunset Route*. Atwell had been travelling and preparing the book for most of 1887, after living and working quietly in the San Joaquin Valley for many years; he was an able writer but, according to one contemporaneous report, never made the most of his talents because of persistent alcoholism. In 1887 the future had appeared to be brighter, but Atwell died suddenly of peritonitis on 18th February 1888, while staying at the El Capitan Hotel in Merced on his promotional trip. He was 56.

64. Included in the Report of the President of the San Diego Chamber of Commerce, 3 August 1888. (Figures quoted referred to Southern California as a whole.)

A detailed account of the hour-by-hour climax to the rate-cutting war between the Southern Pacific and the Santa Fe on 6 March 1886 appeared in the *Los Angeles Times* on 7 March, under the headline—"The War ... Terrific Rate-Cutting Yesterday ... The Combat Deepens: On, Ye Brave!".

65. James M. Guinn, "The Great Real Estate Boom of 1887", *Publications of the Historical Society of Southern California*, Los Angeles, vol. 1 (1884-91), 1890, pp. 13-21; also Glenn S. Dumke, *The Boom of the Eighties in Southern California*, San Marino, Cal., Huntington Library, 1944.

66. Judge Goodwin, *The Salt Lake Daily Tribune*, 20 May 1888.

67. Walter Raymond outlined his plans in the *Pasadena Chronicle*, 22 November 1883.

68. Reported in Walter Lindley and Joseph Pomeroy Widney, *California of the South*, New York, 1888, p. 152.

69. Charles Frederick Holder, *All About Pasadena and its Vicinity*, Boston and New York, 1889, p. 17.

70. Kate A. Sanborn, *A Truthful Woman in Southern California*, New York, 1893, p. 12.

71. Reported in W. Lindley and J.P. Widney, *op. cit.*, 3rd edit., 1896, p. 210. See also hotel archives, Hotel del Coronado, Coronado, Cal.

72. Walter Lindley, *op. cit.*, 1888, p. 213.

73. Franklin Walker, *A Literary History of Southern California*, Univ. of California Press, Berkeley and Los Angeles, 1950, p. 109.

74. Reports in *Cook's Excursionist*, American edition, *passim*, Thomas Cook and Son company archives, London; also in various company pamphlets and prospectuses held in American public and university library collections, particularly in the northeastern United States and in California.

75. Act of 1 March 1872, *U.S. Statutes at Large*, vol. 17, pp. 32-3; *An Act to set apart a certain Tract of Land lying near the Head-waters of the Yellowstone River as a public Park.*

76. J. Rudyard Kipling, *From Sea to Sea: Letters of Travel*, New York, 1899, London, 1900, vol. 2, pp. 74, 85.

77. *Ibid.*, p. 72.

78. "The Yellowstone National Park", *Scribner's Monthly*, vol. 4, 1872, pp. 120-1. This reference p. 121.

79. John James Aubertin, *A Fight with Distances*, London, 1888, p. 86.

80. *Boston Globe*, 16 April 1907.

81. This analysis of the Raymond & Whitcomb tour programs is based entirely on a study of the company's own prospectuses, notices and timetables. These survive mainly in university, special research and public library collections in Massachusetts, New York, and California. The Raymond & Whitcomb Co. has maintained no archive collection of its own.

82. J.J. Aubertin, *op. cit.*, p. 210.

83. Mary H. Wills, *A Winter in California*, Norristown, Pennsylvania, 1889, pp. 43-5.

84. Susie C. Clark, *The Round Trip from The Hub to the Golden Gate*, Boston and New York, 1890, pp. 144-5.

Chapter Eight. The 1890s: Competition Intensifies In The Transport, Tourist, and Information Industries.
The New Age of Diversification.
California and Colorado Increase Their Rivalry and Expand Their Markets.

1. Production Statistics by value, *Bulletin No. 3*, Bureau of Mines, State of Colorado, Denver, 1899.

2. Amos Steck to E.O. Carpenter in New York, Denver, 29 August 1897; in Nolie Mumey, *Amos Steck (1822-1908)*, Denver, 1981, pp. 173, 176.

3. Quoted by Mumey, *ibid.*, p. 170. Material on Amos Steck is also located in the *Special Research Collections*, Colorado Historical Society, Denver. It includes the diaries of his Overland Journey to California (1849), also reprinted by Mumey.

4. Colorado Springs City Directories, and Business Directory Index, 1894 and 1896. (No Directories were published in 1893 and 1895.)

5. Harry Alexander MacFadden, *Rambles in the Far West*, Hollidaysburg, Pa., 1906, p. 251.

6. Hotel archives, The Antlers, Colorado Springs.

7. Records, Cripple Creek Museum.

8. William Henry Jackson (1843-1942), originally from Troy, N.Y., was one of that distinguished group of early travel photographers employed by the railroad companies, as well as by official government surveys. See Jackson's autobiography *Time Exposure*, New York, 1940; also W.H. Jackson, "Photographing the Colorado Rockies Fifty Years Ago", *The Colorado Magazine*, vol. 3, 1926, pp. 11-22.

   Influential nineteenth-century photographers of the West included, in addition to W.H. Jackson, Andrew J. Russell, Charles R. Savage, Carleton E. Watkins, Eadweard Muybridge, George M. Ottinger, Alfred A. Hart, Thomas Houseworth and William G. Chamberlain. Their work, and others', made an indispensable pictorial contribution to the western tourist industry, where it was widely used for railroad and hotel advertising, for engraved illustrations in guidebooks and magazines, for postcards, souvenir 'view cards' and lantern slides, and for stereo sets.

9. Archives, Los Angeles Chamber of Commerce, *passim*.

10. William N. Byers was appointed President of the Festival but acknowledged that the idea had originated with Hooper. The Festival of Mountain and Plain was held annually 1895-9, then again in 1901 and 1912, after which it was discontinued (See *Special Collections*, Colorado Historical Society).

    However, following proposals in the mid-1980s to revive the Festival as a major regional attraction, it was reintroduced as an annual event in 1986.

11. *Rocky Mountain News*, 8 September 1898.

12. Needles *Eye*, 12 May 1894; John C. Frémont, *Los Angeles Tribune*, 11 March 1888. Both quoted by John E. Baur, *The Health Seekers of Southern California, 1870-1900*, San Marino, Cal., Huntington Library, 1959, pp. 47, 143.

13. Quoted by Earl Pomeroy, *In Search of the Golden West*, New York, 1957, preliminary caption.

14. Frederick Henry Harvey, a Londoner, arrived in America in 1850 at the age of fifteen. After working on the railroads, and in restaurants in New York and New Orleans, he opened his first railroad restaurant at the Santa Fe's Topeka depot in 1876. After that, Harvey's hotels, restaurants, and dining cars became an outstanding feature of the A.T. & S.F. routes, famous for their good food, spotless dining rooms, fine china, cutlery and linen, and not least for their waitresses — nationally advertised for as "young women of good character, attractive and intelligent, 18-30" — the widely respected Harvey Girls.

15. K. Sanborn, *op. cit.*, p. 5.

16. Ratcliffe Hicks, *Southern California; or, The Land of the Afternoon*, Springfield, Mass., 1898, pp. 40-1, 9, 65-6.

    Travelling in 1872, J.E. Lester had found that "The designation is rather indefinite, but Southern California seems to include all that part of the State which lies to the south of Stockton." See *The Atlantic to the Pacific*, Boston and London, 1873, p. 209. By the late 1880s-1890s, however, Southern California was identified as the region south of the Tehachapi Mountains.

17. John Wesley Hanson, *The American Italy: the scenic wonderland . . .*, Chicago, 1896, p. 201.

18. John Muir, *Our National Parks*, Boston and New York, 1901, p. 56. This extract first published in "The Yellowstone National Park", *The Atlantic Monthly*, vol. 81, 1898, pp. 509-22.

19. E. Pomeroy, *op. cit.*, p. 125.

20. *Crofutt's Grip-Sack Guide of Colorado* (1885), p. 100.

21. "Camping Out", in W.G.M. Stone, *Denver and its Outings*, Denver, 1892, pp. 102-3.

22. W. Lindley and J.P. Widney, *California of the South, op. cit.*, 3rd edit. 1896, p. 259.

23. John Muir, *Our National Parks, op. cit.*, p. 1. (*The Atlantic Monthly*, vol. 81, 1898, pp. 15-28).

24. John Muir, *Our National Parks, op. cit.*, p. 34. (*The Atlantic Monthly*, ibid.).

25. Quoted by Glenn Chesney Quiett, *They Built the West: An Epic of Rails and Cities*, New York and London, 1934, pp. 288-9.

26. Sara White Isaman, *Tourist Tales of California*, Los Angeles, 1907, p. 13.

27. Isaac B. Potter, President of the League of American Wheelmen, "The Bicycle Outlook", *The Century Magazine*, vol. 52, 1896, p. 789. (Quoted by Gary Allan Tobin, "The Bicycle Boom of the 1890s", *Journal of Popular Culture*, vol. 7, 1973-4, pp. 838-49. This reference p. 839.)

28. J.E. Baur, *op. cit.*, p. 26. See also, M. Cerf, "The Wheel in California", *The Overland Monthly*, vol. 22 (Second Series), 1893, pp. 391-400.

29. Charles Dudley Warner, *Our Italy*, New York, 1891, pp. 150, 153, 199, and *passim*.

30. John Muir, on Tioga Road, 21 August 1895, in *John of the Mountains: the unpublished journals of John Muir*, edit. by Linnie M. Wolfe, Boston, 1938, p. 347.

31. W. Finley Thompson, *A Brief Description of Palmer Lake and its Environs, as a Health and Pleasure Resort*, Denver, 1884, p. 6.

32. E. Chapin Gard, *Palmer Lake, the Gem of the Rockies*, Palmer Lake, 1894, p. 31.

33. The Chautauqua Movement, founded by Methodists John H. Vincent and Lewis Miller, had originally been planned as a program for training Sunday School teachers, but while maintaining the traditional Bible classes, the Movement soon broadened its interests into a wide range of educational activities. California Methodists established the Pacific Grove Retreat on the Monterey peninsula in 1875, and Chautauqua Summer Schools expanded right across the United States in the 1880s and 1890s. The Colorado Assembly also took place at Boulder, and in the Garden of the Gods in the early 1900s. Nationally, the Chautauqua Movement had a significant and lasting influence on North American adult education, particularly the growth of Summer Schools, University Extension, and Correspondence Courses.

34. *Crofutt's Grip-Sack Guide of Colorado* (1885), p. 32.

35. See Table of Bicycle and Tricycle Repair Establishments, Manufactures: Special Reports on Selected Industries, in U.S. Department of the Interior, *Twelfth Census of the United States, 1900*.

36. *Crofutt's Grip-Sack Guide of Colorado* (1885), pp. 37-41.

37. H.A. MacFadden, *op. cit.*, p. 248. In 1890-1, the first steps had also been taken to create the Broadmoor resort region at Colorado Springs. Although Count James Pourtales' Broadmoor Casino burned in 1897, the Broadmoor Hotel and adjacent area were afterwards developed into a highly successful resort complex by the wealthy local entrepreneur, Spencer Penrose.

38. C.D. Warner, *op. cit.*, p. 184.

39. *Salt Lake Chamber of Commerce, Sixth Annual Report, for the Year 1892*, Salt Lake City, 1893, p. 23.

40. Frances Fuller Victor, "Northern Seaside Resorts", *The Overland Monthly*, vol. 23 (Second Series), 1894, pp. 138-49. These references pp. 138, 140, 149.

41. S.W. Isaman, *op. cit.*, p. 18.

42. James Fullarton Muirhead, *The Land of Contrasts*, Boston, New York, London, 1898, pp. 229-30.

43. *Ibid.*, p. 219.

44. *Ibid.*, p. 161.

45. Henry Gannett, *Statistical Atlas of the United States, based upon results of the Eleventh Census* (1890), U.S. Department of the Interior, Census Office, Washington, D.C., 1898, p. 14.

    The Superintendent of the Census (1890) had reported: "Up to and including 1880 the country had a frontier of settlement, but at present the unsettled area has been so broken into by isolated bodies of settlement that there can hardly be said to be a frontier line. In the discussion of its extent, its westward movement, etc., it can not, therefore, any longer have a place in the census reports." Frederick Jackson Turner took these words as his text for his influential paper read in Chicago in July 1893 entitled "The Significance of the Frontier in American History."

    After Henry Gannett's introduction to Colorado as a student in 1869 (see Note 11, Chap. VII), he was appointed as topographer to the Hayden Surveys of Colorado and Wyoming in 1872, and later became the Geographer of the Tenth (1880), Eleventh (1890) and Twelfth (1900) Censuses of the United States. In a long and distinguished career, Gannett was also associated with the founding, *inter alia*, of the National Geographic Society in 1888, and the Association of American Geographers in 1904.

Epilogue.   Closing The Frontier

1. R.H. Davis, *op. cit.*, p. 226.

2. William Newton Byers, *Encyclopedia of Biography of Colorado*, vol. 1, Chicago, 1901, p. 283. Only one volume was ever published; Byers died in 1903. There is no biographical entry for Crofutt in this, or any other, encyclopedia.

3. See *List of Officers of El Paso Lodge No. 13, A.F.A.M., 1866 to 1967*, Colorado Springs Public Library records. For general background, see George B. Clark, *Masonry Came to Colorado, 1858-1956*, Colorado Historical Society, Denver.

   Crofutt was never a Mason, either in the Eastern or Western States.

4. F. Fossett, *Colorado*, New York, 1879, p. 461.

5. *Ibid.*, 2nd edit. 1880, pp. 458-9.

6. List compiled by E.A. Willoughby, Secretary of the Colorado Pioneer Association, and included in William Byers' *Encyclopedia of Biography of Colorado, op. cit.*, p. 165.

7. *Rocky Mountain News*, 26 December 1900.

8. *The Denver Field and Farm*, 4 August 1888, reporting their arrival on Monday, 30 July 1888.

9. *The Denver Times*, 25 March 1902.

10. Now in the *Special Collections*, Palmer Wing, Colorado Springs Public Library (Pikes Peak Regional Library District, Local History Division).

11. Articles of Incorporation, *Company Registrations*, Colorado State Archives and Public Records, Denver.

12. *United States Patent Office Records*, Patent Nos. 741,631 and 741,632.

13. Although a number of the entries are correct, Crofutt's death certificate (George A. Crofutt; State of New York) also contains several demonstrable inaccuracies (e.g. length of residence in New York City, 50 years) — probably the result of confusion on Crofutt's, or the hospital authorities', part.

14. The individual most frequently credited with making the first transcontinental automobile trip is Dr. Horatio Nelson Jackson, a surgeon from Vermont who left San Francisco on 23rd May and arrived in New York City on 26th July 1903, travelling in his own regular model Winton automobile, 20 h.p. See *New York Times*, 2 August 1903. Although the trip was not a special promotion, the Winton Motor Carriage Co. of Cleveland subsequently published an account of the journey in a book entitled *The Transcontinental Automobile Record*. Two more transcontinental automobile trips from San Francisco to New York City were also completed in 1903. See F.E. Brimmer, *Motor Campcraft*, New York, 1923, pp. 206-9. Claims to earlier transcontinental motor trips (by J.M. Murdock in 1898, and T. Fetch in 1902) are recorded in the Lincoln Highway Association's *The Lincoln Highway: the Story of a Crusade that made Transportation History*, New York, 1935, pp. 6-7.

LIST OF SOURCES

*   *   *   *   *

I U.S. GOVERNMENT PUBLICATIONS AND NATIONAL COLLECTIONS

National Archives, Washington, D.C.:
> U.S. Bureau of the Census
> U.S. Bureau of Land Management
> Post Office Department Records

U.S. District Court Records for the Southern District of New York, Federal Archives and Records Center, Bayonne, New Jersey.

U.S. Patent Office Records, Crystal City, Virginia.

Smithsonian Institution, Washington, D.C.:
> National Museum of American Art
> National Museum of American History, Division of
>   Transportation

Library of Congress, Washington, D.C.:
> Main, Rare Book and Special Collections
> Copyright Office
> Geography and Map Division
> Law Library; House and Senate Executive Documents
>   *U.S. Statutes at Large*
>   *The Congressional Globe, 1833-73*
> Local History and Genealogy Room
> Newspaper Collection
> Prints and Photographs Collection

II OTHER PRINTED, MANUSCRIPT, AND CARTOGRAPHIC COLLECTIONS

Harvard University; the Baker, Kress, and Widener Libraries.

Yale University; the Beinecke Rare Book and Manuscript Library, Western
   Americana Collection.

Boston Public Library; the Research Library.

New York Public Library.

The New-York Historical Society.

Museum of the City of New York.

The Historical Society of Pennsylvania, Philadelphia.

The Library Company of Philadelphia.
The Presbyterian Historical Society, Philadelphia.
The Historical Society of Berks County, Reading, Pennsylvania.

The Danbury Scott-Fanton Museum and Historical Society, Danbury, Connecticut.
Danbury Public Library; Special Collections.
City Hall Archives, Danbury, Connecticut.

University of Kansas, Lawrence; the Kenneth Spencer Research Library, Kansas Collection.
The Elizabeth M. Watkins Community Museum and Archive Collection, Lawrence, Kansas.

Colorado State Archives and Public Records, Denver.
Colorado State Historical Society, Denver.
Denver Public Library; Western History Department
                          Genealogical Department.
University of Colorado, Boulder; Western History Collection.
University of Denver Library.
Pikes Peak Regional Library, Colorado Springs; Local History Division.
Colorado College, Colorado Springs; Tutt Library Special Collections.
Pueblo Regional Library; Western Research Collection.
Douglas County Clerk and Records Division, Castle Rock, Colorado.

Utah State Historical Society and Division of State History, Salt Lake City.
Salt Lake City Public Library; Local History Collection.
University of Utah, Special Collections.

Oregon Historical Society, Portland, Oregon.
The Library Association of Portland, Oregon; the John Wilson Collection.

The Huntington Library, San Marino, California.
The Bancroft Library, University of California, Berkeley.
California State Library, Sacramento.
California Historical Society, San Francisco and Los Angeles.
San Francisco Archives, San Francisco Public Library Collection.
University of California, Los Angeles; Research Library and Special Collections.
Seaver Center for Western History Research, Natural History Museum of Los Angeles County.
Los Angeles County Public Library, Rosemead; the Californiana Collection.
Pasadena Public Library; Local History Department.
San Diego Public Library; the California Collection.

The British Library, London.
The Royal Geographical Society, London.
University of London Library, and the Institute of Historical Research.
Thomas Cook Ltd, London; Company Archives.

III NEWSPAPERS

Extensive study has been made of western newspaper files, and of the major New York, Boston, and Philadelphia newspapers, among others, at selected periods. This list includes only those cited in the Notes to the text.

Boston Globe, 16 April 1907.
Buffalo Commercial Advertiser, 25 June 1845.
Colorado City Iris, 1 January 1898; 8 January 1898; 8 July 1904.
Colorado City Journal, 28 November 1861.
Colorado Episcopalian (Denver), June 1959.
Colorado Springs Gazette, 7 August 1880. (Weekly edition begins as *Out West*, 23 March 1872-26 December 1872. *Out West* (New Series), monthly, begins July 1873).
Daily Missouri Republican (St. Louis, Mo.), 10 March 1859.
Daily Morning Chronicle (San Francisco), 11 May 1869.
Danbury Times (Danbury, Conn.), 1845-70; continued as the *Danbury News*.
Denver Field and Farm, 4 August 1888; 20 May 1905.
Denver Post, 20 October 1908.
Denver Republican, 14 September 1883.
Denver Times, 1 June 1896; 25 March 1902.
Denver Tribune, 9 January 1881.
Deseret News (Salt Lake City), 19 May 1869.
Eye (Needles, California), 12 May 1894.
Fowler Tribune (Fowler, Colorado), 24 July 1936.
Kansas Herald of Freedom (Lawrence, Kansas), 24 April 1858-17 December 1859.
Lawrence Republican, 28 May 1857-13 November 1862.
Los Angeles Times, 7 March 1886.
Los Angeles Tribune, 11 March 1888.
Missouri Democrat (St. Louis, Mo.), 10 and 12 December 1859.
New-York Mirror, 15 November 1828.
New York Times, 2 August 1903.
New-York Tribune, 29 May; 5, 22, 25, 26 June; 12, 19, 28 July; 2 August 1869.
Pasadena Chronicle, 22 November 1883.
Rochester Daily Advertiser, 19 April 1830.
Rochester Daily Democrat, 24 April 1843; 5 September 1846.
Rochester Union and Advertiser, 2 October 1876.
Rocky Mountain News (Denver; begins 23 April 1859), 14 May 1859; June 1860; 20 April 1863; 25 and 27 September 1865; 1 and 26 March 1866; 12 March 1871; 13 May 1882; 8 September 1898; 26 and 30 December 1900.
Rocky Mountain Presbyterian (Denver), June 1872.
St. Louis Evening News, 17 March 1859.
Salt Lake Daily Tribune (Salt Lake City), 20 May 1888.
Salt Lake Herald (Salt Lake City), 2 August 1885.

IV BOOKS AND ARTICLES

This list includes references cited in the Notes to the text, and other selected material having a bearing on the theme and the period.

Abbott, Carl. *Colorado, a history of the Centennial State*, Boulder: Colorado Associated Univ. Press, 1976. Rev. edit. with Leonard, S.J. and McComb, D., 1982.

Adams, Percy G. *Travel Literature and the Evolution of the Novel*, Lexington: Kentucky Univ. Press, 1983.

"The American Press", *The British Quarterly Review*, London, vol. 53, 1871, pp. 1-26.

Anderson, George LaVerne. *General William J. Palmer: a decade of Colorado Railroad Building, 1870-1880*, Colorado Springs, 1936.

Appletons' Northern and Eastern Traveller's Guide, edit. by W. Williams, New York, 1850, 1851.

Appletons' Southern and Western Traveller's Guide, edit. by W. Williams, New York, 1850, 1851.

Appletons' New and Complete United States Guide Book for Travellers, edit. by W. Williams, New York, 1853.

Appletons' Illustrated Hand-Book of American Travel . . . in the United States and the British Provinces, edit. by T. Addison Richards, New York, 1st publ. 1857. Title varies slightly in later editions, some of which edit. by Edward H. Hall.

Appletons' Illustrated Hand-Book of American Cities, New York, 1st publ. 1876.

Appletons' Hand-Book of Summer Resorts, illustrated, New York, 1st publ. 1876.

Appletons' Hand-Book of Winter Resorts, illustrated, New York, 1st publ. 1876.

Appletons' General Guide to the United States and Canada, New York, 1st publ. in newly revised and expanded form, 1879.

Archer, William. *America Today; observations and reflections*, New York, 1899. (Based on a journey from San Francisco to Chicago in 1877).

Arrington, Leonard J. *Great Basin Kingdom; an economic history of the Latter-Day Saints, 1830-1900*, Cambridge: Harvard Univ. Press, 1958.

Ashley, Susan Riley. "Reminiscences of Colorado in the Early 'Sixties", *The Colorado Magazine*, Denver, vol. 13, 1936, pp. 219-30.

Ashton, Wendell J. *Voice in the West; biography of a pioneer newspaper* (the *Deseret News*, Salt Lake City), New York, 1950.

Athearn, Robert G. *Westward the Briton*, New York, 1953.

— "The Denver and Rio Grande and the Panic of 1873", *The Colorado Magazine*, vol. 35, 1958, pp. 121-38.

— *High Country Empire. The High Plains and the Rockies*, New York, 1960.

— *Rebel of the Rockies: a history of the Denver and Rio Grande Western Railroad*, New Haven: Yale Univ. Press, 1962.

— *Union Pacific Country*, New York, 1971.

Atwell, H. Wallace ("Bill Dadd, the Scribe"). With George A. Crofutt (qv), *Great Trans-Continental Railroad Guide*, Chicago, 1869.

— *The Western Shore Gazetteer and Commercial Directory for the State of California, ... Yolo County*, Woodland, Cal., 1870. No further vols published.

— *Trades Magazine, devoted to California Interests. Immigrants' Land Guide for Tulare County*, San Francisco, 1885.

— , Creede and Ebbets. *San Francisco and North Pacific Sketch Book. A Brief Description of the Health and Pleasure Resorts along the line of the San Francisco & North Pacific Railroad*, San Francisco, 1888.

— *The Sunset Route. A Tourists' Guide and Immigrants' Land Directory from New Orleans to San Francisco*, San Francisco, 1888.

Aubertin, John James. *A Fight with Distances; the States, the Hawaiian Islands, Canada, British Columbia, Cuba, the Bahamas*, London, 1888.

— *Wanderings and Wonderings*, London, 1892.

Ault, Phil. *Wires West*, New York, 1974.

Ayer, I. Winslow. *Life in the Wilds of America, and Wonders of the West in and beyond the bounds of civilization*, Grand Rapids, Mich., 1880.

Bachelder, John Badger. *Bachelder's Illustrated Tourist's Guide of the United States. Popular Resorts and how to reach them*, Boston, 1873, 1874, 1875, 1876.

Badè, William F. (ed.) *The Life and Letters of John Muir*, 2 vols, Boston and New York, 1924.

Baedeker, Karl (ed.) *The United States, with an Excursion into Mexico. Handbook for Travellers* (compiled by J.F. Muirhead), Leipzig and London, 1st publ. 1893.

— *The Dominion of Canada, with Newfoundland and an Excursion to Alaska. Handbook for Travellers* (compiled by J.F. Muirhead), Leipzig and London, 1st publ. 1894.

Bailey, James Montgomery. *History of Danbury, Conn., 1684-1896*, compiled by Susan Benedict Hill, New York, 1896.

Baillie-Grohman, William Adolph. *Camps in the Rockies. Being a narrative of life on the frontier, and sport in the Rocky Mountains, with an account of the cattle ranches of the West*, London and New York, 1882.

— *Fifteen Years' Sport and Life in the Hunting Grounds of Western America and British Columbia*, London, 1900.

Baldwin, Alice Blackwood. *An Army Wife on the Frontier: the Memoirs of Alice Blackwood Baldwin*, edit. by R.C. and E.R. Carriker, Salt Lake City: Univ. of Utah Press, 1975.

Ballantine, William. *The Old World and the New*, London, 1884.

Bancroft, Hubert Howe. *The Works of Hubert Howe Bancroft*, 39 vols, San Francisco and New York, 1874-90. Histories of: Arizona and New Mexico (vol. 17); California (18-24); Nevada, Colorado and Wyoming (25); Utah (26); Northwest Coast (27-28); Oregon (29-30); Washington, Idaho and Montana (31).

Barber, John Warner. *Connecticut Historical Collections, containing a general collection of interesting facts, traditions, biographical sketches, anecdotes, etc. relating to the history and antiquities of every town in Connecticut, with geographical descriptions*, New Haven, Conn., 1836.

Barclay, James William. *The Denver and Rio Grande Railway of Colorado*, London, 1877.

Barnes, Demas. *From the Atlantic to the Pacific, Overland*, New York, 1866.

Barnum, Phineas Taylor. *The Life of P.T. Barnum, Written by Himself*, New York and London, 1855. Also, *Struggles and Triumphs; or, the Life of P.T. Barnum, Written by Himself* (covering period 1855-89), edit. by George S. Bryan, 2 vols, New York and London, 1927.

Barth, Gunther. *Instant Cities: Urbanization and the rise of San Francisco and Denver*, New York, 1975.

Bates, Henry Walter (ed.) "A Year's Tramp in Colorado", *Illustrated Travels: a record of Discovery, Geography, and Adventure*, London and New York, vol. 5, 1873, pp. 318-20, 342-8, 357-9.

Baur, John E. *The Health Seekers of Southern California, 1870-1900*, San Marino, Cal.: Huntington Library, 1959.

Beadle, John Hanson. *The Undeveloped West: or, Five Years in the Territories*, Philadelphia, Chicago, etc., 1873.

— *Western Wilds, and the men who redeem them*, Cincinnati, Philadelphia, Chicago, etc., 1878.

Beck, Joseph. *Rambling Rhymes on Western Travel*, London, 1874.

Beebe, Lucius Morris and Clegg, Charles M. *Hear the train blow; a pictorial epic of America in the railroad age*, New York, 1952.

— *The American West; the pictorial epic of a continent*, New York, 1955.

— *Narrow Gauge in the Rockies*, Berkeley, Cal., 1958.

Bell, William Abraham. *New Tracks in North America: A Journal of Travel and Adventure whilst engaged in the Survey for a Southern Railroad to the Pacific Ocean during 1867-8*, 2 vols, London and New York, 1869.

— *The Colonies of Colorado in their relations to English Enterprise and Settlement*, London, 1874.

Berger, William M. *Berger's Tourists' Guide to New Mexico, including description of towns, pueblos, churches, pictures, statues, ruins and antiquities; together with mountains, cañons, springs, and other places of interest*, Kansas City, Mo., 1883.

Billington, Ray Allen. *Westward Expansion: a History of the American Frontier*, New York and London, 1949, 4th edit. 1974.

— *America's Frontier Heritage*, New York, 1966.

— *America's Frontier Culture*, College Station: Texas A. & M. Univ. Press, and London, 1977.

— *Land of Savagery, Land of Promise: the European Image of the American Frontier in the Nineteenth Century*, New York and London, 1981.

Bird, Isabella Lucy. *A Lady's Life in the Rocky Mountains*, London, 1879.

Blaikie, William Garden. *Summer Suns in the Far West; a holiday trip to the Pacific slope*, London and New York, 1890.

Bland, David. *A History of Book Illustration*. Berkeley and Los Angeles: Univ. of California Press, 1969.

Blodgett, R. "The Colorado Territorial Board of Immigration", *The Colorado Magazine*, vol. 46, 1969, pp. 245-56.

Boorstin, Daniel Joseph. *The Image; or, What Happened to the American Dream*, New York and London, 1962.

— *The Americans*. Vol. 2, *The National Experience*, New York, 1965.

Borchert, John R. "American Metropolitan Evolution", *The Geographical Review*, New York, vol. 57, 1967, pp. 301-32.

Bowles, Samuel. *Across the Continent*, Springfield, Mass. and New York, 1865.

— *Our New West*, Hartford, Conn., 1869.

— *The Pacific Railroad — Open*, Boston, 1869.

— *The Switzerland of America: a summer vacation in the Parks and Mountains of Colorado*, Springfield, Mass., 1869.

Bowman, J.N. "Driving the Last Spike at Promontory, 1869", *California Historical Society Quarterly*, San Francisco, Vol. 36, 1957, pp. 97-106, 263-74.

Boyle, Regis Louise. *Mrs. E.D.E.N. Southworth, Novelist*, Washington, D.C.: Catholic Univ. of America Press, 1939.

Brace, Charles Loring. *The New West; or, California in 1867-1868*, New York, 1869.

Brewer, William Henry. *Rocky Mountain Letters, 1869; "Letters written to my wife during a trip to the Rocky Mountains, July to September, 1869"*, Denver, 1930.

— *Up and Down California in 1860-1864; the Journal of William H. Brewer*, edit. by Francis P. Farquhar, New Haven: Yale Univ. Press, 1930.

Brimmer, Frank Everett. *Motor Campcraft*, New York, 1923.

Brockett, Linus Pierpont. *Our Western Empire; or, the New West Beyond the Mississippi*, Philadelphia, etc., 1881.

Bromley, Isaac H. "The Wonders of the West, I. The Big Trees and the Yosemite", *Scribner's Monthly*, New York, vol. 3, 1872, pp. 261-77.

Brown, Dee Alexander. *Hear That Lonesome Whistle Blow: railroads in the West*, New York, 1977.

Bryant, Keith L. *History of the Atchison, Topeka & Santa Fe Railway*, New York, 1974.

Bryant, William Cullen (ed.) *Picturesque America*, 2 vols, New York, 1872-74.

Bryce, James. *The American Commonwealth*, 3 vols, London and New York, 1st publ. 1888.

Buckman, George Rex. "Colorado Springs", *Lippincott's Magazine*, Philadelphia, vol. 31, 1883, pp. 9-20.

— *A few words about Colorado Springs and its new hotel, The Antlers*, Chicago, 1884.

— *Colorado Springs, Colorado, and its famous scenic environs*, Colorado Springs, 1892, 2nd edit. New York, 1893.

Buel, James William. *America's Wonderlands. A Pictorial and Descriptive History of Our Country's Scenic Marvels as delineated by Pen and Camera*, New York, Boston, Philadelphia, San Francisco, etc., 1893.

Burkart, Arthur John and Medlik, S. *Tourism: Past, Present, and Future*, London, 1974.

Burroughs, John. "The Spell of the Yosemite", *The Century Illustrated Monthly Magazine*, New York, vol. 81, 1910, pp. 47-53.

Burton, Sir Richard Francis. *The City of the Saints, and across the Rocky Mountains to California*, London, 1861, New York, 1862.

Buss, Henry. *Wanderings in the West, during the year 1870*, London, 1871.

Byers, William Newton. *Encyclopedia of Biography of Colorado*, vol. 1, Chicago, 1901.

— and Kellom, J.H. *A Hand Book to the Gold Fields of Nebraska and Kansas*, Chicago and New York, 1859.

Cerf, M. "The Wheel in California", *The Overland Monthly*, San Francisco, vol. 22 (Second Series), 1893, pp. 391-400.

Chamblin, Thomas S. (ed.) *The Historical Encyclopedia of Colorado*, 2 vols, Denver, 1960.

Chapin, Frederick H. *Mountaineering in Colorado. The Peaks about Estes Park*, Boston: The Appalachian Mountain Club, 1889.

Chittenden, Newton H. *The Climate, Watering Places, Health and Pleasure Resorts of the Pacific Coast*, Santa Barbara, Cal., 1881.

— *Homes, Health and Pleasure in Southern California*, San Buenaventura, Cal., 1883.

— *Health seekers', Tourists', and Sportsmen's guide to the sea-side, lake-side, foothill, mountain and mineral spring, health and pleasure resorts of the Pacific Coast*, San Francisco, 1884.

Clark, Susie Champney. *The Round Trip from The Hub to the Golden Gate*, Boston and New York, 1890.

Clarke, Charles M. *A Trip to Pike's Peak, and Notes by the way*, Chicago, 1861.

Clay, John. *My Life on the Range* (1st publ. 1924), Norman: Univ. of Oklahoma Press, 1962.

Cleland, Robert Glass. *The Cattle on a Thousand Hills: Southern California, 1850-1870*, San Marino, Cal.: Huntington Library, 1941, 2nd edit. 1951.

— *From Wilderness to Empire: A History of California, 1542-1900*, New York, 1944.

Codman, John. *The Round Trip, by way of Panama through California, Oregon, Nevada, Utah, Idaho and Colorado*, New York, 1879.

The Colorado Springs Region as a Health Resort: High Altitudes for Invalids, Chamber of Commerce, Colorado Springs, 1898.

Conklin, Enoch. *Picturesque Arizona. Being the result of travels and observations in Arizona during the Fall and Winter of 1877*, New York, 1878.

Conway, John. *Tourists' Guide from the Yosemite Valley to Eagle Peak, for the Spring and Summer of 1879*, San Francisco, 1878, 3rd edit. 1881.

Cook, Thomas and Son. *Our American Relations*, London, New York and Boston, 1874.

— *Cook's Excursionist, American edition*, monthly beg. March 1873, New York. (In 1873-78, pub. by Cook, Son, and Jenkins; thereafter, by Thomas Cook and Son.)

Coolidge, Susan *pseud.* (Sarah Chauncy Woolsey). "A Few Hints on the California Journey", *Scribner's Monthly*, New York, vol. 6, 1873, pp. 25-31.

— *Clover*, Boston, 1888.

— *In the High Valley*, Boston, 1896.

Cordley, Richard. *A History of Lawrence, Kansas, from the first settlement to the close of the rebellion*, Lawrence, 1895.

— *Pioneer Days in Kansas*, Boston, 1903.

Crofutt, George Andrews. See full list of publications, pp. 403-5.

Cromwell, George R. (ed.) *America, Scenic and Descriptive. From Alaska to the Gulf of Mexico*, New York, 1894.

Crump, Spencer. *Ride the Big Red Cars; how trolleys helped build Southern California*, Los Angeles, 1962, 2nd edit. 1965.

Daggett, Stuart. *Chapters on the History of the Southern Pacific*, New York, 1922.

Dale, Matthew H. "Life in the Pike's Peak Region: the letters of Matthew H. Dale", edit. by R.G. Athearn, *The Colorado Magazine*, vol. 32, 1955, pp. 1-24.

Dall, Caroline Wells Healey. *My First Holiday; or, Letters Home from Colorado, Utah, and California*, Boston, 1881.

Dana, Charles Anderson. *The Scenery of the United States, illustrated in a series of forty engravings*, New York, 1855.

Darrah, William Culp. *Stereo Views: A History of Stereographs in America and their collection*, Gettysburg, Pa, 1964.

Davidson, Lillias Campbell. *Hints to Lady Travellers at Home and Abroad*, London, 1889.

Davis, Richard Harding. *The West from a Car-Window*, New York, 1892.

Davison, Gideon Miner. *The Fashionable Tour. A Guide to Travellers visiting the Middle and Northern States, and the provinces of Canada*, Saratoga Springs and New York, 4th edit. enlarged and improved, 1830, 8th edit. 1840.

Denison, Charles. *The Influence of the Climate of Colorado on the Nervous System*, Denver, 1875.

— *Rocky Mountain Health Resorts*, Boston, 1880, 2nd edit. 1881.

— *The Climatic Treatment of Pulmonary Consumption*, Denver, 1883.

— *Dryness and Elevation, the most important elements in the treatment of phthisis*, New York, 1884.

— *Exercise for Pulmonary Invalids*, Denver, 1893.

Dillon, Sidney. "Historic Moments: Driving the Last Spike of the Union Pacific", *Scribner's Magazine*, New York, vol. 12, 1892, pp. 253-9.

Dimsdale, Thomas Josiah. *The Vigilantes of Montana; or, Popular Justice in the Rocky Mountains*, Virginia City, Montana, 1865.

Dixon, William Hepworth. *New America*, 2 vols, London, 1867.

— *White Conquest*, 2 vols, London, 1876.

Dodge, Grenville Mellen. "How We Built the Union Pacific Railway", *Senate Documents*, 61st Congress, 2nd Session, vol. 59, Serial No. 5658, Washington, D.C., 1910.

Dorsett, Lyle W. *The Queen City: a history of Denver*, Boulder, Colorado, 1977.

Duke, Donald. "Pacific Electric Railway: a pictorial album of electric railroading", *Pacific Railway Journal*, San Marino, Cal., vol. 2, Sept. 1958.

Dulles, Foster Rhea. *A History of Recreation: America Learns to Play*, New York, 1940, 2nd edit. 1965.

Dumke, Glenn S. *The Boom of the Eighties in Southern California*, San Marino, Cal.: Huntington Library, 1944.

Dunbar, Seymour. *A History of Travel in America*, 4 vols, Indianapolis, 1915.

Dunbar, Mrs. Simeon J. *Colorado Springs and Manitou*, Colorado Springs, 1883.

Dunraven, Windham Thomas Wyndham-Quin, 4th Earl of. *The Great Divide. Travels in the Upper Yellowstone in the Summer of 1874*, London, 1876.

— *Past Times and Pastimes*, 2 vols, London, 1922.

Dwight, Timothy. *Travels; in New-England and New-York*, 4 vols, New Haven, Conn., 1821-22.

Edwards, Sir Henry. *A Two Months' Tour in Canada and the United States, in the autumn of 1889*, London, 1889.

Edwards, William A. and Harraden, Beatrice. *Two Health-Seekers in Southern California*, Philadelphia, 1897.

Eitel, Edward E. *The Southern Pacific Sketch Book; Illustrated Sketches of the Principal Health and Pleasure Resorts of California and the South-West, embracing Pacific Grove, Yosemite, Los Angeles, New Orleans and the Chief Points of Interest*, San Francisco, 1887.

Ellis, Amanda M. *The Strange, Uncertain Years. An informal account of life in six Colorado communities*, Hamden, Conn., 1959.

Emerson, Ralph Waldo. *Nature*, 1st publ. Boston, 1836. Also, *Nature; An Essay. And Lectures on the Times*, London, 1844.

Enock, Charles Reginald. *The Great Pacific Coast; Twelve Thousand Miles in the Golden West*, London, 1909, New York, 1910.

— *Farthest West; Life and Travel in the United States*, London and New York, 1910.

Evans, Cerinda W. *Collis Potter Huntington*, 2 vols, Newport News, Va, 1954.

Fabian, Rainier and Adam, Hans-Christian. *Masters of Early Travel Photography*, Hamburg, Paris and New York, 1981.

Faithfull, Emily. *Three Visits to America*, Edinburgh and New York, 1884.

Fergusson, J.C. *The Alta California Pacific Coast and Trans-Continental Rail-Road Guide*, San Francisco, 1871.

Finck, Henry T. "Southern California Revisited", *The Nation*, New York, 19 Oct. 1893, pp. 282-4.

Fisher, John S. *A Builder of the West: the Life of General William Jackson Palmer*, Caldwell, Idaho, 1939.

Fisher, Sidney George. *A Philadelphia Perspective. The Diary of Sidney George Fisher, 1834-71*, edit. by N.B. Wainwright, Philadelphia: The Historical Society of Pennsylvania, 1962.

Fite, Gilbert Courtland. *The Farmer's Frontier, 1865-1900*, New York, 1966.

Flake, Chad J. (ed.) *A Mormon Bibliography, 1830-1930*, Salt Lake City, 1978.

Fogel, Robert William. *Railroads and American Economic Growth: Essays on Econometric History*, Baltimore and London: Johns Hopkins Press, 1964.

"Fortunes in Colorado — the Atlantic-Pacific Tunnel", *St. Louis Illustrated Magazine*, St. Louis, Mo., Oct. 1881, pp. 375-82.

Fossett, Frank. *Colorado; a historical, descriptive, and statistical work on the Rocky Mountain gold and silver mining region*, Denver, 1876.

— *Colorado; its Gold and Silver Mines, Farms and Stock Ranges, and Health and Pleasure Resorts. Tourist's guide to the Rocky Mountains*, New York, 1879, 2nd edit. 1880.

Freedley, Edwin Troxell. *Philadelphia and its Manufactures: . . . in 1857*, Philadelphia, 1858.

Frémont, John Charles. *A Report of an Exploration of the Country lying between the Missouri River and the Rocky Mountains on the line of the Kansas and Great Platte Rivers*, Washington, D.C., 1843.

— *Report of the Exploring Expedition to the Rocky Mountains in the Year 1842, and to Oregon and North California in the Years 1843-'44*, Washington, D.C., 1845. Also, *Narratives of Exploration and Adventure*, edit. by Allan Nevins (incl. the first three expeditions and Frémont's "Geographical Memoir upon Upper California"), New York, 1956.

Frewen, Moreton. *Melton Mowbray and Other Memories*, London, 1924.

Frost, Max and Walter, Paul A.F. (eds) *The Land of Sunshine: A Handbook of the Resources, Industries and Climate of New Mexico*, Santa Fe, 1904, 1906.

Fuller (Ossoli), Sarah Margaret. *At Home and Abroad; or, Things and Thoughts in America and Europe*, edit. by Arthur B. Fuller, Boston, 1874.

Gage, Emma Abbott. *Western Wanderings and Summer Saunterings through Picturesque Colorado*, Baltimore, 1900.

Galloway, John Debo. *The First Transcontinental Railroad, Central Pacific Union Pacific*, New York, 1950.

Gannett, Henry. *Statistical Atlas of the United States, based upon results of the Eleventh Census (1890)*, U.S. Department of the Interior, Census Office, Washington, D.C., 1898.

Gard, E. Chapin. *Palmer Lake, the Gem of the Rockies*, Palmer Lake, Colorado, 1894.

Gardner, S.A. "A Trip to Colorado in 1878", *Peoria Evening Call*, Illinois, 27, 29 July; 1, 10 Aug. 1878.

Gatchell, Horatio P. *The Invalid's Guide: or, Where to go in search of Health*, Atlanta, Ga, 1880.

Giddings, Jennie Hollingsworth. *I Can Remember Early Pasadena*, Los Angeles, 1949.

Gilpin, William. *Notes on Colorado*, London, 1870.

— *The Mission of the North American People: Geographical, Social, and Political*, Philadelphia, 1873, 2nd edit. 1874. (1st publ. as *The Central Gold Region*, Philadelphia and St. Louis, 1860).

Gleed, Charles Sumner. *From River to Sea; a tourists' and miners' guide from the Missouri River to the Pacific Ocean*, Chicago, 1882.

— (ed.) *Rand, McNally & Co.'s Overland Guide from the Missouri River to the Pacific Ocean, via Kansas, Colorado, New Mexico, Arizona, and California. The Southern Route*, Chicago, 1883, rev. edit. 1885.

Goetzmann, William H. *Exploration and Empire. The Explorer and the Scientist in the Winning of the American West, 1805-1900*, New York, 1966.

Goode, William H. *Outposts of Zion, with Limnings of Mission Life*, Cincinnati, 1863.

Goodrich, Carter. *Government Promotion of American Canals and Railroads, 1800-1890*, New York, 1960.

Goodrich, Samuel Griswold. *Peter Parley's Own Story*, New York, 1864.

Gordon, S. Anna. *Camping in Colorado*, New York, 1879.

Greatorex, Eliza. *Summer Etchings in Colorado*, New York, 1873.

Greeley, Horace. *An Overland Journey, from New York to San Francisco, in the Summer of 1859*, New York and San Francisco, 1860.

Greenwood, Grace *pseud.* (Mrs. Sara Jane Clarke Lippincott). *New Life in New Lands: Notes of Travel*, New York, 1873.

Greever, William S. *Arid Domain: The Santa Fe Railway and its Western Land Grant*, Stanford Univ. Press, 1954.

Griswold, Wesley S. *The Work of Giants: Building the first Transcontinental Railroad*, London, 1963.

Grodinsky, Julius. *Jay Gould: his business career, 1867-1892*, Philadelphia: Univ. of Pennsylvania Press, 1957.

— *Transcontinental Railway Strategy, 1869-1893: a study of businessmen*, Philadelphia: Univ. of Pennsylvania Press, 1962.

Guinn, James M. "The Great Real Estate Boom of 1887", *Publications of the Historical Society of Southern California*, Los Angeles, vol.1 (1884-91), 1890, pp. 13-21.

Hafen, LeRoy R. "Pioneer Struggles for a Colorado Road across the Rockies", *The Colorado Magazine*, vol. 3, 1926, pp. 1-10.

— *The Overland Mail, 1849-1869*, Cleveland, Ohio, 1926.

— (ed.) *The Pike's Peak Goldrush Guidebooks of 1859*, Glendale, Cal., 1941.

— (ed.) *Overland Routes to the Gold Fields, from contemporary diaries*, Glendale, Cal., 1942.

— and Hafen, Ann Woodbury (eds) *Reports from Colorado; The Wildman Letters, 1859-1865, with other related letters and newspaper reports, 1859*, Glendale, Cal., 1961.

Halaas, David Fridtjof. *Boom Town Newspapers: Journalism on the Rocky Mountain Mining Frontier, 1859-1881*, Albuquerque: Univ. of New Mexico Press, 1981.

Hale, Edward Everett. *A New England Boyhood*, New York, 1893.

Hale, Sarah Josepha Buell. *Sketches of American Character*, Boston, 1829.

— *Traits of American Life*, Philadelphia, 1835.

Hall, Edward Hepple. *The Great West. Emigrants', Settlers', and Travellers' Guide and Hand-Book to the States of California and Oregon, and the Territories of Nebraska, Utah, Colorado, Idaho, Montana, Nevada, Wash-*

ington and Arizona. With a Full and Accurate Account of their Climate, Soil, Resources, and Products, New York, 1st publ. 1864. Sub-title varies slightly in later editions.

Hall, Frank. *History of the State of Colorado*, 4 vols, Chicago, 1889-95.

Hamer, P.W. *From Ocean to Ocean, being a Diary of a Three Months' Expedition from Liverpool to California and Back, from the Atlantic to the Pacific by the Overland Route*, London, 1871.

Handlin, Oscar. *This Was America: true accounts of people and places, manners and customs, as recorded by European travelers to the western shore in the eighteenth, nineteenth, and twentieth centuries*, Cambridge: Harvard Univ. Press., 1949.

Hanson, John Wesley. *The American Italy: the scenic wonderland of perfect climate, golden sunshine, ever-blooming flowers and always-ripening fruits. Southern California*, Chicago, 1896.

Hardy, Lady Duffus. *Through Cities and Prairie Lands; Sketches of an American Tour*, London and New York, 1881.

Harper's New York and Erie Rail-Road Guide Book, New York, 1st publ. 1851.

Harriman, Karl Edwin. "The Trolley Car as a Social Factor", *The World To-day*, Chicago, vol.10, 1906, pp.137-44.

Hatton, Joseph. *Today in America. Studies for the Old World and the New*, 2 vols, London, 1881.

Hayden, Ferdinand Vandeveer. *Sun Pictures of Rocky Mountain Scenery, with a description of the geographical and geological features, and some account of the resources of the Great West*, New York, 1870.

— "The Wonders of the West, II. More about the Yellowstone", *Scribner's Monthly*, New York, vol. 3, 1872, pp. 388-96.

— *Catalogue of the Publications of the United States Geological Survey of the Territories*, F.V. Hayden, geologist in charge, Washington, D.C., 1874, 2nd edit. 1877, 3rd edit. 1879.

— *Geological and Geographical Atlas of Colorado and portions of adjacent territory*, New York, 1877.

— *The Great West; its attractions and resources*, Bloomington, Ill., 1880.

Hayes, Jr., Augustus Allen. "Vacation Aspects of Colorado", *Harper's New Monthly Magazine*, New York, vol. 60, 1880, pp. 542-57.

—*New Colorado and the Santa Fe Trail*, New York, 1880.

Hayes, H. Wilbur. *The Great Resorts of America*, Portland, Maine, 1893.

Hazard, Lucy Lockwood. *The Frontier in American Literature*, New York, 1927.

Hedges, James Blaine. *Henry Villard and the Railways of the Northwest*, New Haven: Yale Univ. Press, 1930.

Herndon, Mrs. Sarah Raymond. *Days on the road; crossing the plains in 1865*, New York, 1902.

Hicks, Ratcliffe. *Southern California; or, The Land of the Afternoon*, Springfield, Mass., 1898.

Hinton, Richard Josiah. *The Hand-book to Arizona; its Resources, History, Towns, Mines, Ruins, and Scenery*, San Francisco and New York, 1878.

447

History of the Arkansas Valley, Colorado, Chicago: O.L. Baskin, 1881.

Hittell, John Shertzer. *The Resources of California, comprising the Society, Climate, Salubrity, Scenery, Commerce and Industry of the State*, San Francisco and New York, 1st publ. 1863, 6th edit. rewritten, 1874, 7th edit. 1879.

Hoig, Stan. *The Sand Creek Massacre*, Norman: Univ. of Okla. Press, 1961.

Holder, Charles Frederick. *All About Pasadena and its Vicinity*, Boston and New York, 1889.

Hollister, Ovando. *The Mines of Colorado*, Springfield, Mass., 1867.

Hollon, William Eugene. *The Southwest: Old and New*, New York, 1961.

Home Comforts. The Tourists' Guide and Directory to the Hotels, Boarding and Rooming Places of Los Angeles and Pasadena, Los Angeles, 1894.

Hooper, Shadrach Kemp (Denver & Rio Grande Railroad). See selected list of company publications (1885-1909) of which Hooper was sole or joint author, p. 322.

Howbert, Irving. *Memories of a Lifetime in the Pike's Peak Region*, New York and London, 1925.

Hoyt, A.W. "Over the Plains to Colorado", *Harper's New Monthly Magazine*, New York, vol. 35, 1867, pp. 1-21.

Hudson, T.S. *A Scamper through America; or, Fifteen Thousand Miles of Ocean and Continent in Sixty Days*, London and New York, 1882.

Humason, William Lawrence. *From the Atlantic Surf to the Golden Gate*, Hartford, Conn., 1869.

Hutchings, James Mason. *Scenes of Wonder and Curiosity in California*, San Francisco, 1st publ. 1860.

— *Hutchings' Tourist's Guide to the Yosemite Valley and the Big Tree Groves for the Spring and Summer of 1877*, San Francisco, 1877.

— *In the Heart of the Sierras; the Yosemite Valley, both historical and descriptive; and scenes by the way*, Oakland, Cal., 1st publ. 1883.

— *Souvenir of California, Yosemite and the Big Trees; what to see and how to see it*, San Francisco, 1894, 1895.

Huth, Hans. *Nature and the American: three centuries of changing attitudes*, Berkeley: Univ. of California Press, 1957.

Iddings, Lewis Morris. "Life in the Altitudes: Colorado's Health Plateau", *Scribner's Magazine*, New York, vol. 19, 1896, pp. 136-51.

Ingersoll, Ernest. *Knocking Round the Rockies*, New York, 1883.

— *The Crest of the Continent: a Record of a Summer's Ramble in the Rocky Mountains and Beyond*, Chicago, 1885.

Isaman, Sara White. *Tourist Tales of California*, Los Angeles, 1907.

Isely, Elise Dubach. *Sunbonnet Days*, as told to her son Bliss Isely, Caldwell, Idaho, 1935.

Jackson, Helen Maria Fiske Hunt (H.H.). *Bits of Travel at Home*, Boston, 1st publ. 1878.

— "Echoes in the City of Angels", *The Century Magazine*, New York, vol. 27, 1883, pp. 194-210.

— *Glimpses of California and the Missions* (1st publ. 1883), Boston, 1902.

Jackson, William Henry. "Photographing the Colorado Rockies Fifty Years Ago", *The Colorado Magazine*, vol. 3, 1926, pp. 11-22.

— *Time Exposure*, New York, 1940.

Jackson, William Turrentine. *Wagon Roads West; a study of Federal Road Surveys and Construction in the Trans-Mississippi West, 1846-1869*, Berkeley and Los Angeles: Univ. of California Press, 1952.

James, Bushrod Washington. *American Resorts; with Notes upon their Climate*, Philadelphia and London, 1889.

James, Edwin (comp.). *Account of an Expedition from Pittsburgh to the Rocky Mountains, performed in the years 1819 and 1820, ... under the command of Major Stephen H. Long. From the notes of Major Long, (et al.) ...* , 2 vols, Philadelphia, 1822-23.

James, George Wharton. *Pasadena and the Mount Lowe Railway. The ideal health and pleasure resort of the world*, Echo Mountain, Cal., 1894. (*Scenic Mount Lowe and its wonderful railway*, Los Angeles, 5th edit., 1905).

— *Tourists' Guide Book to South California for the Traveler, Invalid, Pleasurist, and Homeseeker*, Los Angeles, 1st publ. 1894.

— *In and Around the Grand Canyon; the Grand Canyon of the Colorado River in Arizona*, Boston, 1st publ. 1900.

— *Travelers' Handbook to Southern California*, Pasadena, Cal., 1904.

— *The 1910 trip of the Hotel Men's Mutual Benefit Association to California and the Pacific Coast*, San Francisco, 1911.

— *The Lake of the Sky, Lake Tahoe, in the High Sierras of California and Nevada*, Pasadena, Cal., 1st publ. 1915.

James, Henry. *The American Scene*, London and New York, 1907.

Jeffrey, Julie Roy. *Frontier Women: the Trans-Mississippi West, 1840-1880*, New York, 1979.

Jocknick, Sidney. *Early Days on the Western Slope of Colorado, and Campfire Chats with Otto Mears, the Pathfinder, from 1870 to 1883 inclusive*, Denver, 1913.

Jones, Billy Mac. *Health-Seekers in the Southwest, 1817-1900*, Norman: Univ. of Oklahoma Press, 1967.

King, Doris Elizabeth. "The First-Class Hotel and the Age of the Common Man", *The Journal of Southern History*, Southern Historical Assoc., vol. 23, 1957, pp. 173-88.

Kingsley, Charles. *Charles Kingsley's American Notes; Letters from a Lecture Tour, 1874*, edit. by Robert Bernard Martin, Princeton, N.J.: Princeton Univ. Library, 1958.

See also, *Charles Kingsley: His Letters and Memories of His Life, edited by his wife*, London, 1st publ. 1876.

Kingsley, Rose Georgina. *South by West; or, Winter in the Rocky Mountains and Spring in Mexico*, with a preface by Rev. Charles Kingsley, London, 1874.

Kipling, J. Rudyard. *From Sea to Sea; Letters of Travel*, 2 vols, New York, 1899, London, 1900.

Lamar, Howard Roberts. *The Far Southwest, 1846-1912: A Territorial History*, New Haven: Yale Univ. Press, 1966.

— (ed.) *The Reader's Encyclopedia of the American West*, New York, 1977.

Lamb, Grace I. "History of Douglas County Schools from Early Records", *Record-Journal, Douglas County*, Castle Rock, Colorado, March 1949.

Langford, Nathaniel Pitt. "The Wonders of Yellowstone", *Scribner's Monthly*, New York, vol. 2, 1871, pp. 1-17, 113-28.

— *Vigilante Days and Ways; the Pioneers of the Rockies; The Makers and Making of Montana, Idaho, Washington, and Wyoming*, 2 vols, Boston, 1890, New York, 1893.

Larson, Henrietta Melia. *Jay Cooke, private banker*, Cambridge: Harvard Univ. Press, 1936.

Lass, William E. *From the Missouri to the Great Salt Lake: an account of Overland Freighting*, Lincoln, Nebr.: Nebraska State Historical Society Publications, vol. 26, 1972.

Lavelett, Lucille. *Monument's Faded Neighbor Communities and its Folk Lore*, Monument, Colorado, 1979.

Lavender, David Sievert. *The Rockies*, New York, 1968.

— *The Great Persuader* (Collis Potter Huntington), Garden City, N.Y., 1970.

Leclercq, Jules. *La Terre des Merveilles. Promenade au Parc National de l'Amerique du Nord*, Paris, 1886.

Legard, Allayne Beaumont. *Colorado*, 1872.

Leighton, Caroline C. *Life at Puget Sound, with Sketches of Travel in Washington Territory, British Columbia, Oregon, and California, 1865-1881*, Boston and New York, 1884.

Leng, Sir John. *America in 1876. Pencillings during a tour in the Centennial Year; with a chapter on the aspects of American Life*, Dundee and London, 1877.

Leslie, Frank. "Out West on the Overland Train—The Frank Leslie Transcontinental Excursion to the Pacific Coast", *Frank Leslie's Illustrated Newspaper*, New York, 7 July 1877 - 6 July 1878.

Leslie, Miriam Florence Folline Squier. *California. A Pleasure Trip from Gotham to the Golden Gate* (10 April - 7 June 1877). By Mrs. Frank Leslie, New York and London, 1877.

Lester, John Erastus. *The Atlantic to the Pacific. What to See, and How to See it*, Boston and London, 1873.

— *The Yosemite*, Providence, R.I., 1873.

Lewis, Oscar. *The Big Four: the story of Huntington, Stanford, Hopkins, and Crocker, and the building of the Central Pacific*, New York and London, 1938.

— and Hall, Carroll Douglas. *Bonanza Inn; America's first luxury hotel* (The Palace Hotel, San Francisco), New York and London, 1939.

Lincoln Highway Association. *The Lincoln Highway; the story of a crusade that made transportation history*, New York, 1935.

Lindley, Walter and Widney, Joseph Pomeroy. *California of the South; its Physical Geography, Climate, Resources, Routes of Travel, and Health-*

Resorts, being a complete guide-book to Southern California, New York, 1888, 3rd edit. 1896.

Linville, Leslie and Bertha. *Up the Smoky Hill Trail in 1867*, Osborne, Kansas, 1983.

Lipsey, J.J. "How Hagerman sold the Colorado Midland in 1890", *The Brand Book of Denver Westerners*, Denver, 1956, pp. 267-86.

Long, Margaret. *The Smoky Hill Trail*, Denver, 1943, 3rd edit. 1953.

Lovett, Richard. *United States Pictures drawn with pen and pencil*, London, 1891.

Low, Alfred Maurice. *America at Home*, London, 1908.

Low, Edith Parker. "History of the Twenty-Mile House on Cherry Creek", *The Colorado Magazine*, vol. 12, 1935, pp.142-4.

Ludlow, Fitz Hugh. *The Heart of the Continent*, New York and London, 1870.

Ludy, Robert Borneman. *Historic Hotels of the World, Past and Present*, Philadelphia, 1927.

Lynde, Francis. *A Romance in Transit*, New York, 1897.

Lynes, Russell. *The Taste-makers*, New York, 1954.

MacCannell, Dean. *The Tourist: a new theory of the leisure class*, New York, 1976.

McClure, Alexander Kelly. *Three Thousand Miles through the Rocky Mountains*, Philadelphia, 1869.

MacFadden, Henry Alexander. *Rambles in the Far West*, Hollidaysburg, Pennsylvania, 1906.

McFarland, Edward M. *The Midland Route: a Colorado Midland Guide and Data Book*, Boulder, Colo., 1980.

—*The Cripple Creek Road: A Midland Terminal Guide and Data Book*, Boulder, Colo., 1984.

McGowan, Joseph Aloysius. *History of the Sacramento Valley*, 3 vols, New York, 1961.

McIntosh, Robert Woodrow. *Tourism: Principles, Practices and Philosophies*, Columbus, Ohio, 1972.

McMechen, Edgar Carlisle. *The Moffat Tunnel of Colorado*, 2 vols, Denver, 1927.

McWilliams, Carey. *Southern California Country: An Island on the Land*, New York, 1946.

Majors, Alexander. *Seventy Years on the Frontier*, Chicago and New York, 1893.

"Man, Time, and Space in Southern California. A Symposium", *Annals of the Association of American Geographers*, Washington, D.C., vol. 49, 1959; Supplement.

Mandeville, Frank H. *Tourists' Guide to San Diego and Vicinity*, San Diego, 1888.

Manning, Samuel. *American Pictures drawn with pen and pencil*, London, 1876.

Marcy, Capt. Randolph Barnes. *The Prairie Traveler. A Hand-book for Overland Expeditions*, New York, 1st publ. 1859.

Marr, Josephine Lowell and Kaiser, Joan Marr. *Douglas County; A Historical Journey*, Castle Rock, Colo., 1983.

Marshall, Walter Gore. *Through America; or, Nine Months in the United States*, London, 1881.

Marx, Leo. *The Machine in the Garden: Technology and the Pastoral Ideal in America*, New York, 1964.

Mather, E. Cotton. "The American Great Plains", *Annals of the Association of American Geographers*, Washington, D.C., vol. 62, 1972, pp. 237-57.

Mayer, Lynne Rhodes and Vose, Kenneth E. *Makin' Tracks: a history of the transcontinental railroad in the pictures and words of the men who were there*, New York, 1975.

Meinig, Donald William. "The Mormon Culture Region: Strategies and Patterns in the Geography of the American West, 1847-1964", *Annals of the Association of American Geographers*, Washington, D.C., vol. 55, 1965, pp. 191-220.

— *Southwest: Three Peoples in Geographical Change, 1600-1970*, New York, 1971.

— "American Wests: Preface to a Geographical Interpretation", *Annals of the Association of American Geographers*, Washington, D.C., vol. 62, 1972, pp. 159-84.

Meline, James Florant. *Two Thousand Miles on Horseback. Santa Fe and Back; a Summer Tour through Kansas, Nebraska, Colorado, and New Mexico, in the year 1866*, New York, 1867, London, 1868.

Melvin, Jane. "The Twelve Mile House", *The Colorado Magazine*, vol. 12, 1935, pp. 173-8.

Mencken, August. *The Railroad Passenger Car*, Baltimore: Johns Hopkins Univ. Press, 1957.

Merk, Frederick. *Manifest Destiny and Mission in American History: a reinterpretation*, New York, 1963.

— *History of the Westward Movement*, New York, 1978.

Middleton, Dorothy. *Victorian Lady Travellers*, London, 1965.

Moir, Esther. *The Discovery of Britain: English Tourists, 1540-1840*, London, 1964.

Money, Edward. *The Truth about America*, London, 1886.

Morris, Maurice O'Connor. *Rambles in the Rocky Mountains; with a visit to the Gold Fields of Colorado*, London, 1864.

Morrison, Sidney B. "Letters from Colorado, 1860-63", *The Colorado Magazine*, vol. 16, 1939, pp. 90-96.

Mott, Frank Luther. *A History of American Magazines*, 5 vols, Cambridge: Harvard Univ. Press, 1938-68. (Vol. 1 1st publ. New York, 1930).

— *Golden Multitudes: the story of Best Sellers in the United States*, New York, 1947.

— *American Journalism. A History: 1690-1960*, New York, rev. 3rd edit. 1962.

Muir, John (ed.) *Picturesque California and the region west of the Rocky*

Mountains, from Alaska to Mexico, 2 vols, San Francisco and New York, 1st publ. 1888.

— *Our National Parks*, Boston and New York, 1901.

— *John of the Mountains; the unpublished journals of John Muir*, edit. by Linnie Marsh Wolfe, Boston, 1938.

— See also, Badè, William F. (ed.)

Muirhead, James Fullarton. *The Land of Contrasts. A Briton's View of his American Kin*, Boston, New York and London, 1898.

— See also, Baedeker, Karl (ed.)

Mulvey, Christopher. *Anglo-American Landscapes, a study of nineteenth-century Anglo-American Travel literature*, Cambridge: Camb. Univ. Press, 1983.

Mumey, Nolie. *History of the Early Settlements of Denver*, Glendale, Cal., 1942.

— *Amos Steck (1822-1908)*, Denver, 1981.

Murphy, John Mortimer. *Rambles in North-Western America, from the Pacific Ocean to the Rocky Mountains*, London, 1879.

— *Sporting Adventures in the Far West*, London, 1879, New York, 1880.

Nash, Roderick. *Wilderness and the American Mind*, New Haven: Yale Univ. Press, 1967, rev. edit. 1973.

Newmark, Harris. *Sixty Years in Southern California, 1853-1913*, New York, 1916, 3rd edit. 1930.

Newmark, Marco Ross. *Jottings in Southern California History*, Los Angeles, 1955.

Nims, F.C. (Denver & Rio Grande Railroad). *Health, Wealth and Pleasure in Colorado and New Mexico*, Chicago, 1881.

Nordhoff, Charles. *California: for Health, Pleasure, and Residence*, New York, 1st publ. 1872.

Norris, Frank. *The Octopus: A Story of California. The Epic of Wheat*, New York, 1901.

Notes by a Wanderer from Demerara, in the United States, Demerara, British Guiana, 1885.

Nuhn, Ferner Rall. *The Wind Blew from the East: a study in the orientation of American culture*, New York, 1940; reissued 1967.

Oberholtzer, Ellis Paxson. *Jay Cooke, financier of the Civil War*, 2 vols, Philadelphia, 1907.

Oehlerts, Donald E. (comp.) *Guide to Colorado Newspapers, 1859-1963*, Denver, 1964.

Off-hand Sketches; a companion for the Tourist and Traveller over the Philadelphia, Pottsville, and Reading Railroad, Philadelphia, 1854.

(The Travelers') Official Guide of the Railway and Steam Navigation Lines in the United States, Canada and Mexico, monthly, New York: The National Railway Publication Co., begins 1868. Title varies slightly.

O'Neil, Hugh F. "List of Persons Present, Promontory, Utah, May 10, 1869", *Utah Historical Quarterly*, Utah State Historical Society, vol. 24, 1956, pp. 157-64.

O'Rell, Max *pseud.* (Leon Paul Blouët). *Jonathan and his Continent. Rambles through American Society*, Bristol, London and New York, 1889.

Ormes, Manly Dayton and Eleanor Reddie. *The Book of Colorado Springs*, Colorado Springs, 1933.

Overton, Grant Martin. *Portrait of a Publisher, and the First Hundred Years of the House of Appleton, 1825-1925*, New York and London, 1925.

Overton, Richard Cleghorn. *Gulf to Rockies: the heritage of the Fort Worth and Denver-Colorado and Southern Railways, 1861-1898*, Austin: Univ. of Texas Press, 1953.

Pabor, William Edgar. *Colorado as an Agricultural State. Its Farms, Fields, and Garden Lands*, New York, 1883.

Palmer, William Jackson. *Report of Surveys across the Continent in 1867-'68, on the thirty-fifth and thirty-second parallels, for a route extending the Kansas Pacific Railway to the Pacific Ocean at San Francisco and San Diego*, by Gen. William J. Palmer, Dec. 1, 1868; Philadelphia, 1869.

— *The Westward Current of Population in the United States*, London, 1874.

Parkman, Francis. *The California and Oregon Trail; being sketches of Prairie and Rocky Mountain Life*, New York and London, 1849.

Pattison, William D. "Westward by Rail with Professor Sedgwick: a Lantern Journey of 1873", *Quarterly*, Historical Society of Southern California, Los Angeles, vol. 42, 1960, pp. 335-49.

Paul, Rodman Wilson. *Mining Frontiers of the Far West, 1848-1880*, New York, 1963.

— and Etulain, Richard W. (eds) *The Frontier and the American West*, Arlington Heights, Ill., 1977.

"The People at Play. The Growth of the Summer Vacation as a Social Habit and as a Business Investment — A Continent of Summer Homes and Resorts — The Mountains, The Seashore, The Lakes, The Forests — Outdoor Life for the Millions", *The World's Work*, New York, vol. 4, 1902, pp. 2373-2426.

Perkin, Robert L. *The First Hundred Years: an informal history of Denver and the Rocky Mountain News*, Garden City, N.Y., 1959.

Perkins, J.R. *Trails, Rails and War: the Life of General G.M. Dodge*, Indianapolis, 1929.

Peters, Harry Twyford. *Currier & Ives, printmakers to the American people*, Garden City, N.Y., 1942.

Pidgeon, Daniel. *An Engineer's Holiday, or Notes of a Round Trip from Longitude 0° to 0°*, 2 vols, London, 1882.

Pike, Zebulon Montgomery. *Exploratory travels through the western territories of North America; comprising a voyage from St. Louis, on the Mississippi, to the source of that river, and a journey through the interior of Louisiana, and the north-eastern provinces of New Spain. Performed in the years 1805, 1806, 1807, by order of the government of the United States*, London, 1811. (Pike's Journal 1st publ. Philadelphia, 1810; title begins *An Account of Expeditions* . . .).

Plunkett, Mrs. H.M. "Modern Hotels", *Scribner's Monthly*, New York, vol. 6, 1873, pp. 483-92.

Pomeroy, Earl. *In Search of the Golden West: the Tourist in Western America*, New York, 1957.

— *The Pacific Slope: A History of California, Oregon, Washington, Idaho, Utah, and Nevada*, New York, 1965.

Poor, Henry Varnum. *Poor's Manual of the Railroads of the United States*, 57 vols, annual publ. New York, 1868-1924.

Porter, Robert P. (asstd by Henry Gannett and William P. Jones). *The West; from the Census of 1880*, Chicago and London, 1882.

Potter, Isaac B. "The Bicycle Outlook", *The Century Magazine*, New York, vol. 52, 1896, pp. 785-90.

Powers, Stephen. *Afoot and Alone; a Walk from Sea to Sea by the Southern Route*, Hartford, Conn., 1872.

Price, Morgan Philips. *America after Sixty Years. The Travel Diaries of Two Generations of Englishmen*, London, 1936.

Prior, Melton. "Across America — Express Railway Trip", sketched for *The Illustrated London News*, 15 July 1876, pp. 56-8.

Pudney, John. *The Thomas Cook Story*, London, 1953.

Quiett, Glenn Chesney. *They Built the West: An Epic of Rails and Cities*, New York and London, 1934.

Rae, William Fraser. *Westward by Rail; the New Route to the East*, London, 1870; 2nd edit. 1871 entitled *Westward by Rail; a Journey to San Francisco and Back, and a visit to the Mormons*.

— *The Business of Travel; a fifty years' record of progress* (Thomas Cook & Son), London and New York, 1891.

Rand, McNally & Co's Western Railway Guide. The Travelers' Hand Book to all Western Railway and Steamboat Lines, Chicago, rev. edit. 1871.

— *Business Atlas of the Great Mississippi Valley and Pacific Slope*, Chicago, 1876.

— *Guide map of Colorado; with a compilation showing the railroads in the State, and the express company doing business over each*, Chicago, 1876.

— *Illustrated Guide to Colorado, New Mexico and Arizona*, Chicago, 1879.

— See also, Gleed, Charles Sumner (ed.)

— See also, Steele, James William (ed.)

Rapson, Richard Lawrence. *Britons View America: Travel Commentary, 1860-1935*, Seattle and London: Univ. of Washington Press, 1971.

Remondino, Peter Charles. *The Mediterranean Shores of America. Southern California: its climatic, physical, and meteorological conditions*, Philadelphia and London, 1892.

Reps, John William. *Cities of the American West: A History of Frontier Urban Planning*, Princeton Univ. Press, 1979.

Richards, T. Addison. *American Scenery, Illustrated*, New York, 1854.

— See also, *Appletons' Illustrated Hand-Book of American Travel ...*

Richardson, Albert Deane. *Our New States and Territories, being notes of a recent tour of observation through Colorado, Utah, Idaho, Nevada, Oregon, Montana, Washington Territory, and California*, New York, 1866.

— *Beyond the Mississippi, from the great River to the Great Ocean. Life and Adventure on the Prairies, Mountains, and Pacific Coast . . . 1857-1867*, Hartford, Conn., 1867.

— *Garnered Sheaves, from the writings of Albert D. Richardson*, collected and arranged by his wife, Hartford, Conn., 1871.

Rideing, William Henry. *Scenery of the Pacific Railways, and Colorado*, New York, 1878.

— *A-Saddle in the Wild West*, New York and London, 1879.

Ridgway, Arthur. "The Mission of Colorado Toll Roads", *The Colorado Magazine*, vol. 9, 1932, pp. 161-9.

Riegel, Robert Edgar. *The Story of the Western Railroads*, New York, 1926.

Roberts, Edwards. *Santa Barbara and Around There*, Boston, 1886.

Robinson, Philip Stewart. *Sinners and Saints. A Tour Across the States, and Round Them; with Three Months among the Mormons*, London, 1883.

Rusling, James Fowler. *Across America: or, The Great West and the Pacific Coast*, New York, 1874.

Russell, Carl Parcher. *One Hundred Years in Yosemite*, 1st publ. Stanford Univ. Press, Cal., 1931.

Russell, William Howard. *Hesperothen; Notes from the West. A Record of a Ramble in the United States and Canada in the Spring and Summer of 1881*, 2 vols, London, 1882.

Ruxton, George Frederick Augustus. *Adventures in Mexico and the Rocky Mountains*, London, 1847.

— *Life in the Far West*, Edinburgh and London, 1849.

Sabin, Edwin Legrand. *Building the Pacific Railway*, Philadelphia and London, 1919.

Sage, Rufus B. *Rocky Mountain Life; or, Startling Scenes and Perilous Adventures in the Far West during an expedition of three years*, Boston, 1857.

Sala, George Augustus. *America Revisited*, 2 vols, London, 1882.

Sanborn, Katherine (Kate) Abbott. *A Truthful Woman in Southern California*, New York, 1893.

Sanborn, Margaret. *Yosemite: its discovery, its wonders, and its people*, New York, 1981.

Sanford, Mrs. Byron N. "Life at Camp Weld and Fort Lyon in 1861-62: an extract from the diary of Mrs. Byron N. Sanford", edit. by Albert B. Sanford, *The Colorado Magazine*, vol. 7, 1930, pp. 132-9.

— *Mollie. The Journal of Mollie Dorsey Sanford* (Mrs. Byron N. Sanford) *in Nebraska and Colorado Territories, 1857-1866*, Lincoln: Univ. of Nebraska Press, 1959.

The San Francisco Chronicle and its History, 1865-1879, San Francisco, 1879.

Settle, Raymond W. and Mary Lund. *Empire on Wheels* (Russell, Majors & Waddell), Stanford Univ. Press, Cal., 1949.

Seyd, Ernest. *California and its Resources. A Work for the Merchant, the Capitalist, and the Emigrant*, London, 1858.

Seymour, Silas. *Incidents of a Trip through the Great Platte Valley, to the Rocky Mountains and Laramie Plains, in the Fall of 1866. With a synoptical statement of the various Pacific Railroads, and an account of the Great Union Pacific Railroad Excursion to the One Hundredth Meridian of Longitude*, New York, 1867.

Shaw, Milton M. *Nine Thousand Miles on a Pullman train; an account of a tour of railroad conductors from Philadelphia to the Pacific Coast and return*, Philadelphia, 1898.

Shaw, Ronald E. *Erie Water West: a History of the Erie Canal, 1792-1854*, Lexington: Univ. of Kentucky Press, 1966.

Sheldon, Albinus Z. et al. *Statement, Reports, and Examination of the St. Luis Park Grant in Colorado Territory; its title and resources in gold, silver, and other mineral wealth*, New York, 1865.

— "El Paso County", in *History of the Arkansas Valley, Colorado*, Chicago, 1881, pp. 415-76.

Shepard, Jr., Paul. "The Nature of Tourism", *Landscape*, Santa Fe, N.M., vol. 5, 1955, pp. 29-33.

Simonin, Louis Laurent. *Les Pays Lointains. Notes de Voyage*, Paris, 1867.

— *Le Grand-Ouest des Etats-Unis*, Paris, 1869. (Trs. by W.O. Clough as *The Rocky Mountain West in 1867*, Lincoln: Univ. of Nebraska Press, 1966.)

Smiles, Jr., Samuel. *(A Boy's Voyage) Round the World; including a residence in Victoria, and a journey by rail across North America*, London and New York, 1871.

Smiley, Jerome Constant (ed.) *History of Denver, with outlines of the earlier history of the Rocky Mountain Country*, Denver, 1901.

Smith, Duane A. *Rocky Mountain Mining Camps, the Urban Frontier*, Bloomington, Indiana, 1967.

Smith, Henry Nash. *Virgin Land: the American West as Symbol and Myth*, Cambridge: Harvard Univ. Press, 1950.

Smith, R.A. *Philadelphia as it is, in 1852*, Philadelphia, 1852.

Smith, Wallace P.V. *Garden of the Sun: a history of the San Joaquin Valley, 1772-1939*, Los Angeles, 1939.

Smythe, William Ellsworth. "Social Influence of Electric Lines", *Out West*, Los Angeles, vol. 19, 1903, pp. 694-5.

Solly, Samuel Edwin. *Manitou, Colorado, U.S.A.; Its Mineral Waters and Climate*, St. Louis, 1875.

— *The Health Resorts of Colorado Springs and Manitou*, Colorado Springs, 1883.

— *A Handbook of Medical Climatology*, Philadelphia and New York, 1897.

South, Colon. *Out West; or, from London to Salt Lake City and Back*, London, 1884.

Spain, David F. "The Letters of David F. Spain", edit. by John D. Morrison, *The Colorado Magazine*, vol. 35, 1958, pp. 81-112.

Spengemann, William C. *Adventurous Muse: the Poetics of American Fiction, 1789-1900*, New Haven: Yale Univ. Press, 1977.

Sprague, Marshall. *Money Mountain; the Story of Cripple Creek Gold*, Boston, 1953.

— *Newport in the Rockies; the Life and Good Times of Colorado Springs*, Denver, 1961.

Stanley, Sir Henry Morton. *My Early Travels and Adventures in America and Asia*, 2 vols, New York and London, 1895.

Steele, James William (ed.) *Rand, McNally & Co's Guide to Southern California*, Chicago, 1886.

— *Rand, McNally & Co.'s New Overland Guide to the Pacific Coast, Santa Fe Route. California, Arizona, New Mexico, Colorado and Kansas*, Chicago and New York, 1st publ. 1888.

— *Colorado Outings*, Chicago: Burlington & Quincy Railroad Co., 1898.

— *Colorado, the Burlington Route*, Chicago: Burlington & Quincy Railroad Co., 1900.

— *Colorado the magnificent*, Chicago: Chicago, Rock Island & Pacific Railway, 1900.

Stevenson, Robert Louis. *Across the Plains; leaves from the notebook of an emigrant between New York and San Francisco*, London, 1892. (Also in *The Amateur Emigrant*, London, 1895).

Stone, Wilbur Fiske (ed.) *History of Colorado*, 5 vols, Chicago, 1918-19.

Stone, William G.M. *The Colorado Hand-book; Denver and its Outings*, Denver, 1892.

Storey, Samuel. *To the Golden Land. Sketches of a Trip to Southern California*, London, 1889.

Storke, Thomas More. *California Editor*, Los Angeles, 1958.

Storm, Colton (comp.) *A Catalogue of the Everett D. Graff Collection of Western Americana*, pub. for the Newberry Library by Univ. of Chicago Press, Chicago, 1968.

Stover, John F. *American Railroads*, Chicago: Univ. of Chicago Press, 1961.

— *The Life and Decline of the American Railroad*, New York, 1970.

Strahorn, Robert Edmund. *To the Rockies and beyond; or, A Summer on the Union Pacific railroad and branches*, Omaha, 1878.

Strong, Josiah. *Our Country: its possible future and its present crisis*, New York, 1885.

Sutton, Horace. *Travelers. The American Tourist from Stagecoach to Space Shuttle*, New York, 1980.

Swinglehurst, Edmund. *Cook's Tours. The Story of Popular Travel*, Poole, Dorset, 1982.

Synge, Georgina M. *A Ride through Wonderland*, London, 1892.

Taaffe, E.J., Morrill, R.L. and Gould, P.R. "Transport Expansion in Underdeveloped Countries: a comparative analysis", *The Geographical Review*, New York, vol. 53, 1963, pp. 503-29.

Taft, Robert. *Artists and Illustrators of the Old West, 1850-1900*, New York, 1953.

Tallman, Elizabeth J. "Early Days in Colorado", *The Colorado Magazine*, vol. 13, 1936, pp. 141-9.

— "Early History of Parker and Vicinity, *ibid.*, vol. 23, 1946, pp. 184-6.

Taylor, Bayard. *Eldorado; or, Adventures in the Path of Empire*, New York and London, 1st publ. 1850.

— *At Home and Abroad; a Sketch-Book of Life, Scenery, and Men*, New York and London, 1st publ. 1860.

— *Colorado. A Summer Trip*, New York, 1867.

Taylor, Benjamin Franklin. *Between the Gates*, Chicago, 1878, 13th edit., 1888.

Taylor, Joseph. *A Fast Life on the Modern Highway; being a glance into the Railroad World from a new point of view*, New York, 1874.

Taylor, Joshua Charles. *America as Art*, Washington, D.C.: Smithsonian Institution, 1976.

Tenney, Edward Payson. *Colorado: New Homes in the West*, Boston, 1880.

Thacher (Higginson), Mary Potter. *Seashore and Prairie*, Boston, 1877, New York, 1878.

Thayer, William Makepeace. *Marvels of the New West*, Norwich, Conn., 1887.

Thompson, Kenneth. "Irrigation as a menace to health in California: a nineteenth century view", *The Geographical Review*, New York, vol. 59, 1967, pp. 195-214.

Thompson, Mary Emma Dartt. *On the Plains, and Among the Peaks; or, How Mrs. Maxwell made her Natural History Collection*, Philadelphia, 1879.

Thompson, W. Finley. *A Brief Description of Palmer Lake and its Environs, as a Health and Pleasure Resort*, Denver, 1884.

"Through-Tickets to San Francisco: a prophecy", *The Atlantic Monthly*, Boston, Vol. 14, 1864, pp. 604-17.

Tice, John H. *Over the Plains, On the Mountains; or, Kansas, Colorado, and the Rocky Mountains; agriculturally, mineralogically, and aesthetically described*, St. Louis, Mo., 1872.

To San Francisco and Back. By a London Parson, London: Society for Promoting Christian Knowledge, n.d. (c.1870).

Tobin, Gary Allan. "The Bicycle Boom of the 1890s", *Journal of Popular Culture*, Bowling Green State University, Ohio, vol. 7, 1973-4, pp. 838-49.

Todd, Mabel Loomis. "Pike's Peak and Colorado Springs", *The Nation*, New York, 5 Oct. 1893, pp. 245-6.

Townshend, Frederick Trench. *Ten Thousand Miles of Travel, Sport, and Adventure*, London, 1869.

Townshend, Richard Baxter. *A Tenderfoot in Colorado*, London, 1923.

Townshend, Samuel Nugent. *Colorado; its Agriculture, Stock-Feeding, Scenery, and Shooting*, London, 1879.

— *The New Southern Route from San Francisco through Southern California, Arizona, New Mexico, Colorado and Kansas to New York and the Atlantic Seaboard*, Chicago, 1881.

Tracy, Joshua L. (with B.D.M. Eaton). *Guide to the Great West*, St. Louis, Mo., 1870.

Train, George Francis. *My Life in Many States and in Foreign Lands, dictated in my seventy-fourth year*, New York and London, 1902.

Truman, Benjamin Cummings. *Semi-Tropical California: its Climate, Healthfulness, Productiveness, and Scenery*, San Francisco, 1874.

— *Occidental Sketches*, San Francisco, 1881.

— *Homes and Happiness in the Golden State of California*, San Francisco, 1883.

— *Tourists' Illustrated Guide to the celebrated Summer and Winter Resorts of California adjacent to and upon the lines of the Central and Southern Pacific Railroads*, San Francisco, 1883.

— *From the Crescent City to the Golden Gate; via the Sunset Route of the Southern Pacific Co.*, New York, 1886.

— *Southern California*, Los Angeles, 1903.

Tryon, Warren Stenson. *A Mirror for Americans; Life and Manners in the United States, 1790-1870, as recorded by American travelers*, 3 vols, Chicago: Univ. of Chicago Press, 1952. Vol. 3, *The Frontier Moves West.*

Tuckerman, Henry Theodore. *America and her Commentators; with a Critical Sketch of Travel in the United States*, New York, 1864.

Turner, Frederick Jackson. "The Significance of the Frontier in American History", *Annual Report of the American Historical Association for 1893*, Washington, D.C., 1894.

Twain, Mark *pseud.* (Samuel Langhorne Clemens). *Roughing It*, Hartford, Conn., Chicago, etc., 1871.

Uhlhorn, John F. *Tourists' Guide to Picturesque California*, San Francisco, 1887.

Ullman, Edward L. "Amenities as a factor in regional growth", *The Geographical Review*, New York, vol. 44, 1954, pp. 119-32.

Union Pacific Railroad Co. *The Colorado Tourist and Illustrated Guide to the Rocky Mountain Resorts, via the "Golden Belt"*, Kansas City, Mo., 1880.

—*The Union Pacific Tourist. Illustrated Sketches of the Principal Health and Pleasure Resorts of the Great West and Northwest, embracing Yellowstone Park and Yosemite and the chief points of interest in the Rocky Mountain Region, all most easily reached via the Union Pacific Railway*, Buffalo, N.Y., 1884.

— *Colorado. A Complete and Comprehensive Description; the Resources and Attractions of Colorado for the Home-Seeker, Capitalist, and Tourist*, Omaha, Neb., 1890.

— *Souvenir and Views of the Union Pacific, "the Overland Route", the world's pictorial line*, edit. by E.L. Lomax, Chicago, 1897.

Utah State Historical Society, National Golden Spike Centennial Commission Official Publication. *The Last Spike is Driven, Utah Historical Quarterly*, Salt Lake City, vol. 37, 1969.

Utley, Robert M. "The Dash to Promontory", *Utah Historical Quarterly*, Salt Lake City, vol. 29, 1961, pp. 99-117.

Vance, Jr., James E. "California and the Search for the Ideal", *Annals of the Association of American Geographers*, Washington, D.C., vol. 62, 1972, pp. 185-210.

Vandewater, Robert J. *The Tourist, or Pocket Manual for Travellers on the Hudson River, the Western Canal, and Stage Road, to Niagara Falls. Comprising also the routes to Lebanon, Ballston and Saratoga Springs,*

New York, etc., 1830, 2nd edit. enlarged and improved 1831, 9th edit. 1841.

Vickers, William B. *History of the City of Denver, Arapahoe County, and the State of Colorado*, Chicago, 1880.

Victor, Frances Fuller. "Northern Seaside Resorts", *The Overland Monthly*, San Francisco, vol. 23 (Second Series), 1894, pp. 138-49.

Villard, Henry. *The Past and Present of the Pike's Peak Gold Regions*, St. Louis, Mo., 1860.

Vivian, Arthur Pendarves. *Wanderings in the Western Land*, London, 1879.

Vivian, Henry Hussey. *Notes of a Tour in America*, London, 1878.

Wagner, Henry Raup (ed.) *The Plains and the Rockies: a bibliography of original narratives of travel and adventure, 1800-1865*, San Francisco, 1920. (Revised by Charles L. Cramp, 1937, 1953; and by Robert H. Becker, 1982).

Walker, Franklin Dickerson. *San Francisco's Literary Frontier*, New York, 1939.

— *A Literary History of Southern California*, Berkeley and Los Angeles: Univ. of California Press, 1950.

Walker, Henry Pickering. *The Wagonmasters: High Plains Freighting from the earliest days of the Santa Fe Trail to 1880*, Norman: Univ. of Oklahoma Press, 1966.

Walsh, Margaret. *The American Frontier revisited*, London, 1981.

Warner, Charles Dudley. *Our Italy*, New York, 1891.

Webb, Walter Prescott. *The Great Plains*, Boston, 1931.

Wells, A.J. "California Summer Resorts", *Out West*, Los Angeles, vol. 19, 1903, pp. 115-27.

Wharton, Junius E. *History of the City of Denver*, Denver, 1866.

Wheat, Carl Irving. *Mapping the Trans-Mississippi West, 1540-1861*, 2 vols, San Francisco, 1957-8.

White, Arthur Stanley. *Palaces of the People: a social history of commercial hospitality*, London, 1968, New York, 1970.

White, Jr., John H. *The American Railroad Passenger Car*, Baltimore and London: Johns Hopkins Univ. Press, 1978.

Whitman, Walt. "America's Characteristic Landscape"; *Walt Whitman: complete poetry and selected prose and letters*, edit. by E. Holloway, London, 1938, 8th impr. 1971.

Whitney, Josiah Dwight. *The Yosemite Guide-Book*, Sacramento, Cal. and Cambridge, Mass., 1870.

Whitney, Orson Ferguson. *History of Utah*, 4 vols, Salt Lake City, 1892-1904.

Whymper, Frederick. "From Ocean to Ocean — The Pacific Railway", *Illustrated Travels: a record of Discovery, Geography, and Adventure*, London and New York, vol. 2, 1869-70, pp. 1-12, 35-40, 65-71.

Wilde, Oscar. *Impressions of America* (1883), Sunderland, 1906.

Willard, James Field (ed.) *The Union Colony at Greeley, Colorado, 1869-71*, Boulder, Colo., 1918.

— and Goodykoontz, Colin B. (eds) *Experiments in Colorado Colonization, 1869-1872*, Boulder, Colo., 1926.

Williams, Henry T. (ed.) *The Pacific Tourist. Williams' Illustrated Trans-Continental Guide of Travel, from the Atlantic to the Pacific Ocean*, New York, 1876, repr. until 1884. (see pp. 246-7).

— *Williams' Tourists' Guide and Map of the San Juan Mines of Colorado*, New York, 1877.

Williamson, Jefferson. *The American Hotel*, New York, 1930.

Willis, Nathaniel Parker. *American Scenery; or, Land, Lake, and River. Illustrations of Transatlantic Nature*, 2 vols, London, 1840.

Wills, Mary H. *A Winter in California*, Norristown, Pennsylvania, 1889.

Wilson, John. *Health and Health Resorts*, Philadelphia, 1880.

Winther, Oscar Osburn. *The Transportation Frontier: Trans-Mississippi West, 1865-1890*, New York, 1964.

Wolcott, Frances Metcalfe. *Heritage of Years; kaleidoscopic memories, 1851-1889*, New York, 1932.

Wood, Ruth Kedzie. *The Tourist's California*, New York, 1914.

Wood, Stanley. *Over the Range to the Golden Gate. A Complete Tourist's Guide to Colorado, New Mexico, Utah, Nevada, California, Oregon, Puget Sound and the Great North-West*, Chicago, 1st publ. 1894.

Wyman, Mary Alice. *Two American Pioneers; Seba Smith and Elizabeth Oakes Smith*, New York: Columbia Univ. Press, 1927.

Yates, Raymond F. "The Old Lockport and Niagara Falls Strap Railroad", *Occasional Contributions of the Niagara County Historical Society*, Lockport, N.Y., No. 4, 1950.

"The Yellowstone National Park", *Scribner's Monthly*, New York, vol. 4, 1872, pp. 120-1.

Zelinsky, Wilbur. *The Cultural Geography of the United States*, Englewood Cliffs, N.J., 1973.

V ILLUSTRATIONS

Author, 2 (lower), 3, 5, 19, 34, 50, 76 (upper), 78b; *Baker Library, Harvard Business School*, 45; *Boston Public Library*, 76 (lower); *British Library*, 2 (upper), 14, 15, 24, 27, 42, 43, 49, 51, 56, 70; *California Historical Society/Ticor Title Insurance (Los Angeles)*, 52, 69, 71, 72, 86, 88, 91, 92, 93, 94; *Colorado Historical Society*, 13, 18, 21, 22, 23, 28, 31, 32, 55; *Danbury Scott-Fanton Museum and Historical Society*, 4; *Denver Public Library, Western History Department*, 33, 53, 80, 96, 98, 99, 102, 104, 105, 106, 107; *Department of Special Collections, University Research Library, UCLA*, 73, 87, 89; *Elizabeth M. Watkins Community Museum, Lawrence, Kansas*, 16; *Erie Canal Museum, Syracuse, N.Y.*, 6; *Kansas Collection, University of Kansas Libraries*, 17; *Library Company of Philadelphia*, 9, 10; *Library of Congress*, 8, 25, 26, 30, 35, 36, 37, 38, 40, 57, 60, 64, 75, 77, 108-116; *Metropolitan Museum of Art, Edward C. Arnold Collection, courtesy Museum of the City of New York*, 46; *New York Public Library*, 1, 7; *Philadelphia Museum of Art*, 11; *Pikes Peak Regional Library, Local History Division*, 61, 65, 66, 79, 81, 103; *Royal Geographical Society*, 67, 68; *Santa Monica Public Library Historical Photograph Archives*, 90; *Smithsonian Institution #3835*, 85; *Thomas Cook Company Archives*, 78a; *Union Pacific Railroad Museum Collection*, 29; *University of Colorado Western Historical Collections*, 20, 48, 54, 62, 63, 100, 101; *Utah State Historical Society*, 12

INDEX